Dictionary of American Government
and Politics

Dictionary of American Government and Politics

Duncan Watts

Edinburgh University Press

© Duncan Watts, 2010

Edinburgh University Press Ltd
22 George Square, Edinburgh
www.euppublishing.com

Typeset in 10 on 12pt Ehrhardt
by Servis Filmsetting Limited, Stockport, Cheshire, and
printed and bound in Great Britain by
CPI Antony Rowe, Chippenham and Eastbourne

A CIP record for this book is available from the British Library

ISBN 978 0 7486 3501 6 (hardback)

1006613331

Contents

Preface

The United States of America is a fascinating – but at the same time complex – area of study for many students of politics and interested observers of the contemporary political scene. It is a vast liberal democracy of more than 300 million people of great diversity: it covers a huge landmass, exceeding that of all but three nations of the world, Canada, China and Russia: it has the oldest written constitution in the world, but one which has been flexible enough to adapt to circumstances very different from those known to the Founding Fathers back in 1787: it has a separated system of government which fragments the exercise of political power and in which there are overlapping jurisdictions and a series of checks and balances: it is based on federalism so that the role and influence of the states and local government assume considerable significance, as well as the central government in Washington: and it has a system for choosing its president that is remote from British experience and puzzling to many observers who are amazed at how long the process seems to last.

Yet however confusing and remote from British experience the American practice of government may be, the significance of the United States in global terms is apparent to most people. Decisions taken in Washington have an impact on us all, be they in foreign policy or in the effort to stimulate the economy. Moreover, as the leading country of the Western world, the United States proclaims many attitudes and values that are widely recognised and in many cases admired as well.

Given its governing arrangements, diversity and size, the United States is not an easy country to study. But it is hoped that this dictionary will explain many of the terms and clear up many of the confusions that may make American politics difficult to understand. As a result of its usage, readers may acquire a broad understanding of the American system of government and the forces that influence its operation. The task may seem daunting for, although the United Kingdom and the United States share a common commitment to liberal democracy, their political systems are different. Some of these differences derive from the operation of the federal system in America but in the area of elections, too, there are many aspects of American life that are largely unfamiliar to students of British politics, ranging from primary elections to the election of judges in several states, from the use of initiatives to votes to recall public officials.

The nature of this study

This is not an exhaustive, twelve-volume encyclopedia but neither is it a short glossary. Nor is it a general political dictionary surveying the terms covered in many courses dealing with comparative government and political thought. It is a dictionary concerned specifically with the government and politics of the United States. Many of the entries will be similar in title to those likely to be found in a more general political dictionary but the coverage of them is strictly related to American experience. The discussion of concepts such as democracy and socialism is rooted in consideration of how they function and with what success in the United States, although the terms will initially be briefly defined to inform the discussion.

By its very nature as a one-volume work, this dictionary cannot be encyclopedic in its coverage of the references included. An attempt has been made, however, to ensure that the amount of space devoted to particular references is broadly proportional to their importance in the US political system. It may be that some references seem briefer than might be expected but, in those cases, there should be cross-references that will further illuminate the subject. In other cases, though references may seem surprisingly lengthy, there may be few cross-references to follow up.

Invariably, many writers on the American scene may quibble with the choice of topics for inclusion or the length or amount of detail and elaboration provided. That is their prerogative. But as a broad approach, the intention here is to provide a useful explanation of the key concepts, events, institutions, issues and personnel that have become part of the American political system – and in suitable cases, to point readers in the direction of other interesting lines of enquiry.

British students of American politics are often required to delve further back into history than the terms government and politics usually imply. In part, this is because, whereas when studying the British system they may possess some broad knowledge and understanding of developments in the past, such information may be unfamiliar in the case of the United States. More often, it is because decisions taken at various stages in American history still have an impact and relevance in political life and controversy today. The written Constitution may now be very elderly but reference to it is relevant to the study of how the Executive, Legislature and Judiciary have operated in recent decades. Again, analysis of the state of civil rights for minority groups in the present day inevitably leads to references to segregation and the civil rights struggles of the past.

The general canvas of this work concerns government and politics of the post-1945 era, with the greatest emphasis being on the period of the Clinton and G. W. Bush presidencies. But, wherever appropriate, presidential or Supreme Court decisions of the late eighteenth, nineteenth or early mid-twentieth centuries are explored in sufficient detail to make concepts such as segregation and desegregation, dual federalism and new

federalism, meaningful. If historical references sometimes seem to be generously catered for, so too are very up-to-date issues such as the financial and economic problems associated with the onset of recession in America and much of the rest of the world from 2007 onwards, and the impact of international terrorism and the wars fought to combat it.

A mere listing of the areas to be covered – key personalities, court judgments, institutions and how they operate, and national and international developments – must illustrate how difficult the task of selecting items for inclusion has been. The question of selectivity is most evident in regard to personalities. My initial listing of past and present-day people in public life with a claim to be included has been pruned, for one can soon find that the number of available candidates runs into hundreds. My reduced list narrowed the range of possible contenders, confining it to post-1933 presidents (in the eyes of many writers, 1933 marked the beginning of modern American government); recent presidential candidates such as Al Gore, John Kerry and John McCain, whose names are likely to be familiar; those who hold or have relatively recently held key positions of authority in Congress or on the Supreme Court; and prominent figures involved in the various movements to bring about civil rights for all Americans. All those included are figures who have featured prominently in important debates of recent decades and who – by their actions or inactions, or the controversies associated with them – have influenced and sometimes greatly modified the course of events. (N.b. Readers at any level may benefit from the listing of the dates of presidents and recent chief justices of the Supreme Court, in the same way that up-to-date figures for party control of state governorships and Congress might also act as a useful aide-memoire and enable the reader to extract more use out of the discussion.)

Inevitably some key figures and other references will have been left out, doubtless a few of which are of considerable importance. It is to be hoped that after delving further into the book and looking up particular references, readers will at least appreciate the reasons for my choice even if their own would have been different. For any omissions that disturb readers, I apologise in advance. Their omission may reflect an error on my part or it may reflect my need to be selective – highly selective – as to what can be included in a book of this length and scale. It is intended that the book can be an accessible and manageable volume. Some dictionaries are considerably longer and more detailed. They have their value but their bulk in terms of size and content can detract from their utility as a source of reference.

A guide such as this can be very useful as readers peruse some specialist tomes and in so doing come across references that mean little or nothing to them. My hope is that, though the list of entries is not totally exhaustive, readers will be able to find out more about the issue or person on which they are seeking information. In some cases, the accounts are very brief but the cross references may enable interested students to pursue their enquiries in greater detail. In others, there is scope for reference – where appropriate

– to leading academic theories and/or viewpoints. The controversies surrounding issues of political debate, such as the nature of presidential power, the value of political parties and the politics of abortion, are appropriately aired, with due attention paid to some of the most important and sometimes pioneering recent political thinking.

From a personal point of view, I have much enjoyed writing this dictionary. It has made me think carefully about the institutions, issues, events and personnel that might be regarded as significant when people examine and assess the post-1945 era. It has forced me to curb my natural inclination to write at length and made me concentrate on the aspects that matter most.I have tried, however, to indicate how and why the various items included have assumed importance and trust that enough coverage has been given to make use of this study very worthwhile.

Duncan Watts

Useful Background Information

US presidents from Washington to Obama

President	Party	Term
1 George Washington (1732–99)	Federalist	1789–97
2 John Adams (1735–1826)	Federalist	1797–1801
3 Thomas Jefferson (1743–1826)	Democratic-Republican	1801–09
4 James Madison (1751–1836)	Democratic-Republican	1809–17
5 James Monroe (1758–1831)	Democratic-Republican	1817–25
6 John Quincy Adams (1767–1848)	Democratic-Republican	1825–29
7 Andrew Jackson (1767–1845)	Democrat	1829–37
8 Martin Van Buren (1782–1862)	Democrat	1837–41
9 William Henry Harrison (1773–1841)	Whig	1841
10 John Tyler (1790–1862)	Whig	1841–45
11 James K. Polk (1795–1849)	Democrat	1845–49
12 Zachary Taylor (1784–1850)	Whig	1849–50
13 Millard Fillmore (1800–74)	Whig	1850–53
14 Franklin Pierce (1804–69)	Democrat	1853–57
15 James Buchanan (1791–1868)	Democrat	1857–61
16 Abraham Lincoln (1809–65)	Republican	1861–65
17 Andrew Johnson (1808–75)	Union	1865–69
18 Ulysses S. Grant (1822–85)	Republican	1869–77
19 Rutherford B. Hayes (1822–93)	Republican	1877–81
20 James A. Garfield (1831–81)	Republican	1881
21 Chester A. Arthur (1830–86)	Republican	1881–85
22 Grover Cleveland (1837–1908)	Democrat	1885–89
23 Benjamin Harrison (1833–1901)	Republican	1889–93
24 Grover Cleveland (1837–1908)	Democrat	1893–97
25 William McKinley (1843–1901)	Republican	1897–1901
26 Theodore Roosevelt (1858–1919)	Republican	1901–09
27 William Howard Taft (1857–1930)	Republican	1909–13
28 Woodrow Wilson (1856–1924)	Democrat	1913–21
29 Warren G. Harding (1865–1923)	Republican	1921–23
30 Calvin Coolidge (1871–1933)	Republican	1923–29
31 Herbert Hoover (1874–1964)	Republican	1929–33
32 Franklin Delano Roosevelt (1882–1945)	Democrat	1933–45
33 Harry S. Truman (1884–1972)	Democrat	1945–53

34 Dwight D. Eisenhower (1890–1969)	Republican	1953–61
35 John F. Kennedy (1917–63)	Democrat	1961–63
36 Lyndon B. Johnson (1908–73)	Democrat	1963–69
38 Gerald R. Ford (1913–2006)	Republican	1974–77
39 Jimmy Carter (b. 1924)	Democrat	1977–81
40 Ronald Reagan (1911–2004)	Republican	1981–89
41 George H. W. Bush (b. 1924)	Republican	1989–93
42 William Jefferson Clinton (b. 1946)	Democrat	1993–2001
43 George Walton Bush (b. 1946)	Republican	2001–09
44 Barack Obama (b. 1961)	Democrat	2009–

Membership of the Supreme Court (2009)

Justice	Year of birth	Year of appointment	President who made the appointment
Chief Justice			
John Roberts	1955	2005	G. W. Bush
Associate justices			
John Stevens	1920	1975	G. Ford
Antonin Scalia	1936	1986	R. Reagan
Anthony Kennedy	1936	1988	R. Reagan
Clarence Thomas	1948	1991	G. H. Bush
Ruth Ginsburg	1933	1993	W. Clinton
Stephen Breyer	1938	1994	W. Clinton
Samuel Alito	1950	2006	G. W. Bush
Sonia Sotomayor	1954	2009	B. Obama

N.B. As of September 2009, the average age of the nine justices is sixty-seven.

Party control of Congress (2009)

Party	House	Senate
Democrats	256	57
Independents	0	2
Republicans	178	40
Vacancies	1	1

Party control of state governorships (2009)

Party	Governorships held
Democrats	28
Republicans	22

All figures correct as in September 2009.

A

Abolitionists/Abolition Movement

Abolitionists agitated for the immediate, unconditional and total abolition of slavery in the United States. Abolitionist groups existed before the founding of the Republic. Some of those involved at Philadelphia were involved in the cause, Alexander Hamilton and Benjamin Franklin being among those who founded the Pennsylvania Society for the Abolition of Slavery. By the early 1790s, anti-slavery groups existed in almost every state. Their approach was known as *gradualism*, involving petitioning Congress to develop plans for the end of slavery. In the early to mid-nineteenth century, some who argued for the freedom of black Americans – Lincoln and Madison among them – were interested in the idea of transporting freed slaves back to Africa, making emancipation a more attractive prospect to whites.

Black Americans protested against their circumstances throughout the period of their enslavement, sometimes in the form of work slowdowns and, on occasion, in more open rebellion. In the North, free blacks were able to organise and protest although they often ran into resistance from whites. White protests could more easily be organised in any part of the country, as whites had greater freedom of travel, opportunity to organise and resources to employ, in order to advance the abolitionist cause. Many abolitionists joined the American Anti-Slavery Society (AASS) which urged *immediatism*, immediate emancipation. The AASS engaged in an active campaign of petitions and pamphleteering, their activities provoking a powerful – and sometimes violent – reaction in the South, in Congress and even in parts of the North.

Tensions rose in the 1830s and 1840s, with violence committed by abolitionists against slaveholders and vice versa. By the 1850s, the abolition movement was becoming much more aggressive in its approach, as abolitionists increasingly demanded that slavery be ended immediately and everywhere. John Brown was the only abolitionist known to have actually planned a violent insurrection. In 1859, he and some twenty associates, black and white, attacked the federal arsenal at Harper's Ferry, Virginia, in a bid to seize weapons and free the slaves. It resulted in the execution of Brown and six others. By that time, there was a sense of crisis. Much depended on the outcome of the 1860 election which Lincoln won with virtually no southern votes. Finally, the issue of slavery was resolved on the battlefields during the Civil War.

The efforts of the abolitionists culminated in Lincoln's Emancipation Proclamation of 22 September 1862 and in the post-Civil War amendments (Thirteenth, Fourteenth and Fifteenth) to the US Constitution. Some former abolitionists continued the work to better the living and working conditions of black Americans generally.

See also *Civil War*; *Emancipation Proclamation*; *Lincoln, Abraham*

Abortion

Abortion, the deliberate termination of a pregnancy, is a highly controversial issue in the United States. It has on occasion been referred to as the 'new Vietnam' because of the way in which it has

1

so sharply polarised popular opinion. What makes it different from most other questions is that it involves a clash of absolutes. To its supporters, it is a matter of a woman's fundamental right to do what she wishes with her own body. To its opponents, it is about the fundamental right to life of the as-yet unborn child. Opponents, be they Roman Catholics or the Christian Right, regard abortion not just as another symptom of a general decline in moral standards, but as a sin. For them, it is a contravention of the divine law of the Scriptures and, for the more militant, one they cannot accept.

Abortion is sometimes portrayed as a defining issue between liberals and conservatives and to a broad extent this is true. But there is more to the issue than this straightforward division. The degree of religious involvement in the debate about abortion makes such a categorisation less clear-cut. Many Catholics who might be liberal on social questions such as employment rights, would find themselves in the conservative camp in discussion of the rights of the unborn to life itself.

Abortion before and after the Roe v. Wade judgment (1973)

In the nineteenth century, many states had introduced laws against abortion but, by the early 1970s, nineteen states permitted the practice. The American Law Institute and the American Medical Association came out in favour of abortion in certain situations, such as foetal abnormality. Their members were also worried about the danger to desperate women who resorted to dubious back-street treatments. They were joined by elements in the growing women's movement who also campaigned for the removal of restrictive state laws. On the other side of the argument, there were important developments, too. Foremost among them was the increasing involvement of the Roman Catholic Church in the debate. Its role was crucial to the anti-abortion movement that resisted any liberalisation of the law. It established the National Right to Life Committee (NRLC) in 1971. Abortion, originally a state concern, had come to assume national importance.

Then, the Supreme Court adjudicated, in the much-quoted *Roe* v. *Wade* case of 1973 (and again, in *Doe* v. *Bolton*). It found that state laws against abortion were unconstitutional, in that they violated the right of a woman to terminate her pregnancy and thereby have control over her own person. This denied a woman her right to privacy, as laid down in the Fourteenth Amendment. As a result of the judgment, there was a constitutional right to have an abortion. Abortion thereafter became legal everywhere in the United States.

Opponents and supporters of abortion were galvanised into action by this Court judgment. Supporters formed the National Association for the Repeal of Abortion Laws, now known as the National Abortion and Reproductive Rights Action League (NARAL). They soon realised that it was necessary to mount a defence of the newly proclaimed right to abortion in order to fend off the attacks of those who would seek to undermine it. Although many of the foremost opponents were to be found in the Catholic Church, there were soon stirrings among religious evangelicals such as Dr Billy Graham who strongly opposed what the nine justices had decided. Opposition to abortion became a key issue in the emergence of what was to become the Christian Right.

Limitations upon abortion by the judiciary and legislature

Since 1973, there have been numerous attempts to reverse the legal position, mostly through the courts. In 1989 the Rehnquist Court made a significant inroad into the 'right to choose', in the *Webster* v. *Reproductive Services* case. Instead of overruling the 1973 decision, the justices reduced its impact by acknowledging the constitutional right to an abortion but also granting more power to individual states to impose restrictions (though not to ban the operation completely).

Some states began to make cuts in their allocation of funding to meet the costs of an abortion but it was still in the Supreme Court where the key decisions were being taken. The conservative majority created by the appointments of justices during the Republican ascendancy made further limitations possible. In 1992, in *Casey* v. *Planned*

Parenthood, states were given the power to regulate abortion even in the first three months of pregnancy (the period in which the *Roe* v. *Wade* judgment had denied any right of interference) and to ban it once the foetus was deemed to be 'viable'. Yet the fundamental right was upheld, and state regulations were not to infringe that right unduly. Thereafter, Clinton's two appointments to the Supreme Court tilted its balance in a more moderate direction, making further Court restrictions less likely.

In the 1990s the pressure to limit abortion further came from the legislative branch, following the change of party control in 1994. In late 1995, the House voted to ban a rare, late-term abortion procedure (partial birth abortion) and to jail doctors who carried it out. The Senate similarly gave the bill a speedy passage. Twice, Bill Clinton used his veto to prevent the measure from reaching the statute book and in 2000 the Supreme Court ruled against a state law that sought to ban such abortions. The issue remained contentious, for the anti-abortion movement saw it as one on which it could make progress with its campaign to impose further inroads into the constitutional right to have an abortion.

In 2003, George Bush (who opposed abortion except in cases of incest, rape or any threat to the life of the mother) signed into law a ban on partial birth abortions. The procedure involved is a means of last resort where there is a severe foetal abnormality or the health of the mother is under threat. Because of its special nature, the pro-choice groups were outraged at what the National Abortion and Reproductive Rights Action League called 'the most devastating and appalling attack on a woman's freedom to choose in the history of the House'. Anti-abortionists portrayed the operation as being tantamount to infanticide.

Polls show that Americans are more or less evenly divided on the rights and wrongs of abortion. Even many women who favour women's rights in other areas may take a pro-life stance. Both parties – but especially the Republicans – have suffered from internal fission over the issue. Democrats tend to favour the right to legal abortions and most feminists who campaign for it are firmly committed to them.

See also *Christian Coalition*; *Fourteenth Amendment*; *National Organization for Women*; **Planned Parenthood of Southeastern Pennsylvania** v. **Casey** *(1992)*; *Pro-Life Movement*; *Religious Right*; **Roe** v. **Wade** *(1973)*; **Webster** v. **Reproductive Services** *(1989)*

Abortion Rights Movement

The abortion rights movement comprises a number of organisations involved in the campaign to ensure that women should continue to have access to safe and legal abortion. Some were established before the 1973 *Roe* v. *Wade* decision in order to campaign for the right to have a termination. Others were set up after that landmark decision to uphold the constitutional right that had been won and oppose any erosion of it.

The origins of the modern abortion rights movement can be found in the work of various groups that campaigned for at least limited abortion rights. In 1959, the American Law Institute proposed allowing abortion on grounds of foetal abnormality and a threat to women's health. The American Medical Association (AMA) declared itself in favour of reform eight years later. In some states the demand for legal change was rebuffed but, between 1966 and 1971, eighteen states had liberalised their law.

In the late 1960s, abortion rights campaigners formed the National Association for the Repeal of Abortion Laws (NARAL). NARAL widened its agenda to become the National Abortion and Reproductive Rights Action League (NARRAL, although it now usually styles itself as NARAL Pro-Choice). Planned Parenthood and its predecessor organisations have long advocated reproductive rights, including the right to abortion. This advocacy includes contributing to sponsorship of abortion rights and women's rights events. NARAL Pro-Choice America and Planned Parenthood are the leading pro-choice advocacy and lobbying groups in the United States. Most major feminist groups also support pro-choice positions, however. The National Organization for Women (NOW) also became actively involved in the cause and has continued to play a central role over recent decades.

Of the two main political parties, the Democratic

Party's platform endorses the pro-choice position, stating that abortion should be 'safe, legal, and rare'. Although the 2008 Republican platform was pro-life (employing some of its strongest language ever in condemnation of abortion and supporting legal protections for unborn children) a few nationally prominent Republicans identify themselves as pro-choice, including California Governor Arnold Schwarzenegger. Within the churches (usually associated with resistance to abortion) the Religious Coalition for Reproductive Choice and Catholics for Free Choice have also supported the maintenance of the Roe judgment.

Common to all the organisations mentioned above is a belief in the right of a women to choose what happens to her own body, a central plank of the women's rights platform. Pro-choice describes the political and ethical view that a woman should have complete control over her fertility and pregnancy.

The pro-choice movement strongly opposed many of the attitudes and positions advanced by the Bush administration and many Republican-dominated state legislatures on matters relating to abortion and human embryos. Its methods included supporting the election of more pro-choice candidates to public office, mobilising pro-choice Americans and encouraging activists at grass-roots level to stop anti-choice legislation, lobbying Congress and providing up-to-the-minute information about state bills, the enactment of new laws and decisions handed down by state and federal courts related to reproductive rights.

See also *Abortion*; *National Organization for Women*; *Pro-life Movement*

Advice and Consent

The 'advice and consent' clause of the Constitution (Article 2, Section 2) requires that, for international treaties and presidential nominations for executive and judicial positions to become effective, they must be approved by the Senate on the basis of a two-thirds vote. A similar 'advice and consent' power is also held by several state senates that are consulted on, and approve, various appointments made by the state's governor, such as some statewide officials, departmental heads in the governor's cabinet and state judges.

The clause represents a compromise by the Founding Fathers who included the phrase as part of a delicate balancing act concerning the balance of power in the federal government. Many delegates preferred to develop a strong executive control vested in the president. Others, worried at the prospect of authoritarian control, preferred to strengthen the Congress. Requiring the president to gain the advice and consent of the Senate achieved both goals without seriously impeding the business of government.

See also *Senate*

Affirmative Action

Affirmative-action policies and programmes (better known in Britain as means of positive discrimination) are designed to increase the chances of specified disadvantaged racial, ethnic and sexual groups being selected for positions in public life, such as on university courses or in management jobs. They are designed to make up for the effects of past individual and societal discrimination by giving compensatory treatment today to women and minorities. The rights and wrongs of such methods have been a topic of fierce debate in the last decade.

In the 1960s, many affirmative programmes were adopted by national, state and local governments, by public institutions such as state colleges and universities, and by some private employers and organisations. Sometimes backed by federal money, they were introduced to help promote an improved racial and/or gender balance.

These affirmative-action programmes usually involved a special effort to recruit and promote members of these groups. They could be of the 'hard' or 'soft' kind. Hard forms involved setting specific targets or quotas as to how many people of a certain type should be recruited to an organisation, irrespective of whether they have the appropriate qualifications (e.g., 20 per cent of a police force had to be black). Soft forms involved measures to encourage minority applications. They were intended to boost minority representation by ensuring that, when people of equal qualifications presented themselves, the member of the disadvantaged group would then usually be chosen. This would increase diversity.

The debate over affirmative-action programmes

Although segregation and discrimination had already been made illegal by the mid-1960s, many supporters of equal rights saw this as insufficient. Neutral treatment would do little or nothing to equip women and racial minorities (primarily African Americans, Hispanics and Native Americans) with genuine opportunities, and they would still be denied the chance to participate fully in American life. In particular, because African Americans had suffered from the continuing burden of disadvantage for so long, they would never have equal openings in areas such as access to education or medical school, skilled employment or winning government contracts. Affirmative action was, then, a well-intentioned – and not unsuccessful – attempt to give modest preferences to those long denied their full citizenship and a fair chance in life. In the process, it might have other benefits, such as improving the nation's economic and social life (enriching it by bringing in a diversity of talents and experience) and removing a cause of disaffection and thereby promoting social order and stability. It might also help create a black middle class which could provide a useful role model for any aspirational African American.

Affirmative action became highly contentious in the 1990s and remains controversial today. Its opponents believe that it is a form of reverse discrimination that replaces one form of discrimination with another. They feel that appointment, progress and promotion should be organised on the basis of merit rather than on any other consideration. In particular, they dislike the quotas that are often written into programmes and which establish a target number of women or members of a minority group who must be employed. When there is work for everyone, the quota might seem more acceptable. When it is in short supply or when a few particular jobs are much in demand, there tends to be a backlash against the concept. Similar controversy is stirred over educational provision. To achieve the target of a certain number of minority representatives in universities involves allowing some students to be enrolled who may be less academically qualified than others who were being rejected.

Northern whites began to be upset by the policies designed to promote opportunities for black people, such as busing and affirmative action. Many of the programmes derived from the Civil Rights Act (1964) and the way it was to be interpreted. It was the Supreme Court that had to decide whether the Act was constitutional. Could equality of treatment be obtained by providing opportunities for some groups that were themselves inherently unequal?

The legality of affirmative action

Within the Supreme Court there has been uncertainty over affirmative action, just as there has been throughout the nation. The Fourteenth Amendment to the Constitution laid down the notion of 'equal protection' before the law. The Court has, on occasion, argued that quota programmes in government, or instigated by it, are a violation of that idea. The Burger Court (1969–86) generally approved the principle of affirmative action (e.g., *Regents of the University of California* v. *Baake*, 1978) but was unhappy with the details of particular programmes. The details can vary and the variations may be very important in their constitutional implications. In *Firefighters* v. *Stotts*, 1984, it would not accept the principle as the only, or even most, important consideration.

In subsequent cases, a division of opinion arose in the attempt to apply the 'equal protection' clause of the Constitution. Justice Sandra Day O'Connor, herself the first woman to make it on to the Bench, expressed grave doubts as to whether race-sensitive remedial measures could ever be justified, whereas others have taken the view that they can be necessary if the commitment to equality is to be honoured and past injustice righted.

Many Court votes have been very close, 5–4 or 6–3. In 1990, by five votes to four, the Court upheld the right of Congress to adopt 'benign race-conscious measures' designed to increase the number of minority-held radio and television licences issued by the, Federal Communications Commission. Similarly, with regard to women, the Supreme Court has often been willing to accept policies designed to help women overcome past disadvantages. In 1987, it upheld the California county agency's scheme allowing consideration of gender in making appointments to positions where women had fared badly in earlier years. It recognised that there had in the past been unfairness in representation, and that it was therefore fair to use the issue of gender to correct the imbalance.

Bill Clinton was aware of the unpopularity of affirmative action but generally resisted the temptation to trim his support, and tried to encourage a 'mend it, don't end it' approach. His appointments to the judiciary helped to ensure that the policy continued despite the doubts and hesitancy revealed by members of the Rehnquist Court. Rehnquist was highly sceptical of the policy, arguing in a dissenting submission in the case of *Fullilovev* v. *Klutznick* (1980) that

> The Fourteenth Amendment was adopted to ensure that every person must be treated equally by each state regardless the color of his skin . . . Today, the Court derails this achievement and places its imprimatur on the creation once again by government of privilege based on birth.

In the 1990s, there was increasing scrutiny of affirmative action at all levels in the political system. Some states, meanwhile, took their own line on affirmative action. Via a 1996 proposition (209), Californians voted to end it in education and the public services. There was a year-long delay in the state courts before the policy was enacted (1997). In 1998, Washington became the second state to outlaw affirmative action, passing the *Initiative 200* law. In 2000, Governor Jeb Bush's *One Florida* initiative succeeded in banning race as a factor in college admissions policies. Such moves reflected a growing hostility to the whole idea. Conservatives in many states were resistant to the idea, opposition that was not confined to white Americans. Some successful African Americans shared the sense of resentment about programmes that tended to devalue success achieved on the basis of merit. In *The Content of our Character*, a black commentator, Shelby Steele, argued that, not only

was the value of qualifications being undermined but, more seriously, affirmative action tended to reinforce feelings of black inferiority to white Americans.

From time to time, a particular issue arises that brings the matter into national prominence once again. The case of *Taxman* v. *Township Board of Education* (1997) concerned events in Piscataway, New Jersey. The school board, faced with the need to make economies, sacked a white teacher, Sharon Taxman, rather than her black colleague, and made the racial basis for the decision explicit. The Supreme Court decided that diversity was not a sufficient rationale for considering race, except 'to remedy past discrimination or as the result of a manifest imbalance in the employment of minorities'. The governmental review accepted that 'a simple desire to promote diversity for its own sake . . . is not a permissible basis for taking race into account'.

Bill Clinton called for a modification of affirmative-action programmes in the light of court judgments. But, in the private sector, such programmes continued to be popular with many large companies that see them as a means of winning or maintaining a market share for their products among minority communities. Their approach was a relevant factor in the policy of the University of Michigan over admissions. By its rulings in 2003, the Supreme Court maintained its commitment to diversity as a laudable goal and accepted that race could be a factor, among others, in making decisions over recruitment. In *Gratz* v. *Bollinger* and *Grutter* v. *Bollinger*, the justices reaffirmed the spirit of the Baake judgment. They found against the admissions policy of the university (based as it was on additional points for being a member of an ethnic minority) but allowed the approach adopted by the Law School (considering issues of race and diversity on a practical basis) to continue.

Affirmative action remains contentious. Its opponents are aware of ambiguities in recent Court judgments, and are likely to feel encouraged to continue their campaign to put the policy finally to rest.

See also **Regents of the University of California Regents** *v.* **Baake** *(1978)*; **Gratz** *v.* **Bollinger** *and*

Grutter *v.* Bollinger *(2003)*; Piscataway Board of Education *v.* Taxman *(1989)*

Afghanistan

The War in Afghanistan (2001–present) was launched in response to the attack on the World Trade Center on 11 September 2001. It began on 7 October with the invasion of NATO-backed troops, *Operation Enduring Freedom* (*OEF*) marking the beginning of the Bush administration's War on Terrorism campaign. The stated purpose of the invasion was to capture Osama Bin Laden, destroy al-Qaeda forces and oust the Taliban regime which had provided support and safe harbour to al-Qaeda.

The United States and Britain led the aerial bombing campaign, with ground forces supplied primarily by the Afghan Northern Alliance. In 2002, US and British infantry joined the attack. In December 2001, NATO-led troops were added, as part of the Coalition of the Willing. These operated under the name of the *International Security Assistance Force* (*ISAF*), an international stabilisation force authorised by the United Nations Security Council. Apart from America and Britain, troops and aircraft have been sent to Afghanistan by Australia, Canada, Denmark, France and Norway, among several other countries. After the initial attack, the Taliban's conventional force dissolved and the war turned into an insurgency that has continued ever since. In July 2006, the ISAF assumed command of the south of the country and, in October, also of east Afghanistan.

In his election campaign, Barack Obama promised to end the hostilities in Iraq and switch the focus to Afghanistan. Soon after becoming president, he pledged to send an additional 21,000 troops (bringing the total to some 68,000) and to intensify counter-insurgency efforts. But in 2009 casualties have been rising and many politicians in Washington have lost faith in the Afghan president, Hamid Karzai, especially after the presidential elections of August 2009, which were tainted by evidence of widespread fraud and malpractice. In these circumstances, public support for the war has dropped dramatically and there is a clear division between those who feel that it is imperative

that the West protects its interests and security by continuing the war for as long as it takes and those who say that it is becoming an increasing muddle in which the objectives have become confused.

The campaign in Afghanistan successfully unseated the Taliban from power but has been significantly less successful at achieving the primary policy goal of ensuring that al-Qaeda can no longer operate there. A resurgence of Taliban violence, growing illegal drug production (a major source of funding for the Taliban) and fragile governmental institutions point to the weakness of the state. The increase in Taliban power has led to increased human rights violations against women in Afghanistan. According to Amnesty International, the Taliban commit war crimes by targeting civilians, killing teachers, abducting aid workers and burning school buildings.

The link between Afghanistan and al-Qaeda has dimmed in memory in the years since the 9/11 attacks and Osama bin Laden remains at large. Meanwhile, the fighting grinds on, leaving the Administration with key decisions to take over the coming months.

See also *al-Qaeda*; *Coalition of the Willing*; *Guantánamo Bay*; *War on Terrorism*

AFL/CIO see *American Federation of Labor and Congress of Industrial Organizations*

African Americans

African Americans are Black Americans of African ancestry. Most Black Americans are descendants of captive Africans who survived the era of US slavery, although some are – or are descended from – voluntary immigrants from Africa, the Caribbean, Central America, South America or elsewhere. In total, they account for about 13 per cent of the US population. Their numbers have increased significantly over the last few decades, the 23 million of 1970 rising to more than 36 million today. Until the twentieth century, most blacks lived in the South and 54 per cent still do so; 19 per cent live in the Midwest, 18 per cent in the Northeast and 10 per cent in the West. In the

South, ten states have black populations of over a million and the population of four states is more than a quarter black. Many cities have a large African American population, much of which is often to be found in poorer quarters (e.g., New York has 2.3 million and Chicago 1.1 million). Gary (Indiana) and Detroit (Michigan) have the largest black majorities, in both cases exceeding 80 per cent.

The black population has for much of the last one hundred years sought to improve its position in American society. Freed as a result of the Civil War, it was long denied full participation and recognition. Its struggle to advance its position and achieve civil rights has been an important feature of post-war politics. The freedom rides and sit-ins, the marches and boycotts, posed problems for white Americans as they finally had to concede a greater measure of equal treatment than they had ever contemplated before.

Issues of racial division and race relations have bedevilled America for much of its short history and, though blacks have achieved greater rights and political power, they tend to be worse off, with an average income substantially below that of the white population; one-third of the black population lives below the poverty line. In places as far apart as Los Angeles and Detroit, riots have from time to time broken out in the ghettos as a result of deprivation and discrimination. It is a matter of political contention as to whether the black population should be helped by policies, such as affirmative action, which provide certain groups with greater opportunities to achieve a range of positions long denied them.

See also *Affirmative Action*; *Black Power*; *Civil Rights Movement*; *King, Martin Luther*

Agenda-setting Theory

Agenda-setting theory is concerned with explaining the extent to which the amount of media coverage of an an issue has an impact upon the public's attention to, and interest in, that issue. It was pioneered in 1972 by Maxwell McCombs and Donald Shaw in their study (1972) of the role of the media in the 1968 presidential campaign. Agenda-setting theorists argue that organs of mass communication have a large influence on audiences by their choice of the stories they consider newsworthy and the prominence and space they allocate to them.

Increasingly over recent decades, the media have influenced the political agenda. They cannot directly tell people what to think but they can tell them what to think about. They influence the public by determining what is shown or read so that many of the viewers/readers come to accept what is offered as a representation of the main things that are really happening.

Television in particular helps to set the agenda for discussion. Journalists (or more particularly their editors) and producers of television and radio programmes decide on what they consider to be the key issues worthy of investigation and follow-up reporting and commentary. If they choose to highlight the character of a candidate, the budget deficit or the problems of the ghettos, then these may well become influential factors in shaping the image that Americans have of personalities or events.

When members of the public are familiar with issues and events, the media may have less impact on their attitudes. A study conducted in 1981–82 found that, as people were exposed to media information alleging that the national defences were weak, they became increasingly concerned about the subject. Stories relating to inflation, however, had little impact on the views of those who read or heard them because inflation affects people personally and those surveyed were in a position to reach their own conclusions. Thus, the media wield the most influence in shaping the agenda when the issues raised are beyond individual experience or new topics with which people have yet to become familiar.

See also *Television and Politics*

Alito, Samuel (1950–)

Samuel Alito is the junior and 110th Associate Justice of the Supreme Court, having previously served as a United States attorney and a judge on the Court of Appeals for the Third Circuit. Of Italian descent, he is a practising Roman Catholic.

President Bush's nomination of Alito proved highly controversial. Whereas the ABA's Standing Committee on Federal Judiciary rated him as 'well qualified', the American Civil Liberties Union argued that his record was one of limiting freedoms, and pro-life activists claimed that his confirmation would be a victory for the anti-abortion cause. In the January Senate hearings, Democrat senators characterised him as a hard right conservative in the mould of a Clarence Thomas or Robert Bork. After a failed filibuster attempt by Senator Kerry in the Senate hearings, his nomination was confirmed by a narrow vote of 58 to 42, making it one of the most controversial in American history.

Since becoming an associate justice, Alito has often voted with conservative members of the Court. On the abortion issue, he has supported some restrictions on the procedure, but has not stated a willingness to overturn *Roe* v. *Wade*. In the landmark free speech case *Morse* v. *Frederick* (2007), Alito joined Roberts' majority decision that speech advocating drug use can be banned in public schools. He also warned, however, that the ruling must be circumscribed so that it does not interfere with political speech, such as the discussion of the medical marijuana debate.

al-Qaeda

This is the name given to a network of radical Islamic fundamentalists intensely opposed to the United States, whose supporters wish to reduce outside influence upon Islamic affairs. It comprises independent and collaborative cells in more than fifty countries, to which it dispenses funding and logistical support. Classified by the United States State Department, the United Nations and the United Kingdom as an international terrorist organisation, al-Qaeda is believed to have been responsible for a large number of high-profile, violent attacks against civilians, military targets and commercial institutions in the West and in the Muslim world, most notably the 9/11 attacks on the World Trade Center in New York and the London bombings of July 2005.

See also *Attack on World Trade Center; Terrorism*

American Civil Liberties Union (ACLU)

The American Civil Liberties Union was established in 1920 as a non-profit and non-partisan organisation committed to defending the individual rights and liberties guaranteed to every person in the United States by the Constitution, Bill of Rights and laws of the United States. The mission of the ACLU today remains the same, to preserve all of the protections and guarantees proclaimed in the Constitution and the Bill of Rights, including:

- First Amendment rights – freedom of speech, association and assembly; freedom of the press, and freedom of religion
- The right to equal protection under the law – equal treatment regardless of race, sex, religion or national origin
- The right to due process – fair treatment by the government whenever the loss of liberty or property is at stake
- The right to privacy – freedom from unwarranted government intrusion into personal and private affairs.

The ACLU claims to have more than 500,000 members and supporters. It engages in lobbying elected officials and in providing legal assistance in cases in which civil liberties are deemed to be in jeopardy. On occasion, it brings lawsuits on behalf of those groups and individuals whose freedoms are under threat. Other than providing direct legal assistance, it also submits amicus curiae briefs on matters of concern. It handles nearly 6,000 court cases annually from the offices it occupies in almost every state.

The ACLU has maintained the position that civil liberties must be respected even in times of national emergency. This has led it to criticise individuals and policies of both main political parties, particularly any president whose actions appear to show insufficient respect for basic freedoms. In recent years, it has been particularly critical of the detention of terrorist suspects at Guantánamo Bay. It has also taken up issues involving due process and voting rights, and been active in its opposition to the law signed by President

Bush in 2007 that gave the administration virtually substantial powers to monitor Americans'
international phone calls and e-mails and granted
immunity to telecommunications companies that
illegally aided in the wiretapping programme.

American Dream

The phrase 'the American Dream' encapsulates
the widespread belief that, by hard work and individual enterprise, even the most poor and lowly
Americans can achieve economic success, a better
way of life and enhanced social status in a land of
immense opportunity. According to the Dream,
there are no insurmountable barriers that prevent
Americans from fulfilling their potential. All have
the chance to prosper, even if many individuals
and groups do not do so.

The term appears to have first been used in
a sentence in a history book by James Truslow
Adams entitled *The Epic of America* (1931):

> If, as I have said, the things already listed were all we
> had to contribute, America would have made no dis-
> tinctive and unique gift to mankind. But there has
> been also the *American dream*, that dream of a land
> in which life should be better and richer and fuller
> for every man, with opportunity for each according
> to his ability or achievement.

The Dream is often referred to in American liter-
ature and has been a theme of many a Hollywood
film. In a speech to the Democratic Leadership
Council (1993), former President Clinton spoke
of it as the 'dream that we were all raised on'. It
was one based on a simple and powerful idea: that
'if you work hard and play by the rules you should
be given a chance to go as far as your God-given
ability will take you'. Americans tend to be valued
as individuals, according to what they make of
their chances in life.

American Exceptionalism

American exceptionalism is the belief that
American society and culture are exceptional in
comparison with those of other advanced industrial countries. In a sense, this is true of all
societies and cultures, and commentators might
equally point out that there are several things

that they have in common. But supporters of the
'exceptionalist' viewpoint suggest that several features distinguish the country from other Western
democracies. It was the Frenchman, Alexis de
Tocqueville (1805–59), who, in 1835, first wrote
of 'American exceptionalism'. He saw the United
States as 'a society uniquely different from the
more traditional societies and status-bound
nations of the Old World'. It was 'qualitively different in its organising principles and political and
religious institutions from . . . other western societies', some of its distinguishing features being a
relatively high level of social egalitarianism and
social mobility, enthusiasm for religion, love of
country, and ethnic and racial diversity.

A number of politicians and writers have reinforced this idea that theirs is a 'chosen people'
that has made a special contribution to humankind and whose actions have been guided by a
'special providence'. Such thinking leads some
Americans to claim that their country has a superior culture to that of other nations. They see it as
a bastion of liberty and democracy, qualities that
ideally should be exported abroad so that other
peoples might share in the experience.

In his second inaugural address, Bill Clinton
echoed 'exceptionalist' thinking, in his listing of
his country's many achievements:

> What a century it has been. America became the
> world's mightiest industrial power, saved the world
> from tyranny in two world wars and a long cold
> war, and time and time again reached across the
> globe to millions who longed for the blessings of lib-
> erty. Along the way, Americans produced the great
> middle class and security in old age; built unrivaled
> centers of learning and opened public schools to all;
> split the atom and explored the heavens; invented
> the computer and the microchip; made a revolution
> in civil rights for minorities; and extended the circle
> of citizenship, giving opportunity and dignity to
> women.

American Federation of Labor and Congress of Industrial Organizations (AFL/CIO)

The AFL/CIO is a voluntary federation of fifty-
six national and international labour organisations,

with approaching eleven million members. It was established in 1955 as the outcome of a merger between the American Federation of Labor, a craft union federation representing skilled workers founded in 1866, and the Congress of Industrial Organizations, an alliance of mass industrial unions set up in 1935. It includes most large unions representing the interests of organised labour, although between 2003 and 2005 an intense internal debate over the future of the labour movement in the United States resulted in the secession of three of the four largest unions, including the International Brotherhood of Teamsters (the truckers' union). This left the American Federation of State, County and Municipal Employees (AFSCME), as the most sizeable affiliate, with more than a million members.

The peak years of membership of the AFL/CIO lasted from the Great Depression to the 1960s. Thereafter, it was hit by the decline in the percentage of the workforce engaged in heavy industry union membership and the loss of esteem that unions in general experienced. It is still regarded as a powerful pressure group because of its financial resources, large number of paid organisers and sizeable mass membership. It has been active in recent elections in supporting Democratic candidates, spending heavily on advertising campaigns and seeking to mobilise union members and their families to vote. In 2008, it pledged its energy, funding and grassroots membership to work towards the election of Barack Obama.

See also *Trade Unions*

American Medical Association (AMA)

Originally founded in 1847, the American Medical Association is the largest association of medical doctors and medical students in the United States. Its declared mission is to promote the art and science of medicine for the betterment of the public health, to advance the interests of physicians and their patients, to promote public health, to lobby for legislation favourable to physicians and patients, and to raise money for medical education. It also publishes the *Journal of the*

American Medical Association (JAMA), which has the largest circulation of any weekly medical journal in the world.

The AMA has long been regarded as a highly influential professional group, its strong position deriving from the respect that society awards to its members and from the expertise or specialised knowledge that they possess. It has at times become embroiled in political and social controversy. It campaigned strongly against the introduction of Medicare in the 1950s and 1960s, but came round to support it. In the 1990s, it was part of the coalition that defeated the health care reform proposed by President Clinton. It originally opposed abortion in the nineteenth and early twentieth centuries, but changed its position and, in 1967, declared its support for reform of the abortion laws. More recently, it has supported a ban on partial birth abortions.

The Association now acknowledges the need for reform of health care provision and has endorsed the Obama goal of a massive overhaul of the system. It is involved in discussions with the Administration and Congress to expand health insurance coverage to the uninsured, but is wary of 'public option' schemes.

At one time, the AMA dominated discussion of medical provision but today it is one of many medical interests organised to represent medical specialisms and the employers and insurance companies which pay for, and underwrite, most medical care.

American Taliban

The American Taliban is a pejorative term used in relation to some American conservative fundamentalist Christians by their opponents. It was coined shortly after the overthrow of the Islamic fundamentalist Taliban regime in Afghanistan (2001) as a means of drawing attention to alleged parallels between that regime and what was portrayed as the American equivalent. It implied that both were characterised by a fear of change and modernity, exhibiting similar opposition to progressive social policies involving such issues as the rights of ethnic minorities, women and gays. Those who use the phrase fear that such attitudes are deeply ingrained within American politics.

They claim that under the Republican regime of George W. Bush fundamentalist Christians had undue political significance and were in a position to influence political decisions via their position in or around government.

See also *Christian Coalition*; *Fundamentalism*; *Religious Right*

Amicus Curiae Briefs

Amicus curiae is a Latin term translated as 'friend of the court'. It refers to written briefs submitted to the Supreme Court by individuals or organisations that are not themselves party to a lawsuit but wish to express their opinions. They may offer information on their interpretation of a point of law or some other aspect of the case to assist the court in deciding the matter before it. More often, they do so in the hope of influencing feelings among the justices towards their viewpoint. The information may be a legal opinion in the form of a testimony that has not been solicited by any of the parties, or it may be a learned treatise on some matter relevant to the case.

Amicus curiae briefs are much favoured by powerful pressure groups that have a sizeable legal budget. Bodies such as the American Civil Liberties Union frequently submit such briefs to advocate for or against a particular legal change or interpretation. If a decision could affect an entire industry, companies other than the litigant(s) may wish to air their concerns.

See also *Supreme Court*

Anti-federalists

Anti-federalism is the name given to a movement in the late eighteenth-century US politics that opposed the Constitution proposed at the Philadelphia Convention. Many anti-federalists sought to leave intact the government under the Articles of Confederation. Others believed that, while the existing national government was too weak, the national government under the Constitution would be excessively strong. They noted the warning given by James Monroe of Virginia: 'Never grant to Rulers an atom of power

that is not most clearly and inispensably necessary for the safety and wellbeing of Society.'

Anti-federalists emphasised five major themes:

1. the need for a bill of rights;
2. the danger of a centralised government which would chip away at states' rights;
3. the belief that the document was geared to the needs of aristocratic interests;
4. fear of the Congressional power to tax;
5. fear of the possibility of a standing army.

Anti-federalists comprised three main groups: backcountry farmers and artisans, the middling sort (there was no definitive middle class then) and an elite including Eldridge Gerry of Massachusetts, George Mason of Virginia and Luther Martin of Maryland. The leading spokesmen were largely state-centred men with regional and local interests and loyalties. Madison wrote of the Massachusetts anti-federalists that 'there was not a single character capable of uniting their wills or directing their measures . . . They had no plan whatever.'

Many anti-federalists believed that the Constitution represented the work of aristocratic politicians who were bent on protecting their own class interests. At the Massachusetts convention one delegate declared:

> These lawyers, and men of learning and moneyed men, that . . . make us poor illiterate people swallow down the pill . . . they will swallow up all us little folks like the great Leviathan; yes, just as the whale swallowed up Jonah!

During the course of debate over the ratification, numerous independent local speeches and articles were published all across the country. Initially, many of the articles were written under pseudonyms, such as 'Brutus' and 'Federal Farmer'. They produced a vast range of political writing, however, the best and most influential of which was gathered by historians into a collection known as the *Anti-Federalist Papers*.

The inclusion of the Bill of Rights within the Constitution was a concession to the fears of the anti-federalists, to counter their anxieties that it would – unless modified – lead to a process of centralisation and the imposition of elite rule.

Arms for Hostages Scandal see *Irangate*

Articles of Confederation

Written in 1776–7, the Articles of Confederation and Perpetual Union, commonly known as the Articles of Confederation, was the first governing document or constitution of the newly independent United States. The final draft was written in the summer of 1777 and adopted by the Second Continental Congress in November 1777, in York, Pennsylvania. In practice, the Articles served as the de facto system of government until they were adopted and became *de jure* following final ratification in March 1781. At that point Congress became the Congress of the Confederation.

The thirteen Articles laid out the way in which the United States confederation would function, establishing a national legislature, the Continental Congress, but with most authority resting with state legislatures. (Congress served as the final court for disputes between states.) Article 2 asserted the precedence of the separate states over the confederation government: 'Each state retains its sovereignty, freedom, and independence, and every power, jurisdiction, and right, which is not by this Confederation expressly delegated.' The confederation government was granted only a limited role, being able to wage war, negotiate diplomatic agreements, resolve issues regarding the western territories, and print and borrow money inside and outside the United States.

Those who favoured a more powerful central state argued that that the confederation government lacked taxing authority, having to request funds from the states. A second concern was its one-state, one-vote plank which was resented by larger states which were expected to contribute more than smaller states but still carried the same voting strength. Again, while the Articles created a mutual defence confederation designed to manage the American Revolutionary War, the Articles provided no mechanism to ensure states complied with requests for troops. At times, this left the military in a precarious position.

The Articles of Confederation were in force from 1 March 1781 until 4 March 1789, when the new constitutional arrangements hammered out at the Philadelphia Convention came into effect. This first constitution came into being at a time when Americans had a deep-seated fear of a central authority and long-standing loyalty to the state in which they lived and often called their 'country'. Ultimately, the Articles proved unwieldy and inadequate to resolve the issues that faced the United States in its earliest years but, in granting any federal powers to a central authority – the Confederation Congress – they marked a crucial step towards nationhood.

Asian Americans

The term 'Asian American' generally refers to those who are of Asian ancestry and held American citizenship although it may be extended to include non-citizen resident Asians as well, be they living in the United States legally or illegally. It replaces the earlier term 'oriental' (commonly used until the 1960s) which is now viewed as being derogatory or having colonialist implications.

Many of the American Asians originally settled in California and the Western states having journeyed from China and Japan. More recent immigrants have come from the Philippines, South Korea and South-east Asia (especially Cambodia and Vietnam) but the area of settlement remains broadly the same: California and Hawaii, as well as the capital, Washington DC. Approximately half of the heavily urbanised American Asian population lives in the West (49 per cent), followed by 20 per cent in the Northeast and 19 per cent in the Midwest.

Today, there are more than ten million Asian Americans, nearly twelve million if we include those who reported Asian and at least one other race. They arrived in substantial numbers in the 1970s and 1980s but the rate of increase has accelerated so that today they are among the fastest growing racial/ethnic groups and constitute some 5 per cent of the US population. The number of

'Asian alones' rose by nearly 50 per cent in the decade to 2000. The largest ethnic subgroups are in descending order, Chinese, Filipinos, Asian Indians, Koreans, Vietnamese and Japanese, all of whom number in excess of one million. Inevitably, much of the discussion of the place of American Asians in US society focuses on these largest ethnic groups that represent the vast majority of the Asian American population.

With a majority Asian–Pacific American population for most of its history, Hawaii has a long history of Asian political participation at all levels of government. The first Asian American to win election at federal level in Washington, however, was elected to the House of Representatives in 1956, the first to the Senate in 1976. Norman Mineta, born of Japanese parents, went on to become Secretary of Transportation between 2001 and 2006. In the 111th Congress there are ten Asian members of the House and two in the Senate.

Sometimes, Asian Americans are referred to as a 'model minority' because the Asian American culture emphasises the work ethic, respect for elders and high valuation of family. Statistics, such as household income and low rate of criminality, are also seen by many white Americans as encouraging indicators of the Asian contribution to American society. A study published by the Committee of 100 (2001) found several positive perceptions of Chinese Americans in particular, with strong family values being mentioned by 91 per cent, honesty as business people by 77 per cent and high value on education by 67 per cent. Yet there remains a widespread perception that Asian Americans are not 'American' but are instead 'perpetual foreigners'. Asian Americans typically report being asked the question 'Where are you really from?' by other Americans, regardless of how long they or their ancestors have lived in United States.

Most Asian groups have advanced in American society, though there are occasional outbreaks of hostile feeling towards their members. In the past, the Chinese, and especially the Japanese, were the victims of regular discrimination; in 1942 many of the latter were interned in camps because of their 'doubtful' allegiance. Since then, much of the anti-Asian prejudice has disappeared.

Attack on World Trade Center (9/11 Attacks)

On 11 September 2001, there were two sudden, suicide aircraft attacks on the 110-storey World Trade Center in New York, a building that symbolised the business life of America. An aeroplane, reportedly a hijacked American Airlines jet, slammed into one of the 'twin towers', at the height of a morning rush hour in the nation's largest city. As smoke and flames poured out of the building and rescue workers battled to save victims, a second plane hit the second tower. The two towers soon collapsed. Huge clouds of smoke hung over Manhattan. The nearby Wall Street financial markets were shut down. A short time later, another aircraft struck the Pentagon, touching off a massive explosion and fire, and tearing a hole in one side of the historic building. There was immediate chaos, confusion and massive destruction. In total, the terrorist attacks were shown to have caused 2,993 deaths (including nineteen hijackers). Another twenty-four people went 'missing, presumed dead'. The victims were predominantly civilians.

Earlier in the morning the nineteen terrorists had hijacked four commercial passenger jet airliners. The passengers and members of the flight crew of the fourth aircraft attempted to retake control of their plane from the hijackers, and the plane crashed into a field in rural Somerset County, Pennsylvania.

Rescue and recovery efforts took months to complete. It took several weeks simply to put out the fires burning in the rubble of the buildings, the smouldering and smoke lasting for ninety-nine days before the fire was completely out. The final clearance and clean-up of the site was not completed until May 2002. The immediate response of the public was one of gratitude towards uniformed public-safety workers and especially towards firefighters involved in the rescue work. Many police officers and rescue workers from elsewhere in the country took leaves of absence to travel to New York City to assist in the grim process of recovering bodies from the twisted remnants of the Twin Towers. Over the following weeks, incidents of harassment and hate crimes against Middle Easterners were reported and there were reports of verbal abuse and attacks on mosques and other religious buildings.

President Bush vowed that 'terrorism will not stand' and immediately broke off a visit to Florida to return to Washington. In the days following the attacks, his approval ratings soared to 86 per cent. He spoke to the nation on 20 September and addressed a joint session of the United States Congress, regarding the events of 9/11, the intervening days of rescue and recovery efforts, and how he intended to respond. The high-profile role played by New York City Mayor, Rudy Giuliani, won him high praise as well, both in New York and in the nation at large.

Intelligence sources immediately pointed to Islamic extremists as being responsible. Osama Bin Laden and his al-Qaeda organisation were named as the guilty parties. Once the aggressor was confirmed, President Bush was under strong pressure from elements within the United States to act swiftly but he did not take any drastic measures straight away. Acting in concert with the British government, he attempted to create an international coalition to wage war on international terrorism. In the immediate aftermath of the attacks, US officials publicly speculated on possible involvement by Saddam Hussein. Although this proved to be unfounded, the association in the public mind between terrorism and the Iraqi dictator later contributed to public acceptance of the invasion of Iraq in March 2003.

The collapse of the twin towers jolted the Bush presidency into what was then uncharacteristic vigour. It moved into a higher gear and Bush became more focused and purposeful. Washington reorganised itself around the executive branch and Bush reorganised his administration around the struggle against terrorism. Almost at once, he persuaded Congress to approve a substantial recovery package that also made additional provision to allow for the strengthening of the intelligence and security services. It also quickly passed an anti-terrorism bill that greatly increased the potential of executive power.

See also *Afghanistan*; *al-Qaeda*; *Terrorism*

Axis of Evil

The 'axis of evil' was a term used by George W. Bush during his State of the Union speech (2002) in reference to three countries, Iran, Iraq and Korea which were accused of sponsoring terrorism and developing weapons of mass destruction. He claimed that their ruling regimes posed 'a grave and growing danger'.

At the time and subsequently, there was mounting international concern – even among some of America's allies – that the Bush regime was preparing to open a new front in its war against terrorism. Critics pointed out that the three countries were very unlike one another. Also, whereas the Axis powers that opposed the Allies in World War II had co-ordinated their public policy, this was not true of Iran, Iraq and North Korea, making the term 'axis' technically inappropriate.

See also *Rogue States*

B

Baby Boomers

In the United States baby boomers is the term used for those people who were born there between 1946 and 1964. Following World War II, there was a temporary peak in the birth rate in several countries (including the United Kingdom) known as the baby boom. The term was coined in the United States, several years after the phenomenon had ended, to describe Americans of that generation. Over time, the connotations of the term have widened beyond the post-war spike in the birth rate. Some of the 'boomers' developed rebellious, anti-establishment attitudes that have been carried on into older age and stand in marked contrast with an earlier, more deferential society.

Former president Bill Clinton is perhaps the archetypal baby boomer. With his penchant for playing the saxophone, feeling everyone's pain and his admission that he flirted with marijuana (without inhaling), Clinton has come to symbolise a generation that shook up Western society. Some younger and more environmentally minded commentators have noted that the baby boomers' fondness for conspicuous consumption and foreign travel has led to many a modern-day ill, from rising debt to environmental woes.

The major economic, social and demographic changes through which the baby boomers have lived have given them a unique position. Healthier and wealthier than previous generations, many of them can look forward to an active old age that was denied to their forebears and may also be denied to future ones as western economies struggle to maintain pension and welfare provision. The Brookings Institution calculates that by 2030 the generation dominated by largely white boomers will be making away for a younger and much more diverse American population.

Bail-out

A bail-out refers to a situation in which government develops a rescue package through which it offers money to a failing business or businesses, in order to prevent the consequences that would arise from its failure. The Bush administration's Emergency Economic Stabilization Act of 2008 was commonly referred to as a bail-out of the United States's financial system. The Obama Treasury Secretary Timothy Geithner offered a further programme to bail out the very banks whose mistakes were widely believed to have contributed to the financial crisis in the United States and many other parts of the globe. He announced a massive package and envisioned a far greater government role in markets and banks than at any time since the 1930s. Administration officials committed the government to flooding the financial system with as much as $2.5 trillion, $350 billion of that coming from the bail-out fund and the rest from the Federal Reserve and private investors.

See also *Credit Crunch (Squeeze)*; *Financial Crisis*; *Fiscal Stimulus*; *Paulson Plan*

Baker v. *Carr* (1962) and *Reynold* v. *Sims* (1964)

Baker v. *Carr* (1962) was a landmark case that came before the Warren Court. The Court ruled that the districts used as a basis for elections to state legislatures must be drawn in an equitable way. It established the one man, one vote, one value principle which, in practice, means that electoral districts used for state legislatures and the House of Representatives in Washington should have a broadly comparable number of voters.

Apportionment issues had long been controversial. Previously, minorities and urban and suburban residents had been discriminated against in the districting process, for the malapportioned legislatures had reflected the dominance of conservative rural and small-town interests. The particular case concerned Tennessee which had failed to reapportion the state legislature for sixty years, in spite of its population growth and changing distribution. Charles Baker, a voter, brought a suit against the state (Joe Carr was the state official in charge of elections) in the federal district court, claiming that the dilution of his vote because of the failure to reapportion was a violation of the equal protection clause of the Fourteenth Amendment to the Constitution. The court dismissed the complaint on the grounds that it could not decide a political question. Baker appealed to the Supreme Court which ruled that a case raising a political issue would be heard. This landmark decision opened the way for many further cases on legislative apportionment. Reapportionment issues were no longer to be regarded as purely political questions but also as justiciable ones so that, in future, federal courts would be able to intervene and decide in reapportionment cases.

The decision was important in changing the whole nature of state legislatures and state and local politics not just in the South but throughout the country. It also marked a growing willingness on the part of the Supreme Court to become involved in matters that had traditionally been a state prerogative.

Having declared reapportionment issues justiciable in the Baker case, the Court laid out a new test for evaluating such claims in *Reynolds* v. *Sims* (1964). In that case, the Court formulated the 'one-man, one-vote' standard for legislative districting, holding that each individual had to be weighted equally in legislative apportionment. The Court decided that in states with bicameral legislatures both houses had to be apportioned on this standard. It thereby voided the provision of the Arizona constitution which had provided for two state senators from each county, the California constitution providing for one senator from each county, and similar provisions elsewhere.

See also *Reapportionment; Warren, Earl (1891–1974)/Warren Court*

Balanced Budget Amendment

The Balanced Budget Amendment can refer to any one of various proposed amendments to the Constitution which would require a balance in the projected revenues and expenditures of the US government. Most such proposals make an exception allowable in times of war or national emergency. The Balanced Budget Amendment advanced in 1995 was proposed as a means of forcing Congress to tackle the national debt problem. If successful, the amendment would have required federal spending not to exceed the government's own revenue each year, except in the exemptions mentioned above.

Congress had already introduced a number of reforms to the budgetary process in an attempt to control levels of government spending. The 1988 Gramm–Rudman–Hollings Act included a plan to eliminate the annual budget deficit to zero by 1993 but the attempt was unsuccessful and was replaced by a series of agreements that met with a similar lack of success. The issue of reducing or eliminating the national debt had played a key role in the 1992 presidential election in which Ross Perot had made the issue of deficit reduction ('balancing the books') the central item in his platform. When the Republicans took control of Congress in 1995, there was increased public and congressional support for a Balanced Budget Amendment to the Constitution which, it was hoped, would force Congress to keep annual expenditure below government revenues.

Introduction of the Balanced Budget Amendment was an important part of the Contract with America. A resolution quickly passed through the House of Representatives but was defeated by one vote in the Senate (as happened again in 1997). Democratic opposition to the

Amendment was stronger in the Senate than in the House. Moreover, the rules and procedures of the Senate provided more opportunities to block its passage. Whereas Republicans argued that without such an amendment, Congress would never have the backbone to balance the budget, Democrats – including the Clinton administration – counter-argued that courage could not be written into the Constitution. Moreover, they felt that insisting on reduced expenditure – even during an economic downturn – would harm the poor and the elderly who were dependent on government programmes. They claimed that the Republicans had not adequately explained which programmes would be trimmed to achieve a budgetary balance.

Bible Belt

The term 'Bible Belt' describes an area of the United States of America noted for its socially conservative Christian Evangelical Protestantism. Exact boundaries do not exist, but the Belt is usually considered to cover the area stretching from Texas in the Southwest, northwest to Kansas, north to most of Missouri, northeast to Virginia and southeast to northern Florida. Originally an Anglican stronghold, the region was transformed into a bastion of conservative Protestantism in the nineteenth century as it became the base for highly popular religious revivalist movements often associated with the Southern Baptist denomination. The phrase 'Bible Belt' was reputedly coined by the American journalist and social commentator H. L. Mencken in the early 1920s in his reporting of the Scopes ('monkey') Trial in Dayton, Tennessee in July 1925.

The term has subsequently been deployed by a range of social and political commentators, to suggest that discussion of education, politics and social change in the region is greatly influenced by religious faith and observance. Many of the social conservatives are religious fundamentalists who interpret every word of the Bible as being literally true, a position that influences their approach to issues such as abortion and gay rights. Many are also strongly Republican and, in presidential elections, states such as Alabama, Kansas, Mississippi, North Carolina, Oklahoma, South Carolina, Texas and Virginia have consistently supported the Republicans in the elections of the last thirty years.

'Big Mo'/'Little Mo'

'Big mo' refers to the beneficial momentum of events and feelings that derives from success in an election campaign. Traditionally, the momentum that comes with victory (or a surprisingly strong finish) magically transforms itself into more media coverage, more campaign contributions and higher national poll ratings. This is the moment when perception and reality merge, as looking and behaving like a winner are nearly synonymous to being one.

The term was first used in 1980 by an exultant George H. Bush who had just gained success in Iowa's caucus precinct contests. Then, and in subsequent campaigns, the term has been used to describe the drive, mounting confidence and self-belief that derive from a substantial amount of success.

By contrast, 'Little mo' refers to the relative lack of momentum that derives from a flat campaign.

Bill of Rights

The Bill of Rights comprises the first ten amendments to the United States Constitution that were proposed by the first Congress, ratified by eleven states in 1791 and intended to protect individual liberties and rights from actions of the new national government.

Much of the early opposition to the Constitution itself was not centred on resistance to increased federal power at the expense of the states but more on anxiety that the rights of individuals were insufficiently protected. There was widespread agreement that a set of constitutional amendments must be drafted to provide specific guarantees of individual rights, although this would not happen until after a government under the new Constitution had been established.

The contents of the Bill of Rights

James Madison was much involved in the drafting of the ten amendments. At a time of ideological

---

The Bill of Rights: a summary of the first ten amendments to the Constitution and their purpose

Protections afforded fundamental rights and freedoms

Amendment 1: Freedom of religion, speech, press, and assembly; the right to petition the government

Protections against arbitrary military action

Amendment 2: The right to bear arms and maintain state militias (National Guard)
Amendment 3: Troops may not be quartered in homes in peacetime

Protection against arbitrary police and court action

Amendment 4: There can be no unreasonable searches or seizures
Amendment 5: Grand Jury indictment is required to prosecute a person for a serious crime. No 'double jeopardy' – a person cannot be tried twice for the same offence. It is prohibited to force a person to testify against himself or herself. There can be no loss of life, liberty or property without due process.
Amendment 6: The right to speedy, public, impartial trial with defence counsel, and the right to cross-examine witnesses.
Amendment 7: Jury trials in civil suits where the value exceeds 20 dollars.
Amendment 8: No excessive bail or fines; no cruel and unusual punishments.

Protections of states' rights and unnamed rights of the people

Amendment 9: Unlisted rights are not necessarily denied
Amendment 10: Powers not delegated to the United States or denied to states are reserved for the states or for the people.

The Bill of Rights was ratified in 1791 but its application was broadened significantly by the Fourteenth Amendment to the Constitution which was ratified in 1868. A key phrase in the Fourteenth Amendment – 'nor shall any state deprive any person of life, liberty, or property, without due process of law' – has been interpreted by the Supreme Court as forbidding the states from violating most of the rights and freedoms protected by the Bill of Rights.

N.b. The document originally proposed by Congress contained twelve amendments. The first, however (concerned with the number and apportionment of members of the House of Representatives) never became part of the Constitution, and the second (limiting the ability of Congress to increase the salaries of its members) was not ratified until the passage of the Twenty-seventh Amendment in 1992. The term 'Bill of Rights' has traditionally referred only to the ten amendments that became part of the Constitution in 1791, and not the first two dealing with Congress itself rather than with the rights of the people.

---

conflict between federalists and anti-federalists, he was unconvinced about the adequacy of the existing protection of liberties and rights and wanted to see them accorded clear constitutional guarantees. Those that he laid down in 1791 included a list of civil, religious and legal rights that remains intact today, in the same form in which it was originally set out. The first four establish individual rights; the next four concern the system of justice; and the last two are broader statements of constitutional intention.

The new document applied to the federal government only, for many Americans were unworried about possible tyranny in their own states. It was the central government of which they were suspicious although this fear has proved largely unfounded and many infringements of liberty have occurred at state and local level.

The Fourteenth Amendment was seen as meaning that states were bound by the Bill of Rights in the same way that the national government was. For many years, the Supreme Court did not so rule but, in 1925, in a landmark judgment in *Gitlow* v. *New York*, it was decided that:

> For present purposes, we may and do assume that freedom of speech and of the press – which are protected by the First Amendment from abridgement by Congress – are among the fundamental personal rights and liberties protected by the due process clause of the Fourteenth Amendment from impairment by the States.

The ruling was of profound importance and, once it had been accepted that freedom of speech and of the press were protected at state and local level by the First Amendment, so it was inevitable that other provisions of that same Amendment would be enforceable in the same way. Those rights laid down in 1791 – including rights of religion, assembly and petition – are now applicable to all levels of government.

Although the First Amendment has been accepted as binding, this is not true of all the other nine. A minority on the Supreme Court wished to proceed from the 1925 decision to make all freedoms protected by the Bill of Rights binding on the states. In other words, this would mean that the Bill of Rights would be incorporated fully into the Fourteenth Amendment.

This has not been the predominant opinion. The majority has taken the view that some provisions of the Bill of Rights should be included, in other words that there should be selective incorporation. Gradually the number of those original amendments that have come within the scope of the Fourteenth Amendment has been extended. Today, only the Second, Third, Seventh and Tenth do not apply at state and local levels – along with the Grand Jury requirements of the fifth. Other liberties not in the Bill of Rights also receive protection today – among these are the right of association, the right of privacy, the right to be presumed innocent and the right to travel freely.

Once much of the Bill of Rights was interpreted as being applicable at all levels, judges in state courts began to place more emphasis upon its provisions than upon those set out in state constitutions. More recently, however, there has been a more conservative leaning among the Supreme Court justices, and this has led to a greater interest in the protection offered by state guarantees. Justice Brennan (1977) became concerned about the way in which the Court was narrowly interpreting the scope of the Bill of Rights. He urged judges in state supreme courts to take up the challenge, noting that: 'State constitutions . . . are a font of individual liberties, their protection often extending beyond those required by the Supreme Court's interpretation of federal law.'

Bills

Public bills are those that set standards for the whole community in such matters as civil rights, environmental regulation and welfare, as opposed to private ones which set standards for interaction between individuals in such areas as contracts, divorce and personal injury. Here we are concerned with public bills.

Article I of the Constitution charges Congress with the duty of making binding laws. Section 8 of that article lists a series of specific congressional powers ('enumerated powers') such as coining money and establishing post offices, and gives Congress the power 'to make all laws which shall be necessary and proper for carrying into Execution the foregoing Powers, and all other Powers vested by this Constitution in the Government of the United States'. The effect of this 'necessary and proper' clause is that Congress can now legislate over a vast area of American life.

The process by which bills pass into law (see pp. 171–4) resembles an obstacle race for, of the many bills and resolutions introduced, only a small number are enacted, as the figures indicate. Any bill must pass through the process within the two years of a Congress, more being passed into the second session as members complete their consideration, and there is pressure to pass legislation before the next congressional elections.

Bills are introduced by a variety of methods.

	Bills/resolutions introduced in both chambers	Bills enacted
93rd Congress (1973–74)	23,396	649
98th Congress (1983–84)	10,559	623
103rd Congress (1993–94)	8,554	465
108th Congress (2003–04)	8,621	498

Some are drawn up in standing committees, some by special committees created to examine specific legislative issues, and some may be urged by the president or other executive offices. Individuals and outside organisations may suggest legislation to member of Congress, and individual members may themselves have ideas they wish to see pass into law.

See also *Legislation and Lawmaking*

Bipartisan Campaign Reform Act see *McCain–Feingold Campaign Finance Reform Act*

Black Panther Party

The Black Panther Party was an organisation that believed in armed revolution, an open war with white society. When it began to grow in the late 1960s, it became the largest organisation advocating Black Power. Supporters demanded full employment, decent housing, 'black' history in schools, the release of all black prisoners and exemption from military service. While firmly grounded in black nationalism and initially an organisation that accepted African American membership exclusively, the party reconsidered its position as it grew to national prominence. Members ultimately condemned black nationalism as 'black racism' and became more focused on the pursuit of socialist goals than racial exclusivity.

Panthers carried guns and were considered a serious threat to civil order, the more so as they attracted a wide variety of left-wing revolutionaries and political activists. Police and FBI harassment and imprisonment effectively destroyed the organisation in the early mid-1970s. There have been subsequent attempts to reform it in a new form but they have tended to be denounced by those involved in the original body.

Black Power

Black Power was a movement that was concerned with developing a sense of black consciousness in the United States. Supporters rejected the earlier ethnic term 'negro' which was associated by many white Americans with the idea of 'subservient niggers' and past humiliations.

Many black leaders were more confrontationalist than Dr King, among them Stokely Carmichael who rejected the NAACP approach to campaigning for civil rights. He and fellow militant activists felt that the whites would never surrender their supremacy. They rejected the integrationist ideas of King who was concerned not to alienate white liberals. They argued that integration was no longer possible or even desirable. Instead, they wanted to reject white society and urged the cause of black and white separation. In their view, the only route to attaining equality in positions of power was to oppose the evils of white authority by every possible means, including violence.

Carmichael urged the burning of 'every court house in Mississippi' and proclaimed the term 'black power', which was taken up by his supporters. They wanted to see black children taught pride in their black culture so that a generation would grow up willing to challenge those who suppressed them. Their stance was for the most part in direct conflict with that of the leadership of the mainstream Civil Rights Movement so that the two movements have often been viewed as inherently antagonistic. Yet certain groups and individuals participated in the crusade for civil rights and in black power activism.

The Nation of Islam is perhaps the best-known contemporary Black Power group. Another, espousing many of the philosophies common to Black Power, is the New Black Panthers who have become home to many former Nation of Islam members. Members of the original Black Panther Party of the 1960s–70s have insisted that this party is illegitimate, insisting that it promotes principles counter to their own revolutionary ideas.

See also *Blank Panther Party*; *Nation of Islam*

Block Grants

Block grants are discretionary grants handed over by the federal government to states or communities to be spent on broad functional areas such as counter-terrorism, education, health care, transport or welfare. Recipients can choose how the money is spent within the broad area covered by the transfer of funds. Few conditions attach to their use, so that federal oversight is less effectively maintained.

Conservatives have generally preferred this form of central funding. President Nixon – as part of his New Federalist approach – believed that black grants were an important element in his bid to recast the relationship between the tiers of government. His approach was not so much about curtailing the amount of money that reached the states and localities but more about how it got there. The need was identified locally, the money was provided by a block grant and then spent. President Reagan also favoured this approach. In 1981, dozens of categorical grants were consolidated into nine block grants.

According to the General Accounting Office, the number of federal block grant programmes increased from 450 to 700 between 1980 and 2001. The formulas by which they are calculated favour small states at the expense of large ones, for most allow a minimum amount per state.

Blogging

A blog (derived from amalgamating web log) is a website that provides news and commentary on a particular subject, a kind of on-line diary in which entries are written in chronological order and commonly displayed in reverse chronological order. A typical blog combines text, images and links to other blogs and web pages which deal with its topic. A political blog comments on politics.

Political bloggers often have a clearly stated political leaning. They tend to argue that mainstream news media have their own bias, but one which – particularly in the case of broadcasting – is often concealed, the material being presented as impartial. Bloggers prefer to state their political bias at the outset, which they see as being more open. Their blogs serve as a kind of soapbox for

opinions not always represented by the press and television. So popular has blogging become that journalists and politicians often engage in their own blogging.

Blogs helped to draw attention to and keep alive the scandal that developed following remarks made by then Senate Majority Leader Trent Lott. In 2002, he observed that senator and former presidential candidate, Strom Thurmond, who ran on a segregationist platform in 1948, would have made a good president. Bloggers uncovered information concerning Lott's previous observations and drew media attention to his links with various right-wing bodies less known outside his home state.

In 2003, blogs were used by two presidential hopefuls, Howard Dean and Wesley Clark, whose names and qualities were much discussed among bloggers before they were taken seriously as candidates by the traditional media outlets. During the 2004 election, John Kerry and George W. Bush both maintained a blog on their respective campaign sites.

One of the most significant instances of blogs influencing politics occurred during the 2006 Virginia Senate campaign. In that campaign, a video recording was made of incumbent Republican Senator George Allen casting an ethnic slur. The video was posted on the popular video-sharing site You Tube and the story picked up by local and then national media because of the heavy attention by blogs such as the liberal-leaning *Daily Kos*.

At best, political blogs can offer new information, accurate reporting and fresh insights. At their worst, they peddle in muckraking and openly slander public figures, ridiculing their performances and dwelling on their mishaps and misdemeanours. They have unquestionably had a political impact, transforming political communication between the voters (and non-voters) and influencing political leaders and ultimately members of the public at large.

Blue Dog Democrats

The Blue Dog Democrats, collectively known as the Blue Dog Coalition, are a grouping in Congress of conservative and moderate Democrats.

The term 'Blue Dog' derives from the old

description of the Southern party loyalists as those who would vote for a yellow dog if it were described on the ballot paper as a Democrat. They opted for the label 'Blue Dog' because they claimed that their more conservative views had been 'choked blue' by the liberal leadership of their party in the years leading up to the 1994 election.

Blue Dog Democrats are concentrated in the South, particularly in those states where tobacco is a major cash crop, and they have often voted as a block alongside the Republications in both chambers of Congress to defeat attempted legislative curbs on the tobacco industry. Other policy attitudes include: a preference for low levels of government spending; minimal government; and local decision-making; as well as opposition to measures of gun control and funding for the National Endowment for the Arts.

See also *Boll Weevils*

Boll Weevils

'Boll Weevils' was a term in popular use in the mid- and late twentieth century to describe conservative Southern Democrats. They had been broadly able to support the New and Fair Deals of Roosevelt and Truman, respectively, but were very unhappy about the post-1945 trend towards desegregation and support for the civil rights movements. On occasion, a prominent Democrat from the South broke from the main party to run a third party campaign in presidential elections – for example, George Wallace in 1968. The term was sometimes used as a pejorative political epithet by party leaders, the implications being that the Boll Weevils were unreliable in their voting patterns and not team players.

Most erstwhile members of the grouping have now retired from the political scene or switched to the Republican Party. Accordingly, the label is less often used than in the past. More conservative Democrats are now likely to be found in the Democratic Leadership Council or Blue Dog Coalition. They tend to be more moderate on racial issues than the original Boll Weevils and less exclusively concentrated in the South.

See also *Blue Dog Democrats*

Brown v. Board of Education (1954)

Brown v. *Board of Education* of Topeka, Kansas, was a landmark case in which the Supreme Court overturned the *Plessy* v. *Ferguson* judgment (1896) and declared that separate educational facilities were 'inherently unequal'. As such, they breached the Fourteenth Amendment which declared that no state could 'deny to any person within its jurisdiction the equal protection of the laws'.

Prior to the ruling, black children were denied admission to public schools attended by white children under laws requiring or permitting segregation according to the races. An African American minister, Oliver Brown, decided to challenge the segregated educational system in Topeka which meant that he could not send his daughter to the whites-only school five blocks away but only to the all-black one twenty blocks away. The National Association for the Advancement of Colored People (NAACP) took up the case, having already fought several court battles against segregated education. Its leading lawyer, Thurgood Marshall (later to become a Supreme Court justice), represented Brown before the nine justices, as part of a formidable legal team. He had an impressive record of court challenges to state-sponsored discrimination (In all, he went on to win twenty-nine out of the thirty-two cases he argued before the Supreme Court.)

In the Brown case, the Court decided – on a unanimous basis – that, despite the equalisation of the schools by 'objective' factors, intangible issues fostered and maintained inequality. Racial segregation in public education had a detrimental effect on minority children because it was interpreted as a sign of inferiority and therefore psychologically detrimental.

The ruling of the Warren Court provoked widespread white resistance, with White Citizens Councils being formed across the South to fight to preserve segregation. In Virginia, a massive campaign of resistance involved the closure of some schools. Elsewhere, however, the response was more patchy, with places such as Washington DC and some towns and cities in states such as Arkansas, Florida and North Carolina, acting more quickly to desegregate the provision of education.

Even though it laid down no date by which desegregation had to be achieved, the Brown ruling represented a milestone. The NAACP returned to the courts a year later and secured a further judgment in its favour. Again, no time limit was imposed but integration was to be accomplished 'with all deliberate speed'. The 1954 judgment paved the way for integration, racial equality and the advance of the civil rights movements. Although it applied only to segregation in schools, it soon became apparent in other decisions that no service offered by the states could continue to be provided on a segregated basis. Several discriminatory practices in the public services had become open to legal challenge, so that the case marked a decisive step in the gradual – but slow – process of desegregation.

See also *Civil Rights Movement*; *Desegregation*; *Marshall, Thurgood*; *National Association for the Advancement of Colored People (NAACP)*

Buckley v. *Valeo* (1976) see *FECA Legislation*

Budget and Impoundment Control Act 1974

The Budget and Impoundment Control Act was passed by Congress as part of an attempt to provide a more effective check on the president's budgetary and economic planning. Members of Congress objected to the way in which the president impounded (refused to spend) huge sums of money set aside for social programmes. Generally, presidents have used impoundment sparingly but President Nixon used it regularly against the Democratic-controlled legislature, both as a means of controlling spending and as a means of controlling its behaviour.

The Act also established a budget committee in both houses of Congress and a structured framework for the budget-making process. It also created the Congressional Budget Office (CBO) with its own specialist staff, to boost expertise in this area and enable members of both houses to

seek out and acquire the sort of information that presidents tended to deny them. This made the CBO a more effective counterweight to the Office of Management and the Budget in the executive branch.

Budget (Federal)

The United States federal budget is a federal document that outlines its funding recommendations for the next fiscal year. It is a kind of masterplan that translates revenues into policy goals.

The outcome of the bugetary process is that Congress develops a budget resolution based on recommendations from the president. It also approves individual appropriations bills which allocate fundings to various federal programmes recommended in the budget. But, before the outcome can be reached, there are extended battles between the president and Congress over how the necessary revenue will be raised and how spending will be distributed across government areas of responsibility.

Congress's 'power of the purse' was written into the US Constitution. But it was always an area over which Congress found it difficult to establish control. The large number of congressional committees and power bases made it hard to ensure that overall spending was related to revenues from taxation. Because of the difficulties of establishing a coherent national economic policy, the responsibility for framing the federal budget and national economic policy increasingly fell into presidential hands. In recent decades, however, Congress has struggled to re-establish control.

In 1974 it passed the Congressional Budget and Impoundment Control Act (see adjacent column) which enabled the legislature to propose an alternative to the president's budget based on an examination of all spending and tax measures, as well as an assessment of the overall needs of the economy. It made it easier for Congress to examine and to evaluate formerly isolated parts of the budget, rather than merely debating the merits of individual government programmes. It did this in several ways:

1. It established the House and Senate Budget committees. Members of the House Budget

Committee are drawn from the Ways and Means and Appropriations committees, along with one member from each of the standing committees. Members of the Senate Budget Committee are selected via the same process used to select members of other senatorial committees. These committees are responsible for drafting Congress's annual budget plan and monitoring action on the budget for the federal government.

2. It also established the Congressional Budget Office, a non-partisan body that provides expert analysis of the presidential proposals and seeks to match congressional spending decisions with established budget targets.

The federal government, once small and unobtrusive, now has an impact upon almost every aspect of the nation's life. Such are its responsibilities that the scale of expenditure is enormous. The budgetary process is concerned to finance these spending plans and ensure that revenues relate to expenditure. It is inevitably difficult and contentious bcause the people tend to have conflicting requirements of their elected representatives. They have a preference for low taxes but like to see spending on areas of importance to themselves. They also like the idea of balanced budgets.

The budget process

On the revenue side, the key issues are the amount of money to be raised, the forms of taxation to be employed and the way in which this taxation will be allocated between people of varying wealth in the community. On the spending side, the key issues are the total amount to be spent, the sort of programmes on which expenditure is necessary and desirable, and the groups and interests that need help. The revenues and expenditure must then be matched. If more money is raised than is spent, there is a government surplus in the national coffers. If more is spent than is raised, there is a deficit that will be have to be filled by borrowing.

The budgetary process is seldom completed smoothly. Usually, it involves a tussle – sometimes a serious conflict – between the president and Congress on all of these issues before a budget can become effective. Within the budgetary procedure, there is a series of deadlines which culminates in the completion of a budget to operate from the beginning of the government's fiscal year on 1 October.

The budget is prepared in two key phases, the first of which takes place within the Executive branch, the second within the Legislature. Within the Executive, preparation begins in April–May of the year before the budget is due to become effective, as a set of structured discussions between the president, the Office of the Management and Budget (OMB) and the various executive departments. The OMB presents the president with an analysis of the state of the economy and its forecasts for the coming year. On the basis of broad guidance from the president about his priorities, the OMB sets the broad parameters for spending and communicates them to the departments and agencies. They respond in the light of their priorities and needs, enabling the OMB to make an analysis of the situation and advise the president on his response. Over the coming months, the departments and agencies revise their projections and submit revised requests to the OMB which is then in a position to formulate the presidential message to Congress and the budget document itself. The president then makes any final adjustments. Thereafter, the next phase – deliberation in Congress – can begin, starting with delivery of the presidential speech:

- The president initiates the presidential–congressional bargaining process on the first Monday in February by submitting his budget request for the following year to Congress. In 2006, President Bush submitted a federal budget of \$2.8 trillion for the following year, in 2007 a \$2.9 one for 2008. This covers spending on education, job training, national security, social security, transport and dozens of other worthy purposes.
- All the committees in Congress then submit their estimates and views of the budget to the Budget Committee in their chamber. The committee gathers them into a first resolution that sets overall spending and tax levels on which Congress must vote by 15 April.

- The various parts of this first resolution are reutrned to the standing committees concerned with the particular subject or programme. By mid-June their recommendations return to the Budget Committees which draw up a reconciliation bill that is voted on by Congress. The aim is to reconcile the decisions of the standing committees with the targets contained within the first resolution. On 30 June, the House completes action on all appropriate bills.
- Assuing that agreement by the Senate and the president is secured, the budget becomes effective although sometimes the process overruns and throws the 1 October deadline into doubt.

Balancing the budget

The sources of revenue have changed over the last two hundred or so years. In the nineteenth century, the chief sources of federal revenues were tariffs levied on imported goods and excise taxes on tobacco and alcohol ('sin taxes'). In the twentieth century, taxes on individual and corporate income became the major sources of revenue. In particular, the passage of the Sixteenth Amendment in 1913 allowed Congress to impose a tax on income.

Spending patterns have also changed dramatically over the same period. In the nineteenth and early twentieth centuries, defence loomed largely in the pattern of expenditure, accounting for some half of the peacetime budget and even more in wartime. After World War II, defence spending declined as a percentage of the federal budget – though not in real terms – whereas domestic social spending, on programmes such as Medicare, consumed a larger share of the available money. By the mid-1970s, social welfare provision was costing four times the amount spent on national defence.

Revenue and spending both grew at an unprecedented rate in the early twentieth century but it was not until the mid-twentieth century that expenditures began systematically to outstrip revenues. From the mid-1960s, the US government regularly spent more money than it received in taxation, almost every year recording another budget deficit. In the 1980s and 1990s there was much talk of the need to balance the budget but only in the mid-1990s did the scale of deficits begin to

decline. President Clinton introduced an ambitious deficit-reduction package, that promised to reduce the defiicit by $500 billion over five years, by taxing the wealthy more heavily and making cuts in government programmes. Republicans in Congres disliked its emphasis on tax increases but, after some congressional changes, a version of the legislation was passed in August 1993. When the Republicans gained control after the midterm elections, they swiftly moved to restrain government expenditure, faced as they were with a budget deficit of $176 billion and an accumulated deficit of almost $5 trillion. They introduced their proposal for a Balanced Budget Amendment to the Constitution. In the year 2000, the goal of a budget surplus briefly became a reality although, since then, there have been regular deficits again.

Bureaucracy

Bureaucracy refers to what Burns et al. describe as a 'professional corps of officials organised in a pyramidal structure, and functioning under impersonal, uniform rules and procedures'. By the term 'bureaucrats', we refer to people who operate in the Executive branch, whose career is based in government service and who normally work there as a result of appointment rather than by election; they work for presidents and their political appointees. They serve in government departments and in the more than fifty independent agencies embracing some 2,000 bureaux which are sub-units of the agencies.

Some five million people work in the executive branch; 60 per cent of them are civilians, the rest being military personnel. About 12 per cent of them operate in Washington, the rest are based around the country. In California alone, there are more than a quarter of a million federal employees. Of the three million civilians, about a million work in the area of national security for bodies such as the air force, army, navy and various defence organisations. Nearly half a million work for the welfare agencies.

There are some 15,000 different categories of federal employee. The majority are white-collar workers, ranging from inspectors and engineers to secretaries and clerks. Key positions in the American bureaucracy are held by persons appointed by the president and, because these are normally people who share his or her outlook, this might be expected to result in presidential control of the bureaucratic process. Yet this often does not happen for, once in position, those appointed may 'go native' and become part of the administrative machine rather than agents of the president's will. As with relations with Congress, presidents soon find out that it is important to persuade, for they lack the power to command. In the frustrated words of President Truman: 'I thought I was the President, but when it comes to these bureaucracies I can't make 'em do a damn thing.'

Burger, Warren (1907–95)

Warren Earl Burger served as Chief Justice of the United States from 1969 to 1986. He was nominated by Richard Nixon who had been impressed by a series of speeches in which Burger revealed himself as a prominent critic of the Warren Court and argued in favour of a very literal reading of the Constitution. Because of these views, in 1969 President Richard Nixon appointed Burger to succeed Warren, having in his election campaign pledged to appoint a strict constructionist as Chief Justice.

Under Burger's leadership, the Supreme Court delivered major decisions on abortion, capital punishment, religious establishment and school desegregation. It had been widely anticipated that his Court would be a consolidating one which would differ markedly from its predecessor. The counter-revolution favoured by Nixon never really took place, however, for, although the new nominees made in this period were generally conservative, they did not seek to undo the work of the Warren Court in their decisions. Several key Burger judgments were to prove disappointing to the president and to other American conservatives. By the early 1970s, it was clear that Burger's Court was not going to turn the clock back. Indeed, in some areas it might even extend some Warren Court doctrines.

Liberal and conservative judgments

The Burger Court may not have been as innovative as its predecessor but it produced some surprisingly bold judgments. If its decisions on the criminal law were more cautious than those of the Warren era, none the less on racial matters (*Swann* v. *Charlotte–Mecklenburg Board of Education* 1971), abortion (*Roe* v. *Wade* 1973) and over Watergate (*United States* v. *Nixon* 1974) in particular, it acted adventurously.

On some other issues, Burger remained reliably conservative, his approach leaning towards extending police powers. In *Miller* v. *California* (1973), the Court (by then made more conservative in composition by the four Nixon appointees) moved to limit the spread of sexually explicit materials. He joined the Court majority in voting to reinstate the death penalty in *Gregg* v. *Georgia* (1976) which approved new death penalty statutes that were said to be less arbitrary in their operation than earlier laws. In 1983, he vigorously dissented from the Court's finding in the case of *Solem* v. *Helm* that a sentence of life imprisonment for issuing a fraudulent cheque in the amount of $100 constituted cruel and unusual punishment. Also, as a strong opponent of gay rights, he wrote a famous concurring opinion in the Court's 1986 decision upholding a Georgia law criminalising sodomy (*Bowers* v. *Hardwick*), in which Burger purported to marshal historical evidence that laws criminalising homosexuality were of ancient vintage.

Summary

Overall, Burger devoted much of his time and energy into administering and examining the mechanics of the judicial system. He initiated the National Center for State Courts (now located in Williamsburg, Virginia), the Institute for Court Management, and National Institute of Corrections to provide professional training for judges, clerks and prison guards. He initiated the annual *State of the Judiciary* speech given by the Chief Justice to the American Bar Association.

Despite his best efforts to shun controversy while in the Court (often writing straightforward and uncontroversial opinions) Burger was a contentious figure throughout his tenure. Some portrayed him as a weak Chief Justice who was not seriously respected by his colleagues, on account of his lack of legal acumen. Among his colleagues, he sometimes caused irritation by switching his vote in conference or simply not announcing his position, so that he was able to control the allocation of opinion assignments.

Burger retired on 26 September 1986, in part to lead the campaign to mark the 1987 bicentennial of the United States Constitution.

Bus Boycotts

Bus boycotts were a technique of popular protest first used in the 1940s by black political activists to challenge segregation in South Africa. The method was borrowed by black American activists in the United States, against a backdrop of both heightened civil rights activity and a rising tide of massive resistance. The main boycotts were in Tallahassee, Baton Rouge and – most famously – in Montgomery.

The Montgomery Bus Boycott was a political and social protest campaign started in 1955 in Montgomery, Alabama, in protest against the city's policy of racial segregation on its public transport system. The boycott began after Rosa Parks defied the regulation requiring black people to give up their seats if a white person was standing. She refused, was arrested and charged with a violation of the Montomery city bus segregation ordinance. Blacks subsequently boycotted buses on the day of the Parks trial and, when the city commissioners refused to yield to popular demands (which did not at first go as far as demanding an end to segregation in the transit system), the day-long action became a year-long one.

The boycott had its origins in grassroots black activism which was backed by the National Association for the Advancement of Colored People (NAACP) and the Church. As a local Church leader, Dr Martin Luther King became prominently involved, using tactics which had proved successful in Baton Rouge. He and other leaders understood that boycotts hit white pockets and were an effective mass weapon. They faced opposition from Montgomery whites who used Alabama's anti-boycott law against the black community, their mass indictments attracting national media coverage. The federal district court found segregation on buses unconstitutional, a position backed by the Supreme Court.

The boycott was called off when desegregated buses began operating in December 1956. It was a limited victory in that, other than on the buses, the city remained segregated.

The events in Montgomery however, are usually regarded as the real start of the American civil rights movement, and Rosa Parks as one of its key pioneers.

See also *King, Martin Luther; National Association for the Advancement of Colored People; Parks, Rosa*

Bush, George H. W.

George Herbert Walker Bush was the forty-first president, in office from 1989 to 1993. Before his presidency, Bush served as the forty-third vice president during the Reagan administrations (1981–89). He is the oldest living former president and the father of George W. Bush and of Jeb, the Governor of Florida.

Bush was born into a family with a tradition of public service. He was the son of a United States senator and inherited a strong belief in his obligation to make a contribution to American society both in times of war and of peace. In World War II he flew combat missions and, in one bombing mission over the Pacific, he was shot down by Japanese anti-aircraft fire and had to be rescued by an American submarine. For his dedication and bravery in action, he was awarded the Distinguished Flying Cross.

On leaving the armed forces, Bush became part of the West Texan oil industry before embarking on a political career. He served two terms in Congress as a Republican Representative for Texas but his two bids for a Senate seat were unsuccessful. There followed a series of high-profile positions, notably US Ambassador to the United Nations (1971–73), Chairman of the Republican National Committee (1973–74), Chief of the US Liaison Office in the People's Republic of China (1974–76) and Director of the Central Intelligence Agency (1976–77).

In 1980 Bush campaigned for the Republican nomination for president, stressing his wide range of government experience. He represented the centrist wing in the Grand Old Party (GOP), whereas Ronald Reagan represented its conservative wing. In the contest Bush criticised Reaganite plans for massive tax cuts as 'voodoo economics'. His bid failed but Reagan chose him as his running mate. As vice president, he was given responsibility over several domestic areas, including Federal deregulation and anti-drug programmes. He travelled widely and met many world leaders. When the Iran Contra scandal broke in 1986, Bush stated that he had been 'out of the loop' and unaware of the Iran initiatives related to arms trading. In his second term, he became the first vice president to serve as acting president under the Twenty-fifth Amendment when, in July 1985, President Reagan underwent surgery. Much of the eight-hour presidency was spent playing tennis.

In 1988, Bush won the Republican nomination. Often criticised for his lack of eloquence when compared with Reagan, he surprised many by giving perhaps the best speech of his public career at the Republican Convention, widely known as the 'Thousand points of light' speech for his use of that phrase to describe his vision of the American community. He spoke of his dedication to traditional American values and his determination to direct them towards making the United States 'a kinder and gentler nation'. He decisively defeated his Democratic rival from Massachusetts, Governor Michael Dukakis, in the presidential election, after a campaign noted for its highly negative television advertisements. In his Inaugural Address, Bush pledged to use American strength as 'a force for good', observing that:

> We live in a peaceful, prosperous time, but we can make it better. For a new breeze is blowing, and a world refreshed by freedom seems reborn; for in man's heart, if not in fact, the day of the dictator is over. The totalitarian era is passing, its old ideas blown away like leaves from an ancient, lifeless tree. A new breeze is blowing, and a nation refreshed by freedom stands ready to push on. There is new ground to be broken, and new action to be taken.

President 1989–93

Bush faced a changing world order, confronted as he was by the break-up of the communist empire in Eastern Europe and the fall of the reformist president of the USSR, Mikhail Gorbachev. He urged restraint in the handling of the new situation but, in other areas of foreign policy, he was more active. He sent American troops into Panama to overthrow the corrupt regime of General Manuel Noriega who was threatening the security of the canal and the Americans living there. (Noriega was taken to America to be tried for drug trafficking.) The most important episode of his foreign policy, however, was his handling of the situation in Iraq and of the First Gulf War (1990–91). The Iraqi president, Saddam Hussein, invaded the country's oil-rich neighbour, Kuwait, then threatened to move into Saudi Arabia. Bush rallied opinion at home and abroad in support of an operation to liberate Kuwait, sending in 425,000 American troops who were joined by troops from allied nations. After weeks of air and missile bombardment, the 100-hour land battle, dubbed Desert Storm, defeated Iraq's million-strong army.

Bush was less interested in the domestic political scene, and his administration faced discontent at home over the faltering economy, rising level of violence in the inner cities and continuing high-deficit spending. In his acceptance speech at the convention, he had made the famous pledge, 'read my lips, no new taxes'. In spite of the unprecedented popularity that he had earlier gained from the military and diplomatic triumph over Iraq, he lost the presidential election of November 1992 to Democrat Bill Clinton.

Following his defeat, Bush retired to the family's exclusive neighbourhood in Houston, Texas with a presidential office nearby. He has made many public appearances and undertaken fact-finding missions during his son's presidency.

See also *First Gulf War*; *Vice Presidency*

Bush, George W. A. (1946–)

George Walker Bush was the forty-third president of the United States. He was sworn into office on 20 January 2001, re-elected on 2 November 2004 and sworn in for a second term on 20 January 2005.

Bush was born in Connecticut as the eldest son of former President George Herbert Walker Bush and grew up in Midland and Houston, Texas. He received a bachelor's degree in history from Yale University in 1968 before serving as a fighter pilot in the Texas Air National Guard. He received a Master of Business Administration from Harvard Business School in 1975. Following graduation, he moved back to Midland and began a career in the oil business. He assembled a group of partners who purchased the Texas Rangers baseball franchise in 1989. Having made an unsuccessful run for the House of Representatives in 1978, he later worked on his father's successful 1988 presidential campaign before making another bid for a political career. In November 1994, he was elected Governor of Texas, having defeated the incumbent Governor Ann Richards, a popular Democrat who was widely considered the favourite.

As governor, Bush successfully sponsored legislation for tort reform, increased education funding, set higher standards for schools and reformed the criminal justice system. Under his leadership, Texas executed a record 152 prisoners. Bush used a budget surplus to push through a $2 billion tax-cut plan, the largest in Texas's history, which cemented his credentials as a pro-business fiscal conservative. Bush also pioneered faith-based welfare programmes by extending government funding and support for religious organisations that provide social services such as education, alcohol- and drug-abuse prevention, and reduction of domestic violence. He was re-elected by a landslide, gaining nearly 69 per cent of the vote.

In his six years as governor, he earned a reputation for bipartisanship and as a compassionate conservative who shaped public policy based on the principles of limited government, personal responsibility, strong families and local control. He became the first governor in his state's history to be elected to consecutive four-year terms when he was re-elected in 1998.

He soon decided on a presidential bid. In an Iowan televised Republican presidential debate in December 1999, all the participating candidates were asked which political philosopher or thinker they most identified with and why. Whereas his rivals all quoted political figures, Bush's response pointed to his evangelical Christianity: 'Christ, because he changed my heart.' His appeal to religious values was to help him with the support

of the Religious Right in the presidential election. During the election cycle, Bush labelled himself a 'compassionate conservative' and his political campaign promised to 'restore honor and dignity to the White House', a reference to the scandals and impeachment of his predecessor, Bill Clinton.

Bush won the presidency in 2000 as the Republican candidate in a close and controversial contest in which he lost the nationwide popular vote but won the vote in the Electoral College.

The George W. Bush presidency: the first term 2001–05

In 2001, critics were quick to caricature the new president as a know-nothing, verbally challenged and not-very-industrious politician who had risen well beyond his abilities. They also detected plenty of evidence to suggest that he was shifting American politics sharply to the right. If this was so, it seemed a far cry from the 'compassionate conservatism' that George W. Bush had advanced in the election campaign. At the time, the allegation was frequently made that there would be little to choose between the two candidates; whoever won, little would change.

After polling day, many Americans indeed hoped that Bush would recognise his limited mandate and seek to govern from the centre, as a man of the consensus. This did not prove to be the case, for he and his supporters were serious in their intent to mark a distinct break from the Clinton years. They soon won the support of the ultra-conservative Heritage Foundation, whose members were pleased to find that many items on the Republican wish list were becoming reality. Its head detected that the new team was 'more Reaganite than the Reagan administration'.

Bush employed the rhetoric of bipartisanship, humility and healing as a cover for the pursuit of a radically conservative agenda. His charm and seeming reasonableness earned him some admiration, as did some of his early initiatives. For instance, his:

- appointment of Colin Powell, widely seen as a moderate, as his first Secretary of State, and of a black American, Condoleezza Rice, as his national security adviser and then – in his second term – as Powell's successor

- selection of an ethnically diverse first cabinet which included two black and two Asian Americans (one of the Asians was a Democrat, Norman Mineta), a Cuban American, an Arab American, and four women
- attempt to break down social barriers in Washington by inviting liberal critics to the White House, and also his willingness to meet black American political leaders and visit black churches and schools.

The early charm offensive helped to blunt some Democrat criticism of the Bush agenda and performance, a task made easier because the last, scandal-ridden days of the Clinton administration had demoralised the opposition. But behind the handshakes and smiles, the actions were tougher than the tone would suggest. Critics pointed out that the cabinet might have been socially well balanced but that its members were in several cases deeply conservative. They also noted the importance of business in the administration, with millionaires at the cabinet table; for instance, Condoleezza Rice had a Chevron oil tanker named after her and former chief of staff, Andrew Card, was a former leading lobbyist for General Motors. More partisan and controversial actions included:

- appointing hardliners such as John Ashcroft as his first Attorney General (his record included strong backing for those who opposed abortion rights and affirmative action) and the hawkish Donald Rumsfeld as his defense secretary
- widening the already large gap between the position of the haves and have-nots, by a redistribution of wealth in favour of the rich. Key measures included a programme of $1,600 billion tax cuts, which primarily benefited more affluent Americans, and the proposal to drop inheritance tax (to the benefit of the top 2 per cent of Americans, who have estates worth more than $675,000)
- halting foreign-aid spending on abortions so that, in future, there would be no federal spending in support of international family planning organisations which backed abortion

- allowing prospectors to open up the Alaskan National Wildlife Refuge and relaxing environmental controls on old power plants
- repudiating the Kyoto protocol signed by Bill Clinton on pegging greenhouse gas emissions
- renouncing American support for the nuclear test-ban treaty, the anti-ballistic missile treaty and the ban on chemical weapons, and pursuing a costly and highly controversial national missile defence system known as Star Wars Two. Opponents claimed that narrowly defined national security interests and the commercial interests of the biotechnology sector were being allowed to take precedence over responsible multilateral agreements and global collaboration.

A more assertive presidency

The terrorist attack on the World Trade Center in New York (9/11) jolted the presidency into uncharacteristic vigour. It moved into a higher gear, and Bush became more focused and purposeful. Washington reorganised itself around the Executive branch, and Bush reorganised his administration around the struggle against terrorism. Almost at once, he persuaded Congress to approve a substantial recovery package that also made additional provision to allow for strengthening of the intelligence and security services. It also quickly passed an antiterrorism bill that greatly increased the potential of Executive power.

Having long been suspicious of the power exercised by 'big government' in Washington, many Americans rallied behind President Bush. They were in a mood to accept more assertive presidential leadership. They were unsure of what was happening to them and yearned for a sense of direction. This gave the president a chance to take a firmer grip upon events. He began to shape the political agenda, and his early actions were accepted with little dissent. Some commentators began to use phrases such as 'the revived presidency' or 'the re-imperialised presidency'. War – in this case on terrorism – was the catalyst for change. It demanded personalised control from the man who symbolised the unity of the country.

In seeking to wage war on terrorism, the president engaged on a daunting task. In the short term, the crisis of 11 September served to boost presidential prestige. It matured the new incumbent of the White House into an international statesman. In its early days, what was an American tragedy proved to be the making of George Bush. In the words of Washington correspondent, Ed Vullami (2001), 'the sharpest learning curve in the history of the presidency has seen Bush mutate into a figurehead who has the people behind him'.

But the short and successful war against the Taliban proved to be the first stage of a wider war on terror. Vice president Cheney and others in the White House became obsessed with the link between international terrorism and the existence of weapons of mass destruction (WMD). He became the administration's most aggressive voice in favour of confronting Iraq, hyping the nuclear threat from Saddam Hussein. Saddam had long been a thorn in America's side, and Cheney and other hawks were keen to see America launch a pre-emptive strike against one of American's enemies. A 'coalition of the willing' was assembled to fight in Iraq, consisting primarily of American and British forces. On this occasion, world opinion was much less united behind the president, and at home the war soon generated opposition.

Many early supporters of military action against Iraq later became alarmed at the seeming lack of a plan for peacekeeping after the cessation of hostilities. The failure to find WMD, the excesses of some American troops and the continuation of insurgency against the occupation caused continuing disquiet. Bush nevertheless continued to assert that the war had been worthwhile and confirmed he would have made the same decision if he had known more.

The president faced internal criticism not just over Iraq. Many Americans were concerned that the administration was undermining the constitutional rights and liberties of American citizens. The passage of the Patriot Act enabled him to imprison citizens without charge and clamp down on a range of established freedoms. Conditions at Guantánamo Bay were a regular cause of dissent.

Yet running as a self-described 'war president' in November 2004, George Bush was re-elected, in the process winning more votes than any other presidential candidate had done before. His victory was decisive, not just in the battle for the White House but also in the congressional elections in which Republicans tightened their grip, adding seats in both the House and the Senate. Whatever the anxieties over Iraq and the war on terrorism, the victory illustrated how difficult it was for any challenger to defeat a sitting president at a time when the country has troops abroad and national security was a live political issue. Allegations that, during the Bush presidency, nearly a million jobs had been lost, the budget surplus squandered, record deficits created and 4.5 million Americans left without health insurance, made less impact than might otherwise have been the case.

Bush, the election campaigner

Some of the president's critics underestimated his ability as an election campaigner. Those with more insight recognised that, however much they doubted his competence and policies, he was a strong performer on the campaign trail. If his style did not travel well across the Atlantic, it went down well in parts of the United States. A liberal critic in Britain, Jonathan Freedland (2002), noted in the midterm election contest some of his qualities and was surprised to find himself admitting to them. In particular, he:

- spoke fluently and without notes
- mastered the common touch and – in his folksy, accessible way, mouthing rather simple sentiments – was surprisingly effective
- looked and sounded relaxed
- seemed surprisingly knowledgeable, whether talking about education or the war on terrorism
- could be humorous
- inspired loyalty among his followers who admired him as a 'tough guy'.

The second term 2005–09

Iraqi elections and a referendum to approve a constitution were held in January and December 2005. From 2004 to 2007, however, the situation in Iraq deteriorated further, with some observers arguing that the country was heading towards a full-scale civil war. Bush's policies regarding the war in Iraq met increasing criticism, with demands within the United States to set a timetable to withdraw troops from Iraq. The 2006 report of the bipartisan Iraq Study Group led by James Baker concluded that the situation in Iraq was 'grave and deteriorating'. While Bush admitted that there were strategic mistakes made with regard to the stability of Iraq, he maintained he would not change his overall strategy. In a speech in January, he addressed the nation on Iraq and he announced the surge of 21,500 more troops for Iraq as well as a job programme for Iraqis, more reconstruction proposals and $1.2 billion for these programmes. On 1 May 2007, Bush used his veto to reject a congressional bill setting a deadline for the withdrawal of American troops from Iraq.

Bush was also criticised for what was widely seen as the slow and inadequate response to the devastation caused by Hurricane Katrina in Louisiana, Mississippi and Alabama in late August 2005. On 13 September, in a vague answer to his critics, Bush admitted responsibility to the extent that the federal government had failed to perform its job properly.

Prior to the midterm elections (2006), Bush went on the campaign trail, stressing that the Republicans were strong on national security and would keep taxes low, unlike the Democrats. His party suffered a serious rebuff, losing the majority of state governorships and control of both houses of the bicameral Legislature to the Democrats. Thereafter, he never again exercised the same power, as his administration became engulfed in growing problems as the recession deepened and his personal reputation declined. Of course, the constitutional means by which he has sought to circumvent Congress (see the adjacent box) still existed and continued to be used but the political circumstances had become markedly less favourable to a display of presidential leadership.

A verdict

As a lame-duck president in his final years in office, the popular reputation of George Bush descended to its lowest ebb. At one point in late October 2008, a CBS poll placed the approval rate at 20 per cent, the lowest figure since polling began in the 1930s. According to a poll taken in early 2009, a majority of Americans thought he would be remembered as a below-average or poor president. A mere 17 per cent believed he would go down in history as an outstanding or above-average president a figure at variance with Bush's own confidence that his presidency would be appreciated over a longer period of time. Another 23 per cent predicted that he would be remembered as 'average', while 59 per cent labelled the likely verdict as being 'below average' or 'poor'.

George W. Bush and presidential power

Seeing the office as having been seriously undermined by the Watergate scandal and surrounding revelations about presidential misuse of powers, George Bush consciously set out to reassert the powers of the office in a way that most of his predecessors had been unable to do.

Some members of the administration advanced the unitary executive theory that addressed aspects of the separation of powers and argued for strict limits to the power of Congress to deprive the president of control of the Executive branch. They suggested that the Constitution created a hierarchical, unified Executive department under the direct control of the president. George Bush was an exponent of the theory and in pursuit of his unilateral policy objectives used this broad remit in various ways, such as by the use of signing statements, executive orders, National Security Directives, Executive agreements, proclamations and recess appointments.

Bush's employment of such devices shed an interesting insight on to the debate on presidential power.

Americans were not ambivalent about George Bush as president. People tended to like or dislike him with an unusual intensity. To some, he represented the ideal of presidential leadership whereas others regarded him as an embarrassing usurper who had no right to be in the White House in the first place.

Republican and Democrat voters found themselves in sharp disagreement about almost all aspects of the Bush presidency – on America's standing in the world, whether he was too partisan, whether he had a good grasp of the issues and whether he was too willing to inject his own moral and religious beliefs into politics. Whereas the pollsters found that Republicans saw a man who was decisive, determined and strong, opponents detected a person who was arrogant, cocky and bone headed.

Bush represented the politics of certainty. He did not flinch when the arguments and numbers seemed to be against him for, in his view, government was about truth which he claimed to represent. He tended to paint stark visions of enemies and good guys. This simplicity appealed to some people very much who, in uncertain times, were content to know that the person in the White House knew the answers.

Those who disliked him were deeply suspicious about his abilities and his motives. What to his admirers seemed like moral clarity, to his detractors seems like simple-mindedness: certitude seemed like self-righteousness, and piety like sanctimoniousness. As for his policies, even many Americans who originally backed the invasion of Iraq subsequently developed doubts about not only the credibility but also the competence of the administration. Whether the war came about because of a thirst for oil or out of crusading interventionist zeal, they were uneasy about the reasons for, and direction of, policy.

See also *Bush, George H. W.*; **Bush v. Gore** *(2000)*; *Iraq War: the Second Gulf War (2003–)*; *War on Terrorism*

Bush v. *Gore* (2000)

Bush v. *Gore* was a Supreme Court case heard on 11 December 2000, following the unclear outcome of the presidential election of November 2000. Although Democrat Al Gore scored more popular votes than his rival, he needed the twenty-five votes of Florida to win in the Electoral College. If Republican George W. Bush was victorious in that state, he would win the presidency. Everything depended on the outcome of the contest in Florida.

At first, the news media declared in favour of Gore but they then gave the election to Bush before deciding the race was too close to call. By the morning of Wednesday, 8 November, Bush's margin in Florida had dwindled to about 500 votes, small enough to trigger a mandatory recount in the state. In addition, Gore asked for hand recounts in four counties, as provided for under Florida state law. This set into motion a series of recounts (some by machine, and some by hand), questions about the validity of some votes and finally lawsuits. A month of controversial court challenges and recounts followed until the Supreme Court in *Bush* v. *Gore* ruled in favour of Bush. As a result, Bush was certified as the winner in Florida by a margin of 537 votes, thereby being credited with more seats in the Electoral College.

The Supreme Court judgment and its importance

The final decision of the Court in the *George W. Bush* v. *Albert Gore Jnr* case was among the most momentous of its history. In addition to deciding this particular presidency, it could have the effect in future of pushing the nation's highest court into more election battles – an area it has traditionally avoided.

The Court was dealing with an appeal by George W. Bush against a ruling in the Florida Supreme Court to order a manual recount in the state. The nine justices basically had three options:

1. It could have found for Bush on the grounds that the only votes usually counted in Florida are those clearly marked, so that the state's Supreme Court decision to allow other votes to be included was a departure from normal practice. Justices Rehnquist, Scalia and Thomas were supporters of this viewpoint which,

if handed down, would have been final and stopped all recounts without qualification.

2. It could have ruled clearly for Gore, deferring – as federal courts normally would do – to state courts on matters of state law. This might have involved issuing guidance to the Florida Supreme Court on how the recount should proceed. Justices Breyer and Ginsburg wanted to do this. To do so would have made the process lengthier but would have meant that, ultimately, the choice lay with the voters.

3. The third option, which it actually took, was to seem to do the second while actually doing something akin to the first. By 7–2, it sent the case back to the Florida Supreme Court (FSC) 'for further proceedings not inconsistent with this opinion'. In practice, as the various dissenting opinions made clear, this meant that, five votes to four, by the FSC had to have the votes counted, allow sufficient time for judicial review of these proceedings and do it all by midnight on 12 December, two hours after the Supreme Court issued its ruling but the date when the Electoral College votes were supposed to be over. By opting for the impossible, this meant that the Court effectively handed victory to Bush.

In its defence, seven justices had found serious constitutional violations in the way that the manual recounts had been conducted. Even Associate Justice Ginsburg, a Democrat appointment, called the process 'flawed'. They were uneasy about the way in which decisions on vote counting were being taken away from the officials whom the legislature had appointed for the task of managing the election, and handing them over to the judiciary. Neither was the recount to include 'all ballots', a requirement of state law. All in all, the Court had brought finality to a messy business and produced a result.

To Gore sympathisers, any outcome of the Court's deliberations would have been questionable but the final decision seemed to be intellectually less than rigorous. Doubts were expressed about the reasoning and remedy that led to the verdict. The verdict expressed implied that the Supreme Court knew better than the Florida Supreme Court what was meant by Florida state law, a strange judgment from a largely constructionist court which has generally been very sympathetic to states' rights. As Justice Breyer pointed out, the Florida Supreme Court would have preferred a recount finished on 18 December (when Electoral College votes were due to be certified) for it had stressed in its decision 'the will of the voters' and its willingness to recount ballots.

By rejecting some ballots, as it effectively did, and acting in a way that seemed to reflect its Republican majority, the Supreme Court has involved itself in controversy. The case created intense excitement and partisan feeling, and Americans and observers worldwide were waiting to see how the verdict would go. By its judgment, it risked eroding public confidence in its collective wisdom and fairness, what Justice Breyer – in a dissenting verdict – called 'a public treasure that has been built up over many years'.

Busing

Busing refers to the assignment and transport of children to schools beyond their immediate neighbourhoods in order to obtain racial balance. It involves an effort to counteract discriminatory school construction and district assignments. As this was free transport by school bus, the term 'busing' came into use to describe the plans. Opponents tended to speak of 'forced busing'.

Brown v. *Board of Education* and other federal cases had overturned racial segregation but it was the landmark ruling by the US Supreme Court in *Swann* v. *Charlotte–Mecklenburg Board of Education* (1971) that cleared the way for Charlotte – and districts nationwide – to use mandatory busing and race-based pupil assignment as means of achieving integration. Following the Swann judgment, many court-supervised desegregation busing plans were implemented in the 1970s and 1980s.

Faced with the reality of integration, some white middle-class families in some communities began to move to the suburbs of metropolitan areas with a less mixed population, a process known as 'white flight'. After several years of court supervision of schools, however, busing programmes in several areas fell into disuse as the courts released districts from orders under old lawsuits and in some cases ordered an end to busing. The trend in recent years has been back to neighbourhood schools. In some cases, the public school system is now 75 per cent or more black, so that busing increasingly came to involve the transport of black students from one part of a city to be with black students in other another part. The practice continues in the Boston area where the *Controlled Choice* programme allows any student to go to a school outside his or her own neighbourhood as long as the move helps to fulfil the goal of achieving a racial balance.

C

Cabinet

The Cabinet is the body, comprising department secretaries and other officials designated by the president, that is available to consult with the president and offer him advice. The tradition of the Cabinet dates back to the beginnings of the presidency itself. It is not mentioned in the Constitution but derives its legitimacy from Article II, Section 2 of the Constitution that allows the president to 'require the opinion . . . of the principal officer in each of the executive departments, upon any subject relating to the duties of their respective offices'. It is accepted that any president needs aides who can give advice and monitor the implementation of policies in the federal executive departments. Every president has had a Cabinet though the membership and use vary from incumbent to incumbent.

George Washington created the Cabinet by frequently meeting with his Attorney General and the secretaries of state, treasury and war. James Madison referred to such gatherings as meetings of the 'president's cabinet'. It has always been a loosely designated body and it is sometimes unclear who is entitled to belong to it. In recent years, the Cabinet has included all the department heads and others whom a president considers cabinet-level officials – notably the occupants of offices such as the Ambassador to the United Nations and Director of the Office of Management. For instance, in 1996, Clinton decided to elevate the director of the Federal Emergency Management Agency. Choosing the Cabinet is one of the first jobs of any president-elect.

The Obama Cabinet

The Obama Cabinet comprises the vice president, the heads of the fifteen departments and six others of Cabinet rank.

The departments represented were:
Agriculture
Commerce
Defense
Education
Energy
Health and Human Services
Homeland Security
Housing and Urban Development
Interior
Justice
Labor
State
Transportation
Treasury
Veterans' Affairs

The six offices of Cabinet rank are:
Ambassador to the United Nations
Council of Economic Advisers
Environmental Protection Agency
Office of Management and the Budget
United States Trade Representative
White House Chief of Staff

Use of the Cabinet

It is up to each president to decide how much he or she uses the Cabinet. Kennedy and Johnson made little use of it, preferring small conferences of people directly involved in a problem requiring resolution. Kennedy was particularly critical, seeing Cabinet meetings as a waste of time for busy people. As he asked: 'Why should the postmaster sit there and listen to a discussion of the problems of Laos?' George Bush was similarly dismissive of the Cabinet, its meetings being often rather meaningless.

A number of presidents – Nixon, Carter, Reagan and Clinton among them – promised on entering office that they would use the Cabinet more and equip it with more power but usually it has not worked out that way. Under Nixon, the regularity of meetings declined as Watergate enveloped his administration, and he came to regard his appointees with much distrust. Carter held sixty Cabinet meetings in the first two years but then grew disenchanted. Reagan promised to restore Cabinet government but, by the end of his first year in office, the meetings had become largely ceremonial occasions. Clinton rarely used the Cabinet as a whole, other than for photo opportunities. On occasion, he consulted individuals or a group of Cabinet secretaries to help in the decision-making process but generally their status sank to a new low and they were denied much influence under his administrations. Although he did not wish to listen to them collectively, he sometimes discussed policy issues on a bilateral basis with Cabinet officials, and was generally willing to allow his members wide power over decisions specific to their departments.

The Cabinet is an advisory body with little power or influence. The attitude of many presidents towards their Cabinets was illustrated in a story about President Lincoln who – on being opposed by all of his Cabinet colleagues – is supposed to have been so undisturbed that he remarked: 'seven nays, one aye: the ayes have it'.

Of course, presidents may make greater use of a few members of the Cabinet who are close to them. John Kennedy relied heavily on brother Robert, his Attorney General, and most presidents have a close relationship with the secretaries of defense, state and the treasury. This has led Cronin (2004) to describe this grouping as an 'inner cabinet', a body of important counsellors to the president.

Why do American Cabinets play so limited a role?

- Cabinets have no fixed membership, individual presidents bringing in additional figures to work alongside heads of department as they wish.
- Cabinets are large and unwieldy. Clinton's Cabinet was made up of twenty-five members, fourteen secretaries and eleven other officials accorded Cabinet rank. (Note that British prime ministers often make extensive use of cabinet committees and bilateral discussions, rather than using the cabinet as a whole to make policy – one reason being that the British cabinet is considered too large a body for the efficient making of policy.)
- Members serve for a short time, perhaps coming from relative obscurity as a business person or academic and returning to it – often having served less than a full presidential term.
- Members hold no position of political influence, not being members of Congress or individuals with a party standing – as they are in Britain.
- The loyalty of Cabinet members to the president is questionable. Secretaries may be capable of managing their departments well but often they feel that they have little to contribute in other areas of policy.

As with other presidents, under George W. Bush the Cabinet was not primarily a collective decision-making body. From time to time it discussed the policy agenda of the administration but it rarely reached a collective opinion on which all could agree and to which all felt bound. The president and his immediate advisers made all major decisions.

California Democratic Party v. Jones (2000)

In 1996, Californian voters approved Proposition 198 to change the state's primaries from being closed (allowing only a political party's members to vote on its nominees) to open or blanket primary (in which each voter's ballot lists every candidate regardless of party affiliation and allows the voter to choose freely among them). The California Democratic, Republican, Libertarian and Peace and Freedom parties, which had historically prohibited non-members from voting in their party's primary, each filed suit against Bill Jones, the Californian Secretary of State, alleging that the blanket primary violated their First Amendment right of association. Jones argued that a blanket primary would intensify interest in the election and allow for better representation in elected office. The state courts upheld his position.

The Supreme Court held in a 7–2 ruling delivered by Justice Antonin Scalia that California's blanket primary did violate a party's First Amendment right of association. It argued that the Proposition removed a party's 'basic function' to choose its own leaders and was 'both severe and unnecessary'. Indeed, the opinion went as far as to say that: 'A single election in which the party nominee is selected by non-party members could be enough to destroy the party.' In essence, then, the ruling made it clear that a state could not prevent a political party from having a closed primary that limited voting to members of the party.

Campaign Finance Reform

Campaign finance reform is the common term for the political effort to regulate the involvement of money in political campaigns. Attempts to regulate funding by legislation date back to 1867 but the first successful attempts nationally to change the law on campaign finance go back to the FECA legislation of the 1970s. The Bipartisan Campaign Reform (McCain–Feingold) Act (BCRA) of 2002 revised some of the legal limits of expenditure set in 1974 and prohibited unregulated 'soft money' contributions to national political parties. 'Soft money' also refers to funds spent by independent organisations that do not specifically advocate the election or defeat of candidates, and are not contributed directly to candidate campaigns.

McCain–Feingold's two major pillars – the ban on party soft money and the regulation of electioneering communications (issue ads) – have been generally successful in achieving their purpose. The legislation imposed no new restrictions on large individual donors, however, beyond the existing limit of $5,000 for individual contributions to non-party political committees. Indeed, it was agnostic about the total amount of money raised and spent in federal elections even though some of the bill's supporters in Congress and outside reformers made clear they favoured further controls.

In 2005, the Committee for Economic Development (CED) released a report on key post-BCRA issues entitled *Building on Reform: A Business Proposal to Strengthen Election Finance*. To address other shortcomings in current election finance law, CED made three sets of recommendations: to strengthen the soft-money ban by closing the so-called '527' loophole; to ensure effective enforcement of regulations by restructuring the Federal Election Commission (FEC) and creating an appointment system to attract individuals willing to make decisions independent of partisan politics and in the public interest; and to strengthen the presidential public funding system in both the primary and general election through voluntary public financing for campaign funding and limits on campaign spending and the use of personal funds.

Those who criticise campaign finance reform belive that controls infringe upon the right of free speech and thereby violate the First Amendment. They claim that the purpose of the clause is to guarantee that people have the right to publish their political views. When laws prohibit people from advocating for or against political candidates by limiting the content or the amount of political advertising, the laws are in conflict with those constitutional guarantees.

See also *FECA Legislation; 527s; McCain–Feingold Campaign Finance Reform Act; Soft Money*

Candidate-centred Electioneering

Nowadays, elections focus far more on the candidate and on his or her positive qualities and/or failings than on party labels. What candidates must do is to put together a winning coalition of support – they do this by making sure that there are sufficient funds to allow them to get the message across as widely as possible so that everyone knows who they are and what they stand for.

Once candidates are chosen, parties are obviously concerned to help them to sell themselves and their message. They send out their voluntary workers to canvass on the doorstep; they use the telephone to call possible voters; they arrange lifts for those who otherwise might not make it to the polling booth they involve themselves in fund-raising, commissioning and studying opinion polls and advertising. The role of parties in electioneering has been downgraded, however, for increasingly – with the breakdown of the party machines after the reform of the arrangements for financial contributions in the early 1970s – it is the individual candidate and the team of supporters he or she puts together which have become important. With the backing of Political Action Committees (whose primary function is to help finance election contests) candidates now tend to run their own campaigning. They employ professional opinion pollsters and media gurus, specialists who are able to advise on the best means of exploiting their potential as candidates and playing down or destroying the qualities and reputation of their opponents.

The process of electioneering has always demanded certain qualities from the person chosen – a pleasing voice, a gift for public speaking, the ability to sell one's personality and to persuade people of the merits of a particular case. Today, however, deficiencies in any of these aspects can be a serious liability exposed before the whole nation whereas, previously, many voters did not know about them. Other personal failings are also highlighted in the blaze of publicity surrounding a modern election campaign.

Capital Punishment (Death Penalty)

Capital punishment is the death sentence awarded for capital offences usually, in practice, murder. In 1976, the Supreme Court lifted a bar on capital punishment. Since then, there have been 1,119 executions in the United States (August 2008), there being forty-two carried out in the last year for which figures are available (2007). Many of those convicted wait for several years while their case is subject to appeal. More than 3,000 inmates await their fate on 'death rows' across the country.

Capital punishment has been on the increase in the United States, reflecting an increasing emphasis on tough 'law and order' policies as Americans confront the growth in violent crime. Politicians have had to react to this strong public feeling. Even those of generally liberal persuasion have been forced to make concessions to the tide of opinion. In Clinton's anti-crime legislation, the death penalty was reintroduced for a number of federal offences, including espionage and kidnapping where a death is involved.

States vary in their practice but each year the list of those refusing to employ capital punishment diminishes in length. Even states in the traditionally more liberal Northeast have reintroduced it while, in the South, executions are relatively common. In Texas alone, there were 146 during the Governorship of George W. Bush, the state then and now leading the nation for the number of its executions. More disturbing to those opposed to capital punishment than the varying practice of different states is the inconsistency with which the death penalty is applied. It is employed differently to different sections of the population. Whereas African Americans make up about 12 per cent of the population and whites 74 per cent, on death rows nearly 40 per cent of the inmates executed are black and only 55 per cent are white. This is not because blacks commit many more offences carrying the death penalty. Rather, according to studies by the US General Accounting Office, it is because the chances of a black defendant being executed are much greater than those of a white one – especially if the victim involved is white. Moreover, the inmates who inhabit death rows are invariably very ill-educated and poor (at least 90 per cent of those currently detained were unable to pay for their own legal representation).

Carter, James Earl (Jimmy) (1924–)

James Earl Carter, better known by his preferred name, Jimmy, was the thirty-ninth president of the United States. He grew up in Plains, Georgia in a family where the conversation often revolved around the family's peanut farm, the Baptist faith and politics. In 1946, he graduated from the Naval Academy in Annapolis, Maryland but, on his father's death, he resigned his naval commission and returned with his family to Georgia where he soon became prominent in the community, serving on county boards supervising education, the hospital authority, and the library. In 1962 he was elected to the state senate, where he served for two terms before becoming Georgia's seventy-sixth governor in 1971 He was the Democratic National Committee campaign chairman for the 1974 congressional and gubernatorial elections.

In December of that year, Carter announced his candidacy for the presidency and began a two-year campaign that gradually gained momentum. He was nominated on the first ballot at the party convention (1976) and then chose Senator Mondale of Minnesota as his running mate. In the Electoral College, he received 297 votes to 241 for President Ford.

The Carter presidency 1977–81

In domestic policy, the Carter administration's achievements included: measures to combat the continuing economic problems of inflation and unemployment; an ambitious programme of job creation; the creation of a comprehensive national energy programme conducted by a new Department of Energy, and decontrol of domestic petroleum prices to stimulate production and tackle the energy shortage; deregulation in energy, transport, communications, and finance; major educational initiatives via the new Department of Education; and major environmental protection legislation, including the expansion of the national park system, particularly that achieved by passage of the Alaska National Interest Lands Conservation Act. Over the four years of his presidency, he appointed record numbers of women, blacks and Hispanics to government positions.

In foreign policy, Carter continued the work of his two immediate predecessors by establishing full diplomatic relations with the People's Republic of China; completed negotiation of a nuclear limitation treaty with the USSR; and made a significant contribution to peace in the Middle East by securing the signatures of Egypt and Israel to the Camp David Accords (1978). His championship of human rights, however, was badly received by the USSR and some other

nations. Relations with the Soviet Union deteriorated markedly in the latter stages of his administration, following its invasion of Afghanistan. In addition, the seizure as hostages of the US embassy staff in Iran and the inability to free the captives in an abortive rescue attempt led to recurring bad headlines. (Iran finally released the fifty-two Americans the same day Carter left office.)

Continuing inflation and high interest rates at home, and frustration in his foreign policy goals abroad seriously damaged Carter's reputation. With polls showing that more Americans disapproved than approved of his performance, he was challenged for the Democratic nomination in 1980 by Edward Kennedy. Although the president defeated the challenge, he lost the November election to Republican Ronald Reagan.

After leaving office, Carter founded the Carter Center to work for the advancement of human rights and in achieving conflict resolution across the world. He has travelled widely to observe the conduct of elections, involved himself in peace negotiations and worked in the area of disease eradication and prevention in developing nations. He is the second oldest living former president, a few months younger than George H. Bush.

Categorical Grants

Categorical grants are grants made from the central government to states and to localities for specific, often narrow, purposes and to be used in specified ways. Recipients of categorical grants are often required to match a portion of the federal funds. It is money 'with strings attached'. There is normally a clear procedure for applying, implementing and reporting back on the use of such funding.

Categorical grants were rarely employed in the early twentieth century but, by the end of the New Deal, their use was becoming more widespread. It was in the 1960s, however, that they became commonly used to finance a range of governmental policies. The '1960s witnessed a marked expansion of the role of the federal government in initiating programmes and gaining state/local compliance. President Kennedy had promised to 'get the country moving again'

The growing use of categorical grants

Year	Number of grants
1900	5
1930	15
1960	132
1971	530

with the use of federal money. The policy was vigorously taken up by his successor. In his Great Society programme (including such initiatives as the War on Poverty scheme), President Johnson spoke of 'creative federalism', a more active form of co-operative federalism. This involved a massive expansion of federal aid, with grants to state governments increasing from nearly $7.5billion in 1960 to $32 billion by the end of the 1970s. Much of the increase in this funding came in the form of categorical grants, money being offered with the proviso that the recipient organisation carried out a specific task in such a way as to comply with detailed federal requirements.

During the Reagan years and after, the number of categorical grants was reduced. In the days of the New Federalism, there was a preference for block grants that allowed recipients much greater flexibility and discretion over how they spent money within the broad allocation substantive area covered by the funding.

Caucus

A caucus is a face-to-face meeting of party members, literally 'a gathering of neighbours'. In the United States it can refer to the members of the legislative body as, for instance, when a group belonging to a certain category meet in a forum in which they regularly discuss their ideas and decide how they can best promote their goals – for example, the Congressional Black Caucus and the Dairy Caucus.

More usually, the term is used in connection with the way in which the parties in the fifty states select their presidential candidates. Some states use a caucus system as an alternative to staging primary elections, the choice of candidate resting in the hands of party activists rather than with the wider public. Presidential caucuses are held by at

least one major party in thirteen states which tend to be the geographically large but thinly populated ones. The local party activists meet as a 'gathering of neighbours' on a precinct-by-precinct basis within the state, perhaps in a school or local hall. They discuss the merits of the nominees and then, in some cases orally, declare their preference, in others use a secret ballot. They choose delegates from among themselves who are pledged to individual candidates in the county-, district- and state-wide conventions that follow. When the choice is made, delegates pledged to the successful candidate can then cast their votes at the national party nominating conventions in July–August.

Iowa is the most well-known caucus for it is the contest which 'kicks off' the primary/caucus season. Residents of the 1,784 precincts meet in their local caucus and elect delegates to the ninety-nine county conventions. These county conventions then select delegates for both Iowa's Congressional District Convention and the State Convention which eventually choose the delegates for the national conventions. The outcome in Iowa offers an early indication of a particular candidate's prospects. The result may be misleading, however, for those who attend them tend to be strong party identifiers who are unrepresentative of those who may vote for a party in a general election. Moreover, turnout is usually low. In 2008, the Iowan Democrats backed the ultimate party choice in choosing Barack Obama, whereas the Republicans chose Mike Huckabee who represented many of their views but did not go on to win the party nomination.

Census

The Constitution requires that there should be a population count every decade. Since the first census in 1790, however, the need for further information about the United States's population and economy has became increasingly evident. As a reuslt, the decennial census steadily expanded in scope throughout the nineteenth century. By the turn of the century, the demographic, agricultural, and economic segments of the decennial census collected information on hundreds of topics. In recognition of the growing scale and complexity of the decennial census, President

Theodore Roosevelt asked Congress to convert the temporary Census Office into a permanent agency in 1902.

The census findings are used to allocate congressional seats (apportionment), electoral votes and funding for government programmes. Some states or local authorities also conduct their own censuses.

Chads

Chads refer to the paper fragments that result when a small piece of paper is punched out of punch-card ballot papers. They became a topic of national – indeed worldwide – interest in 2000 during the closely fought presidential election. The voting machines in Florida were unable to 'read' chads where the hole had not been properly pierced so that votes had, in some cases, not been recorded. Where machines had incompletely punched chads (leaving one or more parts still attached) those who checked the ballot papers had to decide on whether or not to count 'hanging chads', 'dimpled chads' and 'pregnant chads', names which became phrases of everyday conversation.

After a period of legal wrangling in the lower courts, the issue was decided by the Supreme Court in its ruling in *Bush* v. *Gore* (2000).

See also Bush *v.* Gore *(2000)*

Checks and Balances

A series of checks and balances was written into the Constitution, the idea being that governmental powers should be distributed to permit each branch to participate in, and thereby check and balance, the powers of the other branches. In this way, the potential for tyranny is avoided for excessive power does not reside in the hands of one agency or person. For instance, the Founding Fathers gave the president a power of veto over congressional legislation and the Senate the power of advice and consent on senior executive appointments. In the case of the appointment of Supreme Court judges, the president nominates his choice but the Senate has to approve the nomination.

Some checks have developed subsequent to the drafting of the Constitution. For example:

Political parties: The president and members of Congress belong to political parties and therefore there are bonds between those who share the same affiliation. This may help the president pass his or her legislative programme if Congress has a majority of members who share the president's political allegiance but make life difficult for a president facing a hostile Legislature (Bill Clinton, after November 1994).

Congressional committees: Although neither the president nor the Cabinet secretaries may belong to Congress, executive branch officers may be questioned in committee about their work and responsibilities. Like parties, committees do not feature in the American Constitution.

Over the years, the system of checks and balances can be seen to have been effective in several ways: presidents have vetoed more than 2550 acts of Congress: Congress has overridden more than 100 of these (some 4%); the Supreme Court has ruled more than 125 federal laws and more than 1200 state and municipal laws and ordinances 'unconstitutional'; the House has impeached seventeen federal officials; and the Senate has refused to confirm several nominations.

Cheney, Dick (1941–)

Brought up in Wyoming, Richard Cheney fist entered public service in 1969 when he joined the Nixon administration, serving in a number of positions at the Cost of Living Council, at the Office of Economic Opportunity, and within the White House. In a long career in public services, he went on to serve three other presidents: Gerald Ford (initially as Deputy Assistant to the President and later Assistant to the President and White House Chief of Staff); George H. Bush (as Secretary of Defence)' and George W. Bush (as Vice President in the period 2001–09).

In the events leading up to the war in Iraq, Dick Cheney was on occasion described as 'probably the most influential vice-president in American history' and 'the power behind the throne'. His is an unusual case of vice-presidential influence for, if he qualifies as the most powerful ever vice president, he is also among the least visible. As a running mate, he was a surprise choice and had several apparent disadvantages. He was an uninspiring and rare public speaker, a mediocre election campaigner and lacked an obviously warm and appealing personality to charm the electorate. In electoral terms, he appeared to bring little to the presidential ticket, coming from a small, conservative state that almost any Republican presidential candidate would expect to win. Moreover, there were serious doubts about his health, given his history of four heart attacks and the need for a pacemaker. Moreover, according to polls, he was not trusted by a significant element of those interviewed. His recent past as chief executive at the Halliburton oil services company, at a time when it dabbled in questionable accounting, made him appear to be the embodiment of America's corporate ills.

From a Bush point of view, however, Cheney had several assets as vice president. He was uncommonly and fiercely loyal to his boss, a person in whom the president could have absolute confidence. Although he was taciturn and rarely showed his cards in a meeting, he used private opportunities to speak his mind, and his judgement and views commanded his boss's respect.

Cheney's importance in the Bush administrations was recognised by admirers and critics alike. He was useful to the President in several ways:

- At the time of his selection, his appeal was that he had been White House chief of staff and defense secretary for the first President Bush during the 1991 Gulf War. He had the experience of handling foreign affairs and national security issues that the presidential candidate so obviously lacked.
- He was also able to say things that the president may feel but dare not say publicly. Whereas George Bush often speaks in terms of 'compassionate conservatism', his vice president had licence to betray the innermost thinking of some Republicans around the White House. He famously derided environmentalism as a 'personal virtue' and broke the 'no gloating' rule after the fall of Baghdad.
- The president viewed him as a quietly solid man, a heavyweight with *gravitas* who dealt

with day-to-day issues effectively. Bush delegated many administrative matters to Cheney, as well as giving him special responsibilities, such as working on a long-term energy plan. Above all, he leaned on him for advice. This was particularly the case after 11 September, when disaster struck. By nature hawkish on foreign policy, the vice president saw an opportunity to advance his ideas on pre-emptive action over Iraq, an issue that mattered to him because he always regretted that US-led forces had not pushed on to Baghdad during the 1991 Gulf War.

- The fact that he sometimes gave advice that did not confirm the president's own thinking only served to make him more respected. It made his advice seem worthwhile for he was thought to be a person who would say what he truly believed.
- Above all, Cheney had one quality that endeared him to the president. He did not covet his office. He did not need to be often seen in public for he was not seeking to build a popular reputation as part of a build-up to some presidential bid. He had no political ambitions.

In his quiet way, Cheney sometimes appeared to enjoy the image that he developed as an insider who wielded power behind the scenes, sometimes in a rather sinister way. On one occasion (March 2004) he surprised and delighted his audience of journalists when he responded to a question on how he would describe his role: 'I would say that I am a dark, insidious force pushing Bush towards war and confrontation.' That is exactly what his critics alleged.

See also *Vice Presidency*

Christian Coalition

The Christian Coalition is a US advocacy group largely comprising Christian fundamentalists and evangelicals. It is an organisation that identifies, educates and mobilises Christians for effective political action. It is concerned with ensuring that government strengthens and preserves traditional families and family values. According to its mission statement, its brief is to work continuously to:

- represent the pro-family point of view before local councils, school boards, state legislatures and Congress
- speak out in the public arena and in the media
- train leaders for effective social and political action
- inform pro-family voters about timely issues and legislation
- protest anti-Christianity bigotry and defend the rights of people of faith.

Since its inception, the Coalition has specialised in voter education, each year distributing tens of millions of voter guides throughout the fifty states. It also actively lobbies Congress and the White House on numerous issues and holds grassroots training seminars and events all around the country, that draw thousands of pro-family supporters, and helps to organise activists on critical issues facing the country.

The Coalition wielded great power within the Republican Party and helped shape the Republican majority in Congress in the mid- to late 1990s. It has, however, suffered from some internal disruption and schism in the years following the departure of Ralph Reed in 1997. Faced by breakaways and disaffiliations, declining membership and contributions, its critics claim that the Coalition has been on the verge of bankruptcy.

See also *Religious Right*

Citizenship

Citizenship refers to the status of being a citizen with its attendant duties, rights and privileges. The original Constitution did not define US citizenship but the Fourteenth Amendment remedied this deficiency by proclaiming that:

All persons born or naturalized in the United States, and subject to the jurisdiction thereof, are citizens of the United States and of the state wherein they reside. No state shall make or enforce any law which shall abridge the privileges or immunities of citizens of the United States; nor shall any state deprive any person of life, liberty, or property, without due process of law; nor deny to any person within its jurisdiction the equal protection of the laws.

Citizenship is one of the most coveted gifts that the US government can bestow. It is acquired in one of two ways:

- By birth, either within the territory of the United States or to American citizen parents, or
- By naturalisation; all applicants (with some exceptions) must pass a citizenship test before taking the Oath of Allegiance and officially becoming United States citizens.

In addition, the Child Citizenship Act (2000) allows any child under the age of eighteen who is adopted by an American citizen and immigrates to the United States, to acquire immediate citizenship.

Civil Liberties and Civil Rights

Civil liberties refer to those areas in which governmental power should rarely intrude on the free choice of individuals, such as free speech and freedom of worship. In these cases, citizens are protected against arbitrary or excessive governmental interference.

Civil rights cover those areas of social life in which the Constitution requires government to ensure that everyone is treated fairly and that opportunities are available to all who are able and prepared to seize them. Here, government is acting positively to protect individuals against discrimination or unreasonable treatment by other individuals or groups.

Whereas civil liberties (sometimes known as negative rights) are legal protections against governmental restriction of First Amendment freedoms, civil rights are legal protections against discrimination because of such things as ethnicity, gender or religion. In these cases, the government positively confers rights on disadvantaged groups, by passing anti-discriminatory legislation.

Most Americans are theoretically comfortable with the two concepts of liberties and rights which combine to ensure that they can do as they please unless they discriminate against others. Yet, in a society in which its Constitution proclaims 'equal protection of the laws', some have seen their rights denied. In particular, members of ethnic minorities and women have long experienced disadvantage, even if much has been done to redress the balance in recent decades. It remains the case that, on average, they earn much less than white males. They also find that, when they seek to advance up the occupational hierarchy, all too often they hit a 'glass ceiling' that limits their progress. As part of the attempt to reverse historical disadvantages, the Great Society programme contained measures of affirmative action. Today, critics of the idea see this as 'reverse discrimination'.

Civil Rights Legislation

The passage of the Thirteenth and Fourteenth Amendments marked a significant step towards the attainment of civil rights for all Americans. Yet, in spite of their passage, African Americans suffered from discrimination, intimidation and segregation for almost another hundred years.

It was not until the Eisenhower (1953–61) and more especially the Johnson (1963–69) presidency that significant progress was made towards equality.

The Civil Rights Act (1957) made it a federal offence to seek to prevent persons from voting in federal elections, and authorised the Attorney General to take legal action when a person was deprived or his or her voting rights. The legislation was targeted primarily at ethnic minorities.

The Civil Rights Act (1964), passed during the Johnson era, prohibited discrimination on grounds of race, religion or national origin, and in public accommodation and federally funded programmes. It also created the Equal Employment Opportunity Commission and addressed how states granted the franchise to their citizens. It was the most sweeping federal anti-discriminatory act passed by the US Congress. It had a significant impact on the position of ethnic minorities and women in American society.

In particular, the statute tackled the issue of segregation. It was passed at the height of the civil rights campaign as part of a bid to establish equality in the United States for black Americans. At the time, southern states still opposed integration, many of its politicians still being elected on an overtly segregationist ticket. Indeed, after

the failure to halt the passage of the legislation in Congress, a legal challenge was mounted. But the Supreme Court upheld the Act in *Heart of Atlanta Motel* v. *United States* (1964). Taken in conjunction with the *Brown* v. *Board of Education* ruling (1954) and the Voting Rights Act (1965), the statute was part of the trio of events that removed segregation from the United States.

The Civil Rights Act (1968) was a follow-up to the 1964 and other legislation. It made it illegal to discriminate in the sale, rental, and financing of housing, on grounds of race, religion, national origin, and (as amended in 1974) sex and (1988) the handicapped and families with children. The Act is commonly known as the Fair Housing Act.

The Civil Rights Act (1991) placed the onus on employers to justify any practices that had a negative impact upon ethnic minorities and women. Employers were required to defend any such practices as being necessary for the job in question, there being no alternative approach available. Compensatory damages could be awarded for intentional discrimination, and punitive damages in the case of employers found guilty of acting with malice or reckless indifference to rights based on sex, religion or disability (they could already be awarded in cases of racial discrimination, under earlier legislation).

The 1991 legislation also established a commission to enquire into the issue of 'glass ceilings', those invisible barriers that served to prevent minorities and women from becoming executives or assuming other important positions in management.

See also *Civil Rights Movement*; *Great Society*; *Johnson, Lyndon*

Civil Rights Movement

The Civil Rights Movement in the United States refers to the political, legal, and social campaign by black Americans to achieve racial equality and to gain rights of citizenship. It was primarily a challenge to the segregation that operated in the South although it moved on to address wider issues of racial discrimination across the whole country.

During the civil rights movement, individuals and civil rights organisations challenged segregation and discrimination via a variety of activities, including protest marches, boycotts and a refusal to abide by unjust laws. There is no precise agreement on when it began and when it ended – or, indeed, whether it has ended yet.

Already by 1945, there had been a clear and dramatic increase in black consciousness and activism, with black organisations using a combination of co-operation, coercion and confrontation in their dealings with whites. The number of significant black leaders was increasing although these leaders had frequent disagreements over the means of achieving their desired end of greater equality for blacks. Most commentators believe, however, that the real start of the civil rights movement was the Montgomery bus boycott (1955) which gave the movement one of its first 'heroes', Rosa Parks; served to unite Northern and Southern blacks, and helped it to win Northern white support.

Many of those who were most active in the Civil Rights Movement belonged to organisations such as the Congress of Racial Equality (CORE) founded in 1942, the Southern Christian Leadership Conference (SCLC), founded in 1957 in the aftermath of the events in Montgomery, and the Student Nonviolent Coordinating Committee (SNCC), founded in 1960. The oldest of them was the National Association for the Advancement of Colored People (NAACP) which had been formed in 1909 'to make 11,000,000 Americans physically free from peonage, mentally free from ignorance, politically free from disenfranchisement and socially free from insult'. The NAACP worked alongside local church leaders, especially Dr Martin Luther King, in the Montgomery dispute. Supporters sometimes spoke of the 'Southern Freedom Movement', rather than the more usual title, because this emphasised that the struggle was about more than civil rights under the law; it included fundamental issues of freedom, respect, dignity, and economic and social equality.

Some would see the ending of the Civil Rights Movement as coinciding with the passage of key legislation such as the Civil Rights Act (1964) and the Voting Rights Act (1965) or the Civil Rights Act (1968). Others would think of the death of Martin Luther King as representing the time by when the main phase of its work had been accomplished and the methods associated with him had lost much of their impact and influence. By then, the emergence of the Black Power Movement, which lasted from the mid-1960s to the mid-1970s, had broadened the aims of the Civil Rights Movement to include wider issues of racial dignity, economic and political self-sufficiency and freedom from oppression by the majority white population. Even among some black activists within SNCC and CORE, there was a feeling that, for too long, liberal white advisers to civil rights organisations had been allowed excessive prominence. The idea of co-operation between white and black Americans, that King had championed, was coming under closer scrutiny.

See also *King, Martin Luther*; *National Association for the Advancement of Colored People*

Civil War (1861–65)

The Civil War was the war fought between the federal government and the eleven southern states that seceded from the Union to form their own independent Confederate States of America (the Confederacy).

Tension between the Northern and Southern states had been developing for some time over issues such as the amount of control the federal government should have over the states, industrialisation (the North was developing a manufacturing economy, the South was more agrarian), trade and above all, slavery. Slavery was basic to the Southern economy for the plantations relied heavily on slave labour. As it became a more controversial issue, southerners became increasingly alarmed by the campaigning of the abolitionists and the calls from the North to end slavery altogether. Slavery raised the whole question of the relationship between the federal government and the states, their being growing resentment in the South over Washington's willingness to ignore states' rights and what was widely perceived as its general lack of sympathy for the Southern way of life.

In the 1860 presidential election, the

Lincoln-led Republicans had campaigned against the expansion of slavery beyond the states in which it already existed. On his election, seven Southern states withdrew from the United States, thereby provoking hostilities. The central government denounced the secession as illegal, making civil war inevitable. When a Confederate force attacked a US military installation in South Carolina, Lincoln called for a volunteer army from each state, leading to declarations of secession by four more slave states.

Four years of bloody, brutal hostilities ensued between the Northern forces led by Ulysses S. Grant and the southern troops of Jefferson Davis. The larger and better-equipped federal army was eventually victorious, Confederate resistance finally collapsing with Lee's surrender to General Ulysses Grant at Appomattox Court House in April 1865.

As a result of the Southern defeat, the Union was preserved. The cost of war had been enormous, how ever. More than six hundred thousand lives were lost, in addition to an undetermined number of civilian casualties, before the war ended. Slavery was abolished via the Proclamation of Emancipation (1862) and the Thirteenth Amendment (1865). The social, political, economic and racial issues of the war decisively shaped the era of reconstruction that followed and lingered into the twentieth century.

See also *Abolitionists/Abolition Movement*; *Confederacy*; *Lincoln, Abraham*

Clinton, Bill (1946–)

Brought up in Hope, Arkansas, Bill Clinton went on to graduate from Georgetown University prior to being awarded a Rhodes Scholarship to Oxford. He received a law degree from Yale in 1973. After graduation, he returned to his home state and taught law at the University of Arkansas before entering politics within the Democratic Party.

Bill Clinton married Hillary Rodham (1975) whom he had met at Yale. He was elected as the Arkansas Attorney General (1976) and then as state governor (1978) but lost his bid for re-election two years later. He regained the governorship (1983) and served until 1993. During his twelve years in office, Governor Clinton earned national recognition for his broadly progressive programmes, especially his efforts to improve the quality of public education.

In 1992, Bill Clinton won the Democratic nomination and went on to defeat incumbent George H. Bush and Ross Perot in the November presidential contest and become the forty-second President of the United States, the third youngest person, after Theodore Roosevelt and John F. Kennedy, to reach the White House. Clinton and his vice president, Albert Gore – both forty-four at the time of their inauguration (January 1993) – represented a new generation in American political leadership. The omens seemed encouraging because, for the first time in twelve years, the same party controlled the White House and Congress. That political advantage was brief for his opponents won both houses of Congress in the 'Republican Revolution' of November 1994. When the president won re-election in 1996, however, he became the first Democrat since Franklin D. Roosevelt to win a second term.

Policies and events in the Clinton presidency 1993–2001

The advantage of dealing with a Democrat-controlled Congress soon proved to be more apparent than real, as a number of presidential initiatives were soon rebuffed. In particular, Clinton's early years in office were noted for the abortive attempt to achieve a major change in the provision of health care. After the setback and the Republican successes in November 1994, his relations with Congress were especially strained, the more so as the president's personal life came under close scrutiny. Faced with the change of party control, he shifted emphasis, recognising that 'the era of big government is over'.

At the end of his term, his admirers could point to the achievements that resulted from his programme of moderate but progressive politics: the first balanced budget in decades (a massive deficit being turned into a surplus); the lowest unemployment rate in modern times; the lowest inflation in thirty years; the highest home ownership in the country's history; the strengthened environmental regulations; the restrictions on the sale of handguns; falling crime rates in many places; and reduced welfare rolls as a result of the reform of the welfare system. As part of a plan to celebrate the millennium in 2000, Clinton called for a great national initiative to end racial discrimination.

On the international scene, the Clinton administration expanded international trade; launched peace and trade initiatives in Africa and the Middle East; supported a worldwide campaign against drug trafficking; argued the case for an expanded NATO; intervened militarily to end 'ethnic cleansing' in war-torn Bosnia; bombed Iraq when Saddam Hussein blocked UN inspections for evidence of nuclear, chemical, and biological weapons; and supported the framework for peace being developed for Northern Ireland aimed at ending the sectarian strife in the province. On his global travels, he drew huge crowds who saw him as a strong upholder of American-style freedom.

The main blot on the Clinton record was his impeachment, only the second time this had happened to a president in American history. It came about when his indiscreet relationship with a young White House intern resulted in the decision of the House of Representatives to lay articles of impeachment (1998). He was found not guilty of the charges made but apologised for his personal conduct. As the proceedings unfolded, he basked in unprecedented levels of popular approval and, when he left office, he continued to enjoy historically high approval ratings for the job he had done.

Assessment of the presidency

For many Americans, much of the Clinton presidency was a serious disappointment. His political opponents claimed to disapprove of him and of his lifestyle. But many fellow progressives also felt disappointment. Not only had the universal scheme of health coverage not been achieved but some of the hopes the president engendered of a fairer society seemed to evaporate early on as he embraced the Republican agenda in a modified way to win his second term. Even some sympathisers saw the second administration as a time of missed opportunities and felt that, if months had

not been wasted on the long investigations into tales of dissembling, lying and sexual/financial misconduct, then more could have been achieved. In the later years in office, he proved to be a lame-duck president, bereft of bold, significant achievement. The frustration was all the greater for Democrats to bear as they had not been in control of the White House for most of the previous thirty years.

Yet there were many Americans who continued to like him, as an individual and as a president. In their eyes, he remained a likeable and attractive figure, whatever his personal lapses. They accepted that he lied and obstructed justice, and many found this reprehensible, but they were also unattracted by the behaviour of the moral puritans who assailed him. The venom of some of his adversaries rallied people into his corner. Whatever the letter of the law, many preferred to act on their own beliefs and were unwilling to condemn him for personal weaknesses. They were willing to praise aspects of his presidency. They looked at the Clinton years and knew that, as America entered the new millennium, it was enjoying an era of general economic prosperity and social peace for which the president could – and did – take some credit.

When Clinton left office, the state of the Union was seemingly strong. A mountain of statistics could be assembled to point to the robust good health of the country. As the presidency reached its conclusion, supporters could claim that the Clinton presidency had reasserted a role for government, and preached and practised a form of practical progressivism. If some progressives lamented the lack of clear doctrinal beliefs in his Democratic philosophy, many others would see his blend of pragmatism and prosperity as a very acceptable combination.

Clinton is a resourceful politician with a deft political touch. He is a fine election campaigner who possesses a rare facility for relating to ordinary people. As a communicator, he scores particularly highly. But his legacy will always be controversial, for the character issue dogged his presidency. He was a man of huge appetites that he did not seek to control. He behaved surprisingly imprudently for a man equipped with such astute political skills. His affairs and his evasiveness with the truth may be seen as character flaws. More seriously, they damaged his presidency and, some would say, the institution as well.

Since 2001, Clinton has been involved in public speaking and humanitarian work, addressing such issues as the prevention of HIV/AIDs and global warning. He has also created the William J. Clinton Foundation, the stated mission of which is 'strengthen the capacity of people throughout the world to meet the challenges of global interdependence'. More recently, he was involved in his wife's presidential bid. When she withdrew from the race at the 2008 convention, he was persuaded to support Barack Obama.

See also *Clinton and Impeachment*; *Clinton, Hillary*; *Health Provision*; *New Covenant*; *New Democrats*; *Television and Politics*

Clinton and Impeachment

The case against Bill Clinton originated in a case of sexual harassment concerning Paula Jones although he was not impeached for sexual misconduct. As part of the Clinton deposition (testimony) in the Jones case, he was asked about his relationship with Monica Lewinsky, a former White House intern. His answers were untruthful, and the perjury involved enabled the [Republican] prosecutor, Kenneth Starr, to recommend that the president be impeached. (The Jones case was eventually settled out of court and, if this had happened earlier in the proceedings, impeachment might have been avoided.)

Four articles of impeachment were laid before the House Judiciary Committee which, in December 1998, voted to approve further action on all of them, namely:

Article 1 Charging perjury before Ken Starr's Federal Grand Jury
Article 2 Charging perjury in the Paula Jones deposition
Article 3 Charging obstruction of justice in the Paula Jones case
Article 4 Charging failure to respond to the eighty-one questions posed by the House Judiciary Committee during the impeachment enquiry.

The whole House decided to go ahead on two counts, Articles 1 and 3. House Representatives handling the prosecution in the Senate emphasised how the obstruction of justice involved in the third article involved a threat to the rule of law that the president had sworn to uphold. They professed concern that, if he was allowed to escape punishment, this set a bad precedent. It would permit one system of justice for the powerful, another for other people. Some Democrats might have agreed with the view that he had behaved badly and violated his oath but the majority of them – and a few Republican moderates – were unconvinced that this amounted to 'high crimes and misdemeanours'. As Senator Jeffords put it:

I am gravely concerned that a vote to convict the President on these articles may establish a low threshold that would make every president subject to removal for the slightest indiscretion, or that a vote to convict may impale every president who faces a Congress controlled by the opposing party.

In other words, this would be a potentially devastating precedent.

The Senate agreed and voted to reject both articles, with ten Republicans defecting on the perjury count and five on Article 3.

Why did the impeachment proceedings fail? As we have seen, some Republicans could not accept that the gravity of the offences merited such a drastic punishment as was being proposed. They realized, too, that the way in which the charges were brought by a near-obsessed special prosecutor and passed by a Republican-dominated House smacked of undue partisanship. It seemed like a Republican witch-hunt against Clinton. If this was the public perception, then their party might suffer for its behaviour at the polls. Beyond this, senators were only too aware of the public mood. The president's personal popularity was increasing at the very time impeachment proceedings were being debated. To impeach him would have been particularly risky for the Republicans, bearing in mind that many Americans did not seem sufficiently troubled to want to be rid of him. They were able to distinguish between the flawed man (whose failings were well known to them at the time of his re-election in 1996) and the successful president who was presiding over a seemingly strong economy.

See also **Clinton** *v.* **Jones** *(1997)*; *Impeachment*; *Lewinsky, Monica*

Clinton, Hillary (1947–)

Hillary Clinton is a leading member of the Obama administration, serving as the sixty-seventh Secretary of State. She had previously served as the senator for New York 2001–09.

Born and brought up in Illinois, Hillary Clinton is a graduate of Wellesley College and Yale Law School. She is married to former President William Jefferson Clinton. They have one daughter, Chelsea.

As First Lady (1993–2001), Hillary Clinton balanced public service with private life. Her active public role began in 1993 when the president asked her to chair the Task Force on National Health Care Reform. She advocated expanding health insurance coverage, ensuring children are properly immunised, and raising public awareness of health issues. Her Health Care Plan failed to gain approval from in Congress in 1994, however.

During her husband's presidency, she became the only First Lady to be subpoenaed, testifying before a federal grand jury as a result of the Whitewatergate episode (1996). She was not charged with any wrongdoing in this or any of the several other investigations that were carried out in her eight years in the White House. There was some public sympathy for her endurance as the Lewinsky revelations unfolded and the president was impeached.

Clinton was elected to the Senate in November 2000, the first First Lady subsequently elected to public office. She serves on the Health, Education, Labor, and Pensions Committee; the Environment and Public Works Committee; the Special Committee on Aging; and the Armed Services Committee. She was re-elected in 2006 by a wide margin. As a senator, she initially supported the Bush administration on some foreign policy issues, most obviously by voting for the Iraq War Resolution. She subsequently opposed its conduct of the war and was a strong critic on most domestic issues.

In the contest for the Democratic nomination, polls showed that Hillary Clinton led the field of candidates throughout 2007. Once the campaign for delegates got underway in 2008, she won more primaries and delegates than any other female candidate in American history. She scored well in primaries where Hispanics or older, non-college-educated or working-class white voters predominated. She lost much of the support she may have expected from among African Americans, however, after some ill-chosen words that she – but more especially her husband – made about Barack Obama being limited in his appeal beyond the black community. After a long and fiercely fought battle, she was defeated by Obama whom she subsequently endorsed at the convention. In recognition of her qualities and political weight, he offered her the Secretaryship of State. At the time of her assumption of the office, her popularity ratings climbed to 65 per cent, the highest point attained since the Lewinsky scandal.

See also *Clinton, Bill*

Clinton v. Jones (1997)

Clinton v. *Jones* was a landmark case in which the Supreme Court had to decide whether a civil case brought against President Clinton could be heard until after his term as president had expired, since the suit would disrupt the performance of his duties as chief executive. In *Nixon* v. *Fitzgerald* (1982), the high court had held that a president has absolute immunity from civil lawsuits over actions taken in his official capacity.

Only three other presidents had been the subject of civil lawsuits involving incidents before they took office, Theodore Roosevelt, Harry Truman and John F. Kennedy. Clinton's case was also unrelated to his performance in the White House for it concerned claims concerning his alleged behaviour before he became president. Paula Jones claimed that Clinton had sexually harassed her while he was serving as Governor of Arkansas and that this was a violation of her civil rights.

In a unanimous decision, the Supreme Court rejected claims that a sitting president should, because of the pressures imposed by office, be protected from civil actions brought by other citizens. This opened the way for Paula Jones to seek damages from President Clinton.

See also *Clinton and Impeachment*

Clinton v. New York City (1998)

By a 6–3 majority, the Supreme Court struck down the line-item veto (as granted in the Line Item Veto Act, 1998) which had allowed the president to delete individual items of expenditure from bills passed by both houses of Congress.

The City of New York and other parties challenged the president's cancellation of an item of new direct spending in a section of the Balanced Budget Act (1997) that reduced federal subsidies paid to states to help finance medical care for the needy poor. The Snake River Potato Growers, Inc. and other parties challenged the president's cancellation of a limited tax benefit in the Taxpayer Relief Act (1997). In a consolidated ruling, the Court asserted in a 6–3 majority ruling that the president could not unilaterally amend or repeal parts of statutes that had been passed by Congress but must, rather, either accept or veto them in their entirety. To allow such discretion would be a violation of the 'finely wrought' legislative procedures of Article 1, as envisioned by the Founding Fathers.

Closed Primary see *Primaries*

Coalition of the Willing

A Coalition of the Willing is a term used in recent years to describe military or military/humanitarian interventions for which the United Nations Security Council cannot agree to mount a full UN peacekeeping operation.

It was used in relation to the forces sent to Afghanistan to fight the Taliban and root out al-Qaeda in the aftermath of 9/11. On that occasion, the US-led Coalition of the Willing included some, but not all, NATO nations, as well as many others from outside, whether they participated in a military, diplomatic or economic way. It was later employed by President Bush in relation to those states ready to confront Saddam Hussein and which were willing to be publicly associated with the US-led invasion and occupation of Iraq. The backing ranged from military and/or economic involvement to allowing fly-over rights or offering verbal endorsement.

See also *Afghanistan*; *al-Qaeda*; *War on Terrorism*

Coercive Federalism

Coercive federalism is a pejorative term used particularly by those opposed to the Great Society vision to suggest that, in the creative federalism of the 1960s, the central government was using its fiscal muscle to coerce and intimidate states into following national rather than local dictates. In other words, creative federalism had become coercive federalism, a situation in which there was, according to Kincaid (1990), 'unprecedented federal reliance on conditions of aid, pre-emptions of state and local authority, mandates, court orders, and other devices intended to ensure state and local compliance with federal policies'.

Cold War

The Cold War is a term that refers to the state of constant rivalry, suspicion and sometimes extreme tension in the post-1945 era between the Communist countries of eastern Europe (which were under the controlling influence of the Soviet Union) and the Western nations (led by the United States). The Cold War began in 1947, peaked at the time of the Cuban Missile Crisis in 1962, and was finally ended by the fall of the Berlin Wall in 1989, the subsequent breakdown of the Soviet system and the establishment of new democracies, such as those of Hungary and Poland. At times the conflict was acute, at other times there was a thaw in diplomatic relations. It was a 'cold' war as opposed to a 'hot' all-out one: protracted tension rather than direct military confrontation.

See also *Cuban Missile Crisis (1962)*

Concurrent Powers

Concurrent powers are those shared between two or more governments. They usually refer to those powers, such as that to levy and collect taxation, that are available to both levels of the federal system, and to national and state governments. They may be exercised simultaneously within the same territory and in relation to the same body of citizens. In the case of road transport, both Washington and the states are involved in creating an integrated national road system.

See also *Federalism*

Confederacy

The Confederacy is the collective name for those states that seceded from the Union in 1860 and 1861, thereby bringing about the Civil War. Eleven Confederate states actually seceded and two others, Missouri and Kentucky, sent delegates to the Confederate Congress, raised military forces for the Confederate Army and, from time to time, had state governments which favoured the Confederacy but did not formally secede from the Union. The federal government argued that the activities of these thirteen states were illegal.

The Confederate states were able to withstand the federal onslaught for four years but were eventually overwhelmed by superior numbers and resources. Their army surrendered at Appomattox in Virginia in 1865, and the states rejoined the Union after a period of reconstruction.

See also *Civil War*

Confederations

Confederations are loose organisations of states whose members yield some powers to a higher body while retaining their own autonomy and independence, including the right to leave the federation. Central control is modest with the component elements retaining primary power. The Articles of Confederation created such a situation in 1781 that lasted until the Articles were superseded by the implementation of the Constitution in 1789.

See also *Articles of Confederation*

Congress

Congress is the legislative branch of the United States federal government. It is the collective name for two elected chambers, the Senate and the House of Representatives, of broadly equal powers which, together, have responsibility for making federal law in the areas set out in the Constitution: namely, to collect taxes, borrow money on behalf of the United States, regulate commerce, coin money, declare war, raise and support armies and make all laws necessary and proper for the execution of its powers. The 'commerce' and 'necessary and proper' clauses have subsequently been interpreted broadly to enable Congress to expand its legislative role.

In addition, Congress acts as a watchdog over the other branches of the federal government, the Executive and the Judiciary. Oversight and scrutiny of the Executive involve approving presidential appointments, holding congressional hearings and the possession of a strong committee system. The floors of the chambers are inappropriate venues for detailed control of executive actions, so that much work is done in committee. The sheer extent of committee engagement in US government is remarkable, enabling Congress to achieve a unique level of oversight and cast light on matters that the Executive might prefer to conceal.

The changing significance of Congress

The Founding Fathers placed Congress at the centre of their deliberations. A leading role for the Legislature was judged an essential defence against executive tyranny. Hence, the list of powers that the Constitution allocates to Congress is longer and more detailed than that awarded to the president. In America as elsewhere, however, there has been a broad trend to executive power throughout the country's history.

In the nineteenth century, Congress normally dominated presidential-congressional relations so that only three presidents – Jefferson, Jackson and Lincoln – were able to alter the balance of power in their favour. Indeed, writing in the 1880s, Woodrow Wilson observed that 'in the practical conduct of the federal government . . . unquestionably, the predominant and controlling force,

the centre and source of all motive and of all regulatory power, is Congress'. With only a very few
exceptions, greater power resided on Capitol Hill
than in the White House right down to 1933.

Since the days of Franklin Roosevelt, Americans
have become used to a more assertive presidency,
for his assumption of the highest office led to a
massive extension of federal power as he sought
to implement his New Deal proposals to lift the
United States out of economic depression. By the
1960s, some academics and commentators were
beginning to write of an 'imperial presidency', in
which presidents were acting too independently
of Congress in both the domestic and foreign
policy spheres. It seemed that Congress could not
act effectively in an age when federal activity had
expanded so rapidly.

Since then, there has been a reaction against an
over-powerful presidency, and Congress has reasserted itself and streamlined its operations. Attempts
were made in the 1970s to impose more control
over the presidency (e.g., by the War Powers Act,
1973) and changes were made which were more to
do with the internal organisation of Congress itself
(e.g., the creation of the Congressional Budget
Office). As a result, Congress has been more willing
and able to challenge presidential policy. When the
party in the White House lacks control of Capitol
Hill, the opportunities for conflict between the two
branches soon become apparent.

Congress is one of the very few national legislatures that have become resurgent in recent
decades. Today, it remains the most influential
legislature in the world.

See also *Congressional Budget Office*; *Congressional
Committee Chairpersons*; *Congressional Committees*;
Congressional District; *Congressional Elections*;
House of Representatives; *Senate*

Congressional Budget Office (CBO)

The Congressional Budget Office is an advisory and
research agency within the Legislature of the federal
government. It was founded in July 1974 as a result
of the enactment of the Congressional Budget and
Impoundment Control Act. It was given a specialist
staff, whose expertise would enable congressmen
to seek out and acquire the sort of information that

presidents tended to deny them. This would enable
it to counter the perceived advantage of the president over Congress in recommending the annual
federal budget and thereby facilitate careful and
detailed scrutiny of the Executive.

The specific role of the CBO is to provide the
Congress with:

- objective, non-partisan and timely analyses to
  aid in economic and budgetary decisions on
  the wide array of programmes covered by the
  federal budget
- the information and estimates required for the
  Congressional budget process.

Congressional Committee Chairpersons

Committee chairpersons are selected by a caucus
of party members or by specially designated
groups of members. They occupy an important
position in American government, being key figures in the work of Congress. The chairmanship
of the most prestigious committees, such as the
House Rules Committee and the Senate Foreign
Relations Committee and several others, is highly
prized and much sought after.

In the days of the seniority rule, committee chairmanships had great security of tenure,
for the incumbent was usually experienced and
respected and often served for several years.
Today, that situation has changed, and there
are some able, younger persons who achieve the
chair. Neither can it be assumed that the chair
will be reappointed from session to session, sur-
vival in part depending on the ability to command
support within the ruling circles of the party. As
there is media coverage of committee hearings
and media scrutiny of what goes on in committee
(particularly in cases where there is a high-profile
investigation underway) committee chairs have to
be careful with regard to their personal behaviour
and performance in office. Their power has also
been diluted by the greater number of subcommittee chairs, rival sources of influence.

Nonetheless, chairpersons remain important in
the legislative process:

- They tend to be active and effective legislators,
  often experienced in making the system work

- They appoint members to subcommittees
- They have a major influence over the legislative agenda, determining the bills that will be considered and the priority attached to them
- They also have influence over the amendments called and the order in which they are discussed
- They direct financial resources
- In the days of the iron triangles of the past, the significance of the role was even greater for, between them, the relevant departmental secretary, interest-group representative and long-serving committee chair could largely shape policy in areas such as agriculture, tobacco and nuclear power.

Congressional Committees

Committees form an important feature of each chamber's organisation. They have assumed their present-day importance by evolution, not by constitutional design, for the Constitution makes no provision for their establishment.

Writing in *Congressional Government*, Woodrow Wilson stated that 'Congress in session is Congress on public exhibition, whilst Congress in its committee rooms is Congress at work.' Committees are the principal means via which the House and Senate carry out their legislative duties. The committee system divides the work of processing legislation and enables members to specialise in particular types of issues. The majority party in each chamber elects the head of each committee and holds a majority of the seats on most committees.

Early in the 111th Congress there were twenty committees in the Senate (sixteen standing and four special or select) and twenty-two in the House of Representatives (twenty standing and two special or select). The largest committee in the Senate was the Appropriations Committee (twenty-nine) and in the house the Transportation and Infrastructure Committee (seventy-five). The smallest in the Senate was the Ethics Committee (six) and in the house the Administration Committee (nine).

Types of congressional committee

There are several types of committee, notably:

Standing committees Standing committees are permanent, having fixed jurisdictions that operate from one session of Congress to another. These are the most important committees and the focus of much of the work performed by the Legislature. In the House, the Rules Committee has a crucial role with the power to delay or even stop legislation. The Ways and Means Committee raises money; the Appropriations Committee deals with how government spends that money. Many members of the House Budget Committee are drawn from these two bodies, with one member from each of the other standing committees. In the Senate, the Appropriations, Budget, Finance, and Foreign Affairs Committees are prestigious. Membership of the committees mentioned is highly prized, and congressmen and senators may have to wait years to be assigned to them, Usually, congressmen serve on one or two standing committees only whereas, in the smaller Senate, members are expected to serve on three or four.

Most standing committees spawn subcommittees. The House and Senate Appropriations Committees each has thirteen of them. The standing committees carry out the committee stage of the legislative process, holding hearings and taking evidence from witnesses who might be representatives of the administration, pressure groups or even ordinary members of the public. They also conduct investigations within their broad policy area, ascertaining – among other things – why problems occurred, whether legislation is working and what action might be taken. In the Senate, they additionally carry out the role of Advice and Consent.

Select committees These are temporary committees that cease to exist unless specifically renewed at the beginning of each new Congress. They may be asked to study or report on a particular topic but they do not receive or report on bills. Their investigations are often time-consuming and detailed, and tend to cover areas that would not be catered for in the investigative capacity of standing committees. An example taken from the Clinton years is the Senate Committee on Whitewater, established in the 104th Congress. It was given the task of uncovering any illegal activity in the president's involvement in a failed Arkansas real estate project in the 1980s.

Joint committees Permanent bodies, these include members drawn from both houses, and have continuing oversight over a particular area of policy. The Joint Economic Committee has the important tasks of studying and reporting on the president's annual economic report. Joint committees may also initiate legislation.

Conference committees Again drawn from both houses, these are temporary committees charged with resolving the differences between legislative proposals dealing with the same topic. These differences come about because of amendments attached to the bill by one chamber but not by the other, or because the two houses have passed different bills relating to the same subject. Before a bill goes to the president, it must be passed in identical language by both chambers.

Congressional District

A congressional district is an area established by law for the election of representatives to the United States Congress.

The fundamental purpose of the decennial census is to ensure that number of seats each state has in the House of Representatives reflects the relative size of its population as compared with other states. Each congressional district is to be as equal in population to all other congressional districts in the state as practicable. After the number of seats assigned to the individual states is determined (apportionment) the task of drawing the new congressional districts (redistricting) is generally given to each state legislature. Congressional district boundaries may be changed more than once during a decade.

See also *Reapportionment*

Congressional Elections

Congressional elections are held every two years. In the November of the even years, there are elections for thirty-nine (a third) members of the Senate and for all 435 members of the House of Representatives. They coincide with presidential elections every four years. Those held midway through a president's term in office are called midterm elections. Midterms serve as an indicator of what the electorate thinks about the president's performance so that their outcome is of considerable interest to any incumbent of the White House.

Elections for membership of Congress can be highly competitive and costly because of the central role that Congress plays in making laws. Many of the seats are won by incumbents, however, and, in non-presidential years, turnout is relatively low, often at around 30 to 35 per cent.

The 2008 congressional elections took place on Tuesday, 4 November 2008.

Conservatism

American conservatism contains many strands, among them fiscal conservatism, libertarian conservatism, religious conservatism and social conservatism. Among the organisations that seek to advance the conservative cause are Eagle Forum, the Heritage Foundation think tank and the American Conservative Union.

In the 1980s, traditional conservatism increasingly gave way to a new variety of ultra-conservatism, its adherents often known collectively as the New or Radical Right. Its members shared much of the ground occupied by other conservatives but they became associated with particular causes which they wished to see become accepted as public policy. They sought to achieve their programme via greater representation in Congress and, in November 1994, the *Contract with America* was based upon the New Right's philosophical approach.

As president, Ronald Reagan was successful in uniting the diverse elements, and he is widely viewed as a symbol of American conservatism. He espoused many conservative attitudes. His belief that 'government is the problem' and that, where necessary, government was better operated at local or state level wherever possible, appeal to many conservatives in America whatever their particular interpretation of conservatism.

The division between the two main parties is sometimes portrayed in terms of a distinction between liberals and conservatives. Since 1932 the

Republicans have generally adopted a more conservative stance than their opponents although the party has always had a liberal or moderate wing. In recent years, the centre of gravity of United States politics has moved well to the right so that, for many Americans, liberalism has gone out of fashion. Nevertheless, there are some party supporters who remain proud to be more liberal or moderate than the mainstream of the party.

Examples of the likely beliefs of American conservatives

Fiscal conservatives argue for small government, emphasising laissez-faire economics with minimum government interventionism in the economy; low governmental expenditure and taxation; balanced budgets; and narrowly tailored, focused welfare programmes.

Libertarian conservatives seek to blend libertarian and conservative ideas. They support economic freedom of the type favoured by fiscal conservatives but are likely to shrink from the social conservatism of many on the Religious Right. Libertarians oppose laws that restrict consensual and private sexual relationships between adults (e.g., gay sex, non-marital sex, and deviant sex) and drug use, and which impose religious views or practices on individuals. The hero of libertarian conservatives is Ronald Reagan who is quoted as saying: 'I believe the very heart and soul of conservatism is libertarianism.' Yet he did not agree with some of the freedoms supported by many libertarians.

See also *Blue Dog Democrats*; *Boll Weevils*; *Social Conservatives*; *Solid South*

Constitution

The Founding Fathers who devised the Constitution had several clear-cut objectives in mind, and these were set down in the fifty-two-word Preamble to the principal document. They may be summarised as:

- 'to form a more perfect Union'
- 'to establish justice'
- 'to insure domestic tranquility'
- 'to provide for the common defense'
- 'to promote the general welfare'
- 'to secure the blessings of liberty to ourselves and our posterity'.

The US Constitution is written and explicit. The document is relatively short and straightforward. It sets out the basic structure and functions of the various branches of government – executive, legislative and judicial – and the relationship between them. The Constitution is designated as the 'supreme law of the land', and this was taken to mean that, in any conflict with state constitutions or state laws, the federal Constitution and federal laws take precedence. Over the succeeding two centuries, decisions by the Supreme Court have confirmed and reinforced this idea of constitutional supremacy.

The Constitution is the framework against which all political activity occurs. It provides the answers to key questions of governmental

Issue	Attitude of many conservatives
Role of government	Distrust big government, prefer operation of free market
Industry	Pro-business, often alarmed by power of organised labour
Spending	Wish to keep spending down
Taxation	Wish to reduce taxes
Abortion	Support right to life
Affirmative action	Wary, wish to make inroads to undermine its operation
Crime/rights of accused	Tough on criminals, sympathetic to victims
Minorities	Many are WASPs (White Anglo-Saxon Protestants), suspicious of newer arrivals
School prayer	In favour
Foreign policy	Often sharp critics of active involvement overseas, some deeply isolationist (though neoconservatives support pre-emptive action)

organisation. Among other things, it explains the method of election for the federal Executive and Legislature, and the system of appointment to federal offices (including the Supreme Court). It itemises the powers of the central government, and denies certain powers to the states while giving them others. It provides certain civil, legal and political rights for the citizens that may not be taken away. It sets out the procedure for its own amendment.

Since its introduction, the Constitution has changed in a number of respects, but its underlying principles remain unaltered. These are:

- The three branches of government are separate and distinct, and the powers given to each of them are carefully balanced by the powers granted to the other two. Each branch therefore acts as a check upon the potential excesses of the other.
- The Constitution, and the laws passed under its provisions, and any treaties entered into by the president which have the approval of the Senate, take precedence over all other laws, executive acts and regulations.
- All free men are equal before the law and are equally entitled to its protection (but not slaves and women, until the passage of the Fourteenth Amendment). Similarly, all states are equal, none being entitled to special treatment from the federal government.
- Each state must acknowledge the laws passed by other states.
- State government must be republican in form, with final authority resting in the hands of the people.
- The people must have the right to change their form of government by legal means defined in the Constitution itself.
- Final authority rests with the people who can change the fundamental law should they so wish by amending or replacing the Constitution. They express their views through the ballot box.

Overall, amendment of the Constitution has been rare. Relatively few amendments have been introduced and fewer still ratified. There have been twenty-seven amendments to the original document.

Why has so little constitutional change come about? One answer is that, in comparison with peoples of other nations, Americans have been broadly contented with that which the Founding Fathers devised. Many regard their Constitution with considerable awe and reverence. Such deference is indicated by poll findings and other statements of popular opinion. These indicate that Americans are both familiar and content with their constitutional arrangements. Indeed, according to US historian, Theodore White, the nation is more united by its commonly accepted ideas about government, as embodied in the Constitution, than it is by geography.

On becoming president in 1974, Gerald Ford observed that 'our constitution works'. He was speaking in the aftermath of the Watergate Crisis that led to the downfall and ultimate resignation of President Nixon. Nixon was judged to have been involved with a cover-up, and various illegal operations, and thereby to have abused his position. As Americans firmly believe in the idea that 'we have a government of laws, not of men', Ford and many other Americans saw Nixon's removal as a vindication of their Constitution. It had served to protect freedom, restrain the behaviour of those in high office and define the limits of executive power.

Given such widespread approval of the form of government, it is not surprising that America has not shown the same interest in constitutional reform that has characterised other nations. Very few people publicly advocate radical changes in the structure of government established in 1787. Those who would tamper with it have to make a strong case for change and tend to talk in terms of restoring it to its original glory rather than making fundamental alterations.

Other than a broad measure of popular satisfaction with the Constitution, there are other factors that help to explain the fact that the original document has survived more or less intact:

- The most obvious factor is the relative difficulty of achieving change. The fate of the Equal Rights Amendment shows that the hurdles created more than two hundred years ago are difficult to surmount. In the two attempts to outlaw flag desecration in the Senate, it was possible to muster sixty-two and sixty-three votes in favour, in 1995 and 2000 respectively. This was an impressive figure but still five and four votes short of what was needed. Even if the Senate had passed the measure, then the hurdle of getting thirty-eight states to ratify the change would have been a hard one to achieve.

- The very lack of clarity in the wording of the Constitution means that the vague phrases can be interpreted over time in accordance with the needs of the day. The language is retained but the values mean different things in different eras. Congress is allowed to 'provide for the common defence and general welfare of the United States', a broad remit that enables the document to adapt to changing circumstances without formal amendment to its language.
- In particular, the ability of the Supreme Court to make 'interpretative amendments' means that the Constitution is kept up to date. When the Bill of Rights (the first ten amendments to the Constitution) was introduced, it applied only to the national government. But, over time, its provisions were extended by Court judgments to the states. Phrases such as 'due process' and the 'equal protection of the law' have been instrumental in allowing this adaptation to changing circumstances.

Assessment of the Constitution

Without flexibility of the type we have seen, it is unlikely that the arrangements made more than two hundred years ago would have survived in a country that has changed dramatically. The diversity of the nation has increased; the country has spread westwards across the entire continent; a stream of migrants has been absorbed; the population has soared; new resources have been exploited; and all sorts of differing interests have developed, be they those of the east-coast shipowners, who favoured free trade, the midwest manufacturers, who wanted protection for their goods from foreign competition, farmers, who wanted low freight charges or rail operators, who wanted high ones; Texas ranchers and Oregon lumbermen all have their own priorities and concerns. Yet the essential unity of the nation has grown stronger. That this has happened is in

no small part because of the success of the working arrangements drawn up in 1787 which had enough built-in flexibility to cater for changing circumstances.

Americans pride themselves on having the world's oldest written constitution, and many still marvel at the wisdom of the Founding Fathers in devising a document that has stood the test of time and been capable of adaptation to changing conditions and circumstances. One American writer has captured some of the appeal that the Constitution has for many Americans:

> Along with the flag, the Constitution stands alone as a symbol of national unity. America has no royal family, no heritage of timeless and integrative state institutions or symbols and no national church. Add to that America's history of being peopled by diverse religious, national and racial stocks, many of whom came long after the founding, and one can see how the Constitution could become such a focus of national identity and loyalty. There is precious little else to compete with it as an integrative symbol and evocation of America . . . Unlike the flag . . . which has changed dramatically over the years, with the constantly expanding number of states, the Constitution has endured virtually unchanged . . . This is, surely, another important source of its status as the focus of American identity, its stability and unchanging quality.

Disadvantages and advantages of the Constitution

Not all writers have supported the various provisions of the Constitution. It has been found deficient by some critics who have been exasperated with the diffusion of power that was basic to its operation. The young Woodrow Wilson, then a professor of government but a future president, wrote his analysis, *Congressional Government*, in 1890, and therefore before the extension of federal and presidential power occurred in the 1930s. He argued that the American arrangements made it difficult to achieve coherence in policymaking or responsible government. In his view, there were too many people involved in the evolution of policy and there was too little likelihood of progress being achieved.

Wilson lamented the absence of strong parties. He particularly disliked the low quality of Congressional debate that – largely because of party discipline – in his view lacked coherence. Too much discussion took place in obscure committees, headed by entrenched and autocratic senior members – a point not effectively addressed until the 1970s. He much preferred the British system of government with its clear allocation of power and responsibility.

A common point of criticism is the failure of the Constitution to permit quick and decisive action, except in times of crisis. One can understand why an American president might envy a British prime minister whose ability to achieve his programme within a parliamentary session is so much greater. But this was how the Founding Fathers wanted it. They were not looking for speedy action. They preferred to create machinery that would function at a slower pace, once all interests had had a chance to expound their viewpoints and to influence the outcome of the debate on any issue. This is what characterises the American approach, the fact that particular groups can frustrate the pace of advance where they think that change would damage their interests.

A contemporary of Wilson, the British Liberal statesman William Gladstone, saw things differently. He described the American Constitution 'as the most wonderful work ever struck off at a given time by the brain and purpose of man'. For all its alleged defects, many writers and commentators might still agree with him more than a century later. The Constitution has now survived for more than two hundred years, and proved its endurability over years of extensive and often rapid economic and social change. It may have been amended twenty-seven times but, after all, ten of these modifications were made at the beginning of its existence and, in any case, the amendments and their subject matter suggest that there has been no fundamental alteration in its character.

In other words, the Constitution remains much as it was originally written. The whole *New Deal* was carried through with no attempt to amend the Constitution, and leaders who wish to innovate use the wording of the Constitution rather than seek to get it changed. Political fashion and

practices have made the system viable in the twenty-first century, and presidents now rely on the Supreme Court to interpret their actions favourably.

It may well be that if the framers of the Constitution were alive today, they might be surprised at the way in which its practical operation has evolved, for it has provided the political framework for a society immeasurably different from the one they knew. For instance:

- The Founding Fathers had fears about democracy and felt that the principle needed to be controlled but, subsequently, the American system has become markedly more democratic. Politicians quickly saw merit in accepting the guidance of the electorate, and the importance of the popular will has become much greater than was ever intended.
- The balance of power has tipped in favour of the federal government at the expense of the states, most evidently since 1933 when President Roosevelt began his New Deal programme to lift the country out of serious economic depression.
- The presidency has become more powerful and, although it was envisaged as being remote and above the political fray, the Constitution has in fact become the most identifiable institution and an essential part of the political battleground. However rigid a written constitution may appear to be, in the American case, it is as flexible as most citizens wish it to be.

What has remained, as the Fathers envisaged, is the built-in conflict between the various institutions. They wanted no part of the machinery to acquire excessive power at the expense of the others, and created a system in which it was difficult to get all parts moving in the same direction and at the same speed. They were happy at the prospect of disputation between the federal government and the states, and between the institutions of the federal government. In this, their wishes have remained intact.

See also *Constitutional Amendment*; *Constitutional (Philadelphia) Convention*; *Constitutional Conventions*; *Founding Fathers*

Constitutional Amendment

The Founding Fathers recognised the need to make provision for amendment of the document should this become necessary. As the nation developed and circumstances altered, change would become necessary but it must not be so easy that it opened up the possibility of ill-conceived changes nor so unduly difficult that any proposal could be blocked by a minority of the nation. The answer was a dual process. Congress was given the right to initiate an amendment by a two-thirds majority vote in each chamber. Or the legislatures of two-thirds of the states could request Congress to summon a national convention to discuss and draft amendments, a method never yet employed. Whichever procedure was adopted, there must be approval from three-quarters of the states before any amendment entered into force. This has usually been granted by state legislatures but it can be done via ratifying conventions.

More than 5,000 amendments have been suggested but only thirty-three have been submitted to the states. Twenty-seven alterations to the Constitution have been made so far. In twenty-six cases, constitutional amendment was brought about by congressional action and state legislature ratification. The Twenty-first Amendment, which ended the experiment of Prohibition, was proposed by Congress but ratified by state conventions.

Most of the twenty-seven changes were made in the very early period after it was adopted: the first ten were made in the first two years. Subsequent amendments have covered a wider range of topics, among them the method of electing the president, the outlawing of slavery, the right of Congress to levy income tax and the direct election of US senators. Most recently:

- **The 25th Amendment (1967)** provided for filling the office of vice president when it becomes vacant in midterm. The president must make a nomination which then requires majority approval in both chambers. (The procedure was to be used shortly afterwards, in 1973, when President Nixon required a new vice president on the resignation of Spiro T. Agnew, and again the following year when, on the elevation of that vice president – Ford – to the presidency, a new second in command was needed.)
- **The 26th Amendment (1971)** lowered the voting age to eighteen.
- **The 27th Amendment (1992)** concerned congressional salaries; no payrise under consideration can come about until an election has intervened.

Indirect means of amending the Constitution

We have outlined the formal means of constitutional amendment. The Constitution can also be changed by judicial interpretation for, in a landmark ruling, *Marbury* v. *Madison* (1803), the Supreme Court established the doctrine of judicial review which is the power of the Court to interpret acts of Congress and decide on their constitutionality or otherwise. This doctrine enables the Court to offer its verdict on the meaning of various sections of the Constitution as they apply in changing economic, social and political circumstances over a period of time. In other words, without any substantive changes in the Constitution itself, the thrust of constitutional law can be changed.

In the same way, congressional legislation can also broaden and change the scope of the Constitution, as also can rules and regulations of the various agencies of the federal government. Everything depends upon whether such legislation and rules conform to the intentions of those who devised the Constitution.

See also Marbury v. Madison *(1803)*

Constitutional (Philadelphia) Convention

In 1787, the legislative body of the Republic, the Continental Congress, put out a call to all the states inviting them to send delegates to Philadelphia on 25 May 1787. The meeting was to be held in Independence Hall where the Declaration of Independence had been adopted eleven years earlier. The delegates met to consider 'the situation of the United States, to devise such further Provisions as shall appear to them necessary to render the Constitution of the federal Government adequate to the emergency of the Union'. They were authorised to amend the Articles but, in the event, they cast them aside and proceeded to draw up a charter for a more central-ised form of government. It was this Constitution that was completed on 17 September 1787 and formally adopted on 4 March 1789.

Inevitably, there were disappointments with the outcome of the deliberations, and some del-egates departed before the signing ceremony (of the thirty-nine who did sign, few were completely satisfied with what had been accomplished). The settlement had to be a compromise, given the obvious differences between large and small states, and those between who wanted and those who baulked at an extension of federal power. Benjamin Franklin articulated the viewpoint of those who had doubts but still gave their acquies-cence: 'There are several parts of this Constitution which I do not at present approve, but I am not sure I shall never approve them.' Acceptance was justified because 'I expect no better and because I am not sure that it is not the best.'

It was, in theory, desirable for every state to ratify (give formal approval to) the new docu-ment but the convention delegates realised that this would be difficult to achieve quickly. They boldly declared that the proposed Constitution should become effective when nine had given their approval. Delaware was the first to sign, followed by Pennsylvania and New Jersey, and then by Georgia and Connecticut where com-fortable majorities were achieved. There was a fiercely contested struggle in Massachusetts over the absence of any Bill of Rights but, in early 1788, it, too, narrowly endorsed the document. In June 1788, the ratification by Maryland, New Hampshire and South Carolina meant that nine states had given their support, enough to see the document accepted.

Constitutional Conventions

Constitutional conventions are unwritten and non-legal rules of constitutional behaviour, cus-toms of political practice that are usually accepted and observed. They are more relevant to British than to American constitutional practice but they are not totally unknown. It is a convention that electors in the Electoral College will cast their votes for the presidential candidate to whom they were pledged on polling day in November. Normally this is the case but, on occasion, this has not happened. Electors have switched their allegiance (as in 1988 when a Democrat voted for Lloyd Bentsen, the vice-presidential nominee rather than for Michael Dukakis, the candidate for the presidency) or withheld their vote to make a protest (as in 2000 when a Gore-supporting Democrat from the District of Columbia cast a blank vote to make a point about the city's lack of representation in Congress).

When American conventions are flouted, they can be turned into law. The Americans passed an amendment to limit the period for which a president could serve in office. Until 1940, it had been assumed that presidents would withdraw after two terms. Franklin Roosevelt had not done so, standing for a third and then a fourth term. The Twenty-second Amendment (1947) restored the situation to what had always been assumed.

Containment

Containment was the goal of the foreign policy pursued by the United States in the Cold War. It was based on the idea of containing Communist – particularly Soviet – aggression and expansion by strengthening US allies on the periphery of the Soviet empire. It was laid down as part of the Truman Doctrine which outlined America's place in the world and was to become the founda-tion of foreign policy up to the late 1960s and/or early 1970s.

See also *Cold War; Truman, Harry; Truman Doctrine*

Contract with America

The Contract with America was the policy plat-form agreed by House Republican candidates in the run-up to the elections of November 1994. Strongly influenced by the Heritage Foundation, its provisions represented the view of many con-servative Republicans on the issues of shrink-ing the size of government, promoting lower taxes and greater entrepreneurial activity, and welfare reform. It comprised ten bills that the Republicans promised to bring to a vote on the floor of the House during their first hundred days in office, should they be elected. They were:

- The Fiscal Responsibility Act, a constitutional amendment requiring a balanced budget
- The Taking Back Our Streets Act, an anti-crime package
- The Personal Responsibility Act, designed to cut welfare spending and discourage dependency
- The Family Reinforcement Act, to strengthen family life
- The American Dream Restoration Act, to provide tax relief for the middle classes
- The National Security Restoration Act, to limit US commitment to the United Nations
- The Senior Citizens Fairness Act, to remove the restrictions on what elderly people could earn
- The 'Common Sense' Legal Reform Act, to prevent frivolous litigation
- The Job Creation and Wage Enhancement Act, a package to help business and promote employment
- The Citizen Legislature Act, a constitutional amendment to impose twelve-year term limits on members of the two chambers of Congress.

This was an unusually clearly defined programme of action for an American party. As Speaker, Newt Gingrich was influential in smoothing its passage through the House, aided as he was by a more united and disciplined party than had usually been the case in the past. All ten items in the Contract were brought to a vote, as promised. Nine passed, the sole exception being the provision for Term Limits which received a plurality but required a two-thirds majority as it was a constitutional amendment. Most of the measures successfully passed through the chamber. In the highly partisan atmosphere created at the time, congressional Democrats successfully blocked the passage of several of the Republican initiatives, thereby blunting its impact as a major issue in the 1996 elections.

See also *Gingrich, Newt; Republican Party*

Co-operative Federalism

Co-operative federalism was a mid-twentieth-century view of federalism in which national, state and local governments acted as partners, their powers becoming intertwined as they exercised responsibility for a range of key functions.

The New Deal programme inaugurated the era of co-operative federalism, which emphasised the partnership of different levels of government in providing effective public services for the nation. As Cummings and Wise (2000) put it: '[The two levels] were related parts of a single government system, characterised more by cooperation and shared functions than by conflict and competition.' Writing a few decades previously, Grodzins (1966) did not view the American system as a 'layer cake' of three distinct and separate planes, but rather as a 'marble cake', an inseparable mixture of differently coloured ingredients. In the nature of the relationship, the federal government supplemented, stimulated and assisted states, rather than pre-empting them.

See also *Federalism*

Court-packing Scheme

The court-packing scheme refers to a plan of President Franklin Roosevelt to increase the size of the Supreme Court and then bring in several new justices with the intention of changing its balance of opinion.

Overwhelmingly elected in 1932, Roosevelt promised a New Deal of social and economic involvement by the government in an America ravaged by the Great Depression. But the Supreme Court, most of whose justices were appointed by the Republican presidents of the 1920s, soon began to undo his work by ruling his New Deal laws unconstitutional on a vote of 5 to 4. In May 1935, the Court invalidated the Railroad Retirement Act of 1934 (a law that had established pensions for railway workers) and the National Industrial Recovery Act of 1933. In January 1936, it ruled the Agricultural Adjustment Act of 1933 unconstitutional. Roosevelt lambasted the justices for these rulings, his animosity rapidly increasing towards the business-oriented and conservative-minded court of 'Nine Old Men' in which six justices were age seventy or older and the youngest was sixty-one.

Re-elected in 1936 by an even larger majority than in 1932, Roosevelt (at that time the only twentieth-century president not to have appointed a Supreme Court justice in four years) began to contemplate 'the court problem' publicly. A confrontation of some sort seemed inevitable but, even among those closest to Roosevelt, few expected what came next. In 1937, he disclosed a Judiciary Reorganization Bill to reorganise the federal judiciary. The measure called for all federal judges to retire by the age of seventy. If they failed to do so, the president could appoint another judge to serve in tandem with each one older than seventy. The practical effect of the proposal would have been to allow Roosevelt to have appointed immediately six associate justices sympathetic to his ideas, thereby increasing membership of the Court to fifteen and tipping its ideological balance in his direction. A Congress dominated by Democrats would have undoubtedly appointed judges friendly to Roosevelt and his New Deal agenda.

This proposal provoked a storm of protest, even among some members of the Democratic Party. The newly re-elected vice president John Nance Garner led the opposition to what opponents referred to as the court-packing bill. It was rejected in Congress in July 1937 yet, in spite of the antagonism it had aroused, Roosevelt's initiative did in one sense succeed. Justice Owen Roberts began to switch his position, voting to uphold New Deal measures thereby, in effect, creating a liberal majority. Journalists wrote of 'the switch in time that saved nine'. Thereafter, the opinions handed down by the Court (which had sometimes previously resulted in 9–0 defeats for New Deal measures) were more favourable to the government, and key legislation was allowed to pass on to the statute book.

President Roosevelt was eventually able to appoint nine justices to the Supreme Court and by 1941 eight of its members were Roosevelt appointees.

See also *New Deal*; *Roosevelt, Franklin*

Courts

There are today two parallel systems of courts in the United States that, between them, cover the range of civil and criminal cases. There are the state court systems established under the individual state constitutions: these decide actions and settle disputes concerning state laws. Secondly, there is the federal judicial system which has become relatively more important as the country has expanded and the amount of legislation passed by Congress has increased. In effect, there are therefore fifty-one different judicial structures.

State courts

The practice of state courts may vary significantly for it is the essence of federalism that the states may run their own affairs in the way best suited to their own wishes and requirements. Differences of operation and terminology are inevitable, and this makes general comment on their structure more difficult. For instance, judges are elected in approximately three-quarters of the states while in others, they are appointed.

States are responsible for passing and enforcing most of the civil and criminal law of the United States. For every person in a federal prison, there are at least eight times more in a state one. The vast majority of cases is resolved in state municipal or justice courts in towns and cities, with a right of appeal to the state appeals courts or, in a small minority of cases, involving the interpretation of the state constitution or basic constitutional rights, to the state Supreme Court.

Federal courts

Federal courts enforce federal law and state courts enforce state law but the relationship between the two systems is more complex than this. The federal Constitution is the supreme law of the land and, if state law conflicts with it or with federal laws made under that Constitution, then state law gives way. This is made clear in the 'supremacy clause' of the Constitution (Article VI). Because of it, decisions made in the federal courts can have a broad impact on those made in the state courts. The federal courts are often called the guardians of the Constitution because their rulings protect rights and liberties guaranteed by it.

The structure of the federal judicial system is relatively simple. There are three layers of courts. At the bottom of the pyramid are the district courts, above them are the circuit courts of appeal and at the apex of the system is the Supreme Court, the highest court in the land.

The District Courts The United States district courts are the trial courts of the federal court system. The district courts have jurisdiction to hear nearly all categories of federal cases, both civil and criminal. Every day hundreds of people across the nation are selected for jury duty to help decide some of these cases.

There are ninety-four federal judicial districts, including at least one district in each state, the District of Columbia and Puerto Rico. Three territories of the United States – the Virgin Islands, Guam, and the Northern Mariana Islands – have district courts that hear federal cases, including bankruptcy cases.

Bankruptcy courts are separate units of the district courts. Federal courts have exclusive jurisdiction over bankruptcy cases, so that they cannot be filed in state courts.

Courts of Appeals The ninety-four US judicial districts are organised into twelve regional circuits, each of which has a United Court of Appeals. A court of appeals hears appeals from the district courts located within its circuit, as well as appeals from decisions of federal administrative agencies.

In addition, the Court of Appeals for the Federal Circuit has nationwide jurisdiction to hear appeals in specialised cases, such as those involving patent laws and cases decided by the Court of International Trade and the Court of Federal Claims.

Creative Federalism

Creative federalism was a term coined by President Johnson to describe his own view of the relationship between Washington and the states.

Creative federalism was not supposed to be a means of imposing programmes from the centre although it did involve a great expansion in the role of the federal layer. The idea was that Washington, the top tier, would seek out and respond to local ideas and demands, and be able therefore to provide the type of service and the money which was wanted by those who lived in each locality. The role of state governments and legislatures was of less importance, the wide-ranging series of civil rights and other measures imposing a greater degree of regulation upon state capitals.

See also *Federalism*

Credit Crunch (or Squeeze)

A credit crunch (or squeeze) is a situation in which there is a dramatic reduction in the availability of loans and other types of credit which banks and capital markets can lend to businesses and consumers. Lenders become reluctant to lend funds and they tighten their borrowing requirements.

A credit crunch is often brought about by a sustained period of inappropriate or even reckless lending that results in losses for lending institutions and investors in debt when the loans turn sour and the full extent of bad debts becomes known. In the case of the United States, the problems in the sub-prime market (which enables borrowers to gain access to loans despite having bard credit history) created turmoil in the American credit markets in 2007. The problems turned global and forced central banks in Europe and the United States to pump a massive injection of funding into the financial system to keep it operating smoothly.

The tightening credit market proved to be a drag on the economy as a whole, seriously affecting the housing market, and companies reliant on credit, who found it harder to get loans for business needs.

See also *Bail-out*; *Emergency Economic Stabilization Act*; *Financial Crisis (2007)*; *Fiscal Stimulus*; *Paulson Plan (2008)*

Crisis Management

A crisis is a sudden unpredictable and potentially dangerous event. Most occur in the realm of foreign policy. Crises often involve hot tempers and high risks. Quick judgements are needed despite the availability of only sketchy information.

Whether it is American hostages held in Iran or the discovery of Soviet missiles in Cuba, a crisis challenges the president to make difficult decisions. In origin, crises are rarely the president's doing but, handled incorrectly, they can be the president's undoing. Crisis management is fundamental to the presidential roles of Chief Diplomat and Commander-in-Chief.

Early in American history, there were fewer immediate crises. By the time officials were aware of a problem, it had often been resolved. Communication could take weeks or even months to reach Washington. Similarly, officials' decisions often took weeks or months to reach those who were to implement them. The most famous battle of the War of 1812, the Battle of New Orleans, was fought after the United States had signed a peace treaty with Great Britain. Word of the treaty did not reach the battlefield and so General Andrew Jackson won a victory for the United States that contributed nothing towards ending the war, though it did help to put him in the White House as the seventh president.

With modern communications, however, the president can instantly monitor events almost anywhere. Moreover, because situations develop more rapidly today, there is a premium on rapid action, secrecy, constant management, consistent judgement, and expert advice. Congress usually moves slowly (one might say deliberatively) and is large (making it difficult to keep secrets), decentralised (requiring continual compromising) and composed of generalists. As a result, the president who can come to quick and consistent decisions, confine information to a small group, carefully oversee developments, and call upon experts in the Executive branch, has become more prominent in handling crises.

Throughout the century, crises have allowed presidents to become more powerful, and crisis management is a natural role for most who assume the presidential role. Most have been only too willing to step in to the vacuum and seize their chance to lead. Postwar examples of crisis management have included Truman and the Berlin Blockade, Kennedy and Cuba, Bush Senior and Iraq, and Clinton and Iraq/Bosnia.

Most recently, George W. Bush confronted the gravest immediate threat to the United States since Pearl Harbor, the 11 September attacks on New York and Washington.

See also *Cuban Missile Crisis (1962)*

Cuban Missile Crisis (1962)

The Cuban Missile Crisis was a major confrontation between the superpowers, the United States and the Soviet Union, during the era of Cold War.

The crisis came about when the Kennedy administration received intelligence gathered by U-2 spy planes flying over Cuba of the installation of missile-launching sites on the Communist island, then ruled by the pro-Soviet Fidel Castro. Faced with the threat posed by atomic warheads targeted at the United States, the president reinforced the US naval base at Guantánamo, ordered a naval quarantine or blockade against Soviet military shipments to Cuba and demanded that the Soviet Union remove its missiles and bases from the island. The crisis intensified as Soviet merchant vessels, thought to be carrying missiles, approached the US blockade. Tension was at its height with the rival forces by then placed on full alert. On 28 October the Soviet ships were ordered by Premier Khrushchev to turn back. The Soviet Union agreed to Kennedy's demand that the missile bases be dismantled in return for a pledge not to attack Cuba and the removal of some obsolete US Jupiter missiles in Turkey. The naval blockade was lifted on 20 November and, by the end of the year, the missiles and bombers were removed from Cuba

One outcome of the crisis was the establishment of a direct, exclusive line (the 'hot line') of communication, to be used in an emergency between the two world leaders. Another was the retreat from brinkmanship and the signing of a Nuclear Test Ban Treaty which led to an easing of the Cold War.

The crisis ranks with the Berlin Blockade as one of the major episodes of the Cold War. It is often regarded as the moment in which the Cold War came closest to global nuclear confrontation, coming as it did as the climax to an acutely antagonistic period in US–Soviet relations.

D

Declaration of Independence (4 July 1776)

The Declaration of Independence is the name given to the document adopted by the Second Continental Congress which declared that the thirteen colonies were independent of Great Britain. An elaboration of Richard Henry Lee's Resolution of 7 June, which first proclaimed independence and was passed on 2 July, the Declaration – written primarily by Thomas Jefferson and formally entitled The Unanimous Declaration of the thirteen United States of America – explained and justified the decision made by the colonies to declare their independence from Britain. John Hancock was its first signatory.

The Declaration and the US Constitution are considered to be the founding documents of the United States of America where 4 July (the day the wording of the Declaration was approved by Congress) is celebrated as Independence Day. Not only did the Declaration declare the colonies to be free and independent states, it also articulated the fundamental principles under which the new nation would be governed. It established the goals of American politics, whereas the Constitution outlined the means by which they were to be attained. At the time it was issued, the American colonies were 'united' in declaring their independence from Great Britain but were not yet declaring themselves to be a single nation. That union would evolve and take shape during the next few years after the Declaration was proclaimed.

The Declaration advances two fundamental principles under which the newly formed nation would be governed. It holds that governments have one primary purpose, to secure the 'unalienable' rights' of their citizens. It also makes it clear that governments derive their powers and authority from the 'consent of the governed'. It bears the imprint of the writings of the English liberal philosopher, John Locke. His social contract theory was highly influential upon, and inspirational to, those who drew up the Declaration which begins with resounding words highly reminiscent of Lockean individualism:

> We hold these truths to be self-evident, that all men are created equal, that they are endowed by their Creator with certain unalienable Rights, that among these are Life, Liberty and the pursuit of Happiness. – That to secure these rights, Governments are instituted among Men, deriving their just powers from the consent of the governed . . .

The document argues that via a process of social contract free men create governments to serve their interests and that, if any government fails to serve them, then it can be rightfully replaced: 'it is the Right of the People to alter or to abolish it' and to create a new government in its place. George III had breached or violated the contract by his arbitrary acts and tyrannous behaviour. Hence the colonists must sever relations with Britain and its monarchy, and establish alternative governments of their own creation.

United States President Abraham Lincoln succinctly explained the central importance of the Declaration in his Gettysburg Address (1863): 'Four score and seven years ago our fathers brought forth on this continent, a new nation, conceived in liberty, and dedicated to the proposition that *all men are created equal.*' The exalted and unforgettable phrases of the Declaration make it at once the nation's most cherished symbol of liberty and Jefferson's most enduring monument.

See also *Constitution*; *Founding Fathers*; *Jefferson, Thomas*

Defense Department

The United States Department of Defense (DoD) is the federal department charged with co-ordinating and supervising all agencies and functions of the government relating directly to national security and the military. The National Military Establishment (NME) was set up under the terms of the National Security Act of July 1947. The first Secretary of Defense assumed office in 1947 at approximately the same time and, within two years, the DoD was established under that name, it being by then realised that NME had as its obvious pronunciation a sound too reminiscent of 'enemy'.

The Department is based in The Pentagon, in Arlington County, Virginia, across the Potomac River from Washington DC. It has three major components – the Department of the Army, the Department of the Navy, and the Department of the Air Force. Among its many agencies are the Missile Defense Agency, the Defense Advanced Research Projects Agency (DARPA) the National Geospatial-Intelligence Agency (NGA) and the National Security Agency (NSA).

With over 1.3 million men and women on active duty, and 669,281 civilian personnel, the department is the nation's largest employer. Another 1.1 million serve in the National Guard and Reserve forces. About two million military retirees and their family members receive benefits.

Democracy

The term 'democracy' derives from two Greek words, *demos* meaning 'people' and *kratia*, signifying 'rule of' or 'rule by'. Many people therefore see democracy as meaning 'people power', with government resting on the consent of the governed. According to Abraham Lincoln, democracy is 'government of the people, by the people and for the people'.

Athenian democracy was practised in a small city-state; the citizens made some political decisions directly and controlled others. This was direct democracy in action with people coming together to make decisions whenever necessary. After the Greeks, the notion of democracy went out of fashion, being associated in the eyes of many rulers with factional conflict and violence. Until the early nineteenth century, far from government being rule by the many, it was actually in effect rule by the very few who were not subject to popular control. The majority of people were seen as unfit to rule, and members of the nobility who possessed governing skills did not feel that they should be subject to the whims of the illiterate and ill-informed majority. In *The Federalist*, James Madison echoed the outlook of many of his co-framers of the American Constitution when he wrote: 'Such democracies [as the Greek and Roman] have ever been found incompatible with personal security of the rights of property; and have in general been as short in their lives, as they have been violent in their deaths.'

The word 'democracy' is not used in the US Constitution. The framers preferred the term 'republic' to describe the form of government that they wished to create. It lacked the connection with direct democracy, with its possible associations with demagogues, mass rule and the mob. The vision of the Founding Fathers was of a representative system, a republic in Plato's sense, by which all those in power obtain and retain their positions as a result of winning elections in which all free adults are allowed to take part. Today, America is a representative democracy in which the people play a part in decision-making indirectly, through their elected representatives. The nineteenth century saw the spread of representative democracy which is today widely accepted as the only viable form of democracy in such a vast country.

America has long been regarded as a model democracy but some commentators believe that, today, the system is not working well. Indeed, Kenneth Dolbeare (1996) has written of 'the decay of American democracy' and asks whether the condition is a terminal one. He sees the problem as one compounded by the sheer scale and power of the government in Washington, for this has meant that it is 'increasingly connected only to a steadily shrinking proportion of its affluent citizens'. He discerns several factors that have contributed to the 'decay':

- the decline of political parties
- the rise of television
- the dominance of money as a means of access to television and electioneering in general
- the rise of political action committees
- near-permanent incumbency in Congress
- a general abandonment of leadership to the latest opinion poll.

More serious than any of the above factors, however, he sees the 'thirty-year trend toward abandoning political participation' as the most alarming indication of decay. In particular, this means a more or less continuous decline in voter participation, particularly a problem for those in the bottom one-third of the social pyramid. He notes the paradox that has emerged:

> The growing underclass has rising needs for education, jobs, training, health care etc., but these very services are being held to a minimum or even cut – and yet the voting participation of this same underclass is declining faster than that of any other population group.

Other writers have also noted that, at the very time that the Soviet control of eastern Europe has broken down and given rise to the creation of 'new democracies', the American version of that same system has shown severe signs of fatigue. Paul Taylor (1990) is an exponent of this viewpoint: 'As democracy flourishes around the globe, it is losing ground in the United States.'

Democracy is seen as a pre-eminently American value. Yet the United States has not always acknowledged the democratic rights of all its citizens, and some of the developments in the twentieth century have cast doubt upon the genuine attachment to democratic values. For instance, the existence of the right to vote is seen as a major criterion of any democracy. If broad categories of the public are denied the opportunity to express their preference between candidates, then this must be a blot on the landscape. Women obtained the vote in 1920 and, in theory, all men had the vote from the time the Constitution was created, subject originally to a property qualification. Yet slaves were not allowed to participate in elections and, when slavery ended, ruses were adopted in various Southern states to prevent blacks from exercising their democratic rights. It was not until the 1960s that the majority of black Americans was able to use their entitlement, if they so wished.

On the score of recognising and respecting minority rights, the Americans again fare well in theory. Crucial liberties were granted in the Constitution, most obviously in the first ten amendments that make up the Bill of Rights. These are inviolable unless there is a further constitutional amendment to change them. Yet, again, there have been blemishes upon the record. Three sets of factors ruin the record of the Americans in protecting and respecting such rights:

1. **In the 1920s and in the 1950s, anti-Communist hysteria was at a high level**. The 1920s was a markedly intolerant decade in which the liberties of many individuals were infringed, and anyone whose views were mildly progressive was liable to be branded as a 'red'. Similarly, the McCarthy witch-hunt against those portrayed as Communists was at a fever pitch in the early 1950s. McCarthy's techniques of investigation, with their emphasis upon smear and innuendo, displayed little respect for constitutional niceties. 'Un-American activity' was interpreted very widely, and there was much harassment of individuals and groups. There was in both eras a desperate desire for conformity, and those who did not conform to the American ideal of white Anglo-Saxon Protestants (WASPs) were hounded.

2. **The treatment of minority groups.** The ideal of equality, as proclaimed in Jefferson's resounding cry 'We hold these truths to be self evident, that all men are created equal', is seen as an American contribution to humankind. Certainly, privilege and rank count for less in America than in western Europe, and

an egalitarian fervour is in a way a part of the American Dream – allowing each person to go out and make a fortune by using his or her gifts and exhibiting a pioneering spirit. But the position of black Americans until comparatively recently suggested that, in practice, not everyone benefited from the Jeffersonian dream. Other minorities have also faced discrimination and other barriers to their economic and social progress. States adopted many differing rules to prevent political and legal equality of white and black from becoming a reality. Segregation and racial discrimination may be particularly associated with the Deep South but, in many northern cities, there was much de facto segregation well into the 1960s. Even today the opportunities available to many black Americans are more theoretical than real.

3. **Measures taken to tackle the threat to national security.** Some people who feel little or no sympathy for the actions taken by terrorists nonetheless question whether it is right to ignore the rights of those seen as dangerous. They believe that the Bush administration has been so understandably keen to combat terrorism effectively that it has been willing to sacrifice traditional values of justice and liberty, particularly via the passage of the Patriot Act and the treatment of prisoners at Guantánamo Bay.

Yet, if in several respects, reality has sometimes fallen short of the democratic ideal, the commitment to democracy for many Americans has always been apparent and, to their credit, many have always felt uneasy about lapses from that ideal. It would also be fair to point to other areas of political life in which the theory and practice of democracy have been evident:

1. In the Progressive era, the introduction of direct election of senators and the spread of primary elections to defeat the power of the machine bosses were moves that reflected a true concern for democracy.
2. The United States has also practised direct democracy as well as the representative form. Devices such as the referendum, the initiative and the recall are practical demonstrations of direct democracy in action, whatever their weaknesses. More unusual is the use of the town meeting in small rural areas of New England. Originally, such meetings were vehicles through which the mainly Puritan religious leaders informed and led other members of the community – a means of seeking a consensus via a guided discussion. They were not opportunities for the expression of majority will on issues of the day, and those who declined to agree to the general will were likely to be driven out of the area. Such meetings have developed into a more acceptable democratic form, however, and in them citizens gather together to make decisions for their community.

Democratic Party

The Democratic Party is the oldest political party in the United States and, arguably, the oldest party in the world. It traces its origins to the Democratic Republican Party, founded by Jefferson, Madison and other influential opponents of the Federalists in 1792.

In the twentieth century, the Democrats consistently positioned themselves to the left of the Republican Party in economic as well as in social matters. Rossiter (1960) was right in suggesting that a usual characteristic of Democratic rule has been a willingness to embrace change. The party accepts innovation and has, since the days of Woodrow Wilson, been more willing to extend governmental intervention and welfare programmes. The very names given by presidential contenders for their party platform suggest an acceptance of the need to embrace innovation and move forward with the task of reform. Woodrow Wilson offered the 'New Freedom', Franklin Roosevelt the 'New Deal', Harry Truman the 'Fair Deal', John Kennedy the 'New Frontiers', Lyndon Johnson the 'Great Society', and Bill Clinton the 'New Covenant'.

The activist philosophy of Franklin D. Roosevelt strongly influenced American liberalism and has also shaped much of the Democrats' economic agenda since 1932. Roosevelt's New Deal coalition usually controlled the national government until 1964. Since the New Deal, the Democrats have been the party associated with more positive government action to promote social welfare and regulate business activity. They were seen as standing for some redistribution of income, the extension of welfare measures and increased governmental expenditure. The Civil Rights Movement of the 1960s, championed by the party despite opposition at the time from its Southern wing, has continued to inspire the party's liberal principles. Yet, in the last two decades, Democrats have gone some way to shed this image. Bill Clinton's programme in 1992 sounded a far cry from the more liberal ones of some of his party predecessors. It was notably more cautious than the platform adopted by Kennedy and Johnson. From an electoral point of view, it does not pay to advertise liberal credentials.

Clinton attempted to blend features of the liberal tradition of positive government with elements of the traditional Republican programme such as controlling the budget deficit. He knew that Americans were growing weary of the problems posed by the urban centres, with such things as the breakdown of law and order, the preoccupation with civil rights and the use of affirmative action. Their anxieties about particular programmes combined with a feeling that government was growing 'too big'. They disliked the spiralling cost of welfare and other public spending, and warmed to promises to 'get Washington off their backs' and of lower taxes. In his New Covenant programme, Clinton was responding to profound changes in American attitudes.

Within the present Democratic Party, several tendencies can be distinguished:

1. The *New Left* is the most liberal faction and it represents the minorities who inhabit the party. It supports interventionist policies to help the disadvantaged – blacks, Latinos, gays and the disabled. It is generally pacific in its approach to foreign policy, and its attitudes are popular on university campuses. The Reverend Jesse Jackson belongs in this camp.
2. *Neo-liberals* broke away from the New Left and therefore share the same ancestry. Supporters stress competence rather than traditional 'tax-and-spend' policies and are generally sympathetic to civil liberties and

minority rights. Their approach appeals to professional suburbanites.
3. *Regulars* represent the mainstream party tradition with its emphasis on governmental intervention in economic and welfare matters; they also tend to be more 'hawkish' on foreign policy. 'Regular' attitudes are more appealing to labour (unions) and to Roman Catholics.
4. *Southerners*, such as Bill Clinton and Al Gore, tend to take a more conservative stance on a range of issues. They are less enthusiastic about government intervention and labour, pro-free market in economics, and tend to take a robust stance in foreign policy. Traditional liberal nostrums have little appeal but, on civil rights, they are more sympathetic than Southern Democrats of the past; they rely heavily on black votes. They appeal otherwise to the white working class and rural voters. After the 1984 defeat, many Southern Democrats joined together to form the Democratic Leadership Council (DLC). It seeks to organise and co-ordinate the more centrist elements within the Democratic coalition. It serves as a forum for debate on policy, and has a Washington 'think tank' – the Progressive Policy Unit (PPU) – and a magazine, the *New Democrat*. Although its New Democrat members accepted much of the Reagan Revolution and called for cuts in government spending, free trade, welfare reform, strong national defence and adherence to the moral and cultural values that most Americans share, they remain clearly distinct from most American conservatives, particularly in their backing for gun control and support for abortion rights.

Other than the DLC, another coalition of moderate and conservative Democrats on Capitol Hill is the Blue Dog Coalition whose members are drawn mainly from the South, are committed to low levels of government spending and a balanced budget, minimal government and local decision-making. On some occasions, it has broken with the majority of Democrats; for instance, in joining Republican congressmen in opposing restrictive laws on gun purchase and attempts to increase funding for the National Endowment for the Arts.

In terms of voter identification, Democrats

still tend to be associated in the public mind with positive action as necessary to promote social welfare and control the worst operation of big business. Since the New Deal and subsequent programmes of leading Democrats, such as Truman, Kennedy and Johnson, workers tend to look to the Democrats as being more helpful to them, 'the party of the little man'. Roosevelt's New Deal Coalition embraced labour unions, minority groups (racial, ethnic and religious), liberal farm groups, intellectuals and the South. It fell apart after 1966 and later lost much of its strength in the South. It remains the model that party activists seek to replicate, however, the party's base currently comprising two widely diverging groups within the electorate. There is the working class which includes many millions of black Americans, many Hispanics and other minorities in the cities. There are also well-educated and relatively affluent liberals who espouse a range of causes from the advancement of civil rights to environmental issues.

The Democrats are the party preferred by many members of the National Farmers Union (NFU), the American Federation of Labor and Congress of Industrial Organisations (AFL/CIO), and the American Political Science Association.

As a consequence of the elections of November 2008, the Democratic Party controls the White House; is the majority party in both chambers of the 111th Congress; holds a majority of state governorships; controls a plurality of state legislatures; and is currently the largest political party with seventy-two million registered members, 42.6 per cent of the electorate.

See also *Clinton, Bill*; *Johnson, Lyndon*; *Obama, Barack*; *Roosevelt, Franklin*

Democratic Republicans

The Democratic Republican Party (DRP) – also known as the Republicans (but not related to the present-day Republican Party), Jeffersonians, Democrats or combinations of these (such as Jeffersonian Republicans) – was one of the first two American political parties, the other being the Federalist Party. It was the first American opposition party.

Founded by Thomas Jefferson and James Madison, the DRP was the dominant political party in the United States from 1801 until the 1820s, Jefferson, Madison and James Monroe all being Democratic Republican presidents. They opposed the economic and foreign policies of the Federalists and resisted their continued attempts to expand the powers of the federal government. Democratic Republicans believed that a strong federal government would weaken, and not respect the rights of, the states and the people. Its members often represented agricultural and state interests against the claims of mercantile, commercial, and federal interests.

Eventually, the DRP disbanded in the 1820s, splintering into two competing factions, the Democratic Party and the Whig Party. It is usually regarded as the direct antecedent of the present Democratic Party.

See also *Jefferson, Thomas*; *Madison, James*

Desegregation

Desegregation is the process of eliminating racial segregation, most commonly used in reference to the United States. It usually refers to the moves to end the provision of separate facilities in a school, workplace or the military, so that members of all races or ethnic groups can experience the same opportunities. The process was for many years the focus of the Civil Rights Movement, both before and after the Supreme Court's decision in *Brown* v. *Board of Education* (1954), as a prior move to achieving the more ambitious goal of racial integration.

The Brown decision applied only to schools and, even in this respect, it was not initially time limited. Even so, acceptance of the ruling varied. In the peripheral and urban South it was introduced quite quickly for, in places such as Washington DC and some towns and cities in Arkansas, Florida, Maryland, North Carolina, Tennessee, Texas and Virginia, whites reluctantly accepted the law of the land. In the heart of the old Confederacy, in Alabama, Georgia, Louisiana, Mississippi and South Carolina, feeling was much stronger and resistance more determined. Some of those who wished to defend segregation formed White Citizens Councils to defend and challenge desegregation. Overall, the pace of desegregation was painfully slow because of the powerful white backlash. In 1960, still only 6.4 per cent of black Americans went to integrated schools in the South, only 2 per cent in the Deep South. Yet, twenty years later, the South had been transformed, in the words of Martin Luther King's old friend, Bayard Rustin (Anderson [1998]) 'from a reactionary bastion into a region moderate in racial outlook and more enlightened in social and economic policy'.

See also Brown *v.* Board of Education *(1954)*; *Civil Rights Movement*; *Segregation*

Devolutionary Federalism

Devolutionary federalism is a variant of 'new federalism', the emphasis being on devolving responsibility for once federally run programmes to the states which – being closer to the people – are thought to be better placed to respond to local needs.

The concept of devolution is in some ways a dubious one to apply to the United States for it is traditionally associated with the idea of transferring specific powers to a subordinate tier of government under a unitary system such as that of the UK. But, in as much as the term points to a rebalancing of the federal system in such a way as to boost the power of the states, its use has been accepted by several writers.

Direct Action

By direct action we mean doing for yourself what the government has refused to do. This may mean that homeless people find a home by occupying unoccupied property. By extension, the term has been used more widely to allude to any attempt to coerce those in authority into changing their viewpoint – as when the homeless might occupy a council office until they are housed. These activities invariably involve law-breaking which may be passive (e.g., obstruction, trespass) or violent (if a person is threatened or the furniture is broken up).

Today, the usual meaning of the term is 'action taken outside the constitutional and legal framework'. It describes a situation when, in order to resolve a problem, a group decides to take matters into its own hands rather than rely on established methods of decision-making. Those who employ it seek immediate remedy for the perceived ills with which they are confronted, as opposed to indirect actions, such as electing representatives who promise to provide remedy at some later date.

Direct action does not have to be violent. It can be militant without being violent. If violence is used, it may be against property rather than against a person. Non-payment of a portion of taxation, by people opposed to American defence policy based on the willingness to use force, is non-violent but illegal. Vandalism is illegal whereas, in most constitutional democracies, demonstrations are not illegal although they can easily become so.

Campaigns of direct action may start off as peaceful protests but easily become violent. Many people might choose to engage in an orderly demonstration against some motorway development or the export of live animals. They might find that, as passions become inflamed, so disorder creeps in. Protest marches have often turned out to be occasions in which violence erupts, and the demonstrators become locked into confrontation with the police who are seeking to maintain law and order. Of course, this does not necessarily happen, and the right to peaceful protest is one that civil libertarians strongly defend.

Operating at the extreme end of the spectrum of forms of direct action, hijackers and terrorists, among others, have shown how effective techniques of law-breaking can be. Fortunately, few groups are willing to resort to such tactics in order to obtain their desired goals. Because they operate beyond the realms of democratic politics, many consider that they cannot be included within the scope of any study of direct action.

Resort to direct action has a long history but the theory of direct action developed primarily in the context of labour struggles. In his book, *Direct Action*, William Mellor (1920) defined direct action 'as the use of some form of economic power for securing of ends desired by those who possess that power'. He placed direct action firmly in the struggle between worker and employer for control 'over the economic life of society'. Mellor considered direct action to be a tool of owners and of workers and, for this reason, he included within his definition lockouts as well as strikes and sabotage. By this time, how ever, the American anarchist and feminist, Voltairine de Cleyre (1912), had already given a strong defence of direct action, linking it with struggles for civil rights:

> The Salvation Army was vigorously practising direct action in the maintenance of the freedom of its members to speak, assemble, and pray. Over and over they were arrested, fined, and imprisoned . . . till they finally compelled their persecutors to let them alone.

Various forms of direct action have been employed by the Civil Rights Movement. In the pre-World War II years, some black Americans were inspired by Gandhi's confrontational but non-violent tactics against the British in India. Among them, Christian Socialist, James Farmer, thought such tactics would be particularly effective in time of war and advocated a campaign of 'relentless non-cooperation, economic boycott, civil disobedience'. In the Montgomery Bus Boycott, such methods were put into effect, the refusal of Rosa Parks to move from her seat triggering a year of non-violent protest which was not so much 'passive resistance' but more – in King's words – 'active non-violent resistance to evil'. In 1963, civil rights leader, Martin Luther King Jnr described the goal of non-violent direct action (NVDA) in his *Letter from Birmingham Jail*:

> Non-violent direct action seeks to create such a crisis and foster such a tension that a community which has constantly refused to negotiate is forced to confront the issue. It seeks so to dramatize the issue that it can no longer be ignored.

In the last two or three decades, there has been an upsurge in the growth of forms of direct action by individuals and groups. Groups committed to opposing abortion in the United States have often been willing to resort to forms of direct action to voice their protest. Operation Rescue/Operation Save America is a Christian pro-life organisation

based in Dallas which promotes an anti-abortion agenda by conducting mass protests at abortion clinics. It is a large-scale civil-disobedience organisation but, over the years, there has been violence at some of their protests. In the early 1990s, it began to target clinics across the country.

The Iraq War has inspired national and more localised protest. One of the largest direct actions in recent years took place in San Francisco the day after the war began in 2003. Twenty thousand people occupied the streets and over two thousand people were arrested in actions throughout downtown San Francisco, home to military-related corporations such as Bechtel. Similarly, the Chicago Coalition Against War and Racism (CCAWR), formed in September 2001 to protest against the imminent invasion of Afghanistan, gained prominence when it organised the rally at Federal Plaza the day after the invasion. During that protest, some fifteen thousand Chicagoans marched and eventually took over Lake Shore Drive in a massive action that received extensive media coverage on the major networks. Since then, CCAWR has organised and collaborated on projects ranging from conferences, to street protests, to national mobilisations, to counter-recruitment against the military.

On a global scale, the 1990s saw the emergence of a widespread movement of opposition to globalisation in which a wide variety of groups – environmentalists, campaigners for debt relief, human rights activists and so on – took part in a series of demonstrations. One of the first international anti-globalisation protests was organised in dozens of cities around the world in June 1999 (the Carnival Against Capitalism) with those in London and Eugene, Oregon most often noted. The Eugene protest turned into a riot in which local anarchists drove police out of a small park.

See also *Globalisation and Anti-globalisation Protest*

Direct Democracy

Direct democracy is a form of government in which citizens come together in one place to make laws. Today, the term is often used to refer to populist measures such as the initiative and referendum. By whatever method it is practised, direct democracy involves 'people power' or the self-government of the people.

The Ancient Greeks were the first people to develop democratic ideas, Athenian democracy being practised in a small city-state. Pericles (*c.* 490–429 BC) observed: 'Our constitution is named a democracy, because it is in the hands not of the few but of the many.' Democracy then involved the direct involvement of all male citizens in making decisions, meeting as they did in some large public place. At that time, it was feasible for people who lived in a relatively small city-state or *polis* to come together and make decisions. As conducted in Ancient Greece, democracy is largely impractical today. Scarcely any modern industrial society can claim to practise it in the original form though elements of it survive in the town meetings held in parts of New England. Referendums, initiatives and the recall are methods of direct democracy that enable the electorate to vote on single issues. They keep alive the flame of direct popular involvement in decision-making, enabling voters to decide issues for themselves.

Direct democracy was strongly opposed by the Founding Fathers. They saw a danger in majorities forcing their will on minorities. As a result, they advocated a representative democracy rather than a direct democracy. John Witherspoon, one of the signers of the Declaration of Independence, articulated a view prevalent at the time: 'Pure democracy cannot subsist long nor be carried far into the departments of state – it is very subject to caprice and the madness of popular rage.' An alternative view was advanced many years later by President Theodore Roosevelt, in his 'Charter of Democracy' speech to an Ohio constitutional convention in 1912: 'I believe in the initiative and referendum, which should be used not to destroy representative government, but to correct it whenever it becomes misrepresentative.'

No form of direct democracy exists at the federal level, the US never having had a nation-wide referendum. Yet, despite the doubts of the Founding Fathers, ballot measures have been widely used at the state and sub-state levels. There is much state and federal case law, from the early 1900s to the present day, that protects the people's right to participate in ballots on single issues. The first Supreme Court ruling in favour of citizen lawmaking was in *Pacific States*

Oregon and direct democracy: *Pacific States Telephone and Telegraph Company* v. *Oregon* (1912)

In the early twentieth century, political and social reform was sweeping across America. Progressives reformers stressed direct democracy, giving more political powers to the voters, and included the initiative and the referendum. With the initiative, voters of a state could introduce new laws, bypassing the Legislature. A referendum allowed citizens to accept or reject laws passed by the government. The use of the initiative and the referendum was popular in the Great Plains and Far West, and in 1902, Oregon amended its constitution to include these reform measures. The reforms, however, were not popular with some companies, which were often the target of laws passed through initiative and referendum.

In Oregon, the Pacific States Telephone and Telegraph Company disliked a law that levied a 2 per cent tax on the profits of telegraph and telephone companies doing business in the state. Oregon voters had initiated the law in 1906; it went into effect the following year. Pacific States refused to pay the tax, and Oregon sued for its money. In court, the company cited Article IV, Section 4 of the Constitution for its defence. By introducing the initiative and referendum, Pacific States claimed that Oregon had ceased to have a republican government, because it gave citizens the right to pass laws by initiative and referendum rather than rely on elected representative to make legislation. Oregon's courts upheld the state's tax, and Pacific States took its claim to the Supreme Court in Washington.

In a unanimous decision, the Court dismissed Pacific States's argument. Citing a clear precedent, the Court reaffirmed that it had no constitutional authority to decide a political issue, such as the validity of a state government, thereby upholding a state's right to introduce initiative and referendum reforms.

Telephone and Telegraph Company v. *Oregon* 1912 (see previous page).

Some commentators argue that, even in modern industrial states, it is possible to break down governing structures in such a way that people see themselves as belonging to small units. According to this view, voters in their communities could take more decisions at the local level. This idea has little chance of ever being implemented, however, for national political leaders are unlikely to surrender their powers of decision-making. Another possibility in the future would be the greater development of direct personal involvement by the voters via the new media of Internet websites, interactive television and mobile phones.

Disability Rights

Many Americans with disabilities have in the past suffered from discrimination, often being denied education, jobs and rehabilitation services. Throughout much of the country's history, the blind, deaf and mobility impaired found buses, stairs, telephones and other necessities of life designed in such a way as to make it impossible for them to use them to full advantage, if at all. As one campaigning slogan put it: 'Once, blacks had to ride at the back of the bus. We can't even get on the bus.'

The American disability rights movement became a significant force in the 1970s, encouraged by the examples of the African American civil rights and women's rights movements which began in the late 1960s. In 1973, the Rehabilitation Act (twice vetoed by President Nixon) added people with disabilities to the list of those protected against discrimination and, two years later, an education act entitled all children to a free public education appropriate to their needs. The real breakthrough, however, came during the presidency of George H. Bush. In 1990, Congress passed the Americans with Disabilities Act (ADA). The law defined a disabled person as anyone possessing a mental or physical impediment 'that substantially limits one or more activities of life'. Among other things, the ADA prohibits discrimination based on disability in employment, state and local government, places of public accommodations and public services

(e.g., buses, trains and undergrounds) commercial facilities and telecommunications; requires that facilities be designed to make them accessible and usable by those with disabilities; and, to the extent feasible, be redesigned to do so.

The introduction of the ADA was a key legislative achievement of the Bush era, an example of federal action to remove disadvantages suffered by many Americans across the country and allow them to participate more fully in daily life. It has resulted in dramatic improvements in wheelchair access to facilities ranging from churches to hotels, from restaurants to universities. Telephone companies have provided special facilities for those with speech and hearing impairments.

The attainment of civil rights for the disabled has not been achieved without encountering substantial opposition. While few people would wish to seem to be in outright opposition to a group already enduring emotional and/or physical handicaps, the good will has not always been apparent in their attitudes and actions. Even when passed into law (sometimes in the face of considerable opposition) enforcement has sometimes been sporadic and sluggish. The problem is the same one that influenced President Nixon, namely cost. Others who argued for full civil rights made the point that short-term expense might eventually benefit society for, if the handicapped can become wage earners, spenders and taxpayers, then they might become a net gain for the economy.

Dissenting Opinions

Dissenting opinions are delivered to record the disagreement with the majority view of a justice or justices on the Supreme Court. Often they are accompanied by an explanation of why they disagree and often they present an alternative viewpoint. Most dissenting justices wish to explain why they disagree with the majority decision. Famously, in *Plessy* v. *Ferguson* (1896), the Court let stand a state law requiring trains to provide 'separate but equal' facilities for black and white passengers. Justice John Marshall Harlan wrote a dissenting opinion in which he said that 'the Constitution is color-blind, and neither knows nor tolerates classes among citizens'.

The dissenting opinion is not an intended to change the minds of the Court's majority, for the final decision has already been reached by the time the dissenting opinion is written. Rather, the dissenter hopes to arouse public opinion against the majority view, in the hope that ultimately the Court will reconsider the majority opinion and overrule it. Chief Justice Charles Evans Hughes (Ransom, 1916) explained the situation in this way:

> A dissent in a court of last resort is an appeal to the brooding spirit of the law, to the intelligence of a future day, when a later decision may possibly correct the error into which the dissenting judge believes the court to have been betrayed.

Justice Harlan's dissent in *Plessy* v. *Ferguson* was eventually vindicated by the majority opinion in *Brown* v. *Board of Education* (1954) in which the Court unanimously rejected the 'separate but equal' doctrine, and ruled that racially segregated public schools were inherently unequal. Justice Oliver Wendell Holmes, who was known as the Great Dissenter, wrote 173 dissenting opinions during thirty years on the Supreme Court.

See also *Supreme Court*

District of Columbia

Washington DC is an American city named after George Washington (1732–99) and the national capital of the United States. It is an area of 68.3 square miles (176.8 sq. km) situated within the District of Columbia, to keep the capital distinct from the states. It is located on the banks of the Potomac River and bordered by Virginia to the west and Maryland to the east, north and south. 'Columbia' was used as an early poetic name for the United States, a reference to Christopher Columbus (1451–1504), the early European explorer of the Americas.

The three branches of the US government are based in Washington DC, other key headquarters being those for the World Bank and the International Monetary Fund, as well as a myriad of other national and international institutions including labour unions and professional associations. Given its importance in the worlds of business and politics, it is unsurprisingly the frequent location for political demonstrations and protests.

The District of Columbia and the city of Washington are governed by a single municipal government and, for most practical purposes, are considered to be the same entity. Although there is an elected municipal government and an elected mayor, Congress has the supreme authority over the city and district, and intervenes from time to time in local affairs on issues ranging from gun control to schools. The governing arrangements mean that citizens have less self-governance than residents of the states. Citizens of the national capital have no voting representation in Congress. In the House, they are represented by a delegate who sits on committees and participates in debate but who has no vote. Citizens have no representation in the Senate.

Citizens of DC are fully taxed and subject to all US laws, as are the inhabitants of the fifty states, hence they can legitimately argue the case for 'no taxation without representation'. Attempts to change the situation to provide for representation in Congress have included proposals for statehood and the introduction of the District of Columbia Voting Rights Amendment but these have been abortive. With the passage of the Twenty-third Amendment (1961) residents did become eligible to vote in presidential elections, DC having three votes in the Electoral College, the same level of representation as states with the smallest populations (e.g., Delaware, Montana, Vermont and the two Dakotas). In 2000, one elector pledged to vote for Gore in the Electoral College abstained in protest at the lack of effective representation for the city on Capitol Hill.

See also *Washington DC*

Diversity

Diversity means difference. People's differences can be many and varied. Diversity in a social and political sense means recognising those differences and encouraging tolerance for people of different backgrounds and experiences which may derive, among other things, from culture to

disability, ethnicity to gender, and sexual orientation to family structure. In particular, the term is
often used in reference to national origin and the
ideology of providing opportunities to people of
diverse cultural and religious backgrounds.

Those who argue for diversity seek to build a
safe, just and tolerant society for everyone in the
United States, irrespective of their background,
religion or gender. They urge the need to promote equality of opportunity, for instance by
policies of affirmative action.

See also *Ethnicity and Race*

Double Jeopardy

In the United States double jeopardy is both
a procedural defence and a constitutional right
which means that a defendant cannot be tried
twice for the same crime. The phrase derives
from the wording of the Fifth Amendment, specifically the words 'twice put in jeopardy' in the
clause 'nor shall any person be subject for the
same offense to be twice put in jeopardy of life
or limb'. The amendment initially applied only
to the federal government but, in the case of
Benton v. *Maryland* (1969) the Supreme Court
overruled an earlier landmark decision *Palko* v.
Connecticut (1937) and ruled that it applies to the
states as well, through incorporation under the
Fourteenth Amendment.

The concept is designed to prevent repeated
prosecution for the same offence, which could be
seen as a means of harassment and/or oppression.
It combines three key elements: protection from
being retried for the same crime after an acquit-
tal; protection from retrial after a conviction; and
protection from being punished multiple times
for the same offence.

Dred Scott v. *Sandford* (1857)

Dred Scott v. *Sandford*, better known as the 'Dred
Scott Case' or 'Dred Scott Decision', was a lawsuit decided by the Supreme Court in 1857. In
a pivotal ruling written by Chief Justice Roger
Taney, it ruled that people of African descent,
whether or not they were slaves, were not and
could never be citizens of the United States.

In addition, the Court concluded that Congress
lacked the constitutional authority to exclude
slavery in federal territories.

Dred Scott was a slave owned by John Sanford
whose name was misspelt in Court records. The
ruling against Scott was significant both as an
example of judicial review and as a factor that
fuelled sectional tensions during the lead-up to the
Civil War. Those parts of the judgment relating
to the citizenship and rights of African Americans
were later explicitly overturned by the passage
of the Thirteenth, Fourteenth and Fifteeenth
Amendments, following the Civil War.

Dual Federalism

Dual federalism was the original concept of
American federalism which envisaged a federal
system in which the national and state governments are coequal, sovereign in fairly distinct areas
of responsibility, with little overlap or sharing of
authority. Specifically, dual federalism discusses

The division of power in American federalism, as set out in the Constitution

Delegated powers (powers delegated to federal government)

- Declare war
- Make treaties
- Coin money
- Regulate interstate and foreign commerce

Concurrent powers (powers shared by the federal and state governments)

- Taxes
- Public health
- Vehicle safety
- Drugs

Reserved powers (powers reserved for state governments)

- Draw electoral districts
- Intrastate commerce
- Creation of local units
- Police powers

the relationship between the national government and the states' governments. According to its narrow interpretation, a very large group of powers belongs to the states, and the federal government is limited to only those powers explicitly listed in the Constitution. Limits are placed on the federal government to ensure that it rules only by enumerated powers and for a limited set of constitutional purposes. The relationship between nation and states tends to be one of tension rather than co-operation.

Dual federalism existed in the nineteenth and early twentieth centuries. Such a model is a conservative one, for those who have supported it (right through until the present day) would prefer to see a strictly limited role for Washington. Supporters stress the importance of 'states' rights', a large and secure place for the states within the federal system. Some writers would argue that such a situation never really existed in anything like its pure form for, from the early days, there was a distinction between those who wanted a more nation-centred form of federalism and those who wanted a more state-based form.

From the early mid-nineteenth century, the federal government on occasion 'stepped in' to provide grants for improvements on expensive and necessary items such as road building. It was the nation-centred view that emerged triumphant, a significant step towards its resolution being taken on the battlefields of the Civil War in the 1860s when the Lincoln approach of keeping the country united was vindicated. By the early twentieth century, a combination of economic and social factors had brought about change to constitutional relationships within the federal system. Several developments had by then occurred which served to increase the influence of Washington over the states:

1. **Constitutional amendments.** Some amendments since 1787 affected the federal system – for example, the Fourteenth Amendment provided 'equal protection' of the law to all citizens, and the Sixteenth gave the federal government the right to raise graduated income tax.
2. **Decisions of the Supreme Court.** At times, Court decisions allowed a considerable expansion of national intervention by emphasising

the broad and permissive character of some clauses in the Constitution – for example, the Congressional power to 'tax for the common defence and general welfare of the United States'.
3. **The financial relationship.** After the passage of the Sixteenth Amendment on income tax, the financial base of the federal government expanded. This led to a considerable increase in the size of its budget. (Americans now pay most of their taxation to Washington, a smaller amount to the states and slightly less again to their local governments).

Despite the broad drift of power towards the centre, the term 'dual federalism' is still normally used to describe the type of federalism in operation until the introduction of the New Deal. By then, however, dual federalism had proved to be inadequate to meet the needs of the Great Depression of the early 1930s. Roosevelt's energetic response to the deteriorating economic situation was to deploy the resources of the central government in a series of interventionist measures known as the New Deal, in 'an extraordinary assumption of federal authority over the nation's economy and a major expansion of its commerce and taxing powers'. More and more decision-making moved to Washington, with numerous grant-in-aid programmes bringing federal, state and local tiers into close, if not always harmonious, co-operation.

See also *Federalism*

Due Process Clause

Due process is the principle that, before a government deprives a person of life, liberty or property, it must have respected all of the individual's legal rights, not just some or most of them. It imposes certain *procedural* requirements on governments when they impair life, liberty, or property. It also limits the *substantive power* of the states to regulate certain areas of human life. There is a due process clause in the Fifth Amendment, binding on the *federal* government: 'No person shall be . . . deprived of life, liberty, or property, without due process of law . . .' The Fourteenth

Amendment says: 'No State shall . . . deprive any person of life, liberty, or property, without due process of law . . .'

The term 'due process' existed before its insertion into the US Constitution in 1791. In the early United States, the terms *law of the land* and *due process* were used somewhat interchangeably. New York was the only state that asked Congress to add 'due process' language to the Constitution, proposing the following amendment in 1788: 'No Person ought to be taken imprisoned or disseised of his freehold, or be exiled or deprived of his Privileges, Franchises, Life, Liberty or Property but by due process of Law.' In response to this request, James Madison drafted and Congress adopted a Due Process Clause which removed some wording and inserted *without*. No state or federal constitution in the United States had ever previously utilised the phrase 'due process'.

The Fifth Amendment guarantee of due process applies only to federal actions. The Fourteenth expressly applies to the states. The Supreme Court has interpreted both clauses identically, as Justice Felix Frankfurter once explained in a concurring opinion: 'To suppose that "due process of law" meant one thing in the Fifth Amendment and another in the Fourteenth is too frivolous to require elaborate rejection.'

Due process acts as a restraint upon the executive, judicial and legislative branches of government. Where a person is deprived of liberty by a process that conflicts with some provision of the Constitution, then the Due Process Clause normally prescribes the remedy, restoration of that person's liberty.

E

Egalitarianism

Egalitarianism is a political philosophy that believes in equality. Deriving from the French *égal* ('equal' or 'level') its adherents support the notion that all people should be treated as equals from birth because all human persons are equal in fundamental worth or moral status whatever their nation, ethnic group, or gender. This view is heavily influenced by the writings of eighteenth-century philosopher Immanuel Kant (1724–1804), who arged that human beings are equally due the right to be treated morally and ethically. In this sense, the Declaration of Independence includes a kind of moral and legal egalitarianism. Because 'all men are created equal', all are entitled to be treated equally under the law. It was a long time before black Americans, women and other groups were accorded this degree of consideration but the belief in egalitarianism has today won wide support and is a key element of modern policies concerned with the promotion of civil rights.

See also *Equality*

Eisenhower, Dwight (1890–1969)

Born in Texas in 1890 and brought up in Abilene, Kansas, Dwight Eisenhower received an appointment to West Point. He soon made his mark in what was to be a distinguished military career. After Pearl Harbor, General George Marshall called him to Washington for a war plans assignment. He commanded the Allied Forces landing in North Africa in November 1942. As Supreme Commander of the Allied Forces in Europe, he was involved in planning the successful liberation of France and Germany and on D-Day, 1944 led the invasion of France. Given his personal prestige, his services were in great demand. He became President of Columbia University but took leave to assume supreme command over the new NATO forces being assembled in 1951.

Eisenhower then turned to a political career. He had been courted by representatives of both parties to run as their presidential candidate in 1948 but had declined to run. As a 'draft Eisenhower' movement developed among senior Republicans, however, party emissaries to his military headquarters near Paris persuaded him to stand in November 1952. He campaigned against the Truman administration's policies on 'Korea, Communism and Corruption', even promising to go to Korea himself in a bid to end the fighting. He and his running mate, Richard Nixon, promised a corruption-free and frugal administration at home. They won a sweeping victory against the Democratic opponent, Adlai Stevenson. On becoming the thirty-fourth president (1953–61) and the first general to enter the White House in the twentieth century, he ended a twenty-year Republican absence from the presidency.

White House years 1953–61

As president, Eisenhower oversaw the truce that brought an armed peace along the border in South Korea in 1953. Negotiating on the basis of America's immense military arsenal, over the next few years he worked to ease the tensions of the Cold War and concentrated much of his attention on maintaining world peace. He was concerned to maintain American security and, in doing so, accorded nuclear weapons a higher defence priority. For a time, the death of Stalin eased the strains with the Soviet Union but, during his years in office, there was little thawing in the relationship. Shortly after the Suez Crisis (1956), he proclaimed that America intended to act as the guarantor of Western interests in the Middle East. This was part of the 'Eisenhower Doctrine' (1957) which stressed that – in relation to that region and elsewhere – America was 'prepared to use armed force . . . [to counter] aggression from any country controlled by international communism'.

In domestic policy, Eisenhower was supportive of the business community, including a preponderance of businessmen in his Cabinet that was said to contain 'eight millionaires and a plumber'. Like many contemporary Republicans, he emphasised the need for a balanced budget. But he also appealed beyond the party's traditional constituency, by his pursuit of a moderate, middle-of-the-road 'me-tooist' course. He accepted the bulk of the New Deal and Fair Deal programmes as accomplished facts and sought to build on the broad postwar consensus that covered a range of economic and social issues. He expanded the federal social security programme, extending benefits to an additional ten million workers and creating a new Cabinet-level agency, the Department of Health, Education and Welfare.

On racial issues, he was much less inclined than his predecessor to move America towards greater equality. He had been brought up in an all-white town in the South, and spent much of his life in Southern states and in the company of segregated armed forces. He shared typical white anxieties about miscegenation, believing that his support for equality of opportunity did not mean that black and white had to mingle socially. Moreover, as a traditional Republican, he was ideologically opposed to large-scale federal intervention and saw little benefit for his party in adopting a firmly pro-civil rights platform. Yet, as desegregation of schools began following the 1954 Supreme Court ruling (*Brown* v. *Board of Education, Topeka, Kansas*), he was the president who sent troops into Little Rock, Arkansas (1957) to ensure compliance with the orders of a federal court. He also ordered the complete desegregation of the armed forces and drew up civil rights legislation that passed through Congress in a weakened form, with Eisenhower (1957) acknowledging in a press conference that 'there were certain phrases I did not completely understand' and many black Americans seeing it as irrelevant to their struggle.

Eisenhower was unable to stand again in November 1960. He was the first president to have no choice but to leave office, having served the maximum two terms allowed by the Twenty-second Amendment. In his farewell televised address, Eisenhower urged the necessity of maintaining an adequate military strength but 'warned against the industrial-military complex'. He argued that vast, long-continued military expenditures could breed potential dangers to the American way of life. He concluded with a prayer for peace 'in the goodness of time'. He reassured his countrymen that 'America is today the strongest, most influential, and most productive nation in the world'. Many of them warmed to his style, 'I like Ike' being an irresistible slogan.

Eisenhower's reputation declined over the following years for, in contrast to the presidency of his young activist successor, John F. Kennedy, his own seemed to have been a period of inactivity. In the liberal climate of the 1960s and 1970s, he was seen as a president who had been insufficiently concerned to assist in the struggle for civil rights. More recently, his reputation has considerably improved, as writers recall his wartime leadership, lack of partisanship, willingness – however reluctant – to send troops to Little Rock and concern for world peace.

Election Campaigns

An election campaign is the process by which democracies choose the direction they will take into the future. Usually, campaigns are designed to enable the voters to make the choice of which party or person can best represent their interests and opinions although, in the cases of initiatives and referendums, they offer a choice of policy in a vote on a single issue.

The United States has a huge number of elected offices, and there is wide variation between different states, counties, and municipalities on which offices are elected and under what procedures. Campaigns for minor office may be relatively simple and inexpensive – talking to local newspapers, giving out campaign signs and greeting people in the local square. In the cities and at the congressional, state and national levels the contests are far more high profile, however, and are phenomenally costly and last over a much longer period. Such campaigns are not merely a civic ritual and occasion for political debate. They are a multibillion dollar industry, dominated by professional political consultants using sophisticated campaign-management tools, to an extent far greater than elsewhere in the world.

The US has relatively weak parties. While parties play a significant role in fund-raising and occasionally in drafting people to run, American election campaigns are ultimately controlled by the individual candidates themselves. Their ideas and characters are the focus of elections, rather than national party strategies and manifestos. Hence we talk of candidate-centred electioneering.

Campaigns for election to the presidency

Compared with the relatively short political campaigns of other democracies, such as the United Kingdom, major campaigns in the United States can be marathons. They start any time from several months to several years before election day. They enable parties to choose their candidates at the primary stage and the mass of voters to choose who they wish to represent them in the main election fought against their party opponents.

Campaigning for the party nomination in the primaries and caucuses

The first part of any campaign for a candidate is deciding to run. Prospective candidates will often consult family, friends, professional associates, elected officials, community leaders and the leaders of political parties before deciding to run. They will consider their ability to develop the fund-raising, organisation and public appeal needed to get elected.

If they decide to run, would-be candidates will make a public announcement which may be anything from a simple press release to a major media event. Campaigns are often not formally announced, however, until several months after active campaigning has already started. Such coyness enables candidates to 'test the waters' and retain media interest.

One of the most important aspects of the major American political campaign is the ability to raise large sums of money, especially early on in the race. Political insiders and donors often judge candidates based on their ability to raise funds. Not raising enough money early on can lead to problems later, as donors are not willing to fund candidates they perceive to be losing.

Also during this period, candidates travel around the district for which they are running to show an interest in, and identify with, its characteristics and inhabitants. They address voters in large crowds, small groups or even one to one, seeking opportunities to meet as many as possible. Campaign managers launch expensive media campaigns on their behalf during this period to introduce the candidate to voters. The intensity of the media gathers momentum as election day draws closer, via the use of television advertising and direct-mail campaigns designed to persuade voters to support the candidate or belittling the qualities of opponents. In the final weeks before polling day, campaigners also intensify their grassroots campaigning, in a final effort to build up a sufficient total of votes to enable them to win nomination at the party convention.

The campaign proper

The purpose of the general election campaign is not only to reach as many people as possible but to ensure that those who are sympathetically disposed actually turn out and vote. Given the relatively low turnouts in the United States, it is important for the parties and political action committees (PACs) to do anything they can to assist in the process of voter registration and to encourage those who are registered to go to the polls. Postal ballots are a commonly used voting method so that voting for some people starts weeks before election day. Campaign organisers

will therefore often run two persuasion programmes, one aimed at postal voters and one
aimed at the overwhelming majority of more
traditional poll voters.

In the mid-twentieth century, candidates
needed to be effective 'on the stump', addressing
a gathering in the local marketplace or school hall.
Sometimes those running for office addressed
electors from a platform at the back of a train,
most famously Harry Truman whose 'whistle-
stop' tours involved the train pulling up at every
local station. He was the last campaigner to
deploy this method of electioneering on such a
scale, though others subsequently (e.g., John F.
Kennedy) conducted very active speech-making
tours and sometimes spoke from the rear of a
railway carriage.

At that time, presidential campaigns were
built around senior elected officials, top party
bosses and the party's senior fund-raisers.
Contemporary campaigns are built around pollsters, media consultants, issue strategists and a
range of other specialists unimaginable a half-
century ago. Today, a presidential nominee may
have a campaign: team comprising: a chairperson
who organises the broad operation and liaises with
party officials; a manager who assists in organising
broad strategy and co-ordinates state campaigns;
a political director who is responsible for day-to-
day operations and manages the election team,
responding to opposition charges, seizing media
opportunities and deploying resources as seems
appropriate; a lead pollster, focus group analysts,
media consultants, communications stategists,
speechwriters, fund-raisers and schedulers. The
ready response team has a key role in the campaign. Its members respond quickly to any attacks
from the other side, ensuring that no comments
that might harm the candidate go unchallenged.
The Clinton and G.W. Bush teams were notably
effective in handling any allegations, inaccuracies
or slips, developing ready response into something of an art form.

The trend is towards far greater professionalism than ever before. Those who run campaigns
are skilled in the new campaign technology. They
use texting or direct mail shot to target individual
voters, computers to analyse the voters of a specific precinct, and the services of all the specialists

referred to above to advise on the best means of
exploiting the potential of the candidate and playing down or destroying the qualities and reputation of an opponent.

Much depends on the qualities of the candidates themselves, however. Their own characteristics are important: a pleasing voice, a gift for
communication, appealing looks and a persuasive
personality all help to create a favourable image.
Deficiencies in any of these respects can be a
serious liability when exposed before the whole
nation. Any personal failings are highlighted in
the blaze of publicity surrounding a modern
election campaign.

To be successful, candidates need to be able to
put together a winning coalition of support. They
do this by making sure that there are sufficient
funds to allow them to get the message across as
widely as possible, so that everyone knows who
they are and what they stand for. An ability to
arouse the loyalty and belief of members of the
campaign team is essential, for they need their
support in explaining and selling the candidature.
In the United States, the campaign emphasis on
the marketing of individual politicians has been
highly developed.

Skilful use of mass communications is today
fundamental to election campaigns which are
created around opportunities for media coverage,
especially on television. Like the cinema, television is a medium for entertainment, so politicians
have seen the need to attune performances to
its demands. Whereas, once, candidates set out
to convince their audiences by a reasoned statement of their views, the emphasis is now increasingly upon broad themes rather than on detailed
policies, emotion rather than rational debate.
Campaigns are managed and orchestrated, many
of the skills used in selling goods and services now
being applied to the electorate.

If, today, television has taken over election
campaigning, its purpose remains fundamentally
the same as it always was, to encourage the
electorate to support the candidate and policy
platform on polling day. Reaching the maximum
number of voters has always been a priority but,
whereas the whistle-stop tour could last weeks
and enable the candidate to address an audience
that could be counted in tens or hundreds, now

that audience can be counted in millions for a single programme.

See also *Turnout*

Elections

An election is a competition for office based on a formal expression of preferences by a designated body of people at the ballot box. Such a contest holds those in office to account and, if necessary, provides a means for their replacement. In a democracy, in which elections are held to provide the voter with a meaningful choice of candidates, they are distinguished by several characteristics, including a universal franchise, a secret ballot, the involvement of political parties, contests in every, or almost every, constituency and campaigns regulated by strict and fair rules.

Elections are basic to the democratic process. In America, at almost every tier of political life, the incumbent is chosen by election, examples being the president and members of Congress at national level, the governor and representatives at state level, and city mayors and town councillors at local level. Depending on the state, town or township, a variety of other relatively low-profile community positions, including those of municipal judge and registrar of wills is elective. In Massachusetts, Bay State voters even vote for their tree wardens who are charged with the removal of hazardous trees on town property. Altogether, according to official census figures, there are well over half a million elective offices, though elections for many of them fail to make the headlines and the turnout is low in many cases. About 96 per cent of such contests are at the local level.

Elected officers serve terms of varying lengths. Senators serve for six years, presidents and most elected officials four years, but members of Congress serve for only two years. The tree wardens of Massachusetts serve for three years. The elections are staggered rather than all being held at the same time. Presidential and congressional ones are held in the November of even years but local elections often take place in the spring of odd-numbered years. Because of this 'staggering' and the different lengths of incumbency, there is no occasion when there is a total 'clean sweep' in which all office holders are changed.

The vast number of elections is a natural expression of the democratic principle to which Americans strongly adhere. They have traditionally believed that the greater the involvement of the citizen, the better the likely policy outcome; more participation equals superior government. But there is another explanation for the frequency of elections. This is the long-standing belief in limited government. Americans have a fear of concentrating an excess of power in too few hands. Elected officers should not be trusted too much or for too long. It is desirable to retain as much power as possible under voter control.

Electoral College

An electoral college refers to a system under which a body is elected with the expressed purpose of itself electing a higher body. In the United States, the Founding Fathers provided for the people of each state to elect a number of electors who will vote in the Electoral College to choose the candidate who will enter the White House as president. Therefore, it is the electors in the College who formally choose the president, just as they separately decide on the vice presidency, too. The choice is not made by the ordinary voter who, when he or she went to the polling station in November 2008, actually voted for electors who were pledged to Obama/Biden or McCain/Palin. In each state, the candidate who received the largest popular vote won the entire electoral vote, though Maine and Nebraska have a slightly different procedure.

To win the presidency, a presidential candidate needs to acquire 270 votes in the Electoral College, out of the 538 available. Each state is apportioned a number of votes according to the number of seats it possesses in Congress: two for the Senate and a variable number for the House of Representatives. Thus, in 2004, California had fifty-five, Texas thirty-four, New York State thirty-one, Florida twenty-seven, and Illinois and Pennsylvania twenty-one each. Because of the equal representation of each state in the Senate, the smaller states are overrepresented in the Electoral College, so that Delaware and Vermont, with well under a million people each, still have three votes each.

If, when the electors in the College are making their choice for president, no candidate gains a majority, then the choice is thrown open to the House of Representatives which chooses from among the top three candidates. If there is no majority for the position of vice president, then the choice goes to the Senate which chooses between the first two candidates. If it became necessary to use this process, then it is the new Congress just elected (e.g., the 111th one elected in November 2008) rather than the old one (the 110th elected in November 2006) that makes the choice. Theoretically, it would be possible for the two houses to choose candidates from different parties so that, under the procedure, the House could have opted for Biden, the Senate for Palin.

The importance of the Electoral College

From this short account, it becomes apparent that it is essential for any presidential candidate to win a majority in the Electoral College. To achieve this, he or she needs to perform strongly in the large urban and suburban states that have so much influence. Indeed, it has often been said that, to become president, it is necessary to win in California; its fifty-five votes are a greater number than the twelve least populated states and the District of Columbia all combined. Texas, New York, and Illinois and Pennsylvania have a significant number of votes and – as the 2000 result indicated – so does Florida. The candidate is likely to focus attention particularly on such large states and on those where he or she can expect to fare well.

The importance of certain individual states dictates the strategy of any would-be contender. A candidate who can win in California or New York is more important than one who can do fairly well in every state, for most candidates do not aim to win across the nation and often fight less than enthusiastically in some hostile territory. For this reason, it is important for the main parties to have a candidate of wide appeal in the states that are liable to go one way or the other. If they choose a candidate from a safe state, then this wastes the possible bonus of choosing a local

person in a state or region in which there is a chance of success. For the Democrats in 1992, the choice of Clinton was a useful way of trying to restore the party's fortunes in a region where support had been eroded over the Reagan years.

Yet, as we have seen, winning the November election is not the end of the process. The result of the contest may be known within a few hours of the close of polling but it is another month before the actual election of the president takes place – when the members of the Electoral College cast their votes. The event is largely unnoticed in the outside world, yet it is of profound importance even if the actual outcome is a formality in almost every case.

Problems associated with the College

Much of the anxiety about the American system of choosing its president relates to the use of the Electoral College, for it is from the use of this approach that several potential problems derive. Criticism centres on several aspects, notably:

- the overrepresentation of very small states and the excessive concentration on those which have many College votes
- the use of the simple plurality method of voting
- the possibility that members of the College may vote for a person other than the one to whom they were pledged
- the fact that it is possible to win the popular vote and yet lose the election
- the fact that there may be no clear victor in the College if no one emerges with a majority. This could have happened in 1992 if Ross Perot had actually managed to carry some states. It was the strategy of George Wallace in 1968 to aim for deadlock and thereby throw the decision into the House. A choice made in Congress could be contrary to the people's will as expressed in the ballot box in November.

Because the smaller states are proportionally overrepresented in the College, it is possible for a candidate to win a greater share of the popular vote than his rival but not acquire the majority of the votes in the Electoral College. In 2000, intense controversy centred upon the choice of George W. Bush who won less votes in the country than Al Gore, particularly because the outcome in Florida was hotly disputed. This was not the first time that this had happened for, in 1824, 1876 and 1888, the candidate with the largest number of votes nationally failed to gain a majority of the delegates' votes in the College count. It nearly happened in 1960 and 1976, elections that were closely contested. Neither of the men elected in those years, Kennedy nor Carter, received a popular majority of the votes cast, and neither did Bill Clinton in either of his two victories.

Why have an Electoral College? Does the system work well?

The Founding Fathers wanted a method of choosing their president that would shun 'mob politics'. Democracy was then not yet in fashion and, as they were creating an elected office, they wanted to ensure that they were not handing power to demagogues who could manipulate popular opinion. They were suspicious of the mass of the people. Choice by college, after the voters had expressed their feelings, could be conducted in a more leisurely and rational manner. As Hamilton put it in *The Federalist Papers,* 'The immediate election [of the President] should be made by men most capable of analysing the qualities needed for the office.' In this spirit, the Founding Fathers set up a system in which the electorate actually chooses between two competing lists or 'slates' of Electoral College candidates although, on the ballot papers, it is the names of the candidates for the presidential office that are actually given.

There was never any serious likelihood that members of the Electoral College meeting in December would ignore the expression of public feeling in early November, and candidates for the College soon became pledged to cast their votes for one of the presidential challengers. In other words, they do not use their individual discretion but reflect the feelings of voters in their state. In fact, the college does not even meet as one deliberating body. Members meet in their state capitals and their choices are conveyed to Washington. Very rarely, an elector in the Electoral College has changed his or her mind and not voted for the person to whom he or she was pledged. In 1948 a Tennessee elector did not vote for Truman, who had carried the state, but opted instead for the States Rights candidate. Twenty years later, an elector in North Carolina switched from Richard Nixon to the Third Party candidature of George Wallace. In 1988, a Democrat voted for Lloyd Bentsen, the vice presidential nominee, rather than for Michael Dukakis, the candidate for the presidency.

Some writers have also drawn attention to the way in which balloting takes place. Instead of there being a proportional split in the Electoral College vote of a particular state to reflect the division of the popular vote, the candidate who gets the most votes carries the whole state allocation. This simple plurality or 'winner takes all' method may seem unfair, especially when the result is very close. In 1960, Kennedy obtained all of New York's forty-five College votes, despite the fact that he only obtained 52.5 per cent support; a proportional split would have given him twenty-four votes, to twenty-one for his opponent. This method makes the impact of geography very important on the outcome for, as we have seen, a candidate who can carry California and other populous states has an enormous advantage. This would not be the case if the College vote was divided. The importance of urban states with dense populations is unduly emphasised under this process.

For all of its disadvantages, the system has so far worked tolerably well. When there is a close popular vote, as in 1960, the outcome in the College makes the result clear cut. Until 2000, the same was true in other contests where the gap between the main candidates was a narrow one.

Is there a better alternative to the Electoral College?

There have been many suggestions for the use of an amended college system, and others for its total abolition. Modifications could take the form of using a different electoral system from 'winner takes all'. A proportional division of the College votes is an alternative to the simple plurality.

The most obvious change would be to jettison the Electoral College and opt for a straight popular election of the president by the voters instead of using the present indirect process of election. If it proved to be the case that no candidate could overcome a 40 per cent hurdle on the first round of voting, then there could be a replay, a run-off between the two candidates who had scored most successfully. The person elected could then claim to have wide national backing and not be unduly beholden to the voters in especially populous states. No longer is there the same apprehension about democracy as prevailed when the Founding Fathers made their choice.

It is true that such a method could further enhance the power of television, for few candidates could ever get across the nation to tour every state to encourage popular support. Yet effectively this is what happens now; the campaign is already organised for its television impact. More seriously for some critics of reform along these lines, it might weaken further the two main parties and encourage the candidature of third-party nominees.

For defenders of states' rights, such a proposal might seem to be a threat to the federal system for it undermines the importance of each state and region in the contest. In particular, the smaller states may feel uneasy, for their influence in deciding the outcome would be diminished compared with the current situation.

Is change likely?

It is far more likely that the present system will continue indefinitely for, although there is periodic unease about the Electoral College, this mainly coincides with the prospect of an indecisive outcome in the next presidential election. When a clear winner emerges, as eventually happened in 1992, much of the earlier talk of change vanishes.

There is no agreement on any alternative. Jimmy Carter supported direct election early in the life of his presidency when he described the existing arrangements as 'archaic'. Many analysts might concur with such a view but there are strong forces ranged against it. The federal system was designed to protect the influence of the states, especially small ones, and they would not readily vote for a change, either via their members of Congress or in their state legislatures. For the

Dakotas or Vermont, the Electoral College gives them an influence beyond their size, and why should they wish to surrender it?

See also Bush *v.* Gore *(2000)*

Electoral System

For almost all American elections, the method of choosing candidates is the one employed in Britain and Canada, the 'first-past-the-post' or simple majority system. In other words, the candidate with the most votes in a single-member constituency is elected. It is a straightforward and familiar means of deciding the outcome but one that is becoming increasingly rare around the world. In several countries, plurality or 'winner-takes-all' systems are out of favour, the preference being for systems in which candidates and parties are to some degree rewarded in proportion to the share of the vote they obtain.

The United States has always had a tradition of single-member district, winner-takes-all elections. This method is widely seen as making it more likely that a two-party system will result, for third parties are discouraged; they may win many votes in an area but, unless they can win in an individual constituency, they get no tangible reward. By comparison, proportional methods of voting, such as those used in most of continental Europe, are said to encourage the formation and development of small parties. They have a chance of gaining representation in the legislature, even on the basis of relatively small support.

In elections to Congress, there is an overwhelming preponderance of two main parties that totally dominate the Legislature. The same applies in state legislatures, as well. The use of 'winner takes all' has worked against the development of minor parties which usually obtain scant reward for their efforts. Plurality systems convert seats into votes in a way that damages the interests of small parties, particularly if their limited support is spread across many constituencies. The effects of the system are evident in the fortunes of the American Socialist Party. Even during its peak years of electoral support (1912–20) when it won 3 to 6 per cent of the national vote in presidential elections, it was barely represented in

Congress. At its high point of 1912 (6 per cent) it failed to elect a single representative to Congress. The evidence suggests that it makes more sense for an existing or would-be third party to form an alliance with a major one than to struggle on its own with little hope.

The American situation is different in one respect from that of Britain for, under its presidential system, no government is being formed out of either chamber in Congress. When electing presidents, there is only one prize available. The presidency cannot be shared, so that a proportional system would not work. In presidential elections the party with a plurality in a state receives all the electoral votes of that state, other than in Maine. In 2000, there was much disquiet about the outcome of the presidential election in America, in which George W. Bush defeated Al Gore. For the fourth time in American history, more people voted against the eventual winner than for him.

In single-member constituencies there can be a close relationship between the elected representative and his/her constituency. One member alone has responsibility for an area that he/she can get to know well. He or she represents all who live in it, not just those who voted for one particular party; all citizens know whom to approach if they have a problem or grievance needing resolution. This is very different from what happens under some more proportional systems in which several elected members represent a broad geographical area. This relationship between individual legislators and their constituencies is highly valued by many commentators in Britain and America where these local relationships are highly significant. In the United States, elected representatives are judged according to their ability to 'bring home the pork'.

There is little pressure for reform in America. Proportional representation (PR) could be used only in limited circumstances. As we have seen, it could not be used for the presidency and, as individual states elect only one senator at a time, it would not work for these elections either. Six states return only one Representative and would therefore be unable to employ multi-member constituencies. PR could be used for congressional districts in larger states but their average

size is already around 600,000, so that a multi-member constituency of five representatives would be one of three million. Moreover, except in small states, the geographical areas which the successful candidates would have to represent would be a very large one, destroying much hope of keeping that sense of connection with a district and making electioneering particularly exhausting and expensive.

Experimentation with proportional representation in America

During the early part of the twentieth century two dozen American cities for a time employed the single transferable vote (STV). Its use was urged by the Progressive Movement which sought to clean up government in the major cities and blunt the power of the party bosses. Progressives argued that winner-take-all, single-member district elections served to reinforce the power of – often Democratic – urban political machines, sometimes enabling them to win almost all the seats on city councils, on the basis of only 50 to 60 per cent of the popular vote. PR was seen was a way to break these one-party monopolies and to allow for the fair representation of a variety of political parties.

The Proportional Representation League – founded in 1893 – was also instrumental in promoting the use of PR. As an attainable goal, it urged the adoption of PR at city level, for cities could easily introduce PR elections by a change of charter following a referendum, without the need to persuade government officials of the case for reform. Ashtabula, Ohio (1915) was the first American city to introduce STV but the major boost was its adoption in large urban areas, such as Cleveland and Cincinnati, in the mid-1920s. In 1936, voters in New York City approved by a large margin the adoption of PR elections, a development that inspired several other cities to take up the cause.

Why was the flirtation with PR abandoned?

In several cities, the system came under attack from the politicians and parties who lost power and privileges. Legal challenges were mounted in

Michigan and California, the courts ruling that PR violated their constitutions. More usually, change was brought about by popular referendum. Just as its use had made it easy to get PR adopted, so too was it a tool deployed by well-financed opponents who eventually succeeded in some cities. In New York City, a 'red scare' campaign was mounted by the Democrats who attempted to link PR with Soviet Communism. A handful of Communists had served on the STV-elected city council since 1941 but it was the onset of the Cold War that enabled party leaders to exploit this issue and portray the method as essentially an un-American practice. The voters opted to end the use of proportional representation by a solid margin, their example soon being followed in the 1950s in other cities.

By 1962, only Cambridge, Massachusetts retained this system. It is still used in elections to its nine-member city council and a six-member School Committee. Representatives are elected every two years by STV, making it currently the only governing body in the United States still to use the system. Once a laborious process that took several days to complete by hand, vote counting is now done by computer.

See also *Political Parties*; *Third Parties*; *and individual third parties such as the Socialist Party of America/Socialist Party USA*

Electronic Media

The term 'electronic media' refers to forms of the media that use electronics to enable the audience to access the content, as opposed to print media which may be created electronically but do not require electronic intervention to enable the recipient to access the final form. The term has traditionally referred to the broadcast media, radio and television (including cable) and, since the 1970s, to video recordings as well. Today, however, use of the term has widened so that it includes CD-ROMs, DVDs and other forms that are not film or paper based. Of the 'new media', the Internet has made a large impact, creating a massive resource of easily accessible online information.

In US politics, the most important form of

electronic media is broadcasting by radio and especially television. But other forms of electronic communication have been used by local communicates to enable them to exercise some political muscle. These have ranged from the familiar to the uncommon. In New Jersey, those who opposed a tax increase organised a mass phone-in to a radio station to attract attention to their grievance, as part of a general revolt against their growing burden of taxation. By contrast, landlords in California, who objected to the introduction of rent control, decided to circulate videotapes which depicted pro-control members of the Santa Monica city council in an unflattering light.

Electronic Voting Machines

The term 'electronic' or 'e' voting is used to embrace several different types of voting methods, and can refer either to electronic means of casting a vote and/or electronic means of counting votes. Electronic technology includes punch cards, optical-scan voting systems and the use of direct-recording electronic (DRE) voting machines. It can also cover the transmission of votes and ballot papers via telephones, personal computers and the Internet.

The first electronic voting machines were used for a real election in Illinois in 1975 since when, in their various forms, they have become more familiar. They made the headlines because of problems with punch-card voting machines in Florida (and to a much less extent in some other states) in the 2000 presidential election between George W. Bush and Al Gore. Voting technology became the object of national and worldwide attention, because of the problems with unclear ballot designs and, particularly, spoiled ballots. The issue of voter intent on cards where the chad was not fully punched caused some of the most serious problems. 'Hanging chads', 'dimpled chads', and 'pregnant chads' were phrases that entered everyday conversation.

Following the 2000 election debacle in Florida and the difficulties experienced in some other states, Congress passed the Help America Vote Act in 2002 which – among other things – provided $4 billion of federal funding to assist states in updating their often antiquated voting equipment. With federal money available and the cautionary experience of inadequate punch-card voting systems as a warning, states began turning in droves to DRE voting machines. In 2004, 17 per cent more voters were using electronic voting machines than four years earlier, the largest rise of a specific voting system from one election to the next since 1980.

A good system must include several key criteria. The machine must be able to guarantee the anonymity of a voter's ballot, be tamper resistant, and allow for the possibility of human error. It must also be comprehensible to, and usable by, the entire voting population, regardless of age, infirmity or disability. Many of the current electronic machines are made by Ohio-based Diebold Election Systems, in states ranging from California to Georgia, Maryland to Texas. The voter is typically given a PIN, a smartcard, or some other token that allows them to approach a voting terminal, enter the token and then vote for their candidates of choice. When the voter's selection is complete, DRE systems will typically present a summary of the voter's selections, giving him or her a final chance to make changes.

There is no federal agency with regulatory authority or oversight over the voting machine industry. Much depends on the performance of two companies, Diebold and ES&S, whose machines now count the majority of votes cast in American elections. Some commentators have warned against the speedy introduction of electronic voting using this type of technology, the most fundamental problem being that that the entire election hinges on the correctness, robustness and security of the software within the voting terminal.

For its study of e-voting vulnerabilities, the Brennan Center for Justice, a New York City-based non-partisan think tank, convened a task force of election officials, computer scientists and security experts. They examined the three most commonly purchased systems, optical scanners and touch-screen machines with and without paper trails. They expressed alarm at the possibility that the security of votes could be imperilled by software attacks and urged the case for regular auditing of the machines by state election officials.

See also Bush *v.* Gore *(2000)*; *Chads*

Emancipation Proclamation

The Emancipation Proclamation was an executive order issued in 1863 by President Abraham Lincoln, during the American Civil War, which declared the freedom of all slaves in those areas of the rebellious Confederate States of America that had not already returned to Union control.

As the Union armies proceeded to conquer the Confederacy, thousands of slaves were freed each day until, by July 1865, nearly all (around four million) were freed. As the Proclamation was a war measure, abolitionists were concerned that it had not secured the final end of slavery. Accordingly, they urged the passage of the Thirteenth Amendment – ratified in 1865 – which brought about a permanent end to the institution.

Emergency Economic Stabilization Fact see *Paulson Plan (2008)*

EMILY's List see *Women's Movement: the Fight for Female Equality*

Enumerated Powers see *Delegated Powers*

Environmental Politics see *Green Movement*

Environmental Protection Agency (EPA)

The Environmental Protection Agency is the agency of the federal government that leads the nation's environmental science, research, education and assessment efforts. Originally proposed by President Nixon at a time of mounting concern about pollution and other environment hazards, the EPA was given the task of protecting human health and the environment by regulating chemicals and safeguarding the supplies of air, land and water upon which life depends.

The EPA was assigned the daunting task of repairing the damage already done to the natural environment and to establish new criteria to guide Americans in making a cleaner environment a reality. Its establishment was a recognition of the need to consolidate in one agency a variety of federal research, monitoring, standard-setting and enforcement activities. It is not a Cabinet agency but it is headed by an administrator who is usually accorded Cabinet rank.

Equal Rights Amendment (ERA)

The Equal Rights Amendment was a constitutional amendment intended to prohibit discrimination based on gender and guarantee 'equality of rights' under the law for both sexes. An ambitious project, widely supported by feminist organisations such as NOW in the 1970s, it provoked a backlash, not just from men, but from socially conservative groups such as religious evangelicals and powerful business interests. Passed by both chambers of Congress in 1972, the ERA was never ratified by enough states to become part of the Constitution. Thirty-five had approved it by 1978 but, by then, three of them were seeking to withdraw their support. With little prospect of wider ratification, it lapsed in 1982. Ultimately, many Americans were too anxious about the extent of social change that the Amendment might unleash to allow their support.

See also *Constitutional Amendment*; *National Organization for Women*

Equality

Equality is about making sure people are treated fairly and given fair chances. It is not about treating everyone in the same way but it recognises that their needs are met in different ways.

All people are not equal in any descriptive sense. For instance, they are not equal physically or intellectually. In a prescriptive sense, we might say they should be treated equally, as long as there are not grounds for treating them differently. Their entitlement is to equal consideration. They should be treated equally unless there are good reasons for not doing so. The principle of equality, understood in this way, does not say that all human beings must be treated alike. We presume that they should be unless there are grounds for making distinctions.

Equality has traditionally been a political issue in many democracies. Those on the politically progressive side tend to dislike the degree of economic inequality in society and point to the vast discrepancies in wealth and income. They note the extent to which affluence confers social advantage in education, health and other forms of social provision. Many emphasise the importance of equality of outcome, wanting to see not absolute economic equality but decisive moves towards the creation of a more equal society in which the distinctions of rich and poor are less apparent. Those who are more conservative stress that people are born unequal. They have different abilities and some will flourish. We therefore need a 'ladder and a safety net' so that, in life's competitive race, the enterprising can flourish and those who cannot make it can be rescued.

In the Declaration of Independence, Thomas Jefferson decreed that 'all men are created equal'. By this, he was not saying that everybody was alike and that there were no differences between human beings. Indeed, throughout his life, he clearly believed that there were differences for he took the view that black Americans were genetically inferior to whites. But a further clue to his meaning is to be found in the same declaration when it speaks of the 'unalienable rights' to which all were entitled. What he wanted was that everyone should have the same chance, in other words, equality of opportunity. What individuals made of that chance was, in his view, a matter dependent on their abilities and efforts. He did not favour equality of outcome, with its emphasis on equal rewards, but he did think that, in a moral sense, all had the right to equal examination of their needs and situations.

The struggle for equality has been the rallying point for all groups demanding an end to discrimination against them and the attainment of their full civil rights – among them African Americans, women and others, such as gays and lesbians, and the disabled. The list could be extended to cover the victims of discrimination on grounds of age (the old and the young), people with AIDS, and the homeless.

See also *Egalitarianism*

Establishment Clause

This is the clause in the First Amendment which lays down that 'Congress shall make no law respecting an establishment of religion' and thus makes it clear that the government – and Congress in particular – cannot establish an official national religion nor show preference to one religion over any other. Under the Incorporation Doctrine, the Supreme Court has applied the clause to state and local, as well as federal, government. Subsequently, the Bill of Rights has been broadly applied to limit state and local government as well. In the *Board of Education of Kiryas Joel Village School District* v. *Grumet* (1994) the majority of the court agreed with the opinion set out by Justice David Souter, which stated that 'government should not prefer one religion to another, or religion to irreligion'.

There is an ongoing debate about how much, if any, contact is allowed between religion and government. It is clear what the establishment clause does not permit but less clear what it allows. There is doubt over whether government can use public money or facilities, or resort to moral persuasion, to support and co-operate with religious groups, assuming it treats all other groups in the same way. The issue is raised in the controversy over whether or not parents of children who attend religious schools are entitled to receive state aid in the form of health, lunch, special education and transport programmes or provision of textbooks for their offspring. Those who support such assistance argue that the help is being given to children rather than to the schools and that, in effect, some children are receiving their normal level of state support but in a religious school setting. In its judgments, the Supreme Court has evolved a threefold test for the constitutionality of any form of aid: whether it has a 'secular purpose'; whether it has a 'primary effect' of advancing or impeding religion; and whether it encourages 'excessive entanglement' of church and state.

Further controversy has concerned the issue of school prayer. One of the most controversial decisions of the Warren Court was made in the case of *Engel* v. *Vitale* (1962). Although a prayer written by the New York Board of Regents was non-denominational, the Supreme Court struck it down, Justice Black writing that 'it is no part of the official business of government to compose official prayers for any group of American people to recite as part of a religious program carried out by the Government'. In a further ruling in 1963 (*Abington Township* v. *Schempp*) the reading of the Lord's Prayer or of the Bible in the classroom of a public school by the teacher was ruled unconstitutional, a decision much criticised by many evangelical Protestants and also the then Chief Justice, William Rehnquist. In this case, the Court introduced its 'secular purpose' and 'primary effect' tests as means of determining compatibility with the establishment clause. As the law requiring the recital of the Lord's Prayer violated these tests, it was unacceptable. The 'excessive entanglement' test was added in *Lemon* v. *Kurtzman* (1971) which established the 'Lemon test' of legislation based on the three prongs mentioned above.

In *Wallace* v. *Jaffree* (1985) the Supreme Court struck down an Alabama law whereby students in public schools would observe a daily period of silence for private prayer, not because the moment of silence was itself unconstitutional but rather because, in introducing it, Alabama lawmakers had violated the secular purpose test because they were acting solely to advance religion. Further controversies followed in the 1990s. In *Lee* v. *Weisman* (1992) the Court ruled unconstitutional the offering of prayers by religious officials before voluntarily attended ceremonies such as graduation, thereby establishing that the state could not conduct religious exercises at public occasions, voluntary or otherwise. Eight years later, in *Santa Fe Independent School District* v. *Doe*, it decided that even a vote of the student body could not authorise student-led prayer prior to school events.

Ethnicity and Race

Ethnicity refers to membership of an ethnic group, especially a minority one with common ancestry, racial and sometimes linguistic characteristics, as well as distinctive cultural and religious traditions. The mixture of physical traits and social characteristics gives a social group a common consciousness and separates them from other social groups. As a result of many years of sharing the same land and intermarriage, however, such differences may become blurred.

Ethnicity and race are related concepts. Whereas ethnicity generally refers to shared cultural, linguistic, or religious traits, race refers to shared biological characteristics. If writers are referring to a group marked by longstanding culture, kinship, geography and often religion, it is now more usual to use ethnicity rather than race, for the latter concept has overtones and has in any case been undermined by modern thinking in genetics.

In asking questions about race, the United States Census Bureau and the Office of Management and Budget (OMB) use the concept to imply not just scientific or anthropological features but social and cultural characteristics as well. Race and ethnicity were considered as separate and distinct identities, Hispanic origin or otherwise being asked as a separate question. This meant that, in addition to their race, respondents were also categorised according to whether or not they were of Hispanic or Latino origin, or not.

For the 2000 Census, questions of race were asked differently from the way they had been in previous surveys, respondents being given the

Category	Population	Percentage
One race	293,285,839	98.0
White	221,331,507	73.9
Black or African American	37,051,483	12.4
American Indian and Alaskan Native	2,369,431	0.8
Asian	13,100,095	4.5
Native Hawaiian and Other Pacific Islander	426,194	0.1
Some other race	19,007,129	6.3
Two or more races	6,112,646	2.0
Hispanic or Latino (of any race)	44,252,278	14.8

Source: US Census Bureau, 2006 American Community Survey

option of selecting one or more race categories to indicate their racial identities. This means that direct comparison with the findings of previous census returns is difficult to achieve. Data show that nearly seven million Americans identified themselves as members of two or more races.

Data shows that nearly seven million Americans identified themselves as members of two or more races. In order to identify their race, Americans were provided with seven categories into which to place themselves: white; Black or African American; American Indian and Alaskan Native; Asian; Native Hawaiian and Other Pacific Islander; some other race (e.g., not the others listed and including groups such as Creoles and mulattoes, but primarily those of Hispanic origin); and those of two or more races.

According to the Census Bureau's 2006 American Community Survey, the minority population had just reached 100 million, with the Hispanic element the fastest growing. It categorised the US population in this way:

See also *Diversity*

Executive

The term 'executive' derives from the Latin *ex sequi*, meaning to 'follow out' or 'carry out'. The role of the executive branch of government is then to carry out the political system's policies, laws or directives. As long as there have been political systems, there have been individuals or small groups who assume the role of leadership. They have formulated and implemented public policy. At the apex of this executive structure, there is usually a single chief executive, be that person known as a president, prime minister, chief minister, supreme leader or monarch.

The Executive is, then, the branch of government mainly responsible for the day-to-day management of the state, a role that includes initiating government action, making and implementing public policy and co-ordinating state activities. In the United States, it includes the president, vice president, departments of state and the various independent agencies.

In Article II, Section 1, of the United States

Constitution it is stated that, 'the executive power shall be vested in a president of the United States of America'. This makes the president the head of the executive branch of the federal government. The president appoints the Cabinet and oversees the various agencies and departments of the federal government.

Executive Agreements

Executive agreements are agreements negotiated between the executive branch of the US government and a foreign government that do not require confirmation by the Senate. They are less formal than treaties but have the same legal force. The distinction between them is only of domestic significance. International law regards both as binding, whatever their designation under domestic law. Unlike treaties, agreements are not binding on succeeding presidents.

In recent years, presidents have concluded more agreements than treaties. Their growing use is in part attributable to the sheer volume of business and contacts between the United States and other countries, coupled with the already heavy workload of the Senate. Many international agreements are of relatively minor importance and would needlessly overburden the Senate if they were submitted to it as treaties for advice and consent. Another factor has been the passage of legislation by Congress authorising the executive branch to conclude international agreements in certain fields, such as agriculture, foreign aid and trade. Treaties have also been approved implicitly authorising further agreements between the parties.

The Constitution does not provide for executive agreements but several presidents have found them useful because they can be agreed speedily, in secret and without running the risk of Senate rejection. Examples include the agreement that ended the fighting and provided for prisoner exchange between North Vietnam and the US in 1973, and most trade agreements. Their use peaked in the Reagan years, when 2,840 agreements were made, as opposed to 125 treaties. The United States is currently a party to nearly nine hundred treaties and more than five thousand executive agreements.

Although they appear to offer wide-ranging scope to the president, sometimes the implementation of agreements requires the spending of appropriated money and therefore congressional involvement and action. This is why presidents have increasingly made greater use of congressional–executive agreements (often on trade matters) via which the president concludes an agreement and then submits it for congressional assent (a majority vote in the two chambers sufficient for it to pass). Clinton's North American Free Trade Agreement (NAFTA) was passed under this procedure, an example of an agreement that might not have received ratification if it had been concluded as a treaty.

Executive Office of the President

As a result of the recommendations of the 1937 Committee, Roosevelt agreed that new machinery should be established. Two years after it reported, an enlarged presidential office was created, far larger in scale than had existed previously. Instead of a few clerks and secretaries, there was to be a new Executive Office of the President. In the words of Clinton Rossiter (1960), the presidency was converted 'into an instrument of twentieth century government . . . it gives the incumbent a sporting chance to stand the strain and fulfil the constitutional mandate as a one-man branch of our three-part government'. In Rossiter's opinion, the innovation saved the presidency from paralysis and the Constitution from radical amendment.

From the earliest days, it was obvious that the new Office would be highly significant but, even so, the extent of its eventual impact on American government could not have been judged. At the time, it comprised barely a thousand staff whereas, at the beginning of the twenty-first century, the total exceeds five thousand. But the extent of its operations and of its importance is not to be judged by numbers alone but more by the centrality of its position in the workings of the executive branch. It has become what Maidment and McGrew (1992) call 'the principal instrument of presidential government'.

The modern president relies on the Executive Office to come up with the background information, detailed analyses and informed policy recommendations that are needed to enable him or her to master the complexities of a task. It has taken its place at the heart of the administration, giving the president the advice he or she depends upon, conducting many dealings with Congress, and helping to publicise and supervise the implementation of presidential decisions. The president is freed to deal with top-level matters of the moment and to engage in future planning.

The component parts of the Executive Office change from president to president for it is the president's personal bureaucracy. Individuals have varied in the use made of it and amended its internal organisation to reflect their own priorities, interests and needs. New parts of the Office have been established; some have been developed or transformed from their original character; and others have become redundant.

> The Executive Office is an umbrella under which exist a number of key agencies that cover the whole range of policy areas and that serve him directly. The Office of Management and the Budget already existed in 1939 but, otherwise, only the White House Office has been there since the original machinery was set up. Elements have changed in different administrations but central to the work of the Office are the White House staff, personal appointees who are likely to be the closest advisers for general and particular policies.

Assessment of the Executive Office

It was because of the growing demands on the president that some help was necessary if he or she was to be adequately equipped for the necessary tasks. As the president's responsibilities grew so did his or her need for expert assistance. At the time of the creation of the Executive Office, few commentators realised just how important it would become. It is now far larger than in the year after its establishment, and its influence has grown even more dramatically than its number of personnel. What makes it so important for the president is that it is beholden only to him or her. The president appoints its members, and they

know that they owe their position to him or her and therefore seek to serve him or her loyally.

The Executive Office is the main instrument of presidential government, and all modern presidents rely upon it to a greater or lesser degree, for information, analysis and policy recommendations. In some cases, their dependence is greater than others, and certain key aides emerge as the linchpins of the administration. For them, their focus of attention is inevitably the presidency, as it must be. It is easy for them to become so obsessed by the protection of the president that they ignore the limitations of the office designed by the framers of the Constitution. In other words, the Executive Office – and especially those assistants who serve in the White House Office – can become out of touch with the viewpoints and requirements of those who inhabit other areas of the system of government.

The danger can be that, having appointed an advisory team of people who share his or her personal and political preferences, the president receives advice only from those who share the same outlook. Other people in different branches of the governmental process also have insights worthy of an audience, and some members of Congress and bureaucrats may find that their route to the president is barred. Presidents can come to rely too much on those around them and, in that way, allow themselves to become out of touch with the views of a wider section of the American public.

See also *West Wing*

Executive Orders

Executive orders are regulations or rules issued by the president that have the effect of law. Such orders must either be derived from the president's constitutional powers or based on laws passed by Congress. They were first used by President Washington in 1789 and were regularly employed thereafter. But many of the early ones covered relatively minor administrative and rule-making functions. Over time they have become an important and often contentious weapon by which the president can initiate policy. Many orders have had far-reaching importance – for example, the integration of the armed forces under Harry Truman, the desegration of public schools under Eisenhower, and Kennedy's instruction prohibiting racial discrimination in housing subsidised by the federal government.

Those commentators who believe that the president holds broad power cite Article II, Section 1 of the Constitution: 'The executive Power shall be vested in a President of the United States of America' and from Section 3: ' . . . he shall take Care that the Laws be faithfully executed, and shall Commission all the Officers of the United States'. The view that the president holds total control over the executive branch is referred to as the unitary executive theory, as supported by George W. Bush who made substantial use of executive orders. One of his most controversial uses of them was his decision (July 2008) to mount counter-terrorist operations inside Pakistani territory, following an intense internal administration debate.

Critics – many of whom disapprove of the unitary executive theory – dislike the way in which executive orders are used by presidents to make laws without the approval of the Legislature and sometimes even against the will of Congress, as when existing laws are redirected away from their original mandates. The Supreme Court has upheld the validity of executive order, however, and accorded them under most circumstances the force of law.

See also *Unitary Executive Theory*

Executive Privilege

Executive privilege refers to the right claimed by presidents to refuse to appear before, or withhold information from, Congress, the courts and the public. Although it does not feature in the Constitution, it has been asserted by presidents since Washington, several of whom exercised the power without facing any serious congressional challenge. They portrayed it as necessary in order to maintain secrecy in the conduct of foreign affairs and to ensure the confidentiality of advice they receive. The courts have accepted the case for executive privilege but limited the circumstances under which it can be advanced and

made it clear that its extent is subject to judicial determination.

Executive privilege was recognised for the first time only in the Supreme Court's 1974 ruling in *US* v. *Richard M. Nixon*. President Nixon had tried to extend its meaning so that it was applicable to all executive officials, even those who no longer worked within the Executive. When the special prosecutor pursued the matter in the federal courts, the Supreme Court ruled that presidents can legitimately claim executive privilege but not when facing a criminal investigation. In this case, the judgment imposed strict parameters on executive privilege by ruling that the president had to release tape recordings of his conversations at the White House to those investigating the Watergate scandal. A further limitation was made by the Court during the Clinton presidency when it was decided that presidents could not invoke executive privilege to avoid or delay civil proceedings for actions that occurred before they became president.

Exit Polls

Exit polls are surveys of selected voters taken soon after they leave their voting locations. Unlike opinion polls, which ask voters for which party they would vote in some forthcoming or hypothetical election, exit polls are concerned with how voters actually voted and why they voted as they did. They are conducted by private companies working on behalf of newspapers or broadcasters, with a view to being in a position to provide an early indication of the outcome of an election well before the actual result will become apparent.

Exit polls benefit from dealing with what has happened rather than what might happen. As with opinion polls, however, they are based on a small fraction of the electorate and there is a margin of error. In addition, in order to provide an early forecast of what the outcome of an election might be, they tend not to sample late-hour voters. The undersampled groups may be among the most active sections of the population, as opposed to the elderly and women who stay at home to bring up the children, and are more likely to vote earlier in the day. Finally, there is the problem that some voters may not be willing to participate in the exit polls or, if they do, they may distort the findings by deliberately giving a false indication of the party for which they voted.

Some exit polls have given false impressions of the relative performances of American presidential candidates, most obviously in the 2004 presidential election in which there was a discrepancy between the findings of the early exit polls, indicating a Kerry victory, and the final outcome. One other criticism which has emerged is that the early publication of exit polls may itself influence the voting in different parts of the United States. In 1980, at 8.15 p.m. NBC predicted a victory for Ronald Reagan, based on exit polls of 20,000 voters. The polls were still open on the West coast where it was 5.15 p.m. There was speculation that, on hearing the results, some potential voters were deterred from voting. Since then, projections of the final outcome have been delayed by the television networks until the closure of the polls in Alaska and Hawaii.

F

Fair Deal

The Fair Deal was President Truman's ambitious legislative agenda of measures for social improvement, as outlined in his State of the Union Address to Congress in January 1949. He declared that: 'Every segment of our population, and every individual, has a right to expect from his government a fair deal.' Truman set out to prove that New Deal liberalism was not yet dead and indeed argued that newer initiatives were needed to solve the nation's economic and social problems in the post-war era. He contended that his Fair Deal programme would redistribute income among people of various classes, transferring money from the very rich to the very poor, and tackle many of the nation's most pressing social problems. Truman's Fair Deal included six major federal initiatives:

- New civil rights legislation
- Federal housing programmes
- Unemployment insurance benefits
- New tax cuts for the poor
- Federal funding for education
- A federal health care and health insurance programme.

On first taking office in 1945, Truman had tried to continue FDR's policies and he sent to Congress a host of New Deal-style bills which were not so much bold new endeavours but rather extensions of existing policies. His attempts were thwarted, however, by opposition on Capitol Hill. The same fate befell his Fair Deal changes. In Congress he was confronted by a conservative coalition of Southern Democrats (more conservative fiscally, socially, and politically than Democrats from the Northeast or the Midwest) and Northern Republicans that had arisen out of opposition to New Deal liberalism and Roosevelt's internationalism. They particularly disliked Truman's liberal stance on civil rights for African Americans.

Truman was similarly unable to pass through Congress any major social legislation in his second term, few of his Fair Deal bills ever being enacted. The programme remains significant, however, in that it established the call for universal health care as a rallying cry for the Democratic Party. Lyndon Johnson later credited Truman's unfulfilled programme as a key influence upon the Great Society measures of his own administration, such as Medicare.

FECA Legislation

FECA legislation refers to a series of Federal Election Campaign Acts passed in the 1970s to address the issue of the role of money in US elections and to bring a degree of transparency to the subject. Attempts had been made from the 1960s onwards to legislate on political funding. Commentators were becoming alarmed at the escalating costs of election campaigns, the sources of money and the unequal distribution of the finance available that allowed very rich candidates to outspend their rivals. There was also the possibility of undue influence being exercised by those who handed over money.

The first significant piece of legislation was the Federal Election Campaign Act (1971), which replaced all earlier laws on the subject.

All candidates for political office, as well as the individuals, campaign committees, parties and political action committees (PACs) that backed them, were made to declare the source of their contributions.

As a result of evidence heard in the Watergate hearings, it was felt necessary to tighten up the FECA restrictions by a new measure three years later. The 1974 legislation tackled two themes, the importance of tough limits on contributions and the need for public funding, as well as establishing the Federal Election Commission to oversee the disclosure process.

In *Buckley* v. *Valeo* (1976), the Supreme Court ruled sections of the 1974 legislation unconstitutional, the justices arguing that candidates should not be restricted in the amount of money they could spend on their own campaign (unless they accepted public money), for this posed a threat to freedom of expression. As a result of the decision, wealthy individuals seeking the presidency were allowed to spend their own money without limit.

As a result of the 1974 Act, there was legislation in place to regulate the raising and spending of money. Direct donations to campaigns ('hard money') had been subjected to a ceiling. But in the late twentieth century there were still ways in which the regulations could be evaded, particularly by the collection of so-called 'soft money'. This was money contributed by individuals or organisations, such as businesses and unions, to political action committees. It was unaffected by the restrictions on hard money. A measure passed by Congress in 1979 had allowed parties to raise and spend money on party building, registration drives and getting-out-the-vote activities ('soft money'). These were purposes not always easy to distinguish from supporting party candidates. As the amount of spending on these activities significantly increased over the following years, there was increasing suspicion about the ways in which money was used. By the 1990s, the scale of election spending was increasing dramatically. Parties were using soft money to complement their publicly financed presidential campaigns, in effect bypassing the official 1974 limits. There was therefore a considerable gulf between legislative intention and prevailing practice.

Senator John McCain made several efforts in the late 1990s to ban the raising and spending of soft money but the proposal was blocked by fellow senators, some of whom were concerned that they posed a threat to the First Amendment. In 2002, the McCain–Feingold Campaign Finance Reform Act was passed against the preferences of President Bush who, however, did not use his veto against it.

See also *Federal Election Commission*; *McCain– Feingold Campaign Finance Reform Act*; *Soft Money*

Federal Courts

Federal courts enforce federal law and state courts enforce state law but the relationship between the two systems is more complex than this. The federal Constitution is the supreme law of the land. If state law conflicts with it or with federal laws made under that Constitution, then state law gives way. This is made clear in the 'supremacy clause' of the Constitution (Article vi). Because of it, decisions made in the federal courts can have a broad impact on those made in the state courts. Moreover, the federal court system has become relatively more important as the country has expanded and the amount of legislation passed by Congress has increased.

The first Congress divided the nation into judicial districts and created federal courts for each district. From that beginning has evolved the present structure which is relatively simple. There are three layers of courts. At the bottom of the pyramid are the ninety-fourth district courts; above them are the thirteen circuit courts of appeal and two courts of special jurisdiction; and at the apex of the system is the Supreme Court, the highest court in the land. Congress retains the power to create and abolish federal courts, as well as to determine the number of judges in the federal judiciary system. It cannot, however, abolish the Supreme Court.

The appointment of judges in federal courts

Federal judges are appointed by the president, who is advised by the Department of Justice and the office of the Deputy Attorney General. This power of appointment is highly significant. As Vile has pointed out: 'No president can afford to ignore either the partisan advantages of such appointments or the fact that the men he appoints will be able, to say the least, to give a particular emphasis to the way in which policy is carried out.'

The power of appointment gives the president the opportunity to influence the balance of opinion in the courts. By 1940, Roosevelt had achieved a Democratic majority among federal judges but the high point was reached during the presidency of Johnson when more than 70 per cent were of his party. In his 1980 election campaign, Reagan undertook to choose conservative judges who would abandon the social activism of many earlier appointees. His overt concern with the ideological stance of judges was in line with the Nixon approach but a departure from the usual practice whereby party label was a more important consideration. For Reagan, Republican leanings alone were not a sufficient guarantee of suitability.

In his two terms as president, Ronald Reagan made 368 federal judicial appointments, four to the Supreme Court, six to special courts, seventy-six to circuit courts and the rest to district ones. As with presidents before him, he made partisan appointments but two factors were particularly significant about his choices:

1. He had the opportunity to appoint more lower-court judges than any of his predecessors since Franklin Roosevelt – he filled about half of all the judgeships at that level.
2. His appointees were singularly conservative by nature, much more so than most previous Republican nominations. This was a deliberate decision by the president to choose people of a different legal philosophy to those who had in the past sat on the Bench.

George Bush followed a similar approach in his selection of another 185 judges. The effect of the appointments made in the twelve years from 1981 to 1993 was to transform the type of personnel who sat in judgment on legal issues. Overwhelmingly, the nominees were young, white males who were deeply conservative. Few women, African Americans or members of other minority groups were selected but, in one respect, the choices were unusual for Republican administrations. More Roman Catholics were chosen than usual, probably because the Justice Department was in sympathy with the Catholic stance on the controversial matter of abortion, and saw a chance to win some popularity on the topic with the Christian Right.

Appointments made in the Clinton era were quite distinctive. As a result of a rush of retirements, he was able to nominate almost a quarter of all federal judges, and he used the opportunity to diversify the composition of the judiciary. Almost of his nominees were Democrats but many of them were more moderate and less ideological than some party members would have liked. The figures below illustrate the different approaches of the three presidents since 1981 and give an early indication of the background of judges appointed by George W. Bush:

Presidential appointments to the federal judiciary

1. Party affiliation of appointees under selected presidents

President	Party	Percentage of party appointees
Roosevelt	Democrat	97
Kennedy	Democrat	92
Nixon	Republican	93
Reagan	Republican	94
Bush Snr	Republican	89
Clinton	Democrat	88

2. A profile of appointees under selected presidents

Characteristic	Reagan	Bush Snr	Clinton	Bush Jnr (to Dec. 2002)
Female	28	36	110	18
Black	7	12	62	9
Hispanic	15	8	24	6
Asian	2	0	5	6
Total	368	185	376	100

Figures adapted from those provided by T. Cronin and M. Genovese, *The Paradoxes of the American Presidency*, Oxford University Press, 2004

Federal Election Commission

Congress created the Federal Election Commission (FEC) in 1975 as an independent, non-partisan regulatory agency with a brief to administer and to enforce the Federal Election Campaign Act (FECA), the statute governing the financing of federal elections. The duties of the, FEC are: to disclose campaign finance information; to enforce the provisions of the law, such as the limits and prohibitions on contributions; and to oversee the public funding of presidential elections.

The commission comprises six members appointed by the president and confirmed by the Senate. Each member serves for six years, two seats being subject to appointment every two years. By law, no more than three commissioners can be members of the same political party, and at least four votes are required for any official commission action.

See also *FECA Legislation*

Federal Government

The Constitution forms the foundations of the United States federal government in that it created its basic structure. The federal government carries out roles assigned to it by the Constitution. It has three branches – legislative, judicial, and executive – which, between them, carry out governmental power and functions:

- The executive branch of the government is responsible for enforcing the laws of the land. The president, vice president, department heads (cabinet members), and heads of independent agencies carry out this mission.
- Article I of the Constitution establishes the legislative or law-making branch of government. It has a two-branch Congress – the Senate and the House of Representatives – and agencies that support Congress.
- Courts decide arguments about the meaning of laws and how they are applied. They also decide if laws violate the Constitution – this is known as judicial review, and it is how federal courts provide checks and balances on the legislative and executive branches.

Under the system of separation of powers, each of these branches has some authority to act on its own, some authority to regulate the other two branches, and some of its own authority regulated by the other branches. In addition, the powers of the federal government as a whole are limited by the Constitution which leaves a great deal of authority to the individual states.

Federal Reserve Banks

The Federal Reserve System (aka the Federal Reserve or The Fed) is the US central banking system and note-issuing authority established in 1913 to regulate the country's credit and monetary policy. It is a private banking system comprising twelve regional Federal Reserve banks located in major cities throughout the nation (e.g., Atlanta, Boston and Chicago) and all their member banks. The system is governed by the Federal Reserve Board in Washington DC, appointed by the president with Senate approval.

Federalism

Federalism is a system in which constitutional authority is divided between the central government and the regional or state government, according to a binding written document. The states and the central government are independent. Wheare (1946) put it clearly in his definition, describing federalism as 'the method of dividing powers so that the general and regional governments are each, within a sphere, coordinate and independent'. In many cases, particularly in the United States, there has been a broad historical drift of power from the regions to the centre although, in different periods, that trend undergoes a reversal.

All Americans are then subject to two governments that act directly upon them. As an example, the state of Wyoming has formal authority over its inhabitants but the national government can also pass laws and establish policies that affect Wyoming. The system was not designed as a pyramid structure with the federal government at the apex, the states below it and then local government at the bottom. In constitutional terms, the federal and state governments are seen as being of equal status within their own distinctive realms of authority. The written Constitution lays down the binding division of power, and ultimately federal statutes prevail in the event of conflict with state laws. The Supreme Court settles disputes about divisions of powers. Its judgments are accepted as binding on the federal and state governments. It is a system of shared power between units of government.

The establishment of US federalism

Before the creation of the federal system in the American Constitution, there were governments within the separate colonies (states). One of the early tasks of the settlers had been to devise some system of government and, as the nation pushed westwards, new outposts of government were required for the management of local affairs. When the American Constitution was agreed, this multilayered system of counties and smaller governmental units was left largely untouched for it was appreciated that there was a need for a series of governments which were directly in touch with the people and which were recognised by them. What resulted was really a mosaic comprising a multiplicity of government units or building blocks that together make up the whole.

Against this background, the Founding Fathers established at Philadelphia a system that was the result of compromises necessary to reconcile conflicting political and economic interests. Federalism was seen as a 'halfway house' between the concept of a centralised unitary state that was unacceptable to thirteen states jealous of their independence, and the idea of a confederation that would have been a weak association of autonomous states. In the words of Alan Grant (1994), federalism 'arose out of a desire to bolster national unity whilst . . . accommodating regional diversity'.

One of the attractions of federalism was that it dispersed power. It thereby prevented any excessive concentration of power in the hands of one person or one agency. It was thought likely that the states and the federal government would each jealously guard the powers allocated to them, so that there was little likelihood of either power base dominating the other. Also, federalism had the merit of dealing with the inevitable conflict that arose at the Convention between the most populous states and the smaller ones. Larger delegations were willing to accept a strong central government, as required by the less populated ones, because they thought that they could carry sufficient weight to influence its workings and protect their interests.

The drift of power in American federalism

The system established at Philadelphia was one of *Dual Federalism*, two levels of government supposed to be independent, each with its own clearly defined sphere of influence and responsibility. Some writers argue that dual federalism never really existed in a pure form for, from the early nineteenth century, the federal government was stepping in to provide grants for improvements on expensive and necessary items such as road building.

Well before the early twentieth century there were problems and situations that made new demands on the central government and changed the balance of power between the centre and the states. Over a century-and-a-half, a combination of economic and social factors led to pressure for a change in the political and constitutional relationships within the federal system. For instance, the nation developed from one of mostly towns and isolated farms into one of urban living based around large-scale industry in important areas. In particular, a web of commerce and communication required action beyond the level of states and local communities.

The development of railways and the telegraph also had a significant impact on the federal balance. Before their establishment, businesses were often local or sometimes regional. Once they could operate more widely, advertising delivery over long distances, they rapidly expanded. By the end of the nineteenth century, huge monopolies, known as trusts, controlled products such as banking, communications, railways, steel and sugar, among several others. How were these organisations to be controlled? No level of the federal system was equipped for the task. Localities, even states, found it hard to regulate a railway system which stretched across six or more states, or a railway system that spanned half the states in the United States. State-by-state action would have been complex and inefficient. Grudgingly, the Supreme Court expanded the meaning of commerce to allow the control of railways and telegraphs, as well as the other enterprises they spawned. Gradually, Congress stepped in with regulatory measures.

The influence of the federal government was much strengthened in the twentieth century as the United States became a world power. This led to huge increases in the budget and a massive expansion of personnel, civilian and military. As a major contractor and provider of jobs, the federal government's decisions vitally affected the well-being of the states and the people.

The response to the Great Depression inaugurated a more centralised era of *Co-operative or Concurrent Federalism* in which many Americans increasingly looked to the government to solve their problems. This emphasised the partnership of different levels of government in providing effective public services for the nation. Federal, state and local representatives met together to co-operate on a wider range of substantive programmes. As Cummings and Wise put it, the relationship was characterised 'more by cooperation and shared functions, than by conflict and competition'.

In the post-1945 era some rurally dominated state legislatures neglected the urgent difficulties afflicting the nation's urban areas and, not surprisingly, the city administrations turned to the federal government for a lead. Indeed, the very problems faced in a highly complex industrialised society provided a continuing challenge to the federal system, and Washington stepped in to coordinate governmental problems cutting across state boundaries. The drift of power was away from the states.

Yet, in describing the state of American federalism in *The Report of the President's Committee on National Goals* (1960), Grodzins (1966) did not view the American system as a 'layer cake' of three distinct and separate planes, national, state and local, but rather as a 'marble cake', an inseparable mixture of differently coloured ingredients. As the colours are mixed in a marble cake so were the functions of American federalism: 'There is

no neat horizontal stratification.' In Grodzins's view, the federal government still supplemented, stimulated and assisted states, rather than pre-empting them.

Grodzins wrote before the Kennedy–Johnson years and, arguably, the Great Society programme of LBJ led to a substantial increase in the role of the national government. The changes initiated in these years amounted to *Creative Federalism* in action, clearly a much more active form of co-operative federalism. Indeed, given the conditions of aid, the court orders and other devices intended to ensure state and local compliance with federal policies, many would agree with Kincaid that this was *Coercive Federalism*. States had become ever-more dependent on federal funding which was increasingly provided in the form of categorical grants. The money was granted on condition that state and local governments engaged in a specific activity and did so in compliance with federal requirements concerning such things as programme design, service delivery and reporting.

To Johnson's political opponents, the proliferation of policies and grants had brought about confusion and an excess of bureaucracy. Against such a background, Richard Nixon preached his ideas of a *New Federalism*. This involved a redefinition of the relationship between the different tiers. There was a diminution of categorical grants, money being provided by block grant instead. States were more free to decide how and where to spend their funds. The need was identified locally and the money then spent. There was no major recasting of the distribution of power but this followed in the second era of New Federalism, the Reagan years.

The Reagan version of New Federalism was more radical in its intention and in its impact. It was meant to devolve more power to the states, for the president believed that they knew what needed to be done and could do it in the way most appropriate for their particular area; the dangerously overgrown federal government could increasingly withdraw from its funding and regulatory role. As a conservative, Reagan did not like federal intervention and saw federal programmes as often wasteful and inefficient. Of the war on poverty programme, he was particularly dismissive, remarking: 'I guess you could say poverty won.'

Reagan's intentions were clear from his inaugural address in which he spoke of his intention 'to curb the size and influence of the Federal establishment and to demand recognition of the distinction between the powers granted to the Federal Government and those reserved to the States or the people'. His approach was more reminiscent of Herbert Hoover than of any more recent White House incumbent. His presidency was noted for a further reduction in grants-in-aid, a merging of those directed to specific purposes into block grants, a removal of federal regulations, a recasting of welfare arrangements (with the states left to look after their own programmes) and a broad decentralisation of power and decision-making.

Despite Reagan's efforts, by the last year of his administration, the national government was still spending an estimated $116 billion on grants-in-aid to states and localities, and hundreds of categorical grant programmes remained on the books. But few would deny that he significantly changed the direction of intergovernmental relations. States and localities became less dependent on federal dollars for carrying out their work. For example, in 1978, 26.5 cents of every dollar spent by state and local governments came from the national government. By 1990, the figure was down to 17.9 cents. Peterson was led to remark that the Reagan years represented 'fend-for-yourself federalism'.

George H. Bush's presidency made little impact on the federal–state relationship for he was more of a foreign affairs leader. In general, he did not share Reagan's limited conception of the role of central government and, if anything, there was a very modest swing back to emphasising the role of Washington. The Clinton era was perhaps of greater interest. Democrats, traditionally more keen on an activist centre, wished to ensure that a minimum level of services and certain important policies, in areas such as civil rights, are applicable to all. But Clinton was a New Democrat, less enamoured of government expenditure and unwilling to be labelled as a traditional 'liberal'. His New Covenant programme resumed the effort to redirect financial resources

and programmatic authority to the states in 1993. The process of returning power to the states was intensified when the Republicans captured Congress in November 1994. To many analysts, this 'devolution' of national governmental power marks the most fundamental change in federal relations since the New Deal.

Broadly, in the Clinton years there was no major reversal of the New Federalist approach even though, in certain areas, he was more willing to use the power of the presidency to achieve his goals. He was a more activist president than either of his two predecessors and, to that extent, he was more of a centraliser in intergovernmental relations. He wanted to give a lead in solving problems such as crime and welfare. But as a Southerner, coming from an area where there is a history of resistance to federal demands and a strong commitment to states' rights, it was perhaps inevitable that his solutions often stressed the role of the states, as in welfare policy.

Clinton emphasised the importance he attached to improved co-operation between the federal and state governments, with increased scope for local experiment. For some years, states had acted in a more innovatory manner, and had been a testing ground for experiments which others could follow. The test was a limited one: if it failed, the damage was limited; if it succeeded, it might be worthy of emulation. On the environment and welfare, much pioneering work has been done in recent years.

The impact of the Bush presidency

On entering the White House, George W. Bush labelled himself a 'faithful friend of federalism', as might be expected from a former Republican state governor. In the early days, he leaned on the advice and services of leading state officials and established a study group to see how the role of states might be advanced. Yet there were factors which worked against such a pro-devolution policy: the business community was sometimes unenthusiastic about regulatory state laws; the religious right disliked some features of state autonomy, not least Oregon's suicide law; and sympathetic state governors feared the electoral consequences of trying to impose measures on standards and accountability in schools. More seriously, perhaps, two issues came to the fore on which federal leadership has been needed. Firstly, the 11 September attacks on the twin towers and their aftermath have shifted the focus of attention away from the states and more to Washington. Secondly, after the 'good years' in which the economy had been performing well, recession made it more difficult for states to fund programmes for which they had assumed responsibility.

American government today

The fundamental ideas underlying federalism are that:

1. political power, though necessary, should not be unduly concentrated, rather it should be spread between different levels of government
2. particular responsibilities and powers are best assigned to these different levels. The massive changes in American society over the last hundred years or more, however, have meant that there has been a change in the balance of the relationships.

As we have seen, Bill Clinton favoured a relationship between Washington and the states that was more one of negotiation and compromise, rather than one of coercion. Hence there is much to say for Kincaid's (1990) assessment of the state of federalism today: 'federal dominance and state resurgence'. A number of factors has contributed to this 'resurgence' of the states, among them:

1. Some rulings of the Supreme Court: for instance, those allowing states to regulate the availability of abortion and the conditions under which it takes place
2. The changes made in the Reagan to Clinton period, involving less grants-in-aid and the need for more state self-reliance
3. The decentralisation of decision-making powers in areas such as welfare
4. The greater spirit of innovation in several states, sometimes as a result of the changes outlined above
5. The fact that liberals and conservatives are now ready to support an increased role for the

states, allowing more discretion in the delivery of services.

Clinton was willing to allow federal officials to loosen programme requirements, so that states and localities could be given greater scope for innovation, as part of a general move towards greater devolution. What has happened over the last two decades as a result of the changes described is that there is now a complex system of intergovernmental relations in which the roles of all layers, national, state and local, are liable to change over time, depending on a variety of economic, political and social circumstances. American federalism is a flexible arrangement among the different tiers, adapting as new problems and changing conditions require. There is no finality in the present arrangements.

Popular reactions

In general, Americans are strongly attached to their state and local governments although their attachment can vary from time to time. Polling evidence suggests that confidence in their state representatives has increased over recent years for, in 1997, 81 per cent of those surveyed gave positive replies when asked how they felt about them (up 18 per cent on when the question was asked in the early 1970s). Americans seem to like the public officials who operate closest to them for, whereas confidence in local administration had also increased from 63 per cent to 78 per cent, respect for national government was down from 70 per cent to 60 per cent.

Yet, when difficult, pressing problems arise, Americans turn more to Congress, the Supreme Court and the Washington-based Executive. If new issues of motor car emissions or other environmental concerns develop, the automatic response of many of them is to look to the federal capital rather than to the state capital. Terry Sanford, a former governor of North Carolina, later Senator, noted that 'people seem to conclude that the state vehicle is not so driveable as the federal vehicles'.

Question: In general, who do you think does the best job of spending tax dollars in an efficient and constructive way, Federal Government, State Government or Local Government?

	per cent
Federal Government	12
State Government	32
Local Government	38

Los Angeles Times poll, January 1995

See also *Coercive Federalism; Co-operative Federalism; Creative Federalism; Dual Federalism; Federal Government; New Federalism; States*

Federalist Papers

Shortly after the end of the Constitutional Convention, a huge national debate began about whether or not to ratify the Constitution. Newspapers nationwide published articles and letters both for and against it. The most famous of these letters were the *Federalist Papers* which were written and published during the years 1787 and 1788 in several New York State newspapers (primarily, the *Independent Journal* and the *New York Packet*) to persuade New York voters to approve the document. In total, the papers consist of eighty-five essays outlining how this new government would operate and why this type of government was the best choice for the United States of America.

All of the essays were signed Publius, the actual authors of some being disputed. The general consensus is that Alexander Hamilton wrote fifty-two essays, James Madison twenty-eight, and John Jay the remaining five. In 1788, the essays were published in a bound volume entitled the *Federalist* and eventually became known as the *Federalist Papers*. Today, one of the most highly regarded is paper ten, which discusses the means of preventing faction and warns of the dangers of a democracy. Paper fifty-one provides a clear exposition of federalism. Paper eight-four is also notable for its opposition to a Bill of Rights.

Because two of the authors, Hamilton and Madison, attended the convention, the *Federalist Papers* offer insight into the intentions of those who penned the Constitution and are a primary source for interpretation of it as they outline the philosophy and motivation of the proposed system of government To address fears that it would give the central government too much power and would limit individual freedom, Hamilton, Madison and Jay analysed the proposals in detail and outlined the built-in checks and balances meant to divide power between the three branches of government and to preserve the rights of the people and states. The *Federalist Papers* remain today an excellent reference for anyone who wants to understand the US Constitution. Historian Richard Morris describes them as an 'incomparable exposition of the Constitution, a classic in political science unsurpassed in both breadth and depth by the product of any later American writer'.

Federalist Society

The Federalist Society for Law and Public Policy Studies, usually known simply as the Federalist Society, was formed in 1982 as an organisation that set out to challenge the perceived liberal orthodoxy said to exist at that time in most law schools. The Federalists draw inspiration from James Madison, one of the Founding Fathers, who on occasion railed against the power of central government. Madison had actively supported the cause of a strong central government (as long as there were appropriate checks and balances), but later changed from being a nationally oriented ally of Hamilton in 1787–88 to a states' rights-oriented opponent of an active and strong national government a few years later.

Having a headquarters in Washington, the Society has a membership of over 20,000 practising attorneys and flourishing chapters in many law schools. It serves as a haven for conservatives and libertarians who are interested in preserving the current state of the legal order. According to its mission statement: 'It is founded on the principles that the state exists to preserve freedom, that the separation of governmental powers is central to our Constitution, and that it is emphatically the province and duty of the judiciary to say what the law is, not what it should be.' Today's Federalists are trying to steer the Judiciary away from the judicial activism of the past. As a means of fulfilling this agenda, they seek out ideologically acceptable candidates who might become suitable judges. Most members of George W. Bush's vetting panel for nominees belong to the organisation.

A key figure on the conservative right, Associate Justice Antonin Scalia, is a member of the Federalist Society. Members played an influential role in the impeachment proceedings against President Clinton and in the Florida legal offensive which brought George Bush to power in 2001.

Federalists

The Federalists were those who supported the constitution created at Philadelphia. Sometimes known as Nationalists, because they urged the need for a strong national government, Federalists such as Alexander Hamilton, John Jay and James Madison co-ordinated their efforts and wrote a series of eighty-five letters under the name Publius (now known as the Federalist Papers) which both explained the new Constitution and answered the charges of their opponents, the Anti-federalists. Hamilton et al. had the backing of two national heroes whose support greatly improved the Federalists' prospects of victory, George Washington and Benjamin Franklin.

The Federalists claimed that the creation of a strong federal government would more closely unite the states as one large, continental nation. They tended to come from the wealthier class of merchants and plantation owners. They had been instrumental in the creation of the Constitution, arguing that it was a necessary improvement on the Articles of Confederation, the country's first attempt at unifying the states in a national political arrangement.

Among their ideas, they favoured the protection of private property rights and limits on the extent of popular participation in government. In the debates at Philadephia, among other things they argued for high property qualifications for voting, an indirectly elected Senate and a strong non-elected judiciary, as measures that would 'filter' expression of the popular will.

The Federalists were successful in their effort to get the Constitution ratified by all thirteen states. They later established a party known as the Federalist Party which backed the fiscal views of Hamilton and was a strong force in the early history of the United States, controlling the federal government until 1801.

Fifteenth Amendment

The Fifteenth Amendment said that the right to vote 'shall not be denied . . . on account of race, color, or previous condition of servitude'. To former abolitionists and Radical Republicans in Congress who fashioned Reconstruction after the Civil War, it appeared to signify the fulfilment of all promises made to African Americans. Set free by the Thirteenth Amendment, with citizenship guaranteed by the Fourteenth Amendment, black males were given the vote by the Fifteenth Amendment, the basic purpose of which was to enfranchise former slaves.

The first person to vote under the provisions of the amendment was Thomas Mundy Peterson who cast his ballot in a school-board election in the city of Perth Amboy, in New Jersey, the day after the amendment was ratified. African Americans exercised the franchise and held office in many Southern states through the 1880s but, in the early 1890s, steps were taken to ensure 'white supremacy'. Literacy tests for the vote, 'grandfather clauses' excluding from the franchise all whose ancestors had not voted in the 1860s, and a variety of other devices were used to disenfranchise African Americans and were written into the constitutions of former Confederate states. It was not really until the Voting Rights Act (1965) that the promise of the Fifteenth Amendment was actually delivered in all states. In retrospect, its passage was only the beginning of a struggle for equality that would continue for more than a century before African Americans could begin to participate fully in American public and civic life.

Fifth Amendment

The Fifth Amendment (part of the Bill of Rights) is that part of the US Constitution which guarantees citizens 'due process' of law should they be accused of crime. It protects citizens against abuse of government authority in any legal procedure by – among other things – providing for the right of jury trail, preventing a person from being tried twice for the same crime ('double jeopardy') and ensuring that a person should not be required to incriminate himself or herself. It reads 'No person shall be held to answer for a capital, or otherwise infamous crime, unless on presentment or indictment of a Grand Jury, except in cases arising in the land or naval forces, or in the Militia, when in actual service in time of War or public danger; nor shell any person be subject for the offence to be put twice in jeopardy of life or limb; nor shall be compelled in any criminal case to be a witness against himself, nor be deprived of life, liberty, or property, without due process of law; nor shall private property be taken for public use without just compensation.'

'Taking the fifth' is a shorthand way of claiming one's Fifth Amendment right against self-incrimination.

See also *Double Jeopardy*; *Due Process Clause*

Filibuster

'Filibuster' is the term used for any attempt to stall or block the passage of a bill through the Senate, by one or more speakers debating it at length with a view to preventing a vote on the bill. The word derives from the Spanish word meaning 'pirate', one who plunders freely. Filibusters are part of the normal political process, a means by which a legislative minority can prevent a vote.

As Senate rules contain no motion to force a vote, then a vote can take place only once debate ends. Senate rules permit a senator – or series of senators – to speak for as long as they wish and on any topic they choose, unless a supermajority of 60 per cent brings debate to a close by invoking cloture. Strom Thurmond still holds the record for the longest filibuster; in seeking to delay the 1957 Civil Rights Act, he spoke for 24 hours 18 minutes!

Filibustering in Congress was first employed in the 1850s as a tactic for pirating or hijacking debate At first, it could also refer to the tactics applied by members of the House of Representatives but, as the chamber grew in numbers, revisions to the house rules limited debate. In the smaller Senate, unlimited debate continued on the grounds that any senator should have the right to speak as long as necessary on any issue.

During the 1930s, Louisiana Senator Huey Long used the filibuster in a bid to thwart legislation that effectively used the filibuster against bills that he thought favoured the rich over the poor. On one occasion, he spoke for fifteen hours, using long passages of Shakespeare to embellish his speech. South Carolina's Strom Thurmond achieved the record in 1957, however, when he filibustered to delay and, be hoped, prevent the Civil Rights Act. More recently, Senator John Kerry used the device, in January 2006, in an abortive attempt to block the nomination of Samuel Alito as an Associate Justice.

Filibustering has become more frequent since the 1960s when in no Senate term were there more than seven attempts at obstructing legislation. In the early twenty-first century, the number has been nearer to fifty.

Financial Crisis and Global Recession (2007–09)

The financial crisis of 2007–09 began in July 2007 when there was a loss of confidence by investors in the American housing market, prompted by reckless, sub-prime lending. The sub-prime mortgages were only part of a far more extensive problem, however, the first in which the collapse of the bubble affecting the housing market showed up. The developing crisis in real estate, banking and credit in the United States has had a global reach, affecting a wide range of financial and economic activities and institutions.

In September 2008, the financial crisis deepened as stock markets worldwide crashed and entered a period of high volatility, and a considerable number of banks, mortgage leaders and insurance companies failed in the following weeks. Wall Street bank, Lehman Brothers, filed for Chapter 11 bankruptcy protection; rival Merrill Lynch sought refuge by selling itself to Bank of America; and insurance giant AIG needed emergency funding. In particular, the collapse of Lehman triggered the turmoil in global financial markets.

The financial crisis of 2007–09 has been described by several commentators as the most serious financial crisis since the Great Depression. Its global consequences have included the failure of key businesses, declines in consumer wealth and purchasing power, substantial financial commitments incurred by governments, and a significant downturn in economic activity.

Presidential responses to the crisis

Market-based and regulatory solutions have been implemented or are under consideration in several countries but significant risks remain for the world economy.

Faced with the onset of recession within the United States, George W. Bush signed a $170 billion economic stimulus package (the Paulson Plan) which was intended to improve the economic situation by sending tax-rebate cheques to many Americans and provoking tax breaks for struggling business. Bush's critics have claimed that in the eight years of his presidency, he actively pursued policies of deregulation that caused or encouraged the financial and economic meltdown. He certainly presided over a widespread failure of regulation, the US authorities doing little during his presidency to prevent the sale of millions of mortgages to people who could never afford them or to police the market in mortgage-backed securities which has subsequently collapsed with such devastating consequences. In the blame game for the crisis, Bush has come a close second to the so-called 'greedy and unscrupulous' Wall Street bankers.

There is no doubt that George Bush was a natural supporter of deregulation and that, even though it did not condone them, his administration did nothing to step all sorts of questionable financial activities in the private sector. As president, he bore the ultimate political responsibility, and his party paid the ultimate political price at the polls in November 2008. But deregulation started long before President Bush came to power, and it was a policy enthusiastically pursued by Democratic and by Republican administrations.

Early in his administration, in June 2009, President Barack Obama and his key advisers introduced a series of regulatory proposals designed to address consumer protection, executive pay, bank financial cushions or capital requirements, expanded regulation of the banking system and enhanced authority for the Federal Reserve.

See also *Bail-out; Credit Crunch; Lehman Brothers' Collapse; Paulson Plan (2008); Quantitative Easting*

First Amendment

The First Amendment provides Americans with a range of basic freedoms, including entitlements to freedom of speech, worship and assembly. It also guarantees freedom of the media and prohibits links between Church and State. In the words of the Constitution:

> Congress shall make no law respecting an establishment of religion, or prohibiting the free exercise thereof; or abridging the freedom of speech, or of the press; or the right of the people peaceably to assemble, and to petition the Government for a redress of grievances.

The Founding Fathers were troubled about the possible abuse of governmental power which is why those who called for a Bill of Rights were concerned to see essential civil liberties written into the Constitution. Those in the First Amendment are widely regarded as essential if democracy is to function as it is intended so to do. They enable people to keep informed, to communicate with one another and with the government without fear. Journalists, lobbyists, member of Congress and political parties would find their ability to comment on, and organise to change, existing practice very restricted, should basic freedoms not be protected.

The first ten words of the First Amendment are known as the Establishment Clause which, in Jefferson's words, were designed to create 'a wall of separation between Church and State'. In *Engel* v. *Vitale* (1962), the Supreme Court ruled that the clause prevented prayer and other forms of religious worship in public schools although there are areas of uncertainty such as the status of student-led prayer. The amendment also sought to protect the 'free exercise of religion'. Again, there are areas of controversy, such as whether polygamy is acceptable if it has a religious basis.

Perhaps most well known is the assurance of freedom of speech but this, too, has generated controversy. Speech has been interpreted widely to cover symbolic speech and mediums of expression such as the Internet. There are limits to what is tolerated, however. The Court has permitted restrictions on forms of speech that might incite violence or be considered subversive.

See also *Establishment Clause*; *Free Exercise Clause*; *Symbolic Speech*

Flag Desecration

Flag desecration refers to the intentional defacing of the national flag although other flags can be defaced as well. Usually, it is a gesture intended to make a political point against a government or country and its policies. Desecration of the American flag is legal in the United States but it is illegal to 'deface, defile or contemptuously abuse' the Confederate flag in Florida. Usually, desecration takes the form of flag burning but it includes other forms, such as using the flag for clothing or for making napkins.

Congress first passed a bill to outlaw desecration in 1968, in response to protest burnings of the flag at demonstrations against the war in Vietnam. Within a few years, forty-eight states enacted similar flag-protection laws. These federal and state statutes were overturned by the Supreme Court in the case of *Texas* v. *Johnson* (1989) as unconstitutional restrictions of public expression. Congress quickly passed a new Flag Protection Act which suffered the same fate the following year when the Supreme Court struck down the legislation in the case of *United States* v. *Eichman* (1990). The Court decided that freedom of expression through flag burning was constitutionally protected, as a form of 'symbolic free speech'.

The Court rulings prompted Congress to contemplate using the only avenue available, promotion of a constitutional amendment. The flag-burning amendment is a contentious constitutional proposal that would allow Congress to prohibit expression of political views through the physical desecration of the flag. It generates heated controversy between those who feel that the flag should be protected as a symbol of American patriotism and those who feel that the right to protest by flag desecration is protected under the

First Amendment. In each Congressional term since 1995, the House has considered and passed the flag-desecration amendment which regularly obtains the necessary two-thirds majority. When introduced in the Senate, however, it narrowly fails. The most recent attempt to adopt it in the Senate was lost by one vote in June 2006.

See also *First Amendment*; *Symbolic Speech*; **Texas** v. Johnson *(1989)*

Focus Groups

Focus groups comprise a form of qualitative research in which a group of perhaps ten or fifteen carefully selected individuals are asked about their attitudes towards a product or service. They have been used for two or three decades in politics, as parties and candidates seek to find out the issues of concern to voters and their underlying feelings about them. Questions are asked in an interactive group setting in which participants are free to talk with other group members. The participants are led through an in-depth discussion of their thoughts and reactions to particular policy issues, candidates, or campaign themes and arguments. Focus groups are not really opinion polls but are often used in conjunction with them and provide similar – but more valuable – information. They supplement surveys by uncovering why people think as they do.

Whereas earlier forms of opinion polling had been concerned to research voting behaviour and public attitudes on policy areas, those that began to be employed by political parties in the 1980s were designed to see how they could be used to assist them in their bid for power. Rather than merely finding out what people felt about defence, education or health, the attempt was to understand voters and their concerns more thoroughly. Voters were encouraged to express their feelings so that the strength of their beliefs could be ascertained.

Republicans of the Reagan era were the first to make widespread use of focus groups but the Democrats soon followed. In 1991–92, those backing the Clinton campaign for the presidency wanted to understand their target market better and to adapt their message to the beliefs and values of those whose influence mattered. They asked members of focus groups some projective questions, such as 'If Bill Clinton was a colour, which one would he be?' or – more directly – 'How do you rate Bill Clinton?'

Critics of focus groups believe that focus-group-led campaigning takes politics further away from principles and policies and more towards the most cynical kind of market manipulation. They are suspicious of those who conduct focus groups and who, having sifted through their accumulated findings, come to their own conclusions and report them to those who sponsor the research. They are in a position to convey the message to which they are personally committed.

Ford, Gerald (1913–2006)

When Gerald Ford became the thirty-eighth president, the political circumstances were highly unusual. It was an unprecedented time. The first vice president appointed under the terms of the twenty-fifth Amendment, he succeeded the first president (Richard Nixon) ever forced to resign. He was the first president never to have been elected to the presidency or the vice presidency in his own right.

Born in Nebraska, Ford grew up in Grand Rapids, Michigan where he starred in the University of Michigan football team before going on to Yale, where he served as assistant coach while earning his law degree. After war service in the navy, he returned to Grand Rapids, where he practised law and entered Republican politics. He was elected to Congress in 1948 and served as House Minority Leader (1965–73) before being chosen as Nixon's vice president.

Ford's reputation for integrity and openness had earned him popularity in Congress and was respected during his presidency. He came under intense criticism, however, for his early decision to grant a pre-emptive pardon to his predecessor as part of an attempt to calm earlier controversies and consign the Watergate affair to the past. Otherwise, his administration was scandal-free. He continued to view himself as 'a moderate in domestic affairs, a conservative in fiscal affairs, and a dyed-in-the-wool internationalist in foreign affairs'. In foreign policy, he signed the Helsinki

Accords, marking a move towards détente in the Cold War.

In the 1976 presidential election, Ford lost to the Democratic nominee, Jimmy Carter, who – campaigning as an outsider – gained support from voters dismayed by the Watergate scandal. Carter led consistently in the polls, Ford never being able to shake voter dissatisfaction following Watergate and the Nixon pardon. For that election, presidential debates were reintroduced for the first time since the 1960 election. Ford blundered badly in the second debate when – at a time of Cold War – he stated that 'there is no Soviet domination of Eastern Europe and there never will be under a Ford Administration'. He had to counter a plethora of negative media imagery, not helped by the fact that he had already developed a reputation as president for being accident-prone and ill at ease in interviews.

Shortly before his death, he became the longest-living US president when he reached 93 years and 122 days, passing the record held by Ronald Reagan.

Foreign Policy

According to the State Department's *Foreign Policy Agenda*, the officially stated goal of American foreign policy is 'to create a more secure, democratic, and prosperous world for the benefit of the American people and the international community'. Within that broad goal, priorities are:

1. Promoting democratic values: human rights, political choice, the rule of law, and self-determination
2. Fostering global growth by promoting market principles, involving an active economic agenda, bilaterally with trading partners and multilaterally through the IMF, the World Bank and the World Trade Organisation (formerly GATT)
3. Promoting the global environment that is vital if democratic and market values are to flourish
4. Working with all allies against new transnational threats, such as environmental degradation, narcotics and terrorism
5. Reshaping alliances and the important ties to

the largely favourable conditions that America and its Atlantic and Pacific partners created in the postwar period.

An interesting insight into the values of many Americans about what matters in foreign policy was provided by a poll reported in *Foreign Policy* (1991), entitled 'Public Opinion: The Pulse of the 1990s'. Asked about the most important foreign policy goals, the top responses of members of the public were:

	percentage
Protecting the jobs of American workers	65
Protecting the interests of business abroad	63
Securing adequate supplies of energy	61
Defending our allies' security	61
Preventing the spread of nuclear weapons	59
Promoting and defending human rights	58

Strengthening the United Nations came a poor eleventh, and helping to improve the lot of developing countries followed with 41 per cent. Hopes of spreading the democratic form of government around the world had obviously deteriorated, for only 28 per cent saw this as an important goal.

1945 and after

After 1945, American policy was shaped and dominated by relations with its superpower rival, the USSR. Presidents employed a range of strategies and means of diplomacy in pursuit of their foreign policy goals, such as aid, economic sanctions, political coercion (including the breaking off of diplomatic relations), covert action and military intervention. The competition between the two military giants dominated world politics. This was the age of the Cold War, the period of continuous hostility, short of actual warfare, that existed through to the late 1980s.

For many years there was a large measure of consensus or agreement about American aims abroad. Few raised a voice against the direction of US policy after Truman had laid down the Truman Doctrine of containment which outlined America's place in the world and was to become the foundation of foreign policy to the late 1960s. It was based on the idea of containing Communist aggression and expansion. America was the world's policeman. It had abandoned its pre-war isolationism, stationed troops abroad and adopted an increasingly interventionist role.

Congress willingly accepted presidential leadership, and gave Truman and his successors more or less carte blanche in matters of national security. The nation was united, and congressmen had no desire to create an impression of disunity, so that a bipartisan coalition acquiesced in most presidential initiatives. There were good reasons for this – the nature of the post-war threat, America's involvement in a series of defence treaties under which America was obliged to come to the aid of member nations if they were attacked, and the fact that, after the Korean War, America had ground, naval and air troops stationed around the world, in a position to fulfil commitments or to forestall/respond to conflicts.

For many years, foreign policy was the president's policy, and it received the almost automatic ratification of Congress. Its members accepted that their country was engaged in a worldwide struggle versus Communism, as did the vast majority of their fellow Americans. This being the case, it was only responsible to allow the president to move personnel and equipment around the world as seemed necessary. This left the position wide open for presidents to initiate hostilities and determine their scope and duration, according to their interpretation of the degree of danger involved. Operations, such as the Korean War and the Bay of Pigs fiasco (secretly planned by the Eisenhower administration and executed by Kennedy), were carried out without any significant congressional opposition. Some members of the legislature were slow to appreciate the presidential accretion of power.

This was a use of presidential power very different from that which had originally been intended. Johnson's escalation of the war in Vietnam; Nixon's bombing of Cambodia; and the use of the CIA to topple the elected president of Chile (Allende) and replace him with a military dictatorship – all these seemed to indicate a degree of high-handed presidential leadership which was much disliked by many members of Congress. The years following the conclusion of the Vietnam War and the Watergate Scandal were ones in which presidential supremacy was challenged. In this atmosphere, the War Powers Act was passed in 1973. Since then, Congress has been more vigilant in its response to presidential foreign policy initiatives.

Foreign policy after the end of the Cold War

With the fall of the Berlin Wall in 1989 and the subsequent ending of the Cold War, there were still challenges to America's security and economic well-being. For instance, Communism in eastern Europe may have broken down but former nations, such as Czechoslovakia and Yugoslavia, had broken apart, in the latter case with disastrous results in terms of peace in the region. The Middle East was unsettled with sporadic fighting, terrorism and the rising crisis of Islamic extremism which posed a challenge to the West and threatened American energy supplies. Moreover, although the United States was militarily strong, it faced stiff competition for influence in the world as the power base shifted from military might to economic strength. The United States was the most military power in the world but, in many regions, it was not necessarily the most influential nation.

There has been much debate about US foreign-policy goals. The rise of Europe, and particularly Japan, and the increasing importance of economic and trading interests, have transformed discussion of America's role in world affairs in recent years. There has, too, been an increasing debate about the global environment and the role and value of the United Nations as a peacekeeping force in the world. The UN was expected to play an even greater role in the post-Cold War era but the US also had other commitments, being an active participant in several other international organisations, North Atlantic Treaty Organization (NATO), Southeast Asia Treaty Organization (SEATO), Central Treaty Organization (CENTO), Australia, New Zealand, United States Security Treaty (ANZUS) and the Rio Pact, all of which oblige the United States to come to the aid of member countries under attack.

Critics both in and beyond America pointed to the contradiction between the lofty foreign policy rhetoric of noble causes espoused by the US government and its post-war actions, some of which were seen as Machiavellian and hypocritical. These included:

- The long list of military involvements that stood in contrast to the rhetoric of promoting peace and respect for the sovereignty of nations.
- The many former and current dictatorial governments that had received American financial or military support, especially in Latin America, South-east Asia, and the Middle East, despite claiming to support democracy and democratic principles.
- The lack of support by the United States for international machinery, such as the United Nations, and for environmental treaties, such as the Kyoto Protocol.

The foreign policy of George W. Bush

In the early twenty-first century, Bushite foreign policy marked a departure from existing thinking and practice. The new policy – which came to be known as the Bush Doctrine – was set out in a document known as *The National Security Strategy of the United States* (September 2002). In the wake of the 9/11 attacks and the wider threat of international terrorism, it comprised various foreign-policy principles outlined by President George W. Bush who was much influenced by neoconservative thinking. Bush argued that the 'strategy of deterrence' and 'mutually assured destruction' of states that had prevented the Soviet Union and the United States from annihilating each other had become outdated because of the possibility of stateless terrorists getting hold of weapons of mass destruction.

The president claimed the right to act against countries that harboured or gave aid to terrorists, this being the justification for war in Afghanistan. He reserved the right to wage preventive war (the policy of 'pre-emption') arguing that the United

States should act to depose overseas regimes that represented a threat to US security even if that threat was not imminent (as in the case of Iraq in 2003). He also opened up the possibility of American use of nuclear weapons against non-nuclear states.

The Bush Doctrine has proved contentious, critics noting that the new approach involved the violation of current international obligations and treaties. (For instance, the United States withdrew from the Anti-Ballistic Missile Treaty (1972), widely seen as one of the corner stones of international stability.) Moreover, it opened the way to unilateral action, instead of the more traditional attempt to achieve international agreement and work through changes via the United Nations.

See also *Wildavsky's 'Two Presidencies' Thesis*

Founding Fathers

The Founding Fathers of the United States (aka the Framers) were the political leaders who met at Philadelphia between May and September 1787 and agreed the Constitution. Chaired by the widely respected George Washington, the delegates benefited from the political brilliance and insight of Alexander Hamilton and James Madison, while the eighty-one-year-old Benjamin Franklin added the moderation of age to the proceedings. Overall, the delegates possessed a blend of experience and learning, forty-two of fifty-five having served in the Continental Congress, and more than half having received a college education and studied the classics of political thought. Their average age was only forty and, having matured politically during the revolutionary period, they were less tied to state loyalties than were older men whose outlook was formed before the war. Only six had signed the Declaration of Independence. Those who assembled were nationalists building a nation, not merely defending the interests of their states.

Socially, the Framers were not a representative sample of the population, among them several wealthy bankers, land speculators, lawyers, merchants, planters, and fifteen being slave-holders. They constituted a conservative, propertied group in which small farmers and workers were unrepresented. There were divisions among them during the writing and ratification process, in part reflecting whether the representatives came from large or small states. Those from large states tended to favour a strong national government that they hoped to dominate, whereas those from the smaller states were fearful of a strong centre. The division is often expressed in the distinction between the federalists and the anti-federalists. All delegates supported a republican form of government and all were constitutionalists who opposed arbitrary, unrestrained rule.

The making of foreign policy: who does what? Presidential and congressional roles

In his role as Chief Diplomat, the president negotiates treaties with foreign nations but his or her actions are subject to the 'advice and consent' role of the Senate. Treaties can enter into force only if ratified by two-thirds of the Senate. The president is also Commander-in-Chief of the United States Armed Forces and, as such, has broad authority over the armed forces once they are deployed. Congress has the sole authority to declare war, however, and the civilian and military budget is written by the Congress. In theory, it also has some control over troop deployment, under the War Powers Act. The Secretary of State is the foreign minister of the United States and is the person primarily responsible for state-to-state diplomacy. The Defense Department has assumed increased importance in what some see as an assertive bid to eclipse the State Department as the major location for handling foreign policy.

The Constitution equips the president with a key role in foreign policy, deriving from his constitutional position as Commander-in-Chief and Chief Diplomat. Incumbents of the White House are called upon to make crucial decisions concerning peace and war. In particular, crisis management has been a major challenge to a number of presidents, most recently to George W. Bush following the terrorist attacks on the World Trade Center.

On 27 September 1787, the Founding Fathers assembled for the ceremony of signing the document that they were commending to the nation. All but three of those present signed. By then, those who had doubts about the general tenor of the proposals being made had already departed.

Fourteenth Amendment (1868)

Section 1 *All persons born or naturalized in the United States, and subject to the jurisdiction thereof, are citizens of the United States and of the State wherein they reside. No State shall make or enforce any law which shall abridge the privileges or immunities of citizens of the United States; nor shall any State deprive any person of life, liberty, or property, without due process of law; nor deny to any person within its jurisdiction the equal protection of the laws.*

The Fourteenth Amendment was designed to protect the civil liberties of recently freed slaves and make them full citizens. Section 1 says that no state shall deprive any person of 'life, liberty, or property, without due process of law'. This clause has been used by the Supreme Court to protect the rights of citizens against the powers of the state in a broad range of cases. The section also includes the provision that states may not deny any person the 'equal protection of the laws'. This phrase has been used as the basis of challenges to unfair and discriminatory practices, and the Supreme Court found segregation by race to be unconstitutional in *Brown* v. *Board of Education* (1954). It also required states to reapportion their electoral boundaries in *Baker* v. *Carr* (1962) and both of these decisions rested on the Fourteenth Amendment's 'equal protection' provision. (Section 3 banned former state or federal government officials, who had acted in support of the Confederacy during the Civil War, from holding public office again. It limited the president's ability to pardon those persons. Congress removed this 'disability' in 1898.)

In effect, the amendment means that the laws of a state must treat an individual in the same manner as others in similar conditions and circumstances. A violation would occur, for example, if a state prohibited an individual from entering into an employment contract because he or she was a member of a particular race. The equal protection clause is not intended to provide 'equality' among individuals or classes but only 'equal application' of the laws. The result, therefore, of a law is not relevant so long as there is no discrimination in its application. By denying states the ability to discriminate, the equal protection clause of the Constitution is crucial to the protection of civil rights.

The Thirteenth (banning slavery), Fourteenth and Fifteenth Amendments (banning race-based voting qualifications) are collectively known as the 'Reconstruction Amendments'. According to Associate Justice Noah Swayne (1862–81): 'Fairly construed, these amendments may be said to rise to the dignity of a new Magna Carta.' With its broadly phrased language, the Fourteenth Amendment continues to provide a basis for civil rights claims in the United States. Most Southern states refused to ratify the Fourteenth Amendment and therefore Radical Republicans urged the passing of further legislation to impose these measures on the former Confederacy. The result was the 1867 Reconstruction Acts that divided the South into five military districts controlled by martial law, proclaimed universal manhood suffrage and required new state constitutions to be drawn up.

Free Exercise Clause

The Free Exercise Clause is the accompanying clause with the Establishment Clause of the First Amendment. It says that 'Congress shall make no law respecting an establishment of religion, or prohibiting the free exercise thereof.' The intention is to protect a wide range of religious observance and practice from any governmental interference. The Supreme Court has consistently refused to examine the content of any religious beliefs. There is a difference, however, between religious belief and religious action. An individual can believe in human sacrifice as part of his or her religion but that does not mean that the state does not have a right to make such sacrifice criminal behaviour.

The Supreme Court was first called to interpret the extent of the free exercise clause in *Reynolds* v. *United States* (1867) which concerned the prosecution of polygamy under federal law. In their ruling, the justices took the view that it was a crime to have more than one husband or wife at the same time, on the basis that to decide otherwise would provide constitutional protection for a range of religious beliefs, including those as extreme as human sacrifice. They laid down that: 'Laws are made for the government of actions, and while they cannot interfere with mere religious beliefs and opinions, they may with practices.' The Court has also required children to be vaccinated in spite of parental objections on religious grounds. In other words, the guarantee of free exercise is not absolute.

Occasional exemptions from the law for religious reasoning have been permitted. It is up to a state to show why there is a compelling need for its regulations. Justices may take the view that laws applicable to the general population may be unduly burdensome to a particular group and violate their rights under the Free Exercise Clause. In 1972, Chief Justice Burger decided in the case of *Wisconsin* v. *Yoder* that Wisconsin's requirement for compulsory school attendance in order to create an educated populace constituted insufficient grounds for interfering with the free exercise of Amish religious beliefs.

Freedom of Information

Freedom of information refers to the right of free access to information contained in government records. Knowledge is widely seen as a prerequisite to effective control of the Executive. The ability of people and their elected representatives to extract full and accurate information about the basis on which decision-makers make their decisions enables them to offer informed and effective scrutiny. In the words of Thomas Jefferson: 'Information is the currency of democracy.'

Over seventy countries around the world have implemented some form of freedom of information legislation. These laws, sometimes known as as open records laws, establish rules on access to information or records held by government bodies. America has had freedom of information legislation since 1966, as well as a series of laws and rules (the 'sunshine' acts) that opened

up the vast majority of congressional meetings to public view. The Freedom of Information Act was signed into law by President Johnson and became effective in 1967. It guarantees full or partial disclosure of previously unreleased information, thereby giving the public access to information about bureaucratic activities and policies. Applicable only to federal agencies, the legislation sets out which agency records are subject to disclosure, outlines mandatory disclosure procedures and grants nine exemptions to the statute. All of the states, however, have enacted similar statutes to require disclosures by agencies of the state and of local governments, though they vary significantly in their breadth and extent. Several states also have open meetings legislation which requires government meetings to be held publicly.

Whatever the doubts about the costs of its implementation or its effects on carrying out confidential investigations, most Americans and consumer groups welcome the fact that the freedom of information legislation is strong and effective, giving Americans a 'right to know'. It was extended in October 1996 by the passage of the Electronic Freedom of Information Act Amendments. A limitation was introduced by the declaration of an Executive Order by President Bush in November 2001, shortly after the 9/11 attack. It denies access to the records of former presidents.

Front-loading of Presidential Primaries

Front-loading refers to the practice of scheduling state party caucuses and state primary elections earlier and earlier in advance of the November presidential election in the hope that this will maximise their influence on the Democratic and Republican nomination processes, by adding decisive momentum to the campaigns of one or other of the presidential candidates. A strong performance in the early contests can provide useful momentum to a campaign and help to demoralise rivals who do less well. Underdogs realise this and understand that they have to take maximum advantage of the brief window of opportunity available to them if they are to overtake the front-runner. This means that they – and all candidates – need to have much of their campaign money available as early as possible in order to make an impact.

Campaigning for president often begins a year or more before the Iowa caucus and the New Hampshire primary, almost two years before the presidential election. The results of these early contests receive heavy media attention, so that the winner is considered the front-runner candidate for that party. John Kerry won both the Iowa caucus and New Hampshire primary over heavily favoured Howard Dean to win the 2004 Democratic nomination. (George W. Bush made a poor start in primary elections, however, but ultimately won the Republican Party's nomination in 2000.)

Up to, and including, 2004, several more states staged primaries and caucuses in February. Then, on Super Tuesday (the first Tuesday in March), some of the largest and most important states like California (not in 2004) and New York held their contests. (With more states attempting to front-load their primaries, a Tuesday in early February was designated mini-'Super Tuesday', as several states had their primaries on that day.) As a result, the party's nominee was virtually decided after Super Tuesday, with some 70 per cent of the delegates to the convention having been selected by the end of March.

For the 2008 primary season, several more states wanted to bring their caucuses or primaries forward into February. As a result, Super Tuesday was held on 5 February, when at least one of the main parties in twenty-four states held electoral battles. In a bid to gain a larger role in the nominating process, the state Democratic parties in Florida and Michigan brought their primaries forward ahead of 5 February without permission. Both were penalised by the Democratic National Committee which awarded its delegates only half a vote each at the national convention.

Arguments surrounding front-loading

The most commonly mentioned critiques against the presidential primary front-loading process are:

- that the front-loading process reinforces candidate-centred campaigns throughout the whole election process
- that it places high demands upon the candidates, such as:
  1. a compressed, punishing campaign schedule for the candidates
  2. the need to spend large amounts of money for primary election campaigns well before the general election campaign starts. This means that candidates who can raise great amounts of money very early in the process have an advantage
  3. the need to gain credibility and support very early to obtain a positive media image.

Supporters claim that:

- the compressed primary season prepares candidates for the intense battle they will face with their opponent(s) in the general election campaign
- early competition encourage candidates to reach out and mobilise new supporters during the primary process.

Frost Belt

The Frost Belt is the region of the United States that is known for its cold, frost-producing winters and heavy snowfall. It covers the Northeast, the Great Lakes Region and much of the Upper Midwest. Census findings indicate that there has been a shift in population from the Frost Belt to the Sun Belt.

Furman v. *Georgia* (1972)

Furman v. *Georgia* was a Supreme Court decision that ruled on the requirement for a degree of consistency in the application of the death penalty. By five to four, the justices ruled that capital punishment was unconstitutional in the particular case but could not agree on the reason, each justice writing a separate opinion. Two of the justices in the majority were opposed to capital punishment in all circumstances, believing it fell foul of the Eighth Amendment's rejection of 'cruel and unusual punishments'. The other three were concerned at the arbitrary way in which the death penalty was often being implemented, its victims being primarily those who were African American, poor and/or badly defended in court. As one justice put it, its imposition was 'wanton and freakish'.

After 1972, states began to draft more precise laws on the use of the death penalty, ensuring that their statutes conformed to the Court's guidelines. This enabled the Court to reverse its earlier decision in the *Gregg* v. *Georgia* (1976) case. Although Georgia's death penalty had been declared unconstitutional four years earlier, the death penalty itself was not regarded as being intrinsically so.

G

Gay Rights

The gay rights movement is committed to campaigning for the decriminalisation of homosexuality, and protection and extension of the civil rights of homosexuals. Gay campaigners argue for recognition of their rights under the First Amendment (the right of free speech, and thus of gays to discuss their sexual orientation) and under the Fifth ('equal protection' for all groups). Their views meet with strong resistance from some sections of American society, however, for the degree of tolerance to be accorded to gays and lesbians is a highly contentious issue in the United States, as in many other democracies.

While organised activity on behalf of homosexual rights has its origins in the mid-nineteenth century, the modern gay rights movement began with the Stonewall riot (June 1969) in New York City which was the outcome of a police raid on an illegal gay bar. Gay campaigners began to organise to air their views, several groups allying to work: for the repeal of laws prohibiting consensual homosexual conduct; for legislation barring discrimination against gays in housing and employment; and for greater acceptance of homosexuals among the rest of the population. They presented their case in positive terms, emphasising the discrimination from which they suffered and their entitlement to the full range of civil rights. Their increasing boldness in espousing the cause created a backlash from the Religious Right which was particularly alarmed by the spread of AIDS in the 1980s. Right-wing Christians portrayed AIDS as God's retribution for immoral behaviour.

Gay activists succeeded in obtaining federal funding for AIDS research and treatment although most relevant legislation included clauses designed to prevent such money from being used to advance homosexuality. American gays secured other gains in the 1990s although they could not overturn the ban on gays serving openly in the military. Under Title 10 of the United States Code (1956), which outlines the role of the armed forces, military policy prohibited anyone who 'demonstrate(d) a propensity or intent to engage in homosexual acts' from serving, because it 'would create an unacceptable risk to the high standards of morale, good order and discipline, and unit cohesion that are the essence of military capability'.

'Don't Ask, Don't Tell'

In his election campaign in 1992, Bill Clinton was reassuring to the gay community. He encouraged its members to believe that he would act to remove barriers that prevented them from enjoying their full civil liberties in the military, as in other aspects of public life. Yet, on becoming president, he proved a disappointment to those seeking decisive action to tackle the ban. He lacked determination on the key issue about which gays were troubled. Under pressure from the Pentagon and top military brass, he came up with the 'Don't Ask, Don't Tell' formula.

Under the Clinton compromise, officers could not ask about a soldier's sexual proclivities, but neither could a bisexual or gay person in uniform 'come out' or engage in sexual activities while on duty or special assignments. The effect of the compromise, which has continued to the present day, is that the military does not take an official stance against gay or bisexual desire but it is a punishable offence to disclose such orientation or openly to engage openly in homosexual or lesbian practices.

Constitutional challenges to the behaviour of the military have met with some success. In that same year, a Los Angeles judge barred the services from taking 'any action against gay or lesbian service members' based on homosexual conduct that could not be 'proven to interfere with the military mission of the armed forces'. Yet outright victory on the issue is likely to be hard to achieve for the courts usually attach considerable importance to those involved in making military policy, and defer to their 'expertise'. This means that members of the services have tended to have fewer guarantees of their constitutional rights than have civilians.

Of the presidential candidates in 2008, Barack Obama backed repeal of the 'Don't Ask, Don't Tell' formula, such as to enable gay and lesbian people to serve openly in the armed forces. John McCain made it very clear that he opposed allowing professed lesbians and gays to serve in the military, and declared that if elected he would stand by the 'Don't Ask, Don't Tell policy.

Gains in the Clinton years and beyond

Bill Clinton was willing to appoint known homosexuals to his administration, and gay activists achieved some other gains. He established the first official liaison office for the gay community and, in 1998, signed an executive order prohibiting civilian federal departments and agencies from discriminating on the basis of sexual orientation. Other achievements in recent years have been the repeal of many state laws banning homosexual sex, and court orders and legislation in a small number of states to provide partner benefits for public employees in some areas such as health insurance. But there were reverses, such as the passage of a Defense of Marriage Act (DOMA) in 1996 that banned people in same-sex marriages from eligibility for those federal benefits available to married couples.

The issue of such same-sex liaisons became a controversial one, however, as the new millennium approached. Religious conservatives were determined to achieve a ban on gay marriages. They campaigned to do so at national, state and even local levels. In the late twentieth century, the Supreme Court supported the principle of marital privacy. Whereas in 1986, it decided that a Georgian law that criminalised consensual sodomy as practised by homosexuals was acceptable within the Constitution, in 2003 it overturned all state anti-sodomy laws. It also repudiated the earlier decision in which it had refused to extend the right of privacy to consensual sexual acts, arguing that the state had no right to intrude into the home except in extreme circumstances.

Civil unions and same-sex marriages

In 2000, Vermont became the first state to adopt a civil unions law, providing legal recognition of same-sex partnerships and a number of the legal entitlements and obligations of marriage. The Defense of Marriage Act, however, denies same-sex couples 1,138 rights available to married couples under federal law.

In 2004, Massachusetts went a sizeable step beyond Vermont by becoming the first state to recognise gay marriages, the first taking place in May of that year. The governor himself was against the initiative and invoked an old law to stop same-sex couples from outside the state from coming in to get married although many city clerks said that they intended to ignore his move. It soon became apparent that there was a real doubt as to whether these same-sex marriages would be recognised elsewhere in the country, particularly in the thirty-eight states that had banned them by specifically stating that marriage can only involve a man and a woman.

The events of early 2004 unleashed powerful forces on either side of the debate. Gay marriage became a touchstone social issue in the presidential election. Both candidates were opposed but, whereas John Kerry argued that decisions on such matters should be taken at state level, George W. Bush stated his support for an amendment to change the Constitution to define marriage as a heterosexual institution. Both men supported civil unions, conferring some marriage benefits.

President Bush saw a constitutional amendment

as necessary because 'after more than two centuries of American jurisprudence and millennia of human experience, a few judges and local authorities are presuming to change this most fundamental institution of civilisation'. He was not reassured by the Clinton Defense of Marriage Act or by the state bans. Cynics said his advisers were pushing him to take up the case for an amendment as a political manoeuvre. He knew that the chances of securing an amendment requiring a two-thirds vote by the House and the Senate, as well as ratification by three-quarters of the states, were very small. But, by pushing the issue, he was able to divert attention from more pressing problems and create a useful 'wedge issue' that would serve to unite the Republicans and divide the Democrats. Some commentators pointed out that a president who believed so strongly in states' rights in other contexts should have been prepared to let the states do their jobs and work out their own marriage laws before resorting to a constitutional amendment.

In 2008, Barack Obama and John McCain shared the view that marriage is a union between a man and a woman. Neither backed a constitutional amendment on the matter, arguing instead for the states' right to determine their own positions.

Gender/Gender Gap

In common usage, gender refers to the differences between men and women. Whereas sex refers to the biological and anatomical characteristics that divide them, gender is more concerned with the ways in which differences between men and women, real or perceived, have been valued, used and relied upon to classify them and to assign roles and expectations to them.

The definition of gender has been the subject of exhaustive debate, including at a special United Nations session in connection with the Fourth World Conference on Women in Beijing. It concluded that:

> gender refers to a set of qualities and behaviours expected from a female or male by society. Gender roles are learned and can be affected by factors such as education or economics. They vary widely within and among cultures. While an individual's sex does not change, gender roles are socially determined and can evolve over time.

Gender roles and expectations are often identified as factors hindering the equal rights and status of women with adverse consequences that affect life, family, socio-economic status, and health.

According to the 2000 census, 281.4 million people (50.9 per cent) were counted in the United States, 143.4 million of whom were female and 138.1 million male. Between 1990 and 2000, the male population grew slightly faster (13.9 per cent) than the female population (12.5 per cent). The excess of the female to male population fell to 5.3 million in 2000, compared with 6.2 million in 1990.

Among the regions of the United States, the Northeast had the lowest male–female ratio in 2000, at 93.5. The Midwest and South had male–female ratios in 2000 of 96.1 and 95.9, respectively. The West had the highest male–female ratio, at 99.6, approaching parity between the sexes. The regional male–female ratios in 2000 follow the same pattern as in 1990. Males outnumber females in the early age groups but, starting from age forty upwards, women outnumber men. At eighty-five and over, there are more than twice as many women as men.

At the state level in 2000, women were more numerous than men in all but seven states. Alaska led the states with the highest male–female ratio (107.0), followed by Nevada (103.9), Colorado (101.4), Wyoming (101.2), Hawaii (101.0), Idaho (101.0), and Utah (100.4), all of Western states. In contrast, the lowest male–female ratios were recorded in Rhode Island (92.5), Massachusetts (93.0), and the District of Columbia (89.0).

Women and men have equal rights to vote and hold office, 'equal protection of the laws' extending to all Americans. Gender remains a fault line in US politics, however. There is a significant gender gap in public opinion and voting. In the 1950s and 1960s, women leaned towards the Republicans. In more recent decades, however, political observers have noted the fact that, across all racial and socio-economic groupings, women incline to the Democrats whereas white men are more likely to support the Republican Party.

Polling evidence shows that women are more likely to oppose violence (including the death penalty and possession of handguns), are more compassionate on social issues (e.g., health provision and poverty) and are more concerned about the environment and international peace. Men are more concerned with issue such as the budget deficit, the cost of living and the trade deficit.

Gender issues concerning work and family life have become increasingly important in recent years, especially those topics such as day care, prenatal and post-natal leave policy, and equality of treatment in the workplace.

General Revenue Sharing (GRS)

General revenue sharing was an innovative grants-in-aid programme initiated in 1972. It was designed to provide formula-based funding (dependent on population and related factors) to state and local governments in order to allow them to pursue a wide range of activities. Over a five-year period from its inception in 1972, it made $30.2 billion available to the states and to localities. It was amended in the later years of the decade and, by the late 1980s, it was no longer employed. Unlike categorical – or even block – grants, there were few significant conditions attached. As such, GRS was one means of fulfilling the Nixonian promise of greater devolution as part of the programme of New Federalism.

See also *New Federalism*

Gerrymandering

Gerrymandering refers to the practice by the party in power in a state legislature of devising congressional district boundaries in a way that gains political advantage, maximising its own voting strength and minimising that of the opposing party. It can be done by drawing together in one constituency scattered groups of supporters who are in a minority in each of several existing constituencies or, alternatively, by lumping its opponents' voters together in one constituency, drawing them away from marginal areas where they endanger the control of the governing party.

The effect of either technique is to produce artificial constituencies that may be of extraordinary size and shape. The technique is thought to have been consciously first employed in Massachusetts in 1812 during the administration of Governor Eldridge Gerry. One of the constituencies in the state had the shape of a lizard. One 'wit' is said to have remarked: 'Why, this district looks like a salamander!' An opposition editor responded: 'Say, rather a gerrymander!' Two notable examples of distortion occurred in 1959. The twelfth congressional district in New York State is said to have resembled an elongated sea horse, while the twenty-sixth in California looked like the head and horns of a moose. In both cases, the boundaries had been devised in the interests of the majority party.

Gerrymandering was, for many decades, practised in some Southern states to prevent black Americans from voting, by drawing electoral districts to ensure that they were in a minority in all districts. The Voting Rights Act (1965) made gerrymandering to harm minorities illegal. More recently, manipulation of district boundaries based solely on race has been ruled unconstitutional under the Fourteenth Amendment by the Supreme Court in *Shaw* v. *Reno* (1993) and subsequently by *Miller* v. *Johnson* (1995). The constitutionality of racial considerations in creating districts remains ambiguous, however; in *Hunt* v. *Cromartie* (1999), the Supreme Court approved a racially focused congressional gerrymandering on the grounds that the drawing was not pure racial gerrymandering but instead partisan gerrymandering.

Partisan gerrymandering remains constitutionally permissible and is still carried on in some American states. The Supreme Court has said that grossly partisan gerrymandering can, in certain circumstances, be unconstitutional (e.g., *Davis* v. *Bandemer*, 1986). In June 2006, however, the Court upheld most of a Texas congressional map devised three years earlier by former House Majority Leader, Tom DeLay. The judgment has given greater scope to those who wish to devise their districts in ways that protect their political parties and seats, as long as, in the process, they do not harm racial and ethnic minority groups.

In some states, action has been contemplated or actually taken (e.g., Arizona and Washington) to hand over responsibility for redistricting to some form of neutral commission in order to prevent the repeated abuses.

See also *Congressional District*; *Reapportionment*

Gideon v. Wainwright (1963)

The *Gideon* v. *Wainwright* judgment established that criminal defendants in state courts were entitled to the assistance of legal counsel during their trial, unless they had specifically waived their right.

The case came about after Earl Gideon, charged with breaking into a poolroom in Panama City, Florida, had requested and been denied legal backing, and was convicted of the crime. His appeal was based on violation of the 'due process' clause of the Fourteenth Amendment, it being unfair that an inexperienced and untrained citizen should be confronted with the complexity of the legal system without any support. The Supreme Court justices – citing the Sixth Amendment that guarantees an accused person the right to representation by a lawyer – ruled that the states should pay for legal representation for defendants on low incomes who were charged with a felony. The requirement had been long ignored in many situations concerning trials involving poor Americans.

Subsequent cases in 1964 established the same right to legal counsel at earlier stages in the judicial process of investigation and arrest, so that aid should be available from the moment a person was seen as the key suspect in a criminal case. In 1972, in the case of *Argersinger* v. *Hamlin*, the Court broadened its earlier rulings to include penniless defendants on trial for any offence in which imprisonment was a possible penalty.

Gingrich, Newt (1943–)

A college history professor and prolific author, Gingrich was first elected as a representative for Georgia in November 1978 and subsequently re-elected ten times. He became House Minority Whip in 1989 and was later the main architect of the 1994 *Contract with America* programme. He was widely seen as the leading conservative figure in the so-called Republican Revolution in the House that followed the November 1994 midterm elections which ended forty years of Democratic Party control.

Newt Gingrich achieved eminence as the Speaker of the House of Representatives from 1995 to 1999. During his tenure, he became the public face of Republican opposition to President Clinton which culminated in the impeachment trial that took place after his own resignation following a setback for his party in the 1998 elections.

In recent years, Gingrich has been a political analyst and writer. He did not make a challenge for the presidency in 2008 but has indicated that he may do so in 2012.

Gitlow v. New York (1925)

Gitlow v. *New York* was a Supreme Court ruling that marked a major development in the law on free speech. Gitlow, a member of the Socialist Party, who had advocated the overthrow of capitalism and democracy, was convicted under New York law. His legal team claimed that the law was unconstitutional because the First Amendment entitlement to free speech had been 'incorporated' into the 'due process' clause of the Fourteenth Amendment. The justices accepted this 'incorporation' defence which contended that freedom of speech and the press are 'among the fundamental personal rights and liberties protected . . . from impairment by the states'.

The Court thereby accepted the argument that the First Amendment limited state as well as federal action. It applied, however, a relaxed version of the 'clear and present danger' test previously proclaimed by the justices. Instead, it allowed speech to be punished as long as it created a 'bad tendency' that might encourage people to engage in illegal action, produce political or social turmoil and thereby endanger society, even at some point in the remote future.

Giuliani, Rudolph (1944–)

Rudolph Giuliani is an American lawyer, businessman, and politician from the New York state. A Democrat and Independent in the 1970s, he became a broadly liberal Republican in the 1980s and remains so today.

Giuliani served two terms as mayor of New York City (1994–2001). He gained international recognition during and after the 9/11 attack on the World Trade Center, and he was much praised for his leadership during the crisis. His mayoralty is widely seen as innovative and significant, New York City becoming perhaps the best-known example of the resurgence of urban America. Admirers point out that, at the end of his mayoralty, the city's citizens were left feeling more confident and secure. This was in part because of his adoption of a policy of zero tolerance of criminalitiy, involving crackdowns on minor offences, such as graffiti and turnstile jumping, on the theory that this would send out a message that order would be maintained. Giuliani was criticised by some Republican opponents for his liberal approach to illegal immigration and to gay rights. In 1998, he codified local law by granting all city employees equal benefits for their domestic partners.

After leading in national polls for much of 2007, Giuliani's candidacy for the Republican presidential nomination faltered late in that year. After a poor showing in the caucuses and primaries in early 2008, he withdrew from the race.

Globalisation and Anti-globalisation Protest

Globalisation refers to the increased interconnectedness between nations brought about by the flow of people, ideas, technology and culture in general. It is multifaceted, taking distinct economic, political and cultural forms. As a result of this interconnectedness, countries now influence one another to an extent without historical precedent. National boundaries are losing much of their former importance. Hence Waters's (2000) description of globalisation as 'a process in which the constraints of geography on social and cultural arrangements recede and in which people become increasingly aware that they are receding'.

The media – especially television – have a massive impact on cultural values. On the one hand, there is the worldwide availability of media products to transmit and receive information. On the other, the media play a role in promoting produce familiarity. People can watch the same television programmes or videos on You Tube, buy and sell on ebay, or visit McDonald's. Consumerism and its culture have a powerful grip across the world. Coca-Cola, Gap, Lara Croft and Microsoft have global recognition and universal consumer appeal, created by advertising in transnational media.

Anti-globalisation

The aggressive promotion of Western culture has created widespread resentment across the world. A widespread anti-globalisation movement emerged in the 1990s. It is difficult to characterise but among its key features are:

1. It is diffuse, having self-appointed spokespersons but little formal organisation; it covers a range of groups with a wide range of ideas, from environmentalists to debt-relief campaigners and human rights activists.
2. It is especially directed at economic globalisation, protesters seeing American-style capitalism as the root cause of world poverty, the debt crisis and environmental degradation. It largely equates with anti-capitalism which is why demonstrators have targeted high-level conferences, as in the Battle of Seattle (1999), the site of a World Trade Organization gathering, or Quebec (2001) where a Summit of the Americas was being held.
3. There is a strong thread of anti-Americanism in the protest. The United States is seen as the architect of the international economic order, the world's worst polluter and home to the most powerful multinational corporations (MNCs). Otherwise disparate groups can unite against the US, the more so when the administration in office seems to have close links with MNCs.

Antagonism to globalisation has led to major international protests, some of which have ended violently. However, although many anti-globalisation activists support the use of direct action in furtherance of their goals, this does not mean that they all condone violence and damage to property.

See also *Direct Action*; *Foreign Policy*; *Green Movement*, *Interest Groups*

Gore, Al (1948–)

Albert ('Al') Gore Jnr was a representative for his home state of Tennessee between 1977 and 1985 prior to becoming one of its two senators for the next eight years. He made an unsuccessful bid to be the Democratic Party presidential candidate for the November 1988 election but, four years later, was chosen by Bill Clinton as his running mate. Following the election, he became the forty-fifth vice president, serving from 1993 to 2001. He was the presidential candidate for the Democratic Party in the 2000 election in which he won a plurality of the popular vote but lost in the Electoral College. The legal controversy over the outcome in Florida and the election recount – ultimately resolved in favour of George W. Bush – was one of the most controversial in American history.

Gore has long been interested in the environment and, since the Democrat setback in 2001, has spent much of his time as an activist for the environmental cause, lecturing on the dangers presented by global warming. The release of *An Inconvenient Truth* helped to polish his environmentalist credentials. He shared the 2007 Nobel Peace Prize for his effort 'to build up and disseminate greater knowledge about man-made climate change, and to lay the foundations for the measures that are needed to counteract such change'.

Gore decided not to run as a candidate in 2008, although some Democrats felt that the man 'cheated' out of the presidency in 2000 deserved the chance to uphold the party banner. Neither did he become a member of the Obama administration formed as a result of the November election of that year.

See also **Bush v. Gore** *(2000)*

Governors

Each American state has its own elected governor who serves as its chief executive, the political and ceremonial head of the state. The role and importance of individual governors, however, vary according to the individual state and the personality of the incumbent. In most cases, they have a range of important powers. In some cases, the governor is the commander-in-chief of the National Guard (when not federalised) and possesses the ability to commute or pardon a criminal sentence. In other states, such as Texas, the position is, on paper at least, weaker than elsewhere although a strong incumbent may make his or her mark. As a broad generalisation, the position of governor has assumed greater significance in recent years, the trend being for him or her to serve for a longer period than in the past and, in some cases, for successive terms.

In 1900, fewer that half of the forty-five states granted their chief executive a four-year term, three states allowing only one year. Today, all but two governors serve for four years, New Hampshire and Vermont allowing a two-year period. In most cases, term limits prevent a governor from holding office for more than two consecutive terms although the two states mentioned above, and nine others, impose no limit. In some states, a person cannot serve for more than a certain number of years within a fixed period, Washington state allowing a maximum of eight years in a twelve-year period.

The process of internal reform in many states has also boosted the position of governor. The governor's budgetary control has been increased and streamlining of the administration has tended to enhance his or her personal role and status. In all but two states, governors have the power to veto bills passed by the legislature; in all but seven they can exercise a line-item veto enabling them to block specific sections of a bill. The overall power and influence of governors also depend on the extent to which they share executive power with other elected officials, some states, such as Michigan, having many state-wide elected officials and agencies, others very few. Where there are no other elected officials and agencies (in Maine, New Hampshire and New Jersey) this strengthens the gubernatorial hand; where there are several – particularly if they are under the control of the opposing party – there is less opportunity to co-ordinate and control the executive branch. (Senior executive officials who may be elected rather than appointed are the lieutenant governor, secretary of state, attorney general, comptroller, and members of various boards and commissions. Positions not filled by election are usually filled by appointment by the governor.)

It is tempting to view the office of governor as the state equivalent of the presidency in the federal government. In both cases, the role has expanded considerably from that initially laid down in the relevant constitution. There are differences, between their legal and constitutional authorities, however, the reality of the governors' strength varying from state to state. Much depends on the relationship with the deputy, the lieutenant general. In nineteen states, the two offices are elected separately so that the incumbents may belong to different parties, be political rivals and/or disagree on significant policy questions. In the case of the president, he and his vice president are elected together on the same ticket.

The stock of governors is rising and likely to do so more as reform efforts continue the process of modernising state administrative arrangements so that they are better equipped to assume powers formerly exercised by the federal government. In a media-dominated age, the spotlight of attention falls upon them and there are numerous opportunities for incumbents to command journalistic interest. In several cases, the state governor may give an annual State of the State Address which may be widely covered on television and in the press.

It is significant that, of the presidents from Carter to George W. Bush, all but George H. Bush have had gubernatorial experience. Service as a state governor has become the common background for those who aspire to the presidency or vice presidency whereas, a few decades ago, most presidential candidates tended to have a senatorial background.

See also *State Government*; *States*

Grants-in-aid

Grants-in-aid are transfers of money from federal government to states and localities in order to finance state policies and programmes.

Since the Great Depression (1929 and subsequent years), the main financial assistance has been in the form of grants-in-aid. Some existed before 1900 but most have developed since the 1930s, leading to federal supervision in areas not normally within its orbit. In other words, it is money 'with strings attached'. The federal government began to lay down minimum standards and to inspect the results of its funding, and matching funds had to be provided by the states to qualify for federal aid. The more a state was prepared to develop programmes, the more it was likely to receive national funds or contracts.

The amount of federal money that went to states and localities increased dramatically in the 1960s, as did the number of programmes and regulations concerning their implementation. Categorical grants were developed as the form of grant-in-aid that specified in detail how the money is to be spent, for example, for the building of airports or highways.

Gratz v. *Bollinger and Grutter* v. *Bollinger* (2003)

In *Gratz* v. *Bollinger* and *Grutter* v. *Bollinger*, the Supreme Court justices reaffirmed the spirit of the *Baake* judgment. They maintained its commitment to diversity as a laudable goal and accepted that race could be a factor, among others, in making decisions over recruitment. They found against the admissions policy of the University of Michigan (based, as it was, on additional points for being a member of an ethnic minority) but allowed the approach adopted by the Law School (considering issues of race and diversity on a practical basis) to continue.

Two white students in Michigan claimed that their university had acted unconstitutionally in denying them places in 1995 because of its race-scoring policy, and a third argued that the Law School (which took race into account but did not explicitly score applicants) did the same to her in 1997. The university claimed that its policies were essential to its goal of assembling a diverse student body.

The case was highly controversial, generating a record number of amici curiae from institutional supporters of race preferences. In preparation for the Michigan ruling, the Bush administration filed papers with the Supreme Court, urging it to decide that the university policy was 'unconstitutional'. It wanted a once-and-for-all decision that racial preferences had no place in admissions policy. It accepted that the goal of diversity was a worthy one but argued that it must not supersede equal rights and individual opportunity, for this was reverse discrimination. Moreover, because of the backlash created, any attempt to grant preference on minority grounds could end up harming the people it was intended to support. This stance did not satisfy all members of the administration, some of whom backed the then Secretary of State, Colin Powell, who wanted to see a continuation of affirmative action policies geared to ending racial imbalance.

Supporters of the university's approach saw it as beneficial in promoting diversity. Some (including the National Association for the Advancement of Colored People [NAACP]) argued that affirmative-action policies were needed for a different reason, as a means of remedying past and present discrimination at the institution. Others pointed out that another crucial factor in Michigan admissions policies favours white students – namely, the allocation of extra points to those whose parents attended the institution. Further backing came from the private sector, for affirmative-action programmes were popular with many large companies that saw them as a means of winning or maintaining a market share for their products among minority communities. In particular, General Motors – which employs many graduates from the university – urged that diversity-admissions policies be allowed to continue. As a global enterprise, its spokespersons argued that diversity equipped American students to deal with people from different backgrounds, cultures and races – in effect, to be better business people.

In striking down the rigid, point-based admission policy in the *Gratz* case, the Court was upholding its position in the *Baake* case, for it judged the Michigan system to be in essence a quota system of the type that had been earlier forbidden. However, by supporting the university in the *Grutter* case, it was accepting the validity of certain positive discrimination programmes as being desirable in an inclusive society. As such, judgments left affirmative action intact, *Grutter* being widely hailed as a victory for the cause of diversity.

See also *Affirmative Action*; Gratz v. Bollinger *and* Grutter v. Bollinger *(2003)*; Piscataway Board of Education v. Taxman *(1989)*; Reports of the University of California v. Baake *(1978)*

Great Depression

The Great Depression refers to the period of unemployment, low profits, low prices, high poverty and stagnant trade that affected the entire world in the ten years from 1929 to 1939. The Wall Street Crash (the stock market crash of October 1929) triggered the depression in the United States which then spread across the world's economies.

In America, the depression brought about major changes, most notably the Rooseveltian New Deal programme that involved large-scale federal relief programmes, aid to agriculture, support for labour unions and, in politics, the Democrat Coalition. It greatly increased the expectation that the federal government would intervene to deal with the major social and economic ills of the country, for the states were unable to act themselves as a result of the strain on their finances as well as out of an ideological unwillingness in some cases so to do. Because of the greater concentration of power in Washington, the depression created, or at least certainly accelerated, a fundamental change in political behaviour in the United States. Roosevelt was not reluctant to respond to the economic dislocation and hardship. The scale of his response marked a significant extension of presidential power which is why the 'modern presidency' is often dated from the time of his takeover in 1933.

See also *New Deal*; *Wall Street Crash*

Great Society

The Great Society was a set of domestic programmes proposed or enacted on the initiative of President Johnson in the mid to late 1960s. Two of the main goals of the Great Society social reforms were the elimination of poverty and racial injustice. In addition, major new spending programmes, which addressed education, medical care, urban problems and transport, were launched during this period. In scope and scale, the programmes resembled the New Deal agenda of Franklin Roosevelt although the variety of programmes was considerably different. As a highly focused set of measures, they amounted to a vast expansion in the federal government's role in domestic policy.

During the Johnson administration, Congress enacted two major civil rights acts (1964 and 1965), the Economic Opportunity Act (1964) and two education acts (1965). In addition, legislation was passed that created the Job Corps, Operation Head Start, Volunteers in Service to America (VISTA), Medicaid and Medicare. Some of these measures had been unfulfilled elements of the Kennedy platform. The president's greater success in implementing them was largely due to his remarkable skills at persuasion and arm twisting, coupled with the influx of many new liberals as a result of the 1964 Democratic landslide. Towards the end of the Johnson presidency, some enthusiasts for the Great Society noted that the cost of the measures, at a time when the war in Vietnam was being escalated, was reducing their impact.

In the Reagan years, some of the Great Society legislation was seen as unduly costly and ill-targeted and wasteful, a misguided and failed social experiment that wasted taxpayers' money. Critics claimed that it amounted to 'throwing money' at social problems. Some of the programmes were abandoned or scaled down. Others, however – including Medicare, Medicaid and federal education funding – are still operative today.

See also *Johnson, Lyndon*

Green Movement

Movements comprise large numbers of people who are united but loosely organised around a central idea or interest that is of continuing significance and who are willing to take action on that issue in order to change attitudes, institutions and policies They often arise at the grassroots level and evolve into national groupings. Often, they include individuals and groups who otherwise are 'left out' of government. Movements are different from interest groups or pressure groups but often closely related to them. They contain people who

share common concerns but their views about how to achieve their broad goals – such as care for the environment – may differ sharply.

Environmental concern was born in environmental movements which occupy a political terrain that is often distinct from more established institutionalised political forms, such as parties and pressure groups, and the administrative and legislative systems of the state. It is within these non-institutional, more informal realms of society and their politics that environmental movements emerged. In several countries, they have had a significant effect in greening both government and corporations.

Since the 1970s the green movement in the United States has been working through a whole array of local and national networks and organisations to press its claims. Sometimes, members have employed direct action in the form of blockades, marches and rallies, as well as quieter, more conventional attempts to lobby for policy changes and new initiatives.

There is a difference between the environmental movement in western Europe and the United States. In western Europe, several environmental movements have been of the 'New-Left' variety. They favour fundamental change in which ecological and social needs are seen as more important than the economic concerns of the existing pattern of society, in particular the obsession with economic growth. They are rooted in anti-nuclear energy issues and the politics of human and political ecology. In America, environmental movements have been dominated by wilderness-oriented perspectives. In fact, the US green movement is not unlike several western European nature conservation movements but with less emphasis on the preservation of the built environment and more on the great outdoors. Its main thrust is to protect species in danger of extinction in a modernising world. Members are often in the forefront of the fight against pollution. They are broadly content with, and prepared to operate within, the existing economic order by proposing moderate reforms and ensuring that politics has a green tinge.

At different times and in different places, the American green movement has had different concerns. On the East Coast, with its high population density, there has been an emphasis on the human element of ecology, with air- and water-quality issues assuming particular importance. The prevalence within the movement of many powerful non-governmental organisations has tended to mean that they do not offer a radical critique of existing society and politics but work to make the existing system function more effectively. In the Western regions, wilderness issues prevail, with arguments surrounding forest wilderness issues, such as the reintroduction of large species (e.g., elks, grizzly bears and wolves) and the management of national parks.

Within the American environmental movement, many 'light greens' adopt a slow pace to environmental improvement, with an emphasis on broad policy statements, policy documents and the creation of new institutions. More radical environmentalists or 'dark greens' argue that incremental change is insufficient. They demand a more deepseated, widespread reassessment of our modern way of life, based as it is on conspicuous consumption and a preoccupation with material living standards. Overall, the mainstream environmental movement in the United Stated is less political, and sometimes apolitical, in the way that it views and tackles environmental questions, when compared with the western European tradition. There tends to be limited criticism of the broad direction of the existing political system though there has been campaigning for radical change from groups such as Earth First! which urges direct, sometimes militant, piecemeal actions.

The green movement and political parties

Some environmentalists believe that formal, traditional politics are incapable of resolving ecological problems, and argue that partisan politicians have little interest in tackling difficult environmental problems or pursuing principled activities. Others, sometimes viewed as realists or pragmatists, believe in becoming involved in elections, either putting up green candidates or supporting those of the two main parties who exhibit sympathy for their priorities.

By involving themselves in party politics, they hope to achieve wider political influence and be recognised as significant players on the political scene. If they themselves cannot win, particularly given the existence of the first-past-the-post electoral system, they may have an impact on the outcome. For instance, by standing on a green ticket in California, Ralph Nader felt that he could damage the Democrats' chances of winning and also gain media coverage of green issues if left-leaning voters showed signs of deserting to him. He did not want to see a Republican in the White House but used his campaign as a lever to extract environmental concessions from President Clinton. Following Nader's decision to run, the president became more active in environmental matters and spoke out against increased logging in public forests. Of course, in 2000, the effect of his intervention was damaging to the Gore candidacy and probably cost the Democrats a sufficient number of voters (not least in Florida) to hand victory to George W. Bush.

The Democratic Party has had an uneasy relationship with the politics of environmental concern. Some of its key figures and presidential aspirants have embraced environmental issues as part of their campaigning, often without achieving success. Al Gore was known for his attempts to make the environment an electoral issue before he became vice president and worked hard to get the Clinton administration to adopt environmentally aware policies. The success of the Republicans in November 1994, however, and the adminstrations's need to adjust policies to enable them to work with their opponents, led to some reversals of early stances.

See also *Green Parties*; *Nader, Ralph*

Green Parties

Green, or ecologist, parties base their thinking on the principles of the environmental movement. As such, they include environmentalism, reliance on grassroots democracy, non-violence and support for social justice.

Greens can respond to the political system in one of three ways:

1. they can consciously abstain from electoral politics – perhaps opting for pressure-group activity instead;

2. they can seek to influence existing parties to take on elements of their ideological package (playing the 'normal' political game);
3. they can create distinctive green parties.

Within the United States, as elsewhere, there are greens who favour each of the above strategies.

The Democratic Party has had an uneasy relationship with the politics of environmental concern. Some of its key figures – particularly Al Gore – have embraced environmental issues as part of their campaigns. He consciously set out to persuade members of the Clinton administration to adopt more green policies, a task which became more difficult when he was faced with a Republican majority in Congress that disliked regulatory activity.

Green parties at the local, state and federal levels

Discrete green parties have made little headway in the United States. Several have been formed at local and state levels and achieved occasional success but, on the national scene, the Green Party rarely polls above 2 to 3 per cent in presidential elections. It suffers from the usual difficulties experienced by third parties: the difficulties of getting on the ballot paper in some states; the limitations on the availability of state funding, payable only after the election and then only if they have gained 5 per cent of the vote; and the first-past-the-post electoral system that tends to entrench a two-party system.

Greens have been active at the federal level since 2001, though they first gained widespread public attention during Ralph Nader's presidential bids in 1996 and 2000. Currently, the primary national body is the Green Party of the United States (a federation of state green parties) which has eclipsed the earlier greens/Green Party USA. Cynthia McKinney, a former member of Congress from Georgia, was the official Green candidate in the 2008 presidential election. Standing with the endorsement of the Workers World Party, she won a mere 161,603 votes (0.12 per cent of the vote).

See also *Green Movement*; *Nader, Ralph*; *Third Parties*

Gregg v. *Georgia* (1976)

In the aftermath of the Furman ruling, many of the states whose statutes had been invalidated by the Supreme Court rewrote their laws on the use of the death penalty in order to repair any inherent flaws. To gain acceptance, their legislators wished to ensure that there were institutionalised procedures and that the impact of the imposition of capital punishment would be made less arbitrary. In *Gregg* v. *Georgia*, the Supreme Court decided that the death penalty was not always unconstitutional. It accepted the constitutionality of the revised statutes, a verdict that seemed to many anti-death-penalty campaigners to be a remarkable volte-face. The justices argued that there should be two stages in consideration of the use of the death penalty: the first would establish innocence or guilt, the second would decide whether the death sentence was appropriate, in the light of any mitigating factors.

See also *Capital Punishment*; **Furman** *v.* **Georgia** *(1972)*

Guantánamo Bay

Guantánamo Bay is a bay located in Guantánamo province in the south-east corner of Cuba. In December 1903, the United States leased the 45 square miles (110 sq. km) of land and water for use as a naval base. It is the oldest American base overseas and the only one in a Communist country.

Today, Guantánamo is better known for the US detention camp which has served as a military prison and interrogation camp since 2002. The prison holds people accused by the US government of being al-Qaeda and Taliban operatives, as well as those no longer considered suspects who are being held pending relocation elsewhere. The detainment areas consist of three camps in the base: Camp Delta, Camp Iguana and the now-closed Camp X-Ray.

The detainees were classified as 'enemy combatants' rather than as 'prisoners of war', President Bush having signed a memorandum stating that no al-Qaeda or Taliban detainee qualifies as a prisoner of war and that Article 3 (common to the four Geneva Conventions), which requires fair trial standards and prohibits torture, cruelty, and 'outrages upon personal dignity, in particular humiliating and degrading treatment', does not apply to them either.

Since the fighting in Afghanistan began, of the 775 detainees who were taken to Guantánamo, nearly two thirds have been released, but 229 remain (as at September 2009). Some have been cleared for release but are having to wait for their freedom because government officials have been unable to make arrrangements as to where they should be sent.

In November 2003, the Supreme Court announced that it would listen to cases brought to appeal by Afghan war detainees who challenged their continued detention at the camp as being unlawful. In June 2004, in *Hamdi* v. *Rumsfeld*, the Court ruled that 'illegal combatants', such as those held in Guantánamo, can challenge detentions but can also be held without charges or trial. Two years later, in *Hamdan* v. *Rumsfeld*, it decided that the military commissions, established by Executive order to try detainees, are unlawful and violate the American Uniform Code of Military Justice, the 1949 Geneva Conventions and various human rights standards relating to fair trials. The justices also disagreed with the administration's view that the laws and customs of war did not apply to the armed conflict with al-Qaeda and Taliban fighters in Afghanistan.

In the election campaign of 2008, Barack Obama pledged himself to close down Guantánamo Camp as soon as possible. In January 2009, the White House announced that the detention facility would be shut down within the year. However, finding an alternative has proved difficult. Even Democrats who supported the promise are less than enthusiastic about the prospect of the remaining detainees being transferred to their states for imprisonment or trial.

Gulf War see *Iraq War: the First Gulf War (1990–91)*

Gun Politics

'Gun politics' are concerned with gun control and firearms rights. These have long been among the most controversial, intractable and polarising issues in American politics. At the heart of the debate is the relationship between the government's authority to regulate firearms and its duty to maintain order and provide for the common defence, and the rights of the citizen.

America is noted for having the most heavily armed citizenry in the world. Most Americans do not own guns but one in six possesses a handgun and, altogether, estimates suggest that there are at least 250 million firearms in circulation – not far short of one per person. Gun ownership on this scale makes America distinctive from other countries, hence the popular impression in many countries that guns are part of the American way of life. The impression has been encouraged by many films and television programmes which depict the United States as being a particularly violent society. Indeed, the country was created in violence and, in the nineteenth century, the opening up of the West was accompanied by the destruction of human and animal life. Guns, and their use and abuse, were and remain key features of American society. More Americans have died as a consequence of gun-related violence than have been killed in all of the wars since the War of Independence, 750, 000 in the half century or so since 1960.

Yet, despite this heavy emphasis on gun ownership and use, America does not – contrary to widely held belief – lack gun laws covering the production, distribution and ownership of guns. Neither do most Americans oppose legislation on gun control.

Gun laws

What America lacks is effective gun-control legislation at the federal level. There were only eight laws introduced in the twentieth century, and their overall impact is much less restrictive than laws passed in many other countries. The history of gun-regulation legislation is characterised by repetitive cycles of popular outrage, action and reaction, usually in response to sensational outbreaks of shooting.

The first piece of legislation, the National Firearms Act, was passed in 1934, at a time when many Americans were receptive to restriction following the violent gangsterism of the Prohibition era (1920–33). It imposed penal taxation on the manufacture and distribution of gangster weapons and required that the FBI subjected those who purchased them to background checks. Another measure, the Gun Control Act (1968) was passed following the assassinations of Martin Luther King and Robert Kennedy, when elected representatives were again aware of a widespread public mood to curb gun ownership. Among other things, it banned traffic in firearms between states, required serial numbers to be imprinted on guns and prevented certain groups, such as drug addicts and the mentally ill, from legally acquiring firearms. More recently, the Domestic Violence Offender Gun Ban (1996) prohibited anyone convicted of domestic violence from purchasing or owning a gun. Supporters of individual gun rights have resisted nearly all these regulation efforts, often spearheaded by the National Rifle Association (NRA).

At state and local level, too, numerous measures have been introduced. Their combined impact has been modest, however. In several cases, states have imposed no instant check or waiting period on those who seek to buy guns. Just four states have legislated to prevent the purchase by individuals of more than one gun per month. Many of the restrictive laws that have been introduced have been weak, permissive and easily evaded. The combined effects of the massive volume of legislation have been less dramatic than might have been anticipated. Yet, this is despite the findings of many opinion surveys which show that there is public recognition of the problems associated with gun ownership and support for gun control, especially at the federal level.

The politics of gun control

Many Americans of progressive persuasion, including many activists within the Democratic Party, support effective gun-control legislation. They see a simple equation between widespread and ill-regulated gun ownership and the levels of violence in American society. Traditionalists, many of whom are to be found in – or are supporters of – the Republican Party, doubt this

analysis. They reject the idea that there is a clear linkage between the legal availability of guns for self-defence and recreational use, and the violence endemic in much criminal behaviour. They do not believe that there is anything inherently wrong with guns but rather with those who abuse them, hence the slogan 'guns don't kill people, people kill people'. Rather, they see gun ownership as a traditional right of Americans, whether it be to defend themselves and enable them to feel secure in their homes, or to go shooting and hunting.

In particular, those who support the right of gun ownership tend to quote in their favour the Second Amendment which has been a barrier for those who wish to strengthen and extend gun-control legislation. They quote the clause that lays down that 'the right of the people to keep and bear arms shall not be infringed'. Members of the NRA, and other elements within the gun-rights lobby, have long expressed such a view which is much stronger than the inadequately resourced gun-control lobby. It has been articulated more recently by members of the Bush administration, such as former Attorney General, John Ashcroft, who noted that the amendment 'unequivocally' established an individual's right to gun ownership.

Some measures designed to limit gun ownership and use have fallen foul of the Constitution but not because of the Second Amendment. The Gun-free School Zones Act (1990), which made it a federal offence knowingly to possess firearms within 1,000 feet (300 m) of a school, was rejected in the Supreme Court in *United States* v. *Lopez* (1995) on the grounds that education is a state matter and therefore not subject to regulation under the Commerce Clause of the Constitution. In *Printz* v. *United States* (1997) the background check provision of the Brady law (1993), which required a waiting period of five days in which checks could be carried out on prospective purchasers, was deemed unconstitutional on the basis of the Tenth Amendment, that the federal government lacked the authority to require local officials to execute federal policies.

The reality is that it has not been the Second Amendment as much as the federal–state relationship that has led to the repudiation of congressional legislation. Nonetheless, opponents of gun control still rely heavily on its support. Supporters of control remind Americans of the first part of the amendment, before the phrase quoted above: 'A well-regulated militia, being necessary to the security of a free State'. They make the point that the clause was really concerned with the right of states – rather than of individuals – to establish militias. It supported the arming of the people only when bonded together for communal defence. Supporters of gun rights see the amendment as enshrining an individual right.

See also *National Rifle Association*

H

Hamdan v. Rumsfeld (2006)

Hamdan v. *Rumsfeld* was a case in which, by a 5–3 ruling, the Supreme Court decided that the military commissions established by the Bush administration to try Guantánamo detainees lacked 'the power to proceed because [their] structures and procedures violate both the Uniform Code of Military Justice and the four Geneva Conventions signed in 1949'. Specifically, the ruling stated that the commissions violated Article 3 of the Third Convention.

The justices considered: whether Congress was able to pass legislation preventing the Supreme Court from hearing the case of an accused combatant before his military commission took place (as the government was claiming under the Detainee Treatment Act, DTA); whether the special military commissions violated federal law (including the Uniform Code of Military Justice and treaty obligations); and whether courts are able to enforce the Geneva Conventions. In an opinion for the Court written by Justice Stevens, the Court considered that it did have jurisdiction to hear the case. Its ruling dismissed the government's 'motion to dismiss' under Section 1005 of the DTA which gave the DC Circuit Court of Appeals 'exclusive' jurisdiction to review decisions of cases being tried before military commissions. It argued that Congress did not include language in the DTA that might have precluded Supreme Court jurisdiction.

See also *Guantánamo Bay*

Hamilton, Alexander (1757–1804)

Alexander Hamilton was a political theorist, practising politician, leading statesman and financier in the United States, one of its most prominent Founding Fathers. He was also one of America's first constitutional lawyers, active in summoning the Constitutional Convention in 1787. Along with John Jay and James Madison, he was one of chief authors of the *Federalist Papers*.

Born illegitimately in the British West Indies, Hamilton moved to the United States in 1772 and was educated in New York City. He developed strong political views and wrote a series of pamphlets in defence of the rights of the colonies against Britain. He joined the Continental Army in 1776, became captain of artillery, and also served as aide-de-camp to General George Washington. After the War of Independence, he studied law before becoming a member of the Continental Congress and a member of the New York State Assembly. When Washington became president, Hamilton was appointed as the first Secretary to the Treasury Secretary. He thus became the architect of the structure of the department. He favoured a strong, centrally controlled Treasury and was in constant conflict with Thomas Jefferson and others over the amount of power the department should be allowed to wield. His influence extended to external as well as to financial policy. He assumed the leadership of the Federalist Party, opposed by the Jeffersonian Democratic Republicans.

In 1804, Vice President Aaron Burr asked Hamilton to support his campaign to become governor of New York. Hamilton declined, describing him as 'a man of irregular and insatiable ambition . . . who ought not be trusted with the reins of government'. The furious Burr challenged Hamilton to a duel. Hamilton accepted, was shot by Burr and died the following day.

Few, if any, of the Founding Fathers can have had such a diverse and eventful career as Hamilton. He held his first important public office on George Washington's staff when he was twenty and retired from his last one as inspector general of the army when he was forty-three. None suffered such a spectacular death.

See also *Judicial Review*

Health Provision

Health care in the United States is today provided by a range of separate legal entities. It was once a purely private arrangement, with the most deprived members of the community receiving help from charitable bodies. Now, the government meets their costs, but above that category are many who do not qualify for assistance. In 2008, some forty-seen million Americans (16 per cent of the population) had no health insurance, and a substantial number of those who do have it lose their entitlement each month because they cannot afford the expense and their employers are no longer willing to provide the facility. For those who lack the means to pay, but who do not fall into the lowest social groups, there is a real inadequacy in the present arrangements.

For many years, there has been debate over the merits of the health care available in the United States. The quality of provision is widely regarded as inadequate, especially in parts of rural America, but the service is costly. Health care now consumes about 15 per cent of gross domestic product (GDP), the world's highest figure and nearly three times as much as was spent thirty years ago. The share of GDP is expected to continue its historical upward trend, perhaps climbing to nearly 20 per cent within ten years. This figure includes the costs of the private system which plays a larger role than in other advanced industrialised countries. Less than 40 per cent of expenditure on health is spent through the public sector whereas, in Australia and Japan, the figure is almost 70 per cent, in Britain around 85 per cent and in Norway and Sweden, over 90 per cent. Yet, although private treatment looms large in US arrangements, the provision of it is widely condemned as inefficient and wasteful.

The United States is the only major industrialised nation in the world that lacks universal health-care access. About 84 per cent of Americans have health insurance, via their employer, purchased individually or provided by government programmes. Publicly funded health-care programmes help provide for the elderly, disabled, children, veterans and the poor, with federal law ensuring public access to emergency services regardless of ability to pay. Private health insurance is expensive, medical bills sometimes being the reason for personal bankruptcy.

Attempts at reform

There have been many moves over the last century to establish some form of national health insurance so that there might be nationwide access to health care. In the 1920s, even the American Medical Association (AMA), now a bastion of conservative thinking, was committed to a comprehensive scheme. In the 1960s, when liberal views were in the ascendancy and the frontiers of the Great Society were being advanced, Medicare was created. It was a compromise scheme designed to win as much support as possible. In return for the federal government's assumption of a role in the financing of treatment, the actual provision was left in private hands.

Medicare has done much to improve the health and well-being of millions of Americans, and was and remains a popular governmental initiative. It is not comprehensive, however, for, whereas Part A provides inpatient hospital/hospice insurance funded by a payroll tax split between employers and employees, Part B, optional Supplementary Medical Insurance, pays around 80 per cent of outpatient services. Part A is under serious financial pressure. Moreover, although the 1997 Balanced Budget Act added some extra services to those already provided (including annual cancer screenings and tests for conditions such as diabetes and osteoporosis), other aspects, such as long-term nursing care are not included.

Since the introduction of Medicare and Medicaid (a programme providing health care coverage to more than 40 million poor Americans) liberal Democrats have been keen to improve health facilities. Many support the principle of universal national health insurance but the costs of any such innovation have always proved a deterrent to any new policy to translate the theory into practice.

The Clinton administration promised an attempt to tackle the problem of health care. He favoured such a universal scheme, with the premiums of the least well off being subsidised by the government. He also wanted to see more competition in the system, for the lack of it contributed significantly to the growing financial burden of providing an acceptable level of care. Health reform was to be the keystone of his presidency, with a plan that would be comprehensive, offering guaranteed treatment to all Americans.

Hillary Clinton headed a taskforce on reform. She ran into much opposition in Congress, however, for, while most Americans saw the need for change, there was less agreement on the nature of any new departure in policy. For two years there was wrangling over the Clinton proposals, the plans running into opposition not just from the AMA and Republican opponents but also from some Democrats who felt they would be too expensive and politically dangerous. After the loss of Democratic control of Congress in November 1994, there was no chance that the president would achieve what was to have been the centrepiece of his domestic presidency.

Policy under the Obama Administration

In the primary battle for the Democratic nomination, both Hillary Clinton and Barack Obama took up the issue of reforming America's health care provision. The issue then became a key part of the Democrats' platform in the presidential contest. The new Administration was committed to working with Congress to pass legislation in his first year providing health care stability and security for all Americans. According to the President, comprehensive reform should:

- reduce long-term growth of health care costs for businesses and government

- protect families from bankruptcy or debt because of health care costs
- guarantee choice of doctors and health plans
- invest in prevention and wellness
- improve patient safety and quality of care
- assure affordable, quality health coverage for all Americans
- maintain coverage when people change or lose their job
- end barriers to coverage for people with pre-existing medical conditions
- provide a public health insurance option, as a key element to his plans for lowering costs and improving care.

In July 2009, House Democrat leaders introduced a 1,000-page plan for overhauling the US health care system. The bill would require all Americans and legal residents to obtain health insurance, offer subsidies on a sliding scale to help people buy it, levy fees on health care companies and insurers, and expand Medicaid, the health care system for the poor. A crux issue was whether the extension of health insurance to those Americans who do not at present have any should be done via a federal government scheme – the public option – or left to private insurance companies, who have a stranglehold on the market at present. Obama argued for the public option, but has been careful to avoid saying he would veto any bill that did not contain it. Republicans oppose the public option, but so to do some fiscally conservative Democrats.

At the time of writing, the likelihood was that some health reform bill might be passed through the support of Democrats and moderate Republicans. The federally funded scheme – the public option – might have to be abandoned, but its removal would leave a watered-down bill that would disappoint reformers.

The political debate over health care reform has for several decades revolved around the questions of whether fundamental reform of the system is needed, what form those reforms should take, and how they should be funded. There remains widespread agreement that the present arrangements do not work well. They are subject to the same demographic pressures affecting many countries, for the 'greying' of the American population means that the cost of provision is inevitably going to rise.

Many Americans want to see better and more widespread health care, particularly for those in need. But, in their attitudes to health and welfare provision in general, they are concerned about the impact of any reform on their income taxes and tend to draw a sharp distinction between the entitlements of the deserving and the undeserving poor.

Hispanic Americans

Hispanics is the collective name for people whose origins can be traced back to Hispania, the Roman name for the Iberian Peninsula which now includes Andorra, Gibraltar, Portugal and Spain. Some Hispanics prefer to be called Latinos, a shortened version of the noun 'Latinoamericano', meaning Latin American.

Hispanics are the fastest-growing group in the population of the United States (see below), which grew by 57.9 per cent between 1990 and 2000. There are currently estimated to be 45.5 million (approximately 15.1 per cent) Hispanics who, for the first time, outnumbered the number of black Americans in 2003. Indeed, as a significant minority of black Americans are also Hispanics, the historic primacy of primarily English-speaking black was already at an end by the turn of the last century.

Hispanics tend to be undercounted in surveys, a situation made more possible by the number of illegal immigrants ever year. They are expected to number approximately 105 million by 2050 and will then account for nearly a quarter of America's population.

The increase in the Hispanic population in the US over the last generation (in millions)

1980	15
1990	22
2000	5
2008 (est.)	45

NB A separate listing for Hispanics is no longer included by the Census Bureau in its figure for ethnic groups living in the United States. It considers Hispanic to mean a person of Latin American descent (including persons of Cuban,

Mexican, or Puerto Rican origin) living in the US who may be of any race or ethnic group (white, black, Asian, etc.)

Most Hispanics have a Mexican origin (up 52.9 per cent). Those who reported other origins are the fastest-growing group (up 96.9 per cent) significant rates of increase occurring among the Central and South Americans, and the Dominicans. There are also many Puerto Ricans who have left their overcrowded island for the mainland with the hope of improving their position in life. Those from Cuba compromise another significant group. They, or their parents and grandparents, fled from Castro's Communist revolution in 1959. They tend to be professional and middle class, and do not share many of the social and political attitudes of the Mexican Americans and Puerto Ricans.

The origin of the Hispanic population (percentage)

Mexican	58.5
Puerto Rican	9.6
Cuban	3.5
Others, of whom the largest group includes central American and Dominican	28.4

Mostly better off than African Americans, half of all Hispanics live in just two states, California and Texas. They account for approximately a quarter of the population in the West, the only region in which Hispanics exceeded the national level. Nearly two-thirds of the Cuban element lives in Florida. A majority of Miami residents are Hispanic but, in cities from Dallas to Houston, Los Angeles to New York, they are also well represented.

Influence in US society

Inspired by the example of black activism, Hispanics have drawn more closely together but the diversity of their origins has prevented them from becoming a solid national grouping. They are a young population, their relative youthfulness being reflected in the size of the under-eighteen population (35.0 per cent, against an overall figure of 25.7 per cent) and in its median age (twenty-six, as against thirty-six). They tend to be poorer than whites and many have not qualified as citizens. Their campaigning has been done via local groups that fight for better conditions rather than through large nation-wide associations. But they are becoming more organised and many are now acquiring citizenship. In 2009, for the first time, an Hispanic was chosen as an associate justice on the Supreme Court.

As they now constitute the largest minority group, it is likely that issues of concern to the various Hispanic subgroups will gain greater prominence on the nation's political agenda. They may be still seriously underrepresented in American institutions (e.g., the 29 members of the 111th Congress represent only 5.4% of its total membership) but there have been recent signs of an emerging Latino-led radicalism, particularly among those who carry out many of the lowest-paid and dirtiest jobs in the US. In the words of Davis (2001): 'The long history of political marginality is finally coming to an end. Latinos, all political pundits agree, are the sleeping dragon of US politics.'

The votes of Hispanics are crucial in some states, Texas, California and Florida among them. In the light of what happened in 2000 (see p. 34), Florida became a particularly interesting political battleground, not least because Jeb Bush, the president's brother, was at that time the governor. His articulate son, George P. Bush (born in Mexico to his mother Columba) could well prove to be the next member of the Bush dynasty to take the political stage and enter public life.

Homeland Security, Department of

The United States Department of Homeland Security (DHS) is a Cabinet department of the federal government with responsibility for protecting the territory of the country from terrorist attacks and for reducing America's vulnerability to terrorism. While the department was created to secure the US against those who sought to disrupt the American way of life, its charter also included preparation for, and response to, all hazards and disasters. The department was established as a direct response to the 9/11 attacks, initially as the Office of Homeland Security with a

brief to co-ordinate 'homeland security' efforts. It was merged into a department by the Homeland Security Act (2002) which consolidated into a single body all executive branch organisations relating to homeland security.

House of Representatives

The United States House of Representatives is one of the two chambers of the Congress. Its 435 members are distributed according to population so that the larger the state's population, the more representatives it is allocated. Every state must have at least one house seat. For example, Alabama has seven, Delaware one. Representatives are elected from congressional districts within the states, and each serves for a two-year term. Representatives are often called congressmen or congresswomen though, technically, the term applies to senators as well.

The House is often considered to be the 'lower house' with the Senate as the 'upper house' but this is not the language used by the Founding Fathers in writing the Constitution. Each chamber can introduce legislation on any subject, except revenue bills which must originate in the House of Representatives, and the document provides that the approval of both chambers is necessary for the passage of bills. But if the powers of the house and Senate are broadly coequal, most commentators would argue that the Senate's responsibilities with regard to treaties and ratifications of appointments give it a greater degree of authority. Even the requirement that all bills on revenue raising must originate in the house is hardly a great plus, as the Senate has the same full power of amendment as it has with other types of bills. Two of the distinctive features of the house are that it initiates the impeachment procedure and – in the event of there being a deadlock in the Electoral College – it elects the president.

Members of each party gather as a caucus or conference. Those in the majority party choose the speaker, the presiding officer of the house, from among their members. They also choose a majority leader who is second in command to the speaker. The two office-holders work together to schedule legislation for debate on the floor of the house. They are assisted by majority whips who help co-ordinate party positions on legislation, pass information and directions between the leadership and other party members, make sure members know when particular votes are being held and try to persuade waverers to support the leadership. The minority party has equivalent positions, a minority leader and minority whips. The minority party leader is usually his or her party's candidate for the speakership should it become the majority party. Nancy Pelosi was the Democrat minority leader until the change of control in the November 2006 elections. She then became speaker.

Committees form an important feature of the chamber's organisation, preparing the bills on which members of the House vote. The committee system divides the work of processing legislation and enables members to specialise in particular types of issues. Key committees of the house are the Budget Committee and those dealing with Appropriations, Rules and Ways and Means.

See also *Congress*; *Congressional Budget Office*; *Congressional Committee Chairpersons*; *Congressional Committees*; *Congressional District*; *Congressional Elections*; *Reapportionment*

Immigration

Immigration refers to the movement of non-residents to the United States. It has been a major source of population growth and cultural change throughout much of American history although the proportion of Americans born overseas has never been above 16 per cent of the population since the creation of the Republic.

The United States is literally a nation of immigrants. It comprises more than 300 million people, many of whom have very different backgrounds from their neighbours. At various stages in its history, it has been open to migrants from across the world. Its reputation as a land of political, religious and economic freedom has made it a natural and safe haven for the poor and oppressed. They have seen it as a land of opportunity in which everyone has the chance to share the American Dream. Many – but by no means all – immigrants have been able significantly to improve their economic standing and family well-being.

Except for Native Americans, all other people in the United States are immigrants by descent. Many Irish men and women settled in the mid-nineteenth century, some before the potato famine in Ireland (1846), many more after it. The largest wave of immigration, however, was in the years between 1900 and 1924, during which more than seventeen million people arrived, many of them fleeing from poverty or persecution in Europe (Germans, Greeks, Italians and Poles being prominent among them). Another wave arrived in the twenty or so years after World War II, many of them Europeans displaced by war or political refugees such as those from Hungary after the rising of 1956. Many more

came from other parts of the American, notably Mexicans who went to work on the land in the Southwest and Puerto Ricans who settled by the thousand in New York City. A further wave has arrived since 1980–89, this time from Latin America (in particular, the Caribbean and Mexico) and Asia (particularly China, the Philippines and Vietnam). Of those who have entered the United States in the twenty-first century, more than half have come from Latin America.

Exactly 1,266,264 immigrants were granted legal residence in 2006, up from 1,122,373 in 2005. The top dozen countries from which they derived were, in descending order, Mexico, China, the Philippines, India, Cuba, Colombia, Dominican Republic, El Salvador, Vietnam, Jamaica, South Korea and Guatemala. And 202 Iraqi refugees were allowed to relocate in the United States.

Inevitably more difficult to establish is the number of illegal immigrants who enter every year, many from across the border. In 2000, the Census Bureau estimated that there were 8.7 million illegal immigrants living in the United States, and suggested that the total grows by at least 500,000 every year. Illegal immigration has recently resurfaced as a major issue in American politics. Various congressional bills have been put forward, containing proposals to tackle legalisation and amnesty for those illegally present in the country, crack down on employers who employ undocumented workers and build a wall along the Mexican border.

American reactions to immigration

The Statue of Liberty at the entrance to New York Harbour was the welcoming point for many of the world's dispossessed. The lines inscribed on its base declared:

> Give me your tired, your poor,
> Your huddled masses yearning to breathe free.

Yet, at times in its history, Americans have not celebrated diversity. Policy towards immigrants began to change with World War I. A quota system was established in 1921 to limit numbers that could arrive in any one year, a process that was intensified in succeeding years. In 1924, the National Origins Act more than halved the number to 150,000. The object was not simply to curb numbers entering the United States. It was to favour certain types of immigrants over others. More were permitted entry from western Europe than from central and eastern Europe. Canadians and Latin Americans were not excluded but Japanese were totally denied entry.

An Immigration Act of 1965 abolished the National Origins quota in force for more than forty years so that, henceforward, skills and family relationships were to be the main qualifications for admission. In 1986, the Immigration Reform and Control Act (IRCA) was passed, creating penalties for employers who knowingly hired illegal immigrants and offering an amnesty to some three million illegal immigrants already in the United States. (The penalties are seldom enforced and widespread illegal immigrant employment continues.) More recently, legislation has indicated a harsher, more restrictive approach both to legal and to illegal immigrants. The 1996 Antiterrorism and Effective Death Penalty Act (AEDPA) and Illegal Immigration Reform and Immigrant Responsibility Act (IIRIRA) vastly increased the categories of criminal activity for which immigrants can be deported.

Moreover, some members of the minority groups that have arrived have found themselves excluded from political and economic life and opportunities. Throughout their history, Black Americans have struggled to rise from chattel slavery to full participation in American society. Their ancestors came as slaves and, though many of their descendants were freed as a result of the Civil War, it was to be almost a century before they could achieve recognition of their rights as citizens. Of those who arrived in the nineteenth and twentieth centuries, many experienced the same feelings of initial elation after the flight from their homelands – and then, as they clustered in similar areas to their kinsmen and kinswomen, experienced exploitation and rejection.

The arrival of large numbers of migrants poses problems in most societies. In some American cities, there has been competition for jobs and rights with already long-established groups. As immigrants have sought to attain equal treatment and secure their share of political power and influence, conflict has sometimes been inevitable. Sometimes, adversity has had a unifying impact, as groups from different backgrounds and areas join together to fight a common foe, be it a rival international power or the threat of terrorism at home. The American Dream and American values, too, help secure a sense of common identity that can override ethnic diversity, most Americans being committed to equality and liberty in a land of opportunity.

See also *Melting Pot*

Impeachment

Impeachment is a formal accusation issued by a legislature against a public official charged with crime or other serious misconduct. In the United States, it is the process by which Congress can remove officers of the national government, including the president. The House of Representatives votes on a charge or series of charges and a trial on the charges is then conducted in the Senate. Article II, Section 4 of the Constitution states that: 'The President, Vice President and all civil officers of the United States, shall be removed from Office on Impeachment for, and Conviction of, Treason, Bribery or other high Crimes and Misdemeanours.' Impeachment, then, involves a charge being laid of misconduct against an officer of the national government. In the case of the president, he or she is then committed for trial and, if convicted, removed from office.

In the process of impeachment, the house acts as the prosecutor and the Senate as judge and jury. Any member of the house may initiate impeachment proceedings by introducing a resolution to that effect. The House Judiciary Committee conducts proceedings in the lower chamber and then decides in favour of or against impeachment. It delivers a verdict to the whole house which requires a 50 per cent vote to impeach. If the process goes ahead, the case is then tried in the Senate, the Chief Justice presiding on this occasion. A two-thirds vote of those present is needed to secure a conviction and subsequent removal.

Impeachment is one of the most potent checks upon the abuse of power. It can also be a means of undermining a president's authority. But – as a rather partisan, cumbersome and time-consuming means of ensuring accountability which can fill thousands of pages of testimony and involve conflicting and troublesome political pressures – it has been used only sparingly.

Congress traditionally regards impeachment as a power to use only in extreme cases. Charges have been considered by the House of Representatives against sixty-two officials – including nine presidents – since 1789. Two cases did not come to trial because the individuals had left office. In only seventeen of these cases has the issue resulted in a Senate trial, one involving a cabinet officer (acquitted); one involving a senator (stalled on the grounds that the Senate lacked jurisdiction because – in a separate, unrelated action – it had already expelled the member); and thirteen involving federal judges (six acquitted). The other two cases involved presidents.

Impeachment proceedings against a president

Only two of the nine cases involving a president have resulted in impeachment proceedings, that of Andrew Johnson in 1868 and Bill Clinton in 1999. The Senate failed to convict Johnson by just one vote whereas, in the Clinton case, the Senate was at least twelve votes short of the necessary number. The case of Richard Nixon's obstruction of justice in the Watergate enquiry never reached the Senate. The House Judiciary Committee voted three articles of impeachment against him but he resigned before impeachment proceedings in the full house could begin. Had he not done so, he might well have been the first

incumbent of the White House to be successfully impeached.

During the presidency of George W. Bush, there were moves to impeach him. They were supported by some Democratic and Republican members of Congress, various other politicians, government officials, academics, writers, journalists and a segment of the American people and international community. The reasons advanced for Bush's impeachment included concerns about the legitimacy, legality, and constitutionality of the 2003 invasion of Iraq, and the controversial electronic surveillance of American citizens by the National Security Agency.

Although there seemed to be substantial popular support for impeachment proceedings, neither the house nor its judiciary committee formally considered invoking the procedure. The Democratic leadership indicated that it had no intention of pursuing the matter.

Impeachment at state level

Impeachment can also occur at the state level. State legislatures can impeach state officials, including governors, according to their respective constitutions: all except Oregon provide for the removal of executive and judicial officers. Exact procedures vary from state to state but they are all similar to federal impeachment.

Impeachment and removal of governors has happened occasionally, usually on grounds of corruption. The most recent example was the removal of Governor Evan Mecham of Arizona, in 1988. Mecham was removed from office following conviction in his impeachment trial on charges of obstructing justice and misusing government funds. His governorship was plagued by controversy. He became the first governor simultaneously to face removal from office via impeachment, a scheduled recall vote and a felony indictment.

Repeated attempts in the Congress to amend the procedure, however, have been unsuccessful, partly because impeachment is regarded as an integral part of the system of checks and balances in the United States government.

See also *Clinton and Impeachment*

Implied Powers

Implied powers are those powers exercised by the federal government that are not explicitly delegated to it by the Constitution. The document defines the powers of national government and grants all other authority – the residual powers – to individual states. The framers of the Constitution, however, left open the possibility that the national government had implied powers beyond those expressly written. Article I, Section 8, the so-called 'elastic clause', authorises Congress 'to make all laws which shall be necessary and proper for carrying into execution' the powers vested in any department of the national government. This elastic 'necessary and proper' clause has enabled Congress to engage in activities not specifically mentioned in its listing of enumerated powers, if the activities are a reasonable and appropriate mechanism to realise an enumerated activity or goal. In this way, the broad interpretation of implied powers has altered the position of the states by greatly expanding the powers of the federal government.

The interpretation of the necessary and proper clause was the subject of a heated debate between Alexander Hamilton (who argued that the clause should be read broadly to authorise the exercise of many implied powers) and Thomas Jefferson, Madison and others (who argued that 'necessary' really meant *necessary*). Hamilton's more flexible interpretation favours strong national leadership whereas Jefferson's narrower interpretation strengthens states' rights. Washington required Hamilton to defend the constitutionality of his proposal to incorporate a national bank, in the light of the protests of Jefferson and those who sympathised with him. In his defence, Hamilton employed the doctrine of implied powers. He argued that the sovereign duties of a government implied the right to use means adequate to its ends. Although the federal government was sovereign only as to certain objects, it was impossible to define all the means which it should use because it was impossible for the founders to anticipate all future situations. Hamilton noted that the 'general welfare' and 'necessary and proper' clauses gave elasticity to the Constitution. Hamilton convinced Washington who signed his Bank Bill into law.

In the case of *McCulloch* v. *Maryland* (1819), the Supreme Court resolved the constitutionality of implied powers. It had to consider whether Congress had the right to charter a Bank of the United States. Maryland officials argued that the bank was not a legally constituted agency of the federal government because no constitutional provision gave Congress the power to establish a national bank. The bank's lawyers, however, insisted that the power to charter a bank was implied in the constitutional authority to collect taxes, borrow money and regulate commerce. The Court unanimously sided with the national government.

Income Tax

Income tax was first introduced in the United States in 1862, support the cost of defending the Union in the Civil War. It was eliminated six years later, had a short-lived revival in 1894 and 1895 before the Supreme Court ruled in the case of *Pollock* v. *Farmers' Loan & Trust Co.* that it was unconstitutional because it was not apportioned among the states in conformity with the Constitution. The early efforts amounted to the forerunner of modern income tax, however, in that it was based on the principles of graduated, or progressive taxation and of withholding income at the source. Federal income tax has been a permanent feature ever since. Some state and municipal governments also impose income taxes.

In 1913, the Sixteenth Amendment to the Constitution made income tax a permanent fixture in the tax system. The amendment gave Congress legal authority to tax income and resulted in a revenue law that taxed incomes of individuals and of corporations. Soon, thereafter, Congress adopted a modest tax of 1 per cent on incomes over $3,000, with a surcharge of an additional 6 per cent on very high incomes. The vast majority of Americans were initially unaffected by the new tax, only 2 per cent paying it in the first year. In 1918, however, annual internal revenue collections for the first time passed the billion-dollar mark, rising to $5.4 billion by 1920.

In 1981, Congress enacted the largest tax cut in American history although its impact was partially offset by two tax measures in 1982 and 1984 that attempted to raise approximately $265 billion. In October 1986, President Reagan signed into law the Tax Reform Act of 1986, one of the most far-reaching reforms of the United States tax system since the adoption of income tax. The federal income tax system was completely overhauled. Hailed by its supporters – including President Reagan – the changes promoted a simpler tax system, reducing the number of tax bands and cutting individual tax rates. The top tax rate on individual income was lowered from 50 per cent to 28 per cent, the lowest it had been since 1916. President George W. Bush signed a series of tax cuts into law, the largest being the Economic Growth and Tax Relief Reconciliation Act of 2001 which constituted the third largest programme of tax reduction since World War II.

Republican presidents have generally been enthusiastic tax cutters. Democrats support a progressive tax structure, which means that they are less interested in lifting the tax burden of more affluent Americans. Particularly in the presidencies from Roosevelt to Johnson, they had an ambitious spending programme that had to be financed by taxation on incomes, among other means. This 'tax-and-spend' approach was out of fashion at the time when President Clinton refashioned the party as the New Democrats.

Indirect Democracy

An indirect or representative democracy is one in which the people rule indirectly through elected representatives. The vision of the Founding Fathers was of a representative system, a republic in Plato's sense, by which all those in power obtain and retain their positions as a result of winning elections in which all free adults are allowed to take part.

The nineteenth century saw the spread of representative democracy, a system under which a person stands for, and speaks on behalf of, another. Today, it is widely accepted that this is the only viable form of democracy for a vast country such as America although elements of direct democracy (initiatives, recall votes and referendums) exist in many states. The mass of people cannot rule, in the sense of making binding decisions. Instead, representatives of the people, freely elected, decide. What is crucial is that there should be effective popular control over the rulers

or decision-makers. A system is democratic to the extent that those who have power are subject to the wishes of the electorate. A modern, representative, democratic political system is therefore one in which public policies are made, on a majority basis, by representatives subject to effective popular control at periodic elections which are conducted on the principle of political equality and under conditions of political freedom.

See also *Democracy*; *Direct Democracy*

Individualism

Individualism is a label for the moral, political or social outlook that stresses human independence and the importance of individual liberty and self-reliance. Individualists promote the exercise of individual goals and desires. Such values have long been considered defining criteria of American culture.

Liberal individualism is a key characteristic of the American vision of democracy. It dates back to the idea of the English political philosopher, John Locke (1632–1704), who wrote of people's inalienable natural rights. Locke believed that free men, reasoning together, would produce just political institutions. It was reinforced by events that were happening in Europe in the late eighteenth century. At the time of the formation of the United States, many of its citizens had fled from state or religious oppression in Europe and were influenced by the egalitarian and fraternal ideals that later found expression in the French Revolution (1789–99).

The Founding Fathers set out to establish a political system that would protect individual rights by establishing a limited, moderate, constitutional regime by which people's individual rights could be protected rather than threatened. Such thinking soon found expression later in the Bill of Rights. To Alexis de Tocqueville (1805–59), American individualism represented an essential difference between the Old and New Worlds, the culture of the Old World emphasising ideas of hierarchy and nationality.

Belief in individualism is therefore as old as the nation itself. Prior to the 1960s, it focused mainly on the political domain, emphasising ideas such as freedom to speak and write, freedom to pursue religious beliefs and freedom of location and movement. In the 1950s the United States was a nation of political individualists but social conformists. The 1960s ushered in a radical extension of individualism, broadening it from the political domain to personal lifestyles. There was increased concern for the rights of minorities, be they based on ethnicity, gender, sexual orientation or disability.

See also *Political Culture*

Inherent Powers

Inherent powers are powers over and beyond those expressly granted in the Constitution, which may reasonably be regarded as inferred from explicit powers.

Enumerated powers are specific. Implied powers are somewhat broader but are still regarded as comprising a means towards achieving enumerated goals. By contrast, inherent powers are only loosely related to specific provisions of the Constitution. Some presidents have claimed that the natures of their office and of nationhood allow them to go beyond the powers given them under Article II and provided in law to secure the nation in time of danger. Congress and the Supreme Court have accepted that – particularly on foreign and security policy – there may be a right and duty to deal with other nations on an equal basis without reference to specific clauses of the Constitution. Most famously, early in 1861, President Lincoln took several measures, including summoning additional troops and spending large sums of money. This was at a time when Congress was not in session, the legislature having given no prior assent to any emergency measures. When called upon to justify his actions, Lincoln noted that it was possible 'to lose the nation and yet preserve the Constitution'.

See also *Unitary Executive Theory*

Initiative

The initiative is a device by which an individual citizen or group of citizens can – if they collect a given number of signatures on a petition – have a proposal placed directly on the ballot in a statewide election. As such, the initiative is particularly useful in cases where lawmakers refuse to enact or even to consider a law that the people want. Twenty-four US states and Washington DC allow statewide initiatives. Over 60 per cent of initiative activity has occurred in the states of Arizona, California, Colorado, North Dakota, Oregon and Washington. These states generally have lesser signature requirements than other states. The initiative is also in common use at the local and city government level.

The initiative has been recognised in the United States since at least 1777 when provision was made for it by the first constitution of Georgia. Modern use originated in the state of Oregon (2002), however, when the state's legislators adopted it by an overwhelming majority. Most of the early experiments in direct democracy during the progressive era included proposals which opted for the initiative and referendum. Several of the states that have provided for direct legislation since World War I, however, decided in several cases not to go for the whole package and have included provision for the initiative only. Today, the initiative is much more frequently used, there having been approximately five initiatives for every popular referendum since 1980. The number of such initiatives has been on the rise in recent years, a symptom of increased turbulence in state politics and government. They were used in several Western states in the 1990s, among other things to:

- test how many terms a person could serve in a state legislature or on Capitol Hill
- restrict (or enhance) personal liberty
- reduce (or increase) taxes
- decide fishing rights
- prohibit the trapping of black bears out of season.

In November 2006, there were more initiatives than at any time since the initiative process began in 1902. In descending order of popularity, the most common topics were:

1. **'Eminent domain'** proposals to stop governments from seizing property and transferring it

to private users. Nine of eleven states approved the measure.

2. **Gay marriage.** Seven states approved constitutional amendments restricting marriage to a man and a woman, bringing the total number of states that have approved such an amendment to twenty-three. Only Arizona rejected the proposal, the first state yet to do so. (Defeat was largely because of the inclusion of a provision that would have prevented the state from giving benefits to same-sex couples.)

3. The **minimum wage.** Initiatives to increase the wage and index it to inflation took place in six states and all were approved. These measures were placed on the ballot as part of a carefully co-ordinated campaign to increase support for Democratic candidates and thereby, it was hoped, influence the balance of power in Congress.

4. Abortion and stem-cell research were once again hot topics in particular states.

In 2008, Californian voters supported measures to build a high-speed rail link from Los Angeles to San Francisco; give farm animals more space in their enclosures; hand the task of redrawing state legislative districts to an independent commission; and ban same-sex marriage. However, they rejected a proposal that under-18s should inform their parents before having an abortion.

In the last two decades, initiatives have become more popular for several reasons. Key factors include the following:

1. Activists have discovered their value as a means of advancing particular interests – for liberals, this might be an issue such as environmental protection and for conservatives tax cutting or curbing abortion.

2. Some politicians have been keen to associate themselves with initiative proposals as a useful means of raising public awareness of particular subjects and their own profile. This can win them the backing – and finance – of issue activists.

3. An industry has developed to professionalise the use of initiative. Pollsters, media consultants, petition circulators and others have brought their expertise into the field and thereby made it easier to get an issue 'off the ground'. In many states, signature gathering has become a niche industry in the role of politics. Proponents now pay individuals to collect signatures. The 'initiative industry' operates not just in getting measures on to the ballot but in challenging or defending in the courts measures that have been approved by voters.

4. The news media particularly thrive on initiatives, for the attempts to raise or block contentious issues provide good stories, often with a strong human interest and great headline potential.

Sometimes a contentious issue may provoke an enthusiastic response but, usually, turnout is high only if the initiative is being held at the same time as a general election. Magleby (1994) quotes the example of Maine which stages initiatives in general election years and in the odd-numbered years between, when there is no other vote. Far more people take part in the years when offices are being contested then when there is just an issue or issues up for election. Also, in general election years, he detects a mean drop-off of 15 per cent in the number who cast votes on the propositions compared with the number who cast votes for the candidates.

See also *Direct Democracy*; *Referendum*

Interest Groups

In Britain, an interest group is usually defined as a type of pressure group, such as a business or professional association, that represents occupational interest. Trade unions world also be considered to be interest groups. There is no agreed label for pressure-group activity across the world, however, and Americans tend to speak of interest groups as covering the whole range of pressure groups. Such usage is open to question for it fails adequately to cater for myriad groups which are more concerned to promote a particular idea than to look after any specific interest. Americans often use the term 'public interest groups' to cater for those citizen activist groups that try to represent what they see as the interests of the community at large. These bodies are concerned with issues such as the quality of government, civil rights, consumerism and the environment.

Whatever their nomenclature, all such groups have some autonomy from government and political parties, and seek to influence decision-making and public policy. Here we are primarily concerned with those bodies (aka defensive, protective or sectional groups) that are concerned with one section of the population. They are primarily self-interested organisations which often offer services to their members as well as looking after their sectional interests.

The range of groups

There are thousands of economic interests in modern societies, ranging from the vast to the very small, and covering the activities of powerful groups, such as big business, investment houses and agriculture, and those of small employers who run a plumbing or electrical concern. Many are found in the economic sphere of society among the interests just listed although they are also important in the public sector. Professional associations and trades unions fall into this category, as do several major firms. Most notable among the peak organisations are the business confederations which bring together within one organisation a whole range of other organisations.

Business is the most effective area of group activity because it has the advantage of expertise, organisation and resources. In the world of industry, major US peak or umbrella organisations include the Chamber of Commerce, the National Association of Manufacturers and the Business Roundtable which collectively cater for less than a quarter of American businesses. Many large corporations – Chase Manhattan, Chrysler and American Airlines among them – are formidable in defending their own sectional interests. There are also trade associations such as the American Pharmaceutical Association and the American Electronics Association.

The business lobby is a formidable one but it would be wrong to assume that the large range of groups operates together as a powerful bargaining sector. 'Corporate America' is not a single entity with but one agreed objective. The interests of America's fifteen million businesses may

diverge; for instance, some leading manufacturers favour high protective tariffs to fend off foreign competition while others – operating especially in the export market – fear that high tariffs invite retaliation and damage to their overseas prospects. Moreover, not all these organisations focus on the same areas of decision-making, large companies (e.g., Microsoft and Union Carbide) being well represented in Washington whereas umbrella groups, such as the Chamber of Commerce, often function more strongly at state and local level.

Unions have always been less influential in America than in many European countries, such as the United Kingdom, for the workforce is less unionised than in many democracies. Unions lack the clout of major corporations and, in recent years, have been numerically in decline and generally suffered from diminishing membership. They have more influence in industrial areas, such as the Northeast, than in the traditionally agrarian-dominated South. Among labour organisations, the American Federation of Labor and Congress of Industrial Organisations (AFL/CIO) is the umbrella group of nearly seventy trade unions, such as the Teamsters (lorry drivers), International Brotherhood of Boilermakers, United Auto Workers and the International Ladies Garment Workers Union (ILGWU).

American agrarian organisations were historically influential, the agricultural community having strong connections in the Senate and the House of Representatives. The American Agriculture Movement – with a membership of mainly small farmers – tended to take a more militant line than the more conservative American Farm Bureau Federation (AFBF) while both have often found themselves in disagreement with the broadly liberal National Farmers Union (NFU). As the number of farms declined, so agribusinesses – vast farms owned by large corporations – developed in their place. The arrival of business people, familiar with different and more sophisticated techniques of lobbying, helped to change the image of agriculture.

Professional bodies cater for the needs of accountants, doctors, educators, lawyers, scientists and others, groups that have no interests in common other than their status. They may, as with the doctors and lawyers, sometimes come into conflict as, for example, in a case of medical malpractice. There is a vast array of professional groups, ranging from the powerful American Bankers Association, American Medical Association and American Bar Association to Clowns of America at the smaller end. Clowns has few resources but still operates as an interest group, seeking to protect its members' interests regarding workers' compensation, tax laws and other relevant legislation.

There are, in addition, government-related interest groups. Whereas the various tiers of government are usually the target of lobbying, they can themselves act as lobbies. State and local governments often maintain individual representation in Washington, as well as collective representation via bodies such as the Council of State Governments and the National Association of Counties, respectively, to lobby for funds on everything from new public roads to new airports. So also do organisations representing key figures in government such as the National Governors' Association and the US Conference of Mayors. Many large cities, too, such as Baltimore, Chicago and Newark, maintain an office in the federal capital where there staff represent their interests on issues ranging from budgeting to housing, from health care to transport. Cities also lobby their state capitals for various forms of financial aid and in support of, or against, legislation that has an impact upon them.

Many of the groups discussed above possess economic or professional assets, expertise, resources and, often, large memberships. All comprise groups of individuals or organisations which share common goals and seek to influence government at its various levels, federal, state and local.

Public interest groups

Public interest groups, including a range of campaigning groups and community organisations, look beyond narrow self-interest to the broader public interest. Examples include; Common Cause (which promotes bipartisan government reforms concerned with ethics in administration and open government); Ralph Nader's loose affiliation of Public Citizen groups, of which Congress Watch is the best known; the League of Women Voters; and Americans for Democratic Action. There is less disagreement between the various organisations operating in this area than in some other sectors for all are seeking to achieve goals designed to benefit the entire population.

More divisive, in some cases, are the groups that focus on minority and/or religious concerns, lobbying for civil rights. The National Association for the Advancement of Colored People (NAACP) is one of the most famous; less well-known groups include the League of United Latin American Citizens (LULAC) and the Native American Rights Fund (NARF). Muslim groups include: the Council on American–Islamic Relations (CAIR), the largest Muslim civil rights and advocacy group; the Muslim Public Affairs Council (MPAC); the American Islamic Congress (AIC); and the Free Muslims Coalition.

See also *Iron Triangle*; *Issue Networks*; *Lobbying*; *Movements*

Internet

The Internet, sometimes called simply 'the net', is a global network of computer networks linked by telephone lines that allows for the global dispersal of information. By the early twenty-first century, it had become one of the most talked-about communications channels, not just because of its explosive growth but also because it permits the dissemination of any kinds of data. The CIA handbook figures (2008) showed that 223 million Americans had access to the Internet, with some seventy million logging on each day.

Enthusiasts claim that the Internet is now a key source of political information, as voters seek out news and comment on personalities and issues. The proportion of the electorate who use the net for political purposes is growing rapidly, more concentrated among younger and more educated voters. Young Americans rely much more heavily on the Internet than do their elders. Pew (2004) found that of all Americans, 29 per cent read online news at least three times a week, 34 per cent regularly watch nightly network news on television and 42 per cent regularly read a newspaper. For younger Americans (particularly males), the Internet is second only to television as their main source of daily news.

The Internet is becoming more important as a campaigning tool. Candidates and parties have responded to the challenge it presents, spending vast sums on creating websites and e-mail address lists. In 2000, Republican John McCain employed it as an effective means of raising money, Bush used it as the place to announce his financial backers and, in some battleground states, supporters of Gore and Nader used it as a vehicle via which they could attempt to engage in mutually beneficial tactical voting. In 2004, the Internet was again an important factor in the presidential election but it was e-mail – rather than political websites – that made the biggest impact. The unsuccessful Democratic candidate, Howard Dean, raised millions of dollars in funds on the back of an e-mail campaign.

The transformation of American politics by the Internet accelerated with the approach of the 2008 White House elections. Democrats and Republicans sharply increased their use of e-mail, interactive websites, candidate and party blogs, and text messaging to raise money, organise get-out-the-vote efforts and assemble crowds for rallies. They found that the Internet was far more efficient – and less costly – than the traditional tools of politics, notably door-knocking and telephone banks. Campaigners now study popular Internet social networks, like Friendster and Facebook, as ways of reaching groups of potential supporters with similar political views or cultural interests.

What the parties and the candidates are undergoing now is in many ways similar to what has happened in other sectors of the nation – including the music industry, newspapers and retailing – as they try to adjust to, and take advantage of, the Internet as its influence spreads across American society. To a considerable extent, they are responding to, and playing catch-up with, bloggers who have demonstrated the power of their forums to harness the energy on both sides of the ideological divide.

See also *Mass Media*

Interstate Commerce Commission (ICC)

The Interstate Commerce Commission was the first independent regulatory commission established in the United States. It was set up in 1887 to regulate the interstate rail companies. It had a mandate to develop, implement and adjudicate upon fair and reasonable goods charges and levels of service that might be expected on the railways. Its brief was later extended to cover the haulage industry. The Commission's six members were appointed by the president with the consent of the Senate.

In the second half of the twentieth century, several of its functions were transferred, most notably to the Department of Transportation (created in 1966). It later lost its powers over rates and routes in rail and haulage in 1980 and then almost all of its remaining functions in 1994 before being wound up a year later. It was a victim of the deregulatory spirit of the last two decades of the century.

See also *Regulatory Commissions*

Invisible Primaries

'Invisible primaries' is a term that refers to the period of campaigning that takes place in the year prior to the 'visible' series of party primaries. At this stage, the efforts of would-be candidates are directed to gathering support, raising funds and cultivating the media.

The term was coined by Arthur T. Hadley (1976) in his book of that title. He defined it as 'that period of political time between the election of one president and the start of the first state primary to determine the next political candidates'. It is, then, the pre-primary stage in which candidates jostle to become the front-runners for their parties' nominations and vie to raise the most money.

See also *Party Primaries*

Irangate: aka the Iran–Contra Affair/ Scandal (1987)

Irangate was a major crisis of the Reagan presidency. Two officials within the National Security

Council, John Poindexter and the more junior Lieutenant Colonel Oliver North, were accused of pursuing a policy of selling arms, including Hawk missiles, to Iran in 1985 in return for the release of American hostages detained in the Lebanon by pro-Iranian militias. The proceeds of the arms sales were channelled to the Contras, right-wing rebel forces who were seeking to overthrow the left-wing Sandinista government of Nicaragua which the US administration wished to destabilise.

Both operations, the arms for hostages and the diversion of money to the guerrillas, were illegal. Altogether, at least four main laws were breached, the sale of weapons to states sponsoring terrorism being something that the president himself had publicly denounced. Congress had refused to agree to military aid for the rebel forces though it was willing to grant humanitarian assistance and keen to see the regime toppled.

The Congressional Joint Investigative Committee reported in November 1987 that president Reagan bore 'ultimate responsibility' for allowing a 'cabal of zealots' to seize control of the administration's policy but found no firm evidence that he had actually been aware of the Contra diversion. Reagan persistently claimed to have no recall of events. Some evidence was withheld on grounds of 'national security'.

In December 1993 the independent prosecutor Lawrence Walsh published his final report on Irangate. It asserted that President Reagan and Vice President Bush were fully aware of attempts to free US hostages in the Middle East in 1985–86 by means of unsanctioned arms sales to Iran.

Iraq War: the First Gulf War (1990–91)

The Gulf War or Persian War was a conflict between the Iraq of Saddam Hussein and a coalition force assembled from thirty-five nations, some three-quarters of which comprised US troops. As the Iran–Iraq War (1980–88) is sometimes referred to as the 'Gulf' or 'Persian' War, the 1990–91 fighting is sometimes known as the 'Second Gulf War', but more often simply as the 'Gulf War' or the 'First Gulf War', with the invasion of 2003 being known as the 'Second Gulf War'.

In the 1990–91conflict, the US found itself fighting an enemy to which it had previously been giving economic and military aid. During the Iran–Iraq War, American leaders were concerned about the disruption to Iraqi oil exports. They were also alarmed at the prospect of Iran achieving victory over its opponent and then proceeding to export its own Islamic revolution to other countries in the Middle East. When the war was over, however, US concern became increasingly focused on the fear of a military build-up in Iraq, its hostility to Israel and its record of human rights violations.

In late 1990, the Iraqis claimed that Kuwait was slant-drilling petroleum across its border and used this as a pretext for invasion of the oil-rich kingdom. Their action led to the imposition by the United Nations Security Council of immediate economic sanctions. The western military response – aimed at expelling Iraqi troops and liberating Kuwait – was sanctioned by the UN so that, technically, it was a UN-led invasion rather than one led by the Americans who named their air and land operations Desert Storm. The immediate justification offered for American action was the violation of Kuwaiti territorial integrity. An additional motive, however, was the wish to provide support to its long-time ally, Saudi Arabia, whose geopolitical importance in the region – not least as a key supplier of oil – was widely recognised by American politicians.

Hostilities began in January 1991. Aerial and ground combat was confined largely to Iraq, Kuwait and bordering areas of Saudi Arabia although Iraq fired missiles on Israeli cities. The coalition advance was much swifter than American generals had expected and they soon secured a decisive victory. Iraqi troops retreated from Kuwait, setting fire to Kuwaiti oilfields as they left. Coalition forces from the United States, the United Kingdom, and France pursued Iraqi forces as they fled back into Iraq, moving to within 150 miles (240 km) of Baghdad before withdrawing. Britain and the US agreed that, once the freedom of Kuwait was secured, they would not go further by seeking to remove Saddam Hussein from power. If this had been done, it is unlikely that the unity of the coalition could have been maintained. One hundred hours after the ground campaign started, President Bush declared a ceasefire and, on 27 February 1991 declared that Kuwait had been liberated.

Iraq War: the Second Gulf War (2003–)

Following the conclusion of the First Gulf War (1991), relations between the West and Iraq had remained in a state of low-level conflict marked by American and British air strikes, and sanctions and threats against Saddam Hussein. In the wake of the 11 September attacks on the World Trade Center and the apparent early success of the action in Afghanistan in 2001, the Bush administration felt that it had sufficient military justification and public support in the US for further operations against perceived threats in the Middle East. Throughout 2002, while invasion was being contemplated, it was increasingly apparent that removing Hussein from power was a major goal although the US offered to accept major changes in Iraqi military and foreign policy in lieu of this.

The stated justification for invasion included Iraqi production and use of weapons of mass destruction (WMD) which the US claimed were being stored in violation of United Nations Security Council Resolution 1441. George Bush, supported by the Blair government in Britain, claimed that these weapons posed a grave and imminent threat to the United States and its allies. Critics of the Hussein regime also pointed to the alleged Iraqi links with terrorist organisations and the mass killings and general denial of human rights under the Hussein government.

The invasion and occupation of Iraq

Prior to the invasion of Iraq, UN inspection teams searched Iraq for WMD, and were willing to continue but were forced out by the onset of war in spite of their requests for more time. On 17 March 2003, the US abandoned its failing efforts to get international endorsement for war against Iraq, and began the invasion on 20 March 2003. The invading force comprised 98 per cent United States and United Kingdom troops although several other nations also participated. The Iraqi military was defeated and Baghdad fell on 9 April 2003. On 1 May 2003, President Bush declared the end of major combat operations, terminating the Baath Party's rule and removing Saddam Hussein from office. Coalition forces ultimately captured Hussein on 13 December 2003. Careful inspections after Iraq's capitulation failed to locate any WMD, which has given rise to continued debate about the legitimacy under international law of the invasion.

Post-invasion Iraq has been plagued by violence, initially involving loyalists to the Saddam regime and members of the Baath Party, but soon extending to religious radicals and Iraqis angered by the military occupation of their country. The ongoing fighting between Sunni and Shia Iraqis was exacerbated by the involvement of outside powers and the terrorism of the al-Qaeda militant network. Insurgents employed guerrilla tactics including car bombs, improvised explosive devices, missiles, mortars, rocket-propelled grenades, snipers and suicide attacks, in addition to sabotage against the electrical, oil and water infrastructure.

Post-invasion coalition efforts involved work to establish a stable and democratic state capable of defending itself, holding itself together and overcoming insurgent attacks and internal divisions. The strife and regular killings between rival groups, however, led some commentators to detect signs of an impending civil war. More positive indications have been the tentative growth of democracy, as signified by the country's holding of free elections in 2005 and the creation – after considerable delay – of a broadly supported government based upon them. Iraqi forces begin to take greater responsibility for security, encouraging some members of the coalition to withdraw their forces. The Iraqi administration, however, found difficulty in restoring public confidence in its ability to cope with mounting disorder.

The capture and later execution of Saddam Hussein did not lead to a significant lessening of tension, as occupying coalition forces had hoped. Moreover, the discovery in April 2004 of widespread prisoner abuse by US military personnel at the Abu Ghraib gaol appeared to seriously to undermine the moral case for intervention. Graphic pictures of torture aroused widespread indignation and outrage in America, in Europe and across many parts of the Middle East.

American reactions to US military involvement

Initially, there had been strong American support for the invasion of Iraq from most politicians of both parties and from the public at large. This came under increasing strain, however, as there was mounting evidence of the failure of Iraqi and coalition toops to control the insurgency. In 2005 and 2006 there was growing sectarian violence and an increase in the number of attacks on American and other forces. The failure to improve the political and social situation in Iraq led to increasing opposition within America. The alleged failure of the Bush policy was widely cited as the key explanation for Republican setbacks in the midterm elections of November 2008.

The Iraq Study Group, established by the president in 2006, reported in December. It concluded that the situation in Iraq was 'grave and deteriorating' and that American forces were caught up in a mission that had no foreseeable end. It urged further attempts to intensify the training of Iraqi troops, so that they could assume more control for their country's future, allied to a bold diplomatic bid to improve relations with, and secure assistance from, Iran and Syria, two countries thought to be involved in the insurgency. The president responded in January 2007 with a countermove, a troop surge which involved the sending of an additional 21,000 troops and increased money for job creation and reconstruction in Iraq. Led by General David Petraeus, the new commander of US forces, there was an initial increase in violence before the surge strategy appeared to be contributing to a decline in sectarian attacks by late 2007. He felt able to speculate on the possibility of a limited troop withdrawal within a year.

The war continues to be highly controversial in the United States. Doubts remain about the legality of the initial invasion, the inadequacy of post-invasion planning and attempts at reconstruction, the cost of the war and its adverse impact on the global war against terrorism. Polls have generally pointed to a widespread public desire for an end to US involvement in Iraq at the earliest opportunity, many people wanting to see an early withdrawal of some forces and a phased withdrawal of all of them within a target date. They also indicate that many Americans continue to believe that the world is a safer place now that Saddam is no longer in power in Iraq.

Within Congress, many Democrats and some Republicans have sought to link further appropriations to a specific timetable for withdrawal. All Democratic presidential candidates, whatever their original views about the invasion, urged an early end to US military involvement in Iraq. Barack Obama argued that US troops should be out of Iraq within sixteen months of his becoming president; by the summer 2010, and for a shift in American resources towards fighting the Taliban in Afghanistan. As president, he has reiterated his pledge to bring US involvement to an end and offer financial support to Iraqi refugees in neighbouring countries.

Iron Triangle

An iron triangle is the name given to the stable and co-operative policymaking relationships that often developed between a congressional committee (and its subcommittees), an administrative agency and one or more supportive interest groups. Today, many of these relationships are wider and looser, so that triangular description for them is less often used.

For many years, there were tight bonds within these triangles. The three elements were often in close contact with each other and enjoyed a cosy association based on interdependent self-interest. Sometimes, there was movement of personnel between one position within the triangle to another. Such iron triangles often dominated areas of domestic policymaking, possessing a virtual monopoly of information in their sector. One example was the smoking/tobacco triangle (the Department of Agriculture, the House and Senate agricultural committees, and the tobacco lobby of farmers and manufacturers) in which there was a focus on crop subsidies to tobacco farmers. Others covered areas such as defence, agriculture and more specifically, the sugar industry.

The defence triangle comprised the Pentagon, the relevant committee chairs of the two chambers of Congress, and members with a constituency interest in arms manufacturing and/or the armed forces, and representatives of the arms industry who were keen to see their business benefit from federal purchases of the weapons they produced. In his farewell speech on leaving the White House (1961), President Eisenhower issued a warning about the power of the bonds within the armaments industry. He felt that what was good for those with a vested interest in developing costly armaments and weapons systems was not necessarily beneficial to the country as a whole: 'We must guard against the acquisition of unwarranted influence by the military–industrial complex . . . in order to balance and to integrate these and other forces, new and old, within the principles of our democratic system.'

In the last two decades, the autonomy of such triangles, or sub-governments, in America has been challenged by alternative centres of power, often known as 'issue networks'. As Hague and Harrop (2004) have explained, 'the iron has gone out of the triangle; now influence over decisions depends on what you know, as well as who you know'. The policies supported by the tobacco triangle came under challenge from health authorities that had been excluded from the area of tobacco policymaking. In defence policy, at times when the danger to America seemed to be less evident, expenditure on weaponry was curbed – suggesting that influences other than the elements of the triangle were a factor in determining the level of military capability.

See also *Interest Groups*; *Issue Networks*

Isolationists

Isolationists advocated American neutrality in World War I and avoidance of direct involvement in European affairs in the years that followed. They believed that their country should 'play in its own backyard'. Pure isolationists favour a non-interventionist foreign policy with protectionism and strict border controls to prevent international travel and cultural exchange.

Isolationism had a long history. George Washington echoed the views of many of the Founding Fathers when he warned Americans not to 'entangle our peace and prosperity in the toils of European ambition'. Until the end of the nineteenth century, the United States generally turned a blind eye towards matters elsewhere in the world. This view persisted as a basic tenet of US foreign policy in the 1920s and 1930s. Even when the rise of militarism in Europe and the Pacific became alarming, many Americans strongly opposed involvement in another international war that did not seem directly to threaten them. The Japanese attack on Pearl Harbor (December 1941) showed that America was vulnerable and provided the spur to American involvement in World War II.

World War II and its aftermath finally convinced many Americans that they could not avoid a major role in global affairs, as the country emerged from the hostilities as leader of the free world at a time of Cold War. Today, the United States has moved a long way from its earlier history of non-intervention. Democratic and Republican presidents have, since the late 1940s, often used intervention as a tactic of foreign policy. The events of 9/11 and the subsequent War on Terror served to strengthen the feeling that the US had no option but to engage in not just European, but also global, affairs.

Issue Advertisements (Ads)

Issue ads are similar to the usual political advertisements released on behalf of a candidate but do not use words such as 'support' or 'vote'. Moreover, while candidate ads are sponsored by a candidate or his/her organisation, issue ads are sponsored by individuals not running for office, and corporations, unions and various other pressure groups. Some advocate or oppose the election of a candidate in an implied way (sham issue ads) whereas others seek to mobilise constituents, policymakers or regulators in support of, or in opposition to, legislation (pure issue ads). Perhaps the most well-known examples were the 'Harry and Louise' commercials paid for by the Health Insurance Association of America in 1994. Harry and Louise were an imaginary couple engaged in reading the Clinton plan for health reform and discovering in the process how their health care would deteriorate.

By purporting to be about issues, issue ads evaded restrictions that would have otherwise applied to campaign finance. Until they were banned in 2002, they were widely used to promote particular causes, such as environmental protection or tax reform. They often had the effect of either helping or hurting at-risk candidates fighting for their political lives. But the law specifically said they could not endorse, oppose – or even mention by name – any particular federal candidate. In 2002, however, under the terms of the McCain–Feingold reforms, business and labour unions were prevented from directly funding 'electioneering communications', a term defined as broadcast advertising that identified a federal candidate, within thirty days of a primary or nominating convention, or sixty days of a general election. As originally drafted, the provision in the bill applied only to for-profit corporations but it was extended to incorporated, non-profit issue organisations, such as the Environmental Defense Fund or the National Rifle Association, as part of the 'Wellstone Amendment', sponsored by Senator Paul Wellstone.

In June 2007, the Supreme Court issued two decisions on campaign finance. In a consolidated ruling in the cases of *Federal Election Commission* v. *Wisconsin Right to Life* and *McCain* v. *Wisconsin Right to Life,* it held that the 2002 law was overly restrictive and that certain advertisements might be constitutionally entitled to an exception from the 'electioneering communications' provisions of the McCain–Feingold legislation. The Court's conservative majority was itself split on the issue. Roberts and Alito took a narrow approach, saying only that the issue ads in question were not subject to restrictions based on the earlier Court (2003) ruling upholding the McCain–Feingold law. Three other conservatives – Kennedy, Scalia and Thomas – supported throwing out entirely the issue ad restriction contained in McCain–Feingold.

In an opinion by Chief Justice John Roberts, the Court ruling in 2007 did not overturn the electioneering communications limits in their entirety but established a broad exemption for any ad that could have a reasonable interpretation as an ad about legislative issues. 'The First Amendment requires us to err on the side of protecting political speech rather than suppressing it', Roberts wrote: 'Where the First Amendment is implicated, the tie goes to the speaker, not the censor.' In this case, the Court decided that the ads were not election ads covered by the law but were general issue ads that did not aim to influence voters. Although the justices ruled that the

ads must still avoid explicit calls for the election or defeat of a federal candidate, their decision opened the door for advocacy groups, corporations and labour unions to unleash a barrage of issue ads in the frenetic weeks before voters went to the polls in November 2008.

See also *McCain–Feingold Campaign Finance Reform Act*

Issue Networks

Issue networks are policymaking relationships that involve a large number of participants with different degrees of interest in, and commitment to, the policies and problems that bring them together. They form an open and sometimes highly visible sub-government.

In the last two decades, the autonomy of iron triangles has been challenged by the rise of networks which are wider and looser, and involve more players involved in discussions in a given policy area, including the research institutes and the media. Media scrutiny and the attentions of consumer protest groups have led to a more critical analysis of policymaking processes so that secret deals and mutual back-scratching are now less frequent or effective.

In the issue networks of today, relationships are not continuous or particularly close, and there is less interdependence than was the case in the days of iron triangles. They have lost much of their stranglehold over policymaking, and new participants, be they environmental or human rights activists, research bodies or consumer groups, have come into the equation. Grant and Ashbee (2002) have illustrated the vast array of groups now involved in the development of US health policy, ranging from health care providers (the AMA and the American Dental Association) to the health insurance companies (Health Insurance Association of America, HIAA), pharmaceutical and medical equipment manufacturers (Health Industry Manufacturers' Association), employers (National Federation of Independent Business) and representatives of big business (Chamber of Commerce).

See also *Interest Groups*; *Iron Triangle*

J

Jackson, Andrew (1767–1845)

Andrew Jackson was the seventh president (1829–37). He served in the War against Great Britain (1812–15), acting as commander of the victorious American forces in the Battle of New Orleans (1815). As a soldier, he was said to be as 'tough as old hickory wood' on the battlefield, hence his nickname 'Old Hickory'. He became a national hero as a result of his bravery and success.

Jackson was a dominant – but politically divisive – figure in Tennessee politics in the 1820s and 1830s. He revived the old Republican Party, rechristening it as the Democratic Party. Soon after his election as president in 1829, his supporters wanted to give posts in the federal bureaucracy to party members to strengthen party loyalty – thus, in effect, he was responsible for introducing the 'spoils system'. He later called for the abolition of the Electoral College and a term limit of one term on the presidential office although he himself served for eight years.

Andrew Jackson was a believer in a strong and initiating presidency based on popular support. He was the first president who could claim to be truly elected by the people, hence references to the era of 'Jacksonian democracy'. Whereas in the past, state legislatures had appointed most members of the Electoral College, by 1828, all but those from Delaware and South Carolina were popularly elected. Moreover, the removal of ownership of property as a criterion for voting extended the franchise. As president, by virtue of his popular mandate, he sought to act as the direct representative of the common person. He was able to appeal over the heads of congressmen directly to the American public. This gave him widespread popular backing in his conflict with Congress. He rejected congressional bills, his action being based not on any feeling that they were unconstitutional but rather upon disagreement with what was being proposed.

Jackson, Jesse (1941–)

Jesse Louis Jackson is a Baptist minister, civil rights activist and prominent member of the American Left. He is the father of Congressman Jesse Jackson Jnr.

Jackson was a Democratic presidential candidate in 1984 and 1988. He has never held elective office but has maintained a high profile – largely as a result of media visibility. An effective, passionate orator, he has shown a strong interest in the rights of minority groups and in issues of peace and war. While he was initially critical of the 'Third Way' or more moderate policies of Bill Clinton, he became a key ally in gaining African American support for him and eventually became a close adviser to, and friend of, the Clinton family. Clinton awarded Jesse Jackson the Medal of Freedom, the nation's highest honour bestowed on civilians.

Jackson was highly critical of the Florida election result in 2000, alleging that numerous irregularities and examples of intimidation of potential black voters meant that the outcome was deeply flawed. Four years later, he was prominent in a challenge to the voting results in Ohio, suggesting that the state's voting machines were 'rigged' and that some African Americans were forced to stand in line for six hours in the rain before voting. High-ranking Democrats, including John Kerry, distanced themselves from his claims, despite a personal request for Kerry's assistance. The Senate and the House Judiciary Committee overwhelmingly rejected his findings.

In the movement for civil rights, the black church played an influential role in communicating ideas and information. Black ministers, such as Dr Martin Luther King and Jesse Jackson, became nationally recognised figures.

Jefferson, Thomas (1743–1826)

Thomas Jefferson was the main author of the Declaration of Independence (1776), wartime governor of Virginia (1779–81) and author of the Virginia Statute for Religious Freedom (1779, 1786), one of the most influential of the Founding Fathers, first American secretary of state (1789–93), second vice president (1797–1801), third president 1801–09), and leader of the Democratic Republican Party which dominated American politics for a quarter of a century and was the precursor of the modern-day Democratic Party.

Before becoming president, Jefferson had in the past been in favour of restricting the power of the Executive in the Constitution but, in office, he acted in a way that enhanced its role and influence. He did not share Washington's view of the 'baneful effects of the spirit of party' and instead worked to ensure that the party faithful were elected. He saw the value of co-operating closely with those in Congress – led by Madison – who were sympathetic to him. In this way, he could hope to implement his legislative programme. Apart from this party role, Jefferson is also remembered for negotiating and signing the Louisiana Purchase in 1803. Although the Constitution made no provision for the acquisition of new land, he took action without seeking prior congressional approval and in doing so doubled the landmass of his country.

See also *Judicial Review*; *Louisiana Purchase (1803)*

Jim Crow

The term 'Jim Crow' originated in a song performed in the 1830s by a white minstrel show entertainer Daddy Rice. It concerned a runaway slave who composed a song and dance in which the name was used. Rice covered his face with charcoal paste or burnt cork to resemble a black man, then sang and danced a routine in caricature of a silly black person. The term was taken up by white comics and came into general use as a label for all black Americans. By the 1850s, this Jim Crow character, one of several stereotypical images of black inferiority in the nation's popular culture, was a standard act in the minstrel shows of the day.

In the last quarter of the nineteenth century, the term became identified with racist laws and actions that deprived African Americans of their civil rights by defining blacks as inferior to whites. Several laws were enacted in the American South and border states that allowed persecution and segregation to exist. It became illegal for black people and white people to travel together or to use other public facilities, such as hospitals and swimming baths. The statutes were often known as the Jim Crow laws, a generic name for all laws and practices that enforced segregation. Jim Crow was more than a series of rigid anti-black laws. It was a way of life. Under Jim Crow, African Americans were relegated to the status of second-class citizens.

See also *Segregation*

Johnson, Lyndon (1908–73)

The assassination of John F. Kennedy thrust Lyndon Johnson into the presidency as the thirty-sixth president. He was widely considered to be one of the most able and brilliant politicians of his generation. He left office a little more than five years later as one of the least popular presidents in American history.

Born and brought up in Texas, not far from Johnson City which his family had helped settle, Lyndon Baines Johnson enrolled in Southwest Texas State Teachers' College (now Texas State University–San Marcos). He later wrote of how his experience in teaching mostly Mexican children in La Salle County had made him acutely aware of the disadvantage endured by some groups:

I shall never forget the faces of the boys and the girls in that little Welhausen Mexican School, and I remember even yet the pain of realising and knowing then that college was closed to practically every one of those children because they were too poor. And I think it was then that I made up my mind that this Nation could never rest while the door to knowledge remained closed to any American.

In 1937 Johnson was elected to the House of Representatives on a New Deal platform, where he served six terms. Johnson was elected to the Senate in 1948 and soon achieved prominence. He served on many prestigious committees. In 1951, he was elected minority whip for the Democratic Party and two years later became its minority leader. When the Democrats achieved control of the Senate in 1955, he became Senate majority leader, at forty-six the youngest majority leader ever. He was highly effective, often keeping the Senate in session into the night to complete its work. With rare skills of arm twisting, persuasion and organisation, he obtained passage of a number of key Eisenhower measures. In 1957, he helped engineer the passage of the 1957 Civil Rights Acts. This foreshadowed his future strong position on civil rights.

Johnson was a leading candidate for the Democratic presidential nomination in 1960 but lost to Kennedy who then chose him as his running mate. Johnson reluctantly accepted, although the two men were never close and Johnson was often snubbed by White House staffers who reputedly mocked him behind his back as 'Uncle Cornpone'. In November 1963, he was riding two cars behind the president in the motorcade, on the day when Kennedy was assassinated.

The Johnson presidency (1963–69)

Johnson's most significant and long-lasting policies were part of his mission 'to build a great society, a place where the meaning of man's life matches the marvels of man's labour'. In his first years of office he obtained the passage of one of the most extensive legislative programmes in American history. As part of his attempt to fight poverty, he introduced measures such as: the Job Corps, to provide vocational training for disadvantaged youth; Volunteers in Service of America (VISTA), a domestic Peace Corps; and Head Start, to instruct disadvantaged pre-schoolers. In the area of health provision, Medicare and Medicaid were established to provide medical insurance for those over sixty-five and those too poor to pay. In addition, the first environmental legislation was passed.

Probably the most well-known achievement of the Great Society programme was the successful passage of civil rights legislation which had been blocked in Congress during the period of the Kennedy presidency. The legislation included voting rights legislation that increased minority voting. In addition, the Civil Rights Act – actively enforced by the Justice Department – outlawed discrimination in all aspects of American society. Yet, in spite of such advances, between 1964 and 1967 race riots broke out on a regular basis in some American cities. Nevertheless, two overriding crises had been gaining momentum since 1965. Despite the beginning of new anti-poverty and anti-discrimination programmes, unrest and rioting in black ghettos troubled the nation. President Johnson steadily exerted his influence against segregation and on behalf of law and order but there was no early solution.

Overshadowing much of the Johnson era was increasing US involvement in Vietnam, which came to dominate his administration, following a landslide victory in the 1964 presidential election. In 1964, Johnson won the presidency with 61 per cent of the vote and had the widest popular margin in American history – more than fifteen million votes. He received broad congressional approval to prevent Communist aggression from North Vietnam against US forces and the South Vietnamese people. Following, an attack on an American base, Johnson responded by ordering a sustained air attack, known as 'Rolling Thunder', on targets in North Vietnam and he dispatched American ground troops to defend the South. As the scale of American involvement increased, American opinion became more divided and anti-war demonstrations increased. Despite the president's efforts to achieve a settlement, hostilities continued. Faced with mounting opposition, in March 1968 Johnson announced that he would not seek re-election.

Under Johnson, the country made spectacular explorations of space in a programme he had championed since its beginning. When three astronauts successfully orbited the moon in December 1968, Johnson congratulated them: 'You've taken . . . all of us, all over the world, into a new era.' When he left office, peace talks over Vietnam were underway. He did not live to see their outcome under his successor for he died suddenly of a heart attack at his Texas ranch on 22 January 1973.

Johnson's period in the White House seemed at first to confirm that the presidency had the power to produce notable achievements. A honeymoon period after the death of Kennedy and re-election in 1964 gave him the opportunity to pass much-needed legislation, and his skills in the art of political persuasion (political arm twisting) enabled him to persuade congressional leaders of the importance of working with him, his position helped by the massive majority that his Democratic Party had in both chambers. The power of the presidency to achieve massive social change was at its peak in these days of the 'Imperial Presidency'.

Much of Johnson's success in the domestic era derived from his ability to achieve support on Capitol Hill. He urged his aides and Cabinet members to get to know more about the key figures in Congress and what mattered to them. What was sometimes known as the 'Johnson treatment' 'ran the gamut of human emotions', from accusation and cajolery to tears and threats. Writing of the relationship with members of Congress, two journalists, Evans and Novak (1966), noted the technique:

Johnson anticipated them before [interjections] could be spoken. He moved in close, his face a scant millimetre from his target, his eyes widening and narrowing, his eyebrows rising and falling. From his pockets poured slips, memos, statistics. Mimicry, humor and the genius of analogy made The Treatment an almost hypnotic experience and rendered the target stunned and helpless.

See also *Civil Rights Legislation*; *Great Society*; *Health Provision*; *Vietnam War*; *Voting Rights Act*

Joint Chiefs of Staff

The Joint Chiefs of Staff is the principal military advisory panel to the United States president and other government agencies. It comprises the chiefs of the US Air Force, Army, Navy and the commandant of the Marine Corps.

The Joint Chiefs of Staff do not have operational command of American military forces. Their primary responsibility is to ensure the personnel readiness, policy, planning and training of their respective military services for the combatant commanders to utilise.

Judges

American judges operate in two parallel systems of courts that, between them, cover the range of civil and criminal cases. There are the state court systems, established under individual state constitutions, and the federal judicial system which has gained in importance as the country has expanded and the amount of legislation passed by Congress has increased.

An old adage of American politics states that 'a judge is a lawyer who knows a senator or governor'. Although an oversimplification, the remark does highlight that the selection process of judges is highly political whether at federal or state level. In practice, there are two methods of choosing judges in the United States. Popular election is the means by which most or all judges are chosen in thirty-one states. In other cases, the governor may make the appointment or members of the elected legislature may make the choice. Appointment is used within the federal system.

All federal judges and Supreme Court justices are appointed by the president. The typical Supreme Court justice has generally been white, Protestant, well off, and of high social status although there were two females and one black American member of the Court at the turn of the twenty-first century. Since then, with the death of Chief Justice Rehnquist and the retirement of Justice Sandra Day O'Connor, George W. Bush has been able to make two new appointments, John Roberts to the senior position, and Samuel Alito, an Italian American, as an associate. Many who have served on the Court have come from politically active families and/or been politically active themselves, in several cases having previously held political office.

In the lower federal courts, middle-class appointees are common but there has been an attempt by recent presidents to achieve a more diverse judiciary by appointing more women and members of ethnic minority groups. Bill Clinton appointed 376 justices of whom 110 were women and ninety-one were members of ethnic minorities. George W. Bush also demonstrated an interest in a diversified bench, continuing the pattern established by his recent predecessors.

George Bush did, however, show signs of seeking to adjust the composition of the judiciary in a more conservative way. In so doing, he sought advice from the Federalist Society for Law and Public Policy that was formed in the early 1980s. Its members draw inspiration from James Madison, one of the Founding Fathers, who, on occasion, railed against the power of central government. Members of society played an influential role in the impeachment proceedings against President Clinton and in the Florida legal offensive which brought Bush to power in 2001. They are trying to steer the judiciary away from the liberalism of the past, and as a means of fulfilling this agenda, they seek out ideologically acceptable candidates who might become suitable judges. Most members of George W. Bush's vetting panel for nominees belonged to the organisation.

No special training is required for judges, even for those who serve on the Supreme Court. All associate justices have been lawyers but only since 1957 have all members possessed law degrees.

See also *Federalist Society*; *Judicial Activism*; *Judicial Restraint*; *Judicial Review*

Judicial Activism

Judicial activism refers to the view that the courts should comprise a coequal branch of government and act as active partners in shaping government policy – especially in sensitive cases, such as those dealing with abortion and desegregation. Supporters tend to be more interested in justice, 'doing the right thing', than in the exact letter of the text. They see the courts as having a role to look after the groups with little political influence, such as the poor and minorities. Formally, judicial activism is considered the opposite of judicial restraint but it is also used pejoratively to describe judges who endorse a particular agenda.

Such a conception means that the justices move beyond acting as umpires in the political game and become creative participants. An exponent of judicial activism was Chief Justice Earl Warren. His court was known for a series of liberal judgments on matters ranging from school desegregation to the rights of criminals. In his era, decisions were made which boldly and broadly changed national policy. Although alleged activism may occur in many ways, some of the most debated cases involve courts exercising judicial review to strike down statutes as unconstitutional.

Conservative opinion is generally hostile to judicial activism. Ronald Reagan spoke of his intention 'to go right on appointing highly qualified individuals of the highest personal integrity to the bench, individuals who understand the danger of short-circuiting the electoral process and disenfranchising the people through judicial activism'. Current Chief Justice Roberts, in his confirmation hearing, observed that:

> Judges are like umpires. Umpires don't make the rules; they apply them. The role of an umpire and a judge is critical. They make sure everybody plays by the rules. But it is a limited role. Nobody ever went to a ballgame to see the umpire.

Judicial Restraint

Judicial restraint is the notion that the Supreme Court should not seek to impose its views on other branches of government or on the states unless there is a clear violation of the Constitution. This implies a passive role. Some justices have urged that they should avoid conflicts and that one way of doing so is to leave issues of social improvement to the appropriate parts of the federal and state governments. Advocates of this position have felt that it would be unwise and wrong to dive into the midst of political battles, even to support policies they might personally favour. Associate Justice Anthony Kennedy has taken this view, asking:

'... Was I appointed for life to go around answering ... great questions and suggesting answers to Congress?' He has provided his own answer: 'That's not our function ... it's very dangerous for people who are not elected, who have lifetime positions, to begin taking public stances on issues that political branches of government must wrestle with.'

The reactions of the majority of justices on the Rehnquist and Roberts Courts suggest that they are exponents of judicial restraint. They do not see it as their task to act as the guardians of individual liberties and civil rights for minority groups. Of the former, Biskupic (2000) observed: 'Gone is the self-consciously loud voice the Court once spoke with, boldly stating its position and calling upon the people and other institutions of government to follow.' Yet this view of the Rehnquist Court and its alleged judicial restraint has been questioned by some writers. In the words of one of them, for all of the lip-service paid to judicial self-restraint, 'most of the current justices appear entirely comfortable intervening in all manner of issues, challenging state as well as national power, and underscoring the Court's role as final arbiter of constitutional issues'.

Judicial Review

Judicial review refers to the power of any court to refuse to enforce a law or official act based on law because, in the view of the judges, it conflicts with the Constitution.

Under the doctrine of judicial review, the courts are granted the power to interpret the Constitution and to declare void actions of other branches of government if they are found to breach the document. As explained by Stone (2003) in reference to the situation in the United States, it is 'the power of any judge of any court, in any case at any time, at the behest of any litigant party, to declare a law unconstitutional'. Constitutional issues can therefore be raised at any point in the ordinary judicial system although it is the Supreme Court that arbitrates in any matter which has broad significance. Court pronouncements on issues of constitutionality are final and binding for all other courts and governmental authorities, state or federal.

Judicial review is particularly important in federal systems to ensure that each layer of government keeps to its respective sphere. The function was not written into the American Constitution but the function was acquired gradually by the justices themselves. In particular, the ruling of the Supreme Court in the case of *Marbury* v. *Madison* in 1803 was decisive, for the Marshall Court struck down part of the Judiciary Act of 1789 as unconstitutional, thereby highlighting the key role of the Court in determining the meaning of the Constitution. Seven year later, in *Fletcher* v. *Peck* (1810), it went further, extending the scope of judicial review by assuming the right to decide on the constitutionality of state laws.

Although many of the congressional statutes invalidated by the Court have been relatively minor laws, some major pieces of legislation have been affected. Examples include the Missouri Compromise (an 1820–21 Congressional agreement that saw the territories of Missouri and Maine become states of the Union), a federal income tax law, child labour laws, New Deal economic recovery acts, the post-Watergate campaign finance law, statutes to curb pornography on the Internet, efforts to allow victims of gender-motivated violence to sue their attackers in federal court for compensatory damages, amendments to a landmark age-discrimination law and the line-item veto, among them. President Franklin Roosevelt's New Deal programme provoked an unprecedented clash between the Court and the legislative and executive branches in the 1930s. At his instigation, Congress in the 1930s enacted a series of laws aimed at ending the Great Depression and restoring the nation's economic well-being. Eight major statutes fell foul of the Supreme Court early in the presidency, as did President Truman's seizure of the steel mills in 1952 to prevent a strike. Recent cases have included the following:

- In 1997 the Court threw out a major provision of the Brady Act (a law aimed at some measure of federal gun control) which required state or local law enforcement officials to conduct background checks on prospective gun purchasers. The Court said Congress had no power to require states to implement federal regulatory programmes.

- In the same year, the Court threw out a new federal law aimed at limiting access by minors to sexually oriented material on the Internet (*Reno* v. *American Civil Liberties Union*). The Court said that the Communications Decency Act violated the First Amendment by suppressing constitutionally protected speech for adults.
- In 1998, the Court struck down a law giving the president the power to cancel individual spending items and certain tax benefits contained in laws passed by Congress (*Clinton* v. *City of New York*). The Court said that the line-item veto unconstitutionally gave the president the power to change unilaterally the text of duly enacted laws.

In exercising its power of review, the Court normally decides on the basis of precedent (*stare decisis* – stand by decisions made) but, on occasion, it has spectacularly reversed a previous decision and thus enabled the Court to adapt to changing situations and give a lead. The judgment in *Plessy* v. *Ferguson* (1896), which allowed for segregation on the basis that separate facilities were not necessarily unequal, was reversed in the *Brown* v. *Board of Education (Topeka, Kansas)* ruling (1954) when it was decided that such facilities were 'inherently unequal'. The case referred to public education but campaigners rightly saw its wider implications.

Supporters of judicial review argue that any government based on a written constitution requires some mechanism to prevent laws from being passed that violate that constitution. Otherwise, the document would be meaningless, and the legislature, with the power to enact any laws whatsoever, would be the supreme arm of government. Alexander Hamilton set out the case for review in *The Federalist Papers* (78):

The courts were designed to be an intermediate body between the people and the legislature, in order, among other things, to keep the latter within the limits assigned to their authority. The interpretation of the laws is the proper and peculiar province of the courts. A constitution is, in fact, and must be regarded by the judges, as a fundamental law. It therefore belongs to them to ascertain its meaning,

as well as the meaning of any particular act proceeding from the legislative body. If there should happen to be an irreconcilable variance between the two, that which has the superior obligation and validity ought, of course, to be preferred; or, in other words, the Constitution ought to be preferred to the statute, the intention of the people to the intention of their agents.

In 1820, Thomas Jefferson expressed his profound anxieties about the doctrine, based on his fear of excessive judicial power:

You seem . . . to consider the judges as the ultimate arbiters of all constitutional questions; a very dangerous doctrine indeed, and one which would place us under the despotism of an oligarchy. Our judges are as honest as other men, and not more so. They have, with others, the same passions for party, for power, and the privilege of their corps . . . Their power [is] the more dangerous as they are in office for life, and not responsible, as the other functionaries are, to the elective control. The Constitution has erected no such single tribunal, knowing that to whatever hands confided, with the corruptions of time and party, its members would become despots. It has more wisely made all the departments co-equal and co-sovereign within themselves.

Judicial review is now a firmly established part of American constitutional law. There are are some who disagree with the doctrine, or argue that it is unconstitutional. They do so for two reasons:

1. The power of review is not specifically delegated to the Supreme Court in the Constitution.
2. The Tenth Amendment states that any power that is not delegated by the Constitution is reserved to the states, or people.

Although the Constitution does not explicitly authorise judicial review, neither does it explicitly prevent it. But justices have used judicial review sparingly, particularly with regard to federal statutes, only twice (*Marbury* and the *Dred Scott* v. *Sandford* case) striking down acts of Congress before the Civil War. It became a little more frequent thereafter, particularly in the 1920s but, in the whole history of the country – during which Congress has passed many thousands of statutes – the Court has exercised its power to rule laws or parts of them unconstitutional on only about 150 occasions.

See also *Court-packing Scheme*; Marbury *v.* Madison *(1803)*

Judiciary

The judiciary is the branch of government that determines the outcome of legal disputes. It is responsible for the authoritative interpretation of law and its application to particular cases. Accordingly, judiciaries have three main functions:

- To resolve disputes between individuals, adjudicating in controversies within the law's limits
- To interpret the law, determining what it means and how it applies in particular situations, thereby assessing guilt or innocence of those on trial
- To act as guardians of the law, taking responsibility for applying its rules without fear or favour, as well as securing the liberties of the person and ensuring governments and peoples comply with the 'spirit' of the Constitution.

Liberal democracies such as the United States, along with Australia, Canada, France, Italy, the United Kingdom and many other countries, have independent judiciaries charged with responsibility for upholding the rule of law and ensuring that there exists a *reichstaat*, a state based on law.

Justice Department

The Justice Department was established by congressional act in 1870 as 'an executive department of the government of the United States' with the Attorney General as its head. The department was to handle the legal business of the United States and was given control over all criminal prosecutions and civil suits affecting the whole country. In addition, the act gave the Attorney General and the department control over federal law enforcement. To assist the Attorney General, the 1870 Act created the Office of the Solicitor General.

The 1870 Act is the foundation upon which the Department of Justice still rests although its structure has changed over the years, with the addition of the Deputy Attorneys General and the formation of the Divisions. At one time the Attorney General gave legal advice to Congress as well as to the president but this practice ceased in 1819 because of the workload involved. The attorney has a seat in the US Cabinet. His or her tasks include supervision of the FBI, federal marshals, US attorneys and the team of lawyers who represent the US before the federal courts, as well as overseeing the implementation of US anti-crime and anti-trust policies.

The Department of Justice has become the world's largest law office and the central agency for enforcement of federal laws. Its mission statement sets out its core role:

To enforce the law and defend the interests of the United States according to the law; to ensure public safety against threats foreign and domestic; to provide federal leadership in preventing and controlling crime; to seek just punishment for those guilty of unlawful behavior; and to ensure fair and impartial administration of justice for all Americans.

The building in which the department is housed was renamed in 2001 in honour of former Attorney General Robert F. Kennedy.

K

Kennedy Assassination

On Friday, 22 November 1963, when he was hardly past his first thousand days in office, John Fitzgerald Kennedy was fatally wounded by an assassin's bullets as his presidential motorcade wound through Dallas, Texas. Kennedy was the youngest man elected president. He was also the youngest to die.

Lee Harvey Oswald was charged with the crime but, before he could be put on trial, he also was murdered two days later by Jack Ruby. The ten-month investigation of the Warren Commission concluded that Oswald had acted alone in killing the president. In 1979, however, the House Select Committee on Assassinations (charged with investigating the Kennedy and King assassinations) declared that, although Oswald was responsible, his action may have been part of a conspiracy. Discussion of the subject is still surrounded by much speculation, the circumstances of the shooting having spawned a range of theories. None has gained the general acceptance of mainstream academics, no single compelling alternative to the Warren findings having emerged.

See also *Kennedy, John*

Kennedy, Edward (1932–2009)

Edward (Ted) Kennedy was until 2009 the Senior senator from Massachusetts. He was the younger brother of President John F. Kennedy and Senator Robert F. Kennedy, both of whom were assassinated, and the father of congressman Patrick J. Kennedy. In recent years, he was the most prominent living member of the Kennedy family and one of the most recognisable and influential Senate Democrats.

Elected as a Democrat in 1962 to complete the final two years of John F. Kennedy's term, Edward Kennedy remained in the Senate until his death and was at that time its second longest-serving member. As a staunch and influential supporter of liberal principles and causes, he was active in his efforts to make quality health provision accessible to all Americans. He also advocated education and immigration reform, raising the minimum wage, improving the rights of workers and their families, the extension of civil rights, legalised same-sex marriage, more generous assistance for those with disablities, greater social security and a cleaner and healthier environment. He served on several committees, including the Judiciary Committee, and became one of the most enduring icons of his party. He was noted for his skills as a backroom negotiator and for his ability to make deals with presidents and legislators of either party, for the purpose of achieving a compromise and advancing a cause that he regarded as worthwhile.

In May 2008, doctors announced that Kennedy had a malignant brain tumour for which he underwent brain surgery in the following month. On 20 January 2009, he suffered a seizure during Barack Obama's presidential inaugural luncheon. (He had, over previous months, expressed his strong support for the Obama candidature). He died in August 2009.

Kennedy, Chappaquiddick and its impact

The Chappaquiddick incident refers to the circumstances surrounding a car crash that led to the death in 1969 of Mary Jo Kopechne, a former staff member of Robert Kennedy's 1968 presidential campaign. Edward Kennedy drove the car off a bridge into Poucha Pond and managed to swim to safety but his passenger drowned in the car. He left the scene and did not call the authorities until after her body was discovered the following day. He pleaded guilty to leaving the scene of an accident and received a suspended jail sentence of two months. The circumstances surrounding the event were confused but the incident was to dog Kennedy's political career and seriously damaged his presidential ambitions.

Kennedy was urged to run for the presidency in 1972 and 1976 but chose not to do so for 'family reasons'. He eventually relented and ran against the Democratic incumbent, Jimmy Carter, in 1980. After a promising start to his campaign, in which he won ten primaries, he lost popularity – in part because of doubts about his character and past conduct, both of which were much assailed by his opponents.

Kennedy, John (1917–63)

Born in Massachusetts and of Irish descent, John Fitzgerald Kennedy was the eldest son of Joseph Kennedy and brother of Robert and Edward. Graduating from Harvard in 1940, he entered the Navy and later sustained grave injuries when, as commander of the USS *PT-109* in the South Pacific, his boat was attacked by the Japanese. Back from the war, he became a Democratic congressman from the Boston area, advancing in 1953 to the Senate. In the same year, he married Jacqueline and two years later wrote *Profiles in Courage* which won the Pulitzer Prize in History.

Having almost gained the Democratic nomination for vice president in 1956, he became the Democratic candidate for the presidency in 1960 and argued the case for his New Frontiers platform. Millions watched his assured performance in the television debates against his Republican opponent, Vice President Richard Nixon.

Winning by a narrow margin in the popular vote, Kennedy became the first Roman Catholic and thirty-fifth president, the youngest person ever to be elected to that office.

In his Inaugural Address, he invited Americans to 'Ask not what your country can do for you, ask what you can do for your country.' As president, he set out to redeem his campaign pledge to get America moving again, his economic programmes launching the country on its longest sustained expansion since World War II. On the domestic front, however, Kennedy is better known for responding to the demands of the civil rights movement and for new civil rights legislation. His vision of America extended to the quality of the national culture and the central role of the arts in a vital society.

Kennedy wanted America to resume its old mission as the first nation dedicated to the revolution of human rights. With the Alliance for Progress and the Peace Corps, he brought American idealism to the aid of developing nations. But the hard reality of the Communist challenge remained. Shortly after his inauguration, he permitted a band of Cuban exiles to invade their homeland in a bid to overthrow the Communist regime of Fidel Castro. The 'Bay of Pigs' raid was a fiasco, and the American failure encouraged the Soviet Union to renew its campaign against West Berlin. Kennedy responded by reinforcing the Berlin garrison, by increasing America's military capacity, and by making new efforts in outer space. After the erection of the Berlin Wall, Moscow relaxed its pressure in central Europe.

Instead, however, the Russians sought to install nuclear missiles in Cuba. When this was discovered by air reconnaissance in October 1962, Kennedy imposed a quarantine on all offensive weapons bound for Cuba. While the world trembled on the brink of nuclear war, the Russians backed down and agreed to remove the missiles. Kennedy contended that both sides had a vital interest in stopping the spread of nuclear weapons and slowing the arms race, and signed the test ban treaty in 1963.

Kennedy was assassinated on 22 November 1963 in Dallas, Texas. The event was a highly poignant moment in American history, for many young people in America and around the world regarded the youthful President Kennedy as someone who shared their hopes and aspirations for a better and more just world. In surveys of US presidents, the public continues to rank him as one of the greatest or near-greatest presidents, though academic opinion tends to place him in the above-average category. The circumstances of his death did much for his reputation for, given the short period of his presidency, there was inevitably a limit to what he could achieve. Indeed, his social programme of tackling civil rights issues, reducing poverty and introducing Medicare provision was stalled in Congress at the time of his assassination.

Kennedy contrived to give the impression that he was committed to racial equality, using sympathetic rhetoric and making symbolic gestures of support. He had not planned extensive use of executive authority to help black Americans, however, and, on becoming president, did not immediately tackle the issue of civil rights. There was some disappointment with the lack of progress, and it took black activism to galvanise the administration into action. Similarly, he originally opposed the proposed March on Washington in 1963 although he came to endorse it and tried to ensure that it proceeded peacefully on an interracial basis and could contribute to support for his civil rights legislation. Yet, if Kennedy was slow in promoting change, perhaps this was because of his awareness of the risks involved. He understood the scale of Southern white opposition to his moves on integration and feared that resentment in the South might also inspire a white backlash against the civil rights movement in the North. It took some courage to compromise his party's prospects in the South and his own prospects of re-election but, when prodded into action, he became genuinely committed to the cause.

The early 1960s saw the peak of enthusiasm for presidential power. There was a widespread belief that social ailments were amenable to the application of money, and this confidence in the power of economic growth and social engineering enormously enhanced the presidency. It seemed to be the only institution that could solve problems. Kennedy was an activist president, prepared to use the power of his office to promote social change and seek to improve the well-being of disadvantaged Americans.

See also *Kennedy Assassination*; *Television and Politics*

Kennedy, Robert (1925–68)

Robert ('Bobby') was the seventh of nine children of Ambassador Joseph P. Kennedy and the younger brother of President John F. Kennedy (JFK). Having completed a law degree, he served as counsel to a US Senate committee investigating labour unions in the 1950s, leading to his well-known and highly personal feud with Teamsters leader Jimmy Hoffa. Kennedy relentlessly exposed Hoffa's corruption in financial and electoral actions and eventually faced him in open televised hearings during his period as Attorney General.

Robert Kennedy's political career was closely associated with that of his older brother. He managed JFK's successful campaigns for the Senate (1952) and the presidency (1960), and then became Attorney General during the Kennedy presidency. After his brother's assassination, he briefly served the Johnson administration, then successfully ran as an 'outsider' candidate as Senator from New York. In early 1968, he declared his own candidacy for the presidency in a battle for control of the direction of the Democratic Party. He was shot by a young Palestinian, Sirhan Sirhan, at the Ambassador Hotel in Los Angeles on 5 June 1968, moments after delivering a speech to supporters upon winning the California primary. He died early the next morning. It has been suggested that Sirhan did not act alone and that CIA operatives involved in the Bay of Pigs invasion were present at the hotel at the time of the assassination.

Robert Kennedy was one of the most trusted advisers of JFK, particularly during the Cuban Missile Crisis in which he helped develop the strategy to blockade Cuba instead of initiating a military strike. President Kennedy once remarked that: 'If I want something done and done immediately I rely on the Attorney General. He is very much the doer in this administration, and has an organisational gift I have rarely if ever seen surpassed.' Robert Kennedy was also active in the African American movement for civil rights, a cause that seemed to envelop much of his public and private life. As Attorney General he was instrumental in bringing about the total desegregation of the administration. He was also responsible for many of the initiatives taken by his brother. After initial mutual suspicion, he and Martin Luther King became admirers of each other's contribution and, on King's assassination, he delivered a moving tribute.

Kennedy had initially supported the Vietnam War but later reversed his position, one of several moves that led to his detachment from – and eventual break with – the Johnson administration.

Kerry, John (1943–)

Born in Colorado, John Forbes Kerry was brought up in Massachusetts. On graduating from Yale, he volunteered to serve in Vietnam, seeing this as 'the right thing to do' for 'to whom much is given, much is required'. And he felt he had an obligation to give something back to his country. John Kerry served two tours of duty. On his second tour, he serve on a Swift Boat in the river deltas, one of the most dangerous assignments of the war and was awarded a Silver Star, a Bronze Star with Combat V and three Purple Hearts. On returning from service, however, he became a spokesperson for the Vietnam Veterans Against the War, in April 1971 testifying before the Senate Foreign Relations Committee and posing the question 'How do you ask a man to be the last man to die for a mistake?'

In 1984, Kerry was elected to the Senate, where he is currently serving his fourth term as the junior Democratic representative for his home state. He chairs the Senate Committee on Small Business and Entrepreneurship, serves on three others (including the prestigious Foreign Relations Committee) and twelve subcommittees. In 2003, he announced that he would launch a presidential challenge and came from behind to win his party's nomination. Running against George W. Bush, a wartime incumbent, Kerry came close to winning in November 2004. He was portrayed by his conservative opponents as a staunch liberal and was much criticised by the

president for 'flip-flops' during the campaign, especially over Iraq. In the election, he won more than 59.03 million votes (48.3 per cent), the second-highest number of votes ever for a defeated candidate for the presidency, and 251 electoral votes in the Electoral College.

Kerry is a member of the Democratic Leadership Council which advances centrist and liberal positions on a range of issues. He is broadly seen as being slightly to the left of many of his Senate colleagues. He supports abortion rights, civil unions for same-sex couples and most gun-control laws, and opposes capital punishment other than for terrorists. He spoke out in favour of military action against Saddam Hussein although he voiced the need to exhaust the diplomatic process before resorting to war. Later, when no WMD were found, he became criticial of President Bush, arguing that he had misled the country. He has continued to oppose US policy ever since, backing the call for troop withdrawals by a specified date.

King, Martin Luther (1929–68)

Martin Luther King was a Black American political activist and one of the main leaders of the American civil rights movement. He is widely regarded as one of the country's greatest orators and a model for many people involved in political and social struggle.

Born and educated in Atlanta, Georgia, Martin Luther King attended segregated schools in the state. He received his degree in 1948 from Morehouse College, a distinguished institution of Atlanta from which both his father and grandfather had graduated. Following further theological study, he received his doctorate at Boston University in 1955, having already accepted the pastorate of the Dexter Avenue Baptist Church in Montgomery, Alabama. From 1960 until his death, he acted as co-pastor of the Ebenezer Baptist Church in Atlanta, following in the footsteps of his grandfather and father.

In the mid-1950s, King's interest in the cause of civil rights for members of his race led to his involvement in the leadership of the National Association for the Advancement of Colored People, the leading organisation of its kind in the nation. In December 1955, he accepted the leadership of the bus boycott in Montgomery, the first large non-violent demonstration in modern American history. A year later, after the Supreme Court had declared unconstitutional the laws requiring segregation on buses, black as well as white Americans rode the buses as equals. During these days of boycott, King was arrested, his home bombed, and he was subjected to personal abuse. But he was acquiring a strong reputation among his supporters, becoming recognised as a formidable and inspirational speaker who was gaining a national reputation and prestige. In 1957, he was elected president of the Southern Christian Leadership Conference, an organisation formed to provide new leadership for the now burgeoning civil rights movement. In his approach, his outlook was much influenced by his Christian thinking and values, his operational techniques and belief in the efficacy of non-violent passive resistance influenced by Gandhi.

In the eleven-year period between 1957 and 1968, King travelled over six million miles (9.5 million miles) and spoke on more than 2,500 occasions, appearing wherever there was injustice, protest, and action. He led a massive protest in Birmingham, Alabama, which received widespread attention; he planned the drives in Alabama for the registration of African Americans as voters; he spearheaded the peaceful march on Washington DC of 250,000 people to whom he delivered his most influential and well-known public address 'I Have a Dream'; he conferred with President John F. Kennedy and his brother, and campaigned for President Lyndon B. Johnson; he received the Nobel Peace Prize; he was arrested more than twenty times and assaulted at least four times; he was awarded five honorary degrees; he was named Man of the Year by *Time* magazine in 1963; and he became not only the symbolic leader of black Americans but also a renowned and revered world figure.

King's leadership in the civil rights movement was challenged in the mid-1960s as other black Americans became more militant and attracted to the cause of Black Power. By then, his interests had broadened to include criticism of the Vietnam War and a deeper concern over poverty. His plans for a Poor People's March to Washington were interrupted (1968) for a trip to Memphis, Tennessee, in support of striking sanitation workers. On 4 April 1968, he was shot and killed as he stood on the balcony of the Lorraine Motel. James Earl Ray, a career criminal, pleaded guilty to the murder and was convicted but he soon recanted, claiming he was duped into his plea. Ray's conviction was subsequently upheld but he eventually received support from members of King's family who believed King to have been the victim of a conspiracy. The Justice Department later concluded that there was no evidence of an assassination plot. In 1977, King was posthumously awarded the Presidential Medal of Freedom by President Carter. In 1986, Martin Luther King Day was established as a public holiday. In 2004, King was awarded a Congressional Gold Medal.

By the time of his death, much had already been achieved. The civil rights movement had played a key role in producing the legislation that ended segregation and secured voting rights in 1965. American blacks had by then gained greater self-confidence and acquired a voice in the political process. This was not all King's doing, for many of his supporters – particularly in the churches – and the federal government had played an influential role. But his inspirational leadership helped to provide an impetus for reform. Yet, if he had lived, it is by no means certain that the movement could have progressed any further. For, by the late 1960s, other and more impatient black activists were gaining support. Faced with the continuing and enormous problems experienced by many of their fellows, they were impatient for change and saw King as being too willing to defer to white authority. Their frequent extremism was generating a white backlash. Whereas King's methods were moderate and his dream one of reconciliation between 'the sons of former slaves and the sons of former slave owners', many advocates of Black Power rejected his integrationist message and his support for non-violent protest. Many felt that only physical violence could defeat American racism. King had no sympathy with their 'hate whitey' approach.

See also *Bus Boycotts*; *Civil Rights Movement*, *March on Washington*; *National Association for the Advancement of Colored People*; *Parks, Rosa*

Kitzmiller v. *Dover* (2005)

Tammy Kitzmiller v. *Dover Area School District* was the first case brought in the federal court system which challenged a public school district that required the presentation of the case for 'Intelligent Design' as an alternative to teaching evolution as an explanation of how life began. The plaintiffs, eleven parents of students in Dover, Pennsylvania, led by Tammy Kitzmiller, objected to the decision by the school board in Dover, Pennsylvania to promote the teaching of intelligent design in their children's public school science classes. They successfully argued that intelligent design is a form of creationism and that the board policy violated the Establishment Clause of the First Amendment to the Constitution of United States.

Because those bringing the case sought an equitable remedy, the Seventh Amendment, providing for a right to jury trial, did not apply. The decision was therefore made by District Judge John Jones. He ruled that the Dover mandate was unconstitutional and barred intelligent design from being taught in Pennsylvania's Middle District public school science classrooms. The Dover school board members who voted for the intelligent design requirement were all defeated in a November 2005 election by challengers who opposed the teaching of intelligent design in a science class. The new school board president decided not to appeal against the ruling.

The judgment was an historic one and has – not surprisngly – proved highly controversial. It was a victory not only for the ACLU and Americans United for Separation of Church and State (AU), who led the legal challenge, but for all who believe it is both inappropriate and unconstitutional to advance a particular religious belief at the expense of American science education.

Korean War (1950–53)

The Korean War was a civil war fought between North and South on the Korean Peninsula which had been divided at the 38th parallel by the temporary occupations of the Soviet Union and the United States. The war began in June 1950 when North Korea attacked the South which was militarily unprepared for the assault. The United Nations called for a ceasefire and the withdrawal of North Korean forces. President Truman followed this up by ordering US troops to implement the UN resolution, a stance backed by some other UN members, such as Britain, which sent troops to aid the South. The People's Republic of China and Soviet Union entered the conflict on the side of the North, sending weapons, military pilots and 'volunteers'. The fighting reached a stalemate in 1951 when truce talks began but it was not until after the election of Eisenhower as president that a ceasefire was signed in July 1953 and the conflict ended. As a result of the armistice, Korea was divided again along roughly the same line that had existed before the struggle for control.

Like the earlier Berlin Blockade, the events in Korea were an important stage of the early Cold War years. They made the positions of the two rival superpowers more rigid. American policy at this time was based on the idea of containment, halting Communist aggreession in the west and in the east. The US government officially described the conflict in Korea as a police action which avoided the necessity of a declaration of war by Congress.

Ku Klux Klan

The Ku Klux Klan is the collective name used in reference to several past and present secret terrorist bodies in the United States. They are part of a white supremacist, anti-Semitic movement which shares a commitment to extreme violence to achieve its goals of racial segregation. They act as vigilantes, while concealing their identity behind conical masks and white robes. Of the far right racist groups, the Klan remains the one with the largest number of national and local organisations around the country, membership being variously estimated at 5,000 to 8,000 Klansmen who operate in well over a hundred different Klan chapters around the country.

Support for the Klan tends to increase in times of social turmoil. The movement thrived in the South during the Reconstruction period after the Civil War. It flourished again after World War I, when it became extremely hostile to African Americans, Roman Catholics, Jews, communists,

socialists and any other group that could be identified as in some way 'foreign' or 'un-American'.
By 1925, its membership reached 4,000,000. It
was disbanded in 1944 but groups calling themselves the Ku Klux Klan again sprang up in much
of the South after World War II, particularly in
response to civil rights activity during the 1950s
and 1960s. The most important of these was
the White Knights of the Ku Klux Klan led by
Robert Shelton. In the Deep South, Klansmen
exerted considerable pressure on blacks not to
vote. Lynching was still used as a method of ter-
rorising the local black population.

After a period of relative quiet, Ku Klux Klan
activity has increased in the last few years, as
Klan groups have attempted to exploit fears in
America over gay marriage, perceived 'assaults'
on Christianity, crime and immigration.

L

Lame Duck

A lame duck is an elected official who is approaching the end of his or her tenure; in particular, one whose successor has already been elected. Lame-duck presidents are serving out their final period in office either because they have lost a bid for re-election or are no longer eligible to serve. The term is frequently used to describe sitting presidents who have entered their final year or so of a two-term administration. The 'Lame Duck (Twentieth) Amendment' calls for the new president and Congress to take office in January instead of March (as previously), thereby reducing the lame-duck period.

Lawrence v. *Texas* (2003)

Lawrence v. *Texas* was a landmark ruling of the Supreme Court which established that consensual and private homosexual sex is part of a substantive right to liberty as protected by the Constitution. Second, and less obviously, Lawrence held that 'fundamental rights' (i.e., 'substantive due process' or activities implicitly protected by the Constitution) are really broad principles of liberty under which numerous and disparate activities may be protected. The ruling both protected the privacy of the bedroom and renewed the Court's power to identify individual rights above and beyond those historically protected under the law.

The case concerned two gay men who claimed that the state of Texas deprived them of privacy rights and equal protection under the law when they were arrested in 1998 for having sex in a Houston home. By a 7–2 majority opinion, the Supreme Court ruled that the Homosexual Conduct law was unconstitutional because it violated the Fourteenth Amendment's Due Process Clause which protects a substantive right to personal liberty in intimate decisions. In the words of Justice Kennedy: 'When sexuality finds overt expression in intimate conduct with another person, the conduct can be but one element in a personal bond that is more enduring'. That personal bond between adults, as acted upon in the home, is a liberty protected by the Due Process Clause against the states. As a result of the judgment, all sodomy laws in the US are now unconstitutional and unenforceable when applied to non-commercial consenting adults in private.

See also *Gay Rights*

Legislation and Lawmaking

Legislation is introduced by a variety of methods. Some bills are drawn up in standing committees, some by special committees created to examine specific legislative issues and some may be urged by the president or other executive officers. Individuals and outside organisations may suggest legislation to member of Congress and individual members may themselves have ideas they wish to see pass into law.

Such is the volume of legislation proposed by senators and representatives that much of it has no chance of getting any further. It is introduced in the first place more as a way of securing the goodwill of lobbyists or constituents than with any expectation of further progress. After the initial introduction, bills are sent by the leadership to designated committees where many of them die. Ninety per cent of those before a subcommittee get no further, for lack of time or lack of support. This is the justification for the existence of committees. They act as a screening mechanism for the flood of measures presented, thereby preventing the Senate and House of Representative from being overwhelmed.

For those bills with significant backing, the committee schedules a series of public hearings that may last for weeks or months, allowing for an outside input from interested bodies. The subcommittee then discusses and amends the bill, and – assuming there is a vote in its favour – it is sent ('reported') to the full chamber where it is debated, and again a vote occurs. (In the House, the bill will first go to the Rules Committee which determines the time limits to be allowed and decides whether or not amendments from the floor will be allowed.)

Usually, both chambers consider their own bills at approximately the same time. To succeed, the approval of both the Senate and the House of Representatives is necessary. If there are differences in the versions passed, then a conference committee will seek a compromise. The bill must have successfully endured the procedure of both houses and have been approved in identical form before it can become law. If this does not happen in the lifetime of one Congress, the attempt has failed; the whole process needs to be started again.

At this point, the bill goes to the White House for the approval of the president. He may sign it, veto it or do nothing. If Congress is sitting and he does nothing then, after ten working days, the bill becomes law without his signature. If the Congress has adjourned and the president waits ten days before signing, then this is a pocket veto. Other than in this case, a vetoed bill is returned to the Congress with the reasons for rejection. The presidential veto can be overturned if both chambers can muster a two-thirds majority against it.

The role of the Administration in legislation

The amount and character of legislation have changed significantly over the years. In the 1960s and 1970s, there was a burst of legislative action but, in the following decade, the pace of change – especially on substantive issues – slowed.

In theory, federal governments cannot make laws, their proposals having no priority in congressional procedure. Presidents can propose legislation but, if congressional leaders, prefer their own, then the White House has no means of redress. In consultation with committee chairpersons and party leaders, departments draw up the measures seen as desirable. They are then introduced by sympathetic members.

Although most successful legislation now originates in the Executive branch, the administration cannot be sure of its passage in the form that it favours. Whereas, in Britain, the system of party discipline ensures that a government with a parliamentary majority may get its way, this is not the case in the United States. Presidents cannot depend on congressional support, and Congress remains a major force in determining the shape and timing of legislation.

The President and Congress: co-operation in the legislative arena

The separation of powers and the divided government that it involves present an obstacle to policymaking. They set the scene for a continuous struggle although the Constitution requires the two branches to work together. The administration and Congress can legislate when the president and congressional leaders bargain and compromise.

President Johnson was skilled in this process for, as a former Senate majority leader, he understood the need for the White House to build bridges with his former colleagues. But Johnson had more than personal skills working to his advantage. He was president at a time of strong Democrat majorities in

(cont.)

both chambers. Some of his more recent successors would have been delighted to have received such party backing. Moreover, his opponents were less ideologically driven and cohesive than has been the case over the last decade or so. In today's circumstances, a president needs to be in regular consultation with his opponents as well as with his supporters. Following the Republican victory in the midterm elections of November 1994, the Clinton experience showed that, to rescue his legislative proposals, he needed co-operation and agreement. When he obtained this, his success record improved (other than in the year of impeachment proceedings) as the figures (percentages) indicate:

1993	86.4
1994	86.4
1995	36.2
1996	55.1
1997	56.6
1998	51.0
1999	37.8
2000	55.0

N.b. In his first two years, George W. Bush achieved success rates of 87 per cent and 88 per cent. He had a thin legislative agenda that he pursued with modest vigour whereas his predecessor had a more difficult ride, not least because he had a busy programme on which he was seeking to drive a reluctant Congress to take action.

Problems within the legislative procedure

The legislative process is lengthy and complex, there being so many hurdles that a bill may fail to overcome. It is not surprising that so few bills survive this 'legislative labyrinth' and become law for the odds are stacked heavily against success. Because of the number of bills introduced, the standing committees – to which so much power is given – are overwhelmed. Much depends on the drive and forcefulness of the committee chairpersons. It also helps if the two chambers are under the control of the same party, as in the era of Republic predominance since November 1994. But, even when the majority has been more cohesive, as in recent years, there is no certainty that members will vote with their parties in support of the legislative programme.

The lawmaking procedure has often been described as an 'obstacle course', for bills have to get past the appropriate standing committee, be given time by the Rules Committee and then survive the debate on the floor of the house or Senate. To have got this far, there must have been a substantial degree of support but, in the Senate, this is no mere formality and the bill can always be subject to a filibuster by which senators hold the floor of the chamber, speak at length and seek to delay proceedings to avoid a vote being taken.

It is not surprising that few bills successfully navigate the procedure. In the 106th Congress (1998–2000), 5 per cent of those introduced went on to become law. In the 107th Congress, the success rate dropped to 4 per cent of the 8,948 bills introduced. The procedure is not without advantages. The separation of powers is there to stop the domination of one section of the governmental machinery by another, and the lawmaking process reflects this aim of preventing tyranny. It is impossible for the whips to force through changes at the wish of the Executive branch, and there is no elective dictatorship of the type often said to exist in Britain. Instead, those who seek to get a bill passed on to the statute book need to build a consensus in its support and, if it does pass, it is likely to have substantial backing.

In a crisis, however, the machinery is less responsive than the situation demands. Franklin Roosevelt and Lyndon Johnson, each aided by a Congress controlled by his own party, were able to introduce packages of measures speedily but their experience is atypical. The system offers a built-in advantage to those who would thwart legislation which is why Denenberg (1976) described Congress as 'a bastion of negation'. The legislative procedure enables a dissenting minority to prevent the passage of bills by their obstruction at several access points – and thereby kill off proposals.

See also *Bills*

Lehman Brothers' Collapse

Lehman Brothers Holdings Inc. was a global financial services firm involved in equity sales, investment management and commercial banking. It was also a primary dealer in the Treasury securities market. Based in New York, its operations were worldwide. It was the fourth largest investment bank in the United States.

Lehman Brothers was heavily invested in securities linked to the US sub-prime mortgage market. At a time when these investments were being shunned as high risk, it was inevitable that confidence in the company would be seriously hit. In June to August 2007, the investment bank said it would make write downs of $700 million as it adjusted the value of its investments in residential mortgages and commercial property. A year later, this figure soared to $7.8 billion, which resulted in Lehman reporting the largest net loss in its history. The bank also admitted that it still had $54 billion of exposure to hard-to-value mortgage-backed securities. Such revelations led to drastic losses in its stock, a massive exodus of its clients and the downgrading of its assets by credit agencies. Its share price plummeted by more than 95%.

The Federal Reserve and Treasury Department refused to bail the company out and no other financial house on Wall Street was able or willing to step in and prevent Lehmans' collapse. On 15 September 2008, the company was forced to file for bankruptcy protection. This was the largest bankruptcy in American history. It resulted in such fear and panic in the following days that the already troubled financial markets entered a period of extreme volatility, which in turn precipitated a global financial collapse. Governments on both sides of the Atlantic were forced into making an unprecedented and costly effort to restore

calm and patch up the financial system, in order to avoid the danger that the collapse of confidence would trigger another 'Great Depression'.

See also *Financial Crisis and Global Recession (2007–09)*

Lewinsky, Monica (1973–)

Monica Lewinsky is the American woman with whom Bill Clinton admitted to having had an 'inappropriate relationship' while she worked as an intern in the White House Office of Legislative Affairs in 1995 and 1996. She was questioned as part of the investigation into Paula Jones's claim of sexual harassment against the president. Both Lewinsky and Clinton denied having an affair but tape recordings made by her older colleague and confidante, Linda Tripp, suggested otherwise.

The repercussions of the relationship and the attempt to conceal it led to the impeachment of the president, the surrounding scandals of 1997–99 becoming widely known as the Lewinsky scandal. The episode consumed much time and energy in Clinton's second term and limited its achievements. Among many Americans, his reputation was seriously tarnished yet, according to the polls, he gained in popularity throughout the impeachment proceedings. The events brought Lewinsky significant notoriety.

See also *Clinton, Bill*; *Clinton and Impeachment*

Libel

Libel and slander are legal claims for false statements of fact about a person that are printed, broadcast, spoken or otherwise communicated to others. Libel generally refers to statements or visual depictions in written or other permanent form while slander refers to verbal statements and gestures which, therefore, constitute a temporary attack. The term 'defamation' is often used to encompass both libel and slander thereby covering any comment which is malicious and damaging to a person's reputation.

Until 1964, a plaintiff could win a civil case by showing that the statements in question were substantially false. In *New York Times* v. *Sullivan*

(1964), however, the Court expanded press protection by requiring that public officials who claimed to be libelled need to prove that the statements were made with 'actual malice'. To be awarded damages, he or she needed to prove that the publisher acted 'with knowledge that it was false or with reckless disregard whether it was false or not'. This 'actual malice' standard was later extended to cover public figures, those private citizens whose station in life or whose activities made them newsworthy.

'Actual malice' is difficult to prove so that the ruling effectively immunised the press against libel suits by public figures or officials. In 1988, the Court reaffirmed the standard when it ruled that the Reverend Jerry Falwell was not entitled to compensation for the emotional distress he suffered as a result of a vulgar parody of him published in *Hustler* magazine.

It is unusual for someone to win a libel case in America. The courts tend to err on the side of freedom of expression, taking the view that, if public debate is not free, there can be no democracy. The Supreme Court has allowed considerable latitude to those who make derogatory comments that damage or bruise public reputations.

Liberal Party (New York)

The Liberal Party of New York state claims to be the longest-existing third party in the history of the United States. It was founded in 1944 as an alternative to a state Democratic Party, dominated by local party machines that were rife with corruption, and a Republican Party controlled by special interests. It has a history of nominating – or, more often, supporting – candidates on the basis of independence, merit and a progressive viewpoint, regardless of party affiliations. It is interested primarily in whether candidates are likely to provide good, effective and forward-looking government. Past nominees have included Governor Mario Cuomo, Senator Robert Kennedy and New York City mayors Fiorello LaGuardia, John Wagner and Rudolph Giuliani.

Adopting a broadly centre-left stance on policy issues, the Liberal Party has been for many years an influential force in New York politics, campaigning on such things as:

- reproductive freedom – a woman's right to choose abortion
- health care – the need for a system which is well run and affordable
- democracy involvement – encouraging popular participation in civic life
- environmental progress – a serious attempt to place environmental considerations at the forefront of policymaking
- civil rights – comprehensive legislation to ensure that discrimination on grounds of race, ethnicity, religion, gender, sexual orientation, disability and economic class do not restrict people's lives.

The Liberal Party has declined in influence in recent years. Following a poor showing in the 2002 gubernatorial election, it lost its state recognition and ceased operations at its state offices. Internal dissension and secession damaged its prospects but it also suffered from the impact made by the Working Families Party (formed in 1998) which drew away much of its support, particularly among the trade unions. In 2006, for the first time since the early 1940s, there was no Liberal candidate for governor.

Today, the Liberal Party struggles to keep going although dedicated enthusiasts are still proud to label themselves as Liberals and keep the cause alive. It continues its tradition of supporting aspirants for office who are progressive in their ideas and capable of meeting the challenge of providing good government. In 2005, the *New York Daily News* reported that incumbent New York City Mayor, Michael Bloomberg, a liberal Republican on issues such as abortion and same-sex civil unions, was seeking to revive the Liberal Party, with a view to running on a 'Republican/Liberal' ticket and thereby hopeful to attract Democratic voters in the overwhelmingly Democratic city. He was re-elected in 2005 but there has as yet been little indication of any close co-operation.

Liberalism

Liberalism is a political philosophy that involves recognition of the value of the individual and a tendency to view politics in individualistic terms.

Classical liberals believed in government by consent, limited government, the protection of private property, and opportunity. They also stressed the importance of individual rights, some of which were regarded as 'inalienable'. Everyone should have the chance to fulfil his or her destiny, and no individual or group should be denied recognition of their worth or dignity. Accordingly, individual liberties must be respected and their opportunities for economic advance unimpeded. By contrast, collectivist policies and solutions (those based around the idea of the state – on behalf of its citizens – acknowledging society's collective responsibility to care about those in need) have never been embraced in the United States.

The word 'liberal' derives from the Latin *liber*, meaning 'free' or 'generous', from which we can detect an attachment to qualities such as liberty and tolerance. Americans have a strong attachment to liberty, as symbolised by the statue erected in its name. The War of Independence was fought in its defence, and the Constitution, like the American Revolution, proclaims this commitment. The late Clinton Rossiter (1960), a renowned American political scientist, saw liberty as the pre-eminent value in the American political culture: 'We have always been a nation obsessed with liberty. Liberty over authority, freedom over responsibility, rights over duties – these are our historic preferences.'

If classical liberalism emphasised liberty, individual rights and a minimal role for state intervention, liberalism had by the twentieth century become associated with protecting the individual by regulatory action. Today's liberals see government as having a positive role to promote greater justice in society and more equality of opportunity. They talk of individual rights, including the right to own private property, but they also see a need for measures to control the defects of a market economy. Most accept that inequalities of wealth are inevitable and even desirable but they wish to ensure that everyone has a certain minimum level of wealth so that they can enjoy life and have a fair deal.

Franklin Roosevelt was the model for American liberals with his attempt to steer America out of the depression via the New Deal. President Kennedy is similarly regarded as a liberal hero, many of his speeches echoing liberal values. In one passage, he summed up his creed:

> I believe in human dignity as the source of national purpose, in human liberty as the source of national action, in the human heart as the source of national compassion, and in the human mind as the source of our invention and our ideas. It is, I believe, the faith in our fellow citizens as individuals and as people that lies at the heart of the liberal faith.

The problems of the twenty-first century are very different from those of the Great Depression and the 1930s but there are still those who are left behind. Modern liberals want to provide better education and housing, are alarmed by inadequate and costly health care, and support progressive taxation graduated according to the individual's ability to pay. They are committed to civil rights and affirmative action to overcome the effects of past discrimination against minorities and women; many activists, involved in areas ranging from women's liberation and the pro-abortion campaign to the gay and the disabled movements, come within the liberal fold. These are all examples of the positive use of government to improve society and remove its defects. American liberalism is then, today, a philosophical approach that generally favours the positive use of government to bring about equality of opportunity and justice for all men and women. It rests on the basis that much of the evil in society can be removed or alleviated by change and reform.

Neo-liberalism and the passing of Rooseveltian liberalism

In the last few years there has been talk of neo-liberals who are willing to argue the case for traditional liberal beliefs in justice and liberty and the need for government intervention but who do not endorse the whole liberal agenda. Neo-liberals are more suspicious of union power, welfare provision and big government with its large, Washington-based bureaucracies. Some also have doubts about the increasing concern for minority causes. In the words of Irving Kristol (1983), a leading proponent of the idea, they are 'liberals mugged by reality'.

The growth of neo-liberalism reflects the fact that liberalism has rather gone out of fashion. Even those who believe in it are aware of its allegedly adverse effects. Critics, mainly Republicans and Southern Democrats, have portrayed liberalism as being too concerned with federal action by the government, with costly programmes that require huge bureaucracies to run them, and with penal taxation that hits the voter in his or her pocket and tends to destroy any incentive for individual effort. Welfare is seen as damaging to the qualities that made America what it is; it undermines the work ethic and the entrepreneurial spirit. Neo-liberalism has more in common with classical liberalism – laissez-faire, the minimal state and a strong commitment to economic freedom that is interpreted in a different way from what Roosevelt meant by the term.

In 1992 Clinton was concerned to show himself as a new type of Democrat. In the more conservative climate of that decade, he and others were anxious to show that they, too, believed in the virtues of free enterprise, the perils of communism, the need for tough action against criminals, strong defence and a new emphasis upon traditional patriotism. 'Liberalism' had by then increasingly become a term of abuse used by those on the political right. The 'l' word was later used by George W. Bush against John Kerry whom it was easy to portray as a Massachusetts liberal.

Liberalism still has its advocates and, at a time when politicians are reluctant to use the word, there have been academics and journalists who see merit in what it stands for. Thus, Arthur Schlesinger could write an article entitled 'Hurray for the L-Word', in which he claimed:

The presidents we admire and celebrate most – Jefferson, Jackson, Lincoln, Theodore Roosevelt, Wilson, FDR, Harry Truman and JFK – were all, in the context of their times, vigorous and unashamed liberals. They were all pioneers of new frontiers, seeking out the ways of the future, meeting new problems with new remedies, carrying the message of constructive change in a world that never stops changing. From the start of the Republic, liberalism has always blazed the trail into the future – and conservatism has always deployed all the weapons of caricature and calumny and irrelevance to conceal the historic conservative objective of unchecked rule by those who already have far more than their fair share of the nation's treasure.

See also *Political Culture*

Libertarian Party

Americans are deeply attached to the ideas of personal liberty and limited government. Some of them are attracted to the Libertarian Party formed in 1972. Claiming to be neither left nor right, Libertarians are wary of both parties and feel that neither of them can be trusted to defend the rights of individuals. As their website explains: 'In a nutshell, we are advocates for a smaller government, lower taxes and more freedom.' More specifically, members of the Party:

- espouse a classical laissez-faire (leave-alone) philosophy which, they argue, means 'more freedom, less government and lower taxes'
- wish to see most services run on a private basis so that there is unrestricted freedom in commerce
- disapprove of federal and state welfare programmes and policies which offer subsidies to any group, farmers, businessmen and others
- dislike any regulatory bodies of a federal nature, such as the FBI or CIA, and laws that curb individual freedom, such as those on the wearing of seat belts and helmets
- oppose gun control
- are pro-home schooling
- [in the case of the founders of the party] were committed to allowing free choice on abortion although, today, there is some division of opinion on the issue.

Libertarians believe in and pursue personal freedom while maintaining personal responsibility. Those who belong to the Libertarian Party serve a much larger pro-liberty community and have the specific mission of electing libertarians to public office. They traditionally billed themselves as 'America's largest third party'. They are still active in all fifty states, usually field more state and local candidates than any other third force, and have more than 200,000 registered voters. Their claim has been undermined in recent years, however, by the growth of the Greens who have a larger following and attract more media attention. So, too, does the Reform Party attract more votes. In the presidential elections of 2000 and again in 2004, both parties out-polled the Libertarians. In 2008, as a result of legal controversies, they were only on the ballot paper in one state and secured just 481 votes.

See also *Libertarianism*

Libertarianism

Libertarianism is a political philosophy that stresses the importance of individual liberty. It maintains that all persons are the absolute owners of their own lives and should be free to do whatever they wish with their persons or property. Libertarians uphold the principles of individual liberty of thought and action, believing that political and economic liberty results in the maximum well-being and efficiency in any society. They accept that a limited government is necessary for the maximisation of liberty and the advancement of their goals but strongly oppose any government interfering in their personal, family and business decisions. Essentially, they believe all Americans should be free to live their lives and pursue their interests as they see fit as long as they do no harm to anyone else.

Libertarian thinking has always been popular in the United States where it was the philosophy advocated by several of the Founding Fathers including Thomas Jefferson. Libertarians differentiate themselves from conservatives and liberals. They advocate a high degree of *both* personal and economic liberty. Their creed is sometimes confused with American conservatism because many conservatives aim to uphold the ideas of the Founders. Many conservatives, however, are uncomfortable with libertarianism. Whereas most conservatives take a socially restrictive view and wish to limit the sale of marijuana and other soft drugs, gambling, prostitution and pornography, being socially tolerant, libertarians would leave such things unrestricted. They would abolish all legislation designed to promote a particular view of morality. They do not favour laws or restrictions on other people with whom they disagree because of their chosen personal actions or lifestyles.

Whereas many modern liberals, in their support for progressive causes, see the need for state regulation in some areas of economic and social policy, libertarians advocate freedom in economic matters. They are in favour of lowering taxes, slashing bureaucratic regulation of business, and charitable – rather than government – welfare.

See also *Libertarian Party*

Lincoln, Abraham (1809–65)

Abraham Lincoln was the 16 president, serving from March 1861 until his assassination at Ford's Theatre in Washington by John Wilkes Booth, an actor who thought he was helping the Southern cause. During his presidency: he helped preserve the United States by leading the defeat of the secessionist Confederate states in the Civil War; he introduced measures that resulted in the abolition of slavery; he issued his Emancipation Proclamation in 1863, for which he will always be remembered; and promoted the passage of the Thirteenth Amendment to the Constitution in 1865.

An outspoken opponent of the expansion of slavery, Lincoln won the Republican nomination in 1860 and was elected president later that year. At the time, he seemed ill-prepared for the task he had undertaken. Unlike Washington and Jackson, he lacked military experience, and unlike Jefferson and Monroe, he had no diplomatic background. He had never travelled abroad, had no Executive experience and had received almost no formal education.

Lincoln and presidential power

Lincoln immediately made a significant impact on the presidential office. Having once criticised Executive authority and disapproved of the war with Mexico as an unconstitutional act, as president he used his powers in new and extraordinary ways and with dogged tenacity. He quickly began to make tough and controversial decisions. Without first seeking congressional approval, he spent money, blockaded ports, called up militia, suspended some established rights, such as habeas corpus (also closing opposition newspapers, ordering the arrest of suspected traitors and censoring telegraphs and the mail to 'treasonable correspondence'), issued the emancipation edict and lobbied for an amendment to end slavery. In the Civil War, he took the view that a crisis situation demanded bold and far-reaching action, irrespective of whether this handed the White House almost unlimited powers. He did what he thought was necessary to secure victory and thereby preserve the Union. Congress later approved most of his initiatives but, by his approach, he showed where the power of initiative in American government resided.

In waging the Civil War, he shared the views of most Northerners that the hostitilites were not primarily about the fight for racial justice but for the preservation of the Union. Though willing to oppose any extension of slavery to new states, he was willing to protect the institution where it existed for he did not wish to alienate his supporters in slave states. His views were modified as the war progressed. He had always accepted that there must be the position of 'superior and inferior' and was in favour of having 'the superior position assigned to the white race'. He was never the 'Negro lover' that the Democrats labelled him in the 1864 election; indeed, he had never wanted Blacks and Native Americans in the Union army. As the war progressed, however, his position evolved. He was impressed by the performance of black soldiers and contemplated extending the vote to the most gallant and 'very intelligent' among them.

Qualities and approach to leadership

Lincoln never let the world forget that the Civil War involved more than the abolition of slavery. In his moving address when dedicating the military cemetery at Gettysburg, he spoke of his determination 'that we here highly resolve that these dead shall not have died in vain . . . that this nation, under God, shall have a new birth of freedom . . . and that government of the people,

by the people, for the people, shall not perish from the earth'.

Lincoln won re-election in 1864, as Union military triumphs heralded an end to the war. In planning for peace, he was flexible and generous, encouraging Southerners to lay down their arms and join speedily in reunion. The spirit that guided him was made clear in his second Inaugural Address, now inscribed on one wall of the Lincoln Memorial in Washington DC: 'With malice toward none; with charity for all; with firmness in the right, as God gives us to see the right, let us strive on to finish the work we are in; to bind up the nation's wounds . . .'

According to the Lincoln approach, the president was an active politician who needed to rally Congress and the nation in times of crisis. He was unwilling to interpret narrowly his constitutional role in the manner of his predecessor. For him, the limits of Executive power were only those specifically outlined in the Constitution. How powerful he was as president was largely dependent on his own political abilities. The circumstances were propitious for a display of national leadership, for Lincoln was presented with the greatest crisis that his young nation had yet faced. He rose to the challenge in difficult times, in the process helping to shape the course of American history. He established a precedent of 'crisis leadership' that presidents of a hundred years or so later would to follow.

Academics now regularly rank Lincoln among the top three American presidents, with the majority of those surveyed placing him first. He is commemorated in many ways, among them being the fourth figure in the memorial at Mount Rushmore.

See also *Civil War*; *Confederacy*; *Emancipation Proclamation*

Line-item Veto

A line-item veto is a legal provision that permitted the Executive to reduce or nullify or delete specific provisions of a spending bill without having to veto the whole bill. All but seven state governors have some form of line-item veto, those without being Indiana, Maryland, Nevada, New Hampshire, North Carolina, Rhode Island and

Vermont. The president briefly had one but it was removed by the Supreme Court in 1998.

In 1996, Congress passed a line-item veto, giving the president the power to veto 'objectionable' parts of an appropriations (expenditure) bill while agreeing to the rest of it. This enabled him to control pork-barrel spending that favoured a particular region rather than the nation as a whole. President Bill Clinton used the facility on eleven occasions to strike eighty-two items from the federal budget. This innovation was soon tested in the Supreme Court, however. In *Clinton* v. *New York* (June 1998) in a case brought by former New York City Mayor, Rudy Giuliani, the judges were asked to decide whether President Clinton's rejection of some aspects of a tax bill was legitimate. By 6–3, they concluded that the line-item veto was unconstitutional in that it violated the requirement that any bill must pass both houses and be signed by the president in the same form. If the president was allowed to strike out particular features, then, in effect, a new bill was being created.

Several presidents had asked Congress to give them a line-item veto power. Ronald Reagan urged members of Congress to 'give me a line-item veto this year. Give me the authority to veto waste, and I'll take the responsibility, I'll make the cuts, I'll take the heat.' Bill Clinton echoed the request in his State of the Union address in 1995 and was successful in obtaining it. Well after the Supreme Court ruling, George W. Bush similarly urged such a power:

> A line-item veto would be a vital tool that a president could use to target spending that lawmakers tack on to the large spending bills. That's called earmarking, and that's become quite a controversial subject here in Washington DC.
>
> I happen to believe that a lot of times earmarking results in unnecessary spending. See, part of the job of the President and the leaders in the Congress is to set priorities with the people's money. If you don't set priorities, the tendency is to overspend. And sometimes – a lot of times – the earmark doesn't fit into the priorities that have been sent through the budgetary process. A lot of times earmarks are inserted into bills at the last minute, which leaves no time, or little time, for debate.

Many observers and academics believe the line-item veto would give presidents too much power over government spending compared with the power of Congress.

Little Mo see *Big Mo/Little Mo*

Lobbying

Lobbying refers to the effort to convince public decision-makers to favour a certain cause or take a certain course of action on a subject deemed relevant to those directing or funding the lobbying effort.

By the 'lobby' we mean all those groups that seek to influence public policy whether they are primarily promotional or propaganda bodies or those that seek to defend the interests of their group or organisation. The word 'lobby' originally derives from the location where the process occurred, the anteroom or lobby outside the chambers of Congress where representatives could be intercepted and urged to support a particular cause when they voted. Hotel lobbies have sometimes provided a similar venue, and lobbyists are those who wait there hoping for a chance meeting. To lobby is to seek to influence legislators and officials. Lobbyists are therefore employees of associations who try to influence policy decisions, especially in the Executive and Legislative branches of government.

For many years, lobbyists have played a significant role in the legislative process, a role that has increased with the enlargement of governmental activity in the era since the New Deal. The term 'lobby' includes a vast array of groups, operating at several levels and covering commercial and industrial interests, labour unions, consumer associations, ethnic and racial groups. In the mid-1950s, the *Encyclopaedia of Associations* listed fewer than 5,000 of them. Now, it lists more than 20,000. Representation of companies in Washington has greatly increased but more dramatic has been the explosion in the number of public-interest organisations and grassroots groups. These barely existed at all before the 1960s; today, they number in the tens of thousands and collect more than four billion dollars a year from forty million individuals. More than nine out of every ten Americans belong to at least one voluntary grouping, be it a church, civil rights organisation, social club of some kind, or other public body. On average, every American belongs to four.

Under the Legislative Reorganisation Act (1946), lobbyists were required to register with the relevant offices of the Senate and the House of Representatives, and provide details of their work and funding. At that time, there were fewer than 2,000 registered lobbyists with Congress but now the number registered approaches 9,000. But this figure omits the vast array of individual corporations, state and local governments, universities, think tanks and other organisations in the private sector that engage in lobbying at some level, as well as the myriad Washington representatives ranging from lawyers to public relations agencies which do similar work.

The top twelve lobbying organisations, 2008, based on total spending

Companies and organisations	Amount spent over previous financial year ($)
Chamber of Commerce	206,614,680
Altria Group Inc.	101,220,000
General Electric Group	94,130,000
American Medical Association	92,560,000
Northrop Grumman Corp.	83,405,691
Edison Electric Institute	82,866,628
Venison Communications Inc.	81,870,000
Business Roundtable	80,380,000
American Hospital Association and State Affiliates	79,205,772
Pharmaceutical Research and Manufacturers of America	72,720,000
National Association of Realtors	68,810,000
ExxonMobil Corp.	59,672,742

Source The Centre for Public Integrity – Lobbywatch www. publicintegrity.entry/290/org/projects/

Organisations such as the Ford Motor Company not only belong to the appropriate interest group, they also maintain their own lobbying staff in Washington. Most other business corporations retain a sizeable lobby in the city, partly for reasons of prestige but also as a means of using any opportunity to influence laws and regulations. Similarly, labour unions, and groups representing sections of society such as the elderly and causes such as the environment, maintain well-manned permanent offices. All wish to exert pressure at some level of government, many of them in Washington (either at the White House or on Capitol Hill).

In recent years there has been a marked extension of lobbying activity within the states as well as at federal level. American political culture is tolerant of pressure-group activity, encouraging the creation of an array of organised interests. There are many access points for group representatives to explore. Because of their success, the average citizen looks as much to his or her voluntary groups for political satisfaction as to an elected representative.

See also *Interest Groups*

Local Government

In addition to its fifty state governments, America has a vast and complex maze of local governments numbering nearly 88,000 types of authority. Generalisation is difficult because they range from the extremes of small, rural, sparsely populated townships to huge, densely populated metropolitan areas, with cities, towns, counties and districts between. Every American lives within the jurisdiction of the national government, a state government and perhaps ten to twenty local bodies. For instance, the six-county Chicago–Illinois metropolitan area has more than 1,200 different governments, some serving the people in broad ways, others providing more specialised services.

Since the Reagan era, states have been willing to decentralise their governing arrangements to the local level ('second-order devolution') and the existence of smaller units with worthwhile powers encourages individual participation and promotes the value of individualism. There is a strong tradition of grassroots democracy in America that fits in well with the widely shared belief that government should be kept as close to the people as possible. The very existence of so many governments to deal with so many different and necessary services seems to indicate that democracy flourishes in the localities.

Yet the health of local democracy in America can be overexaggerated. As in Britain, local politics are often poorly covered by the media and, consequently, the public often remains ill-informed about what goes on. This, in turn, makes it difficult to hold to account those who represent them. Moreover, levels of turnout in some elections are often very low. Some cities, such as Birmingham (Alabama), have done much to encourage neighbourhood democracy by creating neighbourhood boards that have meaningful control over important policy decisions. In this way, voters can see that participation is valuable and they feel that it is worthwhile to take their involvement beyond voting alone.

Writing of Britain and the United States, McNaughton (2001) gets the balance about right:

> In the USA, if anything, citizens are more interested in the politics of their state and their community than in the goings-on in Washington. Their daily lives are clearly affected more by the nature and performance of local government than those of British citizens. American local democracy is, therefore, more lively, more meaningful and more cherished than it is in the UK.

Lochner v. *New York* (1905)

Lochner v. *New York* was a landmark Supreme Court ruling that held that the 'right to free contract' was implicit in the due process clause of the Fourteenth Amendment. Lochner was convicted under a New York law that set maximum working hours for bakery workers. He brought this action in protest against the statute. The Court justices narrowly voted by five to four to overrule it, viewing it as 'unreasonable, unnecessary and arbitrary interference' that violated the Fourteenth Amendment freedom of the individual to contract. In other words, the act was not a constitutional regulation of the health and safety of a workplace, so that Lochner was cleared of committing an offence.

Lochner was one of the most controversial decisions in the Supreme Court's history, starting what is now known as the 'Lochner era' in which, over the next three decades, the justices invalidated scores of federal and state statutes that sought to regulate working conditions during the Progressive Era and the Great Depression.

Logrolling

Logrolling is the term applied to the exchange of support or favours (particularly vote trading on bills) that operates between legislators for mutual political gain. They anticipate that, by voting in support of the wishes of fellow congressmen and congresswomen, those colleagues will later vote for a measure in which they themselves have an interest, the idea being that 'you fatten my district, and I'll fatten yours'. Although vote trading is usually designed to enable members to 'bring home the bacon' for their constituents, it may also reflect deference to the superior expertise of others whose judgement they trust.

Louisiana Purchase (1803)

The Louisiana Purchase refers to the treaty with France signed by President Jefferson in 1803 that doubled the size of US territory as a result of buying the area known as Louisiane. It added 5.3 million (822,000 ha) acres of land, which extended the borders of the United States to the Rocky Mountains in the west and to what is now the state of Louisiana in the south. The purchase covered portions of fifteen current American states and two Canadian provinces (now Alberta and Saskatchewan). The deal cost the US Treasury fifteen million dollars.

The purchase was a key feature of the Jefferson presidency. At the time, some domestic critics viewed the transaction as unconstitutional. Jefferson understood that the Constitution made no provision for such an acquisition of territory, but saw merit in a move that would remove the power of France and Spain to block American trade access to the port of New Orleans. (N.b. At the time, the so-called Oklahoma Panhandle, and the south-western portions of Kansas and Louisiana were still claimed by Spain.)

See also *Jefferson, Thomas*

M

Machine Politics

A political machine is an unofficial system of political organisation based on patronage and the ability to do favours in return for votes. It is a method of 'behind-the-scenes' control. Machines sometimes have a boss or leader who directly controls the party workers at lower (city district or ward) levels. (Local leaders obey the boss because he controls party nominations and patronage positions.) Bosses have the allegiance of local business leaders, elected representatives and their appointees. Sometimes, this system is supplemented by threats of violence or harassment towards those who attempt to step outside it.

Machine politics existed in many large American cities, from Boston to Cleveland, New York City to Philadelphia, especially between about 1875 and 1950, a few continuing to survive today. They controlled hundreds – sometimes thousands – of jobs and lucrative city and county contracts. Those who operated them were in the business of winning elections by securing large numbers of voters on election day. Machines are often said to have drawn their strength from, and served as a power base for, ethnic immigrant populations. In particular, the Irish – but also other minority groups – were often willing to trade their votes in return for help with housing and jobs.

In the Progressive Era, civic-minded citizens denounced the corruption of the political machines and campaigned for political reform. By the late 1940s, many of the big city machines had collapsed. A local political machine in Tennessee was forcibly removed in what was known as the Battle of Athens (August 1946), a rebellion led by citizens in Athens and Etowah against their local government, following allegations of corruption and voter intimidation.

The Chicago machine was the most famous example of machine politics. Founded in 1931 and later run by Mayor Richard Daley until his death in 1976, it kept a firm grip on the Democratic Party machine, acting as an informal government and social service agency. At its peak, it controlled some thirty thousand jobs in Chicago and Cook Island. It survived longer than most but, after Daley's death, it subsequently declined. Today, machine politics are generally regarded as a leftover from America's past. Civil service reform, the move towards non-partisan local elections and the advent of technology – with presidential and other candidates now able to contact the voters directly via television and other electronic means – have undermined the need for the powerful traditional party organisations of the past.

American machines can be viewed as effective instruments for managing city governments and keeping powerful local interests under control. They also provided immigrants with political networks that could respond to their needs. On the other hand, they can be regarded as undemocratic and corrupt.

See also *Progressive Era*

Madison, James (1751–1836)

James Madison was one of the Founding Fathers of the United States and also its fourth president (1809–17). He was the principal author of the Constitution. In 1788, he wrote over a third of the *Federalist Papers*, still generally regarded as the most influential commentary on the Constitution.

A student of history and government, and well read in law, Madison participated in the framing of the constitution of Virginia, his home state, in 1776. He served in the Continental Congress and was a leader in the Virginia Assembly. He played a leading and sometimes decisive role in the debates at the Philadelphia Convention in 1787, hence the label sometimes applied to him as the 'Father of the Constitution'. (In his later years, he protested that the document was not 'the off-spring of a single brain', but 'the work of many heads and many hands'). In Congress, he helped frame the Bill of Rights and enact the first revenue legislation. The emergence of the Republican or Jeffersonian Party (later referred to as the Democratic Republicans) arose out of his leadership of the opposition to Hamilton's financial proposals which he felt would grant undue wealth and power to Northern financiers.

As Jefferson's Secretary of State (1801–09), Madison supervised the Louisiana Purchase and sponsored the ill-fated Embargo Act of 1807. As president, he led the nation into the War of 1812 against Great Britain in order to protect American economic rights. The conflict began badly as the US suffered numerous defeats by smaller forces, with the British entering Washington and setting fire to the White House and the Capitol. It ended on a high note, however, with a few victories that enabled Americans to view it as a glorious success, after which a new spirit of nationalism swept the country.

In his retirement, Madison spoke out against those who urged states' rights at the expense of the power and influence of the federal government. In a note opened after his death in 1836, he stated: 'The advice nearest to my heart and deepest in my convictions is that the Union of the States be cherished and perpetuated.'

Majority and Minority Opinions of the Supreme Court

A majority opinion is a controlling decision of the Supreme Court that is approved and signed by a majority of the justices – at least five on the nine-person body.

A minority opinion is one signed by a minority of the Court's members. It states their view of the case and why they disagree with the majority.

At the conclusion of oral argument, the justices retire to another conference at which the preliminary votes are tallied. The most senior justice in the majority assigns the initial draft of the Court's opinion to a colleague on his or her side. Drafts of the Court's opinion, as well as any concurring or dissenting opinions, circulate among the justices until the Court is prepared to announce the judgment in a particular case.

It is possible that, through recusals (see below) or vacancies, the Court divides evenly on a case. If that occurs, then the decision of the court below is affirmed but does not establish binding precedent. In effect, it results in a return to the status quo ante. For a case to be heard, there must be a quorum of at least six justices. If, because of recusals and vacancies, there is no quorum to hear a case and a majority of qualified justices believes that the case cannot be heard and determined in the next term, then the judgment of the court below is affirmed as if the Court had been evenly divided.

N.b. A recusal refers to the act of abstaining from participation in an official action, such as a legal proceeding, because of a conflict of interest. On the Supreme Court, justices typically voluntarily recuse themselves from participating in cases in which they have a financial interest. Justice Sandra Day O'Connor generally did not participate in cases involving telecommunications firms because she owned stock in that sector, while Stephen Breyer has disqualified himself in some cases involving insurance companies because of his participation in a Lloyds of London syndicate. Justices have also declined to participate in cases in which close relatives, such as their children, are lawyers for one of the parties.

Majority Leader: House of Representatives

The majority leader is the leader of the party that has a majority of the seats in the House of Representatives. The incumbent is responsible for managing the house floor and scheduling bills for consideration, as well as gauging the party mood, helping to unify the caucus and deliver its message. He or she works with the speaker and the majority whip to co-ordinate ideas and maintain support for legislation. In addition to distributing the responsibility for running the house, the existence of the majority leader allows the speaker to criticise his or her own party should this prove politically expedient.

The office was created in 1899 by Speaker David Henderson who saw a need for someone to act as a party leader on the house floor in addition to someone fulfilling his own role. This was because the speaker had increasingly become a prominent national figure with responsibilities elsewhere and also because the size of the house had grown from 105 at the beginning of the nineteenth century to 356. The majority Leader is second in command to the speaker. The holder of the office is formally chosen every two years by the party caucus, or – as it is usually known in the case of the Republican Party – the Republican Conference. He or she, however, is normally a close political ally of the speaker.

Congressman Steny Hoyer was elected majority leader in November 2006 by his colleagues in the Democratic Caucus.

Majority Leader: Senate

The Senate majority leader (also called Senate floor leader) is the chief representative and 'face' of the majority party in the Senate. The incumbent is the nearest equivalent to the speaker in the House of Representatives, serving as the chief spokesperson for the party and managing and scheduling the legislative and executive business of the chamber. This involves, among other things, co-ordinating party policy, helping to frame party strategy, determining the timing of debate on bills, assigning bills to committees and appointing members of special committees. In exercising these responsibiilties, the holder of the office is asisted by a whip and assistant whips.

By custom, the presiding officer gives the majority leader priority in obtaining recognition to speak on the floor of the Senate. The holder of the office is elected by the majority party. Normally, he or she will be a person who regularly consults, and can work effectively with, the leadership of the minority party which is all the more important because of the collaborative nature of the Senate's operations. The post can be both demanding and frustrating. This was appreciated by Lyndon Johnson who was a most accomplished majority leader prior to assuming the vice presidency in 1961. As he put it: 'The only real power available to the leader is the power of persuasion. There is no patronage, no power to discipline, no authority to fire Senators like the president can fire his members of Cabinet.'

Harry Reid was elected majority leader in November 2006 by his colleagues in the Democratic Caucus.

Manifest Destiny

This is the notion held by many Americans of the late nineteenth century that it was the 'manifest destiny' of their country to expand across the continent from the Atlantic seaboard to the Pacific Ocean. Given the large and accessible landmass available, it was easy for them to believe that they had the right and duty to secure the continent on behalf of democracy and free enterprise. Advocates of manifest destiny believed that expansion was not just beneficial but it was also obvious ('manifest') and certain ('destiny').

The term was first used to promote the annexation of much of what is now the West, including the Texas Annexation, the Mexican Cession and the incorporation of the Oregon Territory, but it has subsequently been used to advocate or justify other territorial acquisitions. There are echoes of the idea in the belief of some Americans that it is the mission of the United States to promote and sustain democracy throughout the world.

Marbury v. *Madison* (1803)

Marbury v. *Madison* was a landmark ruling in American law. It has become the basis for the exercise of judicial review in the United States, under Article 3 of the United States Constitution. The power of judicial review is not specifically referred to in the document. The doctrine was inferred by the Court, however, from its reading of the Constitution and propounded very clearly in the *Marbury* case, in which the Court for the first time struck down an act of Congress: 'A legislative act contrary to the Constitution is not law . . . it is emphatically the province and duty of the judicial department to say what the law is.'

Shortly before leaving office, President John Adams appointed several minor judicial officials in order to maintain the influence of his party in the incoming administration of his opponent, Thomas Jefferson. When Jefferson took office, he discovered that one of the commissions, that of William Marbury, had not been delivered. He therefore ordered the Secretary of State, James Madison, to hold it up, on the grounds that the appointment had not been officially made. Under a section of the Judicature Act (1789), Marbury sued in the Supreme Court to compel delivery of the commission, arguing that the letter declaring his appointment was being illegally withheld.

The new Chief Justice, John Marshall, was confronted with deciding a case between his political allies and his enemy, Jefferson, who was not only the president but also intent on weakening the power of the conservative Supreme Court. If the Court awarded Marbury a writ of mandamus (an order to force Madison to deliver the commission) the Jefferson administration could simply ignore it, in the process significantly weakening the authority of the courts. On the other hand, if the Court denied the writ, it might well appear that the justices had acted out of fear. Either case would be a denial of the basic principle of the supremacy of the law. Shrewd politician that he was, Marshall dismissed Marbury's case, even though he believed that Marbury deserved his appointment. Marshall ruled that the Court could not order it because the section of the 1789 Act under which he had sued was unconstitutional, and therefore null and void. By so doing, he in effect granted Jefferson what he wanted but the price of this decision was that in future the Supreme Court, on the basis of its reading of the Constitution, could set limits on the actions of Congress and be the final arbiter of what is and is not constitutional.

Marshall's decision in this case has been hailed as a judicial tour de force, establishing the principle of judicial review. Following the 1803 case, the authority of the courts to act as the final arbiter on constitutional matters was confirmed in other cases in 1810 and 1821. It has been accepted ever since.

See also *Judicial Review*; *Marshall, John*

March on Washington (1963)

The March on Washington for Jobs and Freedom was the largest political rally ever seen in the nation's capital and one of the first to have extensive live television coverage at home and abroad. It took place in Washington DC on 28 August, 1963. An estimated quarter of a million people – almost a quarter of whom were white – marched from the Washington Monument to the Lincoln Memorial in what turned out to be both a protest demonstration and a communal celebration. The aim was to encourage passage of a civil rights bill and further action by the administration to help black Americans.

The event included musical performances by several well-known sympathisers with the civil rights movement, Joan Baez, Bob Dylan and Mahalia Jackson among them. Among actors present were Marlon Brando, Sammy Davis Jnr, Paul Newman and Sidney Poitier who read a speech by James Baldwin. The speakers included all the leading civil rights leaders, and among the several 'Negro Women Fighters for Freedom' introduced was Rosa Parks. The most notable contribution was the 'I have a dream' speech of Martin Luther King which drew upon beliefs and documents that were basic to the ideas of white Americans, the Declaration of Independence and the Old Testament among them. By tapping the emotional wellsprings of American history, he appealed to thoughtful and patriotic white Americans, so that they felt inspired to help turn the dream of equality into a reality. It is difficult to quantify the importance of the march but its emotional impact probably prepared the way for the subsequent legislation.

Marches had long been a favourite tactic of civil rights activists, Washington being their favoured location. The heavy police presence turned out to be unnecessary, as the march was noted for its civility and peacefulness.

See also *King, Martin Luther*; *Civil Rights Movement*

Marshall, John (1755–1835)

John Marshall was a statesman and jurist from Virginia who shaped American constitutional law and made the Supreme Court a centre of power. He was the fourth Chief Justice, the longest serving in the history of the Court. He dominated the Court which he led between 1801 and 1835, and is widely regarded as the most influential figure to hold the highest judicial office.

Marshall, a leading figure in the Federalist Party, is one of the few people who have served in all three branches of government. He briefly served in the House of Representatives before becoming Secretary of State under President Adams, prior to his elevation to the Bench. During his three decades or so as Chief Justice, he established the Supreme Court as the ultimate body for interpreting the Constitution. The principle was first demonstrated in the case of *Marbury* v. *Madison* (1803), as the Court established the prerogative of judicial review. Other notable cases included *McCulloch* v. *Maryland*, *Gibbons* v. *Ogden*, *Brown* v. *Maryland*, and *Ogden* v. *Saunders*. Marshall believed that the Constitution was designed to be 'adapted to the various crises of human affairs'.

It was in *Marbury* v. *Madison* that he made his most famous contribution towards establishing the principle of judicial review, the entitlement of the justices to strike down laws that violated the Constitution. In a skilful ruling, his logic seemed to be impeccable. In essence, it was that: 1. the Constitution was superior to any statute; 2. the Judiciary Act of 1789 contradicted the Constitution; and therefore, 3. the Judiciary Act must be unconstitutional. In his judgment, he attacked the administration for its neglect of its constitutional duties but decreed that the Court could not constitutionally issue the writ of mandamus, a court order directing an official, such as the secretary of state, to perform a ministerial duty. This was a third way between issuing the writ of mandamus, which would have been of

no avail as the demand would have been ignored by the Executive, and refusing to issue the writ which would have been an admission of the Court's impotence. As a political balancing act, his decision was a masterpiece. Its key effect was to cement the position of the judiciary as an independent and influential branch of government.

Marshall emphasised national supremacy over the interests of the individual states and the protection of property rights. He made several important decisions relating to the evolution of federalism, shaping the balance of power between the federal government and the states during the early years of the Republic. In particular, he repeatedly confirmed the supremacy of federal over state law, supporting an expansive reading of the enumerated powers.

See also **Marbury** v. **Madison** *(1803)*

Marshall Plan

The Marshall Plan was a package of economic aid provided to Europe to rebuild the continent following the devastation of World War II. It was part of the containment policy developed by the United States under President Truman.

In June 1947 Secretary of State George Marshall announced that America would 'assist in the return of normal economic health in the world'. Billions of dollars were committed to propping up the states of western Europe for, although the aid was available to all countries on the continent, the eastern bloc was uninterested in becoming involved. Whereas British Foreign Secretary Ernest Bevin thought that the Americans were giving an 'inspiring lead', the response of the Communist Party newspaper in Russia (*Pravda*) was less flattering. It discerned an attempt to interfere 'in the domestic affairs of other countries'. The Russian rejection probably made passage of the aid programme through Congress possible.

American motives were mixed. Altruism played a part but so did self-interest. It was in America's economic interests to see Europe prosperous again, for a flourishing continent could afford to buy American goods. In addition, there was a political motive, for Washington understood that hunger and deprivation made for popular discontent and disillusion with the democratic process. If aid could promote recovery, then there was less likelihood of Europeans being tempted by the Communist ideas that were becoming entrenched in eastern Europe. The position of West Germany was especially crucial in this regard for it was geographically adjacent to the Soviet bloc. It was easier to sell the idea of assisting German recovery and rehabilitation to western governments, if it was part of a wider programme of economic assistance.

Altogether, some $13.5 billion were made available. Of this sum, the largest share (over $3 billion) went to Britain, while France, Italy and West Germany also benefited considerably. These countries were helped by the economic boom in the United States, both in the rising demand for manufactured goods and because of heavy investment in European industry by private firms. By the early 1950s, the western European economies were beginning to recover, much helped by the assistance given by the United States through the Marshall Plan.

It was necessary to create an organisation to supervise the administration of this relief. Early in 1948 a number of countries joined together in the Organisation for European Economic Co-operation (OEEC). This was a classic example of intergovernmental co-operation.

The Marshall Plan was one of the key elements of US foreign policy following World War II. The goals and philosophy outlined in 1947 continue to guide America's foreign aid programme. Where once America helped rebuild war-torn nations of western Europe, now the US assists developing countries and newly independent nations of eastern and central Europe and Asia. Today, foreign assistance continues to translate American ideals into concrete actions to help others in need. Its aim is still to build a peaceful, more prosperous world, one that is sympathetic to American values.

See also *Foreign Policy*

Marshall, Thurgood (1908–93)

Thurgood Marshall was the first African American to serve as an associate justice on the Supreme Court. Appointed by President Johnson in 1967, he remained on the Bench until his retirement in 1991, during which time he consistently offered strong backing for the protection of individual rights. His liberal record included support for those challenging racial or sexual discrimination, for abortion rights and for the rights of criminal defendants, and firm opposition to the death penalty. His support for affirmative action led to his strong dissent in the *Baake* case (1978). As the outlook of the Court changed following appointments made by Nixon and Reagan, Marshall found himself increasingly out of sympathy with its general stance. After retiring, he continued to be outspoken in his support for voiceless Americans and became increasingly critical of the judgments the Court delivered.

Prior to his appointment to the Court of Appeals (1961), to the office of Solicitor General (1965) and then to the Supreme Court (1967), Marshall had joined the legal staff of the National Association for the Advancement of Colored People. He was best known for his impressive record in arguing more than thirty cases before the Supreme Court, several of them concerning higher education. It was in his presentation of the challenge to the 'separate but equal' doctrine in *Brown* v. *Board of Education*, however, that he achieved his greatest victory. In his career, he won more cases before the United States Supreme Court than any other American.

Mass Media

By the mass media, we mean those means of communication that permit messages to be conveyed to the public. Media, such as television, radio, newspapers, books, magazines, posters, the cinema, and more recently videos and computers, provide important links connecting people to one another. They allow information to be passed from one person to a vast audience at approximately the same time. Sending a fax or e-mail to a friend is a personal form of communication but, if the message is sent simultaneously to large numbers of people, it becomes part of the mass media. The mass media can reach a large and potentially unlimited number of people at the same time.

The most important forms of the media for

political coverage are newspapers and broadcasting by radio and television but, over the last generation, television has surpassed any other medium as the source from which the majority of people derive their information (see table below) for it provides an easily accessible, easily digested and credible medium available in almost every household. Today, how voters view politics and politicians is much influenced by television. Politicians recognise this and act accordingly, often seeking to influence the television at least as much as they are influenced by it.

But other forms of communication exist, including a number of ways by which local communities can exercise some political muscle. In the United States, these may range from the familiar to the uncommon. In New Jersey, those who opposed a tax increase organised a mass phone-in to a radio station to attract attention to their grievance, as part of a general revolt against their growing burden of taxation. By contrast, landlords in California, who objected to the introduction of rent control, decided to circulate videotapes which depicted pro-control members of the Santa Monica city council in an unflattering light.

The two older technologies, newspapers and the radio, continue to be significant among the American media. Newspapers are the oldest form of mass communication in the United States, with some 80 per cent of adult Americans now reading a paper on a regular basis. America has

traditionally lacked a strong national press, which is not surprising given the divergent interests of people in different parts of the country and the difficulties of transporting morning editions quickly around the country. The middle-market *USA Today* has helped to fill the gap but the likelihood is that, over the next few years, more national papers will be created given the new technology available. In the mean time, however, in most American cities there is only one regular newspaper available although, countrywide, there are some 1,800 titles. Small-town dailies thrive on presenting stories of local interest but may also provide a sketchy coverage of national events.

Americans have always been deeply attached to their free press. Newspapers are often criticised for their bias, on the right there being complaints that they are dominated by a liberal elite and on the left that they are unduly influenced by rich and powerful moguls. They may sometimes be attacked as unduly sensationalist in their coverage of events and too obsessed with the trivia of the personal lives of those who aspire to lead them. But many voters trust their journalists more than their politicians and have a strong suspicion that exposés of corruption and scandal are more than likely to be justified. In episodes, such as Watergate and the Iran–Contra affair, they had reason to be grateful for the investigative instincts of persistent newshounds.

Radio is still extensively used in the United States. It had always remained popular as an outlet for political advertising in some of the smaller states but has recently experienced a surprising revival in the television age. The popularity of chat shows and, particularly, phone-in programmes of the *Talk Radio* variety has aroused considerable interest, as have the new stations which cater for minority groups and tastes. Radio talk shows have been described as the equivalent of 'a 1990s American town meeting', a chance for the voters to listen to and call the candidates. These may have vast audiences, and act as a lively medium for the exchange of views between often-conservative presenters and equally (if not more) right-wing listeners. Individuals can vent their feelings, however blatant, and listen to those of others.

Sources of political information

Source	%
Television	63
Newspapers	22
Radio	12
Other	3

Adapted from the contents of tables in E. Gerber, 'Divided We Watch', *Brills Content* (February 2001).

N.b. Figures provided by the Pew Center (*Trends*, 2005) for the presidential election of 2004 show that 78 per cent named television as their main source, 38 per cent newspapers, 16 per cent radio, 15 per cent the Internet and 4 per cent magazines. The figures in the table do not, of course, take separate account of the Internet, the use of which has subsequently become more widespread.

Television

In the United States television is still dominated by three major commercial networks, CBS, NBC and ABC, although their hold has significantly weakened in recent years. These networks sell programmes to local broadcast stations known as affiliates and, in 1995, the three long–established ones each had more than 200 of these, Fox Broadcasting some 150 or so. What has happened in the last decade is that the hold of the three networks has been challenged, not only by Fox, but also by the development of new technologies that are widening the choice available to viewers. Many Americans now get their television signals not over the air but via cables. Several cable-only channels, such as CNN and C-Span, have emerged.

The impact of new technologies

New technology has had a considerable impact on the media. In the modern communications revolution, four trends have particular significance:

- The continuing improvement in the quality and potential of computers
- The digitisation of data, making possible the integration of computer and telecommunications technologies
- Satellite communications developments
- Fibre optics, which allow many different messages to travel down one line.

Two developments have been of particular significance. The Internet system, the backbone of the information highway, provides a means of extracting a mass of information, political or otherwise. With penetration into many households across Europe and the United States, the worldwide web offers new opportunities for politicians and the public to convey their news and views, and gives all users access to a wealth of stored knowledge. E-mail provides a further

---

Cable television: Fox News and its rivals

The Fox News Channel was created in 1996 by Rupert Murdoch's News Corporation. It promised 'fair and balanced coverage', adopting the slogan 'We report, you decide'. It soon ran into allegations that it had introduced bias into television news bulletins and reporting, however, the suggestion being made that it employed a right-wing bias to assist its commercial success. In the early years, the channel was not regarded as a serious threat to CNN or to the other new operation, MSNBC. The events of 9/11, however, and the subsequent war on terror gave Fox News a new impetus. Viewers – particularly Republicans – responded favourably to its style of reporting which, in an unabashed manner, identified itself with American values such as patriotism and support for the flag. Pew Research found that, in November 2004, 70 per cent of viewers for whom Fox was the main source of election news and information intended to vote for the Grand Old Party. Similarly, CNN catered for Democrat-leaning viewers; 67 per cent of those who tuned into CNN for their election coverage supported Kerry.

New competitors, such as MSNBC and Headline News, have begun to chip away at some of Fox News's audience. CNN and MSNBC have more popular websites which could, in time, draw even more breaking-news audiences away. Yet for all this, Fox News remains the dominant channel, both in terms of overall audience and individual shows. In 2006, more than half the people watching cable news were watching Fox News (as they have since 2001).

The mean viewing figure for Fox News in prime time was 1.4 million in 2006. That is more than triple the viewership of MSNBC (378,000) and almost double that of CNN (739,000). More than half (55 per cent) of all viewers watching prime-time cable news in 2006 were tuned into Fox News. *The O'Reilly Factor* was again the most watched show on cable news, averaging two million viewers a night.

Information derived from research by the Pew Center in its *State of the Nation* survey, 2007.

means of speedy political communication, not only between voters and politicians and vice versa but also between campaigning activists belonging to new popular movements.

In the last few years, the Internet has been one of the most discussed means of communication. Partly this is because it allows the diffusion of several kinds of data, images, speeches, text and video. The level of interest also reflects the speed with which the Internet has been adopted across the world. (see table below). Moreover, young Americans rely much more heavily on the Internet than do their elders. Pew Research (*Trends* 2005) has found that of all Americans, 29 per cent read online news at least three times a week, 34 per cent regularly watch nightly network news on television and 42 per cent regularly read a newspaper. For younger Americans (particularly males), the Internet is second only to television as their main source of daily news, as figures provided by the Carnegie Corporation (2004) reveal:

A further source of information that has rapidly gained a foothold in the last two years is weblogs. Pew found that, in early 2005, there were four million active bloggers, while thirty-two millin regularly read their comments and debates. Bloggers have been prominent in delving into some political scandals. Their findings damaged the reputation of Trent Lott, after the Senate majority leader had seemingly endorsed racist observations in 2002. They have also been involved in political advocacy, some achieving success in organising fundraising on behalf of candidates in the 2004 election.

Overall, the appetite for news has declined in the United States. The traditional channels have lost viewers, and newspaper readership continues its long-term decline. This reduced consumption has been partially offset by the audience for cable and online news but Pew has found that there

has been a general loss of hunger for information about the political situation. This applies especially to young people for whom the more subjective type of coverage, provided by Fox and other cable channels and the Internet, is becoming their main source of information.

The effects of the media

Given the time many people spend viewing, and their constant exposure to a mass of information in news bulletins and current affairs/discussion programmes, it would be surprising if there was no effect on their attitudes and judgements. At the very least, they would be expected to know more about topics on which they already had some knowledge, and to become informed about ones with which they were previously unfamiliar. At election time, one would expect a heightened awareness of key issues. Indeed, some people tend to become mini-pundits on the issues of the day, having watched a programme the night before. One might expect increased interest as well.

The real – as opposed to the imagined – effects of the mass media on popular attitudes are difficult to assess. Viewers may spend hours watching the television or reading a newspaper but this does not necessarily tell us that either or both are their main sources of information. There are many possible ways of obtaining knowledge, and it is impossible to separate that which has been derived from the media from conversations at the workplace or that which has been accumulated from elsewhere. Life is a continuing learning experience in which knowledge and attitudes are liable to be influenced at many points in a person's lifetime.

There are four main theories about the effects of the media on people's attitudes and conduct:

1. The hypodermic theory

Some political scientists, basing their research mainly on the interwar experience of dictatorships in Europe, have suggested that the message carried by the media was like a 'magic bullet' or hypodermic syringe which, on contact with the audience, affected it in a uniform way. People

Most important source of news for American 18–34-year-olds (per cent)

Local television	31
Internet	25
Newspapers	14
Cable television	9
National television	7

soaked up the information they were given, rather as a sponge absorbs water. The survey evidence to substantiate such findings was lacking. In any case, the effect of propaganda in a totalitarian regime was likely to be infinitely greater than in a liberal democracy such as America.

2. The reinforcement theory

Researching in the1960s, Paul Lazarsfeld (1968) found no evidence of decisive influence. He put forward the *minimum effects* model of media influence which recognised that knowledge may increase and attitudes may become clearer in a campaign but that voting behaviour itself was little influenced by television. The reason for this was the *selective exposure theory*, according to which listeners and viewers filtered out and suppressed unwelcome messages while paying particular attention to those they like. The idea was that television functions primarily as a means of reinforcement rather than of fundamental change. People exposed themselves to communications with which they were likely to agree, and tended to remember only information which coincided with their own outlook.

3. The agenda-setting theory

Coverage of the effects of the media moved on from the 'reinforcement' phase to the 'agenda-setting one, according to which the media achieve their aim of influencing people by more subtle means. They can't directly tell people what to think but they can tell them what to think about. They influence the public by determining what is shown or read, and many of the viewers/readers come to accept what is offered as a representation of the main things which are really happening.

4. The independent effect theory

A fourth model is in vogue today. The independent effect theory is now sometimes advocated by sociologists on both sides of the Atlantic. This suggests that the media do have an effect on public attitudes, even if those effects are difficult to monitor and variable in their impact. With the extensive amount of viewing done today, it seems only common sense to assume that the influence of the media must be greater than has been allowed for in the recent past. In particular, what has changed in the last generation is that the traditional identification of many Americans with a particular party has become less firm. It is now a commonplace to speak of declining voter partisanship. If people are more receptive to changes of mind, it seems reasonable to suggest that the media, especially television, may have a greater effect than ever before on their attitudes and voting. There are more votes 'up for grabs'.

The truth is that no one really knows what the effects are, and different research points to different conclusions. People react in several ways. It is misleading to speak of the impact of the media as though this was the same impact on all groups in the population. There are many effects on many different people.

See also *Blogging*; *Internet*; *Press*; *Television*; *You Tube*

McCain, John (1936–)

John McCain is a war veteran who went into politics and became a congressman in 1982 for the first congressional district of Arizona. In 1986, he was elected to the United States Senate, and he is currently the senior senator for Arizona. He serves on the Committee on Armed Services, the Committee on Commerce, Science and Transportation and the Committee on Indian Affairs. As senator, he made several attempts in the late 1990s to ban the raising and spending of soft money but the proposal was blocked in the Senate. He was the co-author of the McCain–Feingold Bipartisan Campaign Reform Act of 2002.

He was a presidential candidate in November 2000, but lost the Republican nomination to George W. Bush. He formally announced his candidature for the 2008 election in April 2007. His strengths as a candidate included national name recognition, his sponsorship of major lobbying and campaign finance reform initiatives, his military service (including years as a tortured prisoner of war), the experience acquired in standing in the 2000 campaign, his extensive fundraising abilities and – initially – his selection of personable Alaskan governor Sarah Palin as his running mate (ultimately, voter reactions to Palin from beyond the Religious Right grew increasingly negative).

The outcome of the election was a heavy defeat for McCain who failed to win most of the swing states and lost some traditionally Republican ones. He won 46 per cent of the national popular vote, compared with Obama's 53 per cent.

Following his defeat, McCain returned to the Senate and indicated that he intended to run for election to that body again in 2010.

See also *McCain–Feingold Campaign Finance Reform Act*

McCain–Feingold Campaign Finance Reform Act

The Bipartisan Campaign Reform Act of 2002 (usually known as the McCain Feingold Act is a federal law that regulated the financing of political campaigns. Its chief sponsors were Senators John McCain of the Republican Party and Russell Feingold of the Democrats. The new legal limits became effective in January 2003 and were therefore in use by the time of the 2004 elections.

McCain made the issue of further reform a plank of his unsuccessful bid for the Republican candidacy in 2000, and thereafter a momentum developed for a further tightening of the law. When the House of Representatives and Senate passed a bipartisan measure of campaign finance reform, President Bush – against his earlier inclinations – did not seek to veto it.

The McCain–Feingold reforms particularly addressed two key issues, the increased role of soft money in campaign financing and the proliferation of issue ads. Among other things, the Act:

- banned the national party committees from raising or spending soft money
- prevented business and labour unions from directly funding issue advertisements
- prohibited the use of business and labour money to broadcast advertisements that named a federal candidate in the thirty days prior to a

primary election and the sixty days prior to a general election
- outlawed any fundraising activities on public property.

Political opponents of the 2002 Act were concerned that, unless there was some control over the structural costs of campaigning (e.g., over advertising), they would find their income restricted and not be able to afford to enter the race, thus benefiting only the wealthiest of candidates. The proposals were also opposed on grounds of free speech, as an affront to the First Amendment.

See also *Soft Money*

McCarthy, Joseph (1908–57) and McCarthyism

Joseph Raymond McCarthy was a conservative Republican senator for Wisconsin (1946–57). In the early Cold War years, he became the most well-known public face of an extreme anti-communist witch-hunt in the United States.

After World War II, there was a developing suspicion of Communist infiltration of the United States government following a series of investigations and espionage trials. Against this background, and after several largely undistinguished years in the Senate, McCarthy suddenly achieved fame or notoriety in February 1950 by making unsubstantiated claims that there were large numbers of Communists and Soviet spies and sympathisers operating a spy ring inside several parts of the federal government, including within President Truman's administrative staff and in the State Department. He alleged that Secretary of State Dean Acheson knew the names of 205 Communists in the State Department, and later claimed to have the names of fifty-seven of them himself. McCarthy's charges caused a furore, and his call for an investigation received extensive media attention, making him the most famous political figure in the nation after the president.

When the Republicans took control of Congress in 1953, McCarthy became chairman of the Committee on Government Operations and the subcommittee on investigations, a post in which he wielded great power. Through widely publicised hearings, the use of unidentified informers and reckless accusations, McCarthy doggedly pursued his prey. His methods came under increasing attack in the press by journalists and his colleagues, the more so as they realised that careers were being ruined on the flimsiest evidence. As chairman, he so angered Democrats that they resigned from the committee in protest. He also antagonised the new president and fellow Republican, Dwight Eisenhower, by accusing his administration of sheltering Communists. Eisenhower refused to issue a public rebuke but worked behind the scenes to isolate him.

In the autumn of 1953, McCarthy investigated the Army Signal Corps but was unable to substantiate further sensational charges and failed to uncover an alleged espionage ring. His frequent interruptions during the proceedings (especially his numerous 'points of order') made him the object of ridicule. Many previous supporters turned against him, and his ratings in opinion polls indicated a sharp decline in public approval. In particular, his treatment of General Ralph Zwicker during the investigation brought McCarthy much discredit. On 9 June, the hearings climaxed when he attacked a young lawyer who worked for the law firm of Joseph Nye Welch, the Army's chief counsel. Welch's reply to McCarthy became famous: 'Have you no sense of decency, sir, at long last? Have you no sense of decency?' After that, the hearings petered out to an inconclusive end but McCarthy's reputation never recovered. Later in 1954, the Senate voted by sixty-seven to twenty-two to censure him for abusing his power, making him one of the few senators ever to be disciplined in this fashion. Though he remained in the Senate, McCarthy now had little power and was ignored by the Congress, the White House and most of the media.

McCarthy's indiscriminate attacks gave rise to the term 'McCarthyism', coined in 1950 in reference to his sensationalist tactics. It was soon applied to similar anti-Communist pursuits. Today, it is used more generally to describe demagogic, reckless and unsubstantiated accusations, as well as public attacks on the character or patriotism of political opponents.

McCreary County v. ACLU (2005)

McCreary County v. *ACLU of Kentucky* and *Van Orden* v. *Perry* were the first cases in which the Supreme Court dealt directly with the display of the Ten Commandments in county courthouses.

Seven individuals and the American Civil Liberties Union (ACLU) sued three Kentucky counties (McCreary, Harlan, and Pulaski) alleging that their erection of framed copies of the Ten Commandments in county courthouses and schools was a violation of the Establishment Clause of the First Amendment. The plaintiffs sought a declaration that the displays were unconstitutional and an injunction preventing the counties from continuing to use them. After the lawsuits were filed, the counties changed their displays to include secular historical and legal documents, some of which were excerpted, in an attempt to bring them within the parameters of the First Amendment. The district court ordered that the displays be removed and that no similar displays be erected, and the Sixth Circuit Court of Appeals affirmed the order, finding that the displays violated the Establishment Clause because their purpose was predominantly religious and that they had the effect of endorsing religion. The court of appeals noted that the displays purported only to have historical and secular purposes; because they did not present the Ten Commandments objectively and integrate them with a secular message, they impermissibly conveyed a religious message.

In June 2005, on a five-to-four vote, the Court ruled in the *McCreary County* case that the several displays of the Ten Commandments in Kentucky courthouses were illegal, on the grounds that they were not clearly integrated with a secular display and therefore were considered to have a religious purpose. By the same margin, however, it upheld the legality of a Ten Commandments display at the Texas state capital in the *Van Orden* case. The six-foot-high monument was deemed to have a 'secular purpose'.

See also *Establishment Clause*; *First Amendment*

Medicaid and Medicare see *Health Provision*

Melting Pot

The 'melting pot' refers to the process by which people of diverse lands, cultures, languages and religions are blended into the host society, mixing with other groups and gradually becoming assimilated into the way of life. The ingredients in the pot are combined so as to develop a multi-ethnic society. The term, which originates in the United States and was coined by an immigrant (Israel Zangwill), is often used to describe countries, in particular the United States, that have experienced large-scale immigration from many parts of the world. Generations of migrants to America became successful by shedding much of their attachment to their historic culture and identity, and adopting the mores of their new country.

Immigration has been a recurring theme throughout America's history, as the country has attracted people in search of a share of 'the American dream'. As a consequence, the 'melting pot' image has been much discussed, many Americans taking pride in the way that their country has successfully assimilated people of different backgrounds and cultures into its society. Others contest the melting-pot image, placing the emphasis on the idea of multiculturalism, which describes the way in which newcomers can retain their own national characteristics while still becoming reasonably integrated. The Canadians describe the result as a 'cultural mosaic'. Some admire the way in which the arrival of immigrants contributes new experiences to the host country without compromising its essential character.

Midterm Elections

Midterm elections take place every two years between presidential elections (e.g., 2002, 2006, 2010, etc.). All members of the House of Representatives are due for re-election, as is a third of the members of the Senate. There are gubernatorial contests and initiative/referendum votes taking place at the same time.

In midterm elections, existing members usually get re-elected, should they decide to stand, because of the incumbency factor. For instance, in 1998, 98.5 per cent of members of the house and 90 per cent of Senators again won re-election. Even in years when there was an anti-incumbency mood (1992, 1994), many more members left office through retirement than because of defeat at the polls.

Midterm elections offer a chance to assess the mood of the country and the president's chance of re-election. They can inspire or demoralise the person in the White House and his would-be challengers. They can be particularly significant during some presidencies. In November 1994, the Republicans scored a convincing victory, capturing both chambers of Congress for the first time for many years and thereby dealing a blow to the future legislative and other prospects of the Clinton presidency. The Republican resurgence proved costly for the president over the following years, for a partisan House was able to pursue him vigorously over the Lewinsky and other scandals. The party's revival significantly reshaped the political agenda, moving it sharply to the right.

In midterm elections, some candidates benefit from a coat-tails effect. When there is a popular president, it can help their cause for they are able to associate themselves with his or her glories. This has not often happened in recent years but, in 2002, many Republicans were delighted to have George W. Bush lend support to their campaign and to bask in his popularity. On that occasion, the party consciously tried to 'nationalise' the campaign, so that candidates could be associated with his success in Afghanistan and the early stages of the war on terrorism. By contrast, in 1994, Democrats were keen to dissociate themselves from President Clinton for his political stock was low at the time after the failure of his health reform project. The president's party often suffers losses in midterm, as the voters express disappointment at, or disapproval of, what has been done over the previous two years.

More usually, local rather than national factors are relevant to voting in midterm elections. Voters assess the performance of the incumbent in 'bringing home the bacon'. Their wants and needs will differ from state to state. For instance, logging is a key issue in Oregon and cross-border immigration in Texas. In all cases, they will want to see ample evidence that their elected representative has pursued every opportunity to achieve economic advantages for the district, perhaps by gaining some defence contracts or public works projects for the area. Midterm elections determine the fate of members of the lower chamber, for their tenure expires with them. Because of the brief period in which they can make a difference, pork-barrel politics assume great importance to them.

See also *Pork/Pork-barrel Politics*

Minority Leader: House of Representatives

The minority leader of the House of Representatives is the floor leader of the opposition party, the minority counterpart to the majority leader. Generally, the minority leader is on the ballot for the speakership during the convening of the Congress. He or she is usually the party's top choice for speaker if party control changes after an election. The minority leader usually meets the majority leader and the speaker to discuss agreements and arrangements on controversial issues.

Minority Leader: Senate

The Senate minority leader is the senator who is elected by the party caucus (or conference) of the minority party to serve as its spokesperson in the chamber, with responsibility for co-ordinating party positions and managing floor strategy. He works with the majority leader in scheduling the legislative and executive business of the Senate.

Unlike the offices of president of the Senate (the vice president of the United States) and the president *pro tempore*, the posts of majority and minority leaders are not included in the Constitution. The task of party floor leadership evolved out of necessity. Both posts carry responsibility rather than specific power. The efficacy of floor leaders largely depends on their individual skill, intelligence and personality.

Minority Opinions see *Majority and Minority Opinions of the Supreme Court*

Miranda Rules

Miranda rules are the guidelines concerning the treatment of people during custodial interrogation, as established by the *Miranda* v. *Arizona* ruling (1966). These rules apply when a person has been taken into custody or otherwise significantly deprived of freedom of movement by the police. Although some exceptions have been created, in essence, they still govern all police interrogations. Courts have often thrown out confessions obtained where the rules have not been followed.

Miranda v. *Arizona* (1966)

Miranda v. *Arizona* was a landmark 5–4 decision of the Supreme Court. The Court held that criminal suspects must be informed of their right to consult with an attorney and of their right against self-incrimination prior to questioning by police.

The case concerned Ernesto Miranda who was arrested at his home in Arizona and taken to the local police station where he was questioned for two hours before confessing to crimes of rape and kidnapping. In the five votes to four decision, the Court held that individuals held for questioning must be clearly informed of their rights to talk with counsel and have a lawyer present during their interrogation. If a lawyer cannot be afforded, then the court must appoint one for the defendant. Furthermore, information obtained from someone who has not been informed of his or her rights cannot be used against them.

Delivering the judgment on behalf of the majority, Earl Warren pronounced that: ' . . . the prosecution may not use statements, whether exculpatory or inculpatory, stemming from custodial interrogation of the defendant unless it demonstrates the use of procedural safeguards effective to secure the privilege against self-incrimination'.

Mondale, Walter (1928–)

Walter 'Fritz' Mondale has been an active figure in national politics for several decades, becoming an influential figure within the leadership of the Democratic Party in the 1970s and 1980s. A two-term senator for Minnesota, he served as the forty-second vice president under President Carter (1977–81). He was party nominee for the presidency in November 1984, standing against the incumbent Republican, Ronald Reagan. Mondale was overwhelmingly defeated, carrying only his home state and the District of Columbia, despite winning 40.6 per cent of the popular vote.

Mondale is perhaps best known for his development of the office of vice president. To a greater extent than most of his predecessors, he enjoyed a close relationship with the president who treated him as a full working partner. Mondale was invited to attend and to participate in any presidential meetings, exercising influence over some areas of policy as well as contributing his ideas. He came to be regarded as a wise adviser and useful troubleshooter for the administration. In this, he was helped by his reputation as an effective team player who did not wish to steal the limelight from Carter. Subsequent vice presidents have tended to follow the 'Mondale model' in the administrations in which they serve.

Monroe Doctrine

The Monroe Doctrine was the policy announced by President James Monroe in December 1823, which stated that any attempts by European powers to interfere with, or establish new colonies, anywhere in the Americas would be considered unfriendly to US interests.

In his State of the Union address, President Monroe was articulating the US position on the new political order developing in the rest of the Americas, and the role of Europe in the western hemisphere. The three main concepts of the doctrine: separate spheres of influence for the Americas and Europe; non-colonisation; and non-intervention; were designed to signify a clear break between the New World and the autocratic realm of Europe. Monroe's statement was little noted by the great powers of Europe at the time but it has subsequently been regarded as a defining moment in US foreign policy in which the country outlined a basic and long-surviving stance.

During the Cold War, the Monroe Doctrine was applied to Latin America by those who formulated American foreign policy. During the Cuban Missile Crisis, it was invoked to prevent the further spreading of Soviet-backed Communism in Latin America. As President Kennedy explained in a news conference (August 1962):

> The Monroe Doctrine means what it has meant since President Monroe and John Quincy Adams [believed to be its prime author] enunciated it, and that is that we would oppose a foreign power extending its power to the Western Hemisphere, and that is why we oppose what is happening in Cuba today.

In the Cold War, there was periodic debate about the interpretation of the Monroe Doctrine. The United States often provided intelligence and military aid to South American governments that appeared to be threatened by Communist subversion. It came to a head in the 1980s during the Iran–Contra Affair, in which CIA Director Robert Gates vigorously defended the Contra operation, arguing that, to avoid intervention in Nicaragua, would be 'totally to abandon the Monroe doctrine'. The Monroe Doctrine was also cited during the American invasion of Grenada (1983).

Motor Voting

Motor voting was the popular name for the National Voter Registration Act (1993) which permitted people to register to vote while they were handling official documentation such as signing up for social services or applying for or renewing their driving licences. Analysts had long argued that one reason for the low voter turnout in the United States was the difficulty in registering to vote. Hopes were high that the simplified procedure would increase registration and encourage more people to exercise the franchise. Several million new voters did register following the passage of the bill although this did not have a beneficial impact on the turnout in the next presidential election for which the figure was disappointingly low.

Mount Rushmore

Mount Rushmore is the location of an epic sculpture that features the faces of four exalted American presidents: George Washington, Thomas Jefferson, Theodore Roosevelt and Abraham Lincoln. Set against the backdrop of South Dakota's Black Hills, the 60-feet-high (18.2 m) mountain carvings – carved in granite – are a lasting memorial to the 'great' or 'near great' presidents.

Some Americans would argue with the choices made but most would agree that they deserve their eminence, even if similar claims could be made for Franklin Roosevelt. But, as the carving started in 1927 and was completed by 1941, FDR was not in serious contention. As the president at the time when the project was conceived, Coolidge insisted that, along with Washington, there should be two Republicans and one Democrat. He and the sculptor, Gutzon Borglum, were united in a shared belief that the four presidents selected represented the first 150 years of American history because of their role in preserving the Republic and expanding its territory.

Movements

Movements comprise large numbers of people who are united but loosely organised around a central idea or interest that is of continuing significance, and who are willing to take action on that issue in order to change attitudes, institutions and policies. They often arise at the grassroots level and evolve into national groupings. Often, they include individuals and groups who otherwise are 'left out' of government. Movements are different from interest groups or pressure groups but are often closely related to them. They contain people who share common concerns but their views about how to achieve their broad goals – such as care for the environment or women's rights – may differ sharply.

See also *Abolitionists/Abolition Movement; Abortion Rights Movement; Civil Rights Movement; Green Movement; Pro-life Movement*

Muckraking Journalists

Muckraking investigative journalists and writers of the late nineteenth and early twentieth centuries were dedicated to uncovering political and corporate corruption and exposing how corporate and partisan political elites operated to their personal advantage at the expense of the public interest. Muckrakers shed light on crime, corruption, fraud, waste and other abuses in the public and private sectors via their articles for popular magazines and newspapers such as *Cosmopolitan*, *The Independent* and *McClure's*. The prevalence of muckraking corresponded with the advent of Progressivism as a political movement, although not all muckrakers were progressives nor all progressives muckrakers. The revelations of the muckrakers provided the Progressive movement with popular support for much-needed and effective reform. The term derives from the word 'muckrake' used by President Theodore Roosevelt in a 1906 speech in which he agreed with many of the charges of the muckrakers but claimed that some of their methods were sensationalist and irresponsible.

Modern tabloid newspapers have continued the muckraking tradition, breaking controversial stories such as that which dealt with the relationship between Gennifer Flowers and Bill Clinton and later became a mainstream news item. Ralph Nader's book, *Unsafe at Any Speed: The Designed-In Dangers of the American Automobile* (1965), which detailed his claims of resistance by car manufacturers to the introduction of safety features, might be regarded as muckraking. A pioneering work of consumer advocacy, it was openly polemical in style.

Nader, Ralph (1934–)

Ralph Nader is an American author, campaigner, lecturer, political activist and frequent campaigner for the presidency. He stood as an independent candidate in 2004 and 2008, having been the Green candidate in 1996 and 2000 when his intervention seriously damaged the prospects of Democrat Al Gore in some states (Nader took more than 97,000 votes in Florida, a state where Bush won the disputed contest by just 537 votes).

Nader is noted for his commitment to the causes of consumer protection, democratic government, environmentalism and humanitarianism. His crusading activities inspired many activists ('Nader's Raiders') to join his movement which pressed for protections for workers, taxpayers and the environment, and fought to stem the power of large corporations. In 1969, he established the Center for the Study of Responsive Law which exposed corporate irresponsibility and the federal government's failure to enforce regulation of business. He founded Public Citizen and US Public Interest Research Group in 1971, an umbrella for many other such groups.

National Abortion and Reproductive Rights Action League (NARAL) see *Abortion Rights Movement*

National Association for the Advancement of Colored People (NAACP)

The NAACP is one of the oldest and most influential civil rights organisations in the United States. It was founded in New York City in 1909 by black, and white, intellectuals at a time when racial inequality was accepted in American society.

The primary focus of the new NAACP was to spread the word about the inequality of African Americans. It engaged in lobbying activities, spoke out about important issues affecting black Americans and publicised issues through the press. In addition to these activities, the NAACP extended its fight by challenging discriminatory practices and inequality in the courts. In 1915, it attacked a grandfather clause that was used against black voters in the South and in 1927 it challenged an all-white primary. It won both cases. In 1939, the organisation set up the NAACP Legal Defense and Education Fund and soon became recognised as a powerful force within the civil rights movement. In 1954, the NAACP's legal council won its greatest legal victory in *Brown* v. *Board of Education* when the Supreme Court declared that school segregation was unconstitutional.

Bolstered by its landmark victory, the NAACP pushed for full desegregation throughout the South. Its activists helped organise the bus boycott in Montgomery (1955), in protest against segregation on the city's buses. It gradually lost some of its influence to more recently formed organisations such as the Southern Christian Leadership Conference (SCLC) and the Student Nonviolent Coordinating Committee (SNCC). These bodies adopted different approaches to activism, relying more on direct action and mass mobilisation, than on working through litigation and for the passage of legislation to advance the rights of African Americans. Roy Wilkins, the

NAACP's executive director, often clashed with Dr King and others in the civil rights movement over issues of leadership and strategy.

The NAACP is still active in rooting out racism and working towards equal rights, highlighting examples of discrimination and speaking out on issues of relevance to the African American community. Its proclaimed mission is to 'to ensure the political, educational, social, and economic equality of rights of all persons and to eliminate racial hatred and racial discrimination'. It retains its original name because of its past achievements and traditions, making it one of the few surviving bodies to employ the term 'colored people'.

See also **Brown** *v.* **Topeka Board of Education *(1954)*; *Bus Boycotts*; *Civil Rights Movement*; *King, Martin Luther*; *Marshall, Thurgood*; *Parks, Rosa***

National Nominating Conventions

The national nominating conventions of the two main parties are held over a four-day period in July and August. By then, the outcome of the contest to be the representative of the party in the November election is usually a foregone conclusion, and normally the successful candidate is chosen on the first ballot. Delegates are now forced to pledge themselves to a definite candidate for at least the first two ballots although, in the past, this was not the case and delegates arrived with varying degrees of commitment.

The convention comprises those delegates elected in primaries, caucuses or state conventions. Their task is to choose the presidential candidate (in effect, already done) and the vice-presidential nominee – a choice actually made by the presidential candidate and invariably ratified by those assembled. Delegates also help to write the party platform and, at this stage, there is often a tussle between different factions seeking to move the party in their direction. The policy statement is not binding on the two men chosen to run for the White House but, as it indicates prevalent feeling in the party, candidates do not usually ignore such an expression of the mood of the faithful.

Once the candidate has been chosen, the nominee makes an acceptance speech and receives homage as the party's standard-bearer for the forthcoming struggle. The conclusion of the national convention season brings to an end a long-drawn-out process for which the candidates have been planning and working for many months, if not years. As a result, the two main presidential candidates have been chosen and are ready for the main battle ahead.

National Organization for Women (NOW)

The National Organization for Women is the largest organisation of feminist activists in the United States. NOW has some 500,000 contributing members and 550 chapters in all fifty states and the District of Columbia. Since its founding in 1966, NOW's goal has been to take action to bring about equality for all women. NOW works to eliminate discrimination and harassment in the workplace, schools, the justice system and all other sectors of society; secure abortion, birth control and reproductive rights for all women; end all forms of violence against women; eradicate racism, sexism and homophobia; and promote equality and justice in our society.

Having been in the forefront of the battle for the Equal Rights Amendment (ERA) and enhanced its reputation and membership in the process, NOW began in 1995 its campaign for a Constitutional Equality Amendment, bolder, lengthier and more explicit than the original proposal. In Article 1, it demands that 'women and men shall have equal rights throughout the US and every place and entity subject to its jurisdiction: through this article, the subordination of women to men is abolished'. Elsewhere, it strikes out discrimination on account of 'sex, race, sexual orientation, marital status, ethnicity, national origin, color or indigence' and prohibits 'pregnancy discrimination and guarantees the absolute right of a woman to make her own reproductive decisions including the termination of pregnancy'. Overall, as its website proclaims, it seeks 'to bring the authority of the Constitution to work on entrenched beliefs about gender difference, as well as equality'.

National Rifle Association (NRA)

The NRA is perhaps the best-known American pressure group and the most successful in lobbying on Capitol Hill. It has over three million members who are enthusiasts for shooting as both recreation and protection. Since the late 1960s, it has successfully resisted most national attempts to limit the ownership of guns even though, on occasion, pressure for gun control has gained ground. In the last few years, it has paid more attention to state governments for it is to that level that supporters of restriction have increasingly turned their attention.

The NRA's Institute for Legislative Action exercises a watching brief over any attempt by the federal or state governments to introduce limitations on the manufacture and sale of guns or on gun ownership. If there are any such initiatives, members are immediately alerted so that they can mount strong resistance, by telephoning or e-mailing relevant officials, writing to newspapers, appearing on television or any other appropriate method.

The NRA is currently seeking to widen its appeal, so that some of its recent propaganda has been targeted at minority groups and women.

See also *Gun Control*

National Right to Life Committee see *Profile Movement*

National Security Council

Established in 1947 by the National Security Act, the council was given the role of advising the president on domestic, foreign and military matters relating to national security. It is meant to bring together all the military, defence and economic considerations which determine the shape of national security policy. Its duty was defined in the Act as being to consider 'policies on matters of common interest to the departments and agencies of the government concerned with national security, and to make recommendations'. As with the Cabinet, the National Security Council meets irregularly and does not make decisions for the president on foreign and defence policy, but it gives him evidence and advice from which he can come to his own conclusions. At times of crisis, the Council does not usually seem to be the place where key assessments are made.

By the terms of the 1947 statute, the National Security Council comprises the president and vice president, the secretaries of state and of defence, and advisers such as the director of the CIA and the joint chiefs of staff. The Special Assistant for National Security Affairs (SA), who is based in the White House and owes his or her prime loyalty to the person who appointed him or her for the position, has a highly significant role in the presidential team. Originally, it was little more than that of a secretary to the NSC but it has grown vastly in scope. Today, some presidents prefer to rely on an informal group of advisers and the SA, rather than on the statutory body.

The NSC has an important role within the Executive, to the extent that it has been described by Destler (1984) as 'the most exalted committee in the federal government'. It can be a major source of support for the president whom it directly serves. Its use varies according to the incumbent of the White House.

National Security Directives

Presidential directives are forms of executive orders issued by the president, having the effect and force of law. All recent presidents have used them though under different names. For Kennedy and Johnson, they were National Security Action Memorandums, for Clinton Presidential Decision (or Review) Directives, and for George W. Bush, National Security Directives, so named because they are issued with the advice and consent of the National Security Council. Bush also issued Homeland Security Directives with the approval of the Homeland Security Council, which he initially created, one being to change immigration policy in the light of the perceived terrorist threat.

National security orders comprise a means by which presidents can act unilaterally and thereby assert the powers they see as being inherent in their office. Their use by President George W.

Bush was in accordance with his support for unitary executive theory.

See also *Executive Orders*; *Unitary Executive Theory*

Native Americans

The Native American population that the explorers and colonists found was the Indian one then known as. By prior usage, the land belonged to the Native Americans, but these tribal peoples were gradually displaced as the settlers moved westwards and the buffalo herds on which Native Americans depended were wiped out. They were eventually granted certain reserved areas, and many of the present Native Americans still live in or near these reservations, in Arizona, New Mexico and Utah. In a sense, it is wrong to group these Native Americans together, for they include representatives of many tribes whose cultures and lifestyles were once very different. Only about 1.5 million remain. Generally, they experience inferior standards of living, their reservations being enclaves of social disadvantage. Native Americans are much more likely to live in poverty. They also earn less and achieve less via the educational system.

Some Native Americans have left their reservations because of the low quality of life there, and now inhabit towns and cities such as Chicago and Los Angeles. Those who have left, however, have, in many cases, yet to become integrated in American society. They often lack the occupational skills and cultural background to sustain themselves. They are prone to a variety of social problems, ranging from alcoholism and family disintegration to, at worst, suicide. Only relatively recently have activist Native Americans begun to organise to press for changes in their quality of life.

Necessary and Proper Clause

The Necessary and Proper Clause refers to the last paragraph of Article 1, Section 8 of the Constitution which states that Congress may make all laws necessary and proper for executing the seventeen powers specifically enumerated in that section. The phrase is not limited to measures that are absolutely necessary. It includes all appropriate means that are conducive to the end to be accomplished and which, in the judgement of Congress, will most advantageously affect it. This is a sweeping power that seemed to defeat the purpose of producing a finite list of enumerated congressional powers. Also known as the 'elastic clause', this clause is one of the most powerful in the Constitution.

In 1791, Congress legislated for the establishment of a national bank, although the Constitution does not specifically give it that power. But the document did enable Congress to regulate the borrowing of money and the minting of currency. The view was taken that creating a bank is an obvious extension of that power.

Neoconservatism

Neoconservatism is a label that embraces a set of right-wing policy attitudes such as support for the free market, limited welfare and traditional cultural values, causes traditionally espoused by members of the New Right and Religious Right. Their key distinction is on international affairs; they prefer a proactive approach internationally that would protect the national interests. In recent years, neoconservatives have argued for US interventionism to spread 'democracy' and 'liberty' abroad. Members of, and writers for, several think tanks and conservative periodicals argue for such policies.

As a candidate in 2000, George W. Bush supported a restrained foreign policy and was criticised by some 'neocons' for pursuing policies too much like those of his predecessor in the White House and for being insufficiently supportive of Israel. The events of 9/11, however, led him to adopt a different approach. In his State of the Union Address in January 2002, written by neoconservative David Frum, he named three states (Iraq, Iran and North Korea) as ones that constituted an 'axis of evil' and posed 'a grave and growing danger'. He also spoke of the possibility of pre-emptive war:

> I will not wait on events, while dangers gather. I will not stand by, as peril draws closer and closer.

The United States of America will not permit the world's most dangerous regimes to threaten us with the world's most destructive weapons.

Neocon attitudes have been much criticised even by some prominent defence and national security figures of conservative persuasion. They are wary of the Bush doctrine of pre-emptive action and believe that foreign policy over recent years has been excessively influenced by an ideological approach. They argue that it led the United States into war with Iraq, a war which was not in the national interest.

See also *Axis of Evil; Foreign Policy*

New Covenant

The New Covenant was a label applied by Bill Clinton to describe his political outlook and platform in the 1992 presidential election. He used the term in his acceptance speech to his party's national convention, claiming that it represented

a new approach to government. A government that offers more empowerment and less entitlement; more choices for young people in public schools and more choices for older people in long-term care. A government that is leaner, not meaner; that expands opportunity, not bureaucracy; that understands that jobs must come from growth in a vibrant and vital system of free enterprise.

Arguing that the traditional relationship between government and people had broken down in the Reagan–Bush years because the Republicans were too beholden to business interests, he wanted to see a new social compact between the two sides.

In the election campaign, Clinton used the term to describe the policies on tax and the economy, health issues, minority rights and defence matters that would be pursued by his administration. Although the phrase was never widely used in the following years in the way that earlier slogans, such as the New Deal or Fair Deal had been, Clinton resurrected it in his State of the Union Address in January 1995 to describe a moderate, centrist approach that offered smaller government, tax

reductions and reduced bureaucracy, and place an emphasis on opportunity balanced by responsibility in the area of welfare policy.

See also *Clinton, Bill; Democratic Party*

New Deal

The New Deal was an ambitious programme introduced by American President Franklin Roosevelt in the 1930s it was designed to combat the depressed condition of the United States by introducing measures to bring about relief, recovery and long-term reform. It included a massive increase in public spending to 'prime the pump' and create an upward spiral of economic activity.

When Roosevelt assumed office in March 1933, America was in deep economic trouble. Many banks were closed, so that no one could get a bank loan or gain access to their deposits; unemployment was alarmingly high, running at 25 per cent and higher in major industrial/mining areas; agricultural was in an even worse shape than much of industry; and many people were in despair about the future. In his Inaugural Speech, the president had sought to counter the prevailing fear and pessimism. and promised 'action and action now'. A series of changes, sometimes known as the alphabet laws (they were commonly known by their initials), were introduced.

In the 'First New Deal' (1933), the immediate target was short-term recovery programmes for all groups, including measures of banking reform, emergency relief for those out of work, and agricultural and industrial reform.

A 'Second New Deal' (1935–36) included programmes for labour union support, the Works Progress Administration (WPA) relief programme, the Social Security Act and aid packages to assist farmers, including tenant farmers and migrant workers. Some of these were judged unconstitutional by the Supreme Court. Most of them were soon restored, however.

Some of the Roosevelt initiatives were overturned during World War II by a conservative coalition of Republicans and Southern Democrats in Congress. Others did not survive the fashion for deregulation in the Reagan years of the 1980s. A number of New Deal programmes still survives, however, in some cases still operating under the original names, among them the Federal Housing Administration (FHA), the Securities and Exchange Commission (SEC) and the Tennessee Valley Authority (TVA).

Controversy remains over the extent to which New Deal measures lifted the country out of depression. The packages of measures were not always systematic and coherent. In some cases, initiatives seemed to be at odds with each other. But Americans in the early 1930s were ready for bold experimentation and new thinking, millions of them regarding their president as a hero.

Sceptics doubted the value of costly and not always well-targeted programmes and disliked the degree of power being concentrated in the White House. When recovery finally came about, they credited the increased production brought about by the demands of war as the main cause of improved economic fortunes.

See also *Roosevelt, Franklin*; *Tennessee Valley Authority*

New Democrats

The New Democrats form a centrist group within the Democratic Party. They emerged in the 1980s as a response to successive defeats at the hands of Republicans Reagan and Bush. They wanted radically to reposition their party and ensure that it became more in touch with the aspirations of middle Americans who had been uneasy about Democratic Party attitudes in the 1970s. They advocated a political 'third way' that embraced neo-liberal fiscal policies and moderate social positions, although they were strong in support of civil rights for all Americans. They were to be found in organisations such as the Democratic Leadership Council (DLC) and the New Democrat Coalitions in the House of Representatives and the Senate.

The label 'New Democrat' had briefly been used by liberal reformists of the late 1980s but it was taken up by the DLC in 1990 when it renamed its bimonthly magazine *The New Democrat*. When Bill Clinton stepped down as DLC chairman to run for president in 1992, he described himself in the same way. His platform

seemed far removed from the more obviously liberal ones of some of his party predecessors, being notably more cautious than those of Kennedy and Johnson on issues such as welfare. He sought to blend some features of the liberal tradition of positive government with elements of the traditional Republican programme, such as control of the budget deficit. He understood that Americans were growing weary of the problems posed by the urban centres, with such things as the breakdown of law and order, the preoccupation with civil rights and the use of affirmative action. Their anxieties about particular programmes combined with a feeling that government was growing 'too big'. They disliked the spiralling costs of welfare and other public spending, and warmed to promises to 'get Washington off their backs'. In his New Coverant programme, he was responding to profound changes in American attitudes.

Founded in 1997, the New Democrat Coalition (NDC) supports policies; to expand economic growth and ensure that all Americans have the opportunity to benefit from that growth; a fiscally responsible and efficient government; a secure home front; and a robust foreign policy that includes trade, constructive American leadership throughout the world, and a modern and strong military. Reorganised under new leadership at the beginning of the 109th Congress, the NDC is a cohesive core of active members of both legislative chambers committed to these legislative goals.

See also *Clinton, Bill*; *Democratic Party*; *New Covenant*

New Europe see *Old Europe*

New Freedom

The New Freedom was the name of a reform programme designed to bring about political and economic liberty, outlined by Woodrow Wilson in his presidential campaign. He called for a series of bold measures, including anti-trust legislation, tariff revision and changes in banking and currency matters. Whereas Roosevelt approved of large corporations that followed the anti-trust laws, Wilson did not favour massive companies being allowed to dominate the economy. Instead, he argued that the federal government should encourage competition among small businesses.

See also *Democratic Party*; *Wilson, Woodrow*

New Frontiers

The New Frontier was the term used by John F. Kennedy to describe the challenges facing the United States. In his acceptance speech for the Democratic nomination at the party convention in 1960, he noted that:

> We stand today on the edge of a new frontier – the frontier of the 1960s, a frontier of unknown opportunities and paths . . . The new frontier of which I speak is not a set of promises – it is a set of challenges. It sums up not what I intend to offer the American people, but what I intend to ask of them.

The phrase, drafted by Kennedy's speechwriter, Theodore Sorenson, was initially an inspirational slogan, a piece of rhetoric. But it came to be used as a label for the programme he set before the American people in the November election. In the campaign, he spoke of moving aggressively into the new decade, for 'the New Frontier is here whether we seek it or not'. Among other things, he promised to boost the economy, to provide international aid and strong national defence, and to boost the space programme. Many of the reforms introduced during his presidency (1961–63) are referred to as New Frontier measures, including the Peace Corps, the Alliance for Progress in Latin America, a trade expansion act, an increase in the minimum wage, a federal housing act and an Area Redevelopment Act to benefit depressed rural areas. Many of his proposals ran into opposition in Congress so that his unfinished business, on such things as civil rights and medical insurance for the elderly, was not actually completed until President Johnson replaced him.

New Social Movements (NSMs)

New social movements have emerged since the 1960s. They deal with a new range of issues and are much less willing to be absorbed into the established political system. Members often provide a radical critique of society and institutions. They are interested in finding different ways of organising political activity.

Whereas the 'old social movements' of the nineteenth century were concerned with issues such as labour conditions and the struggle for factory reform, 'new social movements' are concerned with causes such as environmental and women's issues. Old or new movements have set out to challenge dominant ideas and a given constellation of power. They want to place different priorities on the political agenda.

NSMs have a radical edge and have a vision of a world transformed by their demands. They have what Hague and Harrop (2004) label 'a coating of anti-politics' about them, for they comprise people from beyond the political mainstream who mount an unconventional challenge to the existing political order. They do not seek power but they do seek indirectly to influence governmental decisions; they clearly focus on a single issue, such as feminism, nuclear power, peace or the environment; their methods range from demonstrations and sit-ins to boycotts and political strikes; their structure is loose, for they lack the leadership, membership and subscriptions that characterise political parties and pressure groups: and they are both national and international in scope, the trends towards global interconnectedness making it necessary for them to operate across national boundaries. They have supporters from across the world.

The environmental movements are among the most radical, in that to 'save the planet' supporters seek a major reversal of the existing methods by which we use and distribute economic resources. They want to reverse a way of life built around consumption and the pursuit of material well-being. Because they have post-materialist values, Giddens (2001) refers to such NSMs as representing 'the new politics of lifestyles'.

In the United States, the environmental movement has, at different times and in different locations, had a variety of different concerns. As a broad generalisation, it has been more apolitical than is the case in western Europe, although radical change has been voiced by organisations such as Earth First! Several US environmental movements have been concerned with wilderness issues and conservation whereas west European ecologists have placed more emphasis on the need for wide-ranging social change, campaigning on anti-nuclear-energy issues and the politics of human and political ecology.

New York Times v. United States (1971)

Often known as the Pentagon Papers case, this was the ruling in which the Supreme Court found that prior restraints were a violation of the First Amendment unless imminent danger could be proven. Over the years, members of the Court have disagreed on the limits that can be placed on the constitutional guarantees of freedom of speech and press. In 1971, justices faced these issues again in a case brought by the *New York Times*.

The newspaper – along with the *Washington Post* – had obtained a copy of documents known as the 'Pentagon Papers', an internal Defense Department report that had been illegally copied and then leaked to its staff. It detailed government deception with regard to the Vietnam War. The documents surfaced at a time when there was deep division among the American people over the question of US involvement in the war. The newspaper fought for the right to publish the papers under the umbrella of the First Amendment.

At the government's request, the district court in New York issued a temporary injunction – a court order – that directed the *New York Times* not to publish the documents, for to do so would jeopardise the security of the country. The newspaper appealed to the Supreme Court, arguing that prior restraint – preventing publication – violated the First Amendment. In its view, an informed population was one of the few restraints on Executive power in matters of national defence, and the press was right to seek to provide the public with knowledge of the contents of the Papers. Moreover, the government had failed to show that publication of the *Pentagon Papers* was a threat to national security.

The government claimed that there was no absolute freedom of the press, particularly when the national security was involved. Furthermore, to allow publication of the documents would establish a dangerous precedent for future cases involving national security.

The justices had to strike a balance between the fundamentally important right to a free press and the equally important duty of the Executive to protect the nation. By a 6–3 decision, they ruled in favour of the *New York Times*. In the opinion of the majority: 'Any system of prior restraints of expression comes to this Court bearing a heavy presumption against its constitutional validity.'

See also *Vietnam War*

Nixon, Richard (1913–94)

Richard Milhous Nixon was the thirty-sixth vice president and thirty-seventh president. He is the only person in American history to appear on the Republican Party's presidential ticket five times, to secure the Republican nomination for president three times, and to have been elected twice to both the vice presidency and the presidency. He is also the only president to be forced to resign from office.

Born in California, Nixon graduated from Duke University School of Law before returning to his home state to practise law. After the attack on Pearl Harbor, he joined the US Navy and became a lieutenant commander serving in the Pacific in World War II. In 1946, he was elected to the House of Representatives as a Republican for the state's twelfth congressional district. Four years later, he was elected to the Senate and within two years was the running mate of presidential candidate Dwight Eisenhower, under whom he served as vice president from 1953 to 1961. He was narrowly beaten by John F. Kennedy in his first presidential bid (1960) and, following a further defeat in his campaign to be elected as governor of California (1962), he announced his intention to withdraw from politics. Speaking to journalists, whom he believed had favoured his Democratic opponent, he told them that: 'You won't have Nixon to kick around anymore because, gentlemen, this is my last press conference.' Out of the public eye and in the political wilderness, he still retained support within the core Republican base, for his knowledge of politics and international affairs was widely recognised. He made a remarkable comeback to be elected to the presidency in 1968, defeating the Democratic vice president Hubert Humphrey by a narrow margin in the popular vote but a decisive one in the Electoral College.

Nixon as president (1969–74)

In the campaign, Nixon portrayed himself as a figure of stability at a time of national unrest and upheaval. He won the backing of what he called the 'silent majority' of socially conservative Americans who had wearied of anti-war demonstrations, social unrest and the hippie culture of the 1960s. As president, Nixon made reconciliation of a divided nation his first priority. At the time of his inauguration, the country was divided over the rights and wrongs of the Vietnam War, and there was growing racial tension and unrest in several cities.

Nixon initially escalated the conflict in Vietnam into neighbouring Cambodia, overseeing secret bombing campaigns designed to destroy supply lines to the Vietcong guerillas. But in line with his campaign rhetoric, he implemented what became known as the Nixon Doctrine. This involved implementing a policy of Vietnamisation of the war, encouraging the regime in the South to assume greater responsibility for the country's defence. Yet, while claiming to be seeking an end to American involvement, he ordered the bombing of Laos, a move which strengthened the fears of many Americans who detected a Johnson-like credibility gap in the language used and the action taken; campus protests grew in frequency. Finally, in January 1973, Nixon announced an accord with the North to end American involvement in Vietnam and Indochina as a whole. Troop withdrawal was rapid so that, by the end of the year, there were no American forces in Vietnam.

Nixon also opened up relations with the Communist powers, taking advantage of a Sino-Soviet split to shift the balance of power towards the west in the Cold War. Having arranged contact with the People's Republic of China, he eased trade restrictions and ensured that his presidential team toned down any anti-Chinese rhetoric in the public utterances. During a pioneering visit to Bejing, he met with Mao Zedong and Foreign Minister Zhou Enlai and also viewed the sights of the capital while his wife toured hospitals, schools and other facilities. The tour amounted to a significant breakthrough in foreign policy and led to a significant easing of Sino-American relations. Nixon also sought détente with the Soviet Union, his visit to Moscow resulting in a meeting with Russian leader Brezhnev which led to the signing of a treaty to limit strategic nuclear weapons. In 1974, his Secretary of State, Henry Kissinger, negotiated disengagement agreements between Israel and its opponents, Egypt and Syria, an early move in the long search for a broader Middle Eastern settlement.

One of Nixon's most dramatic events in his first term, a few months into the presidency, was the first moon landing by American astronauts. The first term also saw the ending of the draft, new anti-crime laws, the introduction of revenue sharing, moves to decentralisation as part of a New Federalism, plans for a broad environmental agenda and an acceleation of desegration. As a Quaker, Nixon disapproved of racism and was intent on implementing the desegration that the courts had ordered but he disliked the notion of busing children to satisfy what were viewed by some as the 'capricious meddling of judges'. A judicial constructionist, he appointed justices of conservative persuasion to the Supreme Court in a bid to undermine its liberal inclinations under Chief Justice Warren. (The appointment of Warren Burger as his replacement was to backfire, he later being the person who presided over the Court ruling that Nixon must hand over the White House tapes.)

Nixon's second term was undermined by a serious economic downturn. It was Watergate, however, that posed the most serious – and ultimately ruinous – threat to his presidency.

Re-election, Watergate and resignation

In his bid for re-election in November 1972, Nixon defeated Democratic candidate George McGovern by one of the widest margins on record. It soon became apparent, however, that the presidential team had been so concerned to ensure victory that they had resorted to illegal tactics, knowledge of which Nixon himself tried to conceal. A break in at the offices of the Democratic National Committee was traced to officials of a Nixon support group, the Committee to Re-elect the President (CREEP). As information about the burglary was uncovered, a number of administration officials was forced to resign, some being convicted of offences relating to the attempt to cover up what was developing into a serious scandal.

Nixon denied any personal involvement in Watergate but the courts eventually forced him to hand over tape recordings which indicated that he had tried to divert and mislead the investigation. Faced with almost certain impeachment, Nixon announced his resignation (8 September 1974) in order to allow the 'process of healing which is so desperately needed in America'. In further pursuit of the healing process, Gerald Ford (his successor as president), issued a presidential pardon for any federal crimes committed by the former president while in public office, thereby saving him from possible prosecution.

In his last years, Nixon regained some respect via his role as an elder statesman. By the time of his death (22 April 1994) he had undertaken many overseas trips and written prolifically on foreign policy and his experiences in public life.

Assessment

Nixon was a complex man. He was not easily likeable, his character failings having been exposed in the 1960 campaign when he was referred to as 'tricky Dickie' by his opponents who, in posters, asked if people would buy a second-hand car from him. Satirists and cartoonists found him an easy target, portraying in exaggerated form his unshaven jowls, slumped shoulders and sweaty brow. His poor image had damaged his prospects in the first presidential debate of that year.

Nixon was an awkward and secretive figure, rather uptight and wary of those around him, especially any he suspected of being opposed to his ideas and policies. He tended to distance himself from people so that he was not easily accessible. On occasion, he claimed to be unappreciated and misunderstood, his writings being largely an exercise in self-justification. Yet he was not lacking in ability or industry, and he revealed great stamina in recovering from the setbacks that beset his political career which moved from initial rapid success to striking defeats, from dramatic recovery to personal humiliation.

The abiding legacy of Nixon is of a man who, by his actions over Watergate, seriously damaged not only his own standing but endangered the rule of law and the institution of the presidency as well. Even nearly three decades after his departure, the shadow of that scandal still hangs over his performance in office. There have been other scandals susequently, notably those leading to the Clinton impeachment, but Watergate remains as the touchstone for presidential misdeeds. Yet, for all of the ignominy that surrounded his departure, most fair-minded commentators would accord Nixon praise for his undoubted achievements in the quest for world stability. His pragmatic foreign policy was largely successful, the constructive initiatives with China and the USSR resulting in an easing of international tension in the immediate months afterwards and the prospect of a definite improvement in relations in the future.

Views about Richard Nixon still differ markedly. For some he is a talented man who did much to recast his country's relationships with America's traditional enemies. For others, he is much despised and little lamented, morally lacking and deeply untrustworthy, qualities that were only too apparent in the scandals of his time in office. In any rankings of past presidents, he tends to be placed in the bottom ten, at 'below average' or worse. (See, for instance, that of the Federalist Society and *The Wall Street Journal*, 2005, which rated him at thirty-second of the forty reviewed.)

See also *Watergate*

North Atlantic Treaty Organization (NATO)

NATO was created in April 1949 as a defensive alliance of twelve states (the United States and Canada, along with ten western European nations, the Benelux countries, Denmark, France,

Iceland, Italy, Norway, Portugal and the United Kingdom). By the North Atlantic Treaty, the governments of the day agreed that 'an armed attack against one or more of them in Europe or North America [should] be considered an attack against them all' and consequently that they would take such action as was necessary (including the use of armed force) to cope with any such act of aggression. Although NATO was a mutual defence alliance, each nation was free to decide the form of assistance it provided in the event of an attack, taking 'such action as it deems necessary including the use of armed force, to restore and maintain the security of the North Atlantic area'.

The treaty was prompted by the urgent need to combine against the Communist bloc, at a time when the powerful Russian army was seeking to drive the western allies from West Berlin. America had the vast industrial resources and a monopoly of atomic weapons necessary to counterbalance the military power of the Soviet Union and its satellites. Unsurprisingly, the Soviet Union interpreted developments differently. In their view, NATO was aggressive in intent, rather than defensive.

Once the Cold War ended, NATO's traditional role disappeared. Members recognise the desirability of retaining the tradition of co-operation they have developed, however, and – at the European end – are keen to ensure that the United States retains its commitment to European defence. Now enlarged to twenty-six, NATO serves as a forum in which member states can consult on issues of common concern and agree on action to advance their interests. It sees its primary purpose as to 'safeguard the freedom and security of its member countries by political and military means'. Its main work is in the areas of crisis management and peacekeeping.

See also *Cold War*; *Foreign Policy*

O

Obama, Barack (1961–)

Barack Obama is the forty-fourth and, at the time of writing, current president of the United States. He is the first African American to ascend to the highest office. He was born in Hawaii to a black Kenyan father and a white American mother. He graduated from Harvard Law School where he was the first African American president of the Harvard Law Review. Subsequently, he became involved in public service as a community organiser, civil rights attorney and leader in the Illinois state Senate.

Obama came to national attention at the 2004 Democratic National Convention where he delivered the keynote address. He was elected as the junior senator for Illinois in November 2004 by a landslide 70 per cent of the vote in an election generally noted for Republican gains. He is the fifth African American to gain election to the Senate and the only one currently serving. He currently serves on the Health, Education, Labor and Pensions, Veterans' Affairs and Foreign Relations committees.

Having defeated Hillary Clinton in a closely run primary contest, Obama became the Democratic Party's presidential nominee for the 2008 presidential election. After announcing his candidacy in early 2007, he emphasised ending the Iraq War and implementing universal health care as key campaign themes, as well as capitalising on a mood for change and reform in Washington. He won decisively, defeating Republican John McCain in the first contest between two sitting senators. He secured 365 votes in the Electoral College against McCain's 173, winning the popular vote by 52.9 per cent to 45.7 per cent, on a very strong turnout.

Obama's background is distinctive from that of most African American politicians and civil rights activists of recent decades, on account of the combination of his mixed parentage, his upbringing in Honolulu and Jakarta and his Ivy League education. But he possesses the oratorical skills characteristic of many of them, his use of language having been compared to that of Dr Martin Luther King. There are also echoes of the young John F. Kennedy in his style and approach, with his positive and challenging reiteration in the campaign of the theme 'yes, we can'. In the relatively short time in which he has been a national figure, his rhetoric has seemed able to inspire many Americans who have warmed to his positive leadership and demands of them to act morally and do good by others.

The Obama Administration (2009–): early days

When Barack Obama entered the White House as president in January 2009, there was a period of radiant optimism in which he enjoyed widespread support in the polls. There was always an air of unreality in the expectations that were aroused by the high-flown rhetoric of an election campaign. However, some of the early confidence that problems would be resolved and things were going to get better soon, was quickly eroded and presidential ratings dropped to more realistic levels. Within eight or nine months, Democrats were becoming anxious and Republicans hostile, as conservative opposition became intense. A minority of Republicans were willing variously to denounce Obama as a socialist, a communist or even a fascist.

The Democrats were pleased with the nomination and appointment of the first Hispanic justice, Sonia Sotomayor, to the US Supreme Court. However, although the attempt to reform health provision generally met with approval within the party, it provoked much opposition from the Republicans and special interests. If the president could achieve success in that policy, by demonstrating an ability to persuade Congress to pass a measure such as had eluded Roosevelt, Truman, Clinton and others, then that would provide a more encouraging context for the consideration of other Obama initiatives, such as action on climate change. Meanwhile, a range of other issues required presidential attention, from policy over Afghanistan to US relations with Iran, from the seemingly intractable problems of the Middle East to the future of Guantánamo.

O'Connor, Sandra Day (1930–)

Sandra Day O'Connor was a politician and jurist in Arizona prior to her nomination to serve as the first female and 102nd justice on the Supreme Court from 1981 to 2006. Appointed by President Reagan as a strict constructionist of the type that he admired, she soon made it clear that the Court's role in American society was to interpret the law, not to legislate. Her votes were generally conservative but she frequently surprised observers with her political independence and would frequently author a concurrence that sought to narrow the scope of the majority's opinion.

In her later years on the Bench, O'Connor increasingly became associated with a pragmatic and centrist-oriented conservatism. She was willing to adopt a case-by-case approach, thereby earning herself a reputation as a consummate compromiser and making it difficult for commentators to define her core legal philosophy. Given her relatively moderate political views, she was a pivotal figure among the justices, sometimes determining the balance of the verdict.

Office of Management and Budget (OMB)

Created by President Nixon in 1970, the office replaced the Bureau of the Budget which dated back to 1921. The change of nomenclature indicates its increased role and importance for it now carries out many key managerial, as well as budgetary, functions on behalf of the president. It has become a highly significant element within the Executive branch, its work helping the president: to establish control over the departments and agencies; to assess their success in devising and implementing their programmes; and generally to ensure that the rest of the federal government reflects both the programmatic and budgetary goals of the administration.

The OMB is responsible for, assembling annual budget plans for departments and agencies and drawing them together in proposals that are then submitted to Congress; screening planned executive orders before they are sent to the president for signature; examining proposals for changes in legislation from departments and agencies, and bills passed by Congress, before then advising the president on whether or not they should be signed or vetoed; and – since the days of the Reagan presidency – assessing the rules and regulations issued by departments and agencies, each of which must present an 'impact analysis'.

Old Europe

Through American eyes, Old Europe comprises France, Germany and their traditional western European allies, in particular those who condemned US foreign policy following the 9/11 attacks and the invasion of Iraq. The term was popularised in January 2003 when the then US Secretary of Defense, Donald Rumsfeld, addressed the Washington press corps. He used it in reference to France and Germany:

> Germany has been a problem and France has been a problem . . . But you look at vast numbers of other countries in Europe, they're not with France and Germany . . . they're with the US . . . You're thinking of Europe as Germany and France. I don't. I think that's old Europe.

According to this view, New Europe comprises those central and eastern countries that once belonged to the Communist bloc and which were more supportive of US foreign policy in the Bush years.

Omnibus Bill

An omnibus bill in Congress is a very long piece of legislation that contains several items that are seemingly unrelated but are brought together in a single document. It may include amendments to a number of other laws or even several entirely new ones. The most well-known form would be the omnibus spending bills that group together the budgets of all departments in one year. Although omnibus bills have been used throughout the nation's history, they assumed new importance after Congress adopted its present budgetary arrangements in 1974.

Omnibus bills regularly stretch to more than a thousand pages and often have not even been read in full by the people voting for them. Critics complain that individual provisions of omnibus bills often receive little debate, with members being forced to vote on mammoth measures without fully understanding what is in them. Others say that they contain too much unnecessary and wasteful expenditure, there only because it may be pleasing to groups of constituents ('pork').

Defenders of the omnibus approach argue that members of Congress benefit from the broad overview of government activities that such measures provide. Moreover, several desirable – but politically unpopular – actions might not be taken unless they were lost in an omnibus bill.

Open Government

Open government is the principle that the processes of government should be available for public scrutiny and criticism, based on a free flow of information from those who exercise power and make decisions to the elected representatives, the media and the general public. In the eyes of many people, open government is one of the most basic requirements of any healthy democracy. It allows for taxpayers to see where their money is going; it permits the honest exchange of information that ensures government accountability; and it upholds the ideal that government never rules without the consent of the people. Government

is based not on the need to know but upon the fundamental right to know.

It is recognised that, in any society, there will be some information that has to be kept secret on grounds of national security. In an open system, however, the presumption is in favour of the public's 'right to know'. America has had freedom of information legislation since 1966, as well as a series of 'sunshine laws' designed to ensure public access to government and the information it holds.

Critics of the US political system, and in particular of the presidency of George W. Bush, claim that, since the 1980s, there has been a number of alarming reductions to government access and accountability, noting a series of small but systematic changes to existing laws and the Executive orders. They complain of an obsession with secrecy during the Bush years, with frequent changes to laws and practices that lessen the opportunity for, and impact of, public and congressional scrutiny of the activities of the executive branch. In particular, they argue that government agencies have made extensive and arbitrary use of Freedom of Information (FOIA) exemptions, such as those for classified information, privileged attorney–client documents and certain information compiled for law-enforcement purposes (often inappropriately or with inadequate justification).

Recent legislation on the subject of openness includes the Transparency Act of 2006, which created a publicly accessible online database of all federal funding, with exceptions for classified national security matters. The bipartisan Open Government Act of 2007 was designed to make the most significant reforms to the Freedom of Information Act in more than a decade, reinforcing the view that the Freedom of Information Act establishes a presumption of openness. It: amended parts of the Lobbying Disclosure Act (1995); strengthened public disclosure requirements concerning lobbying activity and funding; placed more restrictions on gifts for members of Congress and their staff; and provided for mandatory disclosure of earmarks (congressional provisions that direct approved funds to be spent on specific projects, or that direct specific exemptions from taxes or mandated fees) in expenditure bills. Formally entitled the Openness Promotes Effectiveness in our National Government Act of 2007, the bill was signed into law by President Bush in December 2007.

Open Primary see *Party Primaries*

Open Rule see *Rules Committee*

Opinion Polls

Opinion polls are enquiries into public opinion conducted by interviewing a sample of people. They apply marketing-research techniques to canvassing public opinion on specific political, social or other issues. In particular, they are frequently used to forecast election results.

Today, polls are essential to high-visibility campaigns, including presidential, congressional and gubernatorial races. Major television stations and newspapers regularly commission polls, particularly in the election season when they help to generate much interest in the campaign. So, too, do most serious candidates use them to survey the voters about their concerns, seeing the considerable cost of the polls expense as being a price worth paying for the feedback on popular attitudes. Once elected to public office, many officials from the president to governors, members of Congress to state legislators, use polls to assess public opinion on a variety of issues and enable them to fine-tune their policy positions.

Opinion polls have a long history, the idea of sounding public opinion dating back to the early nineteenth century when forms of 'straw polls' were carried out prior to elections. Straw polls are very rough attempts to gauge opinion, often taken on an impromptu basis to see how those attending a meeting feel about an issue. (The term derives from the idea of holding up a straw to see in what direction the wind blows, in this case, the wind of group opinion.) Large 'straw polls' were conducted by the *Literary Digest* until the early 1930s but a serious failure in the 1936 presidential election – when it tipped the Republican Alfred Landon to defeat the landslide winner, Franklin Roosevelt – discredited them and began a new era in opinion polling. Straw polls are, however, still

regularly taken and published, most famously that by the Iowan Republicans during the presidential primary season.

The 1936 failure showed the need for a more scientific form of polling, based on a more systematic selection of respondents. George Gallup developed the idea of using a relatively small but scientifically selected sample of voter opinions, using questionnaires to assess voter responses on public issues and individual candidates for public office. As Gallup and other organisations refined their methodology, increased attention was given to question design, question order, the accuracy of sampling, turnout and the margin of error.

Sampling has traditionally been done either in face-to-face interviews with people drawn from a range of categories, including age, ethnicity, gender and social class. These quota samples place a great deal of importance on the skills of the interviewer and can miss the less active sections of the population who are not represented in high numbers in the public places where the polls are usually conducted. Polling can also be done on a random basis, perhaps by mailed surveys or visits to homes, but now usually by telephone interviews. For several years, polling companies have increasingly favoured random sampling, largely because it has a lower probability of error and because it is now possible to get higher response rates. In either method, usually between 1,000 and 1,500 people are surveyed.

Galllup uses random or probability sampling which is the method now used in much survey research. The guiding principle is that a small percentage of the people, randomly selected, can represent the attitudes and likely behaviour of all Americans, the object being to try to ensure that sample results are the same as those that would have been obtained if all of them had been surveyed. The key to this is equal probability which means that, if every member of the public has an equal chance of being selected, the outcome will be representative of the views of the whole population.

The value of survey research

Poll results are viewed with much interest by politicians, the media and many members of the public, especially when an election is looming. Irrespective of its merits, polling is today both inevitable and legitimate. The guarantees of free expression and freedom of the press under the First Amendment ensure that polls can be both conducted and published.

There is a long-running debate about the reliability and usefulness of opinion polling. Those who support the work of the pollsters see them as beneficial to democracy. Polls provide the only systematic information available between elections about the way in which the public views those who govern or aspire to govern.

Critics have two lines of attack. Some worry that they have an effect on the way people vote, creating either a bandwagon movement in favour of the leading candidate or an underdog effect in favour of the ones who trail behind. The alarm is the greater if the survey work is badly done or there are errors in sampling for, in these cases, inaccurate findings may alter election outcomes. Others worry that an obsession with polling data encourages journalists and politicians to think too much in terms of campaign needs and insufficiently about the substance of policy content. This view was expressed by Dottie Lynch (Rees, 1992), a former political editor of CBS News, who began work as a pollster in the 1970s. She has detected a major shift, not just in the influence of pollsters, but in the effects of polls on candidates. When she started, 'the assumption was that an incumbent would run on his record'. A decade later, however, she began to discover 'more and more candidates who either didn't have records or didn't have positions fully formed on issues'. Candidates began to ask: 'What do the polls tell me I ought to believe?' In her view, politicians had moved on from considering what the polls said about his or her beliefs to a situation in which they now thought about what the polls told them they should believe. Forming policy on the basis of poll findings could be said to be a negation of leadership.

The fact that politicians use polls to assess voter reactions, however, does not mean that they are slaves to public opinion. Polls are an important source of feedback in making policy decisions but representatives also rely on their own and others' experience, expertise, instincts and knowledge, as well as their own values, in making a judgement about what policy line should be adopted. They understand that polls are guides but are not always entirely right in discerning the public mood. Moreover, they realise that events, personal and public, can have a significant impact on opinions, making the pollsters' findings liable to change as days and weeks go by.

See also *Election Campaigns*

Originalism

Originalism is the belief that the American Constitution should be interpreted according to the intentions of those who composed and adopted it. It assumes that a fixed and knowable set of meanings was locked into the Constitution at the moment of its adoption and ratification, and that these meanings enjoy a supreme legal authority that should guide and constrain the course of interpretation. Originalists are sometimes called 'textualists' or 'literalists', for they seek to recover the 'original meaning' or the 'original intentions' of its adopters. Today, originalism is popular among political conservatives, its expression being most prominently associated with associate justices Scalia and Thomas, and the rejected Reagan nomination to the Supreme Court, Robert Bork.

To its advocates, originalism promises to prevent politically unaccountable judges from imposing their own values and preferences on the text of the Constitution. For originalists, judges need neutral, objective criteria to make legitimate decisions. The wisdom of the framers and ratifiers of the Constitution provides these neutral criteria. Critics believe that the Constitution was written in flexible terms that are capable of adaptation to the needs of the age, seeing the Constitution as dynamic rather than static. They portray originalism as a retrograde effort to subordinate pressing claims for present justice or adaptations in governance to flawed and obsolete understandings of the past.

Originalism is sometimes used as an interchangeable synonym for strict constructionism, both theories being associated with adherence to the text. There are differences, however. Scalia differentiates the two by pointing out that 'he uses a cane' means 'he walks with a cane', not what a strict use of the words might suggest. He claims to be 'not a strict constructionist', claiming that strict constructionism is 'a degraded form of textualism that brings the whole philosophy into disrepute'. His view is that the Constitution *'should be interpreted [n]either strictly [n]or sloppily; it should be interpreted "reasonably"'*. This involves discovering what the Constitution means (interpretation) and then applying its general provisions to the specifics of a given controversy (construction).

Oval Office

The Oval Office is the president's official office in the complex of offices that makes up the West Wing of the White House, so called because of its distinctive shape.

The president uses the Oval Office as his primary place of work. It is positioned to provide easy access to his staff in the rest of the West Wing and to allow him to retire easily to the White House residence at the end of the day. The Oval Office is the usual location where leaders of overseas nations and delegations from Congress meet the president. It is commonly used as the backdrop for televised addresses to the nation to add a sense of gravity to the occasion. It was from there that President Kennedy presented news of the Cuban Misssile Crisis and George Bush addressed the nation on the evening of 9/11.

The east door opens to the Rose Garden where many presidential press conferences take place.

P

Pariah States see *Rogue States*

Partisan Identification

By partisan identification, we mean the long-standing identification that a person has for a particular party, a preference that will often have been formed over many years. It will have been influenced by family background, education and the influence of peers in the early years, and this sense of attachment stays with people for much of their lives, modified by life experience, especially economic considerations and impressions formed of the effectiveness of particular administrations in delivering the goods and making people feel content.

The idea underlying partisan identification is that most Americans will stick by their normal party affiliation unless there are seemingly good reasons for not doing so. The affiliation may be a strong or a weak one. Research carried out by the *American National Election Study* team has divided responses into seven categories: Strong Democrats, Weak Democrats, Independent-leaning Democrats, the same three categories for the Republican Party, and the Independents who really show no obvious affiliation at all. The apolitical, those who normally would not vote and show little interest in the subject, are not included by the Study team.

The studies have shown that, whereas at the 1960 election when Kennedy was successful 51 per cent could be described as Democrats of one variety or the other and 37 per cent Republican, in 1980 when Ronald Reagan gained the presidency, the figures were 52 per cent and 33 per cent. In other words, comparing a good year for the Democrats in the presidential contest with a bad year shows no significant difference. Indeed, in 1992, the figures remained fairly stable, 50 per cent and 37 per cent. It may be that party identification is the best guide to voting behaviour over the long term but clearly, in the shorter term, there must be other factors which are more important for, otherwise, the Democrats would be regularly more successful than their opponents.

Voting behaviour has become more volatile in recent decades. As Stephen Wayne (1996) has written:

> While class, religion and geography are still related to party identification and voting behaviour, they are not as strongly related as they were in the past. Voters are less influenced by group cues. They exercise a more independent judgement on election day, a judgement that is less predictable and more subject to the influence of the campaign itself.

Political scientists today talk more about these less stable factors, ones that fluctuate from election to election, than in the past. These include the appeal of the candidate and issues. There is, of course, no clear-cut division between them for the party one associates with will often help to determine what one thinks about the candidate and the topic under discussion.

The attractiveness and appeal of the individual candidate are in the forefront of many people's minds. Martin Wattenberg (1991) has detected a change of focus in recent years from party allegiance to concentration on the merits of the nominee: 'The change . . . is an important histori-cal trend, which has been gradually taking place over the last several decades.' Voters now seem to be more interested in the qualities the candi-date possesses: not surprisingly, as these are now featured in the media more than ever before. Via television, they can assess their leadership ability and charisma, their honesty and experience, their knowledge or their ignorance. 'Strength' and 'leadership' are much-admired qualities as is what George Bush Snr called 'the vision thing'; many people like to be led by a person who knows where he or she wishes to lead them.

Issues, too, are also important but rather less so than party identification and candidate appeal. Voters are often ambiguous about where a con-tender stands on a particular issue for politicians realise that clarity can sometimes antagonise the people and groups whom the candidate hopes to attract.

See also *Candidate-Centred Electioneering*; *Presi-dential Elections*; *Voter Behaviour*

Party Primaries

Primaries are preliminary elections held within a party to choose the candidate for that party in the general election. They are common in the United States. Elsewhere in the world, the nomination of candidates is usually the responsibility of political parties and does not make use of the public appa-ratus for holding elections.

At the beginning of the twentieth century, many 'progressives' were concerned at the power exer-cised by party bosses and their political organisa-tions. They wanted to curb the corruption felt to be endemic in public life, and pressed for reforms to break the control of the party machines and the 'bosses' who ran them. In this spirit, they urged the use of primary elections that would transfer power away from the party regulars meeting in smoke-filled rooms to the interested ordinary voter. This was seen as a significant step towards greater democracy.

The presidential primary was first used in the 1912 election, when the Republican incumbent, President William Howard Taft, faced challenges from Theodore Roosevelt and Robert La Follette.

Although Roosevelt proved the most popular can-didate in the non-binding 'preference' primaries, the party nomination went to Taft who control-led the national convention. The use of primaries gradually spread although, for many years, the system was still not widely used for choosing presidential candidates. By the 1970s, however, they had become nationwide for almost all forms of election, local, state and federal.

The impetus for wider use of binding presiden-tial primaries was the chaotic 1968 Democratic National Convention, at which Vice President Hubert Humphrey secured the nomination despite primary victories and other strong demonstrations of support for Senator Eugene McCarthy who was running against Humphrey as an anti-Vietnam War candidate. Thereafter, the Democratic National Committee adopted new rules to assure wider participation in future selec-tion procedures. Faced with the need to comply, several states decided to opt for the presiden-tial primary method of choosing their state's choice to be the party's presidential nominee. The Republicans also adopted many more state presidential primaries.

With the advent of primaries across the coun-try and at so many levels, it was not only the large city machines that lost power. Party organ-isations everywhere lost their hold. Even where there was no suspicion of doubtful propriety, they lost their key nominating function – for any candidate could stand for election whether or not he or she had rendered some service in the local party.

In 2008, New Hampshire was again the first state to hold its presidential primary election although, in recent years, the trend has been for more states to advance their contest in order that they should have more influence over the party's choice. This crowding of primaries and caucuses in the early weeks of the nomination period (frontloading) gives undue weight to those states with early contests. Their results often build momentum for leading candidates and rule out trailing candidates long before the rest of the country has had a chance to have its say.

The scheduling of primaries and caucuses in 2008 was different from that in previous years. The Democrats and the Republicans moved their

Nevada caucuses to 19 January, an earlier date than past election cycles. In response, other states also changed their primary election dates, with several contests held before Super Tuesday (5 February) on which day the two main parties in nineteen states held primaries/caucuses.

Types of primary

Each state makes it own regulations for the conduct of the elections so that the exact procedure varies across the country, practice ranging from the restrictive to the generous. In some states everyone can vote whereas, in others, only those who are registered as members of the party have the right. Where only registered members can vote, this is a *closed primary*. Where anyone, regardless of party affiliation, can vote, then this is an *open primary*. In Connecticut and Delaware in the Northeast, only party members are eligible. In the same region, Vermont holds open primaries. So does Rhode Island which, nonetheless, requires a voter to state his or her affiliation. By contrast, Alaska in the Northwest uses open primaries, allowing voters to vote in both parties should they wish to so do.

Broadly, the position is that:

1. In *open primaries*, the elector is given two ballots, one for each party. He or she fills in one to go in the ballot box and the unused one is discarded in a sealed container. He or she cannot use both and there is no way of knowing which one has been filled in. Some object to this process on the grounds that it is possible for the voter to use their vote not to distinguish between the candidates in his or her favoured party, but rather to seek to 'wreck' the chances of the other party by voting for its least impressive candidate. If that weak person were to be chosen, this might increase the chances of the voter's preferred party.
2. In *closed primaries*, this 'wrecking' cannot occur but neither is the process so secret for, on entering the polling station, the voter must express his or her affiliation. The appropriate ballot paper is then handed over and, if the party officers of one side question the allegiance, it can be challenged.

The merits and disadvantages of primaries

There are obvious benefits in the use of primaries: they are more democratic than the system they replaced; they emphasise the personal qualities of the candidates rather than their party label; and they sometimes produce good candidates who would otherwise not have been chosen. They can provide a chance for the different wings of the parties to air their viewpoints, and so indicate where the preferences of members really lay. They have drawbacks, in that they are an additional expense – often the machine still fights hard to ensure victory for its favoured candidate – and they demand that the voter turns out for yet another election: the frequency of elections is one reason sometimes given for low turnouts for many ordinary voters lack the stamina or interest.

See also *Presidential Elections*

Patriot Act (2001)

The Patriot Act is the shorter name given to the package of measures introduced by the Bush administration to counter terrorism, more fully known as 'Uniting and Strengthening America by Providing Appropriate Tools Required to Intercept and Obstruct Terrorism'. Passed within forty-five days of the 9/11 attacks on the World Trade Center, its purpose was described in the statute as being to 'deter and punish terrorist acts in the United States and around the world, to enhance law enforcement investigatory tools, and for other purposes'.

The Patriot Act substantially expanded the authority of the law enforcement agencies by: increasing their ability to search telephone and e-mail communications and medical, financial and other records; easing restrictions on foreign intelligence gathering within the United States; expanding the Secretary of the Treasury's authority to regulate financial transactions, particularly those involving foreign individuals and entities; and enhancing the discretion of law enforcement and immigration authorities in detaining and deporting immigrants suspected of terrorism-related acts. The act also widened the definition of terrorism to include 'domestic terrorism', thereby enlarging the range of activities to which the Patriot Act can be applied.

The act was passed by wide margins in both chambers of Congress but it has subsequently come under sustained attack from some academics, journalists, politicians and members of the public. Critics have claimed that the measures went far beyond what was necessary to root out terrorists and prevent the danger of further attacks. They detect signs of a serious erosion of accepted freedoms. Their criticism centres on three broad aspects of the measure:

1. The dedication to secrecy, which makes it difficult to find out information relating to the detainees held in federal prisons
2. The tilting of the balance of power towards the Executive, which involves removing from the judicial system some of its opportunities to review the actions of the ainistration. For instance, immigration judges now have less opportunity to prevent unlawful detention or deportation of non-citizens.
3. The undermining of the traditional distinction between foreign intelligence gathering and criminal investigation (e.g., information gathered by domestic law enforcement agencies can now be handed to bodies such as the CIA).

See also *Civil liberties and Civil Rights*; *War on Terrorism*

Paulson Plan (2008)

The Paulson Plan was the bail-out programme devised by US Treasury Secretary, Henry Paulson (1946–), in response to the global financial crisis of 2008. In its original form, it was intended that the federal government should take over responsibility for toxic loans that had been made by financial institutions

Paulson was the designated leader of the Bush administration's policies that were directed towards avoiding a severe economic meltdown in 2008. As part of his programme to restore confidence in the credit markets, he led the attempt to assist firms (mainly US banks) by advancing a scheme to employ $700 billion to purchase bad debts such as non-performing mortgages that

threatened company liquidity and – in its revised form – to make capital injections into banks. The press referred to this as the 'Paulson financial rescue plan'. The plan was eventually enacted into law in the form of the Emergency Economic Stabilization Act (2008).

See also *Bail-out*; *Financial Crisis and Global Recession (2007–09)*

Pelosi, Nancy (1940–)

Nancy Pelosi has represented California in the House of Representatives since 1987 and currently holds the office of speaker. She was the house minority leader from 2002 to 2007, holding the post during the 107th, 108th and 109th Congresses, prior to her elevation in the 110th Congress following the Democratic Party's electoral successes in November 2006.

She is the first woman, the first Californian and the first Italian American to hold the speakership. Second in the line of presidential succession after the vice president, she is therefore the third most senior politician in the United States. This makes her the highest-ranking woman in the history of the American federal government.

Widely respected for her organisational and fundraising skills, Ms Pelosi has previously had a relatively low public profile. But her current position has placed the spotlight on her character and political leanings. In the 2006 elections, the Republicans and their allies in the media attempted to exploit the fears of conservative voters, by portraying her as the embodiment of everything they disliked most about the Democrats. Campaign advertisements suggested that, as a self-confessed liberal, she would raise taxes, help illegal immigrants and back same-sex marriage.

In the early days of the 111th Congress, Speaker Pelosi worked with President Obama to pass the American Recovery and Reinvestment Act to provide relief for American families and to create or save 3.5 million American jobs.

Perot, Ross (1930–)

Ross Perot is a billionaire Texan businessman who twice stood as a candidate for the presidency and, on one occasion, gained considerable support. He is ranked as one of the richest people in America.

Perot founded Electronic Data Systems (EDS) in 1962, later sold the company to General Motors and then founded Perot Systems. In the late 1980s, he began to speak publicly about the state of America and what he perceived as the failings of the United States government. He claimed that his country was losing its pre-eminence and that it was time to get it back on track as the world's most successful nation. He vigorously opposed US involvement in the 1990–91 Gulf War and, in 1992, felt that he could not support President Bush whose administation, he felt, had failed to provide effective leadership, particularly in resolving the budget deficit. He decided to launch his own bid for the presidency instead.

Lacking any party label, he was able to get his name on the ballot paper in every state as a representative of his own creation, the 'United We Stand America' movement. Campaigning on the need to cut the deficit in national finances, he polled impressively, attracting some 19 per cent of the popular vote. He stood again four years later, as the candidate for the newly created Reform Party. On this occasion, he made little impact. He stood aside from those involved in its internal schisms at the end of the decade and, in 2000, backed the candidacy of George W. Bush. Since then, Perot has been largely silent on political issues.

Piscataway Board of Education v. *Taxman* (1989)

Piscataway Board of Education v. *Taxman* was a racial discrimination case begun in 1989. The school board of Piscataway in New Jersey wished to eliminate a teaching position from its high school Business Education department. State law required tenured teachers to be laid off reverse order of seniority. The newest tenured teachers, however, Sharon Taxman and Debra Williams, white and African American respectively, had begun work on the same day. Williams was the only black teacher in the department, however, in a school where 50 per cent of the students belonged to ethnic minority groups. To maintain racial diversity, the school board voted to lay off Taxman even though she possessed a superior qualification. She complained to the Equal Employment Opportunity Commission, citing in her defence Title VII of the Civil Rights Act of 1964.

After the Court of Appeals for the Third Circuit had ruled in Taxman's favour, the Piscataway board appealed to the Supreme Court, where a hearing was scheduled for January 1998. Fearing that a Taxman victory could lead to an outright ban on affirmative action programmes, civil rights groups provided money for an out-of-court settlement, ensuring that the case was never heard. Taxman was subsequently re-hired, through she now teachers elsewhere.

See also *Affirmative Action*

Planned Parenthood of Southeastern Pennsylvania v. *Casey* (1992)

Planned Parenthood of Southeastern Pennsylvania v. *Casey* was a highly controversial case considered by the Supreme Court on the issue of abortion. Its outcome allowed states considerable latitude in regulating abortion, thereby provoking intense clashes of opinion between pro-lifers and pro-choicers in several state legislatures.

The Pennsylvania state legislature amended its abortion control law in 1988 and 1989 to introduce new provisions. Among other requirements, the new law required; informed consent (prior counselling on the risks of, and alternatives to, having an abortion); a twenty-four hour waiting period prior to the procedure for reflection; that a married woman seeking an abortion should have notified her husband of her intention to abort the foetus; that a minor seeking an abortion required the consent of one parent; and the prohibition of abortion after twenty-four weeks of pregnancy unless it was necessary to save the woman's life. These provisions were challenged by several abortion clinics and physicians.

The Supreme Court had to decide whether or not the restrictions imposed violated the right of women to abortions as guaranteed in the *Roe* v. *Wade* ruling. In a controversial and bitterly contested decision, the justices reaffirmed by five votes to four the 'essential holding' of *Roe*, but upheld most of the Pennsylvanian provisions. For the first time, the justices introduced a new criterion for determining whether state limitations on abortion were valid. The new standard would be to consider whether any regulations had the purpose or effect of imposing an 'undue burden', defined as being a 'substantial obstacle in the path of a woman seeking an abortion before the foetus attains viability'. Applying this standard, the Court judged that the only requirement to fail the 'undue burden' test was the husband notification requirement.

In one respect, the opinion of the Court was unique. It was crafted and authored by three justices. *Casey* was a divided judgment, with none of the justices' opinions being joined by a majority of justices. The plurality decision, however, jointly written by Justices Souter, O'Connor and Kennedy, was recognised as the lead opinion carrying precedential weight because each of its parts was concurred with by at least two other justices, albeit different ones for each part. The six justices who did not join the plurality opinion wrote or joined opinions in which they partially concurred and partially dissented from the decision.

The verdict disappointed both sides of the abortion debate. States were granted substantial new powers to regulate abortion but were prohibited from banning it completely. Pro-choicers objected to the restrictions, pro-lifers wanted the overthrow of the *Roe* decision.

See also *Abortion*; *Abortion Rights Movement*; *National Organization for Women*; *Pro-life Movement*; Roe *v.* Wade *(1973)*; Webster *v.* Reproductive Health Services *(1989)*

Pledge of Allegiance

The Pledge of Allegiance is a promise or oath of allegiance to the United States and its national flag. It is commonly recited in unison at public events. It is often a morning ritual in school classrooms. In its present form, it reads: 'I pledge allegiance to the Flag of the United States of America, and to the Republic for which it stands, one Nation under God, indivisible, with liberty and justice for all.' Some states also have pledges of allegiance to their state flags.

The Pledge of Allegiance was first published to celebrate the 400th anniversary of the discovery of America in 1892, and was first used in public schools to celebrate Columbus Day on 12 October. It received official recognition by Congress in an act approved fifty years later. Congress added the phrase 'under God' to the pledge in 1954.

The United States Code states that, when delivering the Pledge of Allegiance, all must be standing to attention, facing the flag with the right hand over the heart. It also states that men not in uniform should remove any non-religious headdress with the right hand and hold it at the left shoulder, the hand being over the heart. Persons in uniform should remain silent, face the flag and render the military salute.

There has been periodic criticism of the promotion – sometimes requirement – that Americans recite the pledge. Legal challenges have been made on the grounds that state sponsoring of its use violates the religious clauses of the First Amendment. The phrase 'under God' seems to indicate that religion is a required part of American life, something which is anathema to atheists, agnostics and polytheists who contend that it contravenes the protections against establishment of religion.

Jehovah's Witnesses have a problem in that their beliefs preclude swearing loyalty to any power lesser than God. They have objected to policies in public schools requiring students to recite the pledge on the grounds that their rights to freedom of religion are guaranteed by the Free Exercise Clause.

In considering a case brought in 2002 by an atheist father who objected to his daughter being asked to take the pledge every morning, the Ninth Circuit Court of Appeals ruled that the phrase 'under God' was an unconstitutional endorsement of monotheism when the pledge was promoted in public school. In 2004, the Supreme Court overruled the Court of Appeals in *Elk Grove Unified School District* v. *Newdow*, deciding that as Newdow (the aggrieved father) was divorced and therefore not the custodial parent, he lacked standing in the case, thereby avoiding ruling on the merits of whether the phrase was constitutional in a school-sponsored recitation. (Chief Justice Rehnquist and justices Sandra Day

O'Connor and Clarence Thomas each wrote separate concurrences, saying that requiring teachers to lead the pledge is constitutional). In a subsequent case (January 2005), before a court in the Eastern District of California, the District Court judge ruled in favour of Newdow and expressed his willingness to require the school district defendants to refrain from requiring children to pledge allegiance to 'one Nation under God'.

In May 2006, in the case of *Frazier* v. *Alexandre*, a federal district court in Florida ruled that a 1942 state law, requiring students to stand and recite the Pledge of Allegiance, violates the First and Fourteenth Amendments even though the law allows students to opt out (on the grounds that they can do so only with written parental permission and are still required to stand during the recitation).

Plessy v. *Ferguson* (1896)

In *Plessy* v. *Ferguson*, the Supreme Court upheld a state law that segregated the races in transport, deciding that it did not violate the Fourteenth Amendment. According to the Court's analysis, the races could be confined to separate spheres within society as long as they were treated equally. The ruling therefore originated the 'separate but equal' doctrine and accepted the constitutionality of institutionalised segregation. In reality, African Americans were consigned to a subordinate role across the Southern states until the 1960s.

See also **Brown** *v.* **Board of Education** *(1954)*; **Segregation**

Pocket Veto

A pocket veto is a special veto power over legislation exercised by a chief executive after the legislative body has adjourned. A legislative manoeuvre in American lawmaking, it is in effect an indirect means of rejecting a bill. By its use, a governor or president is 'putting the bill in his or her pocket' so that it dies.

In the federal government, after passing through both houses of Congress, bills are sent to the White House for the president to sign. If he fails to act within ten days (excepting Sundays) the bill automatically becomes law. But, in the last ten days of a session, a failure to act amounts to a pocket veto; in other words, as Congress is not sitting and cannot fight back, the bill is effectively killed. In 1812, James Madison became the first president to use the pocket veto.

See also *Veto Power*

Political Action Committees (PACs)

Political action committees represent the political wing of business, labour, trade or other pressure groups and are legally permitted to raise funds to distribute to candidates and parties. Business, labour and trade associations, among others, have PACs to further their political goals. They seek to persuade members of Congress to vote as the group wishes, and they offer advice and information to candidates as well as the financial assistance that is their most important role. Elections are expensive, and candidates need substantial funds from their backers for such things as their advertising campaigns.

Groups have always wanted to influence election results, and PACs existed as long ago as the 1930s. It was in the 1970s, however, that they assumed a much greater significance, largely as a result of reforms introduced after Watergate. They have mushroomed in the last two decades, there now being more than 4,500 PACs registered with the Federal Election Commission. Despite concerns about the growing influence of PACs, their numbers have remained fairly constant since the mid-1980s. The scale of their participation in the political process has dramatically increased in recent years, however.

Nearly two-thirds of the PACs represent corporations, trade associations and other business and professional groups. Alliances of bankers, lawyers, doctors, farmers, manufacturers and merchants all sponsor PACs. They range from the American Bankers Association to the National Beer Wholesaler's Association PAC, formerly known as 'SixPAC'. Labour unions also sponsor hundreds of PACs, as do ideological, public interest and non-profit groups seeking to advance a particular cause. For instance, the National Rifle Association and the Sierra Club each operates a PAC, as does EMILY's List (*see* Women's Movement: the Fight for Female Equality), the organisation that has raised and donated millions of dollars to women candidates for political office.

Another recent development has been the way in which congressional and party leaders have also established their own PACs. These high-profile organisations are often the source of controversy because of suspicions that they are simply tools for avoiding federal campaign spending limits. During the mid-1990s, the Federal Election Commission charged that GOPAC, a PAC chaired for many years by Republican Speaker of the House, Newt Gingrich, had violated campaign finance laws by failing to register its activities with the commission in a timely manner and by neglecting to reveal the sources of its money. (In 1996, a federal judge dismissed the allegations against GOPAC.)

In 2004, the five leading PACs, as judged by the money spent by themselves, their affiliates and subsidiaries were:

1. EMILY's List $22,767,521
2. Service Employees International Union $12,899,352
3. American Federation of Teachers $12,789,296
4. American Medical Association $11,901,542
5. National Rifle Association $11,173,358

For and against PACs

In favour

1. They are the modern way to make money available for costly election campaigns. The methods employed are open, and preferable to the situation before they became widespread when the sources of finance were often disguised and unknown to the public. Indeed, it is the very availability of information that has led to criticism of them, criticism that is better directed to the whole system of campaign funding.
2. Such is the cost of campaigning that politicians cannot afford to be unduly beholden to particular PACs. They need a diversity

of sources of funding, and this prevents any undue influence – the more so as the $5,000 a PAC can donate is the level fixed two decades ago.
3. PACs represent a legitimate interest in a pluralist system, and the fact that there are nearly 5,000 of them serves to prevent any one of them from gaining excessive influence. Their actions are open to scrutiny, and the media are constantly on the lookout for examples of undue favours being granted.
4. As with groups in general, they offer an outlet through which people can be involved and express their ideas and opinions. On the one hand, they educate the voters but also they act as a means of communicating their views.

Against

1. The central allegation against PACs revolves around the idea that money can buy influence and power. A members of Congress who has the backing of a PAC is likely to give favours in return, so that they are associated with undue influence. In Griffin's (1992) words, PACs are 'a huge coalition of special interest groups dedicated to perverting the political process for private gain'. The fact that some PACs have actually been willing to back rival candidates is seen as evidence of their determination to gain such influence.
2. Most PACs give money primarily to incumbent members of Congress, and this makes it more difficult for a challenger to mount a successful campaign against a person already in office. In as much as this is true, it is seen as undermining the democratic process, for it makes a contest less meaningful and fair.
3. The costs of campaigning in congressional elections have spiralled out of control, a reflection of the easy availability of money collected by PACs. It is not due to the escalating costs of advertising but more to the fact that members of Congress have used this 'easy money' to equip themselves with needlessly large offices and staffing levels.
4. The usual criticism of pressure groups, the lack of internal democracy, is often mentioned

as well. Grant (1995) quotes the example of the decision of the AFL/CIO to back Mondale as the Democratic presidential nominee in 1984 even though fewer than a quarter of union members were asked their preference.

Political Advertising

Paid political advertising refers to the practice of political parties paying a broadcasting company to purchase advertising time. Such advertising is usually in the form of short broadcasts, much briefer than the party election broadcasts that are allowed to British parties free of charge. Whether or not a country allows paid political advertising in broadcasting is likely to depend heavily on the traditions in its style and ownership of broadcasting and consequently the type of regulatory system that has evolved.

Broadly speaking, countries with a long tradition of public ownership of broadcasting, such as France, the United Kingdom, and Denmark, have tended to be hostile to paid political advertising. Those with a stronger commercial broadcasting tradition – the United States represents the extreme – have tended to regard political advertising as natural.

Political advertising is a highly developed and very costly electoral practice in the USA. Many Americans regard it as an integral part of the right to freedom of expression and information. It is generally assumed that the First Amendment to the Constitution – prohibiting Congress from passing laws 'abridging' free speech – protects paid advertising. Indeed, existing campaign contribution limits are often criticised as being in violation of the First Amendment.

There are almost no restrictions on political advertising in America. A candidate may spend as much as he or she wishes to buy television time. Since the 2007 Supreme Court consolidated judgment in *Federal Election Commission* v. *Wisconsin Right to Life* and *McCain* v. *Wisconsin Right to Life*, the restrictions of the 2002 legislation on issue ads have been substantially watered down.

Adverts place greater emphasis on candidates themselves rather than their party label. Those who make them are concerned to portray their candidate in a flattering light and to stress the demerits of their opponents. There are several types of political ads:

- negative ads, those primarily more about an opponent
- biographic and vision ads, which describe or emphasise the candidate's life or 'vision' for America
- issue ads, which discuss one or more specific issues and the candidate's proposals about them and
- trust ads, those that seek to convince voters that the candidate is someone they can trust to lead them during challenging times.

There are also tailored spots for specific local regions. In 2004, a series of Bush–Cheney campaign ads made mention of specific weapons systems supposedly opposed by Kerry. The Arizona version mentioned Apache helicopters, Tomahawk cruise missiles and F-18 aircraft 'all built here in Arizona'.

The history and development of political advertising

American political advertising began in 1952, with Eisenhower's 30-minute biographical portrait, as 'the man from Abilene'. Its scale has massively increased in recent years and the advertisements have become much shorter. Advertisers know that the public can only absorb so much information at any one time. Whereas in the vice-presidential contest of that same year, Richard Nixon took thirty minutes to answer charges of corruption in front of 58 million viewers, today advertisers specialise in the sixty-second or (more often) the thirty- or even fifteen-second commercial which makes a point briefly, but dramatically.

Adverts can on occasion be longer than the usual current length, particularly when they are portrayals dwelling on the personal assets of the candidate. Americans have often used advertisements which are autobiographical in style. Television is good at handling personalities and stories, and some of the most effective advertisements judiciously combine the two elements. Rees (1992) provides an example:

One of most skilful of such 'endorsement' ads was in Oregon when Joe Slade-White made it for the incumbent governor. An old man was sitting on a bench, and said: 'Some people say Neil Goldschmidt is a big spender, but I happen to know that he was taught about money by one of the toughest economists in this state'. The picture widens to show a grey-haired, smiling lady, 'his Mom'.

The same features were combined in the 'Ron and Nancy' weepie in 1984 and the 'Man from Hope' film about Bill Clinton and his family eight years later. (The former is thought to have provided the model for the 'Kinnock – the Movie' election broadcast used so effectively by the Labour Party in the UK, in 1987.)

Negative advertising

American political adverts are overwhelmingly negative, for research has suggested that this is the most effective approach. In a brief broadcast, it is easier to implant a negative message than a positive one. This is why advertising tends to go for the jugular and expose deficiencies in the moral character of an opponent. Often, ads are used to attack an opponent's financial wheeling and dealing or to remind votes of personal weaknesses, perhaps in a backhanded way. Back in the 1990s, a candidate in Tennessee was congratulated for 'kicking [his] chemical dependency'. Sometimes, adverts are used to highlight inconsistency, as when in 1992 the Bush team showed two politicians expressing directly opposing views on issues from the Gulf War to drug abuse. As the faces became clear, a voice-over observed that: 'One of these politicians is Bill Clinton. Unfortunately, so is the other!'

In 2000, George Bush used one general election ad to promise to be constructive and upbeat in the election, claiming that Americans were tired of negativity and the cynicism it aroused: 'What they want to hear is what's on people's minds and where the candidates' hearts are. I'm going to run a campaign that is hopeful and optimistic and very positive'. Yet in the primaries his supporters had already sought to damage the chances of Senator McCain by claiming – among other attacks – that McCain had fathered a black

child out of wedlock (the McCains' dark-skinned daughter Bridget was adopted from Bangladesh), a misrepresentation that was likely to be an effective slur in a Southern state where race was still a key issue.

In 2004 and 2008, attack advertising was again widely employed. About a third of the pro-Bush ads in 2004 were used to criticise Kerry's version of his war record in Vietnam, his inconsistency over Iraq and other policy 'flip-flops'. In 2008, the McCain team initially claimed that it would not be making personal attacks of Barack Obama of the type that he himself had suffered in 2000. But as the polls looked increasingly discouraging in the later stages of the campaign it set out to destroy the credibility of the Democratic candidate by making reference to alleged past associations with terrorists.

According to *The Wall Street Journal* ('Presidential Election Negative Ads, 2008: The Least Successful Ever', 16 October 2008), *'almost all of McCain's ads and one-third of the Obama ads were negative'*. In defiance of conventional thinking that negative campaigning must be about an issue already worrying voters, both candidates brought up past associations of their rival, such as Obama's use of McCain's involvement in a 1980s savings-and-loan scandal. McCain widened his attacks, for instance (in response to Barack Obama's perceived rise in popularity following his July 2008 trip abroad) by releasing the 'Celeb' ad in which he compared Obama to Paris Hilton and Britney Spears. Members of his team also drew attention to Obama's racial background, often not in an overt way. Attack ads showed Obama playing basketball, an overwhelmingly black sport in the USA. Republican vice presidential nominee Sarah Palin emphasised the importance of electing someone committed to defending true American and Christian values, the implication being that Obama could not be relied upon to so do. This was in line with the advice apparently given to Hillary Clinton during the primary season that she needed to portray Obama as someone whose roots to basic American culture and values were at least limited.

Humour is often used effectively in attack-ads. A Democrat one used against the Nixon campaign in 1968 featured the Republican vice presidential running mate. A caption suddenly appeared on a blank television screen, saying: 'Spiro Agnew for Vice President'. Heard throughout the ad is the sound of uncontrollable laughter. At the end, another caption appears: 'This would be funny if it wasn't serious'. This was a classic example of an ad that plugged into existing voter perceptions. Many people were already doubtful of Agnew's capacity and ability to fulfil the role planned for him. The ad played upon the 'ridiculous' nature of such a prospect.

The impact of political advertising

It is arguable as to whether ads such as this one change people's outlook or voting intention, or whether they simply reinforce existing opinions. In the case of the 'Little Girl and the Daisy' ad used in 1964 by the Johnson team against Republican Barry Goldwater, it skilfully played upon and confirmed feelings and suspicions that many voters already had about Goldwater, who had made intemperate remarks about the possibility of fighting a limited nuclear war. An impression was left in the voter's mind, one which hurt the Goldwater campaign. He lost the election by a landslide margin.

American political scientist Bill Schneider sees negative advertising as a very efficient tool: 'For one thing, it's easier in thirty seconds to turn people off your opponent than to build a positive case for yourself – especially since television is a medium particularly suited for carrying negative, warning-style messages . . . you get more bang for the buck by running negative ads'.

See also *Election Campaigns*; *Issue Advertisements (Ads)*; *Presidential Elections*

Political Consultants

Political participation refers to activity by individuals that is intended to influence who governs and/or the decisions taken by those who do. Political consulting is the industry that has developed around advising and assisting political campaigns, initially in the United States but subsequently in democratic countries around the world. In an age of candidate-centred electioneering, consultants advise candidates as they prepare for elections. In recent decades, political consultants have replaced the traditional campaign managers in the most high-profile campaigns.

Consultants have been increasingly used in election campaigning over the last three decades. Most of them specialise in some aspect of election campaigning, such as fundraising or polling, although others are involved in all aspects of the electoral process, including advising on personal appearance, speech-writing, voice projection, managing the news and 'spinning' stories, the management of pseudo-events, and even policy positions. They tend to work for one party with whom they have political sympathies. In America, the influence of these communications experts is all-pervasive, their numbers having grown dramatically. Their use has now spread to many democracies including Britain. They are all in the business of 'selling politicians'.

According to the Center for Public Integrity website (2007) some 600 professional consultants were paid $1.78 billion for 2003–04 political campaign work. Among these, the three groups that consumed most of the expenditure were (in the order of their spending):

- media consultants (who handled advertising and gave strategic advice), $1.2 billion (67 per cent)
- direct mail consultants, $298 million
- fundraising consultants, $59 million.

See also *Election Campaigns*; *Presidential Elections*

Political Culture

The term 'culture' refers to the way of life of a people, the sum of their inherited and cherished ideas, knowledge and values which, together, constitute the shared bases of social action. Political culture is culture in its political aspect. It emphasises those patterns of thought and behaviour associated with politics in different societies, ones that are widely shared and define the relationship of citizens to their government and to each other in matters affecting politics and public affairs. Pye (1968) describes it as 'the sum of the fundamental values, sentiments and knowledge that give [sic] form and substance to political process'. For

Kavanagh (1987), it is 'the set of values in which the political system operates'.

Citizens of any country or major ethnic or religious community tend to have a common or core political culture, a set of long-term ideas and traditions that is passed on from one generation to the next. The survey work of Almond and Verba (1963) led to the publication of *The Civic Culture*, a landmark study in the field of political culture. Based on lengthy interviews conducted in five countries, the researchers pointed to considerable variations in the political beliefs of the societies they explored.

Research inevitably focuses on what the majority of the people appear to think and feel. Some of the surveys carried out since the 1960s, however, have pointed to the differences in the political beliefs of individuals within the same society. It has also shown that political culture is not an unchanging landscape, a fixed background against which the political process operates. Attitudes can evolve and change over time, for there is often in society a number of forces at work which serve to modify popular attitudes, among them migration and the emergence in some of liberal democracies of a substantial underclass. Both can be a cause of greater diversity in popular attitudes, for immigrants and those alienated from majority lifestyles may have a looser attachment to prevailing cultural norms. In the words of one author, 'culture moves'.

The process by which people acquire their central tenets and values, and gain knowledge about politics, is known as political socialisation. It derives from learning and social experience and is strongly influenced by persons with whom individuals have contact from early childhood through adulthood. Political socialisation ensures that important values are passed on from one generation to the next and that the latest influx of immigrants comprehends, accepts and approves the existing political system and the procedures and institutions through which it operates. For this reason, political socialisation is overwhelmingly conservative in its effects, having a tendency to ensure that people conserve the best of the past.

The impressions and survey work of commentators and academics are of interest to those who wish to study politics. They enable us to make comparisons about the approaches that characterise the inhabitants of other democracies.

Political culture in the United States

Political culture in the United States derives from some of the ideas that inspired the pioneers who made the country and the Founding Fathers who wrote its Constitution. It includes faith in democracy and representative government, the ideas of popular sovereignty, limited government, the rule of law, equality, liberty, opportunity, support for the free-market system, freedom of speech and individual rights. But, of course, at different stages in history, the existing political culture and the process of political socialisation serve some individuals and groups better than others. Until the 1960s, the prevailing political culture suggested that women and ethnic minorities were not full members of the political community. Not surprisingly, these two groups sought to change the political culture. They wanted to see ideas of equality and opportunity applied to them as much as to other groups. Since then, there has been a 'rights culture', as activists sought to demand the rights they regarded as their due.

In particular, throughout American history, there has been a strong consensus in support of democracy and the values that underpin it, including:

- *a deep interest in the exercise of power*, who has it, how it was acquired and how those who exercise it can be removed.
- *a general acceptance of majority rule*, but also respect for minority rights so that minorities can have the opportunity to become tomorrow's majority. Pluralism in society, involving the existence and acceptance of distinctive groups and political toleration, has been important as the country has become more ethnically and religiously diverse, and people have adopted new lifestyle arrangements.
- *a firm commitment to popular sovereignty*, the idea that ultimate power resides in the people themselves.
- *strong support for the rule of law*, with government being based upon a body of law applied equally and with just procedures. The principle

of fairness applies, with all individuals entitled to the same rights and level of protection, and expected to abide by the same codes of behaviour. No one is above the law for, in the words of Chief Justice Marshall: 'the government of the United States has been emphatically termed a government of laws, not of men'.

- *a dislike and distrust of government and a fear of the tyrannical rule and exercise of excessive authority that can accompany it,* not surprising in a land whose pioneers tamed the wilderness, created new frontiers and tried to build themselves a better future. Americans have always had a wariness about those who exercise power over them – a distrust which has roots in Lockean liberalism but was primarily based upon the experiences of the colonists in their dealings with King George III. This suspicion of government and things associated with it may be a factor in the low turnouts in many elections.

America is a multilingual, multiracial society of great social diversity. Yet many of the immigrants and their descendants have taken on board many traditional American values, such as a commitment to liberty and equality. There are forces that bring Americans together and give them a sense of common identity. Part of this sense of national unity can be explained by the pursuit of the American Dream via which all may prosper in a land of opportunity.

Adversity, a sense of common danger, has also helped to unify Americans. War and the threat of war often serve to bind a nation. In World War II, Americans of all creeds and backgrounds could recognise the contribution made by people very different from themselves. So, too, in September 2001 and thereafter. The attacks on the World Trade Center, which destroyed the well-known image of the New York skyline and killed nearly 4,000 people, had the effect of bringing New Yorkers and their fellow Americans together. They were determined to hunt down the perpetrators of the outrage and to show the world that their spirits could not be crushed.

Finally, shared ideas, a common culture, the prevalence of the mass media and intermarriage also serve to blur the differences between different groups. Most Americans can accept and embrace American values. They share a common attachment for certain ideals and processes.

Political Participation

Political participatiotn refers to activity by individuals that is intended to influence who governs and/or the decisions taken by those who do. Citizens can be classified both by the extent of their political involvement (using the 1977 Milbrath and Goel division of Americans into a small number of gladiators, an overwhelming number of spectators and a substantial number of apathetics) and by the nature of their engagement (for example, whether they use conventional or unconventional approaches).

Democracy implies participation, with people having the freedom to take part in the formulation, passage or implementation of policies. Democratic standards are more likely to prevail where people are well informed and willing to get involved. In the *polis*, the city-state of Ancient Greece, it was considered natural that people would take part in politics, through this was a privilege confined to make citizens.

The United States has always attached great importance to the ideas and values of democracy. Although the founders of the American Republic were wary of majority rule, they none the less believed that most people would be able to take part in the electoral process and thus be able to play a key role in determining the direction which government policy should take.

The issue of political participation has been one of lively debate. In 1835, the liberal French aristocrat Alexis de Tocqueville visited America and was much impressed by what he saw of the way it was governed and of how society functioned. He observed that 'Americans of all ages, all stations in life, and all types of disposition are forever forming associations.' He portrayed them as belonging to 'the most democratic country in the world', extolling their involvement in groups which helped them pursue 'the objects of common desires'.

Yet, in a recent controversial study, Robert Putnam (2000) suggests that the willingness of Americans to engage in political life has diminished in recent decades. He argues that there is now a 'degree of social disengagement and civic connectedness' which has damaging consequences for political life. He believes that social participation is declining in the United States, observing that today more people spend time watching *Friends* than making them! More seriously, he points to static levels of political knowledge in spite of the development of university education; in addition, fewer people engage in volunteer work (there may be more pressure groups but average membership stands at only 10 per cent of its 1962 level, and members tend to take a less active role), belong to trade unions, attend church or public meetings, and vote in elections and trust government.

Lack of interest and knowledge

Political issues are not the be-all and end-all of most peoples' lives, and – like most people – Americans are concerned with bread-and-butter matters such as making a living, improving their family position and enjoying their leisure. The level of interest varies sharply between different groups of the community but the findings of the 1992 *American National Election Study*, conducted by the University of Michigan, showed that only 26 per cent were interested for 'most of the time', 41 per cent for 'some of the time' and 21 per cent 'only now and then'; 11 per cent were 'hardly at all' committed.

Many people may find politics a complicated process, and certainly surveys of political knowledge and understanding reveal widespread public ignorance. According to a survey by the *American Political Science Review* (September 1980), 40 per cent of those interviewed could not name one of their state's senators. Ignorance covers personalities and policies. Given such a lack of interest and information, participation in the political process is inevitably unlikely to be very high.

Those who possess knowledge and understanding tend to participate more. They are often the better-educated people who read newspapers, watch current affairs programmes and engage in political discourse with their relatives and friends. At the other end, those who participate very little are the least educated who may feel isolated from the political world which they may see as having

let them down. Many of those who are somewhere between, having sporadic interest in politics, will join in from time to time. They will vote in certain elections that seem relevant or interesting to them – as we have seen, more often in presidential ones than the rest. They will occasionally discuss political issues at times of peak media attention but, for much of the time they choose not to read about or view what is going on.

Forms of participation

At the time when the electorate has the opportunity to be more informed about politics than ever before, turnout in elections is low. But there are more opportunities for participation than voting alone. Americans can involve themselves in election campaigns, join political parties and pressure groups, and take part in protest marches and forms of direct action. The American system also offers the citizens of some states an opportunity for direct participation in decision-making, which is generally denied to the British electorate except on rare constitutional issues. This is done via the town meeting in New England, and via the initiative and referendum in many areas of the country.

See also *Turnout*

Participation in various forms of electoral activity (percentage of total US population)

Type of activity	
Discuss politics from time to time	81
Try to persuade others	35
Wear button, sticker or sign	10
Attend meetings, rallies	6
Do other campaign work	3
Contribute to candidate	7
Contribute to political party	6

Adapted from figures produced in the 2000 National Election Study, University of Michigan

Political Parties

Political parties are organisations of broadly like-minded people whose purpose is to win elections and gain office so that they may implement their chosen policies. Their members do not share identical attitudes and interests, for parties are inevitably coalitions of individuals whose approaches on some issues may be widely divergent.

The Founding Fathers had a deep suspicion of parties or, as they called them, 'factions'. James Madison defined a faction in unflattering terms:

> By a faction, I mean a number of citizens, whether amounting to a majority or a minority of the whole, who are united and actuated by some common impulse or passion, or of interest, adverse to the rights of other citizens or to the permanent aggregate interest of the community.

Accordingly, the Constitution does not make provision for political parties, its creators not wishing to become enmeshed in discussion of such a divisive issue. But, in establishing the Bill of Rights, they tried to ensure that parties could freely operate. Today, the Supreme Court is usually wary of any attempts to regulate political activity. Parties are free to organise as they wish, as long as they do not violate explicit constraints, such as those banning racial discrimination.

American parties are actually local or state parties that come together every four years in order to elect a president. Only in recent years have they established permanent national staffs and anything resembling a national party organisation. National parties do not seek to tell state and local organisations what to say or who to choose for office at any level. Away from Washington, parties in each state have their own leaders and programmes, though they may receive national advice on campaign strategies for congressional elections and perhaps training sessions for newly adopted candidates.

In addition to organising elections, parties are instrumental in running the government, creating and implementing shared political goals through the election of officials to the executive and legislative branches of government, and bringing stability to the political system. Parties also serve as a major link between the government and the governed, giving individuals an opportunity to participate in American politics.

Despite initial anxieties about the baneful effect of parties, future president Woodrow Wilson (1908) could speak of them as 'absolutely necessary to . . . give some coherence to the action of political forces'.

A two-party system

A two-party system is one in which only two parties compete meaningfully for political power though several others might exist. Nationally, the Uinted States has had a two-party system throughout its history although, at state and local levels, there are many one-party and multi-party arrangements. At one time, the South was solidly Democratic but this is not the case today. The rural Midwest is a stronghold for the Republicans who often capture key states in that region. In New York, it is possible that there will be five or six parties represented on the ballot paper.

Although numerous third and minor parties have been created from time to time (for instance, the Reform Party and the Greens in recent years) their members have rarely been elected to major office. *Why have two main parties dominated American politics?*

One explanation is the use of the first-past-the-post, 'winner takes all' electoral system for all federal and state – and most local – elections. No matter how close the vote, only one US representative is elected from each congressional district. Third or minor parties may accumulate plenty of votes across the state but their support is not sufficiently concentrated to enable them to gain representation. Recognising that such parties have little chance of success at election time, voters tend to be drawn to the major party coalitions which generally try to advance moderate, middle-of-the-road positions that may appeal widely.

Writers such as Key (1964) and Hartz (1955) have argued that a two-party system coincides with the natural division of interests in the United States. These divisions often coincide with different views over the role and power of national government and over issues of economic and social policies. Some voters are broadly on the side of progress and reform whereas others are more content to stand pat. The absence of a clear social class divide has meant that – unlike the situation in parts of western Europe – parties have not developed around particular class interests. For instance, because many Americans are agreed about the desirability of capitalism and the value of pursuing the American Dream of pioneering individuals, there has been no substantial support for a socialist party. In addition, there are barriers that make it difficult for third and minor parties to get their names on the state ballot paper. In some states, the regulations are restrictive, although court challenges have led to the removal of some constraints.

Where the two-party system functions effectively, it offers a meaningful choice to the voters. Both parties are broad umbrellas, wide enough in span to cater for the widely divergent interests of American society. They welcome support wherever it can be found and, when possible, seek to make inroads into the electoral base of their opponents, as happened when Ronald Reagan managed to appeal to substantial segments of the traditionally blue-collar vote. By assimilating a spectrum of beliefs, the parties generally steer clear of the extremes although highly partisan Democrats and Republicans have opportunities to vent their frustration and keep within the party fold.

The decline and renewal of parties

American political parties are essentially weak, both in an historical and in international perspectives. Among the factors that have contributed to this weakness are:

1. The federal system of government
2. The operation of the idea of the separation of powers
3. The notion of consensus in American politics
4. The ethos of individualism in American society.

As the twentieth century progressed, parties became weaker than ever before, for several reasons:

1. The growth of the system of primary elections
2. The erosion of the North–South divide
3. The development of the mass media
4. The arrival of new issues on the agenda that cut across traditional party lines
5. The increasing importance of pressure groups and political action committees (PACs).

By the 1970s, some commentators and academics were insisting that the Democrats and the Republicans were in a period of serious decline. They were portrayed as 'weak', inconsistent in their policies, lacking accountability for their actions, disorganised in pursuing their goals and less effective than in the past in organising government. They were said to be overwhelmed by the changes and challenges confronting them as the country had moved from an era of party-centred campaigning to one of candidate-centred campaigning. Broder (1972) popularised this thesis of party decline, and suggested that neither party could adapt adequately to the changing political environment. As he memorably put it: 'The party's over.'

Once the 'upheavals' of the 1960s and 1970s had settled down, signs of renewal became evident in the 1980s. Some academics began to question the idea of inevitable party decline. They noted that some of the factors making for 'decline' had lost some of their impact or were being accommodated. They also drew attention to: the rise in importance of the national party committees; the increasing importance of the national party chairpersons; and how the national party headquarters were beginning to play an unprecedented role in fundraising and dispensing services to congressional, state and local candidates (for instance, via the use of direct mail and computer technology in electioneering). Bibby (1981) wrote on *Party Renewal in the Republican Party* and Reichley (1985) on *The Rise of National Parties*. They claimed that the evidence had been largely misinterpreted and that (certainly by the 1980s) parties had begun to adapt successfully. They detected evidence of party vitality, indeed of 'renewal' or 'resurgence'.

American parties may be less significant than those in western Europe, but this does not make them irrelevant. For all their weaknesses, parties have not been displaced. Epstein (1986) argues that they have continued to be important players so that, even if they have become 'frayed . . . they will survive and even moderately prosper in a society evidently unreceptive to strong parties and yet unready, and probably unable, to abandon parties altogether'. Indeed, he observes that parties have regained some importance in the last generation as the 'new issues' have had less of an impact than they did in the 1960s. They have also become more organised at the federal level and have shown a greater ability in recent years to raise money by new techniques of fundraising. As he points out:

1. They are still a reference point for the electors.
2. They are still a reference point for members of Congress, all but two of whom in the 111th Congress belong to one of the two main parties.

Parties are not about to disappear. In some respects they show signs of revival. They will never have the organisational strength – based on state and local machines – that they had a hundred years ago, nor will they develop into European-style, mass party organisations. They play a less important role in the political system than they once did but they are still necessary to organise legislatures and to structure voter choices and make them meaningful.

See also *references to individual parties, past and present*

Populism/Populist Party

Populism refers to a system of thought that sees itself as being on the side of the people and against the political elites who frequent public office. Its adherents wish to see changes in the social and political system that would benefit the common person. Sometimes, it refers to the rhetoric and style of speakers who urged changes in the existing political system.

The People's Party (or Populist Party as it was widely known) comprised many tenant farmers who had fallen deeply into debt as agricultural depression worsened in the early 1880s. This exacerbated long-held grievances against railways, lenders, grain-elevator owners and others with whom farmers did business. By the early 1890s, as the depression worsened, some industrial workers shared these farm families' views on labour and the trusts.

In 1890, Populists won control of the Kansas

state legislature, and Kansan William Peffer became the party's first senator. In 1892 the national party was founded officially through a merger of the Farmers' Alliance and the Knights of Labor. In that year the Populist presidential candidate, James Weaver, won over one million votes. Between 1892 and 1896, however, the party failed to make further gains, in part because of fraud, intimidation and violence by Southern Democrats.

By 1896, the Populist organisation was in even greater turmoil, with two main factions emerging. The fusion Populists sought to merge with the Democrats in the hope that they may bring about changes in the major party's platform. Fusionists argued that a regionally based third party could never hold national power and that therefore the best strategy was to influence a leading party that could. The second group, known as 'mid-roaders', suspected (with good reason) that Democratic leaders wished to destroy the third-party threat and argued that fusion would give them exactly what they wanted. These Populists advocated staying 'in the middle of the road' between the two larger parties, maintaining their independence from both of them.

Over time, there have been various versions of a Populist Party, inspired by the 1890s creation. As an idea, populism lives on, echoes of populist thinking having been apparent in the campaigns to capture the presidency by Ross Perot, Ralph Nader and the Reform Party.

In the early 2000s, new populist parties have been formed, such as the Populist Party of Maryland, which ran candidates for the governorship and other elected state positions in the 2006 elections. It campaigned for tax cuts for working people, employee-owned municipal utilities and government promotion of employee ownership and control of workplaces. The Populist Party of America (2002) and the American Populist Renaissance (2005), the American Moderation Party (2005) all advocate elements of populist ideas. The Populist Party website explains something of the populist outlook in its declaration that 'the time has come for each citizen of the United States to claim true autonomy over his or her own personage, and exclaim, at last, that they are the true sovereign over themselves, and that the People themselves are the constituent sovereign of our nation'.

Pork/Pork-barrel Politics

The term 'pork' originated in the days of plantation slavery in the South in the years before the Civil War via which, on special occasions, slave owners would put out salt pork in big barrels at a certain time on an announced day, and their slaves would rush to grab what they could. The Oxford English Dictionary (1989) describes 'pork-barrel' politics as 'appropriations secured by congressmen for local projects'.

When members of Congress seek to gain federal funds for special projects in their district or state for the benefit of their constituents ('bring home the bacon') they are often accused of playing 'pork-barrel politics'. Examples of 'pork' include measures providing for public works projects, such as: the construction of federal buildings or roads; schemes of flood control and dams; national defence contracts; and agricultural subsidies.

Whereas senators and representatives defend their pork-barrel efforts as a way of more evenly distributing federal money throughout the nation and gaining obvious benefits for inhabitants of their region, critics argue that pork diverts funds from other, more necessary priorities in order to enhance members' chances of re-election.

Powell, Colin (1937–)

Colin Powell was a professional soldier for thirty-five years, during which time he held myriad command and staff positions and rose to the rank of four-star general. After holding the post of National Security Advisor (1987–89), his last assignment was to serve as Chairman of the Joint Chiefs of Staff (1989–93), the highest military position in the Department of Defense. During this time, he oversaw twenty-eight crises, including masterminding the successful Operation Desert Storm in the First Gulf War. On taking up a political career, he became the sixty-fifth US Secretary of State during the first administration of George W. Bush (2001–05). He was widely seen as a moderating influence among more hawkish colleagues. He was keen to carry as

much international support for US policy as possible, particularly in the diplomacy surrounding the invasion of Iraq.

In many ways, Colin Powell seems to be the embodiment of the American Dream. Born in Harlem to immigrant parents from Jamaica, he knew the rough life of the streets and overcame a barely average start at school. Then he joined the US Army and, during the distinguished career in the military that followed, he became the recipient of numerous US and foreign military awards and decorations. He was the first African American to serve as Secretary of State.

Since his departure from high public office, Powell has spoken with increasing openness about the nature of the war in Iraq, about what went wrong and about the limitations of the current strategy. He has apologised for presenting an inaccurate case to the United Nations on Iraqi weapons. At a meeting with President Bush in August 2002, he outlined at length the dangers that would be involved in a conflict with Iraq and of occupying a largely Arab country. He pointed to the likelihood that the invading forces would have to deal with a situation in which there was a broken civil government, and in which the invading armies ceased to be regarded as liberators but were instead viewed as occupiers.

Having donated the maximum allowable amount to the John McCain campaign in the summer of 2007 and in early 2008, Powell was mentioned as a possible running mate for the Republican. In October 2008, however, he disappointed McCain by endorsing Barack Obama, citing 'his ability to inspire, because of the inclusive nature of his campaign, because he is reaching out all across America, because of who he is and his rhetorical abilities', in addition to his 'style and substance'. Moreover, at a time when, in his view, the Republican Party was narrowing its appeal, he praised Obama as a 'transformational figure'.

Presidency, Presidents and Presidential Power

The American Constitution has relatively little to say about what the American president can and should do. What is said is rather vague, key terms such as the Executive not being clearly defined. Furthermore, the functions set out are subject to restraints.

The actual powers outlined in the document are set out in Articles 1 and 2:

- Article 1vii: to veto congressional legislation
- Article 2 ii: to act as commander-in-chief of US armed forces
- Article 2 ii: to grant pardons
- Article 2 ii: to make treaties
- Article 2 ii: to appoint ambassadors
- Article 2 ii: to make judges
- Article 2 ii: to appoint members of the Executive
- Article 2 iii: to comment on the State of the Union
- Article 2 iii: to recommend legislation to Congress
- Article 2 iii: to summon special sessions of Congress

The Founding Fathers had in mind a presidency of which the holder would stand above the political process and act as a symbol of national unity. He would not depend directly on the people or on any political party for his support. This would enable him to act as a kind of gentleman–aristocrat, remote from the political arena. Congress was supreme, as far as the actual government of the country was concerned. In the words of Maidment and McGrew (1992), the presidency would be 'the brake, the restraining hand of the federal government; it would provide the balance for the congress, and the House of Representatives in particular'.

Franklin Roosevelt's assumption of the presidency in 1933 is often said to have ushered in the era of the 'modern presidency', transforming as it did the role of the federal government and of the president who led it. Since then, people have expected more of their leaders although some presidents have found that the powers of the office have fallen far short of the scope and range of their responsibilities and the popular expectations of what should be accomplished. The popular image is that the president is in charge of the national government in Washington but Charles Jones has reminded us that America

has a 'separated' system of government in which constitutional authority and resources are spread across three organs of government, including the Legislature and Judiciary, as well as the Executive. This results in the mismatch identified by Stephen Skowronek (1993) who has distinguished between the popular understanding of the presidency and the authority that attaches to it in the Constitution:

> Formally, there is no central authority. Governing responsibilities are shared, and assertions of power are contentious. Practically, however, it is the presidency that stands out as the chief point of reference . . . it is the executive office that focuses the eyes and draws out the attachments of the people.

Expectations of the presidency in the 'modern era'

For many citizens, the president is the American government. When things go well, it is because the president is exercising leadership. When they go badly, it is because the president is weak and not up to the job. They applaud presidents for successes and blame them when things go wrong. Disasters as well as triumphs are credited to presidents. Wilson's inability to gain support for the League of Nations; Hoover's handling of economic depression; Franklin Roosevelt's implementation of the New Deal; Johnson's leadership of his country into increasing involvement in Vietnam; Nixon's misuse of his authority over Watergate; Carter's difficulties in the Iran hostage crisis; Reagan's budget deficits; Clinton's impeachment; and George W. Bush's invasion of Iraq – all are seen as being down to personal presidential performance. When a specific national problem arises, whether it is rising crime rates, illegal immigration, a hurricane disaster or a stalled economy, the president is expected to respond and will be judged on his handling of the issue. Many Americans think that, if only the president mobilises all the forces at his command, then he will be able to resolve any problem. If the right candidate for office were to be available, a Lincoln or a Franklin Roosevelt, all would be well. This is the popular myth of an all-powerful presidency, sometimes referred to the 'imagined presidency' (Louis Koenig, 1996) or the 'saviour model' of the presidency (Michael Nelson, 2005).

Such a view, fuelled by memories of 'great presidents', suggests that all of the country's problems, economic, political, social or international, can be resolved by a display of effective leadership from the president, endowed as he is with immense powers. Sometimes, the observations of presidents have served to feed the myth, such as when Jimmy Carter (A. Gitelson, R. Dudley and M. Dubnick, 2001) contended that: 'The president is the only person who can speak with a clear voice to the American people and set a standard of ethics and morality, excellence and greatness.'

Because of the expectations that presidents can, and do, make a real difference to the lives of Americans, they are judged harshly when they fail to achieve all that was anticipated of them. For various reasons, it has at times become more difficult for presidents to fulfil their best intentions. Michael Genovese (2001) has written of how 'once seen as the great engine of democracy, the presidency now seems to be "the little train that can't"', and asks where have all the leaders have gone. A system that once enabled Franklin Roosevelt to lead his country out of depression now seems to be 'characterised by gridlock and deadlock, paralysis and roadblocks. From Lyndon Johnson to Bill Clinton, recent presidents have either failed or performed well below expectations.' Thomas Cronin, too (2004), has claimed that 'presidential frustration is far more the rule than presidential triumph'.

Only five of the twelve leaders before Barack Obama have completed two or more terms, the rest being assassinated, defeated, unwilling to run again or having resigned in disgrace. Compared with the 'great' or 'near great' presidents who were tested by war or economic depression and heroically led their country through troubled times, there has seemingly been a lack of similar quality in recent incumbents. Although – as in the case of Truman – today's 'near greats' were not so viewed at the time, it is hard to imagine Ford, Carter, George H. Bush, Bill Clinton and George W. Bush as ever likely to feature at the top end of any ranking of past presidents.

In recent decades, inspirational and/or towering figures have not reached the highest office. Yet in part their difficulties in office may derive not so much from their personal failings as from the weakness inherent in the modern presidency, an institution that has been labelled as 'tethered' and 'constrained'. But, if in the separated system that Charles Jones (2005) has described, those who take a presidency-centred view of government expect too much of the Executive, it remains the case that it is the head of the Executive who is in the best position to give a lead when leadership is required. The research of William Howell (2004) and others shows us some of ways in which George W. Bush was able to act independently and forcefully.

Americans have an ambivalent attitude towards their presidents. They want to be led but, at the same time, are suspicious of forceful leaders who might abuse their positions of power. They admire strength but worry about the possible adverse consequences of that strength. Presidents, therefore, have to tread carefully, being seen to be active and effective but not overpowerful and domineering. There must neither be too much nor too little power in the White House.

The varying extent of presidential power

Power in the White House has ebbed and flowed. The Founding Fathers never intended that the presidency should be a powerhouse. They admired and they feared leadership, recognising the need for effective direction from a central government, yet afraid that any undue use or misuse of power might jeopardise the freedoms for which they had fought for in the War of American Independence. Similar ambiguities exist today. There remains that ambivalence about whether the presidency should be largely above the politics of the day and respond to the views expressed in Congress and by the electorate, or whether the institution should be politically engaged, providing a lead to members of Congress and to the people.

Since the Founding Fathers did their work, there has been a gradual accretion of presidential power so that presidents of the post-1945 era have tended to be markedly more active and assertive than their predecessors a hundred years ago. But the increase has not been at a steady or consistent rate. Power has increased at times of grave emergency and tension while, in calmer periods, Congress has tended to reassert its role and rein in the president.

In other words, there has been a waxing and waning of presidential power. Broadly speaking, in the years between 1789 and 1933, presidents took a rather limited view of their responsibilities. There were notably active presidents in the period, Washington, Jefferson, Jackson, Lincoln, Theodore Roosevelt and Woodrow Wilson being the foremost examples. Domestic and foreign upheaval, often war, created the conditions that enabled them to concentrate authority in the White House. Other presidents, such as Taft and Coolidge, attempted to do remarkably little. Given their limited concept of the office they held, they needed to raise or spend little money and had no significant legislative programme that they wished to implement.

Some presidents of the first 150 years are very forgettable and, indeed, have in several cases long been forgotten. There were thirty presidents in those years, few of whom, made much impact on the presidency. The presidencies of Chester Arthur, Millard Fillmore and Benjamin Harrison today seem inconsequential.

Interpretations of the presidency

Over recent decades, the presidency has been categorised in various ways. When the potential of the office became apparent under Franklin Roosevelt, the extent of presidential power both before and during World War II was apparent to all observers. Hence the label often applied to the post-1933 years as an era of 'modern' government. Yet, under Roosevelt's successor, Congress was unresponsive to the domestic agenda that Truman advanced. In the case of Truman's successors, Eisenhower and Kennedy, there was a similar gulf between the considerable discretion they were allowed to exercise in foreign policy and the limitations at home. Richard Neustadt saw the power of the presidency as being restricted to the 'power to persuade' and, at the time when the first edition of his book on presidential power appeared, he was concerned to

indicate to fellow-Democrat, President Kennedy, how he might overcome the weaknesses inherent in the office. Within a few years, however, Arthur Schlesinger – aware of the performance of Johnson over Vietnam and particularly the experiences of the Nixon presidency – was writing of the overmighty 'imperial presidency'.

Such a view did not last long for, with the ousting of President Nixon, Congress reasserted itself so that, in the days of Ford and Carter, Franck could portray the office as ineffective, 'tethered' or 'imperilled'. In the early years of Ronald Reagan, it was possible to think in terms of the 'restored presidency'. Yet, within a few years, he had experienced a deadlocked second term, and his successors found it difficult to persuade Congress to respond in the days of the 'constrained presidency'. Such nomenclatures came and went remarkably quickly, the turnover in part resulting from the tendency of observers to equate the strengths and successes or otherwise of individual presidents with the powers of the presidency as an institution. Such an overpersonalisation of the office tends to imply that individual presidents provide genuine national leadership and can make the office respond to their goals.

The presidency is, in one sense, the most powerful office on earth for its incumbent has the power to make massive decisions affecting the peace of the world. The responsibility seems awesome, as Truman realised when – on the death of FDR – he implored journalists: 'Boys, if you ever pray, pray for me now.' But some commentators would argue that the presidency is inherently weak in terms of its limited range of powers and the restrictions placed upon the incumbent.

Perceptions of presidential power have varied enormously. There has been a long-running debate about whether there ever was an imperial presidency or whether the notion was an exaggerated response to the circumstances of the time. Similarly, the weakness or strength of the office has been much debated, with two broad views emerging, as represented by Richard Neustadt and William Howell. In *Presidential Power* (1960) Neustadt introduces his major theme that, far from being all-powerful, presidents find that their wishes do not automatically become policy. They cannot depend upon the support of anyone – not even their own appointees. They must rely upon persuasion. In the system of shared powers, they must convince others that what they want is in their interests as well. The invoking of party loyalty, effective lobbying and personal appeal are all potential means of persuasion but the support of the public is particularly useful even though it cannot guarantee presidential success.

Howell's more recent study is a direct attack on the Neustadt argument. He notes the striking ways in which President Bush used presidential powers following the attack on the Twin Towers, often in the absence of congressional legislation. Although the circumstances of late 2001 were extraordinary, Howell argues that Bush's actions are otherwise typical; in his view, presidents often exercise power without persuasion.

A further theory, first advanced by Aaron Wildavsky (1966) and often restated since then, is that there are really 'two presidencies'. He argued that presidents have a much easier time exercising power in foreign policy than on domestic questions. Indeed, he claimed that, for the president, 'foreign policy concerns tend to drive out domestic policy'.

Presidential Election Debates

Televised presidential debates are held a few weeks after the main parties have nominated their candidates at their party conventions and a few weeks before polling day. There are normally three debates between the two candidates for the presidency and one between the challengers for the vice presidency. The gatherings are staged in a large public place, such as a university hall, before an audience of citizens. Questions are usually posed by one or more journalist moderators although, in some cases, members of the public have been able to join in. Depending on the format adopted, the debates can be useful in clarifying the policies of those participating, and they allow the viewer to make a choice between the merits of rival candidates and to assess their effectiveness and sincerity when under pressure.

Debates between presidential candidates have a long history. Seven debates in Illinois (1858) set the stage for Abraham Lincoln's later run for the presidency. There were further debates in

1948, 1956 and 1960 but none between 1960 and 1976. Since then, presidential debates have been a feature of every campaign. They have become the pre-eminent media event of the campaign, attracting at their peak in 1980 a vast audience of eighty million out of 226 million. Since then, audiences have fallen. In 2004, 62.5 million people watched the first debate while 43.6 million watched the vice presidential debate.

The Commission on Presidential Debates (CPD) was established in 1987 to ensure that debates, as a permanent part of every general election, provide the best possible information to viewers and listeners. Its primary purpose is to sponsor and produce debates for the United States presidential and vice presidential candidates and to undertake research and educational activities relating to the debates. It has organised all the debates from 1988 onwards.

The quality of past debates

Presidential and vice presidential debates have been of varying quality, and the rules of engagement have differed from election to election. Some have almost certainly made a difference to the outcome (e.g., Kennedy v. Nixon, in 1960) so that it is crucial for candidates to avoid mistakes. In that particular contest, Nixon was at a disadvantage against the handsome, telegenic Kennedy. His five o'clock shadow (ill-disguised by inadequate make-up) and grey suit (which, on black-and-white television, faded into the backdrop of the set) created a poor image so that viewers were, to some extent, distracted from what he said. According to many accounts, radio listeners thought that Nixon had won the debate whereas viewers inclined to Kennedy. The televised debates were thought to be the difference in what was an extremely close election.

Errors have been made and some have been costly. President Ford committed an infamous gaffe and exposed his ignorance in 1976 when – at a time when the Cold War was still very much a part of the global scene – he said that Poland was not then under Soviet domination. By contrast, other candidates have used debates to advantage. Whereas George Bush froze in front of the cameras in 1992 and Dole in 1996 similarly lumbered in discomfort, their opponent, Bill Clinton, was more relaxed, using body language and eye contact to engage the viewer.

In 2000, George W. Bush also benefited from the debates, his easy manner contrasting markedly with the more aggressive and stiff style adopted by Gore. It was widely anticipated that Bush might suffer at the hands of the experienced Democrat who was better versed on policy issues. But, in the event, simply by his avoidance of potentially costly mistakes, he benefited from the contests.

In 2004, Kerry was widely judged to have won the debates, turning in three confident performances that enhanced his reputation – particularly for his knowledge of the issues – but, of course, he still did not win the presidency. For the 2004 series, the ground rules were that each debate lasted ninety minutes, included a live audience, had no opening statements, could have included follow-up questions from the moderator and ended with closing statements of two minutes in length.

In 2008, the four debates took place in September to early October at various locations around the country. Obama was widely judged to have won the first and second debates comfortably. In the third, simply by avoiding any gaffe, he did enough to emerge with his reputation firmly intact even if his superiority was less evident. He was strong on domestic issues, in particular the economy. McCain inspired some criticism for his habit of wandering aimlessly around the stage and not looking at or addressing his opponent directly.

See also *Election Campaigns*; *Presidential Elections*

Presidential Elections

Elections for the presidency and vice presidency have been held quadrennially since 1792. They take place on the Tuesday after the first Monday of November. Voters cast ballots for a slate of electors who – pledged to one or another candidate in the Electoral College – in turn directly elect the president and vice president. In the event of there being a tie, Congress is the final arbiter of the outcome of the two contests. The last serious dispute over the outcome of a presidential election

occurred in 2000, when the issue was ultimately resolved by a decision of the Supreme Court.

The road to the White House is long, complicated and expensive:

The early stages

Politicians with presidential ambition usually form exploratory committees to test the waters and raise money, sometimes up to two years before the election. They then formally declare their candidacy and campaign in key states for the nomination of their parties by standing for election in several states during the primary season which begins in the January before the election and lasts until June. Voters in each of the fifty states select party delegates who, in most cases, have pledged to support a particular candidate. Some states use a caucus – a local meeting system – rather than primaries.

The party convention

The candidates with the most support are formally nominated at the national party conventions, held a few months before the November election. Delegates who have been chosen during the state primaries pick the nominee though, by this stage, the party normally knows who has won. The winning candidate then picks a running mate, sometimes from among the defeated rivals.

The final lap: the campaign proper

Only now do the candidates fully square up against each other. There is massive spending on advertising, and a major flurry of state-by-state campaigning. Much attention is paid to the televised debates between the candidates. This can, but does not necessarily, involve any independent candidate.

In the final weeks, the contenders typically concentrate their attention on large, so-called 'swing states' where the outcome is uncertain.

The final choice

As we have seen, the voters on polling day in November do not, technically, participate in a direct election of the president. They choose 'electors' pledged to one or other candidate in the Electoral College.

Each state has a certain number of electors to the college based on the size of its population. In almost every state, the winner of the popular vote gets all the college votes in that state. Because of this system, a candidate can take the White House without winning the popular vote, as George W. Bush in the 2000 contest with Al Gore.

See also *Election Campaigns*; *Electoral College*

Presidential Pardon

A presidential pardon removes the legal consequences of a crime or conviction. Article 2, Section ii of the Constitution gives the president the right 'to grant reprieves and pardons for offenses against the United States except in cases of impeachment'. Whereas a reprieve is a temporary postponement of the effect of a judicial decision to allow the Executive time for further consideration, a pardon – whether awarded before or after a formal judicial finding – wipes the slate clean so that the recipient becomes a new person in the eyes of the law, as if no offence had ever been committed. Many states accord their governors the power of pardon for those convicted of state crimes.

The Founding Fathers intended that the president should be able to set aside inappropriate or unjust applications of the law. The power to pardon also gave the president a means of forestalling or negotiating an early end to rebellions in the hope that this might bring about an early end to violent tumult and facilitate reconciliation.

The most high-profile presidential pardon was that granted by President Ford to disgraced former-president Nixon following the Watergate scandal although those granted by President Clinton on leaving office to three people, convicted of racketeering, fraud and cocaine trafficking respectively, caused a political storm. While the Constitution places no significant limitations on them in granting pardons, presidents or former presidents who appear to grant them haphazardly or show obvious partisanship court unpopularity.

See also *Nixon, Richard*; *Watergate*

Presidential Press Conferences

Press conferences are used with varying frequency and value. Woodrow Wilson was the first president to make use of this form of dialogue with journalists but Franklin Roosevelt, a master of communication, developed its form and made more extensive use of it. He provided background information and an elaboration of his policies on the basis that reporters would only quote him directly on those passages for which he had given his authorisation.

Press conferences are of two types, joint and solo. Joint ones are those conducted with another person (often a foreign leader), following a meeting between them. Solo ones involve the president by himself answering questions. They tend to be lengthier than joint conferences.

Eisenhower allowed his conferences to be filmed for television. Instead of a cosy, off-the-record discussion, the press conference became, in Vile's (1978) phrase, 'an unprecedented opportunity for a president to answer, before a national audience, the questions put to him'. Kennedy further developed the process for he saw the advantages of giving a live performance rather than the version being filmed and edited prior to transmission. He was able to pronounce on a wider array of subjects, 'without the intervention of time or editors'.

The importance of press conferences

The impact of conferences is difficult to measure but their significance for presidential leadership is considerable. The president is carefully briefed by the press secretary, the State Department and his other advisers upon likely questions and the answers to be given. He is in a position of considerable superiority over his questioners who treat him with deference and do not attempt to cross-question him. He has the opportunity to inform, persuade, present his most important messages, signal his priorities and portray his leadership style: 'It is in fact an invaluable forum for the president to make opinion, and a great deal of time and effort is devoted by modern presidents and their assistants to these problems of public relations.'

For journalists, press conferences may be among the more effective ways of obtaining 'news' directly from the president. They can gain or confirm information and, in the process, elevate the reputation of their news agencies or themselves. A modern press conference can certainly put the chief executive in the hot seat as he exposes himself or herself to tough questions from the media as the world watches. At the 2002 traditional Thanksgiving Day ceremony, President George W. Bush exercised his authority by granting a pardon to a turkey at the White House. As he stood in the Rose Garden and commented on the bird whose fate had yet to be determined: 'He looks a little nervous, doesn't he? He probably thinks he's going to have a press conference.' The comment was a reminder of the fact that, in such circumstances, the president is most vulnerable and can land himself in political difficulties. As political scientist Martha Kumar (2003) observes: 'The presidency today is on the record and broadcast live to audiences around the world.'

The frequency of presidential press conferences (total number given)

Press conferences with White House correspondents vary widely in form and in the frequency with which they are used. Whereas Nixon and Reagan averaged one every two months and Kennedy nearly two a month, George H. Bush averaged five a month and Franklin Roosevelt nearly 7.

Hoover	268
F. D. Roosevelt	998
Truman	334
Eisenhower	193
Kennedy	64
Johnson	135
Nixon	37
Ford	39
Carter	59
Reagan	44
G. H. Bush	142
Clinton	193
G. W. Bush	208

Figures adapted from T. Cronin and (for G. W. Bush) those provided by M. Kumar

Press

Newspapers comprise the oldest form of mass communication in the United States, with some 80 per cent of adult Americans now reading a paper on a regular basis. America has traditionally lacked a strong national press, which is not surprising given the divergent interests of people in different parts of the country and the difficulties of transporting morning editions quickly around the country. The middle-market *USA Today* has helped to fill the gap but the likelihood is that, over the next few years, more national papers will be created given the new technology available. In the mean time, however, in most American cities there is only one regular newspaper available although, countrywide, there are some 1,800 titles. Small-town dailies thrive on presenting stories of local interest but may also provide a sketchy coverage of national events.

Americans have always been deeply attached to their free press. Newspapers are often criticised for their bias: on the political right there being complaints that they are dominated by a liberal elite; and on the left that they are unduly influenced by rich and powerful moguls. They may sometimes be attacked as unduly sensationalist in their coverage of events and too obsessed with the trivia of the personal lives of those who aspire to lead them. But many voters trust their journalists more than their politicians and have a strong suspicion that exposés of corruption and scandal are more than likely to be justified. In episodes, such as Watergate and the Iran–Contra affair, they had reason to be grateful for the investigative instincts of persistent newshounds.

See also *Mass Media*

Press Conferences see *Presidential Press Conferences*

Pressure Groups see *Interest Groups*

Primaries see *Party Primaries*

Proclamations

Presidential proclamations are orders that carry the same force of law as Executive orders but, whereas Executive orders are targeted at those inside government, proclamations are aimed at those beyond it. Their administrative weight is upheld because they are often specifically author-ised by congressional statute, making them what Rottinghaus (2008) terms 'delegated unilateral powers'. They are sometimes largely ceremonial or symbolic in nature but can assume greater sig-nificance in presidential governance and cannot be dismissed as a practical tool for policymaking. During the Civil War, President Lincoln issued two proclamations that freed slaves from states in secession. In January 2008, George W. Bush issued Proclamation 8217, regarding the National Sanctity of Human Life Day.

Issuing proclamations is one method by which presidents have attempted to squeeze every ounce of advantage from their position in order to overcome the constraints of the constitutional order. Recent incumbents of the presidency have resorted to such unilateral actions as means of cir-cumventing the restrictions that have otherwise limited their effectiveness, using their unitary executive theory as their cover.

See also *Unitary Executive Theory*

Progressive Era

The Progressive Era refers to a broadly based reform movement that reached its height early in the early twentieth century prior to World War I. Progressivism is an umbrella term for a range of economic, political and social reforms among which were the regulation of business practices, protection from health hazards and improvements in working conditions. Progressives directed much of their attention, however, to eliminating cor-ruption in government. They wished to curb the power of party bosses by introducing measures to democratise many aspects of political life and giving the public more control over government. Among the political reforms they advocated were: the use of direct democracy; the direct election of senators; the adoption of primary elections as a means of choosing candidates for public office; and votes for women.

Initially, the Progressive Movement gained momentum in local politics but then progressed to state and national levels. Its largely urban, college-educated, middle-class members were to be found in both main parties as well as in third parties. Key national politicians who embraced aspects of Progressivism included the Republicans, Theodore Roosevelt and Robert La Follette Snr, and the Democrats, William Jennings Bryan and Woodrow Wilson.

See also *Machine Politics*

Prohibition (or Temperance) Movement

Prohibition refers to a ban on the manufacture and sale of intoxicating liquor although, more usually, the term denotes those periods in history when such bans have been in force as well as to the political and social movements which urged their adoption.

The Prohibition Movement in the United States began in the early 1800s and, by 1850, several states had passed laws that restricted or prevented people drinking alcohol. It developed rapidly after the formation of the Anti-Saloon League in 1893. The league (and other organisa-tions such as the Women's Christian Temperance Union) succeeded in enacting further local pro-hibition laws but they were intent on achieving a national ban.

Prohibitionists were alarmed at the drinking behaviour of Americans and feared that immigra-tion from Europe was spreading the culture of drinking throughout the country. In particular, they disliked the influence of the saloons which had significantly increased in number because the brewing industry had entered the retail trade with a view to expanding sales of their products. Saloons were associated not only with drunken-ness and rowdiness but also with other 'vices' of which prohibitionists disapproved, such as gambling and prostitution.

During World War I, prohibitionists found it easy to persuade some people that it was unpatri-otic to use much-needed grain to produce alcohol.

They also found a sympathetic response when they pointed out that several of the large brewers and distillers were of German origin. Many business leaders were also sympathetic to prohibition for they wanted a sober and more productive workforce.

By the beginning of 1919, the required 75 per cent of the states had approved the Eighteenth Amendment which outlawed the 'sale or transportation of intoxicating liquors'. This became the law of the land when the Volstead Act was passed in 1920.

In the 'roaring twenties', enforcement of Prohibition proved a difficult task. Illegal drinking places ('speakeasies') developed, illegally distilled alcohol ('moonshine') became available and bootleggers sold the alcohol and also imported it from abroad. The increase in criminality and gangsterism associated with the ban on drink trafficking caused public opinion to turn against Prohibition. It became increasingly unpopular during the Great Depression, particularly in large towns and cities where repeal was eagerly anticipated. In 1933, this was achieved by the passage of the Twenty-first Amendment.

Prohibition Party

The Prohibition Party claims to be the oldest 'third party' in the United States, having nominated a candidate for president in every election since 1872. It is generally known, because of its campaign in opposition to the manufacture, consumption and sale of alcoholic liquor, as a key part of the wider temperance movement. It was at its most prominent in the late nineteenth and the early twentieth centuries.

Since the repeal of Prohibition in 1933, the party has declined dramatically in its membership and support at the ballot box. Today, it no longer campaigns solely against the alcoholic drinks industry but advocates a variety of other socially conservative causes, such as controls on gambling, illegal drugs, pornography and commercialised vice. It also opposes forced integration in school systems, criticises the income tax system and federal aid to education, and questions the soundness of social security arrangements.

Although the party also advocated female suffrage, currency reform and other plans unrelated to prohibition, it never received more than the 270,000 votes it achieved for the presidential candidate in 1892. It continues to put up candidates for office at the state and federal levels, but its influence is very limited. Its candidate in the 1992 election received only 691 votes. In 2008, the figure was down to 643.

Pro-life Movement

'Pro-life' is a commonly used shorthand to refer to opposition to abortion and to foetal rights. Pro-lifers are those who believe that foetuses and embryos are human beings and therefore have the same right to live as those who have already been born. The term is sometimes also used in reference to opposition to practices such as euthanasia, human cloning and stem cell research.

The Anti-abortion Movement traditionally comprised a number of different elements although the Roman Catholic Church always played a central role. Religion continues to play an important role within the movement but, since the late 1970s, much of the most active opposition to abortion comes from the Christian Right which strongly opposes any manifestations of feminism and has brought a large contingent of pro-lifers into Republican politics.

The main goal of pro-life campaigners is to reverse the *Roe* v. *Wade* judgment (1973) but, in the mean time, they seek legislation to restrict the circumstances under which abortion can take place. They are opposed by pro-choice campaigners who stress what they see as the fundamental right of women to control their fertility and determine what happens to their own bodies, either by terminating the pregnancy or by allowing it to proceed.

Party and pressure-group reactions

The Susan B Anthony List was founded in 1992 by a diverse group of women 'to advance the role of pro-life women in the political process' and work for an increase in pro-life representation in public office, particularly in Congress. Named after a prominent suffragist, it has nearly 145,000 members (2008) and focuses on the task of training activists, supporting legislation and educating.

The two main parties are divided over abortion although most Republicans are pro-life and most Democrats pro-choice. The mission of the Democrats for Life of America is to work:

'to foster respect for life, from the beginning of life to natural death. This includes, but is not limited to, opposition to abortion, capital punishment, and euthanasia. Democrats for Life of America is one of over 200 member organizations of Consistent Life: an international network for peace, justice and life.

Many opponents of abortion belong to the National Right to Life Committee (NRLC) which was founded in 1973 in response to the Supreme Court decision of that year. Since then, the NRLC has grown to represent over 3,000 chapters in all fifty states and the District of Columbia. Although its ultimate goal is to restore legal protection to the unborn child, it has been instrumental in achieving a number of legislative changes, such as a federal conscience clause guaranteeing medical personnel the right to refuse to participate in abortion procedures, and limitations on the use of federal funds to subsidise or promote abortions in the United States and overseas. Other organisations that oppose abortion include the American Life League, Americans United for Life, Feminists for Life, the Pro-Life Action League and the Republican National Coalition for Life.

In the 1980s and early 1990s, militant elements of the Pro-life Movement attempted to close abortion clinics via the use of direct action, such as the bombing of clinics and the killing of two doctors involved in carrying out abortions. Legal changes limited the efficacy of such tactics, however, and the overwhelming majority of opponents of abortion today rely solely on peaceful methods to further their cause.

See also *Abortion Rights Movement*; *Christian Coalition*; *Religious Right*; Roe v. Wade *(1973)*

Proposition

A proposition is the name used in some states for initiatives, which allow voters to propose a legislative measure or state constitutional amendment. For instance, Proposition 187 appeared on the ballot in California in the 1994 congressional elections. It proposed that illegal aliens would be ineligible for social services throughout the state.

See also *Initiative*

Q

Quantitative Easing

Quantitative easing refers to the process of increasing the money supply by a pre-determined quantity via open-market operations. It is a means of stimulating an economy by what non-economists would call 'printing money' or 'flooring the economy with money'. It often involves buying government bonds to reduce long-term interest rates and encourage private banks to lend more.

Quantitative easing was introduced in Japan in 2001 as part of a bid to overcome the country's deflationary recession. In the United States, this rather extreme form of monetary policy was employed in 2008–09 by the Federal Reserve to deal with the credit crisis that was part of the global financial recession. In March 2009, the Fed announced that it would spend an extra $1 trillion (£700 billion) to resuscitate the economy, including buying billions of dollars worth of government debt as part of the policy of quantitative easing; $300 billion were to be spent within six months on the purchase of government bonds.

See also *Bail-out*; *Credit Crunch*; *Financial Crisis and Global Recession (2007–09)*; *Paulson Plan (2008)*

R

Race see *Ethnicity and Race*

Race Relations

Racial awareness and tensions have a long history in the United States. Race relations have been potentially tense ever since whites dispossessed, humiliated and segregated Native Americans, many of whom still live in poverty. Whites imported, enslaved and then gradually 'freed' slaves from their enslavement and conceded political and legal equality. But many African Americans remain economically disadvantaged. So, too, large sections of the Hispanic community are relatively poor by American standards. The causes of such tensions have sometimes been cultural and/or economic but skin colour has been an abiding cause of antagonism.

Most evidently, tension has occurred between whites and non-whites although there has sometimes been hostility between different non-white groups. In the Los Angeles riots (1992), African Americans rioters targeted Asian-owned businesses. In the mid-nineteenth century in New England, signs were displayed in houses and places of employment saying: 'No Irish Wanted'.

Most white Americans have always felt superior to, and yet threatened by, other groups. As the non-white minorities became more assertive, so too whites became increasingly uneasy. Some ethnic groups have for long periods accepted discrimination without significant public protest, in the way that the Chinese Americans have tended to retreat into their own community.

Others, primarily African Americans, have protested with greater frequency and more potency. Throughout much of American history, there has been an uneasy coexistence between whites and African Americans, interspersed by outbreaks of disorder.

The methods by which whites have asserted their control over minority groups have varied over time. Southern blacks were long enslaved. After they were emancipated, they were the victims of *de jure* discrimination in the South where segregation was a way of life. In the North, they often endured de facto discrimination, forms of social segregation that were not enshrined in law. Other than discrimination and segregation, Black Americans have at particular times and in particular states experienced intimidation and violence, the activities of the Ku Klux Klan in the post-Civil War South being especially vicious. So, too, Native Americans were segregated, in their case on their reservations.

Despite the weight of historical evidence of mistreatment, some racial groups have coped and even prospered. None of them endures legal racial discrimination for this has been outlawed by legislation, most notably the Civil Rights Act of 1964. But the legacy of past injustice lingers and tensions erupt from time to time. With slavery, lynchings, Jim Crow and other racial injustices in its rearview mirror, the United States has come a long way but still has a long way to go.

See also *Melting Pot*

A picture of US race relations in recent years

In your view, are racial minorities in the United States today routinely discriminated against?

	Black	White	Other people of color	Other	Female	Male	White male	19 years and younger	20 to 39 years old	40 years and older	East	South	Mid-west	West	Other
Yes	93.0%	79.0%	82.9%	73.4%	85.0%	78.2%	72.4	79.4%	80.5%	89.2%	87.6%	77.2%	85.6%	81.2%	78.6%
No	4.7%	16.4%	13.2%	19.3%	10.8%	17.6%	23.2	13.6%	15.8%	9.9%	9.4%	17.7%	11.5%	14.5%	15.5%
No opinion	2.2%	4.6%	3.9%	7.2%	4.2%	4.3%	9.4	7.0%	3.8%	1.0%	2.9%	5.1%	2.8%	4.3%	6.0%

Over the last 10 years, how has the quality of life changed for minorities?

	Black	White	Other people of color	Other	Female	Male	White male	19 years and younger	20 to 39 years old	40 years and older	East	South	Mid-west	West	Other
Has gotten better	34.5%	54.0%	57.3%	57.8%	50.0%	47.3%	50.5%	59.8%	47.5%	36.6%	42.5%	51.9%	51.8%	45.3%	55.3%
Has gotten worst	28.6%	10.3%	12.0%	9.3%	14.2%	18.0%	13.1%	7.0%	15.5%	27.8%	18.3%	12.1%	15.0%	17.7%	18.8%
Has stayed about the same	35.4%	30.9%	28.0%	27.0%	32.0%	30.7%	30.6%	27.1%	34.0%	33.7%	36.2%	31.8%	30.3%	32.7%	17.6%
No opinion	1.6%	4.8%	2.7%	5.9%	3.8%	3.9%	5.7%	6.2%	2.9%	1.9%	3.0%	4.1%	2.8%	4.3%	8.2%

Do you think that relations between racial minorities and whites will always be a problem for the United States or that a solution will eventually be worked out?

	Black	White	Other people of color	Other	Female	Male	White male	19 years and younger	20 to 39 years old	40 years and older	East	South	Mid-west	West	Other
Will eventually be worked out	23.4%	40.2%	30.1%	33.9%	32.8%	36.4%	39.4%	33.8%	31.5%	36.8%	35.6%	31.7%	29.8%	32.9%	31.3%
Will always be a problem	76.6%	59.8%	69.9%	66.1%	67.2%	63.6%	60.6%	66.2%	68.5%	63.2%	64.4%	68.3%	70.2%	67.1%	68.8%

Adapted from findings of Race Relations survey, *Race, Racism and the Law*, conducted by Vernellia R. Randall and her team at the University of Dayton, 2002 (based upon 1,695 respondents).

Radical Reconstruction

'Reconstruction' refers to the era from 1863 to 1877 in which the federal government established the terms on which rebellious Southern states would be integrated back into the Union. Initially, they were quite moderate but, as Confederate power began to be reasserted, accompanied by the passage of Jim Crow laws undermining African American rights, Northern politicians opted for policies of radical reconstruction to enforce their wishes.

The Radical Republicans felt that extraordinary times called for direct intervention in state affairs and laws designed to protect the emancipated blacks who, in their view, were entitled to the same political rights and opportunities as whites. They focused on the issue of abolishing slavery, destroying all traces of the Confederacy, establishing the rights of freed slaves ('freedmen') and, via the passage of three new constitutional amendments, strengthening the role of the central government in Washington and that of the federal courts.

Reconstruction policies had been debated in the North as soon as the war started, and began in earnest after the Edict of Emancipation (January 1863) and the federal occupation of many of the key states which allowed the formation of new, loyal state governments. Reconstruction began in each state as soon as federal troops controlled most of the state. It addressed highly contentious issues such as, the means by which secessionist states would regain self-government and congressional representation, the civil status of the leaders of the Confederacy, and the constitutional and legal status of former slaves.

The main legislative changes that laid the foundation for the most radical phase of Reconstruction were passed between 1867 and 1871, the Thirteenth, Fourteenth and Fifteenth Amendments being the main constitutional legacy of the period. By the late 1870s, Reconstruction had made some progress in providing former slaves with equal rights under the law, and allowing them to vote and hold political offices. Provision was also made to educate former slaves. However, As civilian rule reutrned to the Southern states, however, so the traditional white power structure began to resurface, too. Conservative white Democrats began to regain power in state capitals. By the mid-1870s, there was a rise in white paramilitary activity, with organisations such as the Red Shirts and White League determined to drive out the Republicans and prevent Black Americans from voting.

Radical Reconstruction ended at different times in different states. But the collapse of the last three Republican state governments in the South in 1877 is the usual date given for its passing.

Reagan Democrats

Reagan Democrats were traditional supporters of the Democratic Party who were won over by the approach to government and the policies of Ronald Reagan. By the early 1980s, these rural and urban lower middle-class and better-off working-class voters no longer viewed the Democratic Party as the champions of their working-class aspirations. Instead, they saw it as being overly concerned with benefiting other groups: the very poor; the unemployed; African Americans; and others. Socially conservative, they were attracted by Reagan's simple message of fiscal responsibility, moral values and national security. Millions fled to the Republicans and stayed with them. The 'Reagan Democrats' were a cornerstone of Republican electoral success for more than two decades.

In the five presidential contests after Reagan's 1980 victory, Democratic candidates managed to win, on average, 45 per cent of the popular vote and 228 electoral votes (270 are needed to win the White House). Reagan also delivered a strategic electoral blow to the Democrats by winning over many white voters in the previously solid South. In 1980, he carried all the Southern and border states except for West Virginia and Carter's native Georgia. Subsequently, only when Southerner Bill Clinton headed the ticket did Democrats win any states in the region; in 2000, Gore, himself from Tennessee, carried no Southern or border states. In 2008, however, many returned to the Democratic fold, with Obama winning their support as the economy turned the blue-collar vote against the Republicans. He won in the Southern states of Florida, Virginia and North Carolina.

Prior to the 2008 election, commentators discussed whether Senator Obama would be able to redraw the electoral map by winning states that had been voting for Republican candidates in recent decades. In many ways, he was successful, winning in every region of the country by double digits, except in the South. Millions of Reagan Democrats had returned home.

Reagan, Ronald (1911–2004)

Ronald Wilson Reagan was the thirty-third governor of California and the fortieth president of the United States.

Born and educated in Illinois, Ronald Reagan became a radio sports announcer before turning to an acting career in which he made fifty-three films. He became interested in politics during his six terms as president of the Screen Actors Guild (1947–51, 1959), a role in which he became involved in the issues of Communism in the movie industry at the time of MacCarthyism in the United States. Having been an enthusiastic admirer of Franklin Roosevelt, liberal in his political inclinations, his views became increasingly conservative. Though a Democrat, he was from its early days favourably disposed towards the Eisenhower presidency. He joined the Republican Party in 1962 and became a spokesman for conservatism as a television host, before taking up a new career in politics. In 1966 he was elected governor of California and was re-elected four years later, his reputation by then having been established as a tax cutter who wished to scale down state support for public welfare programmes.

Reagan made unsuccessful bids for the 1968 and 1976 Republican presidential nominations before becoming the Republican presidential candidate for the November 1980 election. He chose as his running mate former Texas congressman and United Nations ambassador, George H. Bush. At a time when voters were troubled by the year-long confinement of American hostages in Iran and inflation at home, he overwhelmed the Democratic president, Jimmy Carter, by 489 to 49 votes in the Electoral College, in the process carrying forty-four states. Within three months of taking office, he was shot by a would-be assassin, the bullet just missing his heart and instead piercing his lung. He recovered quickly and completely. His grace and good humour about the incident served to increased his popularity for it showed his penchant for asides and his easy charm. In the operating room, he quipped to the surgeons: 'I hope you're all Republicans!', to which his leading doctor responded: 'Today, Mr President, we're all Republicans.' When his wife,

Nancy, came to see him, he famously told her: 'Honey, I forgot to duck.'

The Reagan administration quickly embarked upon a laissez-faire programme which centred on tax cutting and pruning government expenditure on domestic policies (dubbed 'Reaganomics'), refusing to deviate from it when the strengthening of national defence forces led to a large deficit. After undergoing recession in 1982, the country became more prosperous, and many Americans felt good about their life for Reagan appeared to have restored faith in their country after the setbacks of Vietnam, Watergate and the Iranian hostages, all of which had sapped morale. In November 1984 the Reagan–Bush ticket was returned to office, this time with an unprecedented 529 Electoral College votes. He won in all but Walter Mondale's home state of Minnesota and in Washington DC.

In his second term, the Reagan government overhauled the income tax code, in the process exempting from tax millions of people with low incomes. The country was enjoying its longest recorded period of peacetime prosperity without recession or depression. In foreign and security policy, Reagan placed great emphasis on strengthening America's defence capability, overseeing the largest peacetime escalation of military spending in American history. His policy was one of 'peace through strength' and, as part of this programme, he proposed a controversial and expensive space-based defence system known as the Strategic Defense Initiative, often known as the Star Wars project. He declared war against international terrorism, sending US bombers to attack Libya after seeing evidence that Libya had been involved in an attack on American soldiers in a West Berlin nightclub.

It was in his handling of the US relationship with the Soviet Union that Reagan took a major step forward. His reputation prior to becoming president, and developed in the first administration, was that of being a strongly anti-Soviet leader. Turning his back on the previous strategy of détente, he soon ordered a massive military build-up in an arms race with the USSR which he portrayed as an 'Evil Empire'. Yet, in the mid-to-late 1980s he met Mikhail Gorbachev of the USSR on four occasions, in the process negotiating a treaty to eliminate intermediate-range nuclear missiles. In line with the Reagan Doctrine, however, the theme of anti-Communism was an enduring feature of his presidency. The president was noted for his support for anti-Communist movements worldwide and, during his two terms in office, he gave support to anti-Communist insurgencies in Africa, Asia and Central America.

Assessment

At the end of President Reagan's two terms in office, admirers of the president claimed that the country was markedly more prosperous and contented than when he took over. The so-called Reagan Revolution had reinvigorated the people, reducing their reliance upon government. Power had been returned to the states, as part of the Reagan version of devolutionary New Federalism. Abroad, America's honour had been restored, patriotic citizens being proud of their country once more. Moreover, with the Cold War coming to an end, the world seemed a safer place. Supporters could claim that 'the great, confident roar of American progress and growth and optimism' of which he had spoken in 1980, had returned.

Critics point to the huge budget deficits created by Reaganite economic policies, in particular, the quadrupling of the United States national debt. They note the administrative scandals of the second term. In particular, the last years of Reagan's presidency were disrupted by the Iran–Contra Affair which broke in late 1986 and involved the White House's complicity in the illegal diversion of profits from arms-for-hostage deals with Iran to the US-supported Contra guerrillas fighting the left-wing Sandinista government in Nicaragua. In 2006, a survey by presidential historians ranked the Iran–Contra affair as the ninth worst mistake by an American president.

Sceptics also point out his lack of interest in detail and his lack of basic knowledge on key issues. Attempts to provide him with detailed information often failed to work, in the first presidential debate in 1984 making him seem faltering and unconvincing. His media advisers learnt their lesson and advised him to stick to broad themes to which the answer to any question could be related. In the following debate, he also tackled head-on the question which was potentially most damaging to him, that of his age. Many voters who were well disposed to him personally were uneasy about his fitness to operate in demanding situations. When the inevitable question came up, its impact was deflected by the use of a flash of his characteristic humour: 'I want you to know that I will not make age an issue of this campaign. I am not going to exploit for political purposes my opponent's youth and inexperience.'

Few would deny his personal likeability and his communication skills. In a television age, the personality and style of leadership of anyone who would be president have become all-important. The need to perform well is crucial. Reagan, for all his seeming lack of familiarity with some key issues and his occasional verbal stumbles, was a man who embodied the American Dream. His resolute optimism, his old-fashioned values and his promise to help his country 'stand tall' after the malaise of the 1970s were highly popular. He succeeded in capturing the public imagination and won widespread support. His background as a film and television actor enabled him to communicate effectively so that he represented a merger between the worlds of entertainment and politics. As was said at the time, he was 'the Great Communicator'.

Following America's setbacks in the 1970s, Reagan did much to restore faith in the presidency as an institution. Overall, his reputation today stands at a high level. Much liked by the public, he enjoyed high levels of approval for much of his presidency. Although many academics were critical at the time, scholars, too, have been less harsh on him than seemed likely in the 1980s. He secures a place in the top half in most rankings of former US presidents. He has been immortalised in numerous ways, with an airport, an aircraft carrier and roads being named in his honour.

In 1994, in the hope of increasing public awareness of the illness, Reagan disclosed that he had Alzheimer's disease. He died a decade later as the result of complications associated with the disease.

See also *Television and Politics*

Reapportionment

Reapportionment is the process by which, following the decennial census, seats in the House of Representatives are reassigned among the states to reflect population changes. It becomes necessary to accommodate shifts in population between states. Broadly, in recent years, the states in the frost belt have been allocated fewer representatives and those in the sun belt have more.

Apportionment is the process of dividing the 435 seats in the House of Representatives among the fifty states. A state's apportionment population is the total of its resident population and a count of overseas American military and federal civilian employees (and their dependants living with them) allocated to the state, as reported by the employing federal agencies.

The Census Bureau conducts a census at ten-year intervals. While there are numerous other uses for census data, a fundamental reason for conducting the decennial study is to define state legislative districts. The findings are used to calculate the number of house memberships each state is entitled to have.

Based on the Census 2000 apportionment, each member of the House of Representatives represents an average population of 646,952.

See also *Congressional Districts*

Recall

The recall is a method of removing officials from office by a vote of the people. A specified number of voters can demand a vote on whether or not an elected official should be 'recalled'. Fifteen American states have provision for the recall but it has very rarely been employed. In North Dakota the possibility of recall applies to all public officers. In Alaska and Idaho, all but judicial officers are subject to recall.

The most well-known recent example occurred in California in 2003 where the governorship was in question. Following a vote to recall the Democrat incumbent, Gray Davis, for profligacy with state funds, Arnold Schwarzenegger was elected as the new governor. Davis became the first governor to be recalled in the history

of California, and just the second in American history. Four previous Californian governors – including Ronald Reagan – had faced recall attempts but these were unsuccessful.

In California, any elected official may be the target of a recall campaign. But, of the 118 attempts to date, only eight have attracted sufficient support to qualify for the ballot and only five have succeeded. To trigger a recall election, proponents of the recall must gather a number of signatures equal to 12 per cent of the number of votes cast in the previous elections. For the 2003 recall elections, that meant a minimum of 900,000 signatures, based on the November 2002 midterm elections.

Recess Appointments

Recess appointments are appointments made by the president on a temporary basis while Congress is in recess. The person chosen can serve until the end of the following session of Congress without Senate confirmation.

Under the Constitution, the president and the Senate share the power to make appointments to senior policy-making positions in federal departments, agencies, boards, and commissions. Generally, the president nominates individuals to these positions, and the Senate must confirm them before he can appoint them to office. But the Constitution provides for recess appointments as an exception to this process. Article II, Section 2 states that 'the President shall have Power to fill up all Vacancies that may happen during the Recess of the Senate, by granting Commissions which shall expire at the End of their next Session'. The clause was intended to allow the president to maintain the continuity of administrative government for, otherwise, nominees could not be considered or confirmed when the Senate was not sitting. This was particularly important prior to the beginning of the twentieth century for, before then, Congress was, on average, in session for less than half the year. Throughout the history of the Republic, however, presidents have also sometimes used recess appointments for political reasons, usually to install temporarily an appointee who probably would not be confirmed by the Senate.

Hogue's (2008) research indicates that President Clinton made 139 recess appointments during his eight years in office, ninety-five to full-time positions. During his first seven years in office, President George W. Bush made 171 recess appointments, 105 of which were to full-time positions. Such appointments comprise just one method by which presidents may attempt to control the Executive branch, claiming in the process to be a protector of the prerogative of the office while, at the same time, being able to advance their policy agenda.

The technique was used by George W. Bush to appoint John Bolton as the interim US Permanent Representative to the United Nations with the title of ambassador, from August 2005 until December 2006. His letter of resignation from the Bush administration was sent a few days before the formal adjournment of the 109th Congress.

See also *Unitary Executive Theory*

Red Power

The Red Power movement sought equal rights and justice for Native Americans. Inspired by the example of Black Power, it represented the more militant wing of the struggle to achieve civil rights. In the same way that many black leaders despaired of the moderate leadership of the National Association for the Advancement of Colored People (NAACP), so too many Native Americans despised the National Congress of American Indians (NCAI) which was willing to co-operate with the then white-dominated Bureau of Indian Affairs (established in 1824). They were denounced as Apples, red on the outside but white on the inside, or even as Uncle Tomahawks, a variant of the Uncle Tom label used to describe African Americans.

Generally dissatisfied with the slow pace of progress towards equality and improved living conditions, the leaders of Red Power organisations were younger, and intent on achieving rapid change within their communities. Often college educated and influenced by the prevailing culture of campus defiance, in the late 1960s and 1970s, activists became increasingly militant. In the course of their campaigning, several Native Americans occupied

Alcatraz Island, the formal federal prison in San Francisco Bay (and were visited by some 10,000 others during the occupation).

The most militant group was the American Indian Movement (AIM), formed in the ghettos of Minneapolis–St Paul. Its members carefully monitored examples of police racism, worked to improve conditions in education, employment and housing, and strove to gain a more positive image for their peoples. In particular, they attacked the use made by white Americans of names that derived from the term, Red Indian, which they disliked – such as the baseball team, the Atlanta Braves, and the football team, the Washington Redskins. They urged the use of the Native American.

AIM wanted either land returned or financial compensation. Sometimes protests turned violent as when supporters occupied the reservation at Pine Ridge, the site of the 1890 massacre at Wounded Knee, in 1973. Faced with criminal prosecution, it survived by modifying its tactics and increasingly relying on the type of peaceful legal protests against which it had once protested. Its leaders concluded that the best way to improve the legal status of Native Americans and acquire new rights was to work through the system.

Assisted by federal policies in the 1970s (including the Johnson War on Poverty programme) the Red Power movement saw many of its goals accomplished. By 1980, Congress had authorised substantial payments to Native Americans to compensate for previous unjust land loss; many Indian studies programmes had been created in the United States; and tribal museums had opened. AIM continued fighting for rights to land; protesting over athletic team Indian mascots; and seeking the repatriation of sacred objects once removed from Indian land.

See also *Native Americans*

Red States

Red states are those whose electoral votes went to the Republicans in the previous election. In other words, the term is a convenient label for any conservative, Republican-dominated state. On electoral maps in 2000, and subsequently, electoral maps have adopted consistent colouring, Republican states being red, Democratic ones blue. The colour scheme is now part of the lexicon of American political journalism.

Redistricting

Redistricting is the redrawing of congressional and other legislative boundaries that is carried out within a state following publication of each decennial census. In most states, redistricting is carried out by the state legislature, the governor sometimes exercising a power of veto. It becomes necessary because of population shifts within states that result in some districts becoming excessively large or small.

In the process of rearranging boundaries, two problems have periodically arisen, gerrymandering (manipulation of the boundaries in favour of the majority party) and malapportionment (districts being of unequal populations). Rural-dominated legislatures used to be able to arrange the congressional districts so as to overrepresent rural areas. The decision of the Supreme Court in *Baker* v. *Carr* (1962), however, indicated a willingness to enter into consideration of matters that had once been a state prerogative. It said that districts must be drawn in an equitable manner and that malapportionment was justiciable. A further Supreme Court decision in *Wesberry* v. *Sanders* (1964) ruled that all congressional districts in a state must have, as nearly as possible, the same number of people so that every person's vote is of equal value. As a result of the decision, significant population inequalities have ended.

See also *Congressional Districts*; *Reapportionment*

Referendum

A referendum is a vote on a single issue in which all registered electors are eligible to take part. Instead of being asked to give a verdict on the administration as a whole – as in a general election – they are asked their opinion on one measure or act presented to them by the Legislature. In effect, the device amounts to the people's veto power.

The United States is one of the few democracies that has never held a nationwide referendum.

In the majority of states and in many cities, however, there is provision for direct legislation, be it either the referendum or the initiative, or in some cases both. There are far fewer referendums than initiatives.

Referendums may be of two types, popular and legislative:

- Popular referendums, available in twenty-four states, allow the people to petition so that a specific piece of legislation already enacted by the legislature should be put to the people for them to accept or reject. Citizen-initiated referendums are also sometimes known as petition referendums.
- Legislative referendums, possible in all states, occur when the legislature itself or an elected official, state-appointed commission or other government agency, submits propositions to the people for their verdict. This may be required by the state constitution (e.g., other than Delaware, all states require this when constitutional amendments are being discussed) or may be a voluntary decision to ask for a popular 'yes' or 'no' vote.

Massachusetts was the first state to hold a legislative referendum, its citizens being asked to ratify its constitution in 1778. New Hampshire soon followed. It was in the Progressive Era, however, that Oregon began the twentieth-century trend towards greater use of initiatives and referendums, both of which were more frequently in use by the end of the century.

See also *Direct Democracy*, *Initiative*

Regents of the University of California v. Baake (1978)

The Baake judgment was a landmark Supreme Court decision on affirmative action. It stated that race could be taken into account in admissions decisions, as long as the institution did not set aside a specific number of seats for which only minorities were eligible.

Baake, a white American, could not get into medical school, even though his grades were higher than the sixteen Afro-Caribbeans who obtained entry because of a quota. He claimed that this was reverse discrimination. The Court ruled by five votes to four that he had been the victim of discrimination but, by the same margin, judged that positive discrimination was not inherently unlawful.

The Burger Court (1969–86) generally approved the principle of affirmative action but was unhappy with the details of particular programmes. The Baake judgment was an ambiguous one that came to be regarded as favourable to the existence of affirmative action programmes, even if quotas were unacceptable.

See also *Affirmative Action*

Regulatory Commissions

Regulatory commissions are government agencies, headed by bipartisan boards, charged with enforcing particular statutes. Generally, they have quasi-legislative, as well as quasi-judicial, functions as well as executive powers so that they are involved with developing, implementing and adjudicating policy in their areas of responsibility.

Examples of regulatory commissions include: the Federal Communications Commission (FCC) which oversees radio, television and telephone operations; and the Interstate Commerce Commission which regulated buses, railways and road haulage until its recent demise. The president appoints members of the commissions, and chooses their chair, but has only a limited right to remove commissioners who generally serve longer terms than the president; there is no presidential veto over their actions. They function in a way that is independent of all branches of government.

See also *Interstate Commerce Commission*

Rehnquist, William (1924–2005) and the Rehnquist Court (1986–2005)

William Hubbs Rehnquist was an American lawyer who served as an associate and later the chief justice of the Supreme Court. Shortly after receiving his law degree from Stanford University

in 1952, he practised law in Phoenix and became involved in conservative Republican politics. Between 1968 and 1971, he was an assistant US Attorney General, heading the office of legal counsel in the Department of Justice before being appointed to the Supreme Court by President Nixon.

Within the Burger Court, Rehnquist soon established himself as the most conservative of the president's appointees. He acquired a reputation as a firm advocate of law and order, writing several opinions reversing the liberal trend of the Warren Court in criminal cases. He adopted a narrow view of the Fourteenth Amendment and a broad view of state power. He voted against the expansion of school desegregation plans and strongly dissented from the legalisation of abortions in *Roe* v. *Wade*. He was also in favour of capital punishment, school prayer and states' rights. He was the most frequent sole dissenter during the Burger years. President Reagan was determined to appoint justices of conservative persuasion. He opted for Rehnquist on Burger's retirement.

The Rehnquist Court

Although the intellect and diplomatic skill of the new incumbent were not doubted, commentators and politicians of more liberal leanings saw Rehnquist as the most conservative member of the existing nine. Overall, after 1986, there was a markedly less progressive tone than that employed in the judgments delivered by the recent Courts, judgments generally being cautious and less spectacular than some earlier ones. Many observers from the left and the right, however, praised Rehnquist for improving the Court's efficiency and for his effectiveness in dealing with colleagues.

The Rehnquist Court handled fewer cases each term than previous courts and struck down fewer federal and state laws. The majority of its members did not see it as their task to act as the guardian of individual liberties and civil rights for minority groups. But their broad approach was to nibble away at the edges of contentious issues, rather than make a direct challenge to the whole direction of past policy in areas such as abortion and affirmative action. As Biskupic (2000) and some other commentators have noted: 'Gone is the self-consciously loud voice the Court once spoke with, boldly stating its position and calling upon the people and other institutions of government to follow.'

The conservatism of the chief justice and his more ideological associates, Antonin Scalia and Clarence Thomas, was increasingly tempered in the late 1990s by the emergence of a moderate bloc of justices, including associates Breyer, Ginsburg, Souter and Stevens, with Sandra O'Connor holding a pivotal position. Their collective failure to reverse many judgments of an earlier era disappointed a lot of conservatives but, none the less, Schwartz (1993), detected in the Rehnquist Court a series of cumulative decisions

> limiting the use of habeas corpus by prisoners, broadening the power of the police to search automobiles, applying the harmless error doctrine to a constitutional error committed at the trial, and upholding regulations prohibiting abortion counselling, referrals or advocacy by federally funded clinics.

Schwartz's view of the Rehnquist Court and its alleged judicial restraint has been questioned. Its greater ideological conservatism is generally accepted although its record on civil liberties is more mixed than the term might imply. Some commentators have suggested that it has been highly activist in its willingness to challenge the elected branches of government. Rosen, In a comparison of the Warren and Rehnquist eras, Rosen argued that both courts were committed to an increase in judicial power: 'Both combine haughty declarations of judicial supremacy with contempt for the competing views of the political branches.' Others, too, have observed that, for all of the lip service paid to judicial self-restraint, 'most of the current justices appear entirely comfortable intervening in all manner of issues, challenging state as well as national power, and underscoring the Court's role as final arbiter of constitutional issues'.

Rehnquist presided as chief justice for nineteen years, making him the fourth-longest-serving chief justice. The last eleven years of

Rehnquist's term as chief justice (1994–2005) marked the second-longest tenure of one makeup of the Supreme Court, there being no changes in its personnel. Generally considered to be a strict constructionist, in his thirty-three-year Supreme Court career, he oversaw the court's conservative shift, presided over an impeachment trial and helped decide a presidential election.

Religious Right/Christian Coalition

Originally known as the Moral Majority, the Religious or Christian Right is the term used to cover a broad movement of conservatives who advance moral and social values. Active in the Republican Party over many years, it seeks to take America back to its true heritage and to restore the godly principles that made the nation great.

Most of its members emphasise that they have been 'born again', in other words their religious life has been dramatically altered by a conversion experience that has made them see issues very differently. They tend to be fundamentalist (accepting the literal truth of the Bible) and are unquestioning in accepting Christian doctrines. Some 15 per cent of the electorate in the United States tell pollsters they are allied with the Religious Right. Many of its supporters can be found in the Christian Coalition whose values are consistent with those of the Religious Right. The Coalition's website states:

> Christian Coalition of America is a political organization, made up of pro-family Americans who care deeply about becoming active citizens for the purpose of guaranteeing that government acts in ways that strengthen, rather than threaten, families. As such, we work together with Christians of all denominations, as well as with other Americans who agree with our mission and with our ideals.

Supporters of the Religious Right are distinguished by their moral fervour. The telegenic Pat Robertson is a leading spokesperson. He founded the Christian Coalition in 1988 and presided over the organisation until February 2001. Via his daily talk show, the *700 Club* – a mixture of faith healing, hymns and Christian-oriented news – he informs his listeners that, in the outlook of 'liberals' it is wrong to ridicule Hispanics, blacks, the disabled, women, gays and lesbians, but it is 'open season' to ridicule and humiliate, denigrate and insult Christians 'as it was with the Jews in Nazi Germany'. He portrays the women's movement as a 'socialist, anti-family, political movement that encourages women to leave their husbands, kill their children, practice witchcraft and become lesbians'. He thunders that: 'God does not want us to turn America over to radical feminists, militant homosexuals, profligate spenders, humanists or world communists.'

The Religious Right/Christian Coalition opposes abortion, birth control, embryonic stem cell research, evolution, gay rights, and any other developments which they see as damaging to the nations's moral standards. Members stress pro-life policies and take a firm line on issues such as capital punishment. Among other specific Christian Coalition policies are:

- the abolition of federal endorsement for the arts
- the elimination of the federal and state departments of education
- a cap on spending on AIDS research and treatment
- compulsory reporting of AIDS carriers
- the mandatory teaching of Creationism
- the abolition of abortion
- the restriction on pre-school education
- the rejection of gun control.

Among the key figures in the Religious Right is the Reverend Rod Parsley. He is a champion of theocracy ('rule by God' or 'God in power') or what he refers to as a 'christocracy'. At his World Harvest Church in Ohio, he and his followers talk of establishing dominion or control over society in the name of God and 'reclaiming America for Christ'.

History and tactics

Under the leadership of Ralph Reed and Robertson, the Christian Coalition quickly became the most prominent voice in the conservative Christian movement. Reed took control of day-to-day operations of the Coalition in 1989. Under his leadership, its approach became more organised and sophisticated. It was based on building up grassroots support by involving people at the local level on the city council and the school board – as well as aiming for the more obvious congressional targets. Evangelical Christians were encouraged to involve themselves directly in the political process. During sermons, they were exhorted to vote, with the advice usually pointing to the Republicans as the appropriate party for godly Christians to support. Support was made easy, for members of the congregation were often given sample ballot papers showing how and where to mark support for the required candidates. The peak influence of the Coalition culminated in an effort to support the election of a conservative Christian to the presidency in 1996. Since then, the Christian Coalition has made only limited progress. Following Bill Clinton's re-election and Reed's departure in 1997, the organisation declined in influence, financial stability, resources and staffing although it continues to function on a reduced scale.

The wider Religious Right remains active at the local level between presidential elections and influential within the Republican Party when those elections take place. Once in local office, Christian representatives on school boards seek to eliminate 'irreligious' material, particularly books which mentioned alternative lifestyles and such things as abortion or witchcraft: for example, Roald Dahl's *The Witches* has been banned from school library shelves by some boards. Teachers have been told that they should teach 'Creation science' (the story of the world's creation as told in *Genesis*) as well as – or in some cases instead of – Darwinian theories of evolution. The Bible, regarded as literally true, is the prime resource of learning. Other books, which do not meet the necessary criteria, have included works by Martin Luther King, C. S. Lewis, Rudyard Kipling and A. A. Milne. There are now some 2,250 school boards in the United States, and the Religious Right is in control of a significant number of them.

In the presidential elections of 2000 and 2004, enthusiasts for the conservative Christian cause mailed or handed out millions of 'scorecards' issued by bodies such as the Family Research Council and Focus on the Family, showing the voting records of members of Congress on 'issues critical to the family'. Supporters of the Religious

Right were targeted by Karl Rove in 2004, for he realised that many of them had not voted four years earlier. Their mobilisation played a key part in getting President Bush re-elected. But this mobilisation was carried out mainly within the Republican Party rather than by the Christian Coalition. As an example of this more 'in-house' approach to gain the backing of the conservative Christian community, Reed served as Southeast Regional chairman for the Bush–Cheney campaign during the election.

Impact on the Republican Party

In the 1980s, supporters of the Religious Right targeted the Republican Party as the vehicle through which they could advance their agenda. At the same time, a small group of Republican strategists targeted fundamentalist, Pentecostal and Charismatic churches to expand the base of the Republican Party.

The Christian Coalition exercised considerable power within the Republican Party in the 1980s and 1990s, helping to shape the Republican majority in Congress in the mid- to late 1990s. Its supporters were active in pursuing the impeachment of President Clinton. In the 2000 presidential election, the Coalition claims to have distributed over seventy million voter guides in churches all across America, including over five million in Spanish (approximately two million of which were distributed in Florida alone). In 2004, it was again active, but this time in targeted states and congressional districts where the political battle was likely to be close.

The broader Religious Right remains a highly potent electoral force on the American political scene. In 2004, exit polls suggested that 'moral values' had been the most important issue in determining the outcome of the vote. Eight out of ten of those for whom such values were the paramount concern voted for George Bush.

Among Republicans there has been a schism for several years. More traditional mainstream party regulars fear a takeover of the party by religious zealots with their pro-life agenda. They fear that it narrows the breadth of the party's appeal. The Christian Coalition and some other members of the Religious Right are similarly contemptuous

of what it portrays as 'country-club' Republicans of the old type who, somewhere along the way, lost their conservative agenda and became 'me-tooists', too close to the Democrats.

See also *Christian Coalition*

Reno v. *American Civil Liberties Union* (1997)

In *Reno* v. *American Civil Liberties Union*, the Supreme Court struck down the Communications Decency Act (CDA) which had prohibited the transmission over the Internet of any 'patently offensive' material, including 'any . . . image or other communication which is obscene or indecent, knowing that the recipient is . . . under 18 years of age'. It argued that the Act lacked precision and thereby infringed rights under the First Amendment. Writing on behalf of the majority, Justice Stevens accepted the legitimacy of attempting to protect minors from exposure to indecent materials but argued that the CDA went too far, to the extent that it threatened the right of free speech among adult Americans. This was a further example of how the Court has been intolerant of legislation restricting indecent free speech because, as Stevens pointed out, 'the interest in encouraging freedom of expression in a democratic society outweighs any theoretical but unproven benefit of censorship'.

See also *American Civil Liberties Union (ACLU)*

Representative Government

The political idea of representation is based on the idea that some person or institution acts on behalf of the people, by *re-presenting* their beliefs, attitudes and perspectives. Representative government is, therefore, a form of government in which the elected representatives of the people, rather than the people themselves, meet and conduct the business of government. The American political system is one in which the people elect representatives to Congress to *represent* them, hence America has a system of representative government.

See also *Indirect Democracy*

Republic

A republic is a constitutional form of government in which decisions are made democratically by elected or appointed officials. This was similar to the way in which the Greek philosopher Plato (427?–347BC) used the term, his idea being that those in power obtained and retained their positions as a result of winning elections in which all free adults are allowed to take part. The people had sovereign power.

Americans of the colonial period were particularly impressed with the example of Republican Rome. The Founding Fathers liked the term 'republic', preferring it to democracy as a means of describing the form of government they wished to create. They did not believe that governmental authority should be directly in the hands of the people. 'Republic' lacked the connection with direct democracy, with its undesirable overtones of mass rule, demagogues and the mob. What they were creating was an indirect democracy. Instead of direct rule by the majority, with people making rules themselves, in a republic they were choosing representatives who would make them.

N.b. This is a meaning very different from the usual one familiar to British students for whom a republic is a constitutional form in which the head of state is an elected or nominated president, rather than a monarch. The American usage is in line with the historical western usage of the term to describe a representative democracy.

Republican Party

Republicans have traditionally been more cautious than the Democrats in their approach to political and social change. Sometimes they have been deeply conservative, their pro-business, pro-free-enterprise tendencies gaining the upper hand. At other times, in the years of the New Deal and after, party spokespersons often sounded less hostile to government intervention, recognising the popularity of many Democratic initiatives. But there was always a general unease about the direction in which their opponents had taken the country. Many Republicans were lukewarm about the expanding role of the federal government in economic and social matters.

In the 1980s, traditional conservatism – as described – increasingly gave way to a new variety of ultra-conservatism, its adherents often known collectively as the *New* or *Radical Right*. Ronald Reagan said that 'government is the problem'. True to this spirit, the Reagan years saw an emphasis upon the market economy, a relaxation of anti-business controls, hostility to organised trade unionism, and low taxation. In as much as government was accepted as necessary, there was a move towards local or state governmental action over that of the federal government. Reagan's approach appealed to many conservatives in America.

The New Right wrapped itself in the symbols of nationalism and patriotism, and supporters took a strong stand in favour of business, the death penalty and school prayer, issues which struck a chord with many voters. Today, it has a more distinctive social agenda than other conservative forebears, and its restrictive policies include strict control over abortion, drugs and pornography. It dislikes affirmative action and forced busing, and is lukewarm in its support for any legislation to advance civil rights.

Members of the New Right shared much of the ground occupied by other conservatives but they became associated with particular causes which they wished to see become accepted as public policy. They sought to achieve their programme via greater representation in Congress. In November 1994, the Contract with America was based upon the New Right's philosophical approach.

In subsequent years, mainstream Republican thinking has incorporated these New Right attitudes, and the more moderate or liberal element of the party has been largely sidelined. (see, however, the adjacent box on 'Moderate Republicans'). Whereas Reaganite conservatives saw government as 'the problem', however, and wished to curb its influence, Bushite supporters wanted government to act as an enabling force that encourages citizens to assist themselves. The platform of George Bush in 2000 and 2004 was based on what he termed 'compassionate conservatism'. While emphasising the party's traditional concerns, it made reference to the need for a caring and inclusive approach that catered for those disadvantaged by the operation of the free market. 'Comcons' envisaged a triangular relationship between government, charities and faith-based organisations (churches).

The Bush platform owed much to the outlook of the so-called 'Moral Majority', for the influence of Christian fundamentalists (often known as the Religious Right) is fast growing in the United States. Its supporters have been successful at the local level in building a powerful base and, within the Republican Party, their position is a strong one. They contend that religious values are the cement that holds the fabric of society together. They are therefore especially concerned with what is taught in schools for this will influence the attitudes and behaviour of coming generations.

Common Republican attitudes, as expressed in state platforms during the 2004 presidential election, included among other things:

- cutting taxes and public spending
- less government intervention
- government pursuing only those policies which encourage individual initiative and responsibility for economic, political and social well-being
- more scope for individuals and conventional families
- power to be exercised at the lowest possible level
- freedom regarded as inseparable from responsibilities to serve and participate in the life of the community, and work for preservation of our freedom.

In addition, many Republican platforms professed strong faith in God, their dislike of organised labour and resistance to the idea of industrial action, their suspicion of newer arrivals and of the countries from which they arrived, and doubts about active involvement overseas. Some Republicans are deeply isolationist, and even the East-coast establishment tends to be concerned about the scale of commitment made to western

Moderates within the Republican Party

Republican members of Congress who support more moderate ideas and policies may be found in two groupings:

The centrist *Ripon Society*, formed in 1962 in Ripon, Wisconsin (the birthplace of the Republican Party) promotes a 'common-sense' agenda of limited government, a vibrant free-market economy, strong families, civil rights and a foreign policy guided by pursuit of America's national interests. It acts as a source of moderate thinking and stresses the need for the party to reach out to all Americans. It serves as a haven for Republican moderates. It lacks any congressional organisation but prominent Republicans on Capitol Hill and figures such as the former pro-choice Governor Christine Todd Whitman of New Jersey, are leading members of its advisory board. It is wary of the influence of the Christian Coalition, and campaigns against the overrepresentation of small Midwestern states and Western states in the party, seeing these as antagonistic to moderate Republicanism.

The *Republican Main Street Partnership (RMSP)* is a network supporting moderate Republicans for office. Formed following the 1994 House of Representatives elections, it has allied with other moderate Republican groups, including Whitman's It's My Party Too, Ann Stone's Republicans for Choice, the Log Cabin Republicans, the Republican Majority for Choice, The Wish List, Republicans for Environmental Protection and the Republican Leadership Council.

In November 2006, many members of the RMSP were defeated in election outcomes that were generally poor for the Republican Party. This was widely attributed to the fact that moderate Republicans typically hailed from constituencies with large numbers of Democratic voters. Seven members from the House of Representatives were defeated by the Democrats, as were one senator and one governor.

Moderate Republicans do not agree and act in unison on every issue, there being differences over issues such as abortion rights and gun control. But all share a commitment to a more moderate approach to policy issues and are willing to act alongside moderate and conservative Democrats in the party's *Blue Dog Coalition* in a spirit of bipartisanship.

Europe and the use of American troops abroad. There is a strong emphasis upon 'Americanism' and patriotic goals, involving protecting America's status in the world.

Appeal and voter perceptions

The Republican Party is widely seen as the party that does not wish to expand the role of government, especially in Washington. Republicans are viewed as being more lukewarm about innovations. More affluent suburban people (including most business and professional people, and others with a higher level of educational attainment) and large farmers judge that the Republican Party best serves their interests. They have traditionally been keen supporters of the Republicans although a liberal element in the middle class inclines to the Democrats.

The roll of interest groups that are broadly supportive of the main parties also tells us something about their respective leanings. Republicans have long been more associated than the Democrats with the American Farm Bureau Federation, the National Association of Manufacturers, and the American Medical Association (AMA).

See also *Bush, George W. A.*; *Christian Coalition*; *New Right*

Reserved Powers

Reserved (aka residual) powers are those that the Constitution provides for the states, even though it does not list them explicitly. The idea – as clearly set out in the Tenth Amendment – is that powers not expressly granted to the federal government or denied to the states by the provisions of the Constitution are reserved to the states or to the people. Historically, these reserved powers have included such items as providing for the establishment of the building of local roads and highways, and regulating intrastate trade.

Reverse Discrimination

Reverse discrimination is discrimination against members of a dominant or majority group (typically men and whites) especially when resulting from policies established to correct past discrimination against members of a traditionally sociopolitically non-dominant minority group or disadvantaged group. It is said to occur as a result of affirmative action programmes, for instance:

- when an employer favours hiring and promoting possibly underqualified members of protected groups of minorities and women while excluding other candidates from consideration, and
- in the practice of reserving positions for minorities in school admissions programmes.

The claim that affirmative action violates the equal protection clause of the Fourteenth Amendment and Civil Rights legislation has been the cause of differing opinions by members of the Supreme Court.

Rice, Condoleezza (1954–)

Condoleezza Rice was the National Security Advisor and then – in George W. Bush's second administration – Secretary of State, the first African American woman to hold both offices.

Born in Birmingham, Alabama, Condoleezza Rice gained a degree in political science and eventually a doctorate in international studies. She served as a professor of political science and later provost at Stanford. She was the author of several books and articles, notably on Soviet and eastern European foreign and defence policies. She was also a successful businesswoman, becoming a director of the Chevron Corporation as well as serving on the boards of several other organisations.

From 1989 until March 1991, the period of German reunification and the final days of the Soviet Union, Dr Rice served as director, and then senior director, of Soviet and East European Affairs in the National Security Council, under George H. Bush. During the administration of his son, she was widely regarded as a forceful advocate of the policies adopted towards Iraq.

As Secretary of State, she championed the expansion of democratic governments. She took the view that 9/11 was rooted in 'oppression and despair' and concluded that the US should strive to advance democratic reform and support basic rights throughout the greater Middle East. She reformed and restructured the State Department, as well as American diplomacy as a whole. She was committed to 'Transformational Diplomacy', which involved 'work[ing] with our many partners around the world . . . [and] build[ing] and sustain[ing] democratic, well-governed states that will respond to the needs of their people and conduct themselves responsibly in the international system'. She attempted to repair relations with key allies in Europe and elsewhere after the strains caused by the Iraqi invasion, offering negotiations with 'enemy' states, including Iran, and pursuing multilateral diplomatic efforts in the face of North Korea's missile tests in July 2006.

Roberts, John (1955–)

John Roberts is the seventeenth and current chief justice of the Supreme Court. He was appointed as an associate justice by George W. Bush in mid-2005 but, on the death of William Rehnquist, the president nominated him as Rehnquist's successor, thereby making him the youngest person in two hundred years to be appointed as chief justice, since John Marshall took the bench in 1801. He was known to be a Roman Catholic, with generally conservative social and political views.

In his earlier career, Roberts spent fourteen years in private law practice and held positions in Republican administrations in the Department of Justice and Office of the White House Counsel. Immediately prior to joining the Court, he served for two years as a judge on the Court of Appeals for the District of Columbia Circuit.

In the Senate Judiciary Committee Hearings, Roberts spoke of his wish to see the Supreme Court issue more unanimous opinions, something difficult to achieve as the Court sometimes seems as divided as the nation over abortion and other contentious social issues. He indicated his support for some abortion restrictions but did not commit himself to overturning *Roe* v. *Wade*. His nomination was approved by a vote of seventy-eight to twenty-two. He received support from many Democrats as well as Senate Republicans.

Roberts achieved unanimity in over 49 per cent of the cases in his first year, and is similarly on

track today. Since then, there has been the same search for agreement though several rulings have made by divisive 5–4 votes. Of course, there is a limit to his power to obtain consensus. To a greater degree than his predecessors, however, he urges that avoidable disagreements be resolved in the Court's internal conference, rather than being aired in unnecessarily provocative passages or footnotes in an opinion.

Roe v. *Wade* (1973)

The landmark *Roe* v. *Wade* ruling struck down a Texas law, regulating access to abortion, as a violation of a woman's fundamental right to privacy. It thereby established abortion as a constitutional right In a lesser-known companion case, *Doe* v. *Bolton*, the justices overruled a Georgian state law requiring a strict medical procedure before an abortion could be performed and limiting an abortion to residents of the state. Taken together, *Doe* and *Roe* found that the Georgian and Texan legislation violated a constitutional right to privacy under the Due Process Clause of the Fourteenth Amendment. By implication, the justices overturned most laws against abortion in other states.

The central point of the ruling was that abortions are permissible for any reason a woman chooses, up to the point at which the foetus becomes 'viable', in other words potentially able to live outside the mother's uterus. Some conditions were laid down. In the first trimester of a pregnancy (about three months), the decision rested with the woman; in the second period, the right to an abortion remained but state laws could regulate the abortion procedure 'in ways that are reasonably related to maternal health' (by insisting that they were carried out according to a set procedure – e.g., in a hospital); and in the third trimester the state could prohibit an abortion altogether unless it was clearly needed to protect a woman's health. This trimester approach was applied by the Supreme Court for sixteen years, before it signalled a clear change in direction in *Webster* v. *Reproductive Health Services*. Despite a series of modifications to the original ruling, *Roe* v. *Wade* has not been overturned, so that the constitutional right to an abortion remains, circumscribed though it now is in some states.

The *Roe* v. *Wade* decision prompted national debate that continues to this day. Despite significant public backing for the decision in the early 1970s, there was widespread opposition, particularly from those associated with the Christian Right. It led to the greater politicisation of Court appointments, subsequent nominees to the bench having been closely questioned about their attitudes to abortion. It also reshaped national politics, dividing much of the nation into pro-*Roe* (mostly pro-choice) and anti-*Roe* (mostly pro-life) camps, and inspiring grassroots activism on both sides.

See also *Abortion*; *Abortion Rights Movement*; *Christian Coalition*; *Fourteenth Amendment*; *National Organization for Women*; **Planned Parenthood of Southeastern Pennsylvania** *v.* **Casey** *(1992)*; *Pro-life Movement*; *Religious Right*; **Webster** *v.* **Reproductive Health Services** *(1989)*

Rogue States

Rogue states are those nations perceived as acting beyond the international rule of law and which do not fit into the traditional pattern of global alliances. Following the end of the Cold War and the collapse of the Soviet Union, Washington was looking at the new challenges to the interests of the United States and its allies that might emerge. The term 'rogue state' came into use during the Clinton administration as a means of describing those countries – often developing states – considered to be essentially hostile to the United States and a threat to world peace. They did not subscribe to what Washington regarded as the norms of international behaviour. They were often accused of violations of human rights, suspected of pursuing weapons of mass destruction and missile programmes, and even sometimes of sponsoring terrorism. The core 'rogue states' were Afghanistan, Iraq, Iran, North Korea and Libya but, following the regime changes in the first two and the opening of dialogue with Libya, three remained. These were the states seen by George W. Bush as constituting the 'Axis of Evil'.

Rogue states are usually differentiated from 'pariah' states, such as Burma, Sudan, Syria and Zimbabwe, whose rulers are believed regularly to abuse the human rights of their inhabitants but which do not pose a tangible threat beyond their own borders.

Roosevelt, Franklin Delano (1882–1945)

Often referred to by his initials, FDR, Franklin Roosevelt was the thirty-second president of the United States. He remains the only president to be elected to four terms in office, serving from 1933 to 1945. He was a central figure of the twentieth century during a time of worldwide economic crisis and world war.

The fifth cousin of the Republican Theodore Roosevelt, whom he greatly admired, Roosevelt entered political life as a Democrat. He was elected to the New York Senate in 1910. He served as assistant secretary of the Navy during the Wilson presidency and was the Democratic nominee as vice president in 1920. Still only thirty-nine, he was stricken with poliomyelitis in mid-1921. Yet, with great courage and perseverance, he worked hard to regain the use of his legs. In 1928, he became governor of New York and in November 1932 was elected president. He began the first of his four terms in office in March 1933, the last incumbent to commence his term in that month.

Assuming the presidency at the depth of the Great Depression, when there were thirteen million people unemployed and almost every bank was closed, Roosevelt helped Americans to regain faith in themselves. He brought hope with his promise of prompt, vigorous action and, in his Inaugural Address, boldly asserted that 'the only thing we have to fear is fear itself – nameless, unreasoning, unjustified terror which paralyses needed efforts to convert retreat into advance'. In his first 'hundred days', he proposed a sweeping programme based on the '3Rs': *relief* to the unemployed and to those in danger of losing farms and homes; *recovery* to business and agriculture; and longer-term *reform*, especially through the establishment of the Tennessee Valley Authority.

By 1935, recovery was gradually getting underway but opposition from businessmen and bankers was rising. They disliked some of Roosevelt's New Deal experiments and the increases in taxation and budget deficits that accompanied them; they also felt he was too sympathetic to labour. After an overwhelming victory in November 1936, Roosevelt took on the critics in his own party and within the judiciary. In particular, he devised a scheme to enlarge the Supreme Court to fifteen members. Comprising elderly and rather conservative justices, it had invalidated key New Deal measures, declaring them to be unconstitutional. The proposal to 'pack the court' proved contentious and, in the eyes of many commentators, seemed to be an attack on the theory of the separation of powers. But the Court began to decide in favour of New Deal measures.

By 1939, with the outbreak of war in Europe, Roosevelt was increasingly concentrating on foreign affairs. Reforming legislation diminished, and it was to be mobilisation of troops for war that cured the remaining ills of the Depression. During the late 1930s, FDR championed rearmament and led the nation away from its past isolationism towards greater engagement in European and global affairs.

During World War II, Roosevelt tried to maintain neutrality and keep the United States out of the war in Europe while at, the same time, strengthening nations that were threatened or attacked. When France fell and England came under siege in 1940, he sent Britain all possible aid short of actual military involvement. When the Japanese attacked Pearl Harbor on 7 December 1941, Roosevelt directed the war effort. As the war drew to a close, his health deteriorated. He died in April 1945.

Assessment

In scholarly surveys of the 'greatest' presidents, Roosevelt is invariably ranked between first and third. His willingness to use the power of the presidency and the machinery of the federal government marked a decisive break with the past, leading to a concentration of power in Washington that changed the balance of pre–1933 federalism. He is often referred to as the first of the so–called modern presidents. The circumstances allowed – indeed required – him to expand the scope of his

office in a way that none of his immediate predecessors or successors had been able to do. But none of them assumed office at a time of national emergency and neither did they enjoy the level of public support for presidential initiatve and leadership that he possessed. The beneficiary of a landslide victory in a realigning election, a strong coat-tails effect in congressional elections, and as head of a party that was cohesive and dedicated to, and intent upon, taking over the reins in Washington, he inhabited a supportive political environment. Even when he ran into political difficulties in the mid late 1930s, he was aware of the level of backing for his actions among ordinary Americans. As he put it: 'everyone's agin me, except the voters'.

Roosevelt was a model for American liberals, re-energising, realigning and sustaining the Democratic Party for subsequent generations, with his progressive outlook and ideas and the electoral success that he was able to achieve. In the process, he created the New Deal Coalition (based on the support of the labour unions, farmers, the poor and those on relief, ethnic minorities, intellectuals and the South) that was to dominate American politics until the late 1960s

Finally, Roosevelt was also a very fine communicator. He quickly saw the potential for politicians of broadcasting and was adept in handling the new medium which had a popular reach well beyond anything that was formerly available to presidents. From his rooms in the White House, he addressed the American people as though they were his most special friends. What he said seemed personal, both in content and in style. He spoke warmly and informally, allaying the fears of those who listened to him. Moreover, he was a master of more than one form of communication for, as the microphones were turned off, he would then meet the newsreel cameramen with their noisy equipment, understanding as he did that the cinema was just as powerful a medium for his New Deal policies as radio.

He was a master of radio and skilled in sensing the new significance of moving pictures; he was also the politician who first appeared on television, in a little-noticed gathering at the New York World's Fair, in 1939. He was, in all, a 'natural' for the broadcasting age. Having rehearsed his lines with the utmost care and often learnting his speech by heart, he was nonetheless able to make it seem as though he was addressing the individual voter in the intimacy of his or her own home.

See also *Court-packing Scheme*; *Great Depression*; *New Deal*

Roosevelt, Theodore (1858–1919)

Born into a wealthy family in New York City, Theodore Roosevelt (or TR or Teddy, as he was often known) lived an adventurous and strenuous life. In the 1880s, on his ranch in the Badlands of Dakota, he developed his 'cowboy' persona, driving cattle, hunting big game and even capturing an outlaw. He served as lieutenant colonel of the Rough Rider Regiment in the Spanish-American War of 1898, in which he became a conspicuous hero. He entered politics as a Republican but also as a Progressive. He became a governor of New York State in 1898. On the assassination of President McKinley, and still only forty-two, he became the twenty-sixth president, the youngest in American history.

Roosevelt brought new excitement and power to the presidency, vigorously leading Congress and the American public towards progressive reforms. In domestic policy, as a Progressive president, his 'Square Deal' programme promised a fair deal for the average citizen. He saw himself as an arbiter between the conflicting economic forces of capital and labour, guaranteeing justice to each and dispensing favours to neither. He is most famous as the 'trust buster' who forced the dissolution of a great railway combination in the Northwest. Other anti-trust suits under the Sherman Act followed, notably in the area of pure food and drugs. He distrusted wealthy businessmen, dissolving in total some forty monopolistic corporations. He accepted capitalism and trusts in principle but railed against their corrupt, illegal practices.

Roosevelt was an exponent of a forceful and active foreign policy. He wanted to see America engage in world politics. Aware of the strategic need for a shortcut between the Atlantic and Pacific, he ensured the construction of the Panama Canal. He assumed to the United States the sole right of intervention in Latin America,

his motto in foreign policy being 'speak softly and carry a big stick'. He won the Nobel Peace Prize for mediating the Russo–Japanese War.

Roosevelt's conception of the presidential office was that he was a 'steward of the people'. As such, he should take whatever action was necessary for the public good unless expressly forbidden so to do by law or by the Constitution. As he put it: 'I did not usurp power, but I did greatly broaden the use of executive power.'

In 1910, Roosevelt feuded with his friend and anointed successor, William Howard Taft. He was outmanoeuvred by Taft who, in November 1912, defeated him as the Republican nominee for the presidency leaving him to stand on his own Bull Moose platform. Although he lost, Roosevelt diverted so many Progressives from the Republican Party that Woodrow Wilson was able to win the election for the Democrats. Thereafter, the conservative faction regained control of the Republican Party.

Roosevelt is remembered for the force of his personality. He was an all-action man, his energy, range of interests and achievements being extraordinary. Other than being an eminent politician, he was at various times an author, explorer, historian, naturalist and soldier. Some of his most effective work was in the area of conservation. As an outdoorsman, he emphasised the efficient use of natural resources. He added enormously to the national forests in the West, reserved lands for public use and fostered great irrigation projects. He cut a populist figure, crusading endlessly on matters great and small, his performances exciting audiences as he addressed them with his high-pitched voice, jutting jaw, and pounding fist.

Roth v. *United States* (1957)

Roth v. *United States* was a landmark ruling made by the Supreme Court, in which the justices redefined the constitutional test for determining what constitutes obscene material unprotected by the First Amendment. It reasoned that material was obscene and, therefore, unprotected if the 'average person, applying contemporary community standards' found the 'dominant theme of the material' 'appeals to prurient interests' of society or was 'utterly without redeeming social importance'.

This was the first of the modern obscenity cases. Justice Brennan, recognising that sex and obscenity were not synonymous, was attempting to formulate a legal test for obscenity that would protect the right to deal with sexual matters and yet reserve to the government the power to prohibit what was truly obscene. Later cases attempted to clarify the test by describing the community standards as national not local ones, and requiring proof that the work was 'utterly without redeeming social value' (*Memoirs of a Woman of Pleasure* v. *Massachusetts* [1966]).

Rules Committee

The House of Representatives Committee on Rules principally serves to assist the majority party leadership in scheduling bills for floor action in the chamber. Bills are scheduled by means of special 'rules' from the Rules Committee that provide priority status for their consideration in the House and establish procedures for their debate and amendment. If the Committee decides that there can be debate and amendments (subject to the overall time available), then this is an 'open rule'. If it limits debate and insists that only members of the reporting committee may offer amendments, then this is a 'closed rule', an outcome usually reserved only for tax and spending bills. Normally, without any such rule, a bill will not reach the floor.

The Committee on Rules is one of the most powerful committees in the House of Representatives. Its thirteen members include some of the most senior members of the House. It has a 2:1 membership in favour of the majority party and is normally chaired by one of its senior members. The dominance of the majority party reflects the Committee's status in recent decades as an arm of the leadership and legislative gatekeeper.

Before Congress was reformed in the 1970s, the Committee was even more powerful than is the modern committee. The 'old guard' (a coalition of Southern Democrats and Republicans) used their influence to block proceedings. The Committee was then much disliked by liberals and those who wanted to see reform. They saw it as dictatorial and unrepresentative. Today, the Committee is less controversial and more representative of the membership of the majority party. If it wants a bill to be passed the Committee can expedite its passage, by sending it quickly to the floor of the House for immediate debate.

As an arm of the leadership of both parties the Committee is at the centre of both political and legislative battles, performing precarious balancing acts between majority will and minority rights, leadership needs and membership demands, and a wide range of public policy options.

The Senate Committee on Rules and Administration is less powerful than its counterpart in the House, having a more administrative role. In the Senate, there are no official time limits for debate and the legislative procedure is usually determined on a consensual basis between the majority and minority party leaders.

Rumsfeld, Donald (1932–)

Donald Rumsfeld became the twenty-first Secretary of Defense in January 2001, having previously served as a US congressman (1969), Director of the Office of Economic Opportunity and Assistant to the President (1969–70) and US Ambassador to NATO (1973–74) under Richard Nixon, White House Chief of Staff (1974–75) and thirteenth (and youngest ever) Secretary of Defense (1975–77) under Gerald Ford, prior to returning to the world of business. During his business career, he continued his public service by taking a number of federal posts, including:

- member of the President's General Advisory Committee on Arms Control (1982–86)
- Special Presidential Envoy to the Middle East (1983–84), and
- Member of the US Trade Deficit Review Commission (1999–2000).

Secretary Rumsfeld was responsible for directing the actions of the Defense Department in response to the terrorist attacks of 9/11, including Operation Enduring Freedom in Afghanistan and Operation Iraqi Freedom. During his secretaryship, he also oversaw the reform and transformation of America's military, in order to make it better equipped to address the threats of the twenty-first century. Rumsfeld resigned as

Secretary of Defense in December 2006. His resignation came about in the wake of the Republican setback in the November 2006 midterm elections, in which Democrats won control of the House of Representatives and the Senate. His departure was widely regarded as marking a potentially momentous shift in the direction of American foreign and defence policy, for he had been one of the key architects and promoters of the war in Iraq. His handling of Iraqi-related issues had been the subject of intense criticism for several reasons, including: his allegedly misleading statements about the Iraqi regime during the lead up to the war; his failure adequately to plan for post-invasion stabilisation; and his handling of detainee abuse scandals at Abu Ghraib prison and elsewhere.

Rumsfeld is a visiting fellow at the Hoover Institution, a hawkish think tank based at Stanford University that supplied a number of defence and security advisers to the Bush administration.

S

Scalia, Antonin (1936–)

Antonin Scalia is the second most senior associate justice on the Supreme Court. Appointed by Ronald Reagan in 1986, he is usually considered to be a key figure of the Court's conservative wing.

From the beginning of his tenure on the Court, Scalia has continued to argue the case for adherence to the text of the Constitution rather than for attempts to interpret it in a modern-day setting. He does not believe that the document is a living document that can be applied to contemporary reality, for this places judges in the position of lawmakers.

Scalia has always been more sympathetic to national power and to a strong Executive than have some other Court conservatives such as Clarence Thomas. In *Morrison* v. *Olson* (1988) he wrote a dissenting opinion that challenged the constitutionality of an independent counsel established by the judiciary to investigate senior officials in the Executive. In his dissenting opinion he enquired: 'Once we depart from the text of the Constitution, just where short of that do we stop?' For him, the text and any related provisions of statutes that shed light on the meaning of any disputed text are the only guides necessary in judicial interpretation. He is unwilling to discern any constitutional rights that are not clearly set forth so that, in right-to-life cases, he has rejected any constitutional right to an abortion.

School Districts/Boards

School districts are forms of special-purpose districts that administer the local government-funded public schools within a defined geographical areas. They serve one or more towns, often covering districts with similar boundaries to those of a city or country.

A school board – elected by direct popular vote or by appointment by other governmental officials – acts as the legislative body in each district. It appoints a chief executive who has responsibility for carrying out day-to-day decisions and policy implementations. The school board may act in a quasi-judicial capacity in cases of serious discipline involving students or employees. According to the 2002 census, there were 13,506 school boards in existence at the time of the survey.

Some large districts perform tasks that go beyond a strictly educational brief, such as operating medical clinics and campus police patrols. They may also have responsibilities for running recreational and library facilities. In some states, where the Religious Right is influential, Christian representatives on school boards have sought to eliminate from library shelves 'irreligious material' or books that question American values.

The operations and decisions of school boards can be matters of lively controversy in local politics and social life. Districts that are well run and in which schools gain good results can have an impact on house prices and tax revenues, whereas those that are less well rated may be associated with community decline.

Secession see *Confederacy*

Secretary of State

The Secretary of State is the member of the US government responsible for handling the country's external relations. He or she heads the State Department, organising and supervising its work and staff. The secretary is the first Cabinet member and the fourth in line of succession to the presidency after the vice president, speaker of the house and the president *pro tempore* of the Senate. Dr Condoleezza Rice became the sixty-sixth Secretary of State in January 2005, Hillary Clinton the sixty-seventh four years later.

In accordance with the Constitution, the secretary carries out such duties as the president requires. Key tasks include: negotiating with overseas representatives and instructing US embassies or consulates abroad; acting as a principal adviser in the formulation of foreign policy; and, in recent decades, the secretary has become responsible for overall direction, co-ordination and supervision of interdepartmental activities of the US government overseas, except for certain military activities.

In the event of a presidential resignation, there must be a written communication from the president to the Secretary of State. This has occurred just once, when President Nixon had a letter delivered to Henry Kissinger at the time of Nixon's resignation in August 1974.

The importance of the office varies. By its very nature, it has a key role in US government but the impact of different secretaries depends upon the president and the incumbent. In the handling of policy on Iraq, Colin Powell sometimes seemed out of step with other members of the administration whose voices carried greater weight with George Bush.

Some presidents wish to centralise in their own hands decision-making on all aspects of foreign and national security matters, relying for advice primarily on their Special Assistant for National Security Affairs (SA) rather than on a departmental secretary who – once appointed – has a department to represent, the views of which can shape his or her own in a way that the president may not like. Richard Nixon is quoted as observing that 'you need a president for foreign policy; no Secretary of State is really important; the president makes foreign policy'.

See also *Foreign Policy*; *National Security Council*; *State Department*

Segregation

Segregation refers to the practice of creating separate facilities within the same society for the use of a minority group. It may exist as a result of social norms and economic conditions, or be brought about by legal changes. In the United States, it relates to the separation of black and white Americans that existed in the South, in the late nineteenth century, and in particular to the laws that allowed separation to exist. It became illegal for black and white people to travel together, or jointly to use public facilities such as hospitals and swimming pools (the so-called Jim Crow laws). By the turn of the twentieth century, Jim Crow segregation had excluded most black Americans in the South from the electorate and from meaningful economic opportunities. It was associated with the discrimination and intimidation they endured, sometimes being enforced by the threat or the actuality of lynchings or other forms of physical violence.

Historically and socially, segregation was rooted in a desire to preserve the best employment, facilities and status for white Americans and to ensure that there was no dilution of the white race and its culture. Some whites were not totally against change but they feared that any alterations might unleash changes that they could not control. This legalised separation of the races lasted up to the 1960s by when the Civil Rights Movement achieved successes in changing the thinking and practices of many white Americans. It was upheld by the majority in the 'separate but equal' *Plessy* v. *Ferguson* ruling (1896) but was overturned in the *Brown* v. *Topeka Board of Education* case (1954) which viewed separate facilities as 'inherently unequal'. Chief Justice Earl Warren argued that, even if facilities were equal, separate education was psychologically harmful to black children.

The 1954 ruling did not include a date by when desegregation had to be achieved. The process proved painfully slow because of powerful white resistance to further advances, for instance, that of Governor Wallace of Alabama who famously declared in his inaugural address: 'Segregation now! Segregation tomorrow! Segregation forever!' By 1968 all forms of segregation had been declared unconstitutional by the Supreme Court. Not all racial segregation laws have been repealed although Court rulings have rendered them unenforceable and illegal to carry out.

See also **Brown** v. **Board of Education** *(1954)*; *Desegregation*; **Jim Crow**; **Plessy** v. **Ferguson** *(1896)*

Self-incrimination

Self-incrimination means incrimination of oneself, especially by one's own testimony, in a criminal prosecution. Taking advantage of the right against self-incrimination is often referred to as 'taking the Fifth', for the Fifth Amendment guarantees that a person cannot be compelled 'to be a witness against himself'. This applies to investigatory processes, pre-trial disclosures and trials themselves, as well as to testimony in civil, administrative, and legislative proceedings.

The Supreme Court has long acted to ensure that, even in the early days of any case (investigation, arrest and trial), those in custody must be specifically informed that they have a right to silence and cannot be questioned unless they waive that right. The Warren Court reinforced the position in its judgment in *Miranda* v. *Arizona* (1966) that protection from compulsory self-incrimination requires the police to remind criminal suspects of this procedural guarantee.

The issue of self-incrimination had attracted considerable attention in the congressional hearings into Communists within the United States held by Senator McCarthy. Several witnesses had refused to testify on the grounds that they were likely to incriminate themselves. Their assertions were interpreted as admissions of guilt, and the witnesses labelled as 'Fifth Amendment Communists'.

See also *Fifth Amendment*; **Miranda** v. **Arizona** *(1966)*; **McCarthy, Joseph** *(1908–57)* **and McCarthyism**

Senate

The Senate is the legislative chamber that provides for state representation in Congress. In a federal system, there is usually provision to safeguard the individual states against encroachment by the federal government. In the United States, the Senate provides such territorial representation and places a check upon the lower House of Representatives which is, broadly speaking, elected on the basis of population. The size of the country, the need for regional representation and vast geographical cleavages across the territory make a second chamber seem especially desirable.

Role and importance

Formal powers of the Senate, as set out in Article 1, Section 8 of the Constitution

The exclusive powers of the Senate are:

To confirm appointments made by the president
To ratify treaties
To try cases of impeachment
To elect the vice president if the Electoral College is deadlocked.

Its concurrent powers, shared with the house, are:

To pass legislation
To override the president's veto
To initiate constitutional amendments
To declare war
To confirm a newly appointed vice president.

In the United States, the two chambers are of formally equal status but the Senate is the dominant and more prestigious one. Its exclusive powers, with regard to treaties and ratification of appointments, give it a greater degree of authority. Even the restriction that all bills on revenue raising must originate in the house is hardly a limitation as the Senate has the same full power of amendment as it has with other types of bill.

Indicative perhaps of the Senate's higher status is the fact that candidates for the presidency and vice presidency tend to come from the upper house (or after serving a period in office as a state governor). Few come from the House of Representatives. Senators tend to get higher levels of media coverage and so find it easier to build personal reputations. More of them are known nationwide, the names of Elizabeth Dole, Edward Kennedy, John Kerry and John McCain all being recognisable well beyond the confines of their states. Pear (1963) elaborated in this way:

> Great senators have made the Senate great, and have influenced the course of American history in ways which can be recorded in the history books . . . [Some] sitting for safe seats have spent their lives in the Senate, becoming the embodiment of national or regional thinking on certain topics. Great senators are competitors for the limelight with presidents. They know their power and can use it for long term objectives.

An important difference between a senator and a representative is the length of service. Senators have the opportunity to acquire a working knowledge of their subjects of concern without the problem of constantly having to campaign for their return to Washington. They can take part in a genuine debate rather than speaking and listening with the likely reactions of the voters in mind. Also, they have been elected by the whole state rather than by a district of it. (For instance, Edward Kennedy and John Kerry represent Massachusetts and are well known across (as well as beyond) the state, whereas the long-serving Democratic House Representative for the 7th District, Ed Markey, lacks their wider recognition.) Significantly, whereas members of the house may seek a Senate vacancy, the reverse is not true.

Owing to the high volume and complexity of its work, the Senate divides its tasks among twenty standing committees (with a combined total of sixty-eight subcommittees), four select/special/other committees and four joint committees. Because of the smaller size of the Senate, its members are likely to gain the chair of a committee or subcommittee or hold some party position.

Membership

The Senate was originally indirectly elected, members being appointed by state legislatures. As a result of the passage of the Seventeenth Amendment, this changed in 1914 when the first direct elections were held. It now comprises a hundred members, two senators being elected from each of the fifty states. Rhode Island, the smallest state in terms of landmass, with just over 1,000 square miles (2,590 sq. km), therefore has the same senatorial representation as Alaska, the largest state with more than half a million square miles (1,400,000 sq. km). Wyoming, the smallest in terms of population with just over 500,000 inhabitants, has the same number of senators as California with more than 36.5 million.

Each person elected to the Senate must be at least thirty years of age, have had citizenship of the United States for at least nine years and be a current resident of the state from which he or she is elected. Senators are chosen in statewide elections held in even-numbered years. They serve for six years, with one-third of the membership standing for re-election every two years. Hence, two-thirds of the senators are always persons with some legislative experience at the national level.

Senators are paid the same amount as representatives.

See also *Congress*; *Congressional Committees*; *Congressional Elections Senatorial Courtesy*

Senatorial Courtesy

Senatorial courtesy refers to the expectation that the president will clear federal district court judgeship appointments with senators of his party from the state in which the judge will serve, even when his party is not in control of the Senate. If he or she fails to seek their approval, he/she is unlikely to secure Senate approval for his/her nominees. Of course, when he/she does seek it, the practice of senatorial courtesy may lead to rejection of a nominee, if one or both senators from the home state indicate(s) that they strongly oppose the proposed appointment. This is more likely in cases of federal district judge appointments although it has in the past undercut a presidential Supreme Court appointment as well.

Senators see *Senate*

Separate but Equal see Plessy *v.* Ferguson *(1896)*

Separation of Powers

The separation of powers refers to the division of the powers to make, execute and adjudicate upon the law among the three established branches of the US government, the Congress, the presidency and the courts. Article 1, Section 3 of the Constitution states the position clearly:

> The powers of government shall be divided into three distinct departments: legislative, executive and judicial. No person or persons belonging to or constituting one of these departments shall exercise any of the powers properly belonging to either of the others . . .

The French philosopher Montesquieu (1689–1755) who wrote *De l'Esprit des Lois*, argued that each arm needs to be separate so that no one person could take control of all three functions of government. His influence was to be found in the work of the Founding Fathers for they instituted a number of checks and balances to prevent any danger of a powerful individual or group from dominating the whole structure by concentrating power in too few hands. In the forty-seventh Federalist Paper, Madison quotes Montesquieu to that effect: 'There can be no liberty where the legislative and executive powers are united in the same person or body of magistrates, or if the power of judging be not separated from the legislative and executive powers.'

Some writers have questioned the appropriateness of the term 'separation of powers' in the case of the American Constitution. Richard Neustadt (1960) pointed out that, in the United States, it is

the institutions that are separate rather than the powers. In his view, rather than having created a government of 'separated powers', the Founding Fathers created a system of 'separated institutions sharing powers'. The distinction is a valid one for what they did was to devise a system in which each of the three branches of government can act as a brake on, and balance to, the others. In the case of the president and the two houses of Congress, a further check is introduced by virtue of the fact that they each serves for different terms of office and is elected by different constituencies. In the words of Alan Grant (1994): 'Negativity is the chief characteristic of the separation of powers doctrine as it is concerned with producing limitations and constraints on government rather than looking at the positive use to be made of such authority.'

Having separated the three branches of government, the delegates of the Philadelphia Convention allowed a certain amount of participation in, and checking of, the activities of one branch by the others. Thus, key presidential appointments have to be confirmed by a majority of the Senate; all legislation the president wishes to see enacted has to pass through Congress; and the Supreme Court can declare the president's actions and policies (and those of Congress) to be 'unconstitutional' (though this latter idea was not made explicit in the Constitution). The president has the opportunity to reshape the Supreme Court by making nominations in the event of vacancies, and can veto bills passed by Congress that are considered to be unnecessary or undesirable.

Sharpton, Alfred (Al) (1954–)

Al Sharpton is a Baptist minister, chat-show host and political activist with a special interest in issues of civil rights and social justice. In 2004, he sought the Democratic nomination for the presidency but eventually backed John Kerry. In 2007, he doubted whether the country was ready for an African American in the White House and so decided not to run again. He later announced that he was backing the Obama candidacy although he made the strategic decision to keep his support quiet.

Highly controversial and outspoken, Sharpton is strongly disliked by many conservatives who see him as dangerously radical and, in the views of some, anti-Semitic as well. Others are impressed by his leadership skills. Supporters have noted Sharpton's willingness to go to jail in support of the African American cause and claim that he deserves the respect he enjoys within the black community.

Sierra Club

The Sierra Club is America's oldest, largest and most influential grassroots environmental interest group. Its 1.3 million members in chapters across the United States are committed to working to protect communities, wild places, and the planet itself. Its mission statement describes its role as being:

> To explore, enjoy, and protect the wild places of the earth; to practice and promote the responsible use of the earth's ecosystems and resources; to educate and enlist humanity to protect and restore the quality of the natural and human environment; and to use all lawful means to carry out these objectives.

In June 2006, the Sierra Club announced the formation of a Blue–Green Alliance with the United Steelworkers Union. The goal of the partnership is to pursue a joint policy agenda reconciling workers' needs for good jobs with humankind's need for a cleaner environment and safer world.

Signing Statements

Signing statements are written observations made by a president at the time of signing legislation, sometimes being merely comments on a bill's value in fulfilling some pressing need but, in more controversial cases, involving claims by presidents that they believe some part of the legislation is unconstitutional and therefore they intend to ignore it or to implement it only in ways they believe are constitutional.

Only seventy-five signing statements had been issued by the end of the Carter presidency. More use was made of them in the Reagan–Clinton era. Bill Clinton issued more such statements than his successor but the G. W. Bush approach

seemed particularly geared to undermining legislative intent. He routinely asserted that he would not act contrary to the constitutional provisions that direct the president to supervise the unitary executive branch, a formulation originally made in the first signing statement of Ronald Reagan. Basically, it asserts that Congress cannot pass a law that undercuts the constitutionally granted authorities of the president. When signing the contentious Medicare and Prescription Drug Act in 2003, he commented adversely on two sections of the statute that interfered with his constitutional prerogative to 'supervise the unitary executive branch'. He continued to say that

> the executive branch shall construe these provisions in a manner consistent with the President's constitutional authority to supervise the unitary executive branch and to recommend for the consideration of the Congress such measures as the President judges necessary and expedient.

See also *Unitary Executive Theory*

Social Conservatives

Social conservatives believe that the government has an important role in encouraging or enforcing traditional values or behaviours, for these are what keep people civilised and decent. Opinions may differ on exactly which policies ought to be upheld. Most social conservatives in the United States, however,

- are pro-life on abortion and wary of stem cell research
- support restrictions on civil marriage and child adoption by gay couples
- argue for traditional family values, seeing the nuclear family model as the core of society
- are sympathetic to – often supporters of – religious belief and practice.

Many social conservatives are to be found within the Republican Party and/or the Religious Right. Some – mainly white Southern – Democrats may share such values.

See also *Conservatism*

Socialism

Socialists share in common a belief that unrestrained capitalism is responsible for a variety of social evils, including the exploitation of working people, the widespread existence of poverty and unemployment, gross inequality of wealth and the pursuit of greed and selfishness. Socialists would prefer to see a social system based on co-operative values and emphasise the values of community rather than of individualism. They also believe strongly in the need for a more equal and just society based on brotherhood and a sense of social solidarity.

Given the commitment to the American Dream and the ideas that underpin it, it is no surprise that socialism has never taken root in the United States. Indeed, for Seymour Lipset and Gary Marks (2000), its absence is a cornerstone of American exceptionalism. They point out that opinion polls in America continue to reveal a people whose attitudes are different from those of people in Europe and Canada. Many Americans do not favour an active role for government in the economy or a desire for large welfare programmes. They favour private efforts in business and welfare and rely more on philanthropic giving. The two writers point to the absence of those conditions that the left has always seen as a prerequisite for the development of any 'mass allegiance' to socialism, but draw attention to the diversity of explanations given for the failure of American socialism:

> Explanations for [socialism]'s weakness are as numerous as socialists were few. Some . . . attribute the weakness of socialism to the failures of socialist organizations and leaders. Another school ascribes socialism's bankruptcy to its incompatibility with America's core values, while still others cite the American Constitution as the decisive factor.

In their analyses of the development of socialism, Karl Marx and Friedrich Engels contributed a Marxist perspective to the debate on the failure of American socialism. Marx had assumed that the working class was destined to organise revolutionary socialist parties in every capitalist society. He and Engels had, however, noted the respects in which the United States differed from other European societies. Above all, it was a new nation and society, a democratic country lacking many of the institutions and traditions of previously feudal societies. It had a 'modern and purely bourgeois culture'. After Marx's death in 1883, Engels (Lipset and Marks, 2000) gave more thought to the non-emergence of socialist movements on a mass scale. He attributed the 'backwardness' of the American workers to the absence of a feudal past. In his view, 'Americans [were] born conservatives – just because America is so purely bourgeois, so entirely without a feudal past and proud of its purely bourgeois organisation.'

Whatever the reasons involved, America has not proved to be fertile ground for socialist thinkers and their ideas. The main writers and philosophers of socialism have been Europeans, and their ideas and their approach have been developed from European experience. Perhaps because of the influence of German and Jewish believers, socialism has often been regarded as an alien import unsuited to the conditions of American life.

Socialism in its various forms is traditionally associated with the wish to replace private ownership of the means of production, distribution and exchange with a system of greater public ownership. In the ultimate socialist Utopia, property is owned by the state on behalf of the people and, in Marx's phrase, each receives what is necessary for his or her needs: 'From each according to his ability, to each according to his needs.' In America, there is more discussion over the rights of private property than interest in public ownership.

American socialists of whatever disposition broadly favour an increased role for government, and wish to place a greater burden on the rich by higher taxation. They would use the revenue thereby obtained to introduce more redistributive policies, including public works schemes to offer work for the unemployed, and more aid to the least well off.

Socialist doctrine has gained a small but influential following among some middle class intellectuals but the working classes have never taken up the cause with much enthusiasm or in any significant numbers. Groups have developed to represent the various shades of socialism, most notably the American Socialist Party, but as in Europe left-wing organisations have been prone to internal schism, factional strife and secession.

See also *Socialist Party of America/Socialist Party USA*; *Third Parties*

Socialist Party of America/Socialist Party USA

The Socialist Party USA advocates progress via the ballot box rather than militant revolutionary change. It is a breakaway faction that emerged out of the major divisions in the Socialist Party of America (SPA) in the early 1970s and is currently the only countrywide party to use the term socialist in its title.

Staunchly anti-Communist, the Socialist Party of America was established in 1900 by Eugene V. Debs who stood five times for the presidency. In the first twenty years or so of its existence, it was the third largest national party. It elected two members to Congress, was represented in several state legislatures and localities and, at its peak, had more than 100,000 members. But, even at its peak, it never really challenged the supremacy of the major parties.

In the decades after World War II, the Socialist Party suffered from serious internal schism, control passing from left to right and back again. Since 1973, the breakaway Socialist Party USA has focused its attention more on grassroots and local politics, and has dealt with the issue as to whether to stand in presidential elections on a case-by-case basis. It actively campaigns against restrictive state laws that deny the party ballot access and, when it is able to stand, does so primarily in order to educate the public about socialism and the need for electoral democracy in the United States.

Over many years socialist parties have been kept alive by a band of dedicated enthusiasts who ensured that they continued to contest elections of all types in several states. In 2004, Walt Brown and Mary Alice Herbert were the presidential candidates for the Socialist Party USA, standing in fifteen states. Their efforts were rewarded with a meagre national total of around 11,000 votes. Four years later, Brian Moore and Stewart Alexander fared even worse, being on the ballot paper in only eight states and securing 7,315 votes.

According to its own mission statement, the party stands for:

> the abolition of every form of domination and exploitation, whether based on social class, gender, race/ethnicity, sexual orientation or other characteristics . . . and is committed to the transformation of capitalism through the creation of a democratic socialist society . . . It strives to establish a radical democracy that places people's lives under their own control – a non-racist, classless, feminist, socialist society in which people cooperate at work, at home and in the community.

See also *Third Parties*

Soft Money

Soft money is money contributed in ways and for purposes that do not infringe the FECA legislation on limits to contributions and expenditure. It is not contributed directly to candidate campaigns or to political parties but to other bodies and for other purposes which do not 'expressly advocate' the election or defeat of a candidate. It includes money spent on party-building activities, such as registration, as well as mass mailing and issue ads. Soft money may be collected at state and local level but is often used for national purposes.

In practice, there is little to distinguish issue ads from those promoting a candidate which – by law – have to be funded by 'hard money'. The McCain–Feingold reform (2002) prohibited national political parties from raising or spending soft money, but other organisations may still do so.

See also *McCain–Feingold Campaign Finance Reform Act*

Solid South

The Solid South refers to the South as a voting block, in particular to the electoral support of the Southern states for candidates of the Democratic Party, which lasted from the late 1870s to the early 1960s. The Democratic dominance originated in the animosity of many white Southerners towards the Republican Party's support for political rights for black Americans during the era of Reconstruction. It was maintained by the Democrat's willingness to back segregation and the Jim Crow laws that sustained it.

Southern Democrats represented the agrarian interests of the planter elite. They were opposed to the growing power of the industrial North and to what they saw as the growing trend towards centralised government. Their commitment to the Democratic cause began to wane in the 1960s, as the party fell under the grip of the liberal leadership of the Kennedy–Johnson era. Given their social conservatism, many were increasingly attracted by Republican attitudes of the type espoused by Ronald Reagan. Since the 1980s, most states in the region have tended to elect Republican representatives.

See also *Blue Dog Democrats*; *Boll Weevils*; *Social Conservatives*

Sovereign Immunity

Sovereign immunity is the principle that the sovereign body (in the United States, the states or the federal government) cannot commit a legal wrong and is therefore immune from civil suit or criminal court action.

In the nineteenth century, sovereign immunity was used to limit suits by individuals against state and against federal governments. The Eleventh Amendment (1795) prohibited suits against states in federal courts and, in the case of *Gibbons* v. *United States* (1868), the Supreme Court held that the federal government could not be sued without the consent of Congress.

Sovereign immunity has been reduced in recent decades. The states have narrowed the immunity via laws and judicial decisions. By passing the Tort Claims Act (1946), Congress expressly authorised individuals to sue the federal government for specified claims (subject to various exceptions), a reflection of the widely held belief that governments should be accountable for losses they occasion. Moreover, in a further erosion of the principle, in situations where the principle bars action against the government, the injured party may seek damages from any individual officials personally liable for offending decisions.

Speaker of the House

Members of the majority party in the House of Representatives choose the person whom they favour as speaker in a party caucus (gathering of party members) at the beginning of each two-year session of Congress. The person chosen is not necessarily the oldest or longest-serving member but is usually someone who commands respect and has served a lengthy apprenticeship in other party offices in the house.

The speaker's role in the house is the only one mentioned – though not described – in the Constitution. In his/her capacity as presiding officer over the lower chamber, he/she fulfils several functions including opening each session, ruling on procedural matters, deciding who will speak and referring bills to committees. Beyond this, he or she has several powers of appointment, including membership of the Rules Committee and of ad hoc committees that may be created. The speaker is third in line to the presidency, should the president and vice president resign, be impeached or be killed. Because of this, he/she is expected to inform the White House of his/her whereabouts at all times. He or she also represents the house on ceremonial occasions.

The two most recent Republican incumbents were Newt Gingrich and Dennis Hastert. Taking over in January 1995 after the Republican success in the midterm elections of the previous November, Newt Gingrich became the first Republican speaker for forty years. His period was highly influential. He was concerned not only to make the lower chamber operate more efficiently but also to introduce a system of party government within the chamber. Accordingly, he:

- ushered in several rule changes
- tightened the co-ordination of activities among house leaders
- limited the number of subcommittees within each committee and reorganised several committee jurisdictions
- introduced greater cohesion among the Republicans, so that in the first hundred days

of his speakership the *Contract for America* programme was pushed through the house with an average of only five dissenting voices on thirty-three roll-call votes

- handpicked committee and subcommittee chairs, often ignoring the claims of seniority; chairs were to be limited to six years service in future, to prevent them becoming too powerful and independent
- created task forces of carefully chosen colleagues to consider issues and make proposals, and thereby bypass the characteristic blockages often found within the committee system
- freed himself from the day-to-day business of running the house by handing over such tasks to the house majority leader, so that he was able to concentrate on determining the party agenda
- used frequent media appearances to turn his office into a powerful role from which he could advance an alternative and more conservative programme than that of the president.

Via the force of his personality and the fact that several new Republicans had been elected, Gingrich was able to boost the importance of the office. He had been the most powerful speaker of modern times but his tenure did not last long. He did not achieve all that he hoped. In particular, aspects of the *Contract for America* programme stalled because of opposition in the Senate. Moreover, his personal brand of leadership created enemies who disliked the concentrating of power in his hands on which he had embarked. This led to his downfall shortly after disappointing midterm elections in 1998. After four years, the mantle of leadership was taken up by Dennis Hastert, a legislator with no national profile at the time.

The Hastert approach to the speakership was more traditional in its mode of operation. More of a conciliator, he has sought a consensus. By spending more time in the chamber and involving himself in legislative details and procedures, he has opted for a 'return to regular order'. Although at the time, his appointment was expected to be a short-lived affair, he nonetheless outlasted his more high-profile predecessor.

In January 2007, Nancy Pelosi made history by becoming the first woman to serve as speaker of the House of Representatives. As the highest-ranking elected woman in American history, she also became second in the line of presidential succession. Admirers of her performance point to her success in building consensus across the aisle and within the diverse House Democratic Caucus. They portray her as a strong, pragmatic and effective leader. She came under fire from some Democratic activists, however, for not being aggressive enough in confronting Bush.

As we have seen, the speaker is a highly influential figure, possessing considerable power via his or her control over the majority party and his/her influence over how the committee system operates. This is why more powerful holders of the office, such as Gingrich, have often been referred to as the equivalent of prime ministers.

See also *Gingrich, Newt*; *Pelosi, Nancy*

Special Revenue Sharing (SRS)

Special revenue sharing refers to the system of block grants developed by the Nixon administration via which categorical grants were bundled into special revenue sharing grants intended to enhance state and local discretion over programmes and spending.

See also *Block Grants*

Split-ticket Voting

By split-ticket voting, we mean the practice of casting ballots for the candidates of at least two different political parties at the same set of elections; e.g., voting for some Democrats and some Republicans. (By contrast, the habit of voting solely for Democrats or for Republicans is labelled 'straight-ticket voting'.)

Since the days of Democratic ascendancy, which ended in 1968, there has been a clear reduction in voter loyalty. Voters are more willing to vote differently between elections and within them – by split-ticket voting. The trend towards split-ticket voting actually has a longer history, going back to 1952, but it has intensified in recent years. Whereas in 1952, 12 per cent of the electorate voted differently in their choice of party for the president and for their member of the House of Representatives, by 1968 26 per cent did so, and in 1980 the figure was 34 per cent. Voters were enthusiastic about electing Ronald Reagan but less willing to vote for his party in the congressional elections.

The trend is notable at all levels, with more voters behaving differently in choosing a candidate for the White House and ones for Capitol Hill, more voting one way for the Senate and a different way for the house, and – particularly marked – a larger number voting differently in their choice for state and for local representatives.

Among the explanations for split-ticket voting, are:

1. Many Americans want to divide power in order to prevent an undue concentration in the hands of one person or party. For example, they may have preferred Clinton to Dole as their president in 1996 but chose to balance this by electing a Republican-dominated Congress.
2. Voter attachment to one party has declined, there being less strong partisan identification and more voter volatility. There are more votes 'up for grabs' and voters make a judgement on the qualities and policy positions of the candidates, both of which matter more in a media age of candidate-centred electioneering.
3. Some voters may feel that the candidate of one party is better at providing leadership in the White House whereas, in Congress, they prefer to see the other party predominate. For instance, they may feel safer with a Republican president, who might be expected to be tough on America's enemies, but prefer the more progressive Democratic agenda on domestic policy.

Spoils System of Presidential Appointments

The spoils system refers to an informal patronage system that was prominent for several decades in the nineteenth century. The parties that successfully contested presidential and congressional elections were keen to take control of jobs within the bureaucracy and reward those who had worked for victory with government posts.

At one time, political appointees made up the vast majority of the federal bureaucracy. Appointments were made on the basis of patronage, 'who you knew, rather than what you knew', and membership of the successful party was important in gaining government jobs. Andrew Jackson (1829–37) developed the patronage system to its maximum extent, for he believed that 'to the victor go the spoils'. By the 'spoils system', employment was given to members of the party that won political office, not just as a reward for political support but also as a way of ensuring that many offices were opened up to ordinary citizens.

The Jacksonian approach survived for several decades and it helped to make the federal bureaucracy responsive to the needs of the White House. Later, however, it came to be associated with corruption. Congress tackled this problem by passing the Pendleton Act (1883) which limited the number of political appointments that a president could make and established a merit system for about 10 per cent of federal jobs. This stressed ability, education and job performance as the key criteria for appointment, rather than political background. The merit system now applies to some 95 per cent of federal civilian jobs.

The spoils system survived much longer in many states, counties and municipalities but it had largely died out by the 1930s.

Appointments today

Today, the president has an opportunity to influence the nature of the bureaucracy via his power of appointment over the most strategically important positions in government. He or she can nominate more than 3,000 senior civil servants to serve in the administration, and these include the heads of the fourteen major departments (the secretaries), as well as assistant and deputy department secretaries, deputy assistant secretaries and a variety of other appointive positions. Nearly seven hundred of the top presidential appointments have to be confirmed by the Senate. Once in office, their tenure of office depends on how the White House judges their performance.

The president is likely to choose personnel whom he or she regards as loyal and competent, and who share his or her political outlook. Abernach (1991) notes that, whereas in the past many appointees had been people who had established good connections with interest groups or congressional committees, in the Reagan era 'ideology was the key'. Before coming to office, he established an appointment system which ensured that appointees would be faithful to him and pursue his objectives of reduced governmental activity.

See also *Bureaucracy*

State Department

The State Department is the Cabinet-level agency of the US government that handles foreign affairs. It is based in the Harry S. Truman Building, a few blocks from the White House. It is headed by the Secretary of State.

In its original form, the Department of State was not concerned with overseas policy alone but, over the years, most of its domestic workload was gradually transferred elsewhere. The department retains the Great Seal of the United States and, if the president or vice president resigns it is to the Secretary of State that the resignation is officially submitted. The main work of the department is concerned with:

- Promoting the security interests of the United States and its allies.
- Protecting foreign trade and commerce.
- Helping to negotiate and to enforce treaties and other agreements with foreign countries.
- Administering the Agency for International Development, and the Peace Corps, and most non-military aid to foreign nations.
- Maintaining friendly contacts between the US and other countries, including such things as arranging the reception by the president of new foreign ambassadors and advising on the recognition of new foreign countries and governments.
- Informing the American public about developments in the field of foreign policy, by publishing appropriate documents, official papers and other publications.

- Protecting American citizens, their welfare and their property abroad. (This last function involves the supervision of the Foreign Service of the United States, including the ambassadors, and administrative, consular, economic and political officers who manage the country's foreign relations. It is also concerned with the treatment of any Americans abroad, and it issues passports for their visits and processes visa applications for those entering America.)

See also *Foreign Policy*; *National Security Council*; *Secretary of State*

State Government

States are free to organise their state governments as they wish, subject only to the requirement that they maintain a Republican Form of Government. In practice, each state has adopted the three-branch system as used for the federal government.

All the states are bicameral (two legislative chambers) except for Nebraska which is unicameral. As with the federal government, the lower house is normally the larger of the two and generally senators or members of the upper house serve for four years, as against two for members of the lower chamber. Many of the states impose term limits on their legislators, largely because of the movement in recent decades towards greater professionalism in legislatures and the resulting development of career politicians. Until the 1960s, many state legislatures had met only in alternate years and even then had short sessions. Today, their operation varies across America. Some states, such as California, are highly professionalised, and have regular sessions and paid, full-time members. On the other hand, Kansas, Montana and seven other legislatures in rural states do not have annually paid members but make payments for each day when the chambers are in session.

Each state has an elected governor but, again, the substance of the position varies considerably. All but two of the governors serve for four years although, in New Hampshire and Vermont, they have only a two-year term but no limit on the maximum number of consecutive terms for which they can hold their position. There has been a trend in recent years towards greater gubernatorial power. In forty states, the governor has full responsibility for proposing the budget and, to the envy of most recent presidents, forty-one of the fifty also have some version of the line-item veto.

The fact that four of the last six presidents have been former governors suggests the degree of respect that the office now carries. In most states in recent years, there has been a greater recognition of the need to modernise gubernatorial authority, the more so as the states are now assuming some responsibilities that were once the prerogative of the federal government. This changed atmosphere has given governors a greater opportunity to make their mark by introducing, or urging, the use of state-initiated initiatives in economic, environmental and social policies.

State of the Union Address

The State of the Union Address is the title of the speech delivered by the president to a joint session of Congress at the start of each year. It outlines the chief executive's opinion on how the administration is faring and explains any policy initiatives being undertaking or planned for the near future. The speech is a requirement of the Constitution, Article 2, Section 3: 'The President shall from time to time give to Congress information of the State of the Union and recommend to their Consideration such measures as he shall judge necessary and expedient.' An address is generally not given in years in which a new president is inaugurated.

States

The fifty states are subnational entities within the US federal system that share sovereignty with the federal government. Each state has its own distinctive history and traditions. Americans see their states as being very important and relevant to their lives. They identify with their state as well as with the nation as a whole. Indeed, for several decades after the formation of the Republic, they tended to think of their state allegiance first and their national one second. The

motto of Illinois reflects this ambiguity of loyalty even today: 'State Sovereignty, National Union'. States remain a powerful reference point in US culture and it is state laws that citizens encounter more frequently than enactments of the federal government. Many federal laws are actually implemented through the states which modify them to suit their circumstances.

The fifty states vary enormously, all of them having distinctive histories, constitutions, governmental institutions and policies. Each has a substantial degree of autonomy so that the quality of public-service provision, the level of taxation and the degree of tolerance extended on matters sexual and social are very different in liberal Massachusetts from those in conservative Kansas. Singh (2003) points out that, on sexual matters, the variation is marked, there being laws theoretically forbidding adultery in twenty-four states, fornication in seventeen, oral sex fifteen and the sale (but not use) of marital aids eight:

> . . . the state of Alabama allows sex with donkeys and corpses, but punishes oral sex between husbands and wives . . . Most of these laws are unenforced . . . and unenforceable. Nevertheless, the differences illustrate how domestic regulations can differ sharply even on the most intimate and private of matters, according to the particular state's moral traditions and political culture.

In general, matters that lie entirely within the borders of the fifty states are their exclusive concern. These include such things as:

- regulations relating to business, industry, property and utilities
- the state criminal code
- working conditions within the state.

States and Washington

Relations between the states and the centre are at the very heart of federalism, for federalism seems to provide for an in-built tension between the two levels of government. The experience of American history reveals that the nature of federalism has changed over time. There was a broad tendency towards central control from the beginning and it accelerated with the greater state regulation following the establishment of the New Deal. The trend reached its peak in the 1960s. Sometimes this greater central power came about as a result of constitutional amendment; more often it was a response to prevailing economic and social conditions. Sometimes, too, the tendency towards central control was given a push by judicial decisions so that clauses in the Constitution were interpreted widely to provide the federal government with a broad scope for legislation. The result was that, in America, the centre gained power at the expense of the fifty states, especially in the area of major economic policy.

The centralising tendency was arrested in the closing decades of the twentieth century. In practice, American federalism has experienced growing interdependence. There is a developing trend to improve relations between federal, state and local governments, and, find common ground between them. In several areas of policy, such as education and transport, policies are made, funded and applied at all tiers. Hague and Harrop (2004) point out that in the United States:

> The original federal principle . . . was that the national and state governments would operate independently, each tier acting autonomously in its own constitutional sphere. In particular, the federal government was required to confine its activities to functions explicitly allocated to it, such as the power 'to lay and collect taxes, to pay the debts and provide for the common defence and welfare of the United States'. In the circumstances of eighteenth-century America, extensive coordination between federal and state administration was considered neither necessary nor feasible. This model of separated governments . . . has long since disappeared, overwhelmed by the demands of an integrated economy and society.

A resurgence of the state power

The states have enjoyed a resurgence and renewal in recent decades. This has come about as part of a backlash against the activist government of the Great Society years. The Johnson presidency had some important achievements to its credit, not least for the poor and ethnic minorities who were its main recipients. These achievements came at a time when state and local governments often seemed inert and inefficient. But the changes generated opposition and political opinion turned against them. Americans have always been lukewarm about 'big government', and opponents found increasing evidence that too many programmes had been badly run, were wasteful and undermined individual and local initiative.

There were several reasons for the state resurgence in the late twentieth century, among them:

- The strong performance of the Republicans in congressional and gubernatorial elections in recent years, encouraging the adoption of policies based on less federal intervention and more respect for states rights.
- Increased wariness of congressional politicians on Capitol Hill who had responsibility for introducing and passing federal laws. (The choice over the last generation of formen governors rather than members of congress as presidential candidates is an indication of a growing distrust of Washington politicians.) These former governors – Carter, but especially Reagan and Clinton – have been well versed in state perspectives on the appropriate national–state relationship.
- A feeling that the federal government has failed to respond to assorted economic and social problems, so that the states have had to act on their own; the cutting of many grants-in-aid further enhanced the tendency towards state self-reliance, spurring state politicians to reform.
- The handing over of decision-making powers to the states on important subjects such as welfare, especially via the 1996 Welfare Reform Act. From then on, although there was a national framework, it was increasingly left to the states to decide whether to hand over money to individual claimants, and the level at which help should be given.
- Rulings of the Supreme Court, a number

of which have supported the states in their attempts to make important inroads on topics such as the availability of abortion.

- The increased willingness – indeed, enthusiasm – of some states to experiment with new policies; state administrations have been notably more vigorous and creative than they were in the heyday of 'big government'.

Innovation across American states

Several states have been active in Washington DC in recent years, lobbying on their own behalf and employing professional lobbying companies to help them in their bid for federal help. They have also recognised, however, the need to become more self-reliant. This has led to more creative thinking, and some states have been fertile in devising initiatives:

- California has been restrictive on the rights of entry of illegal immigrants and the use of affirmative-action programmes. These and many more policies have resulted from the widespread use of direct legislation.
- Hawaii has introduced a British–style scheme of health care, and Oregon, too, has promoted a new system for the delivery of health provision.
- Wisconsin has experimented with parental choice and a voucher system in state education.
- Several states have tried out different approaches to issues of law and order, the main common factor between them being that policies have generally veered towards 'toughness'. Texas is noted for its frequent use of the death penalty and its 'boot camps' for young offenders; other states have employed policies ranging from 'zero tolerance' to registration of sex offenders.

See also *Governors*; *States' Rights*

States' Rights

The term 'states' rights' refers to the protection and promotion of state government policies over those of the federal government. The fifty states possess certain rights and political powers in relation to the federal government, as laid down in the Constitution. Moreover, as advocates of states' rights often point out, the Tenth Amendment lays down that: 'The powers not delegated to the United States by the Constitution, nor prohibited by it to the States, are reserved to the States respectively, or to the people.'

The states' rights concept is usually used to defend a state law that the federal government seeks to override, or to oppose a perceived violation by the federal government of the bounds of federal authority. States' rights have been especially controversial at certain times in US history, most obviously in the period leading upto the Civil War in which Southern states wished to retain their segregationist stance, and in the 1950s and 1960s when segregation was again under attack.

As a broad trend, federal power has expanded at the expense of that of the states throughout US history, a position supported by the Supreme Court decision in *McCulloch* v. *Maryland* (1819) which declared that the federal government has not only enumerated powers but also implied ones as well.

Advocates of states' rights fear any erosion of the position of the states. Their critics often portray the term as a code word for segregation, for segregation was a symbolic issue in the struggle to ensure that states' rights were preserved.

See also *States*

Strict Constructionists

Strict constructionists favour a narrow interpretation of the Constitution which involves seeking to determine and observe the exact intentions of the Founding Fathers. They favour a literalist interpretation and are unwilling to adapt the Constitution to suit modern principles and values, as is favoured by flexible constructionists.

See also *Originalism*

Sun Belt

The sun belt is the area of southern and southwestern United States extending across fifteen states from Virginia and Florida in the southeast to Nevada in the south-west, and including southern California. It is so-called because of its sunny weather and its rapid economic and population growth since the 1960s. In that time, it has experienced a vast influx of retirees who have moved there to benefit from the warm climate.

As the population of the region increased and its economy expanded, so too did its political influence. All winners of presidential elections, from the time of Lyndon Johnson to George W. Bush (1964 and 2000), were from the sun-belt, reflecting in part its growing importance in the Electoral College (given the increased representation in Congress of key states like Texas, Arizona and Florida). The area has long been characterised by relatively conservative voting patterns although the growth of the African American vote in some cities has assisted the Democrats to gain control.

Super Delegates

Super delegates are those individuals who are invited to attend the national party conventions as a result of their status within the party, rather than by qualifying to do so via primary elections and caucus outcomes. They include the ranks of the party leadership (e.g., members of Congress and the national committees) and employees of relevant interest groups. Unlike the majority of delegates, these groups are not selected by state party members.

Super delegates have the same voting rights as elected delegates, a factor that might have proved significant in 2008. The super delegates made up approximately one-fifth of the total number of delegates to the Democratic Party Convention. At one time, it seemed as though Hillary Clinton might await the outcome of their support before deciding to withdraw from the close race for the Democratic nomination. In the event, Obama won a majority of the pledged delegates as well as of the super delegates so that there was no question of the latter voting against the wishes of the majority of the elected delegates.

The Republicans also include some party officials as delegates without regard to primary or caucus outcomes but the term 'super delegate' is more commonly associated with the Democratic Party.

See also *National Nominating Conventions*

Superpower

A superpower is a world power endowed with enough economic and military might to enable it influence events and to use its strength throughout the world. It is considered to represent a higher level of power than a great power. Historically, the term refers to the United States and the USSR in the age of the Cold War but, subsequent to 1989, it is used in reference only to the US.

The main characteristics of a superpower have been summed up in the definition provided by Nossal:

> generally this term was used to signify a political community that occupied a continental-sized landmass, had a sizable population (relative at least to other major powers); a superordinate economic capacity, including ample indigenous supplies of food and natural resources; enjoyed a high degree of non-dependence on international intercourse; and, most importantly, had a well-developed nuclear capacity (eventually normally defined as second-strike capability).

See also *Cold War*; *Foreign Policy*

Supreme Court

The Supreme Court is the highest federal court in the United States. Its existence is provided for in Article III of the Constitution, although Congress is given the power to determine the size of the Court.

Membership

The Court currently comprises a chief justice and eight associate justices. Members are appointed for life by the president.

Procedure

The Court term begins in early October and runs through until June or July depending on the workload. Throughout the term, it alternates between two weeks of open court, known as sessions, and two weeks of recess, during which the justices read petitions and write opinions. In the period when the Court is in session, the justices attend from Monday to Wednesday to hear oral arguments presented by the attorneys whose presentations are strictly time limited. *Briefs* (written documents) will have been presented before the hearing so that, in the oral sessions, attorneys are supposed to discuss the case rather than read from a prepared text.

The more crucial stage is the *conference work*, during which the justices meet on two occasions a week to discuss and decide cases. The chief justice will initiate the discussion of each case by outlining and commenting on the main issues as he or she sees them. Then, in order of seniority, the other eight members of the Court are invited to comment. If the position of some justices is not clear at this stage, a formal, but still preliminary, vote will be taken. After the vote, the chief justice assigns the writing of the opinion to one of his or her colleagues. Others may decide to write *concurring opinions* (in agreement with the conclusion but not the reasoning of the majority) or *dissenting opinions* (that disagree with the majority conclusion). As the drafts are completed, the others comment upon them and may suggest changes in wording and reasoning. Sometimes this is a time-consuming procedure for opinions may diverge sharply. The opinion-writing stage is completed only when all the justices have decided which opinion they support. When this has happened, the Court judgment is announced.

The Supreme Court decides cases by a majority vote and its decisions are final. It handles some 10,000 petitions per year. In an average year, around ninety are the subject of oral argument and seventy to eighty are decided on the basis of a signed, written opinion.

Role

The Constitution said little about the judiciary, and the status of the Court is only briefly sketched. Judicial power was vested in one Supreme Court 'and in such inferior courts as the Congress may from time to time ordain and establish', but it was unclear how important the main Court was to be. Few specific powers were set out but neither did the document seek to limit its role.

The expectation in the very early days of the Republic was that it would play a lesser role in the newly established governing arrangements than the other two branches of government.

The Court stands at the apex of the federal court system and is the only one specifically created by the Constitution. A decision of the Supreme Court cannot be appealed to any other court. Congress has the power to fix the number of judges sitting on the Court and, within limits, decide what kind of cases it may hear – but it cannot change the powers given to the Supreme Court by the Constitution itself.

The Court has original jurisdiction in only two kinds of cases – those involving foreign dignitaries, and those in which a state is a party. In all other cases, the Court is involved on appeal from lower courts or from the supreme courts of the fifty states. Of the 160 to 170 cases it decides in an average year, most are concerned with the interpretation of a particular law, or the intentions of Congress in passing it.

However, An important part of the work of the Supreme Court however, involves the determination of whether Executive acts or legislation conform to the Constitution. This is the power of *judicial review*, which is not specifically referred to in the original document. It is a doctrine inferred by the Court from its reading of the Constitution, however, and it was propounded very clearly in the *Marbury* v. *Madison* case (1803): 'A legislative act contrary to the Constitution is not law . . . it is emphatically the province and duty of the judicial department to say what the law is.'

The Court and political controversy

Courts tend to have a reputation for conservatism. Often, they resist the tide of innovative enthusiasm, interpreting the law as it is, guarding precedents and securing rights that have been traditionally recognised. The American Supreme Court has not regarded the Constitution as fixed and unalterable but rather as an evolving body of ideals. It has preserved the fundamental principles which underpin the whole political system and create its basic character but it has sought to reformulate them at various times in a way which makes them relevant to the problems of the day. In particular, it was the Court that was instrumental in the drive to establish the rights of American blacks on a firmer footing in the post-war era. By doing so, it was effecting a major change – one resisted by a large section of the population. It was not expected to exhibit such extraordinary influence when the Constitution was devised.

The Supreme Court is a complex body for it is neither a completely judicial nor a completely political/policymaking body. As Grant observes: 'Politics play a crucial role in the appointment, working and decision-making of the . . . Court, and many of its judgements have broad policy implications.' Yet, if its work and personnel are involved in political controversy at various times, it is also supposed to interpret the Constitution, a function that places it above the everyday political fray.

The Court has constantly been involved in political matters even though, in theory, it has generally stayed clear of questions of direct political controversy. Its rulings can, and often have, had political implications so that, when in *Dred Scott* v. *Sandford* (1857) the Court declared that a slave was a property and had no rights, this was a serious blow to those campaigning for an end to slavery. In other words, a judicial judgment had had an impact on the political process.

In the 1930s, a Court reflecting the conservatism of the 1920s overturned programmes aimed at fighting the economic devastation of the Great Depression. Roosevelt was dissatisfied with the Court's performance for its members posed a threat to the New Deal by their willingness to strike down key measures as 'unconstitutional'. The broad objection raised was that the federal government was exceeding its authority, and that the president and his advisers were too willing to play down constitutional considerations. Since then, there has been much debate about the rights and wrongs of the issue, some writers believing that legislation should have been more carefully drafted while others took the view that political malice was involved. Four of the nine justices were hostile to the New Deal, seeing it as a threat to property rights and the powers of the states. Several of them were elderly and conservative.

In the 1950s and 1960s, the judgments of the Warren Court ushered in one of the most liberal periods in the history of the Supreme Court. Some of its decisions aroused intense controversy, as indicated by the abortive movement at one time during Warren's stewardship to replace the existing Court with a new Constitutional Court of fifty members.

The political role of the Court is well established, and the justices are widely recognised as important players in the political process. They are appointed for political reasons and, after their appointment, they inhabit an intensely political atmosphere. It may seem strange to many people that matters affecting the fate of society are ultimately decided by nine unelected justices who, once on the bench, have no direct contact with public opinion. But, as has often been pointed out, 'they read the election returns, too'. In other words, they understand prevailing pressures, and react to changing moods among the population, as in their decisions on affirmative action in recent years.

At various times, the Court runs into difficulties with the left and the right, for both liberals and conservatives sometimes find its decisions controversial and unacceptable. This is because it is charged with handling issues that are of vital importance to democracy and society at large. Yet justices use their powers sparingly for they realise that, if they allow themselves to become out of step with popular opinion for too long, then the reputation of the Court will be damaged. They also wish to avoid open confrontation with the other branches of government. They understand the need to interpret the Constitution in the light of the requirements of today's industrialised society, and thus ensure that it remains a living document which continues to command general assent. The Court has performed its role rather well, and Professor Archibald Cox (1987), the Watergate Special Prosecutor, has explained the reasons for this success:

The Court must know us better than we know ourselves . . . the roots of its decisions must already be in the nation. The aspirations voiced by the Court must be those the community is willing not only to avow but in the end to live by, for the power of the constitutional decisions rests upon the accuracy of the Court's perceptions of this kind of common will and upon the Court's ability, by expressing its perception, ultimately to command a consensus.

Those who serve on the Supreme Court invariably survive those who put them there. This means that there is a thread of judicial continuity from one presidential administration to another and that the Court can act as a powerful counter to the other two branches of government.

See also *Burger, Warren*; *Judicial Activism*; *Judicial Restraint*; *Judicial Review*; *Roberts, John*; *Warren, Earl*; *Writ of Certiorari*

Swann v. *Charlotte-Mecklenburg Board of Education* (1971)

Swann v. *Charlotte-Mecklenburg Board of Education* (1971) was an important Supreme Court case dealing with the busing of students in order to promote integration in schools.

The 1954 Brown ruling had eventually led to the abandonment of *de jure* segretation but de facto segregation remained in operation because states and school boards proved unco-operative. Moreover, the neighbourhoods that schools served were divided by race so that, as a consequence, the schools serving those neighbourhoods were either black or white dominated. In 1971, the justices sanctioned the busing of pupils across cities to ensure a racial mix. This would ensure that schools would be genuinely integrated and that all students would receive equal educational opportunities regardless of their race.

See also *Busing*

Swing States

Swing states are states in which no single party dominates, resulting in intense competition for victory in presidential and other elections. States such as New Jersey are liable to switch from one party to another and therefore have a significant role in determining the outcome of contests. When those states have a large population, they carry sizeable weight in the Electoral College.

They are therefore the focus of strong campaigning for parties and their candidates, with heavy financial and personnel resources being devoted to them.

Political consultants and pundits identify the swing states where close votes might prove crucial to the outcome of the presidential election. Those included are mainly located in and around the southern Mountain States, the Rust Belt (aka the Manufacturing Belt) and Florida. In 2008, they were (Electoral College votes in brackets): Colorado (9), Florida (27), Indiana (11), Michigan (17), Minnesota (10), Missouri (11), Nevada (5), New Hampshire (4), New Jersey (15), New Mexico (5), North Carolina (15), Ohio (20), Pennsylvania (21), Virginia (13), Washington (11) and Wisconsin (10). In total, they accounted for 210 votes in the College.

Symbolic Speech

Symbolic free speech refers to speech-related acts such as picketing or flag burning which, like actual speech, are protected under the First Amendment because they involve the communication of ideas and/or opinions. They are sometimes referred to as 'speech plus', for they exceed the normal understanding of what speech involves. The anti-war student who walked along a Californian court-house corridor with the words 'Fuck the draft' on the back of his jacket was not held to be in contempt of court, the majority opinion of the Supreme Court in the case of *Cohen* v. *California* (1971) explained that: 'While the particular four-letter word being litigated here is perhaps more distasteful than most others of its genre, it nevertheless is often true that one man's vulgarity is another's lyric.' The general position regarding such symbolic speech was outlined in the flag-burning case *Texas* v. *Johnson* (1989) in which the justices proclaimed that: 'If there is a bedrock principle underlying the First Amendment, it is that Government may not prohibit the expression of an idea simply because society finds the idea offensive or disagreeable.'

See also *First Amendment*; Texas *v.* Johnson *(1989)*

T

Tammany Hall

Tammany Hall was the name given to the Democratic Party political machine that controlled New York City politics from the mayoral victory of Fernando Wood in 1854 until the election of John O'Brien in 1932. Tammany Hall was seriously weakened by the election of Fiorello La Guardia on a 'fusion' ticket of reform-inclined Democrats, independents and moderate Republicans in 1934, though it enjoyed a brief resurgence in the 1950s.

The seventy-eight-year period between those two elections marks the time in which Tammany was the city's driving political force although its origins actually date to the late eighteenth century and its fall from power was not truly complete until the mid-1960s. Although the term technically refers to the host building in New York, 'Tammany Hall' became a synonym for the well-organised, urban political machine run by city bosses.

See also *Machine Politics*

Television and Politics

Ninety-nine per cent of American households have at least one television and most have more than one. Today, television is the main source of information about politics and current affairs for the majority of Americans.

For several decades, three network evening news programmes had more than 90 per cent of the viewers for television news, with news being available only at set times in the morning and early evening hours. But the stranglehold of the traditional networks, ABC, CBS and NBC, has been broken with the arrival of new ones such as that run by Rupert Murdoch (Fox TV), nearly 1,000 local commercial stations which – even if the majority of them are linked to the 'big three' – have become increasingly autonomous, and cable television. Cable is now available in more than 60 per cent of American households, and it is this which has had a profound effect on the way in which news is presented. Cable News Network (CNN) and C-Span have transformed coverage of current affairs. In 2006, more than half the people watching cable news were watching Fox News (as they have since 2001) although new competitors, such as MSNBC and Headline News, have begun to chip away at some of Fox's viewing figures.

Political coverage

Political coverage on television is handled in several ways, mostly via programmes which are scheduled by those who control the media. It appears in a variety of different types of programme. These include:

- current affairs programmes and news programmes (of which there are many more than ever before, so that Americans can obtain their news from broadcast sources at any time of the day)
- the newer forms of 'infotainment', which use the techniques of entertainment to present more serious issues. There are many talk shows, with hosts such as Rush Limbaugh, Larry King and Phil Donahue. Others have

less political agendas – such as that featuring Oprah Winfrey. Candidates for political office are keen to appear in programmes such as the *Donohue Show*. Via such outlets, they have a chance to sell themselves and canvass their ideas, and the public has the opportunity to learn more about them.

- the regular broadcasting of the proceedings of the Senate and the House of Representatives
- the special outlets through which presidential candidates gain access to television time, providing detailed coverage of aspects of the campaign. Debates are organised between the main contenders. In addition, the candidates and those who organise their campaigns make extensive use of political advertising as a means of 'getting the message across'.
- Finally, once elected, the president may make use of the televised presidential press conference.

In recent years, the trend has been for most political programmes to be presented in a way that grabs the attention. Rather than the early methods of 'talking heads', round-table discussions between weighty interviewees and a generally serious treatment of heavy issues, the emphasis is on featuring stories which are 'made for television', with good pictorial backup. American viewers now seem to be less 'switched on' to overtly political programmes. Today, viewing of the national conventions is markedly less common than in the early to mid-1970s, whereas the 'talk show' format attracts vast audiences.

Such developments feed the fears of those who feel that television tends to trivialise and sensationalise politics. Producers are always on the lookout for opportunities to stress the confrontational approach, with plenty of personality clashes and scenes of groups and individuals locked in disagreement and sometimes physical conflict. As elections approach, these tendencies become ever more apparent.

Television and electioneering

Television is a medium which is infatuated with personalities and, in particular, political leaders. Parties want their presidential candidates to be 'good on television'. Unsurprisingly, politicians are highly sensitive to the way in which their behaviour and actions are reported. As television is so all-pervasive, its handling of personalities and issues is highly significant in the political process.

Television has now become the most important of the ways via which the candidates seek to gain popular approval and support. Although party managers may still be interviewed and seek to use the medium to promote the party cause, it is the candidate who is the focus of media attention. He or she and the team of consultants are constantly on the lookout for opportunities to ensure that they gain favourable coverage and are vigilant in watching out for any signs of bias against them. They attempt to 'manage the news'. News management involves ensuring that journalists get the right stories (information slanted to their particular viewpoint) backed up with good pictures. It can range from crude political arm-twisting to more subtle means. Advisers dream up sound bites and photo opportunities, and use their spin doctors to put across an appropriate line. They try to book interviews with 'softer' interviewers, rather than undergo a potentially damaging interrogation. They seek to control the agenda, sticking to themes on which they are strong and avoiding (or playing down) embarrassing issues.

Political consultancy is an area that has mushroomed; there are at least some 10,000 consultants in the United States. These media advisers understand the way in which television works and what their candidate needs to do to create the right impression. They know that television is not just another channel of communication. It has changed the very way it has become necessary to communicate political ideas. Television has also made the 'look' of a politician vital. When voters think of Nixon, Reagan or Clinton, it is their image, how they look on television, which is the main memory. Television is a medium in which attractive people flourish. Conventional good looks are an advantage – fatness or baldness quite the opposite.

Television has actually changed what is said, as well as how it is said. The form of debate is influenced by the professional persuaders. As we have seen, politicians increasingly talk in memorable sound bites. The emphasis is on broad themes, the phrases being simple and often repeated. Often political language is couched in emotional terms. If the message can be illustrated by a suitable picture, so much the better.

Politicians and television

Politicians are highly sensitive to the ways in which their behaviour and actions are reported. They realise that television, in particular, can do them great damage. It also provides them with a remarkable opportunity to influence opinion, not least in the presidential debates. Three presidents have been 'naturals' for television, just as Franklin Roosevelt was for radio. John F. Kennedy portrayed an image of youth and glamour, and lifted the horizons of many Americans as he offered them a vision of 'new frontiers'. Ronald Reagan, a trained actor, looked good and sounded sincere. Bill Clinton was effective in speaking directly to the viewers. He was, on occasion, able to use television to launch his comeback after going through a bad patch. His style was, in any case, suited to the modern era but he was also well served by his scriptwriters. They were said to spend much time in his company and, as a result, were able to incorporate words and phrases that he used in his private conversation. By doing so, they were able to convey the character of the person, in Clinton's case one who does not favour ornate rhetoric but likes to tell his story in a relaxed, conversational style.

Television as a means of communication: strengths and weaknesses

Today, television is the main tool for campaigning, to the extent that – as Bowler and Farrell put it – 'free elections in a modern democracy would easily collapse if the mass media . . . were to ignore election campaigning'. Television has had its effect at the local level. The roots of party activity are atrophying, and canvassing and pamphleteering are less in evidence. As the same writers point out: 'Local electioneering has been overtaken by the nationalisation of the campaign and the growth of the mass media.'

The quality of news and current affairs programming matters for the public and for the politicians. Ideally, coverage will be fair, balanced and interesting, straightforward and accessible for those who want a brief review, and clear and comprehensive for those seeking a more detailed understanding. For many people, watching a news bulletin or reading a tabloid newspaper gives them as much information as they require. Others want more searching analysis and reflective comment to enable them to understand the background story behind the news.

Television has weaknesses as a source of political education, some of which relate to the need for balance and impartiality. In interviews with leading television personalities, it is sometimes difficult for politicians to get their views across for their replies can be cut off prematurely or they may not be given a chance to provide an adequate answer. Sometimes a sharp intervention by the chairperson of a discussion is necessary to get a response from professional politicians who are skilled at being evasive but, on occasion, the interview can be dominated by the personality of the interviewer more than by the answer being attempted.

Furthermore, there is a need for speed and brevity on television, and great issues are sometimes not handled at length, arguments are left unexplored and, to keep programmes alive and entertaining, they can be superficial and trivial. In-depth analysis – how events came to be – is often lacking. Yet, at best, discussion can be profound, elucidating the arguments on key issues and exploring the backgrounds of incidents and decisions.

Over the last decade, there has been some disquiet about the standard of news and current affairs coverage on television. Several allegations have been made, notably that:

- Television news was often reduced to the role of running other people's stories. Major issues often derived more from what was gathered from the newspapers than from original research undertaken by a television news operation. Good investigation by television journalists was increasingly a rarity.
- The content and presentation of too many

stories were dictated by the ploys of spin doctors and media experts who know how to manage the news. What resulted was an obsession with sound bites and picture opportunities, while issues were neglected. As President Jimmy Carter once lamented: 'The peripheral aspects become the headlines, but the basic essence of what you stand for and what you hope to accomplish is never reported.'

- Though there were more and more bulletins on different stations and at different times of the day, most national coverage repeated the same stories about the same issues and the same people. The manner of presentation might vary and the information was sometimes regurgitated with a slightly differing slant – depending on the news editor involved – but this did not amount to genuine choice. The range of topics which made up the agenda was too narrow.

See also *Election Campaigns*; *Mass Media*

Tennessee Valley Authority (TVA)

The Tennessee Valley Authority is a federally owned corporation created soon after the Roosevelt administration assumed office. In April 1933, he asked Congress to establish it as a means of providing navigation, flood control, electricity generation, irrigation, and the broad economic development of the Tennessee Valley, a region of the United States that had been adversely affected by the Great Depression. The TVA administered a broad area of seven states, including much of Tennessee, parts of Alabama, Kentucky and Mississippi, as well as small slices of Georgia, North Carolina, and Virginia. The TVA also served several other purposes including: improved use of agricultural land; preservation of wildlife; production of fertiliser; and reforestation.

At Muscle Shoals, Alabama, on the Tennessee River, a \$145-million hydroelectric plant and two munitions factories had been built during World War I. After the war, senators Norris of Nebraska and John Rankin of Mississippi drafted a bill that would enable these facilities to be converted for peacetime purposes. Norris,

a Progressive within the Republican Party, twice persuaded Congress to legislate to this end but, on both occasions, his proposals were vetoed by the president, Calvin Coolidge and then Herbert Hoover. As mainstream Republicans, they both viewed such a scheme as a form of socialist planning that was unacceptable in the United States. By contrast, it was just the sort of innovative idea that appealed to Franklin Roosevelt. He recognised its potential to stimulate the economy of one of the poorest regions in the country.

Some Americans, particularly those who worked in the private utility companies that produced and distributed electricity, were troubled by the concept and development of the TVA. They felt that government should not compete with private enterprise and complained bitterly when it became clear that TVA power was distributed at lower unit costs than the rates they were charging.

In its overall conception, the TVA was one of the most ambitious projects of the New Deal. Its comprehensive nature encompassed many of FDR's own interests in conservation, public utility regulation, regional planning, agricultural development and the social and economic improvement of the 'forgotten Americans'.

Today, the TVA is the nation's largest public power company, with 33,000 megawatts of dependable generating capacity. Through 158 locally owned distributors, TVA provides power to about 8.7 million residents of the Tennessee Valley.

See also *New Deal*; *Roosevelt, Franklin*

Term Limits

Term limits are constitutional restrictions on the number of terms that office holders in the Executive or Legislature may serve in a particular elected position. They tend to be employed in presidential systems as a means of curbing the potential for dictatorship in a situation where a leader might effectively become a 'president for life'. Sometimes, they involve an absolute limit on the number of terms an office holder can serve. In other cases, the limits are on the number of consecutive terms for which an incumbent might remain in office.

The debate on how long any incumbent should serve has a long history. The United States first placed a formal limit on the time a person could hold a public position in 1776, in that case to the governorship of Delaware. The Founding Fathers considered limiting the period for which any member of the Executive or legislature should sit but decided to avoid establishing such a restriction. One hundred and seventy-five years later, a restriction of two terms was imposed on service as president, via the passage of the Twenty-second Amendment. Today, limits are in place on a number of other political offices as well, including thirty-nine governorships and legislators in eighteen states. There is little uniformity in their application.

In the nineteenth century, it was customary for elected politicians to limit themselves. It was only in the twentieth century that member of Congress began to exceed two terms in the House of Representatives and one in the Senate. The development of the seniority rule for committee chairs inspired representatives to seek a longer term. The introduction of direct election for senators in 1912 encouraged them to seek an extra six years. In the 1990s, however, there was renewed interest in 'term limits'. They were seen as a method of preventing individuals from becoming too powerful and as a way of countering the advantages that incumbents enjoyed in the electoral process.

Term limits were approved in the 1990 elections in Colorado, and thereafter in several – mainly western – states. In the 1994 elections, the tenth item in the Contract with America, the Citizen Legislature Act, dealt with the issue. The Republican leadership urged the need for a first-ever congressional vote to place limits on career politicians and replace them with citizen legislators.

Several factors inspired a desire to curb career politicians from staying in power on Capitol Hill. They included the facts that:

1. all politicians – and members of Congress foremost among them – were increasingly viewed with disdain by many voters who had a deep scepticism about the motives of those who served them. They wished to 'throw the rascals out', believing that they could 'clean up' a sleazy Congress by ensuring that fresh faces appear to replace older, seasoned Washington politicians who knew how to 'play the system'. Yet, despite this distaste for Congress and many members of Congress, voters seemed more than happy to re-elect their own representatives in either chamber, a point that leads to the second explanation.

2. in recent years, incumbents have been re-elected with great regularity. In 1994, no Republican incumbent was defeated in any gubernatorial, Senate or house race. Even the Democrats lost only two incumbent scalps in the Senate, although they lost thirty-four in the lower house. For a variety of reasons, incumbency presented an advantage over opponents so that, once elected, some members of Congress were staying on Capitol Hill for a long (too long?) time.

3. allied to the point about long-time career politicians was the feeling that there were too many incentives for members of Congress to stay 'on the Hill'. Perquisites and salaries were widely seen as generous, too lavish for the many Americans who had a much less comfortable life.

In 1993 an Arkansas judge found the term limit approved in that state in 1992 was 'unconstitutional', in that it established a new qualification for congressional membership in addition to age, citizenship and residency which are laid down in Article 1 of the Constitution. The same happened in Washington where the limit would have allowed senators a maximum of twelve years' service and representatives only six. The court would not accept this even though, on the expiry of their official maximum term, there was provision for the voters to 'write in' their names on the ballot paper so that they could serve again. The question was taken to the Supreme Court. In 1995, it ruled in the case of *US Term Limits, Inc.* v. *Thornton* that states could not impose limits on the time *served by their federal legislators*. The ruling did not apply to state legislators.

Should there be term limits for members of Congress?

Against:

- Term limits are unnecessary in that the American system provides a check on those in power through regular (in the case of the House of Representatives, frequent) elections. The incumbent can be challenged from within his/her party in a primary election and by the voters as a whole in the general election.
- It seems undemocratic to impose limits on the electorate's right of choice, for limits on members of Congress are actually limits on voters. They cannot reward able men and women who have given good service.
- If there are problems of low ethics and scandalous or self-interested behaviour, the answer is to legislate against the evil or to vote against the offending members of Congress.

For:

1. Term limits would weaken the stranglehold of long servers in Congress, people who command excessive influence by virtue of their seniority. Fresh faces may be talented, as well as being less 'corrupted' by long service in the system.
2. A 'citizen legislature' would replace a chamber of career politicians. Members of Congress would be more in touch with those who elect them and include 'ordinary people'.
3. Applying term limits to members of Congress is a logical extension of the curbs on presidential service and on governorships and legislators in several states.

Territories

Territories are geographical and political units that are administered by the American government but are not part of any state. These territories were created to govern newly acquired land at a time when the borders of the United States were still evolving. Some territories, which were acquired through annexation, have been *incorporated* as part of the United States, their

system of government having been approved via an Organic Act passed by the Congress. These now-incorporated territories existed from 1789 to 1959 during which time thirty-one territories applied for and won statehood. No *unincorporated territories* (often known as 'overseas possessions') existed until 1898 when the United States acquired possessions as a result of the Spanish-American War, including the Philippines, Guam and Puerto Rico.

The position regarding the status of incorporated and unincorporated territories was established in the Supreme Court ruling in *People of Puerto Rico* v. *Shell Oil Co.* (1937) in which the Court decided that the Sherman Antitrust Act which had referred only to 'territories', applied to Puerto Rico even though it was not an incorporated territory of the United States. Incorporated territory refers to land which has been irrevocably incorporated within the sovereignty of the US and is subject to the American Constitution in its entirety. Unincorporated territory is land held by the United States and to which Congress applies selected parts of the Constitution.

Today there are fourteen territories controlled by the United States:

American Samoa
Baker Island
Guam
Howland Island
Jarvis Island
Johnston Atoll
Kingman Reef
Midway Islands
Navassa Island
Northern Mariana Islands
Palmyra Atoll
Puerto Rico
Virgin Islands
Wake Island

Terrorism

Terrorism refers to the use of methods, such as bombing, hijacking, kidnapping, murder and torture, against non-combatants to spread fear, horror and outrage to promote the political ends of the perpetrators. Those who use, or threaten to use, such political violence tend to see themselves as freedom fighters for a particular cause. For this reason, no one definition of terrorism commands universal acceptance. While most people agree that terrorism exists, few can agree on what it is.

Terrorism is easier to condemn than to define. It is a word of abuse for your enemies and, as such, it is often loosely used or misused. One person's freedom fighter is another person's murderous terrorist. But, since the attack on the World Trade Center and many others worldwide, there is now more consensus that indiscriminate attacks on civilians are intolerable, however the crime is described. After 9/11, many people in Washington DC and elsewhere said that one might not be able to define terrorism but one could recognise it when one sees it. This approach may work for extreme cases but is less useful for lesser ones. Hence the long-running debate in America about Noraid, which raised funds in the United States to be spent on assisting the work of the Provisional IRA in Northern Ireland. The United Kingdom viewed such fund-raising as aiding terrorism while many Americans did not. Only in the wake of the events of September 2001 did the US government finally clamp down on it.

The Department of Defense (DoD) defines terrorism as: 'The calculated use of unlawful violence or threat of unlawful violence to inculcate fear; intended to coerce or to intimidate governments or societies in the pursuit of goals that are generally political, religious, or ideological.' The definition preferred by the State Department is: 'Premeditated, politically motivated violence perpetrated against non-combatant targets by subnational groups or clandestine agents, usually intended to influence an audience.'

Domestic and global terrorism

In the United States, acts classified as domestic terrorism are uncommon. The FBI's Terrorist Research and Analytical Center defined domestic terrorism in 1994 as 'the unlawful use of force or violence, committed by a group(s) of two or more individuals, against persons or property to intimidate or coerce a government, the civilian population, or any segment thereof, in furtherance of

political or social objectives'. On this basis, it found that, of those incidents that were confirmed as or suspected to be terrorist acts between 1980 and 2000, 250 out of 335 were carried out by American citizens.

Under current American law, as laid down in the United States Patriot Act passed after the attacks of 9/11, acts of domestic terrorism are those which:

1. involve acts dangerous to human life that are a violation of the criminal laws of the United States or of any state
2. appear to be intended (a) to intimidate or coerce a civilian population, (b) to influence the policy of a government by intimidation or coercion or (c) to affect the conduct of a government by mass destruction, assassination, or kidnapping and
3. occur primarily within the territorial jurisdiction of the United States.

The term 'global (or international) terrorism' means terrorism involving the territory or the citizens of more than one country. The organisations and governments involved in global terrorism are designated as 'terroristic', all participants involved being labelled as 'terrorists'.

Global terrorism has been a problem for the international community for many years. But, previously, terrorists were limited in their reach and had relatively confined political objectives. Although the general rationale for terrorism remains unchanged – that terrorists believe it is both right and necessary to use terrorism to achieve their aims – the nature of the current threat is different. Osama Bin Laden and al-Qaeda have dominated the headlines but the threat does not always come from one person or from a hierarchical or coherent organisation that is readily identifiable as an opponent. The coherence of the threat lies rather in the ideas which people such as Bin Laden have propagated and which are taken up transnationally by others who find them compelling and attractive. They often use the tools of globalisation to realise their aims: the Internet, mobile communications, the media, the easy covert international movement of people and funds, and opportunities for identity theft all being involved. As a result, the threat has become fluid, global, and relatively unpredictable.

In recent years, the United States has been much preoccupied with international terrorism and the states that sponsor it. State sponsors are those adjudged by the Secretary of State 'to have repeatedly provided support for acts of international terrorism'. The listing of such states began in December 1979 when, with Iraq, Libya, South Yemen and Syria were classified as meeting the criteria. Currently, the list comprises Cuba, Iran, North Korea, Sudan and Syria.

See also *Attack on World Trade Center (9/11 Attacks)*; *War on Terrorism*

Texas v. *Johnson* (1989)

Texas v. *Johnson* was a decision by the Supreme Court that invalidated the laws against flag desecration then in force in forty-eight states. By a vote of five to four, the justices concluded that the burning of the US flag, the 'stars and stripes', represented a form of protected speech under the First Amendment and was therefore a constitutional right.

In 1984, Gregory Johnson had burned an American flag in protest against Reaganite policies. He was tried, convicted and sentenced to one year in jail under a Texas law outlawing such behaviour. After the Texas Court of Criminal Appeals reversed the conviction, the case went to the Supreme Court which had to decide whether desecretion, however committed, was a form of free speech and therefore protected by the Constitution. The Court found that Johnson's act was 'expressive conduct' of a political nature that could be categorised as free speech. Whatever the offence given by the activity, this did not justify any curtailment of the right to free speech 'simply because society finds the idea itself offensive or disagreeable'.

See also *First Amendment*; *Symbolic Speech*

Think Tanks

Think tanks are policy institutes that carry out detailed research and provide analysis of, and information on, a range of policy ideas and programmes. Bodies, such as the Progressive Policy Institute, have taken on much of the work of developing new policy options. The libertarian Cato Institute, the American Enterprise Institute and others similarly wield considerable influence.

Think tanks are often ideologically based, their ideas sometimes being influential with the Executive and Legislature, and with the parties that share a broad affinity of perspective. In recent times, they have become increasingly ideological and partisan in character although, because many of them have tax-exempt status, they are prevented from directly campaigning and lobbying. They have been labelled as 'the shock troops of the conservative revolution' by the Heritage Foundation which is itself a prime and highly influential example of the genre. Through aggressive marketing of its policy papers and via its connections to the Reagan and Bush administrations, the foundation crafted the blueprint for such Reaganite policies as the Star Wars Defense Strategy and trickle-down economic theory. It had substantial input into the writing of the Republican Contract with America.

Third Parties

By a third party, we usually mean one that is capable of gathering a sizeable percentage of popular support and regularly gains seats in the Legislature. On occasion, third parties may win – or threaten to win – enough support to influence the outcome of an election and the control of government and, in particular regions or constituencies, they may consistently break through the usual two-party system. We do not usually refer to parties that poll only a tiny percentage of the vote and almost never gain representation as 'third parties'. Such organisations are really minor parties. The terms are often used interchangeably, in textbooks. Whether we describe them as third parties, minor parties or small parties, we are concerned here with all of those bodies which are parties but which operate outside the mainstream of the two–party battle.

Most small parties in America are minor ones that may or may not be permanent. They rarely gain more than a tiny percentage of the popular vote. From time to time, however, there are those that do erupt on to the national scene, and make headline news as they bid for the presidency. These small parties differ considerably in type and permanence. They range from those formed to propagate a particular doctrine over a long duration, to those that are more or less transient. The Prohibition and Socialist Parties have been kept alive over long periods by bands of dedicated enthusiasts and regularly contest elections of all types and in several states. But American party history is noted for the turbulence generated by the rapid rise and equally rapid decline of minor parties; they may play a significant role at a particular time, and then become extinct.

The American political system is basically a two-party one yet, at various times, third parties have had significants impact. Many have existed throughout American history. In recent years, some third-party candidates win election to public office and, in 1990, both Alaska and Connecticut elected Independents in the battle for the state governorships. Vermont re-elected a Socialist to the House of Representatives in the same year. In 1996, Jesse Ventura, a former professional wrestler known as 'the body', was elected as governor for Minnesota on behalf of the Reform Party.

In the 2004 presidential elections, some seventeen parties had candidates on the ballot papers of enough states to allow them theoretically to win a majority in the Electoral College though, in all elections, thirty-nine parties had candidates standing in more than one state.

Third parties in presidential campaigns

Some third parties arise during presidential elections and continue to have an impact. Often they are based largely around a single person, as with Theodore Roosevelt (Bull Moose) and Perot (United We Stand, America in 1992, the Reform Party in 1996). In 1992, Perot created a high-profile campaign, and won the support of activists normally associated with the two main parties. Given his substantial wealth, he could afford to buy extensive advertising on television. For all of the resources at his disposal, he did not win a single state although he gained an impressive 19

per cent of the popular vote and a couple of good seconds, in Maine and Utah.

Perot's was at first more a personal movement than a formal political grouping but, by 1996, it had been transformed into the Reform Party. The party made little impact in 2000, despite running an expensive campaign. There was a serious clash between hard-line conservative nationalists, such as Pat Buchanan (the official candidate), and more socially liberal figures such as Jesse Ventura. Elements among the Reformists seceded and cast their vote elsewhere, and the internal schism has continued with further splintering of the membership. Such events suggest that the party is now in deep trouble.

Some third parties break away from one of the main parties because of disagreement over aspects of the platform that the party currently adopts. John Anderson stood aside from the Republicans in 1980 because he disagreed with the conservative line taken on social issues by the Reaganites, even though he liked the economic approach of the Republican candidate. Other third parties, such as the Libertarians and the Greens, are more long-standing.

The position of third parties in a two-party system

The late Clinton Rossiter (1960) referred to the 'persistent, obdurate two party system', and went on to note that:

> There exists in this country today the materials – substantial materials in the form of potential leaders, followers, funds, interests and ideological commitments – for at least three important third parties, any one of which could, under the rules of some other system, cut heavily and permanently into the historic Democrat–Republican monopoly. There is no reasonable expectancy, under the rules of our system, that any such party could make a respectable showing in two successive elections. Indeed, if a new party were to make such a showing in just one election, the majority party closest to it would move awkwardly but effectively to absorb it.

As we see in the analysis of the two-party system, third parties are at a clear disadvantage in the United States. There are fundamental explanations of the continued dominance of two parties at national and state level, among them: the fact that America has a single Executive; the broad appeal of the existing parties; the mechanics of the electoral system; the barriers to third or minor party advancement; and the voters' fears of wasting their vote.

The role and importance of third parties

A source of new ideas

Third parties can think more of principles than of power for they are unlikely ever to have to implement their proposals. They can 'think the unthinkable' before it later becomes the fashion of the day. Through them, ideas and interests that are not catered for within the main parties may find expression politically. They can handle contentious issues on which neither party can take, or is willing to take, a clear and decisive line. They provide new ideas and issues for the voters to consider. They are not faced with the difficulty of reconciling several views under one umbrella; they can be clear-cut in the solutions they offer. They suffer no particularly serious consequences if their solutions are, on analysis, found to be wanting for they are not putting them into effect. If the ideas do capture the public imagination, then they may well be adopted by one or other of the main parties. The policy is then translated into established public practice.

At various times the Socialists, Prohibitionists and Progressives have taken up controversial matters, and thereby acted as vehicles for the expression of political discontent. Some of the best ideas have been advanced originally by those outside the political mainstream. The point was well made by the historian, Richard Hofstadter (1955). Writing of third parties, he observed that

> their function has not been to win or govern, but to agitate, educate [and] generate new ideas. When a third party's demands become popular enough, they are appropriated by one or both of the major parties and the third party disappears . . . [They] are like bees; once they have stung, they die.

A healthy democratic outlet

Even if they do not see their ideas adopted and rarely or never win a congressional seat (let alone the ultimate prize of the presidency), small parties have at the very least drawn attention to the way people feel. They form an outlet for those who dislike the character and attitudes of both the main parties and, for those who reject the party battle, they provide a haven. They articulate the thoughts of a section of society, and represent a segment of public sentiment. However incoherent or impractical their view may at times be, they have something to say which needs to be considered if only to be rejected. In a democracy, they have a right to exist and to put forward their ideas, however weird they may seem to the majority of people.

Holding the balance

At rare times, a third party can be in an influential position, holding the balance of power and/or affecting the outcome of an election. This is unusual but, in 1992, the Perot intervention probably cost George Bush Senior the presidency just as the votes won by Nader in states such as Florida kept Al Gore out of the White House in 2000.

See also *Libertarian Party*; *Prohibition Party*; *Reform Party*; *Socialist Party of America/Socialist Party USA*

Third Way

The third way is a strategy for creating a new left-of-centre progressive consensus in the United States, Britain and in other democratic countries. Its exponents share a commitment to practical social democracy. Shunning an excess of ideology, they proclaim that 'what matters is what works'. It represents an attempt to transform the traditional political left–right dichotomy and find a middle route between state socialist planning and free market capitalism. It attaches much importance to the values of community, equality of opportunity, personal responsibility and accountability, as well as to enterprise, entrepreneurship and wealth creation. In the words of one of its gurus, Anthony Giddens (1998) of the London School of Economics, the third way rejects top-down socialism as it rejects traditional neo-liberalism.

The third way appeals those who wish to see an efficient market economy and a decent society. In the words of the Blair/Schroeder Declaration (named after two of its foremost advocates who led a meeting in Washington in July 1999), 'it stands not only for social justice but also for economic dynamism and the unleashing of creativity and innovation'. Adherents argue that markets and state should be disciplined by a public interest test. Legislation should provide redress for consumers and monitor the quality of state services.

In the United States, proponents of the third way emphasise fiscal conservatism, some replacement of welfare with workfare, and a stronger preference for market solutions to traditional problems, while rejecting pure laissez-faire economics and other libertarian positions. The third way style of governing was firmly adopted and partly redefined during the Clinton administration. He, Tony Blair and other leading supporters met in conference at Chequers in 1997 to promote its ideas and possibilities The president summed up its key watchwords as being 'community, opportunity and responsibility'.

Since the passing of the Clinton presidency, the ideas of the third way have continued to be influential among members of the Democratic Leadership Council. In 2004, a number of Democrats came together to form a new Washington-based organisation entitled Third Way, which advertises itself as a 'strategy center for progressives'.

Thurmond, Strom (1902–2003)

Strom Thurmond was an American politician from South Carolina who served as governor of the state and then became one of its senators in 1954, serving as a Democrat until 1964 and, for the remainder of his congressional career, as a Republican. He eventually became the longest-serving member of the Senate in United States history (an honour that later passed to Senator Robert Byrd of Louisiana) and the only one still to be in office at the age of one hundred. He also ran for the presidency in 1948, under the segregationist States Rights Democratic Party banner.

Thurmond conducted the longest filibuster ever mounted by a US senator, in opposition to the Civil Rights Act of 1957. Although he later toned down his public position on race, he continued to defend his early segregationist campaigns on the basis of concern for states' rights. As a Southern Democrat, he led the opposition to Truman over his civil rights and Fair Deal proposals and then later opposed the election of John F. Kennedy as the party's presidential candidate in 1960. He left four years later to support the Republican Barry Goldwater in his abortive attempt to win the presidency from Lyndon Johnson.

Thurmond declined to seek re-election in 2002 and left the Senate in January 2003. At his one-hundredth birthday party in December 2002, Republican Senate Minority Leader Trent Lott provoked a storm of controversy when he praised Thurmond's 1948 candidacy for the presidency on a segregationist platform, leading to his own resignation.

After his death, his name featured in the headlines when a seventy-eight-year-old mixed-race woman announced that she was Thurmond's love child, conceived when her mother was a maid working in the Thurmond household in the 1920s. She claimed that, segregationist though he had been, he had nonetheless recognised his paternity. The Thurmond family accepted her version as broadly accurate.

Timmons v. Twin Cities Area New Party (1997)

Timmons v. *Twin Cities Area New Party* was a bitterly contested decision of the Supreme Court which justified the existence of state anti-fusion statutes. The justices supported the American tendency to preserve and privilege a two-party system by limiting the association rights of minority parties.

In a 6–3 judgment, the Court rejected the argument advanced by the New Party that electoral fusion was a right protected under the freedom of association clause of the First Amendment. The New Party was a progressive, left-leaning third party active in the 1990s. It attempted to reintroduce an electoral practice once common in the United States, electoral fusion, in which the same candidate receives nomination from more than one party and therefore occupies more than one line on the ballot. It did this as a means of helping unions and community groups increase their chances of success.

Under Minnesota state law, candidates for political office are prohibited from appearing on more than one party's ballot. When the Twin Cities Area New Party, a chapter of the national New Party, nominated someone for state representative who was already another political party's candidate, Minnesota election refused to accept its petition. The New Party challenged Minnesota's election laws which were upheld by the District Court. The state's Court of Appeals reversed the decision. The Supreme Court had to decide whether the state's anti-fusion laws violated the association rights protected by the First and Fourteenth Amendments. It decided that prohibiting parties from naming another party's candidate as their own did not overly burden their association rights, as they could still endorse the other party's candidate should they wish to do so. It was 'fusing' another party's candidates that was unacceptable.

The judgment was a victory for Minnesota's concern for ballot integrity and political stability. The justices held that Minnesota's law served to avoid ballot manipulation and factionalism and justifiably maintained a two-party system as well. In essence, the decision did not recognise multiple nominations as a significant, legitimate means by which minor parties might achieve their political interests. Critics – the American Cicil Liberties Union (ACLU) and supporters of minor parties – saw it as a ruling that enshrined the two-party system as a basic feature of American politics. They felt that it robbed third parties of a strategy that, once viable, served to enlarge their influence in the political process. The ACLU argued that, if the two-party system was permanently privileged in the courts, minor political parties would never get an opportunity to achieve political parity.

Town Meetings

Town meetings comprise a form of direct democracy, the nearest present-day equivalent to the gatherings that took place in the city-states of Ancient Greece. They are the usual legislative body in most of the smaller Swiss municipalities. In New England, they have operated ever since the first British settlements.

Town meetings are common in many parts of New England. Of Maine's 493 incorporated municipalities, 440 have a town-meeting form of government, in which residents attend for a morning or a day to chart their communal course. Topics debated range widely, from property taxes to budgets for administration, from same-sex marriages to nuts-and-bolts issues concerning local facilities.

Town meetings have been portrayed by one enthusiast as 'a bedrock form of democratic expression', a means of keeping the flame of democracy alive. They offer scope for political participation by the voters who can attend, hear the arguments on either side of an issue and then cast their vote. They are not without their critics, however, and there are problems with the way they function today. In particular:

- Often meetings are not well attended. Rarely do more than 10 per cent of registered voters turn out to participate, and the trend has been consistently downwards in recent years.
- Those who can attend are often self-employed, retired or otherwise not working at regular daytime jobs and therefore cannot accurately reflect the opinions of local citizens. An article in a local newspaper in Maine carried a report that in Kingfield '65 people are calling the shots for the entire town', and that reports from officials in Eustis and Strong also reported low, unrepresentative turnouts.

Several reasons have been advanced for declining turnout. For instance, it is sometimes claimed that:

- Even at the level of a small New England town, society is now too large and complex for direct democracy to be a complete success. Towns used to be smaller, with more of a sense of community. Urbanisation has affected even New England, and people are now too busy, often travelling some distance to work. Meetings take too long for those with little time available.

They can spend their spare time on various forms of entertainment.

- Voters are frustrated and disenchanted with government at all levels.
- Many people are better off than ever before and therefore feel that it is not a matter of serious personal self-interest whether or not they attend.
- There are fewer stress factors (i.e., no burning issues) in municipal government, important ones being taken elsewhere.

Town meetings have been described as 'alive, but troubled'. In some towns they have actually ceased to exist. Voters are experimenting with alternatives to the traditional open town meeting, some opting for meetings where the time is spent in voting directly on a series of referendum questions, others preferring either representative town meetings for which residents elect representatives to vote on their behalf (anyone can stand and speak but only the representatives can vote), straightforward town councils or citizen-initiated referendums. It is in the smaller towns and more rural areas of northern New England that town meetings continue to function best.

Trade Unions

A trade union or labour union is an organisation of employees which, via its leadership, bargains with employers to defend its interests and and promote improved working conditions. The activities of union leaders may include the negotiation of wages, work rules, complaints procedures, rules governing hiring, firing and promotion of workers, benefits, workplace safety and policies. The agreements negotiated by the union leaders are binding on the rank-and-file members and the employer and, in some cases, on other non-member workers.

Never strong in the United States, labour has lost much of its clout in recent decades, and millions of workers. The unions reached their peak in the 1950s when around a third of the non-agricultural workforce was unionised. Since then the fall has been substantial, with current membership at about 12 per cent, and even lower in the South. Today – particularly in the growth areas of the economy – millions of workers are unorganised. Even so, the largest umbrella body representing organised labour (the loose alliance known as the American Federation for Labor and Congress of Industrial Organizations [AFL/CIO]) still has more affiliated members than any other interest group apart from the thirty-five-million strong American Association of Retired Persons (AARP) and can still mobilise millions of people. Nearly fourteen million workers are members of unions affiliated to the AFL/CIO. Millions of others belong to unions not in the AFL/CIO, among them American teachers. Long-standing individual unions include the United Automobile Workers (UAW), the International Brotherhood of Teamsters (lorry drivers), the International Ladies Garment Workers Union (ILGWU) and the United Steelworkers of America.

Trades unions in many countries have lost much of their former influence and bargaining power. They have suffered from a shrinking membership, partly as a result of the decline of manufacturing in the United States, with new, less-unionised service industries becoming ever more significant. The job market in key manufacturing industries has been hit by imported supplies, from Korea in the case of steel and Japan in the case of cars. Unions have failed to cater for the growing number of office workers and those in services (often small scale and harder to motivate). The position of unions has also been made worse as a result of:

- changing attitudes to unions whose position was undermined as a result of the hostile approach adopted by conservative administrations of the Republican years in the 1980s and 1990s
- the increase in the amount of part-time working, especially by women, which made union activity difficult to organise
- the increased diversity of workforces in terms of qualifications and working conditions.

The decline has not been universal or at the same rate, because of differing economic and social conditions prevailing in different parts of the continent. Some unions have been more skilful than others in making adjustments to their attitudes and appeal.

The US workforce has always been less union-ised than in many other democracies, such as Britain and other European countries. Moreover, American unions lack the clout of many large corporations. In total, they are numerically in decline and, individually, they suffer from dimin-ishing membership. They have more influence in the industrial areas, such as the Northeast, than in the South which has traditionally been domi-nated by agrarian interests. In industrial matters, unions can be militant in defence of workers' interests, but politically they play less of a role than in Britain. They carry more weight with the Democratic Party and may give it funds although there have never been the formal, institutional links that exist between British unions and the Labour Party.

See also *Interest Groups*

Treasury

The Department of the Treasury was estab-lished in 1789 to manage government revenue. A Cabinet department, it remains the primary federal agency responsible for the economic and financial prosperity and security of the United States. It is responsible for a wide range of activi-ties including advising the president on economic and financial issues, promoting the presidential growth agenda and enhancing corporate govern-ance in financial institutions. In the international arena, the Treasury works with other federal agencies, the governments of other nations and international financial institutions to encourage economic growth, raise standards of living, and predict and avert global economic and finan-cial crises. As such, the Treasury acts as the steward of the American economic and financial systems, and as an influential participant in the international economy.

The Treasury comprises two major elements: the departmental offices and the operating bureaux. The offices are primarily responsible for the formulation of policy and management of the department as a whole. The twelve oper-ating bureaux carry out the specific operations and employ 98 per cent of the Treasury work-force. For instance, the Bureau of Engraving

and Printing designs and manufactures US cur-rency, securities and other official certificates and awards. Via the Internal Revenue Service, the Treasury collects all federal taxes.

Triangulation

Triangulation refers to the approach of candi-dates who present their ideology as being 'above' and 'between' the traditional left and right posi-tions on the political spectrum. It involves candi-dates adopting for themselves some of the good or popular ideas of their political opponents, thereby insulating them from attacks on that particular issue. The tactic is associated with third-way politics.

Triangulation was the political strategy origi-nally adopted by advisers to President Clinton following the elections of November 1994. His then close aide, Dick Morris, urged him to come to terms with the Republican victories and respond by positioning himself between the Republican Party and the Democrats. In political terms, this meant that the White House should accept Republican policies that had widespread popular approval, such as welfare reform, tax cuts and balanced budgets, but resist strongly on issues such as budget reductions where there was less public support. On these topics, the Republicans could be portrayed as dangerous extremists.

The approach was disliked by more liberal Democrats who saw it as an abandonment of their traditional ideas and policies. But it served the president effectively and helped him secure his re-election in 1996. He continued with the strategy thereafter, boldly announcing in his 1996 State of the Union Address that the 'era of Big Government is over'.

Many Democrats view triangulation as a failed tactic, blaming its use for their defeats in 2000 and 2004. In the 2008 campaign, Barack Obama refers to the way in which Clinton advis-ers urged him to make policy decisions by split-ting the difference on opposing views. Obama wanted to mark a break with the past, observing: 'We've had enough of . . . triangulation and poll-driven politics. That's not what we need right now.'

Trickle-down Economics

Trickle-down economics refers to the economic theory which states that investing money in companies and giving tax cuts to business and rich individuals are the most effective means of stimulating the economy. Supporters of this theory argue that, when government helps businesses, they will produce more and thereby hire more people and raise salaries. As a consequence, workers in the company will be better off and have more money to spend.

The trickle-down effect is most closely identified with the economic policies of the Reagan era ('Reaganomics') but it remains central to much of the conservative economic theory propounded by right-leaning newspapers such as *The Wall Street Journal* editorial page and libertarian and conservative think tanks such as the American Enterprise Institute and the Cato Institute. Supporters do not claim that concessions granted to the rich will trickle down because of any benevolence or generosity on their part but rather that the benefits occur as a result of the normal workings of unfettered markets.

Truman, Harry (1884–1972)

Harry Truman was the thirty-third president, serving from 1945 to 1953, having previously been the vice president for only a few months. He succeeded to the presidency upon the death of Franklin Roosevelt during his fourth term.

Truman, a prosperous farmer from Missouri, became active in the Democratic Party. He was elected as a judge and then, in 1934, as a senator. In World War II he headed the Senate war investigating committee, checking into waste and corruption.

As president, Truman made some momentous decisions at a time when the west was beset with tensions and crises. Most famously or infamously, he gave the order that, in August 1945, atomic bombs be dropped on Japanese cities devoted to war work, in particular Hiroshima and Nagasaki. Japanese surrender quickly followed. In his few weeks as vice president, he had received no briefing on the development of the atomic bomb or the unfolding difficulties with Soviet Russia.

Suddenly, on taking over on Roosevelt's death, he was confronted with a massive test of judgement and leadership. As he later told reporters: 'I felt like the moon, the stars and all the planets had fallen on me.'

Among the other issues he handled in foreign affairs:

- In June 1945 Truman witnessed the signing of the United Nations Charter, established, it was hoped, to preserve peace.
- In 1947 as the Soviet Union pressurised Turkey and, through guerrillas, threatened to take over Greece, Truman asked Congress to aid the two countries, outlining the programme that bears his name, the Truman Doctrine. The Marshall Plan, named after his Secretary of State, stimulated spectacular economic recovery in war-torn western Europe.
- In 1948, he created the massive airlift to supply Berliners after the Russians had blockaded the western sectors of the city.
- In 1949, he signed the treaty establishing the North Atlantic Treaty Organisation, an agreement by western countries to support each other in opposing Soviet aggression.
- In 1950, when the Communist government of North Korea attacked the South, Truman conferred promptly with his military advisers and decided that the United States must fight to preserve South Korea's freedom. A long, discouraging struggle ensued as UN forces held a line above the old boundary of South Korea. Truman kept the war limited in scope, rather than risk an escalating conflict with China and perhaps Russia.

In home affairs, his general stance on racial isues was bold as he sought to move his country along the long road to racial justice. He used Executive orders to begin desegregation of the armed forces, knowing that Congress, dominated by Republicans, was unwilling to pass meaningful legislation on civil rights. He also forbade racial discrimination in federal employment. On other domestic issues, he pursued a Fair Deal programme which was, at first, a continuation of that of his predecessor but soon developed into something more distinctive. He presented a twenty-one-point programme to Congress, proposing the expansion of social security, a full-employment programme, a permanent Fair Employment Practises Act, and measures to promote public housing and slum clearance. He found his reforming plans opposed, however, by a legislature that did not share his ambition of building upon the New Deal.

In 1948, contrary to the expectations of most commentators and politicians, Truman won re-election. His energy in campaigning and his willingness to confront controversial issues earned him a degree of popular support that his opponents had failed to recognise. His famous 'whistle-stop' campaign tour through the country enabled him to meet many Americans and has passed into political folklore. So, too, has the photograph of Truman holding up the newspaper whose headline proclaimed 'Dewey Defeats Truman'. A late swing in his favour helped him to victory.

Four years later, Truman decided not to run again. His administration had been damaged by the allegation of being 'soft on Communism' at a time of McCarthyite hysteria. He had been willing to introduce loyalty checks on federal employees suspected of Communist sympathies and, as a result, many had lost their jobs. He was strongly opposed to mandatory loyalty oaths, however, which, in eyes of his critics, only served to substantiate their accusation. Corruption in his administration reached the Cabinet and senior White House staff. The Korean War dragged on. In these circumstances, as a president under pressure, he stood aside rather than fight another electoral battle.

Truman is generally highly rated in surveys of American presidents who admire his strong and vigorous approach to leadership. He overcame the low expectations of many observers who, at first, adversely compared him to his well-regarded predecessor. Having endured very low poll ratings when in office, his stock has markedly improved since his retirement. A folksy, unassuming man, he remains highly quotable. He is remembered for such phrases as 'the buck stops here' and 'if you can't stand the heat, you better get out of the kitchen'.

Truman Doctrine

The Truman Doctrine refers to the ideas set out by President Truman in March 1947 on the containment of Communist aggression. In his speech to Congress, he pledged American support for 'free peoples who are resisting attempted subjugation by armed minorities or by outside pressures'. The speech also included a request that Congress agree to provide military and economic aid to Greece in its fight against Communism. The president also explained that he intended to send American military and economic advisers to countries whose political stability was under threat.

By his remarks, it was obvious that the United States had abandoned its pre-war isolationism and was willing to station troops abroad and adopt an increasingly interventionist role. Few raised a voice in protest against the direction of US policy that Truman set out, for it was widely accepted that it was a priority to prevent the Soviet Union from becoming more powerful. His view of America's place in the world and his ideas on containing Communist aggression and expansion were to become the foundation of foreign policy in the era of the Cold War. Truman did not actually employ the word 'containment' in his speech. Neither did many of his contemporaries who often spoke of 'rolling back' Communism. Whatever the term used, there was wide agreement with Truman's reasoning that Communist, totalitarian regimes coerced free peoples and constituted a threat to international peace and US nation security.

See also *Cold War; Foreign Policy*

Turnout

In much of the twentieth century, the successful presidential candidate won an election in which less than half of the eligible electorate turned out to vote, so that the decisions about who should govern the country and the direction in which it should be led lay in the hands of a minority of the population. The 1960 presidential contest had a better turnout than usual but, in the subsequent half century, the percentage voting declined more or less continuously, as the table below indicates. In 2004, however, the interest of the voters was more engaged by the Bush v. Kerry contest, when there seemed to be the prospect of a close race between candidates who were dissimilar in much of their political thinking. The sixty-two million votes cast for Bush were the most individual votes cast for anyone in history, though John Kerry's fifty-nine million ranked second in that category as well. In 2008, a record 131.2 million people voted, the highest turnout since 1960.

Turnout in presidential elections since 1960

Year	Percentage of people voting
1960	63.8
1968	61.0
1976	54.4
1984	53.0
1992	53.0
2000	51.2
2004	59.4
2008	61.6

The figures are unimpressive by European standards, with 55 per cent being good by American standards. Comparisons can, however, be misleading. For instance, whereas British figures (themselves disappointing in 2001 and 2005) relate to the number of registered people who vote, the American ones are based upon the number of Americans over the minimum voting age who actually do so. According to VO Key (1964) the difference may be worth as many as 6 or 7 percentage points.

Turnout in presidential and congressional elections

The US presidential campaign certainly gets massive television exposure for it dominates the media from the time of the first primaries through to November. This might be expected to generate interest and excitement yet, in the media age, we are faced by decline. The fall in turnout rates is the more notable if we bear in mind the increase in the size of the potential electorate since the 1970s. The passage of the 1965 Voting Rights

Act added many black voters to the list of those eligible to vote. Moreover, women have become more politically involved in that period, and their turnout levels have risen to such an extent that more women turned out than men in the 1996, 2000 and 2004 elections. Finally, given the overall increase in education and living standards, one might have expected that more would be inspired to vote, the more so as it is traditionally the least well off who comprise the category which is the most reluctant to vote.

Yet some half the registered electorate does not turn out even in presidential contests. For other elections the number is considerably greater still. In an off year (when there is no presidential contest) the average figure for turnout is 35 to 40 per cent in congressional elections. In primaries, the figure is often below 30 per cent.

Why are turnouts so low?

Several reasons have been given for low turnouts but, among them, registration arrangements have always been seen as important.

Registration emerges as a key issue. In most states it is up to individuals to register themselves as qualified voters before election day. Failure to do so disqualifies anyone from using their right even if, in other respects, they are eligible to do so. Registration involves either meeting a registrar or filling out a form at the county courthouse. When allowances are made for this responsibility and for age and residential qualifications, it is evident that there is built-in discouragement to voting.

A change was introduced in 1993 when President Clinton signed the so-called motor voter bill designed to ease the process of registration. Citizens are now able to register when they apply for a driving licence (hence the name) or some other form of public document. Furthermore, states must designate a public office concerned with providing help to the public, a place where assistance is also available with voter registration – such as a state welfare agency. The effects should have been to enable and encourage more people to turn out on election day for it has long been the case that, in those states with same-day or no registration, turnout is considerably above the national average.

The new legislation operated from 1995 and, within eight months, some 5,000,000 new voters registered. Some commentators predicted that, if this momentum was maintained, almost four out of every five voters would be registered by the end of the century. It was not and, today, some 66 per cent of Americans are registered to vote, a few percentage points up on the situation before 'motor voting' was introduced. Yet, in 1996 and 2000, the turnout figures were disappointingly low. As president, George Bush Snr had vetoed such a measure, perhaps in the belief that the Democrats would benefit more from a higher turnout. His fears seem to have been largely unjustified.

Alternative explanations include the following.

1. *Apathy* Some have used apathy as an explanation but surveys of political interest suggest that, if anything, Americans are rather more politically interested than people in many other democracies. Voting does, however, require more personal effort than elsewhere for the reasons we have given, and the frequency of elections could result in voter fatigue and a loss of interest.

2. *Lack of a meaningful choice between the parties* Some commentators would suggest that voters who are registered fail to detect any real difference between the parties, and that the electors feel that a choice between tweedledum and tweedledee is not one worth attempting to make. They say 'a plague on both your houses', and see parties as increasingly irrelevant to their lives. No party really addresses their concerns.

3. *The lack of an inspiring choice of candidates* Others say that the quality of political leaders fails to inspire, and there are too many unattractive personalities who become candidates. Discontent with the available choice was a much-discussed feature of the Bush v. Dukakis contest, the 'Wimp' v. 'the Shrimp' (1988), the Clinton v. Dole contest in 1996 and the Bush v. Gore contest in 2000.

4. *The composition of the electorate* Broadly speaking, middle-class people, those with a professional education and with a college education, are more likely to turn out than unskilled working people or those whose qualifications are only a high-school diploma or less. Again, family influence may be significant. In those homes where there is a tradition of participation, it is more likely that future generations will turn out to vote and become more generally involved in political life.

Certain groups have been persistently more reluctant to vote. Non-voting is greater in the South and in rural areas, among the young, the less educated and among the minorities such as the black population and Hispanics. Young people (under twenty-four) have regularly been less disposed to involve themselves in the electoral process although those who claim a clear allegiance towards one of the main parties are markedly more willing to vote than those who are apathetic about politics and current affairs. Whites are more likely to vote than blacks, blacks than Hispanics.

An important consideration is that the groups which shun the democratic process are ones that make up an increasing proportion of the electorate.

5. *The nature of electioneering* It may be that negative advertising produces disillusion with the Washington politicians and with the political system in general, and that this contributes to the falling turnouts of the last generation. In the 1994 elections, it was suggested that one of the most toxic campaigns in living memory had left many people turned off politicians. American voters have become more disengaged from political strategy, as the style of advertising increasingly antagonises them. Overall, they are seen in Hames's (1996) words as 'over-long, over-slick and dominated by the mass media with a premium on character attacks on political opponents'.

6. *Other factors* The theory has been advanced by Ginsberg and Shefter (1999) that America is now in a post-electoral era. More and more voters see parties and elections as no longer very significant. Now, major decisions are made by investigating committees and the

courts, and through media revelations. The traditional processes have had their day.

Another idea is that non-voting is broadly a sign of contentment with the political system. If Americans felt worried, because their country was in crisis, they might feel inclined to turn out to avert a national catastrophe. But, in times of peace and prosperity, most Americans are happy to leave the politicians to get on with their task; there is less need to vote.

U

Uncle Tom

Uncle Tom is a pejorative term for a black person who is perceived by others as behaving in a subservient manner to white authority or as seeking to ingratiate with his or her representatives by behaving in a needlessly accommodating manner. It derives from the leading character in Harriet Beecher Stowe's novel, *Uncle Tom's Cabin*, a slave who is seen as long-suffering, overly deferential and too faithful a servant of his white owners. In the 1950s, the book went from being a literary phenomenon to an object of derision, with its slave seen as symbolic of black self-loathing.

Unfounded as the term and the application may be, 'Uncle Tom' is still a common epithet for any black person who is seen as too willing to co-operate with whites and insufficiently militant in his or her advocacy of civil rights. In recent history, the term has been applied to Martin Luther King, Colin Powell and even Barack Obama.

Unfunded Mandates

Mandates are legal orders requiring states and local governments to act in specific ways. They developed in the 1980s, at a time when the budget deficit was rapidly increasing. Accordingly, Congress passed directive legislation in the form of statutes or regulations, but chose not to compensate the authorities so directed for the costs incurred in implementing national policy.

The growth in unfunded mandates became burdensome for the states and was a source of friction between Washington and the state capitals. In the light of state concern, Congress legislated to curb the practice of issuing new unfunded mandates thereafter, by passing the Unfunded Mandates Reform Act. Yet critics of Washington claim that measures, such as the Clean Air Act, the Clean Water Act, the Homeland Security Act, the Individuals with Disabilities Act and the No Child Left Behind Act, are federal laws which states, counties and cities have had to finance.

Unitary Executive Theory

Unitary executive theory argues for strict limits to the power of Congress to deprive the president of control of the Executive branch. Its proponents rely heavily on the clause of Article II which states that: 'The executive Power shall be vested in a President of the United States of America.' They use this language along with the 'take care' clause ('[The President] shall take care that the laws be faithfully executed . . .') to argue that the Constitution creates a hierarchical, unified Executive department under the direct control of the president. They argue that the president possesses all of the executive power and can therefore control subordinate officers and agencies of the Executive branch. This implies that the power of Congress to remove executive agencies or officers from presidential control is limited. Thus, under the unitary executive theory, independent agencies and counsels are unconstitutional to the extent that they exercise discretionary executive power not controlled by the president.

Ryan Barilleaux (2006) explains that the ambiguous language of Article II defines 'a role that is sweeping in its potential', giving rise to incentives for 'venture constitutionalism', a term he uses to describe 'the presidential conundrum – that the

Constitution itself encourages presidents to test the limits of the Constitution'. Terry Moe and William Howell (1999) had earlier elaborated on such thinking, by noting that:

> The Constitution's incomplete contract sets up a governing structure that virtually invites presidential imperialism. Presidents, especially in modern times, are motivated to seek power. And because the Constitution does not say precisely what the proper boundaries of their power are, and because their hold on the executive functions of government gives them pivotal advantages in the political struggle, they have strong incentives to push for expanded authority by moving into grey areas of the law, asserting their rights, and exercising them.

The same two writers make the point that the ambiguous language of the Constitution is not accidental but born out of disagreements among its founders. Madison favoured limiting authority of the president. Hamilton, who pushed to expand it, largely won the argument. But they suggest that, since the 1980s, the opportunities afforded by this choice of language have been exploited more fully than ever before.

Unitary executive theory in practice: the conduct of recent presidents

President G. W. Bush was a strong exponent of the unitary executive theory, Chris Kelley (2005) observing that, until that date, he was known to have employed the term publicly on ninety-five occasions, usually when signing legislation into law, responding to a congressional resolution or issuing an executive order. When signing the contentious Medicare and Prescription Drug Act in 2003, he commented adversely on two sections of the statute that interfered with his constitutional prerogative to 'supervise the unitary executive branch'. He continued to say that

> the executive branch shall construe these provisions in a manner consistent with the President's constitutional authority to supervise the unitary executive branch and to recommend for the consideration of the Congress such measures as the President judges necessary and expedient.

In taking his stance on the unitary Executive, some writers argued that George Bush was formalising a process that really began under Ronald Reagan as a result of the assault on the presidency in the post-Watergate/Vietnam years and continued under Bush Snr and Bill Clinton. Others portrayed his position as representing a more recent development or, at the very least, one that was taken to a new level by the Bush administration. Bush certainly interpreted the theory more expansively than his predecessors. In doing so, he was much influenced by the legal positions promulgated by John Yoo, particularly as recorded in several of his legal memorandums while working at the Department of Justice's Office of Legal Counsel under Bush. Yoo argued that the use of military force, like presidential vetoes and pardons, was not a matter for review. He also contended that the president, rather than Congress or the courts, had the sole authority to interpret interntational treaties such as the Geneva Convention, 'because treaty interpretation is a key feature of the conduct of foreign affairs'. Yoo's highly contentious opinions were widely seen by many legal scholars as being contrary to their understanding of the Constitution.

The ways in which Bush used his broad remit shed an interesting insight into the debate on presidential power. As part of his determination to use the powers of the presidency to their fullest extent, Bush:

- was keen to assert executive privilege over information
- made effective use of executive orders
- regularly used proclamations, signing statements, memorandums and national security directives
- made appointments in the recess to avoid the need for Senate confirmation

See also *Executive Orders*; *National Security Directives Proclamations*; *Recess Appointments*; *Signing Statements*

United Nations Organization (UNO)

The United Nations (UN) is an organisation of 192 states. Its stated goal is to promote international co-operation, peace and security, as well as economic and social development and respect for human rights. The United States played a key role in creating the United Nations. It remains a member of the UN and occupies one of the five permanent seats on the Security Council.

Woodrow Wilson (1856–1924) had championed American membership of the UN's forerunner, the League of Nations but ratification was not supported in the Senate. It was another Democrat, Franklin Roosevelt, who is credited with first using the term 'United Nations', when speaking of the Allies in World War II. The United Nations was the first international governmental organisation to receive significant support from the United States.

Soon after its formation, the United States found itself in confrontation with another permanent member of the Security Council, the Soviet Union, as the Cold War increasingly dominated post-war international relationships. On some important international issues, America has found backing for the position it supported, notably in the Korean War and later in the First Gulf War. Conflict between the United States and the UN has a long history, however, a divisive issue being American support for Israel's position and American attitudes in the Middle East. The US has frequently used its power of veto in the Security Council to block resolutions condemning Israeli actions.

As the world's dominant military power, the United States has been in conflict with many member states in recent years, particularly since the invasion of Iraq in 2003. When the Security Council unanimously adopted Resolution 1441 (November 2002) giving Iraq an ultimatum to co-operate in disarmament within an unstated time frame of a few months, American policymakers later claimed that the resolution justified invasion, as it had promised 'serious consequences' for lack of full compliance and achievement of its objective. Some other leading UN members on the Security Council, including France and Russia, maintained that Resolution 1441 did not authorise the use of force without passage of a further resolution.

The United States has long been, and continues to be, the state levied most heavily by the UN.

For many years, as a means of asserting American influence and compliance with American policy, Congress refused to authorise payment of the US dues. After prolonged negotiations, however, the dispute over payment was resolved by the 1999 Helms–Biden legislation which linked payment of arrears to a series of reforms within UNO, including a reduction its its assessment rate ceiling.

Some Americans have long questioned the role and usefulness of the UN in the modern world. They dislike the notion that America's freedom of manoeuvre in international affairs might be threatened by the criticism and approaches of other member states who are unsympathetic to US interests. A small number of Americans have, from time to time, advocated withdrawal but others voice dissent as a negotiating tactic. Voicing American displeasure and dissatisfaction can be a means of imposing pressure on other countries to support US goals in foreign policy. When President Bush appointed John Bolton, formerly a strong and vocal critic, as the American ambassador to the international body (July 2005) it seemed as though he was indicating his scepticism about its value in international affairs. The later appointment in April 2007 of Zalmay Khalilzad as US ambassador, however, served to allay fears of any signficant change of US policy. He was the highest-ranking Muslim within the Bush administration.

United States v. *Lopez* (1995) and *United States* v. *Morrison* (2000)

United States v. *Lopez* was the first Supreme Court case since the Great Depression to impose limits on Congress's power under the Commerce Clause of the Constitution.

Lopez had carried a handgun and cartridges into his high school in San Antonio, Texas and was charged with violating the Gun-Free School Zones Act of 1990. The government claimed that possession of a firearm in a school adversely affected general economic conditions by limiting travel in the area and undermining children's attempts to learn. His defending counsel argued that the federal government had no authority to regulate firearms in school zones, the law under which Lopez was convicted being unconstitutional. Hence the offence fell within the jurisdiction of the Commerce Clause.

The Rehnquist Court held that, while Congress had broad lawmaking authority under the Commerce Clause, it was not unlimited and could not be applied to something as far removed from commerce as carrying handguns, there being no evidence that carrying them seriously affected the economy. In the opinion of the justices, the possession of a gun in a local school zone is not an economic activity that might, through repetition elsewhere, have a substantial effect on interstate commerce. The law is a criminal statute that has nothing to do with 'commerce' or any sort of economic activity.

In a later case, *United States* v. *Morrison*, the Court again examined the limits of congressional power to make laws under the Commerce Clause, as well as under section 5 of the Fourteenth Amendment. It held that the Violence Against Women Act (1994), which provided a federal civil remedy for gender-motivated violence (giving victims of domestic violence the right to sue their attackers in federal court), was unconstitutional because it was beyond Congress's powers to legislate in this way. Drawing on the *Lopez* case (above), the justices ruled that it had been established that the scope of the Commerce Clause did not extend to activity that was not directly economic in nature even if there were indirect economic consequences. The two judgments marked the first significant limitation on the Commerce Clause powers of Congress for several decades.

United States v. Nixon (1974)

After President Nixon refused to hand over sixty-four tapes and transcripts of recordings of his own discussions in the White House, the ruling by the Supreme Court in the *United States* v. *Nixon* declared his action unconstitutional. The president had claimed executive privilege, his aides arguing that it was essential for presidents to be able to speak freely with their advisers without fear that such conversations would be available for public consumption. The Burger Court decided that, although in matters involving national security considerations there might be a valid claim, this did not extend to data in presidential files or tapes bearing on a criminal prosecution. In effect, the judgment did acknowledge the possible constitutionality of executive privilege.

University of California v. Baake (1978) see Regents of the University of California v. Baake (1978)

V

Veto Power

The veto power refers to the right of the president to veto acts of Congress with which he disagrees. It may also refer to the right of a governor to reject legislation passed by state legislatures.

After passing through both houses of Congress, bills are sent to the White House for the president to sign. If he fails to act within ten days (excepting Sundays) a bill automatically becomes law. But, in the last ten days of a session, his failure to act amounts to a pocket veto; in other words, as Congress is not sitting and cannot fight back, the bill is effectively killed.

When a president vetoes a bill within the allotted time, Congress can override his decision, as long as two-thirds of those present in each chamber support the initiative. Presidents know that Congress only very rarely successfully overrides their vetoes, so that the mere threat of using the power is often enough to enable them to extract concessions from the Legislature. As long as the power is sometimes used, the threat is a credible one. Presidents vary in their use of the veto, some using it extensively, as the figures suggest:

George W. Bush was relatively sparing in his use of the veto, his first being to block legislation expanding embryonic stem cell research (July 2006). After the November 2006 election setbacks, however, he faced an increasingly assertive Congress and began to use the veto power more, in a bid to protect legacy issues. His controversial veto to allow interrogation techniques (March 2008) was still only the ninth of his presidency but it was the eighth since the Democrats had won control of Congress. The increased use

Number of vetoes and overrides for selected presidents 1933–2001

	Number of bills vetoed	Number and percentage of vetoes overridden
F. Roosevelt (1933–45)	635	9 (1.4)
D. Eisenhower (1953–61)	181	2 (1.1)
L. Johnson (1963–69)	30	0 (0.0)
R. Nixon (1969–74)	43	7 (16.3)
R. Reagan (1981–89)	78	9 (11.5)
B. Clinton (1993–2001)	37	2 (5.4)
G. W. Bush (2001–09)	12	4 (33.3)

Figures adapted from those available from the Research Division, Congressional Quarterly, Washington DC.

N.b. Frequency of use does not necessarily indicate success or failure. Mere numbers do not allow for any distinction between vetoes on highly significant issues and those that are of much lesser importance.

underscored his determination to preserve many of the executive prerogatives his administration has claimed in the name of fighting terrorism and to enshrine them into law.

Difficulties faced by presidents in using the veto

In some circumstances, presidential use, or threatened use, of the veto can seem to indicate presidential firmness. President Clinton used the device to extract legislative concessions from Congress. But it can indicate weakness in handling Congress, being evidence of the president's failure to persuade others to coalesce around a particular policy, as was the case in the last two years of his successor's administration.

For many years, critics of the procedure argued that the presidential veto was a blunt weapon for the president either had to sign or reject an entire bill. Knowing this, members of Congress sometimes attached extra (and unpalatable) provisions (riders) to a bill that they knew the president really wanted. By doing so, they were trapping him for he either had to sign the whole bill with the unwanted features or lose it altogether. After much discussion, Congress finally passed a line-item veto in 1996, giving the president the power to veto 'objectionable' parts of an appropriations (expenditure) bill while agreeing to the rest of it. This innovation was soon tested in the Supreme Court. In *Clinton* v. *New York* (June 1998), the judges were asked to decide whether Bill Clinton's rejection of some aspects of a tax bill was legitimate. They concluded that the line-item veto was unconstitutional in that it violated the requirement that any bill must pass both houses and be signed by the president in the same form. If the president was allowed to strike out particular features, then, in effect, a new bill was being created.

The loss of the line-item veto means that presidents are left with one weaker power which they can employ if they are unhappy with a piece of legislation. Having signed the bill, they can withhold the funds (impoundment) appropriated by Congress for its implementation. Generally, impoundment has been used sparingly but President Nixon used it regularly against a Democrat-dominated Congress both as a means of controlling spending and as a means of controlling its behaviour. Congress responded by passing the Budget and Impoundment Control Act in 1974. This laid down restrictions on the presidential use of impoundment. What remains is a much-weakened alternative to the defunct line-item veto.

See also *Line-item Veto*; *Pocket Veto*

Vice Presidency

The Founding Fathers appear to have created the office of vice president as an afterthought. The Constitution simply says that he will be chosen by an Electoral College, outlines the circumstances when he will be acting president and lays down that he will preside over the Senate. Given that there are so few formal responsibilities, some vice presidents have made little of it. One such occupant was Charles Dawes who served under President Coolidge. He declared that his position was 'the easiest job in the world'. For many years the office of vice president was viewed as little more than a joke. Its first incumbent, John Adams, spoke of it derisively: 'My country has in its wisdom contrived for me the most insignificant office that ever the invention of man contrived or his imagination conceived.'

The choice

Presidential candidates choose their nominee to serve as vice president towards the end of the presidential nominating conventions. They are usually looking for running mates who are geographically, ideologically, demographically or in other ways able to 'balance the ticket'. For such reasons:

- In 1960, John F. Kennedy, an intellectual Northern liberal, chose Lyndon Johnson, an experienced and respected Southern conservative with long service in the Senate.
- In 1976, Carter, a Southerner, chose Mondale, a more traditional Democrat from the party's Northern heartlands, with a record of support for the interests of the poor, ethnic minorities and backing among the educated middle class.
- In 1988, Michael Dukakis, a liberal New England governor, chose Lloyd Bentsen, a Southern conservative with a long record of involvement in Washington politics.
- In 1988, George Bush chose T. Dan Quayle, an attempt to calm the party's right wing.
- In 1992, Bill Clinton chose Senator Al Gore from a neighbouring state, an unusual move in that it placed two Southerners on the Democratic ticket – but it helped to reinforce the image of change and youth, and gave added respectability to the campaign. Gore was widely seen as 'Mr Clean', a good family man – in marked contrast to Bill Clinton who, whatever

his strong regard for his family, was not seen as representing wholesome family values.

- In 2000, George W. Bush chose Dick Cheney, a man experienced on matters of foreign and security policy and who had served under Ford and under Bush's father. The choice strengthened the ticket for Bush Jnr was widely viewed as rather ignorant of overseas issues and lacking in experience of that whole area of policy.
- In 2008, Obama chose Jo Biden who became the first Roman Catholic to assume the vice presidency and also the first Delawarean. Biden did not represent a swing state or one with a significant vote in the Electoral College. Neither did his selection sit naturally with the Obama message of change. Yet he brought important strengths to the Democratic ticket, most obviously gravitas, deep foreign policy and national security expertise, a willingness and ability aggressively to attack John McCain (in a way that did not come easily to Obama) and an easy connection with middle-class and blue-collar Americans.

The voters are presented with a team of two people, usually two men (although in 2008 McCain chose the then governor of Alaska, Sarah Palin, as his running mate). They cannot have one without the other. The fortunes of the two candidates are inextricably linked and, between them, they need to be able to appeal to as wide a range of opinion and interests as possible. It might just be that, by carefully choosing a vice-presidential nominee with different assets to offer the voters, more Americans can be swayed to switch their support.

The role

The duties of the vice president are few in number. He or she presides over the Senate, acting as speaker. This involves refereeing its proceedings and interpreting the rules. In reality, he puts in few appearances, mainly when there is an important, close call. He has the casting vote in a closely divided chamber. In 1993, Gore used this reserve power to break the deadlock and ensure that the Clinton budget was passed. Tie-breaking votes are rare, however, as the figures illustrate:

Mondale	1
Bush	7
Quayle	0
Gore	4
Cheney	8

N.b. Since 1789, 244 tie-breaking votes have been cast by vice presidents (September 2009).

Vice presidents also perform such tasks – often ceremonial – as the president allocates to them. They take on ad hoc assignments and normally attend meetings of the Cabinet and National Security Council. Dick Cheney was authorised to nominate individuals to the United States military, naval, and air force academies. Some ceremonial duties derived from this area of responsibility, for instance, attending the graduation ceremonies of the UCoast Guard Academy. Jo Biden was named as the head of a new White House Task Force on Working Families, an initiative aimed at improving the economic position of the middle class.

A position of growing significance: a new vice presidency?

The trend in recent years has been to use vice presidents more. Carter valued Mondale's services and his status as a 'Washington insider'. Reagan made use of Bush's background experience as a former director of the Central Intelligence Agency, using him to make overseas visits, lobby Congress and campaign in midterm elections. Clinton made effective use of Al Gore who was given an important role in the White House. Clinton viewed Gore more as a partner, a kind of deputy president. He was asked to give a lead in the area of governmental reform (the Reinventing Government initiative). He was valued by the president as a trusted adviser on policy issues.

Apart from the increased use made by some presidents of their running mate, other factors have tended to increase the importance of the office. The passage of the Twenty-fifth Amendment means that the vice president is liable to take over the reins of the presidential office in the event of the incumbent's incapacity ('unable to discharge the powers and duties of his office'). This actually happened in 1985 under Reagan, when – for a few hours – Bush assumed the highest office while Reagan was under anaesthetic.

As yet, thirteen vice presidents have gone on to become president and four of the last eight served in that capacity. It is the fact that the vice president is only a 'heartbeat away from the presidency' that gives particular significance to the job. Four presidents have been assassinated and – as with Johnson in November 1963 – vice presidents can suddenly find themselves elevated to the supreme office. Under other circumstances, too, the vice president may have to take over. Ford assumed the presidential role on Nixon's resignation after the events of Watergate had undermined his tenure of office.

For all of the increased importance of the job, leading to talk of a new vice presidency, it remains the fact that many vice presidents have seen their job as frustrating and unrewarding, 'not worth a pitcher of warm spit' according to Franklin Roosevelt's choice, John Nance Garner. Vice presidents can find it difficult to establish an identity, and the position is particularly difficult if he are she wishes to stand as president at the end of a longish presidency:

- Humphrey found difficulty in the later Johnson years, as he felt that he needed to establish that he had his own views and was not totally committed to the president's policy on Vietnam. Yet he still needed to be seen to act loyally in public.
- Gore had a similar difficulty in Clinton's second term. He had benefited from the experience gained as someone who was on the inside and knew how government worked at the highest level. He had had the opportunity to meet foreign statesmen so that he was well known beyond American shores. In other words, he had served a good apprenticeship for the highest role and was a natural choice as the Democratic candidate. But the Clinton presidency was mired in controversy. Gore wanted to distance himself from the president whose personal behaviour could be seen as a liability in the forthcoming election. By keeping his distance, Gore risked being unable to campaign effectively on the Democratic achievements in office which were associated with Clinton.

Vietnam War

The Vietnam War or Conflict occurred in Vietnam and, to a lesser extent, Laos and Cambodia between 1959 and April 1975. It was fought between the Communist North Vietnam, supported by its Communist allies, and South Vietnam, supported primarily by the United States. Within the South, the Vietcong Communist insurgents waged a guerrilla war against anti-Communist forces.

The United States entered the war to prevent the North from taking over the South and to contain the spread of Communism in south–east Asia. The fear was that, if one state in the region fell to the Communists, then there would be a domino-like collapse of anti-Communist regimes. Actual direct military involvement began under President Kennedy and was much escalated under President Johnson. In waging the struggle, US and South Vietnamese forces relied on air superiority and overwhelming firepower to conduct search-and-destroy operations, involving ground forces, artillery and air strikes.

Faced by increasing domestic opposition to the war effort and repeated military setbacks, eventually the Johnson, and then the Nixon, administrations recognised the urgency of a resolution of hostilities, A peace treaty was finally signed by all parties in January 1973 although sporadic fighting continued. In June, Congress passed the Case–Church Amendment to prevent further US military intervention. In April 1975, North Vietnam captured Saigon, the capital of South Vietnam and, in the following year, North and South Vietnam were reunited, as the US had originally feared.

The impact of the war

The war had a major impact on American politics, culture and diplomatic relations. Americans were deeply divided over the government's justification for, and conduct of, the war. Opposition to the war contributed to the growth of a strong and vocal anti-war movement as the 1960s progressed. In diplomatic terms, the American withdrawal was a major setback, marking as it did the country's first military defeat. Concerns over the way in which the presidents – particularly Johnson

– had misled people about what was happening in Vietnam contributed to a growing credibility gap, with many people not believing what their commander-in-chief was telling them. The facts, as reported in the media, seemed to be at variance with what they were being officially told. The growing distrust helped to undermine support for an imperial presidency.

The fighting exacted a huge human cost in terms of fatalities. More than 58,000 US soldiers were killed. Cambodian, Laotian and Vietnamese losses were variously estimated at three to six million.

See also *Johnson, Lyndon*; New York Times *v.* United States *(1971)*

Virginia v. *Black* (2003)

Virginia v. *Black* was a First Amendment case decided by the Supreme Court concerning cross-burning. Barry Black, Richard Elliott and Jonathan O'Mara were separately convicted of violating a Virginia statute that makes it a felony 'for any person . . . with the intent of intimidating any person or group . . . to burn . . . a cross on the property of another, a highway or other public place', and specifies that 'any such burning . . . shall be prima facie evidence of an intent to intimidate a person or group'.

In adjudicating on Black's case, the Supreme Court struck down the statute. In a plurality opinion delivered by Justice Sandra Day O'Connor, the Court held that, while a state, consistent with the First Amendment, might ban cross burning carried out with the intent to intimidate, the provision in the Virginia statute, treating any cross-burning as prima facie evidence of intent to intimidate, rendered the statute unconstitutional in its existing form. O'Connor and four other justices argued that the broad and indiscriminate law blurred the distinction between protected 'messages of shared ideology' and proscribable 'threats of intimidation'. The result of their deliberations is that cross-burning can still be a criminal offence if an intent to intimidate is proven.

Justice Clarence Thomas was one dissentient. He claimed that that the statute 'prohibits only conduct, not expression. And, just as one cannot burn down someone's house to make a political point and then seek refuge in the First Amendment, those who hate cannot terrorise and intimidate to make their point.'

In areas of controversial speech, the Court has frequently sided with those who advocate symbolic forms of free speech but, occasionally, it has sided with the state governments and acknowledged their (limited) power to pass laws protecting citizens from specific types of harmful speech.

See also *First Amendment*; *Symbolic Speech*

Voter Behaviour

Ever since the time of the New Deal, there has been a marked trend for urban workers with low incomes, who generally live in the poorest districts and have a lower level of formal educational qualification, to vote Democrat. In contrast, well-to-do voters, often with a higher level of educational attainment and living in suburban areas, have usually inclined to the Republican side.

The Democrats have had the support of minority groups, such as blacks, who suffered in the Great Depression and regarded the party as the one that conferred benefits and was more likely to be interested in advancing their economic interests. The majority of Roman Catholics, mainly of Irish immigrant stock, have inclined to the same party and so have groups such as the Jews and other minorities who participated. Just as white Southern Democrats were often noted for their deeply ingrained Protestant fundamentalism, however, so Republicans always had some voters who were poor whites, Catholics, Jewish or black. There was never a complete racial, religious or socioeconomic divide.

Party identification

By party identification, we mean the long-standing identification that a person has for a particular party, a preference that will have often been formed over many years. It will have been influenced by family background, education and the influence of peers in the early years, and this sense of attachment stays with people for much of their lives, modified by life experience, especially economic considerations and impressions formed of the effectiveness of particular administrations in delivering the goods and making people feel content.

Various studies have shown that, whereas in the 1960 election when Kennedy was successful, 51 per cent of Americans could be described as Democrats of one variety or the other and 37 per cent Republican, in 1980, when Ronald Reagan gained the presidency, the figures were 52 per cent and 33 per cent. In other words, comparing a good year for the Democrats in the presidential contest with a bad year shows no significant difference. Indeed, in 1992, the figures remained fairly stable, 50 per cent and 37 per cent. It may be that party identification is the best guide to voting behaviour over the long term but, clearly in the shorter term, there must be other factors which are more important for, otherwise, the Democrats would be regularly more successful than their opponents.

Changes in voting behaviour since the 1980s

The pattern of voting behaviour in America has changed over the last generation, and some of the broad traditional generalisations were found to be inadequate by the 1980s and 1990s. The changing class structure, with fewer people working in manufacturing industry, greater prosperity for most classes in the population, and more upward social mobility, challenged some previous assumptions about the way Americans vote. Voting behaviour has become more volatile and as Stephen Wayne (1996) has written:

> While class, religion and geography are still related to party identification and voting behaviour, they are not as strongly related as they were in the past. Voters are less influenced by group cues. They exercise a more independent judgement on election day, a judgement that is less predictable and more liable to be influenced by the campaign itself.

Political scientists today still talk about party identification but they also place more emphasis on less stable factors that are liable to fluctuate from election to election, such as the appeal of the candidate and issues, than they did in the past. There is, of course, no clear-cut division between them, for the party a person associates with will often help to determine what he or she thinks about the candidate and the topic under discussion.

Martin Wattenberg (1991) has argued that what has happened is that there has been a change of focus in recent years from party allegiance to concentration on the merits of the nominee: 'The change . . . is an important historical trend, which has been gradually taking place over the last several decades.' Voters in presidential elections now seem to be more interested in the attractiveness of the candidate and the qualities he or she possesses – not surprisingly, as these are now featured in the media more than ever before. Via television, they can assess their leadership ability and charisma, their honesty and experience, their knowledge or their ignorance. 'Strength' and 'leadership' are much-admired qualities, as is what George Bush Snr called 'the vision thing'; many people like to be led by a person who knows where he or she wishes to lead them.

Issues are also important but rather less so than party identification and candidate appeal. Voters are often ambiguous about where a contender stands on a particular issue for politicians realise that clarity can sometimes antagonise people and groups whom the candidate hopes to attract. If they have taken the trouble to find out rival policy positions and understand them clearly, then it may be that they incline to one side on one issue, the other on a different one.

More broadly, voters think in terms of what the last administration has done for them (retrospective issue voting) and what the candidates are offering for the next four years (prospective issue voting). In 1992, many were unimpressed by the domestic performance of the administration of George H. Bush, particularly his handling of the economy. They felt that Bill Clinton offered a better future – reform of health care, and a new emphasis on recovering from the recession and creating jobs ('It's the economy, stupid!') However much Bush might try to stress the 'character-issue' by suggesting that his opponent was untruthful, evasive and not to be trusted, this appeared to matter less than the promise of movement on the domestic front.

Demographics of voting behaviour in 2008

Characteristic	Obama	McCain
Race		
Black	95	4
Hispanic	67	31
White	43	55
Asian	62	35
Other	66	31
Sex		
Female	56	43
Male	49	48

Source: statistics gathered in a CNN exit poll, 4 November 2008

See also *Candidate-centred Electioneering; Partisan Identification; Split-ticket Voting; Turnout*

Voter Registration

Voter registration refers to the requirement in some democracies for citizens to check in with some central registry for the purpose of being allowed to vote in elections.

The Constitution prohibits any restriction of voting rights on grounds of race (Fifteenth Amendment), sex (Nineteenth Amendment) or age (Twenty-sixth Amendment); no one can be prevented from voting simply because of their age. Apart from these requirements concerning the right to vote, most election laws are decided at the state level, with the result that the arrangements for voter registration can vary across the country. Every state, except North Dakota, requires the registration of voters before they can exercise their votes. Registering to vote is the responsibility of individuals.

In most states, it is up to the individual to register himself or herself as a qualified voter before election day. Failure to do so disqualifies anyone from using their right even if, in other respects, they are eligible as voters. Registration involves either meeting a registrar or filling out a form at the county courthouse. Some commentators see this registration requirement as a built-in discouragement to voting.

A change was introduced in 1993 when President Clinton signed the National Voter Registration Act (the so-called 'motor voter'

legislation) designed to ease the process of registration. Citizens are now able to register when they apply for a driving licence (hence the name) or some other form of public document. Furthermore, states must designate a public office concerned with providing help to the public, a place where assistance is also available with voter registration – for example, a disability centre, library, school or state welfare agency. Provision is also made for registration by post by the use of a standardised form, and the removal of names of irregular voters is disallowed. The effects should have been to enable and to encourage more people to turn out on election day for it has long been the case that, in those states with same day/no registration, turnout is considerably above the national average.

The new legislation operated from 1995 and, within eight months, some five million new voters registered. Some commentators predicted that, if this momentum was maintained, almost four out of every five voters would be registered by the end of the century. It was not, and today some 66 per cent of Americans are registered to vote, a few percentage points up on the situation before 'motor voting' was introduced. Yet, in 1996 and 2000, the figures for turnout on election day were disappointingly low. As president, George H. Bush had vetoed such a measure, perhaps in the belief that the Democrats would benefit more from a higher turnout. His fears seem to have been largely unjustified.

In some states, voters may declare an affiliation with a political party at the time of registering. This does not cost any money, and it is not the same as being a dues-paying member of a party as it is in Britain. For example, an American party cannot prevent anybody from declaring his or her affiliation with them, whereas a British one can refuse a request for full membership. Some states, such as Michigan and Virginia, do not have party affiliation with registration.

See also *Motor Voting; Turnout*

Voting Rights Act (1965)

The National Voting Rights Act outlawed discriminatory voting practices that had been responsible for the widespread disenfranchisement of African Americans. Echoing the language of the Fifteenth Amendment, it prevented states from imposing any 'voting qualification or prerequisite to voting, or standard, practice, or procedure . . . to deny or abridge the right of any citizen of the United States to vote on account of race or color'.

By 1965 concerted efforts to break the grip of state disfranchisement had been under way for some time but had achieved only modest success overall and, in some areas, had proved almost entirely ineffectual. The murder of voting-rights activists in Philadelphia and Mississippi, gained national attention, along with numerous other acts of violence and terrorism. Finally, the unprovoked attack in March 1965 by state troopers on peaceful marchers crossing the Edmund Pettus Bridge in Selma, Alabama, en route to the state capitol in Montgomery, persuaded the president and Congress to overcome the resistance of Southern legislators to effective voting rights legislation.

In March 1965, President Johnson sent a bill to Congress that eventually became the Voting Rights Act when he signed it in August of that year. The 1965 measure was a natural follow-up to the Civil Rights Act of the previous year. Ironically, that legislation had resulted in an outbreak of violence in the South, where white racists were deeply perturbed by the success that Martin Luther King had in getting African Americans to register to vote. The violence reminded President Johnson that further action was needed if the civil rights issue was to be defused. In a famous speech, he issued a call for a strong voting rights law and urged Congress to act with urgency:

> Rarely are we met with a challenge . . . to the values and the purposes and the meaning of our beloved Nation. The issue of equal rights for American Negroes is such as an issue . . . the command of the Constitution is plain. It is wrong – deadly wrong – to deny any of your fellow Americans the right to vote in this country.

With the president's strong commitment to the cause, members of Congress were aware that, if they hindered or failed to back it, the responsibility for, and consequences of, inaction would rest with them alone. Hearings soon began on the bill and the far-reaching act was finally passed in August 1965. It outlawed literacy tests and poll taxes as a way of assessing whether anyone was fit or unfit to vote. In other words, all you needed to be able to vote was American citizenship and the registration of your name on an electoral list. The law courts would tolerate no form of hindrance to this.

In a 1966 ruling (*South Carolina* v. *Katzenbach*), the Supreme Court upheld the constitutionality of the act. The decision was unanimous except for Justice Hugo Black's objection to section 5 as a violation of the Tenth Amendment. In the judgment, justices noted that:

> Congress had found that case-by-case litigation was inadequate to combat widespread and persistent discrimination in voting, because of the inordinate amount of time and energy required to overcome the obstructionist tactics invariably encountered in these lawsuits. After enduring nearly a century of systematic resistance to the Fifteenth Amendment, Congress might well decide to shift the advantage of time and inertia from the perpetrators of the evil to its victims.

The Voting Rights Act is generally considered the most successful piece of civil rights legislation ever adopted by the United States Congress. Its impact was dramatic. By the end of 1966, only four out of the traditional thirteen Southern states had fewer than 50 per cent of African Americans registered to vote. By 1968, even hard-line Mississippi had 59 per cent registered. In the longer term, far more African Americans than ever before were elected into public office.

Congress has amended and extended the temporary sections of the act several times since its original passage, most notably in 1970, 1975, and 1982. The most recent amendment was the twenty-five-year extension to the provisions signed by President Bush in July 2006.

W

Wall Street Crash (October 1929)

The Wall Street Crash of 1929, sometimes referred to as the Great Crash, was the most devastating crash that has ever occurred on the American stock market. It was not a one-day affair. The initial crash occurred on Thursday, 24 October but the catastrophic downturn on the following Monday and Tuesday precipitated widespread alarm and the onset of an unprecedented and long-lasting economic depression for he United States and the World. The Stock market collapse continued for a month.

On 3 September, the stock market had reached an all-time high. In the weeks that followed, prices began to decline. Then, on 24 October, over 12,894,650 shares were sold, a figure that increased to over sixteen million on 29 October. The market lost 47 per cent of its value in twenty-six days.

Although fewer than 1 per cent of Americans actually possessed stocks and shares, the crash had a tremendous impact on the whole population. The fall in share prices made it difficult for entrepreneurs to raise the money needed to run their companies. Within a short time, 100,000 American companies were forced to close and, consequently, many workers became unemployed. As there was no national system of unemployment benefit, the purchasing power of the American people fell dramatically. This in turn led to even more unemployment.

See also *Great Depression*

War Chest

A war chest is a fund used by parties or candidates for fighting political campaigns. Originally the term was used to describe the chest or strongbox containing the money collected to wage a war but, over the years, it acquired the more usual meaning that it has today. A substantial chest is needed by any candidate seeking to run for state, or especially federal, office, to finance advertising, staff salaries, travel and other expenses.

War on Poverty

The War on Poverty comprised a series of measures introduced by President Johnson designed to fulfil his vision of a Great Society in which tackling poverty became a major federal concern. The package included acts creating education, health and welfare programmes such as Head Start, food stamps, work study, Medicare and Medicaid, which still exist today. The programme was announced by the president in his first State of the Union Address, in January 1964, made just weeks after he succeeded to the White House upon the assassination of John F. Kennedy.

The notion of a war on poverty waned after the 1960s. In the 1980s and 1990s, deregulation, growing criticism of welfare provision and an ideological shift away from federal aid for impoverished people culminated in a measure passed by the Clinton administration, the personal Responsibility and Work Opportunity Reconciliation Act (1996) which recast the welfare system. Of the war President Reagan declared: 'I guess you could say that poverty won', a reflection of the changed attitudes to government action in the area of social policy by the 1980s.

See also *Great Society*; *Johnson, Lyndon*

War on Terrorism

The war on Terrorism, sometimes known as the Global War on Terrorism, is the usual term for the ideological, political and military battle against international terrorism, from whatever its source. It was first specifically used in relation to the operations of he United States and its allies in Afghanistan in the attempt to root out the leadership of al-Qaeda which had admitted responsibility for the 9/11 attack on the World Trade Center.

Terrorist cells are to be found in many countries from Afghanistan and Pakistan, to India and parts of the Middle East, among several others. The operations conducted under the guise of combating global terrorism involve the break-up of terrorist cells in a bid to disrupt the activities of those whose activities might endanger the lives of US citizens and threaten American security and the American way of life.

The phrase 'war on terror' has served to emphasise the gravity of the threat, the need for international co-operation and the need to respond to terrorism in an effective manner. But the phrase gives the impression that there exists a unified, transnational enemy, as represented by Osama bin Laden and al-Qaeda. In reality, there is a wide range of terrorist groups, many of which have distinctive goals – as did the Irish Republican Army and Baader–Meinhof in Europe and as do Hezbollah in its resistance to occupation of the Golan Heights, the Shia and Sunni insurgent factions in Iraq, and Lasher-e-Taibi in its demands over Kashmir. Although from time such groups may support each other for opportunist reasons, their causes vary and their co-operation is spasmodic.

Few would deny the need to combat terrorism at its roots but there are differences regarding how this should be achieved. The phrase implies a military response but resolving grievances, winning over hearts and minds, and exposing terrorist methods also have a role in separating moderates from extremists. Moreover, the idea of a 'war on terror' implies an ongoing struggle that could conceivably last for several decades for, by definition wherever there is terrorism there is, according to the label, a need to tackle it. As such, the war appears to have no end in sight when victory or failure can be assessed.

Because of the difficulties outlined and the association in some people's minds of the 'war on terrorism' with the action in Iraq, human rights abuses and other actions and ideas that may not command wide assent, there has been a debate on whether or not the term any longer has any value. Hence the decision by Obama administration to request Pentagon staff to avoid its use and refer instead to Overseas Contingency Operation.

See also *Afghanistan*; *al-Qaeda*; *Coalition of Willing*; *Foreign Policy*; *Iraq War: the Second Gulf War (2003–)*; *Terrorism*

War Powers Act/Resolution (1973)

The War Powers Act, aka the War Powers Resolution, limits the power of the president of the United States to wage war without the approval of Congress. Passed by a Democratic-dominated and liberal Congress, it was designed to check the supposed warmongering tastes of the Executive. In 1973, Congress passed the War Powers Act over President Nixon's veto.

Under the Constitution, war powers are divided. It empowers the president to wage wars as commander-in-chief (Article II, Section 2) giving him responsibility for repelling attacks against the United States and leading the armed forces. Congress has the power to declare wars and fund them (Article I, Section 8). But presidents from both major parties often differ with Congress over their ability to deploy military power.

A number of experts believe that, since the end of World War II, presidents have demonstrated greater power to wage wars. The War Powers Act followed a period of growing congressional concern over the presidential use of military force. As a reaction to disillusionment about Americans fighting in Vietnam and Cambodia, Congress passed the 1973 law to give the Legislature a greater voice on the introduction of American troops into hostilities. It required presidents to consult Congress, whenever possible, prior to using military force, and it imposed a sixty-day limit on the time for which a president can keep American troops abroad without congressional approval. Without such authorisation, the troops have to be withdrawn; overall, ninety days can be allowed, to enable the withdrawal to be carried out successfully.

The War Powers Resolution cannot be regarded as a success for Congress, however. It has been controversial since it became law because it did not settle the question of the constitutional division of powers between the two relevant branches of government with regard to the declaration and the conduct of war. All presidents serving since 1973 have deemed the law an unconstitutional infringement of their powers, and there is reason to believe that the Supreme Court would consider the use of the measure to end American involvement in fighting to be a violation of the doctrine of separation of powers. Presidents have largely ignored the law and sent troops into hostilities, sometimes with heavy loss of life, without effectually consulting Congress. The Legislature has found it difficult to challenge the president, especially when American troops were endangered, and the courts have been reluctant to hear a congressional challenge on what would be construed as a political, rather than a legal, issue.

Bush Snr, Clinton, war powers

Following the numerous precedents, George H. Bush took an expansive view of his powers as commander-in-chief. On his own authority, he ordered the invasion of Panama in 1989 and moved half a million troops to Saudi Arabia to liberate Kuwait following its invasion by Iraq in 1990. Matters came to a head in January 1991. President Bush had given President Saddam Hussein of Iraq until 15 January to pull out of Kuwait. At that point, Bush threatened to move the Iraqis out by force. Debate raged over his power to act unilaterally to engage in war. A constitutional crisis was averted when Congress passed, on 12 January – on a divided vote – a resolution authorising him to use force.

In a sweeping assertion of presidential authority, Bill Clinton moved towards military intervention in Haiti and essentially dared Congress to try to stop him. Congress did nothing – other than complain – to block military action even though a majority of members of both parties clearly opposed an invasion. In the end, an invasion – as opposed to a more peaceful 'intervention' – was avoided but Congress was unlikely to have cut off funds for such an operation had it occurred.

The 2007 showdown over the Iraq supplemental war-funding bill marks one of the most important disputes between the Executive and Legislature during an ongoing war. The House of Representatives and Senate passed measures calling for troops to be pulled out starting in 2008. President Bush vowed to veto either one and called on the Congress to send him a 'clean' funding bill to sign. He argued that, by inserting timelines, Congress was trying to micro-manage the conflict which further ties the hands of the commanders in the field. The Democrat-controlled Congress, taking its mandate from the midterm elections and consistently low public approval ratings for the war, claimed it was acting on the wishes of the American people to end the war in Iraq.

Scholars disagree over the extent of congressional and presidential powers. Some assert that Congress has substantial power to define the scope and nature of a military conflict that it has authorised (e.g., by setting troop limits) even when these restrictions may limit the operations of troops on the ground. But former Bush administration Justice Department official John Yoo (2005) has argued that the main power of Congress was in controlling war funding, not deciding troop deployments or the plan to surge forces in Baghdad. In his view, 'Congress is too fractured, slow, and inflexible to micromanage military decisions that depend on speed, secrecy, and force.'

See also *Foreign Policy*

Warren, Earl (1891–1974)/Warren Court

Earl Warren was the fourteenth chief justice on the Supreme Court, serving from 1953 to 1969.

He proved to be talented and innovative, the Warren Court being noted for its moderately liberal stance. Decisions taken in that era were of fundamental importance, concerning – among other things – the rights of individuals (especially minorities) and equal representation and equality before the law. It was to become recognised as an era in which the majority of justices were willing to employ judicial power to achieve social progress. For this reason, Warren is generally regarded as one of the most significant justices in the history of the Supreme Court, almost certainly its most influential in the twentieth century. There is probably no chief justice of the United States who evoked greater controversy in his time.

Some leading figures on the bench have had a mainly political background. Earl Warren was a Californian politician, state attorney general (1939–43) and governor (1943–53) before his elevation. In 1948, he was Republican Thomas Dewey's vice presidential running mate, his keen ambition being to become president of the United States. He eyed the Republican presidential nomination in 1952 but it went to the popular war hero, Dwight Eisenhower. In fact, Warren nominated him at the Republican Convention and, in the November election, delivered the California vote to him. Whether an explicit deal was made between the two men is unclear but Eisenhower showed his gratitude by appointing him to the Supreme Court. Eisenhower never imagined that a court under Warren's leadership would move in a liberal direction for, by past background, he was not thought of as being particularly progressive. He was widely expected to be a consolidator so, initially, the president could feel relaxed and comfortable with his choice.

The Warren Court

The Warren Court was the high point of judicial activism. It tackled a wide range of issues, including civil rights, racial discrimination, the separation of Church and state and police arrest procedure. It was in the field of civil rights, however, that Warren made his greatest impact, in particular with the landmark judgment in *Brown* v. *Board of Education, Topeka, Kansas* (1954).

The Court later ruled that it was constitutional to bus children across school district lines to achieve racial equality, a decision which upset many Northerners, just as the 1954 ruling was greeted with dismay in the South.

The Warren Court was also willing to show a new spirit of tolerance on other issues of civil liberty. The press was rendered less vulnerable to prosecutions for libel, and the state of New York was prevented from allowing a prayer to be recited in schools, as this was deemed to be a violation of the First Amendment. The Court also produced what was criticised as the 'criminals' charter'. Justices took the view that, in criminal cases, the balance of opinion had swung too much in the direction of the prosecution rather than towards those on trial. New Miranda guidelines were imposed upon the police, especially over powers of search and detention, and, in interrogations, a code of conduct limited the possibility of unfair behaviour by those in charge of the case.

The Warren Court made a huge impact on many aspects of American life, so that the years 1953–69 witnessed what has widely been seen as a constitutional revolution. The Court's judgments aroused dismay and opposition among those of a more conservative persuasion. Many felt that, via the new liberal line, it was becoming too immersed in political controversy. Warren himself became a target of the right in the early to mid-1960s. Although he had been a vocal anti-Communist as governor, he was now denounced by the head of the John Birch Society as a member of a Communist conspiracy. 'Impeach Earl Warren' bumper stickers were affixed to the rears of motor vehicles across the nation. Some used 'Hang' instead of 'Impeach'! In the 1968 election, the performance of the Warren Court came under much scrutiny, Richard Nixon promising to appoint 'strict constructionists' who – he hoped – would confine themselves to the task of interpretation of the Constitution, rather than engage in 'political meddling'.

In 1963, the 'Warren Commission' was formed by President Johnson to investigate the circumstances surrounding the death of John F. Kennedy in 1963 and to see if there was any organised conspiracy. The following year, the commission issued a report that concluded that no conspiracy existed. Those advancing other theories have, through the years, assailed the commission's investigation as superficial.

At a dinner in San Francisco in 1989 commemorating the twentieth anniversary of Warren's retirement, Associate Justice William Brennan hailed the man under whom he had served for thirteen years as a man of 'absolutely granite integrity and fairness'. More liberal Americans might be disposed to echo his enthusiasm.

See also *Judicial Activism*

Washington DC

Washington DC is the capital city of the United States and the location of the three branches of the federal government. Given the importance of the institutions that are based there, the Washington DC label is often used as shorthand for the national government itself.

Washington DC is situated in the federal territory of the District of Columbia, named after Columbus. Located between Virginia and Maryland on the Potomac river, the district covers 68.2 square miles (178.6 sq. km) and has a resident population of almost 600,000. It is governed by an elected mayor and thirteen-member council. It has no voting representation in Congress, although it has one non-voting delegate in the House of Representatives. A constitutional amendment proposed in 1978 was designed to give Washington voting representation but it was not ratified by enough states in the following seven years and therefore 'died' in 1985. A petition requesting admission to the Union as the fifty-first state was filed in Congress in 1983, and new statehood bills were introduced in 1993. The campaign for statehood continues.

Under the Twenty-third Amendment (1961) residents of Washington gained the right to vote in presidential elections. Washington DC is allocated as many electors as it would have if it were a state, but no more electors than the least populous state, Wyoming (with three).

Opponents of DC voting rights propose that the Founding Fathers never intended that District residents should have votes on Congress because the Constitution makes it clear that District residents should have votes in Congress because the Constitution makes clear that representation must come from the states. Those opposed to making DC a sate claim that such a move would destroy the nation of a separate national capital, and that statehood would unfairly grant Senate representation to a single city.

DC residents seek statehood because it is the most appropriate mechanism to grant the US citizens who reside in the District of Columbia the full rights and privileges of American citizenship. These rights would include not only full voting rights in the United States House of Representatives and the Senate but also full control over local affairs.

The United States is the only nation in the World with a representative democratic constitution that denied voting representation in the national legislative to the citizens of the capital.

Mayor Adrian Fenty made the following pledge while delivering his inaugural address on 3 January 2007:

DC elects a delegate to the House of Representatives who can vote in committee and draft legislation, but does not have full voting rights. Congress is considering legislation, however, that will grant DC's delegate full voting rights. The current delegate is Congresswoman Eleanor Holmes Norton.

See also *District of Columbia*

Washington, George (1732–99)

George Washington was a central, critical figure in the formation and early development of the United States. He led the Continental Army to victory over Britain in the War of American Independence (1775–83) and became one of the major Founding Fathers of the nation, before becoming the first president (1789–97). To the overwhelming majority of Americans, he is an exemplary figure who, in any surveys of past presidents, is consistently ranked the top three, along with Abraham Lincoln and Franklin Roosevelt. In the words that Henry Lee wrote for John Marshall in the funeral oration, he was 'first in war, first in peace and first in the hearts of his countrymen'.

Born into the family of a Virginia planter,

Washington became an eighteenth-century Virginia gentleman particularly interested in two interlinked themes, military arts and western expansion. He fought in the first skirmishes of what grew into the French and Indian War. The next year, as an aide to the British General Edward Braddock (1695–1755), he escaped injury although four bullets ripped his coat and two horses were shot from under him. Like his fellow planters, he felt exploited by British merchants and impeded by British regulations. As the quarrel with the mother country grew acute, he voiced his moderate but firm resistance to the restrictions. In 1775, he was elected commander-in-chief of the Continental Army, taking command of his ill-trained troops as his country embarked upon its gruelling struggle.

He realised early that the best strategy was to harass the British. He reported to Congress, 'we should on all Occasions avoid a general Action, or put anything to the Risque, unless compelled by a necessity, into which we ought never to be drawn'. Ensuing battles saw him fall back slowly, then strike unexpectedly. Finally, in 1781, with the aid of French allies, he forced the surrender of General Cornwallis (1738–1805) at Yorktown, Virginia. After the war, he soon realised that the Articles of Confederation were becoming increasingly inadequate as a means of government, and he became a key player in the steps leading to the Philadelphia Convention of 1787. When the new Constitution was ratified, he was unanimously elected president by the Electoral College.

On assuming office as America's first president, George Washington was aware of the dignity of his position and that this dignity must be preserved. He understood that he was moulding the evolution of a new institution and that his actions were likely to be viewed by his successors as a precedent. The Constitution provided him with only limited guidance in handling his relationship with Congress so he was wise to tread carefully, too, did congressmen was. Both sides recognised that the balance between them of initiative and influence was unclear.

Washington's wish for dialogue with the Legislature received a setback when he wished to consult the Senate over details of a treaty then being negotiated with Native American tribes in the South. He attended the Senate so that he might talk directly to its members and hear their advice in person. Senators were less enthusiastic, seeing such a presence as intimidatory and preferring to receive a written submission that they could ponder in their own manner and at the time of their choosing. Chastened by the experience, Washington left the building and never attempted to repeat the exercise.

Guidance to Congress was provided in the form of detailed written reports, and proposals for legislation submitted by the Secretary of the Treasury, Alexander Hamilton. His influence was such that, in the early 1790s, he was viewed by some White House-watchers as, in effect, the president's 'prime minister', the leading member of the Cabinet and the co-ordinator of the administration's supporters in Congress.

In his second term, Washington faced resistance to federal authority from the farmers of Western Pennsylvania who were angered by a tax placed on whiskey. He sent troops to put down the insurrection, the first time under the new United States Constitution that the federal government employed military force over the nation's citizens. His action in the so-called whiskey rebellion was later claimed as precedent for a president's residual powers (sometimes known as inherent ones), those not spelt out in the Constitution but necessary for the president to be able to carry out other responsibilities.

As president, Washington adopted a broad interpretation of executive power. He showed that the incumbent could become directly or indirectly involved in formulating legislation, steering a programme through Congress and responding to internal and international threats. His example was also influential in two other respects. He began the practice of meeting heads of executive departments in a cabinet and he did not seek a third term in office, thereby establishing the precedent of a two-term limit that remained unbroken up to 1940.

To his disappointment, two parties were developing by the end of his first term. In his Farewell Address at the end of the second, he urged his countrymen to foreswear excessive party spirit and geographical distinctions. In foreign affairs, he warned against long-term alliances.

Washington v. *Glucksberg* (1997)

Washington v. *Glucksberg* was a case in which the Supreme Court ruled that a right to assistance in committing suicide was not protected by the Due Process Clause of the Fourteenth Amendment.

Dr Glucksberg, four other physicians and three terminally ill patients challenged the ban on physician-assisted suicide. They were assisted by a non-profit-making organisation operating in the area of counselling for those contemplating the deed. They argued that the state's ban (operative since 1854) was unconstitutional in that it denied terminally ill adults the liberty to choose death over life. The Court decided that the right to assisted suicide is not a fundamental liberty interest protected under the Due Process Clause, for its practise was offensive to the nation's traditions and practices. Moreover, the justices held that Washington's ban reflected the state's legitimate interest in protecting medical ethics, shielding disabled and terminally ill people from prejudice which might encourage them to end their lives, and, above all, the preservation of human life. The final point was deemed particularly important in order to avoid a 'slippery slope' into euthanasia. Justices feared that what was couched as a limited right to 'physician-assisted suicide' was likely, in effect, to lead to 'a much broader license which could prove extremely difficult to police and contain'.

Watergate

Watergate was the collective label for a series of abuses of power and political scandals which began with the arrest of five men who broke into the national headquarters of the Democratic Party in the Watergate Building, Washington DC, in June 1972, as part of an attempt to find out the Democratic Party's election plans and thereby assist the chances of a Republican victory. As the story unfolded, many revelations were uncovered. Several members of the Nixon administration were indicted and convicted on charges ranging from burglary and wiretapping, to 'misleading testimony' and 'political espionage'. It became apparent that President Nixon had been taping conversations in the Oval Office and that he had been tapping the telephones of his political enemies. When parts of the tapes were released, many began to become more than ever suspicious that the president had himself been involved in planning the break-in as well as in the attempted cover-up that followed its discovery.

Nixon's position became increasingly precarious. The House of Representatives began formal investigations into the possible impeachment of the president. Its Judiciary Committee voted to recommend impeachment on three grounds: obstruction of justice; abuse of power; and contempt of Congress. When a further tape, previously unknown to those handling the case, proved to be a recording made in June 1972, in which Nixon and his aide Bob Haldeman were discussing how to block any investigation into what had happened at the Watergate building, this was the 'smoking gun' that brought matters to a head. Many of Nixon's remaining supporters deserted him, including those ten members of Congress who had opposed the three articles of impeachment. It had become almost inevitable that Nixon would be impeached by the House of Representatives and removed from office by the Senate. In the circumstances, he resigned in August 1974, the first president to do so. He left the White House in disgrace.

See also **Nixon, Richard**; **United States** v. **Nixon** *(1974)*

Weapons of Mass Destruction (WMD)

'Weapons of mass destruction' is the term used to describe massive weapons with the capacity to kill indiscriminately large numbers of people. The phrase broadly includes nuclear, biological and chemical weapons. It entered widespread popular usage in relation to the invasion of Iraq in 2003. The threat of potential WMD in Iraq was used by George W. Bush and Tony Blair to generate public support for the 2003 invasion but, to date, coalition forces have found only remnants of chemical weapons from degraded artillery shells. Most observers are deeply cynical of the claim that Saddam Hussein was stockpiling WMD. Others say that they did exist but were transported to Syria before the war.

The US military defines WMD as:

Weapons that are capable of a high order of destruction and/or of being used in such a manner as to destroy large numbers of people. Weapons of mass destruction can be high explosives or nuclear, biological, chemical, and radiological weapons, but exclude the means of transporting or propelling the weapon where such means is a separable and divisible part of the weapon.

In an interview with ABC News (December 2008) President George W. Bush claimed that his greatest regret was the failure of America to find WMD in Iraq. When asked if he would have gone to war had he known there were no weapons of mass destruction, he stated: 'That's a do–over that I can't do.'

See also *Iraq War: the Second Gulf War (2003–)*

Webster v. Reproductive Health Services (1989)

Webster v. *Reproductive Health Services* was a Supreme Court ruling that made inroads into the *Roe* v. *Wade* decision on the constitutional right to have an abortion. Specifically, the justices upheld, by five votes to four, all of the abortion restrictions imposed by a Missouri law. In its preamble, the statute indicated that '[t]he life of each human being begins at conception', before proceding to limit the use of public funds, facilities and employees in performing, assisting with, or counselling on abortions. Lower courts struck down the restrictions.

The Supreme Court justices had to decide whether or not the Missouri law infringed the right to privacy or the Equal Protection Clause of the Fourteenth Amendment. In finding none of the restrictions unconstitutional, the Court in effect conceded the principle that states could legislate in an area that had been previously thought to have been already decided. It took the view that the regulations in Missouri did not prohibit a woman from having an abortion but simply and reasonably furthered the state's interest in encouraging childbirth. The Court emphasised that it was not revisiting the essential portions of the ruling in *Roe* v. *Wade*.

Wedge Issues

Wedge issues are contentious social or political issues that tend to polarise debate and divide parties. They create a 'wedge' in the support base of one political group which will often seek to suppress or play down debate about them. By contrast, opponents – keen to weaken the unity of the divided group – are concerned to publicise wedge issues, thereby keeping the divisions alive, causing maximum disunity and hoping to encourage supporters to break away from the natural base. Typically, such issues deal with cultural or populist controversies, such as those that arise over abortion, gay marriage and national security. The use of wedge issues gives rise to 'wedge politics'.

West Wing

The West Wing is the part of the White House complex that is directly west of the Executive Residence and, on the first floor, houses the Oval Office, the Cabinet Room, the Situation Room and the Roosevelt Room. Besides serving as the day-to-day offices of the the president, the complex includes offices for senior members of the Executive Office of the President (EOP) and their support staff.

The two greatest indicators of status within the presidential entourage are the proximity of the person's office to the president and the quality of the officer's view. But anyone in the West Wing, even with an office on the ground floor, is working near the pinnacle of power.

See also *White House*

Whig Party

The Whig Party was established in 1834 by politicians opposed to the reforms and 'executive tyranny' of President Andrew Jackson and the Democratic Party. It was named after the British Whig Party that, at the time, was advocating democratic reforms in Britain.

The Whigs supported the supremacy of Congress over the Executive branch and favoured a programme of modernisation and economic protectionism. Prominent members of the party included Daniel Webster, William Henry Harrison and the leading figure, Henry Clay, of Kentucky. In addition to Harrison, there were four other war heroes within its ranks, including Generals Zachary Taylor and Winfield Scott. Abraham Lincoln was a Whig leader in frontier Illinois.

In its three decades or so of existence, it was successful in two presidential elections, Harrison and Taylor reaching the White House. John Tyler became president after Harrison's death but was expelled from the party. Millard Fillmore, who became president after Taylor's death, was the last Whig to hold the nation's highest office.

Slavery proved to be a divisive issue for the Whigs. There were deep fissues over whether or not to allow its expansion to the territories. The anti-slavery element within the party prevented the nomination of its own incumbent, President Fillmore, for the November 1852 election but the successful nominee was soundly defeated. Thereafter, Whig leaders either joined another party, in particular the newly formed Republican Party or the Democrats. Others quit politics (as Lincoln did temporarily). By the time of the next presidential election, the party was disintegrating, unable to maintain a national coalition of effective state parties. It came third in the popular vote. Although it was disbanded in that year, some factions remained in existence until 1860.

Whips

The party whips are members of either chamber of the Legislature who support the party leadership by acting as a two-way channel, communicating party positions to the rank-and-file membership and keeping the leaders informed of member's views. They are responsible for encouraging and mobilising party support when bills come up for a vote, notifying party members of the scheduling, preparing summaries, maximising attendance and exerting mild pressure in the house and in the Senate. They generally assist the majority and minority leaders, acting as part of the leadership.

The term 'whip' is a hunting reference, deriving from the 'whippers-in' who keep the hounds bunched in a pack.

Whistle-blowing

Whistle-blowing refers to the disclosure to the public or those in authority, by a person employed in a government agency or private enterprise, of some form of wrongdoing, be it corruption, illegality or some form of mismanagement.

Since the 1960s, whistle-blowing has been increasingly recognised as legitimate, indeed desirable. Federal and state statutes and regulations have been introduced to protect whistle-blowers from various forms of retaliation. Even without a statute, numerous decisions encourage and protect whistle-blowing on grounds of public policy. Moreover, the federal False Claims Act rewards a whistle-blower who brings a lawsuit against a company that makes a false claim. Originally passed in 1863 at the time of the Civil War, it was designed to combat fraud by suppliers to the government. As revised in 1986, the act also protects whistle-blowers from wrongful dismissal, allowing for reinstatement with seniority, double back pay, interest on back pay, compensation for discriminatory treatment and reasonable legal fees.

Many states have enacted whistle-blower statutes but these statutes vary widely in coverage. Some statutes apply only to public employees; some apply to both public and private employees; and others apply to public employees and employees of public contractors.

White House

The White House is the official residence of the president of the United States. Built between 1792 and 1800, the 132-room mansion has been used as a home by every incumbent of the office since John Adams.

The First Family's quarters, located on the second and third floors of the historic White House, provide them with privacy and comfort away from the public spotlight. The West Wing is home to the president's office and those of his senior staff. The East Wing serves principally as offices for the First Lady and her staff.

See also *West Wing*; *White House Office of the President*

White House Office of the President

The White House Office of the President comprises his closest aides and his personal staff. It is the nerve centre of the Executive office. Of those located in the White House, only a few dozen of the most senior advisers will see the president regularly. There are special assistants to advise on foreign and domestic affairs, speechwriters, liaison officers who maintain contact with Congress, and, of course, the press secretary. There is nowadays a special counsellor to the president, and also many whose services are more concerned with basic personal needs, such as a personal secretary, a social secretary and a physician.

The office ensures that urgent priority issues reach the president's desk quickly. Members seek to ensure compliance by the departments with presidential policies and so enable him or her to obtain control over the federal administration. The real authority of these assistants derives from their closeness to the president, and the trust that he places in them. By deciding who should see him and the issues to prioritise, they have much discretionary power. The danger is that the office can so 'protect' the incumbent that he becomes remote from the political world. He becomes surrounded with 'yes-men' who say what they think he or she will want to hear and thus prevent him/her from making a balanced assessment.

Under Kennedy, several members were used more to help the president carry out the tasks he set himself rather than to act as key advisers. In contrast, other presidents have given this inner circle enormous influence, so that some administrations are remembered in terms of the president himself and the immediate associates with whom he surrounded himself – Nixon had Haldeman and Ehrlichman, Carter had Jordan and Powell, and Reagan had Baker (later his Secretary of State), Deaver and Meese. During the Nixon presidency the size of the White House Office grew substantially, with well over five hundred personnel. Having downgraded his Cabinet, Nixon obtained the co-ordination of policy that he required by establishing the post of counsellor to the president. The appointee was given the prime responsibility for co-ordinating the handling of home and overseas affairs, and was included within the Cabinet – a status denied to previous White House aides.

See also *Executive Office of the President*

Whitewatergate (aka Whitewater or the Whitewater scandal)

Whitewatergate was an American political scandal involving the real-estate dealings of Bill and Hillary Clinton and their associates, Jim and Susan McDougal in the Whitewater Development Corporation, a failed Arkansas business venture of the 1970s and 1980s. The issue surfaced in Bill Clinton's 1992 presidential bid and continued to dog the White House for some time afterwards. A Securities and Exchange Commission investigation resulted in criminal charges against the two principals in the project, but the Clintons themselves were never charged. Three separate inquiries found that there was insufficient evidence to charge them with any criminal conduct in the land deal.

Sometimes, the term 'Whitewater' is more broadly used to refer to other controversies of the Clinton administration that were investigated by the Whitewater Independent Counsel. The suffix 'gate' derives from the Watergate scandal of the Nixon era.

See also *Clinton, Bill*; *Clinton, Hillary*

Wickard v. *Filburn* (1942)

Wickard v. *Filburn* was a Supreme Court judgment that interpreted the Commerce Clause of the Constitution which permits the permits Congress to 'regulate Commerce . . . among the several States'.

Filburn was a small farmer in Ohio. He was given a wheat acreage allotment if 11.1 acres (4.5 ha) under a Department of Agriculture directive which authorised the government to set production quotas for wheat. Filburn harvested nearly 12 acres (4.9 ha) of wheat above his allotment. He claimed that he wanted the wheat for use on his farm, including feed for his poultry and livestock. Filburn was penalised. He argued that the excess wheat was unrelated to commerce because he grew it for his own use. His defence counsel argued that Congress had no power to regulate activities such as production and consumption which are purely local in character. The Court claimed, however, that even if an action is local and not regarded as commercial,

> it may still, whatever its nature, be reached by Congress if it exerts a substantial economic effect on interstate commerce, and this irrespective of whether such effect is what might at some earlier time have been defined as direct or indirect.

Wickard has often been seen as marking the end to any limits on Congress's commerce clause powers. In the landmark case of *United States* v. *Lopez* (1995), the first decision in six decades to invalidate a federal statute on the grounds that it exceeded the power of the Congress under the commerce clause, the Court described *Wickard* v. *Filburn* as 'perhaps the most far reaching example of commerce clause authority over intrastate commerce'.

Wildavsky's 'Two Presidencies' Thesis

Aaron Wildavsky's thesis was that presidents have a much easier time when seeking to exercise power in foreign policy than on domestic questions. He argued that, in effect, the United States had one president but 'two presidencies', one for domestic policy and the other for defence and foreign policy. His claim referred to the era following World War II.

Wildavsky was one of several writers in the 1960s and 1970s who pointed out that presidents had more discretion when dealing with foreign affairs than domestic ones. His quantitative evidence was based on the fact that, between 1948 and 1964, Congress enacted 65 per cent of president's foreign policy initiatives and only 40 per cent of domestic ones. He further noted that there had 'not been a single major issue on which presidents, when they were serious and determined, have failed'. The same could not be said for domestic policy.

Wildavsky's view became discredited, to the extent that, by 1980s, the author himself felt they had lost their impact, in part because of changes on the international scene. Some more recent studies, however, have offered support for the idea that

the president has greater difficulty when operating in the domestic field. A recent and wide-ranging re-evaluation of the Wildavsky thesis by Brandice Canes-Wrone et al. gave broad endorsement to his viewpoint. The writers examined data relating to the enactment of budget appropriations and agency creation to see whether presidents have more control over foreign policy agencies. They concluded that 'in both instances, the results suggest that presidents exercise significantly greater influence over foreign than domestic policy'.

See also *Foreign Policy*

Witch-hunt

A witch-hunt is a relentless campaign launched under the pretext of investigating activities considered by the state to be subversive. It takes its name from the hysterical campaigns against witchcraft which culminated in the trials held in Salem, Massachusetts (1692).

The object of a witch-hunt is to denigrate those whose behaviour or views are considered unacceptable by accusing them of misdeeds, often by reliance on the flimsiest of evidence. The term is particularly employed with reference to the McCarthyite allegations against public officials accused of 'softness' on Communism.

See also *McCarthy, Joseph (1908–57)* and *McCarthyism*

Women's Movement: the Fight for Female Equality

The Women's Movement is a broad umbrella. Under it, there are several groups pursuing their own agendas. Even where there is agreement on the goals to be pursued, there may be differences of opinion about the means by which they should be attained. All agree, however, on the need to advance rights for women.

Among those who can be included within the Women's Movement are: some who see women's inferior treatment as part of a more general problem of social disadvantage for minority groups; others who stress the right to work or the need for greater educational opportunity; and yet more whose interest relates to a single controversial issue, such as abortion or lesbianism. Even on abortion, there is a division of opinion for, whereas the majority would stress the mother's right to choose, a minority of activists emphasise the rights of the unborn child. There are also differences over tactics, a variety of approaches having been advocated by campaigners. Some want to change the Constitution. Others are content to work for concrete legislative gains, large or small. Some want to work with sympathetic men. More strident voices sometimes portray men as the enemy and see little hope of winning concessions from them – and may, indeed, find it demeaning to seek them.

The past treatment of women in American society

For many years, American women experienced the same treatment as their counterparts in Europe. It was widely assumed that their responsibilities involved the domestic role of caring for their children and for their husbands for whom they were expected to be attractive and dignified adornments. They were seen as goods and chattels, dependants of their fathers and husbands. They had few legal rights and were unable to vote. Neither was there much opportunity to further their interests through educational advancement. This sense of powerlessness and dependency inspired some pioneering women to involve themselves in the Women's Movement. Under a hundred of them gathered in New York State in 1848, where they proclaimed the *Seneca Falls Declaration of Rights and Sentiments*, and demanded 'the rights and privileges which belong to them as citizens of the United States'.

As elsewhere, the position of the minority of women, who were striving for greater recognition, was a difficult one. They were excluded from a political system dominated by men, and their chances of securing their rights and improving the lot of women in society were therefore dependent upon elected male representatives. Most men were unwilling to share the exercise of power for they took the view that the world of politics and decision-making was one for which they were peculiarly well suited. Those women who tried to involve themselves in political action

to persuade men to allow them to open up the citadels of power, found themselves ridiculed, slandered or even arrested.

In the late nineteenth century, however, some states began to grant women the vote, and this was gradually extended across the country. In 1920, the Nineteenth Amendment made it legally binding for all states to provide for female franchise. The right to vote was an important equality gain in itself. More than that, it empowered women for, once they had a voice in political life, they were able to use it to campaign for other rights – on matters such as child welfare, anti-lynching and prohibition.

In World War II, the labour shortage created a demand for extra workers. Although many female workers were considered to be expendable once hostilities were over, there were still six million in work, many of them wives, rather than single women, and a number of them black. Since then, several factors have helped women advance their position in American society, similar factors to those that apply in Britain:

* the spread of education, especially higher education
* the need for labour in the economy
* the increased availability of labour-saving devices in the home
* the increased ability of women to control their own fertility via birth control
* legislative action in the form of the Civil Rights Acts of 1964 and 1991.

Prominent organisations within the Women's Movement

Created in 1966, the National Organization for Women (NOW) campaigns on a broad front, its interests spanning issues such as abortion access, child-care, employment discrimination, the law on marital property and international women's rights. Several women's organisations are c -concerned with more specific issues, such as the relatively small number of women in key positions in public life. Among these:

* EMILY's List (EMILY = Early Money is Like Yeast – it makes the dough rise) was

formed with the intention of getting more pro-choice women elected as representatives of the Democratic Party. It has been very successful at fund-raising, and is currently one of the largest donors among American political action committees (PACs). Other features of its work include the recruitment and training of candidates and campaign managers. It also acts as a consultancy, offering advice to those interested in its area of concern. EMILY's List targets its money on winnable seats. The Republicans set up a similar (pro-choice) body, the Wish List.

• The Fund for a Feminist Majority targets all seats, whatever the chance of success. It likes to field female candidates at every opportunity.

On the other side of the fence, two right-wing organisations, *Concerned Women for America* and *Eagle Forum*, believe that feminists pose a threat to American society, the more so because of their espousal of the pro-abortion cause. Concerned Women for America actively opposes NOW and its proposed constitutional amendments. Relying mainly on education and the use of the media, it focuses its case on biblical principles. Among its special causes are: education, religious liberty and the sanctity of life (for); and abortions, gay adoptions and pornography (against). Eagle Forum's mission is to: enable Christian, conservative pro-family men and women to participate in the political process; work to expose radical feminists, opposing their goals of 'federally financed and regulated child care and feminisation of the military', tax-funded abortions and same-sex marriage; and honour the institution of marriage and the role of the full-time homemaker.

Progress achieved towards equal rights for, and treatment of, women

Despite the pressure of the Women's Movement for equal rights, in the early twenty-first century, women hold only 7 per cent of public offices and women's wages remain on average considerably lower than those of men. They are more likely to work in white-collar employment, more than a quarter of them performing clerical or office-related work. Their jobs tend to be in sectors that pay less well (such as teaching); management/industrial positions are still dominated by men. The fight to upgrade the level of female incomes is an important plank of the Women's Movement whose members point out that twice as many women as men have incomes around the minimum wage.

The number of women in elected office has traditionally been markedly lower than the proportion of women in the American electorate. Several factors may be involved. They are more reluctant to come forward as candidates; they have difficulty in getting nominated; and the electoral system makes it harder for them to succeed if they are chosen.

In the federal legislatures, women are better represented in the Democratic Party which has been more willing to adopt them as candidates than the Republicans. In the 111th Congress, of the seventeen women in the Senate, thirteen are Democrats and four Republicans. Of the seventy-six in the House of Representatives, the figures are fifty-nine and seventeen respectively. Within the fifty states, women fare better so that some states, which have had little female representation in either Washington chamber, have had many women serving in one of their state bodies. Over the last thirty-five years, there has been a

The progress of women in elective public office (rounded percentages), 1979–2009

Year	US Congress	Statewide executive offices	State legislatures
1979	3	11	10
1989	5	14	17
1999	12	28	23
2009	17	24	24

Figures provided by CAWP, the Centre for American Women and Politics, www.cawp.rutgers.edu/

fourfold increase in the number of women in state legislatures, with Colorado (39 per cent), New Hampshire (38 per cent), Vermont (37 per cent), Minnesota (35 per cent) and Hawaii (33 per cent) currently heading the list.

Women who hold political office in federal or state legislatures tend to view themselves not just as representatives of their local areas. Rather, they see themselves as representing 'all women', not just in other parts of their state but across the country. According to one survey, they tend to be actively involved in promoting legislation to improve women's position in society. They tend to prioritise women's concerns, such as child care, domestic violence, health provision, reproductive rights and the welfare of family and children (even if this was not their original intention), have a strong interest in the policy agenda on equality, and work for more open and participatory government.

See also *Women's Suffrage*

Women's Suffrage

The term 'women's suffrage' refers to the economic and political reform movement aimed at extending the suffrage, or right to vote, to women. Its origins are often traced back to the United States in the 1820s.

As in Britain, the vote was an initial target for many campaigners for female rights. Suffragists (campaigners for the right of women to vote) engaged in a variety of persuasive tactics to gain attention, some peaceful and educational, others militant and more intimidatory. Moderates were willing to argue their case patiently in countless leaflets and public meetings. Militants were more likely to cause a stir by chaining themselves to the railings of the White House. When they did such things, they were liable to be gaoled and force fed, among other indignities.

In 1869, a National Woman Suffrage Association was formed by Susan Anthony and Elizabeth Stanton, with the object of securing an amendment to the Constitution in favour of female suffrage. They opposed the terms of the Fifteenth Amendment, unless it was amended to include women. A more conservative suffrage

organisation, the American Woman Suffrage Association, headed by Lucy Stone, was formed by those who argued that progress should be brought about by amendments to the various state constitutions. In 1890, the two organisations united to form one national body, the National American Woman Suffrage Association, under the leadership of Susan Anthony.

Wyoming (1869) and Utah (1870) led the way in granting women the right to vote. Other territories and states – particularly in the west – followed their example in the late nineteenth and early twentieth centuries, the only opposition being presented by the liquor interests and machine politicians. Eventually, the vote was granted to all American women as a result of the passage of the amendment, ratified in 1920. By granting women the franchise, the electorate was doubled. The presidential election of November 1920 was the first occasion in which women throughout America were allowed to exercise their right to vote. In 1971, passage of the twenty-sixth Amendment lowered the voting age of all Americans to eighteen.

Today, CAWP (the Center for American Women and Politics) maintains the push for more women to continue to participate in political life.

How women have used the vote

The traditional picture of women in politics suggests that they are less likely to vote and participate at all levels of activity, and that they are more partisan and more likely to support right-wing parties. For many years, it was true that they turned out less enthusiastically but, in recent years, there has been much less difference between male and female turnouts. Over the period 1978–88, on average 2.3 per cent fewer women voted than men but, as there are now more females than males, there have actually been more female voters than male ones.

Similarly, there is little evidence today that women are more conservative in their voting allegiance and, in recent presidential elections, it is the Democratic Party that has benefited from their support. Whereas in 1980 47 per cent voted for Ronald Reagan and 45 per cent for Jimmy Carter, twelve years later they supported Bill

Clinton over George Bush by 46 per cent to 37 per cent (17 per cent for Ross Perot). Al Gore and John Kerry maintained the Democrat lead among women voters but, whereas the former won 54 per cent of the female vote, the latter achieved only 51 per cent. President Bush's ability to increase his share of the women's vote to 48 per cent in 2004 (up from 43 per cent in 2000) was a major reason why he substantially increased his share of the popular vote. In 2009, Barack Obama made a particularly strong showing among women, exceeding the normal Democratic advantage, with 56 per cent of their support.

It may be that women have leaned to the left in the last few years because they associated Reagan, Bush and Gingrich with serious cuts in welfare expenditure and, in the case of Reagan, with a hawkish attitude to issues of foreign policy. In contrast to Bush, Clinton appeared more interested in the domestic agenda, as well as being widely seen as a more attractive candidate. John Kerry may have benefited among some women from his generally more dovish approach to the Iraq War although his ambivalence on the issue left others in doubt.

See also *Women's Movement: the Fight for Female Equality*

Wonkism

Wonks are persons who are preoccupied with arcane details or procedures in a specialised field. In politics, they have a deep knowledge of politics, being experts on intricate aspects of the subject, to the extent that they are seemingly obsessed with discussion of policy details.

Writ of Certiorari

A writ of certiorari is a request by a higher court directing a lower court to send up a certified record of a particular case it has tried, in order to determine whether any irregularities or errors occurred that justify review of the case. When a court issues a writ of certiorari, it is referred to as 'granting certiorari', or 'cert'.

Most of the cases brought annually to the Supreme Court come about by means of this form of judicial instrument. Granting a writ of certiorari means merely that four of the justices are convinced that the circumstances described in the petition are sufficient to warrant the full Court reviewing the case and the action of the lower court. The device enables the Court to exercise discretion in selecting the cases it wishes to review.

Y

Yellow Journalism

The term 'yellow journalism' refers to newspaper journalism that includes lurid features, scandal-mongering and sensationalised news to attract readers and increase circulation. It originated in the more serious *New York Press* and was used by way of comment on the over-the-top excesses that characterised the furious competition between Joseph Pulitzer's *New York World* and William Randolph Hearst's *New York Journal* from 1895 to about 1898.

You Tube

You Tube is a video-sharing website that enables users to upload, view and share video clips. It allows unregistered users to view most videos on the site, while registered users can upload any number of videos.

Some political candidates were quick to see the opportunity to advertise their candidacies on You Tube, including some engaged in campaigning in the 2008 presidential election, Hillary Clinton, John McCain and Barack Obama among

them. The technique can backfire, as in the case of Senator George Allen (Republican) in the 2006 congressional elections. A videoclip of him allegedly casting a racial slur was frequently mentioned by his opponents and seriously derailed his campaign and cost him his Senate seat. You Tube is a participatory medium and therefore carries risk to the reputation of politicians. It is not only candidates who can advertise their views via You Tube. So also can those well-known political commentators or ordinary pundits who wish to make observations and offer an assessment on their opinions. Recognition of this inspired Republican presidential candidate Senator John McCain to explain how popular video sharing had 'changed the nature of politics' and he described You Tube as 'every politician's worst nightmare'.

The You Tube system has also been used by those in political office who wish to communicate with the public, especially with younger viewers. The White House Office of National Drug Control Policy has conveyed its anti-drug message via You Tube but its campaign was curtailed when other users began to upload rebuttals of key points in the message.

References

Abernach, J., 'The President and the executive branch' in Campbell, C. and Rockman B. (eds), *The Bush Presidency: First Appraisals* (Chatham House, 1991).

Adams, J., *The Epic of America* (Little, Brown, 1931).

Almond, G. and Verba, S., *The Civic Culture* (Princeton University Press, 1963).

Anderson, J., *Bayard Rustin: Troubles I've Seen* (University of California Press, 1998).

Barilleaux, R., 'Venture Constitutionalism and the Enlargement of the Presidency' in Kelley, C. (ed.) *Executing the Constitution: Putting the President Back into the Constitution* (New York Press, 2006).

Bibby, J., *Politics, Parties and Elections in Britain* (Wadsworth, 2000).

Biskupic, J., 'The Rehnquist Court: Justices Want to be Known as Jurists, not Activists', *Washington Post*, 9 January 2000.

Brennan, W., 'State Constitutions and the Protection of Individual Rights', *Harvard Law Review* 90, 1977.

Broder, D., *The Party's Over* (Harper and Row, 1972).

Chafe, W., *The Unfinished Journey: America Since World War Two* (Oxford University Press, 2003).

Cox, A., *The Court and the Constitution* (Houghton Mifflin, 1987).

Cronin, T., *Government by the People* (Prentice Hall, 2004).

Cronin, T. and Genovese, M., *The Paradoxes of the American Presidency* (Oxford University Press, 2004).

CRS Report 96–727, Congressional Statistics: Bills Introduced and Laws Enacted 1947–2004, 2005.

Cummings, M. and Wise, D., *Democracy under Pressure* (Harcourt College Publishers, 2000).

Davis, M. *Magical Urbanism: Latinos Reinvent the US City* (Verso, 2001).

De Cleyre, V., 'Direct action', as cited in Brigati, A. (ed.) *The Voltairine De Cleyre Reader* (AK Press, 2004).

Denenberg, R., *Understanding American Politics* (Fontana, 1976).

Destler, I., *Our own worst enemy: the unmaking of American foreign policy* (Simon and Schuster, 1984).

De Tocqueville, A., *Democracy in America*, 1835 (reissued by Vintage, 1954).

Dolbeare, K., in Davies, P. and Waldstein, F. (eds) *Political Issues in America: The 1990s Revisited* (Manchester University Press, 1996).

Epstein, L., *Political Parties in the American Mold* (University of Wisconsin Press, 1986).

Evans, R. and Novak, R., *Lyndon B. Johnson: The Exercise of Power* (New American Library, 1966).

Franck, T., *The Tethered Presidency* (New York University Press, 1981).

Freedland, J., *The Guardian*, 5 November 2002

Genovese, M., *The Power of the American Presidency, 1789–2000* (Oxford University Press, 2001).

Giddens, A., *The Third Way: The Renewal of Social Democracy* (Polity Press, 1998).

Giddens, A., *Sociology* (Polity Press, 2001).

Ginsberg, B. and Shefter, M., *Politics by Other Means* (W. W. Norton, 1999).

Gitelson, A., et al., *American Government* (Houghton Mifflin, 2001).

Goldsmith, S., speech to Hoover Institution, Stanford University, 30 April 2000.

Grant, A., *Contemporary American Politics* (Dartmouth, 1995).

Grant, A., and Ashbee, E., *The Politics Today Companion to American Government* (Manchester University Press, 2002).

Griffin, C., *Cleaning out Congress* (Griffin Associates, 1992).

Grodzins, M., *The American System* (Rand McNally, 1966).

Hadley, A., *The Invisible Primaries* (Prentice Hall, 1976).

Hague, R. and Harrop, M., *Comparative Government and Politics: An introductory Guide* (Palgrave, 2004).

Hames, T. and Rae, N., *Governing America* (Manchester University Press, 1996).

Hartz, L., *The Liberal Tradition in America* (Harcourt Brace, 1955).

Hofstadter, R., *The Age of Reform: From Bryan to FDR* (Knopf, 1955).

Hogue, H., 'Recess Appointments', *Congressional Research Quarterly*, 2008.

Hughes, C., *The Statesman as Shown in the Opinions of the Jurist* (W. Ransom, 1914).

Jones, C., *The Presidency in a Separated System* (Brookings Institution, 2005).

Howell, W., *Politics without Persuasion: The Politics of Direct Presidential Action* (Princeton University Press, 2004).

Kavanagh, D., *British Politics: Continuities and Change* (Oxford University Press, 1987).

Kelley, C., *Re-thinking Presidential Power – The Unitary Executive and the George W. Bush Presidency*, paper delivered to the Midwest Political Science Association, April 2005

Key, V., *Politics, Parties and Pressure Groups* (Crowell, 1964).

Kincaid, J., 'American Federalism: The Third Century' in *Annals of the American Academy of Political and Social Science*, May 1990.

Koenig, L., *The Chief Executive* (Harcourt Brace, 1996).

Kramnick, I., 'Editor's Instruction' to Madison, J., Hamilton, A. and Jay, J., *The Federalist Papers*, Penguin, 1987.

Kristol, I., *Reflections of a Neoconservative* (Basic Books, 1983).

Kumar, M., 'The White House and the Press: News organizations as a Presidential Resource and as a Source of Pressure', *Presidential Studies*, September 2003.

Lazarsfeld, P. et al., *The People's Choice* (Columbia University Press, 1968).

Lipset, S. and Marks, G., *Why Socialism Failed in the United States: it Didn't Happen Here* (W. W. Norton, 2000).

McCombs, M. and Shaw, D., 'The Agenda-Setting Function of Mass Media', *Public Opinion Quarterly* 36, 1972.

MacNaughton, N., *Success in Politics* (John Murray, 2001).

Maidment, R. and McGrew, D., *The American Political Process* (Sage/Open University, 1992).

Milbrath, L. and Goel, M., *Political Participation: How and Why DO People Get Involved in Politics?* (Rand McNally, 1977).

Miller, W., *Direct Action* (L. Parsons and Co., 1920).

Moe, T. and Howell, W., 'Unilateral Action and Presidential Power: A Theory of Unilateral Action', *Presidential Studies Quarterly* 29: 4, 1999.

Nelson, M., *The Presidency And The Political System* (CQ Press, 2005).

Neustadt, R., *Presidential Power: The Politics of Leadership* (John Wiley and Sons, 1960).

Pear, R., *American Government* (MacGibbon and Kee, 1963).

Putnam, R., *Bowling Alone: The Collapse and Revival of American Community* (Simon and Schuster, 2000).

Pye, L., 'Political Culture' in Sills, D. (ed.) *International Encyclopedia of the Social Sciences* 12 (Free Press, 1968).

Rees, L., *Selling Politics* (BBC Books, 1992).

Reichley, A., *The Life of the Parties: A History of American Political Parties* (Free Press, 1992).

Schlesinger, A. Jnr, *The Imperial Presidency* (Houghton Mifflin, 1973).

Schlesinger, A. Snr, 'A Yardstick for Presidents' in *Paths to the Present* (Macmillan, 1949).

Schwarz, B., *A History of the Supreme Court* (Oxford University Press, 1993).

Singh, R., *Governing America: The Politics of a Divided Democracy* (Oxford University Press, 2003).

Skowronek, S., *The Politics Presidents Make: Leadership from John Adams to George Bush* (Harvard University Press 1993).

Steele, S., *The Content of our Characters* (Harper Collins, 1990).

Stone, A., 'Why Europe Rejected American Judicial Review and Why it May Not Matter', *Michigan Law Review* 101, 2003.

Taylor, P., 'Democracy and Why Bother Americans', *International Herald Tribune*, 7 July 1990.

Vile, M., *Politics in the USA* (Hutchinson, 1978).

Wasserman, G., *The Basics of American Politics* (Longman, 1997).

Waters, M., *Globalizaton* (Routledge, 2000).

Wattenberg, M., *The Rise of Candidate-Centred Politics* (Harvard University Press, 1991).

Wayne, S., *The Road to the White House* (St. Martin's Press, 1966).

Wheare, K., *Federal Government* (Oxford University Press, 1963).

Wildavsky, A., 'The Two Presidencies' in *Perspectives on the Presidency* (Little, Brown, 1975).

Yoo, J., *The Powers of War and Peace: The Constitution and Foreign Affairs After 9/11* (University of Chicago Press, 2005).